OUT OF THE PAST

A Topical History of the United States

Donald V. Gawronski

Associate Dean of Instruction
Associate Professor
Department of History
Florissant Valley Community College
(St. Louis Junior College System)

GLENCOE PRESS
A Division of The Macmillan Company
Beverly Hills, California
Collier-Macmillan Ltd., London

First printing, 1969
Library of Congress catalog card number: 69-19584

GLENCOE PRESS
A Division of The Macmillan Company
Collier-Macmillan Canada, Ltd., Toronto, Canada

Printed in the United States of America

Preface

This textbook is designed primarily for the one-semester college American history course, and attempts to suit the unique needs and interests of its readers. The two-semester survey in United States history often functions to provide a foundation for more advanced study, and in order to do so must give students a heavier dose of what they have received at least twice earlier in their formal education. The one-semester course, on the other hand, is usually chosen by those students who do not expect to continue their historical studies. This implies that the shorter course must stand on its own merits alone and ought to communicate to the students a sense of the relevence and immediacy of the key issues in American history.

It is a difficulty inherent in the teaching of history that grand generalizations and sweeping analyses can have little meaning unless they are based in humble fact. Yet the instructor seldom has the time to present even those concrete details which he considers essential. The problem, then, is one of picking and choosing

—and organizing the details so that the broad trends emerge in clear focus. Based on the conviction that a chronological structuring is not well suited to effective and interesting teaching in a one-semester history course, this book uses a topical approach.

An effort was made to identify the major areas of contemporary national concern, each of which has become the topic of a chapter. Within itself, every chapter is chronological in approach, tracing a line of development from the colonial era to the present. The book as a whole covers essentially the same material that is discussed in more conventional texts, but closely related facts are presented near each other, not scattered over many pages, whence they can only be brought together by use of an index. The primary intent of this form of presentation is to show the relevance of the past for understanding the nation today. There is a chronological table (after the Contents) which will help identify the pages in the book that deal with contemporaneous events, but the author has not been afraid to repeat himself where this would serve the readers' understanding.

The writing of a book affects many people, not least the author who apprehensively awaits the response of his colleagues. Special appreciation goes to a wife who maintained an understanding attitude throughout the course of this project, and thanks go also to several friends who provided knowledge, ideas, inspiration, and encouragement. Particularly are thanks owed in this regard to Professor Leon Gordon. But in the last analysis, the author alone must be held responsible for any errors or omissions.

D.V.G.

St. Louis, Missouri
November, 1968

Contents

PART THREE ■ GUARANTEES AND BENEFITS
                            FOR THE AMERICAN PEOPLE

PART FOUR ■ PRESERVING AND DEFINING AMERICAN TRADITIONS

Chronological Table

Part One
Setting The Stage
For The American Drama

Chapter One
Populating the Nation

The American nation was founded by people who represented many ethnic, racial, and religious types. These people had brought from the Old World differing value structures and social outlooks. The major impetus, of course, for the development of the nation came primarily from its English roots. However, from the early colonial period forward, other groups of people increasingly influenced and permanently affected the course and development of a gestating American nation. In the final analysis American civilization finds its origins in a composite of European and African cultures, and yet it has developed as something quite distinct from both.

Time and again, public speakers and writers refer to the United States as consisting of a pluralistic society. By "pluralistic society" is meant one made up of many different groups, some in open competition with others, and with some sort of an arbitration board (in this case government) attempting to placate all of them. This concept aptly describes both Ameri-

can constitutional development and the establishment of the nation's party structure. For American pluralism has been highly influential in creating the American form of government both theoretically and in a procedural sense.

In order to understand the stage upon which the American experience has unfolded, the nature of the people themselves must be considered. The written documents that give foundation to a government, and the procedures established to implement these documents, carry little meaning without the individuals who either administer or who are governed by the system. Furthermore, in order to understand the strains and stresses of American civilization, an analysis of the ethnic, racial, and religious groups, along with the value structures upheld by them, is essential.

In the process, the evolving nature of the United States will become more evident. This is particularly true with regard to American immigration policy, which has changed according to the prejudices of the American people and the economic status of the nation. Part of the unrest which characterizes modern America stems from the fact that there was no native American nationality; it has been created out of a hodgepodge of migratory peoples. It was a painful process, and one which is not entirely complete.

This chapter will survey and trace, historically, the various ethnic aggregates who have migrated to the United States. Their values, attitudes, and contributions within the realm of social interaction will be considered. With this, then, the stage will be set for a consideration of major topics and issues within the evolving, historical development of the United States.

English Colonial Motivation

The settlement of the future United States was but one development in Europe's Age of Expansionism. First Spain and Portugal, and then England, France, and Holland were engaged in a worldwide scramble for a network of colonies. England, for reasons which will be outlined below, was destined to initiate the peopling of the area which would eventually become the thirteen colonies. The English possessed many attributes which would make them one of the most successful of all colonial powers.

There were many motives which led to English colonization and settlement of North America, and many of these point to the value structure of the first settlers. For one, the English, possessed of a seafaring tradition, were a very adventurous, restless, and spirited people. This, coupled with geographical proximity, was a strong factor in America's becoming the destination of so many Britons.

The Religious Impulse

Then there was a strong double-edged religious motivation in English expansionism. First of all, Protestant England was engaged in a continuing religious rivalry with Catholic Spain, which already controlled a large portion of the New World, having preceded England in western exploration and colonization by over a century. Secondly, many Englishmen did not go along with the established (English) Anglican Church. The state viewed these "dissenters" as potential troublemakers, and considered the founding of colonies to be an ideal method of disposing of such people. This meant that English settlers, for the most part, would be Protestants who were out of favor with the official religious viewpoint in England, and who also stood in opposition to Spanish Catholicism.

Unemployment in England

The impetus for emigration also gained momentum from a severe unemployment problem in England at the time. The sheep enclosure movement had been dispossessing many tenant farmers. Additionally, peace with Spain in 1604 discharged from military service thousands of personnel. And finally Henry VIII's dissolution of the monasteries turned loose upon society numerous monks, who were placed in the curious position of seeking charity when they had formerly been the benefactors of the poor. Again, colonies would provide an outlet for this surplus labor supply, and at the same time, avoid government aid for the poor. This would mean that many settlers would be of a poorer lot and had much to gain and very little to lose by coming to America. Settlement in the New World presented an opportunity for them, which was almost totally lacking in their native land.

The Theory of Mercantilism

From the sixteenth century and into the seventeenth, English merchants and the government combined interests to promote English trade and colonization. The very rich in England were looking for new avenues in which to invest their surplus wealth, whereas the government was quite envious of the gold and silver which was flowing into Spain. Consequently, merchants combined into profit-motivated trading companies under charter from the king. They would put up the money required to finance colonial ventures and the king would grant them governing rights in the areas they colonized.

The alliance was based on the prevailing theory of mercantilism. This was a politico-economic theory which had as its principal tenet the accumulation of wealth for the nation, especially in the form of gold and silver, by means of a favorable balance of trade. Colonies were the answer because they would provide the nation with the raw materials needed to produce manufactured goods without purchasing them from rival nations, thereby draining gold and silver out of the country. And they would also provide a market area for surplus manufactured goods.

English governmental officials believed that America was ideally suited for these purposes. They believed that America not only contained huge quantities of gold and silver, but that it would also provide timber for English ships, game and fish for English kitchens, a new market for English trade goods, and a possible base from which to launch exploratory voyages seeking the long-sought mythical route to the East. However, while the English government direly wanted New World colonies, it had no intention of establishing them itself. England preferred to encourage private enterprise, regulated by the government, to undertake the task. And many Englishmen were forthcoming to handle the job.

The Desire for Free Land

Superimposed upon the desire for wealth, love of adventure, religious motivation, unemployment problems, and mercantile theorizing, was the glittering possibility of owning land. In Europe, landholding was something reserved for the upper classes; it was not something for ordinary working people. Also, the lesser sons of nobility could not inherit land owing to the law of primogeniture, which passed on the entire landed estate undivided to the eldest son. Too noble to work, and deprived of income-producing lands, their best hope was also in the New World, where they could acquire their own landed estates and also serve their king. Desire for land quickly became a major motivating force in America which lasted well into the twentieth century.

Development of Colonial America

The various stages involved in the development of England's American colonies will be taken up in Chapter Two. The principal concern here is with the types of people who settled in America and their value systems. For descriptive purposes, colonial America may readily be divided into four geographical categories: New England, the middle colonies, the southern colonies, and the frontier. Each of these regions tended to be settled by different types of people, and each made its own distinctive contributions to what became an American civilization.

The New England Colonies

The New England colonies were settled almost entirely by Englishmen, for the most part middle–class religious dissenters, chiefly Puritans and Pilgrims. Their perspective, somewhat out of the mainstream of official English thought, contributed vitally to the development of American ideas.

Life in New England was conducted along the lines of a group enterprise. A group would found a town, and subsequently another group from within the town would settle a new area. The town very quickly became the key political and social unit of New England life. Puritan religious practices allowed the congregation to choose its ministry and often decide upon doctrine. This same practice was extended to the local secular governing institution—the town meeting.

New Englanders relied on small farm agriculture for their economic mainstay, but they supplemented their incomes by fishing. A surplus of fish enabled them to enter the field of trade and commerce, and before long, commerce became an important segment of the New England economy. The commercial impulse became an important part of the developing New England character.

At first trade was centered on the British-held islands in the Caribbean, but by the end of the seventeenth century, the so-called triangular trade had developed. New Englanders manufactured rum which they transported to Africa and traded with native chiefs for slaves. These slaves were carried to the West Indies and exchanged for molasses which was carried back to New England and converted into more rum. In addition, some of the rum was used to build up a thriving fur trade with the American Indian. Many of the slaves, brought to the West Indies eventually were sold in the American colonies. Hand in hand with this commerce and fishing grew the rapidly developing shipbuilding industry. New England was on her way toward becoming the commercial center of the future United States.

The religious life of New England was greatly influenced by the thinking of the great Reformation figure, John Calvin. The cardinal doctrine of Calvinism was predestination, i.e., certain "elect" people were destined to be saved from eternal damnation. The good or evil works of a man actually had nothing to do with whether he would be damned or saved. This was a rather morbid doctrine and

created an obsession for some New Englanders over whether or not they were among the elect. So they carefully watched themselves and each other, hoping to find some evidence, one way or another. This compulsion soon led to the discovery of witches. Nineteen American "witches" were hanged in Salem, Massachusetts in 1692. In certain fundamental aspects, New England life was harsh, austere, and intolerant, but eventually, New Englanders would learn to live with their religious doctrines.

Stemming from the dynamics of their religion, New Englanders were greatly concerned about education. Every town had its public schools, and many laws were passed obligating parents to educate their children. The subject matter of New England schools was primarily religious, and several colleges were established to train future ministers, notably Harvard (1636), Yale (1701), Brown (1764), and Dartmouth (1769).

The Middle Colonies

Between the New England colonies and the southern plantation colonies lay a group of colonies usually referred to as the "middle" or "bread" colonies. These colonies were the most heterogeneous of all, and tended to develop three distinctive types of civilization, in the Hudson, the Delaware, and the Susquehanna River valleys.

In the Hudson River Valley, New York developed under strong Dutch influences. Originally established by the Dutch, but conquered by the English in the 1680's, New York was highly aristocratic. Religion was Protestant, but the people tended to de-emphasize the predestination doctrine. More optimistic than New Englanders, they believed that God's grace was sufficiently powerful to save any righteous man. The colony was fairly tolerant of differing religious beliefs, and people were rarely disturbed in their religious practices, provided they did not become too vocal in their differences.

In the Delaware River Valley a different group of people settled. These were the Quakers, a religious group believing in the "Inner Light" doctrine. They held that God speaks directly to any man who will listen; therefore, there was no need for official ministers or formal church organization. And since God might be talking to anyone, there was complete equality, even in dress and between the sexes. The Quakers were a very tolerant people who emphasized the dignity of every human being, and who reviled such institutions as slavery and such practices as inequality in political rights. Their adherence to equality furthered its spread into American political life.

In the Susquehanna River Valley there settled a somewhat more heterogeneous population. Many Germans, the so-called Pennsylvania Dutch, settled there. They came to America primarily because of religious persecutions in the German states (Lutherans versus Catholics), and the constant warfare being engaged in by the numerous petty German princes. Because of their experiences in the warring, decentralized Germanies, they believed strong central government and religious freedom to be solutions to their former problems. These Germans favored individual political rights, but they did not assimilate readily into their adopted English environment. For the most part, they continued to speak and write German, and operated their own national schools. By the time of the American Revolution, roughly one-third of the population of Pennsylvania was of German extraction, marking the area as having the highest concentration of non-English settlers in all the American colonies.

Also settling in the Susquehanna Valley were some Scotsmen. Being Presbyterians, these people emigrated to America to attain a measure of religious freedom unknown in their native land. In conjunction with the religious factor, economic strife at home also sent them to the colonies in numbers equalling the Germans, but they assimilated better because they had common bonds with their English brethren.

There were also Frenchmen, Scots-Irish, and Jews, settling in the area, but their numbers were rather small during the colonial period. Still, the middle colonies were a hodgepodge of ethnic groups, nationalities, and religious creeds. As a result the region proved to be a breeding ground for American styles of thought. Also, out of the interaction of these disparate groups, came some rather astute politicians.

Local government in the middle colonies provided the prototype for the form of government almost universally used throughout contemporary America. The basic unit was the township, which was nothing more than a town plus the area surrounding it. Several townships were united to form a county. This township–county system was fully developed before the close of the seventeenth century.

Public schools appeared quite early in the middle colonies, but, as in New England, the responsibility for education rested primarily with the various religious groups. For example, the Anglicans established King's College (Columbia) in 1754, while the Presbyterians founded Princeton in 1746, and the Dutch Reformed Church set up Rutgers in 1766. Concurrently, Benjamin Franklin sponsored a secular academy in Philadelphia in 1751 which provided the basis for the University of Pennsylvania (1791).

Farming furnished the principle occupation of most middle-colony inhabitants, the major products being grains and livestock. But manufacturing, due to the presence of numbers of German craftsmen and Scottish businessmen, was also present. Major products were iron, textiles, glass, and paper. Commerce and some shipbuilding rounded out the middle colonies economic scene. The area was the first manufacturing center in colonial America.

The Plantation Colonies

The southern colonies are popularly referred to as the "plantation" colonies. Tobacco was the most important crop, followed by rice and indigo. And since tobacco-growing rapidly depleted the soil, large-scale farming (plantations) became pre-eminent. The region was largely populated by members of the lesser aristocracy, and this gave the South a different social system than New England. Also, many laborers were needed to till the large plantations. This gave the southern colonies an upper and a lower class, but with no intervening middle class of any great significance.

The laboring force in the South was made up of three groups of people. Some were poor Englishmen who managed to scrape up enough money to buy passage to America, but who had every intention of eventually carving out their own plantations. But most lower-class Englishmen could not afford passage to America, so they came as indentured servants. These were people who in exchange for passage to America, agreed to work a specified number of years for the person who paid their way—usually this was a plantation owner. The number of years of service was approximately seven, but many indentured servants fled to the back-country before serving out their time. In addition to the vagaries of an indentured laboring force, there was the belief that white labor did not survive very well in the difficult semi-tropical climate.

So the solution hit upon to alleviate the labor problem was to transport Negro slaves from Africa to the South to work the plantations. Southerners were already preconditioned to slavery because of its presence in the neighboring West Indies, where it had been introduced during the preceding century by Dutch and Portuguese seamen. The importation system was strengthened by the notorious English seaman, John Hawkins, in 1619. Some of these early Africans came as indentured servants; they could not escape as readily as English indentured servants since their skin color was a dead give-away. By the end of the 1660's most Negroes had become slaves. There were close to a half-million Negro slaves in America by the time of the American Revolution. Three-fourths of them lived in the South, and they constituted some 40 percent of the entire southern population.

The plantation system and the institution of slavery placed many planters in the position of feudal lords. Most everyday needs of the plantation were met on the plantation itself, for it possessed its own weaving looms, blacksmith, and carpentry shops. Luxury items, and those necessary items which could not or were not being produced in America were imported from England. The planter would order his goods from English merchants and pledge the crop of the following year in payment. Many times he overestimated his future crops, and as a result found himself progressively more in debt with each passing year. This debt issue was destined to become an important factor in the rise of revolutionary sentiment.

Since most needs were met on the plantation there was no compelling need for cities or towns; southern society was essentially rural. The lowest level of government was the parish, governed by a vestry. A parish was a group of plantations, and the vestry consisted of the chief planters of the region. They governed the local church, levied taxes, and administered the region. Several united parishes were called a county. It was governed by roughly a dozen justices of the peace who were appointed by the Colonial Governor from among the planter class. Their orders were enforced by a local sheriff who was also appointed by the Governor.

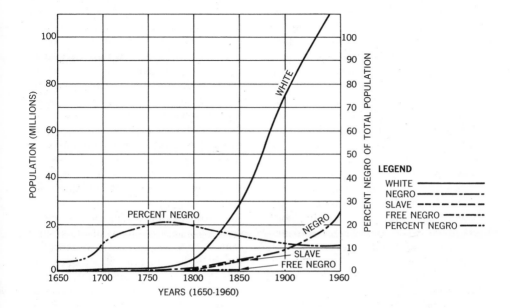

The Negro Population of the United States Compared to the White Population

Each county was also authorized to send representatives to the colonial legislature. These were usually elected from the planter class by those who possessed a prescribed amount of property. Political power heavily favored the planter class.

The Anglican Church was the established religion in the southern colonies. This Church was under the control of the Bishop of London, who never visited America or fully understood colonial problems. This rendered it difficult for effective church administration. One of the most consistent complaints of the southern colonists was directed against this situation. Thus, by the time of the American Revolution, many southerners were Anglicans in name only, and had grown accustomed to violating those laws designed to enforce the established church. This ecclesiastical problem mirrored in certain ways the Imperial muddle and thereby provided an impetus for revolutionary sentiment.

Southern society comprised an aristocracy which rivalled the more ancient ones of Europe. Only the children of the planter class could obtain a formal education, either in Europe or in the new American college, William and Mary, established in 1693. There was no attempt made to establish public schools in the South. Those individuals who could afford it, filled the void by hiring tutors to instruct their children.

The planter class though very small in numbers, directed the entire course of southern life. The planters managed the business functions of their vast landed estates, and the political activities of their areas. They soon began to think of themselves, with some justification, as the paternalistic leaders of the southern people. And this attitude was destined to die a hard death.

The Frontier

The fourth distinctive area in colonial America was the frontier. One point of attraction to the area, for a minority of colonists, was the lucrative fur trade. But the major factor motivating the settlers was the availability of land. Families were very large so some children were forced to look for new areas in order to support themselves. Also, current farming practices rapidly exhausted the soil, thereby necessitating the opening of new lands. The former indentured servant, along with other poor people from the eastern seaboard, also headed for lands available in the backcountry. Occasionally, groups of immigrants moved directly to the frontier in order to preempt lands at no cost. Finally, some groups of American religious dissenters sought greater freedom beyond the pale of civilization. Roger Williams was one such person; in the process he founded Rhode Island.

Living conditions were very difficult in the backcountry. The land was thickly covered with trees, and they had to be cut down and their roots dug out before intensive farming could commence. Transportation was also exceedingly difficult with rivers commonly taking the place of non-existent roads. Isolated then from the rest of colonial America, the frontiersman was forced to rely upon himself for the necessities of life, and he operated strictly on a barter economy. Indians in the backcountry provided him with a potential physical threat, as the intense loneliness, which went with living perhaps a hundred miles from the nearest neighbor, presented a heavy mental burden, especially for the women.

But frontier life was very heterogeneous. People from every colony and practically every country in Europe mixed in this "melting pot" of frontier America. They were destined to aid appreciably in the molding of the American character. Frontier conditions forced and proved congenial to a type of equality and the backcountry became intensely democratic. The frontier pioneer was equally individ-

ualistic—it was a basic characteristic of the frontier type. He had no intention of paying any heed to eastern-imposed regulations on his land, his habits, or his religious convictions. He would, in some cases, literally rather die in order to defend this individualism. A law was obeyed only if it made sense to obey it; a social custom was preserved only if it served a worthwhile purpose. A new social structure was evolving out of the levelling conditions in the backcountry.

The Growth of an Independent Spirit

Most English settlers who came to America had no thoughts of setting up a radically different form of government. In the main they worked within and modelled themselves after the English governmental system. They simply sought greater freedom of opportunity and an escape from the confinement which went with a system composed of privileged classes. Thus, Americans began to view themselves as an independent unit within the British imperial system. English officials, on the other hand, regarded the colonies as dependencies, owing their continued existence to the will and power of Crown and Parliament. Yet the colonies were allowed to pretty much govern themselves during the course of the seventeenth and early eighteenth centuries. During this period progressively more Englishmen came to America, along with increasing numbers of people from other countries in Europe. This would give the colonies the numerical strength to resist any attempts at increased regulation by England in the future.

The French in North America

One of the largest non-English groups absorbed into the English colonies was the

French. Permanent French settlement in North America dates back to the founding of Quebec in 1608. Gradually, such people as Marquette and Joliet penetrated the Mississippi valley. La Salle, another French explorer, dreamed of a French empire extending down the Mississippi to the Gulf of Mexico. By 1699 d'Iberville had established an outpost at Biloxi, near the mouth of the Mississippi, and the French had erected a chain of forts extending throughout the Mississippi Valley. Beginning at the St. Lawrence River, crossing the chain of Great Lakes, and then down the Mississippi, France had loosely settled the interior of the continent long before England was fully aware of the scope of the region.

The French settler was quite different from the English colonist in North America. France in many cases had to force colonization on her people, because there were no obvious advantages for them to realize by coming to America. Some Frenchmen were paid to come to America, while others were literally drafted into the ranks of the pioneer. And on one occasion, French prostitutes were rounded up and forcibly removed to America to provide wives for French settlers, who were in the habit of taking Indian women for their wives. The typical Frenchman rebelled against this type of activity by his government. As a result by 1750, while there were approximately 1.5 million Englishmen in North America, there were only some 80,000 Frenchmen, yet both nations had begun their American colonization at the same time.

French immigration was further curtailed by the existence of a rigidly established Catholic Church. While it was true that England also had established churches in her colonies, there also existed a measure of toleration which was absent in French colonies. French religious practices excluded French Protestants, who were usually skilled craftsmen and mer-

chants of the middle class, from New World settlement. And the French government in North America was absolute; there was no degree of self-government as existed in the English colonies. Also, only French noblemen were permitted to own land in America. This was intolerable to many otherwise prospective French settlers, in the face of thousands of square miles of uninhabited, available lands.

Confronted by these conditions, many of those Frenchmen who did come to America refused to form into settlements. For the most part, these reluctant colonists moved into the wilderness, engaged in the fur trade, and lived with various Indian tribes. In this manner they gained a degree of freedom. But these so-called *coureurs de bois* lived in near isolation and could not be counted on to aid France in the event of any emergencies. The French trapper and trader of the frontier was loyal only to his own breed; he became a prototype of the American rugged frontiersman.

For all their uniqueness, then, these Frenchmen possessed some common characteristics with English settlers. They were entranced by the concept of personal freedom, sought equality of economic opportunity, and deliberately ignored any laws to the contrary. They were unlike most English settlers, however, in that for the most part they came from the lowest social classes in France, as compared to the high percentage of middle-class people in the English colonies.

Before long England and France made their inevitable contact in the New World, and they became involved in a power struggle for North American supremacy. This story will be related in Chapter Two, dealing with expansionism. For the time being, however, it is sufficient to note that England was successful in seizing French territories in the New World as a result of the Seven Years War, known in America as the French and Indian War (1754–1763). This transferred the Frenchmen of the backwoods to English colonial America.

Englishmen Become Americans

The results of the French and Indian War paved the way for a split between England and her American colonies. The economic problems caused by the War, and the subsequent attempts to tighten British administrative control of the colonies, in order to alleviate the problems, resulted in the revolutionary ferment. Additionally, from the English point of view, Americans had been disloyal and disobedient during the war; they required closer control by the mother country. But from the American point of view, the removal of any possible French menace meant that English assistance in America was no longer as vital. Consequently, the colonists developed more independent sentiments than ever.

After 1763 England attempted to regulate and control her American colonies, but it was far too late. Americans were already different from Englishmen. Many did not regard themselves as Englishmen; they were New Yorkers or Virginians, etc. And they might be Irish or German or Scottish. There is a theory, proposed by the historian, James Franklin Jameson, that the American revolution was "in the minds and hearts of men," accomplished in the decade following the French surrender, and that the revolutionary war itself was only fought to preserve an already existing condition in America.

Factors Enhancing Differences

But there were many other reasons why American colonists, regardless of their land of origin, believed themselves to be somewhat different. For one, colonists possessed a unique spirit of independence—many were pioneers, and as such, they had learned to take care of themselves and to think singularly. For another, due to their basic English heritage, most colonists believed that they possessed certain inherent rights, such as trial by jury and the right to assembly. It did not take long for non-English Americans to adopt the "basic rights of Englishmen" notion.

Then there was the geographical factor. A round trip to England required approximately three months, and the colonial environment was different from that of England. This gave the colonists a degree of isolation in which they could put their own theories on life, and its necessities into practice. The unavoidable time lag between British decisions and colonial implementation, furthered American independence, and presented England with already accomplished facts.

And once again there was the increasingly important economic factor. Mercantilism did hurt the American colonies. It caused both a trade deficit and a money shortage in the colonies, which could only be compensated for by engaging in illicit trading practices. The British decision to raise an American revenue, and its subsequent evolution into the problem of taxation, provided the dynamic for the coalescing revolutionary forces. In the process Americans had learned to disrespect English laws by habitually disobeying them.

The Proclamation of 1763

England performed another action at the close of the French and Indian War which alienated Americans. The western lands, the prize that went to England in 1763, prompted a British search for an administrative system that would control the area until a permanent solution could be found for this unsettled region. She did this through the Proclamation of 1763, a hastily drawn temporary expedient, which was greatly resented by the American colonists. The crest of the Appalachian Mountains was set as the boundary limit of colonial settlement from the original English colonies. One of its purposes was to prevent English and French from mixing in the Mississippi Valley until such time as a final determination had been made on how the region would be governed. The colonists, however, were quite embittered over having an artificial limitation placed on their westward expansion, especially since land speculators had already invaded the now closed areas.

The Quebec Act

The supposedly definitive measure was the Quebec Act of 1774, one of the last factors leading to open revolutionary discontent. The act established the Ohio River as the southern boundary of Canadian Quebec, and the Mississippi River and the crest of the Appalachians as the western and eastern boundaries respectively. This region, although English territory, would be governed according to traditional French civil law, and Catholicism would be the established religion. The region was opened to settlement by all colonists, but few Englishmen would willingly place themselves in the position of being forced to adopt Catholicism or to live under the French legal system.

During the Revolutionary War the population pattern shifted somewhat in America. A number of Loyalists, those people who preferred to remain with England, emigrated and were exiled to Canada or England, and many never returned. These people were mainly aristocratic. At the very time when some Englishmen were leaving, non-English immigration was on the upswing. During the course of hostilities England had employed and transported to America a number of German mercenary troops. Not having much personal involvement in

the outcome of the war, many of these mercenaries were more interested in the availability of land in America. So they remained, increasing the percentage of lower-class people. In addition a sprinkling of peoples from other European nations arrived with the termination of hostilities.

The American Nation
Is Established

At the time of the formation of the United States Constitution, most Americans were still, however, Anglo-Saxon in origin, and most spoke the English language. As matters turned out this was propitious for the new nation. A certain sense of unity existed at a critical period in American history. It may be debated whether or not the United States could have survived as a nation had there been a large number of equal sized ethnic groups competing with each other during these early years.

Forming New States

During the decades that followed, the physical growth of the nation was tremendous. This growth is evidenced not only in population figures, but in the number of new western states which came into the Union. By 1820 the states of Ohio, Illinois, Mississippi, Indiana, Alabama, Louisiana, Missouri, and Maine had all entered the Union, joining with the states of Vermont and Kentucky which had been added to the original thirteen states earlier.

In 1800 some 96 percent of the population lived on farms, and the population of the nation was around 5 million. There were only five cities in the entire country which boasted populations over 8,000. By 1820 most Americans still lived on farms, but the population had risen to 10 million, and the urban areas were beginning to develop. During the same period the electorate had changed from a small, wealthy group to a large group composed mainly of common folk.

Population Growth

A better idea of the growth of the nation may be obtained by citing a few specific examples. In 1810 the population of Tennessee was 260,000. By 1820 it had risen to 420,000, and by 1830 it had reached 682,000. Illinois went from 12,000 to 158,000 during the same period. And that area which England had closed off via the Proclamation of 1763 and the Quebec Act, was supporting a population of some 2.4 million additional people between 1810 and 1830. This increase was buttressed by heavy European immigration. The nation did not maintain immigration figures until 1820, but during the first two decades that records were kept, 750,000 new immigrants entered the nation.

By 1840 the population of the nation had increased to 17 million. This was due to a very high birth rate, coupled with a huge influx of Irish and German immigrants. In the first fifty years under the Constitution, the nation had quadrupled the number of its residents.

Despite this growth the nation was still socially quite stable. The so-called "Old Immigration" was predominately Anglo-Saxon. Except for huge increases in the Negro population, due to the rapid expansion of the slavery system, the ethnic and racial composition of the United States had not changed a great deal since the colonial period. There were, however, progressively more poor people from these traditional ethnic groups, especially the Irish, who were coming to America. But the availability of land and opportunity, coupled with hard work and a degree of luck, enabled most of these people to acquire an amount of self-sufficiency within a generation.

Non-European Immigration

The Negro American

During the period under consideration the South had been shifting over to an economy based largely on plantation-grown cotton which was produced by slave labor. At the time the Constitution was being written, many Americans believed that slavery was a dying institution. But in 1793 Eli Whitney invented the cotton gin, rendering cotton growing a very lucrative business. At the time the Negro population of the nation was approximately 817,000. Since the tilling of cotton is a fairly routine but backbreaking process, southerners used their slaves for it. As more cotton was produced more slaves were needed. Negro slaves trained for field work cost around $1500 in 1840, while a highly skilled slave might bring a price as high as $3000, and the cost of slaves progressively increased.

A large number of southern slaveholders felt uncomfortable with the odious slave trade. And some planters sought to avoid splitting up Negro families on the auction block, though profit usually won out over moral scruples and humanitarianism. There was a percentage of planters, traders, and breeders who ignored the barest degree of humanitarianism. As a result, approximately 200,000 slaves were shipped from Virginian and South Carolinian "breeding farms" to the new western plantations between 1830 and 1840. And some of the more unscrupulous of the "breeders" took an active part in the procreative process. In so-called democratic America slaves were auctioned off daily in the streets of the nation's capital. Few people were apparently concerned about the glaring contradiction. As a result, by the eve of

Reading the Emancipation Proclamation

the Civil War the Negro population of over 4.4 million, constituted better than 7 percent of the total population.

As might be expected, slaves did not live in luxury. They were clothed, fed and housed, possessed some security in sickness and old age, and were generally no worse off economically than northern textile workers. But they were not free. Slaves were legally property, and as such, subject to the whims of their owners, and what was more serious, the whims of sadistic slave drivers. A slave could not sue or testify in court against a white man. He could neither own property or make out a will. He was even denied the right of legal marriage. In some states it was a criminal offense to educate him. Only limited religious instruction was allowable, and major emphasis was placed on those passages in the Old Testament which

recognized the existence of slavery. Therefore, while the economic situation of the slave was in some ways comparable to that of northern textile workers, the psychological trauma of slavery exceeded the effects of the basest exploitation of northern labor; the effects of this trauma on slaves and owners alike are profoundly felt today.

Indian and Mexican Minorities

What is true of the American Negro is basically true also of the American Indian. Technically he was a free man, but one of inferior status, and not worthy of citizenship. He could acquire a wife or property, but any white man could take away either of them without much fear of legal intervention. But whereas the Negro population was continually growing, the ranks of the American Indian were progressively diminishing.

During the 1840's the United States acquired another group of people. The Mexican War resulted in huge territorial gains for the nation from former Mexican lands. These lands brought with them a number of Mexicans, and these people for the most part, were of Spanish descent, Negroes, and Indians, plus mixtures of the three groups. The prejudice displayed by the Anglo-Saxon against the Negro and the Indian was very easily passed on to the Mexican-American, with similar results. The Mexican-American was generally regarded as an inferior creature, and in fact, this rationalization had been used to help justify the war itself.

Oriental Americans

Only one other large group of people became a part of the American story during the period prior to the American Civil War. These were the Orientals. There had been a trickle of Oriental immigration to the West Coast during the early nineteenth century owing to American trade and commerce associations with the Far East. But since the numbers were so small, no great attention was paid to them.

However, with the building of the railroads, a development commencing in the 1840's, increasing numbers of Orientals (and Irish) were encouraged to come to the United States to serve as a cheap labor force. This number did not reach its peak until the 1860's with the building of the transcontinentals, and by that time the Oriental problem was considered as a very grave issue by many Americans, particularly those residing on the West Coast.

The Myth of Anglo-Saxon Superiority

Still, for almost the first century of the nation's formal existence, the nation remained basically Anglo-Saxon in its ethnic composition and values. The population of the nation in 1870 was 39.8 million. The total number of people who had migrated to America up to that point was 7.4 million, according to official immigration figures. And, of course, a preponderant number of these immigrants were of Anglo-Saxon origin.

There was a widespread belief that the Anglo-Saxon was a superior being, and all others were not really welcome. They were allowed into America to take on those menial jobs which Anglo-Saxons should not have to bother with. Since their numbers were small in comparison to the total population, a major issue did not develop during the period. However, after the Civil War with the tremendous growth of industrialization, and the subsequent need for workers, the nation experienced a major difficulty. As the labor demand increased dramatically, the void was filled more and more by non–Anglo-Saxon Europeans, and the newly emancipated Negro slaves. The majority's theories of racial superiority would now be faced with an ever growing number of dissidents.

The New Immigration

Up to around 1870 most immigrants had come from northern and western Europe. These people were primarily fair-complected and Protestant. They experienced practically no difficulty in assimilating into American society. They were of the same basic stock as earlier immigrants, and for the most part either spoke or quickly learned the English language. In many instances they were fairly well educated, and what is more important, sincerely desired to belong to American society. Not considered to be a threat to so-called "native Americans," they were generally well received.

However, after 1870 the immigra-

No Luxury in the Hold of an Immigrant Ship

The Vaccination of Immigrants

tion pattern shifted. Because of serious economic difficulties, lack of opportunity, and considerable political instability, the immigrants began to come mainly from various eastern and southern European countries. They were predominantly Mediterranean and Slavic in ethnic origin and practically none of them knew the English language. Also, they were usually Roman Catholic, Greek Orthodox, or Jewish in religion, and as such, did not fit in very well with Protestant America.

What made the situation more difficult was their insistence on what were regarded by many Americans as un-American customs. For example, they preferred parochial schools to the use of public schools. They also worshipped in strange tongues rather than in English. And they built their churches according to strange architectural designs. These people were also generally quite poor and uneducated. They came from a part of the world where only the wealthiest of people could acquire anything remotely resembling a formal education. And these people had been doomed to almost perpetual poverty. These were not the middle-class, Protestant, western Europeans who had founded the United States. These people, it was widely held, would lower the caliber of America and lessen the development of the nation.

Beginning of the Ghetto

Alone and openly hated in a new and alien country, these immigrants tended to form into pockets, preserving their own customs and language as their only source of comfort. This solidarity, aggravated by outside pressures from an intolerant society, produced the modern American ghetto. Practically every major city had its own "Little Poland," or "Little Italy," along with all the other nationalities of eastern and southern Europe. For these people it often took three generations

before the pressures of prejudice appreciably lessened.

What was true of these people was also true of the American Negro who, in his newly freed status, was beginning to migrate to the northern industrial centers. He tended to fit the same pattern as the eastern and southern Europeans. He had his own habits, customs, and beliefs, which were out of the mainstream of white America. He too, found himself in the ghettos; but he could not get out so readily. Unlike the immigrant who could and often did change his name in order to avoid prejudice, the Negro carried a badge of color which he could not disguise.

Prejudice in the New Immigration

There is another reason for the prejudice displayed against the New Immigration, and it goes beyond simple ethnic prejudice. Such prejudice is usually based on two factors: a lack of information about the group, and fears of economic competition. Instead of trying to understand those who are different, hatred offers a much simpler solution. Additionally, charges of racial or ethnic inferiority are often nothing more than a rationalization for an inherent fear of competition in the economic realm. For this New Immigration, and Negroes as well, came from backgrounds which produced a very low standard of living. These ghetto poor were willing to work for very low wages, which to them appeared to be fortunes. Resentment, therefore, arose over this new and dangerous competition in the nation's labor market, particularly for those industrial workers who were attempting to establish collective bargaining rights.

Finally, in the slums (and here the Negro is being excluded from the discussion because he was denied any political rights), the immigrant fell victim to the party boss—his only friend. Because the party boss was popularly held to be corrupt, so the immigrant by association was also considered corrupt. This belief was enhanced by the number of crimes committed in slum areas. Most so-called native Americans believed that the newcomers were willfully debasing the nation's values. They therefore hated the "defiler." Anti-minority violence was not uncommon for a period of about five decades.

Population Increase by Annexation

A further development occurred in the 1890's as the United States, after embarking on a brief, imperialistic spurt, found herself governing large alien populations abroad. One such territory was the Hawaiian Islands. Due mainly to the machinations of American businessmen in the island chain, Congress pushed through a treaty of annexation in 1893. Among those opposed to the annexation were individuals fearing a greater influx of Orientals to the United States. These protestations, combined with certain political developments (see the next chapter) resulted in a delay of the ratification agreement. But in 1898 practical considerations pointed to the value of a large naval base in the Pacific, and the treaty of annexation was ratified. The United States had acquired a large land mass populated with Orientals and Polynesians.

Also, as a result of the Spanish-American War of 1898, the United States acquired the territories of Puerto Rico, Guam, and the Philippine Islands, thus adding large numbers of people of Spanish and Eastern descent to the American domain. The problems relating to this development will be taken up in the next chapter.

Immigration Legislation

Many Americans however, were still primarily concerned with the continuing immigration from eastern and southern Europe, and with venting their hatred on these immigrants, rather than concerning themselves with alien peoples living in faraway territories. These attitudes produced the first general immigration legislation in American history. There had been a number of minor immigration laws passed previously. For instance, the Chinese Exclusion Act of 1882 prohibited the further immigration of Chinese, while another measure of the same year excluded lunatics, paupers, and convicts, and placed a nominal head tax to be paid by the transporters of immigrants to defray the cost of enforcing immigration regulations. In 1891 another law set up a forerunner of the federal Bureau of Immigration, and excluded carriers of contagious diseases and "immoral" persons.

As the influx of southern and eastern Europeans continued, increasing demands were made to exclude such people. One method hit upon was a literacy test which most definitely would have excluded an

From the MINNEAPOLIS JOURNAL

Congress Preserves "Native Americanism"

overwhelming majority of these immigrants. The literacy test law passed Congress in 1893, but was successfully vetoed by the outgoing President Cleveland.

For the next few years, Americans were preoccupied with expansionism and the new problems which it brought. Some immigration controversies continued, but except for the issue with Japan in 1907 and the subsequent Gentleman's Agreement, they were not overly important. However, as Europe became embroiled in the conflicts that preceded World War I, vast numbers of southern and eastern Europeans poured into the United States. The situation was such that Congress was able to pass legislation effectively designed to forestall these alleged "undesirables" from any further migration to the United States. The method employed was the quota system.

The Emergency Quota Act

Not only did the attitudes concerning Anglo-Saxon superiority play a major role in this legislation, but there were also a number of people who felt that the nation's immigration laws were a hodge-podge, in dire need of systematization. The resultant Emergency Quota Act of 1921 superseded and codified all earlier legislation.

The act prohibited the entrance of specified undesirables, such as criminals, paupers, carriers of contagious diseases, and people of moral disrepute. However, the act was also prejudicial to people from southern and eastern Europe, who were to be excluded simply because of national origin. A limit was set on the number of persons who could enter the United States from each foreign country per year. A number equalling 3 per cent of the total number of people from a given

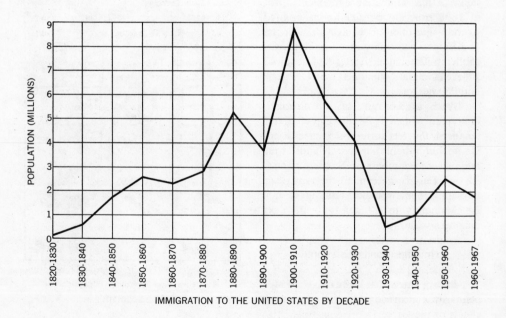

IMMIGRATION TO THE UNITED STATES BY DECADE

country residing in the United States as of 1910 was allowed to enter each year. Since the number of Mediterranean and Slavic peoples was still relatively small as of 1910 (compared with people of western and northern European origin), 3 per cent was a very small yearly quota. The result of the Emergency Quota Act was a two-thirds reduction in the annual immigration rates.

1924 Immigration Act

The act, as the name implies, was intended only as temporary legislation. Congress, in the meanwhile, was busily engaged in devising permanent legislation. The result of these congressional efforts was the Johnson Immigration Act of 1924. This measure excluded practically all immigrants from eastern and southern Europe. Using the same basic principle of the 1921 law, the new measure allowed the annual immigration of a number equalling only 2 per cent of the nationals of a given country residing in the United States as of 1890. Not only was the percentage smaller, but the number of such people living in America in 1890 had been considerably less than it was in 1910.

The act was also aimed quite pointedly at the Japanese. The question of Japanese immigration had erupted during Theodore Roosevelt's administration. It had been quieted by the Gentleman's Agreement, whereby Japan agreed to defer the issuance of passports to the United States, but retained the right to reissue them whenever she desired. But the 1924 act specifically excluded all Orientals from migrating to the United States. The act did not apply to nationals of specified countries within the western hemisphere.

Legislative exclusion was exactly what most Americans desired, and immigration ceased to be a burning issue. In fact during the 1930's, when the United States was experiencing the crippling effects of the Great Depression, immigra-

tion was even further reduced. For the first time in American history there were months when more people left the United States than entered.

The Immigration Acts of 1952 and 1965

Immigration policy has changed very little in basic intent to the present day. However, there was for a time a partial relaxation of the initial stringent quota requirements. Under the Immigration Act of 1952, annual immigration was limited to roughly 155,000 people per year. This figure was based on one-sixth of 1 per cent of the total population of foreign nationals residing in the United States according to the 1920 census. But there have been numerous relaxations of this quota. A Refugee Relief Act in 1953 provided for the admission of refugees over and above quota limits if they met certain basic requirements. Under this measure close to 34,000 refugees from Hungary entered the United States during 1956 and 1957. Also restrictions against Orientals have been eased somewhat. And quota restrictions are not applied to spouses and dependent children of American citizens. But the emergency measures resulted in a large oversubscription of immigrants from certain nations, so a new method was developed.

The national origins quota approach, which has been in effect since 1921, is scheduled to terminate in 1968. Then it will be superseded by the provisions of the Immigration Act of 1965. The measure adds two new dimensions to quota: kinship and skills. An absolute limit of 170,-000 immigrants yearly from outside the western hemisphere is authorized, with no more than 20,000 from any given country. Preference will be given to those potential immigrants who have relatives in the United States or who possess essential skills; an elaborate formula has been worked out to determine qualifications. In addition, a yearly quota of 120,000 has been established for immigration from within the western hemisphere. This is an entirely new feature in American immigration legislation.

The American Family Structure

At the basis of any modern western social system is the family unit. Naturally the settlers who came to America possessed certain preconceived notions of family life. An overwhelming proportion of the colonial settlers, as was stated previously, were of English origin, and they attempted to transplant to the new world their long-standing customs and traditions. But these customs and traditions had been developed in an established nation state. The new pioneer environment forced some important changes.

Courtship and Marriage in New England

In all probability the colonial New England family was required to change the least. New Englanders settled in villages and towns, and their social environment, except for the problems arising from material hardships in a wilderness, was essentially the same as in England. Hence, no unusual degree of adaptation was required.

Adults were expected to marry, and this before reaching their twenties. Oftentimes a bachelor was required to pay special high taxes since he was not supporting a family. Some communities ostracized single adults, who were viewed as irresponsible (and probably immoral) persons.

Women possessed some legal rights, but not many. Socially they were inferior to men, and their lot in life consisted of hard physical labor. Women could enter business, but they could not become actively involved in politics or religion. There are instances of dissenters being banished from their towns for taking a public stand on religion.

The methods of courtship in New England were quite different from those of the modern day. For widows and widowers the proper course was to remarry as quickly as possible. There are many examples of such marriages taking place one or two weeks after a spouse was buried. For younger people the father's consent was always required for the bride. Courtships were very short and exceedingly formal. Marriage was generally regarded as a business contract, and more time was spent negotiating over a dowry for the bride and a determination of the net worth of the groom than on romance. In keeping with this business-like attitude, marriages were usually solemnized in a civil ceremony. Practically all of this was a carry-over from England. However, the role of the bride's father as the giver of consent was rapidly breaking down in America.

Children played a much different role when compared with contemporary standards. One got married in order to beget as many children as was physically possible—and as quickly as possible, it might be added; infant mortality was exceedingly high. The teachings of John Calvin were a heavy weight upon child-raising in colonial New England. According to Calvin children were born depraved; therefore, the strictest of discipline was necessary in order to teach them to overcome their weaknesses. Physical punishment was prevalent. Quite in contrast with modern standards, children were literally frightened out of their wits with picturesque stories of damnation and death. Youngsters were introduced to death and suffering as quickly as possible. No responsible parent passed up the excellent opportunity to instruct his brood by taking them to a funeral or a public execution.

Absolutely no attempts were made to shield children from the harsh realities of life.

The legal structure of New England also reflected prevailing attitudes. Divorce was allowed but only rather sparingly up to the revolutionary era. Then it began its long march to the present high level. Officially, sex was for the procreation of children only, and strictly within the bonds of marriage. Penalties for violating the moral code were quite high; the offenders could be stripped and whipped publicly. Judging from accounts of the period, this did not stop people from running the risk of being caught. Mixed dancing was considered to be sinful. However, the practice of bundling was allowed. Bundling was a quaint American custom, whereby an engaged couple could go to bed together, provided they remained fully dressed.

Southern Chivalry

The attitude in the South was somewhat different. New England society consisted largely of middle-class Calvinists who settled in towns and essentially preserved the English family unit. Southern settlers were usually located on isolated plantations and farms, and developed a different family structure. There existed the same strong belief in marriage as in New England, but the family unit was somewhat broader; it comprised everyone in the household, including domestics, and this sometimes meant quite a few people.

Chivalry was the social code of the aristocratic South. But the notion, widely held, that womanhood was revered throughout the South is somewhat erroneous. Only upper-class women were placed on pedestals and even this was not universal. Lower-class women received little or no respect. Chastity was very important for women, on a sliding scale. Upper-class women were required to be chaste; many lower-class women need hardly have bothered. Men were not required to remain chaste; rather, they were free to take up with any available lower-class white woman and to exploit all Negresses. The well-born southern planter's wife was supposed to conceal her husband's infidelity. He, in turn, was not supposed to be very open about his illicit activities. Unlike New England, the legal system in the South was not very harsh on sex offenders.

The South also believed in early marriages. As in New England, major emphasis during the courting period was on economic factors and bargaining about property rights. But southern marriages were seldom solemnized by civil officials. The Anglican clergy most often presided over such functions. Common law marriage was viewed as being entirely legal in the South, provided no clergyman or civil official was available at the time. There were very few divorces.

Like New Englanders, southerners went in for very large families, and experienced the same high infant mortality rates. Death, however, was viewed rather fatalistically, as just an aspect of marriage. Negroes were rarely allowed to marry, but were encouraged to produce offspring.

The Breakup of Colonial Patterns

Some general observations may now be made on the role of the family in colonial society, even allowing for the differences between the North and South. For one thing, the family was primarily an economic unit; property and money matters received major consideration. Secondly, procreation received major stress as the basic function of a marriage. Such considerations as companionship scarcely received any attention. Thirdly, except for a few individuals, neither the courtship period nor the marriage itself contained much romance. Colonial people were hard realists; their status in life did not usually permit the luxury of romantic activities. Finally, the family was an inclusive structure. It was the center of all activity and it stressed relationships among all kinfolk.

Since colonial times the family structure has been changing rapidly. The change started during the revolutionary period, when Americans began to throw off many of the values of their previous cultural heritage. There were a number of factors responsible and territorial expansion was one. As the land mass of the United States grew the people spread out. As the people spread, the tightly knit family structure of the colonial era began to disintegrate. The masses of immigrants from non-English countries who arrived in the middle of the nineteenth century also brought with them different viewpoints on the role of the family. Of considerable importance here is the fact that cross-ethnic marriages became quite commonplace. Such marriages often meant inter-marriage of religious faiths, and it was likely that the faith of one or the other of the marriage partners would dominate the new family's life to the exclusion of one set of in-laws.

The building of the railroads, making possible greater ease of travel and relocation, was another factor of change. But of even greater significance in this realm was the invention of the automobile which broke down the family structure more than anything else. Ease of movement carried entertainment out of the home, led to absences of certain family members from time to time, and gave the younger generation a degree of freedom unheard of by their ancestors. Quite naturally, this freedom profoundly influenced courting habits.

Despite these changes, however, the official sex code has remained relatively unchanged. There has been a reluctance to change the basic avowed attitude, but an open willingness to change the actual practice. Women are progressively becoming as free as males, and the ready availability of contraceptive devices is a major factor in this development. Some movement is being made in the direction of free-love societies, and this is nothing new in American history. Around the 1830's a number of attempts at communal living were witnessed. Many of them did not emphasize sex, but a few did. None of them, it is to be noted, lasted very long.

The New Look at Marriage

A relatively high national standard of living has brought another important series of changes to the family system. The economics of a marriage contract are not nearly as important as they used to be. With increased leisure, sufficient time is available for a romantic type of courtship. Marriage is now usually based on the free choice of the individuals concerned. Also the role of procreation is not as important as it was at one time. Most young couples desire a family, but there is a growing tendency to postpone the beginning of that family. As a consequence, families are getting smaller, and those couples who have many children are sometimes reproved for contributing to the population explosion.

One reason for the decrease in family size and the postponement of children is that many wives hold jobs outside of the home. Education is another contributory factor, in that marriage is put off by some college students until after they have completed their education. Often marriage is entered into with the understanding that a family will not be started until the husband is well established.

There is an increasing tendency for a marriage to be a companionate arrangement. Many couples marry with the idea of mutual enjoyment and a sharing of responsibility. Also, in many cases there is no longer a single head to a family. The institution has thus become more unstable. Also, since romance plays such a large role in the courtship period, when it wanes there is a difficult period of adjustment which many people are unable to make. Recreation, religion, education, and discipline are all usually outside the modern home. Increasingly, married people go their separate ways, even to the point of separate vacations. No matter what the causes are, however, the end result is a constantly skyrocketing divorce rate, which has caused some social scientists to speculate that marriage as a basic social institution of a permanent nature is on a decline.

The Shift from Farm to City

The Agrarian Myth

When Thomas Jefferson visualized the United States of the future, he prophesied a nation consisting of small farms. This vision added impetus to a certain conception of the farmer known today as the "agrarian myth." The principal tenet of this attitude was that the farmer, being a tiller of the soil, was inherently more virtuous than a non-tiller of the soil.

Jefferson had reasoned that the farmer, being closest to nature, was of all men closest to God. Therefore, the farmer could not help but be the most virtuous. As towns and villages developed into cities, the corollary of the agrarian myth was postulated, which held that the city dweller, by being removed from nature, could not be nearly as virtuous as the farmer.

To support his claims a believer in the "agrarian myth" could readily point out that taverns, houses of ill repute, and other tempting entertainment centers existed primarily in urban areas. He could also raise the claim, dubious as it was, that the farmer exemplified the American tradition of hard work, individualism, and

Rural and Urban Population According to Census Figures

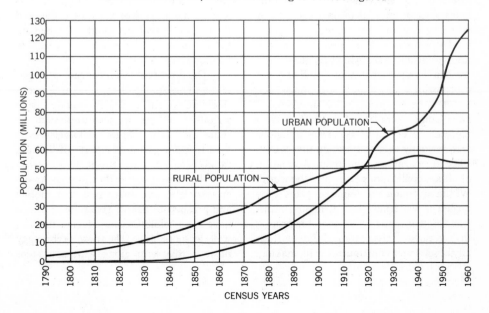

independence, whereas the city dweller was soft, conformist, and dependent. Attitudes often crystallized around the two extremes. The idea of rural virtue was so strong that in the presidential election of 1928, when Al Smith of New York lost to the midwestern farm boy, Herbert Hoover, some political historians claimed that Smith's lifelong habitation of the city was one of the contributory factors.

The Death of a Myth

In contemporary America the trend has somewhat reversed itself. The farmer is now a minority and he necessarily reflects a minority viewpoint. Most Americans live in cities; they are born there and they die there. Many children grow to adulthood without ever having seen a farm. So the opposite view is now more dominant; the good life is in the city. But there is a contradiction in American behavior. Although the good life is supposed to be in the city, there is a rapidly growing trend for the white, middle-class city dweller to remove himself to the suburbs. The two opposing views have merged for many into an attempt to have the best of both the city and the country. But few modern Americans are prepared to give up the conveniences which go along with the hectic impersonality of city living, except during a few annual vacation weeks.

The people who make up America have come from many sources. They represent every country, every religious sect, virtually every culture on this planet. They are a synthesis and an amalgamation of all the civilizations known to the world. Within a couple of hundred years they turned a wilderness into a highly industrialized world power. And in the process they created a civilization different from all those which contributed to its making.

Some Predictions

With this in mind some predictions for the future of American society may be postulated, remembering, of course, that the historian can only posit the future on the basis of known trends. This does not mean that tendencies cannot be reversed or altered, however, for they are created by human beings and controllable by human beings if foresight and wisdom prevail.

Population Growth

The United States is not now overpopulated, and it will not be overpopulated in the year 2000, even with estimates of a population of 325 million compared to the 200 million plus in 1967. There are already areas of dense population, but the major portion of the nation's land mass is actually quite sparsely settled. The whole concept of population is relative to begin with. When the fact is considered that the federal government still pays many farmers *not* to produce foodstuffs and the nation still witnesses commodity surpluses, one need hardly worry about a national population problem in the immediate future, at least in the area of available food and space.

The old Malthusian concept of population increase, however, still carries considerable weight, and it illuminates some serious problems in countries such as India and China. Many sociologists contend that one of the best ways of limiting family size is to raise the standard of living. For confirmation they look to American society, and there find that mobile and prosperous people generally prefer to have fewer children and educate them as well as possible. The new technology plays a role here along with new steps taken by governmental agencies. Contraceptive techniques and devices are well known to most people, and most religious groups are beginning to accept them. Besides, government has begun dispensing them to the economically less fortunate. The American population will continue to increase but at a lesser rate of growth. And immigration will continue to be greatly restricted as the 1965 Immigration Act indicates.

The amalgamation of Americans into something unique will obviously continue. In the past it has been mainly an ethnic amalgamation, but there have been some examples of racial amalgamation. In view of civil rights progress, a better general educational level, and recent court rulings against anti-miscegenation laws, the amalgamation of the future will increasingly be along racial lines. This does not apply to the contemporary generation so much, or necessarily to the next one, but it appears to be a long-range development in American society.

The Rising Megalopolis

American life will become continually more urbanized. And urban centers will take on a different atmosphere. The trend is already clearly present in the direction of planned communities within larger communities. The tendency is away from the traditional home unit and in the direction of apartment complexes and condominium units. Instead of spreading horizontally, the urban areas will expand vertically. But even so, cities which are now twenty or even fifty miles apart will merge into one large unit. It is within the realm of

human reason that there will be three or four megalopolises (giant city areas covering hundreds of square miles) lying in parallel north–south ranges across the nation.

Difficulties of Movement

In the realm of applied technology a serious lag has developed in the area of transportation. The huge difficulties associated with mass travel are reaching major proportions. The public is pleased to hear reports that major cities on opposite sides of the country are only three hours apart —until they make the trip. An additional two hours is usually spent in taking off and landing at already overcrowded airports, and several hours more are spent driving to and from the airports.

Perhaps some day in the not too distant future, people will again be born, live, and die in the same immediate area. But they would not necessarily be isolated from the rest of the world. In fact they might be better informed by staying in the home of the year 2000 than people are in the contemporary era by journeying all over the world; the electronic media help remove the need for travel.

It is exceedingly difficult to ascertain what the world of the future will be like. However, think for a moment how the world has changed just in the past fifty years: electricity, radio, television, aircraft, jets, rockets, atomic power, etc. And what does the future have in store? It will be more complex, more demanding. Perhaps it will also be more interesting, challenging, and rewarding.

For Further Reading

Adamic, Louis. *A Nation of Nations*. New York: Harpers, 1945.

Baker, Gorden E. *Rural versus Urban Political Power: The Nature and Consequences of Unbalanced Representation*. Garden City: Doubleday and Company, 1955.

Divine, Robert A. *American Immigration Policy, 1924–1952*. New Haven: Yale University Press, 1957.

Fishel, Leslie H., Jr., and Quarles, Benjamin. *The Negro American: A Documentary History*. Glenview, Illinois: Scott Foresman, 1967.

Handlin, Oscar (ed.). *Immigration as a Factor in American History*. Englewood Cliffs: Prentice-Hall, 1959.

————. *The Uprooted*. Boston: Little, Brown, 1951.

Kraus, Michael. *Immigration, the American Mosaic*. Princeton: D. Van Nostrand, 1966.

Stephenson, George M. *History of American Immigration, 1820–1924*. Chicago: Ginn and Company, 1926.

Wittke, Carl. *We Who Built America*. New York: Prentice-Hall, 1940.

Wood, Robert C. *Suburbia: Its People and Their Politics*. Boston: Houghton Mifflin, 1959.

Chapter Two
Territorial Expansion

Seldom in the history of man has a nation been able to embark upon a vast expansionistic program, consolidate its gains, and display evidence of territorial stability immediately afterwards. The United States is the only nation to do so in the modern western world.

The fact that the United States began as a tiny settlement on the coast of Virginia in 1607, and then proceeded to populate most of the temperate zone of the North American continent, survive internal attempts at disunification, and wind up possessing territories the world over, is a phenomenal one. Expansion is thus an integral part of American history; it has always taken place.

By a series of giant strides the American people first settled the Atlantic seaboard, then the Mississippi Valley, purchased the vast Louisiana Territory, fought an expansionistic war with Mexico, while negotiating with Great Britain for other continental territories, and added more territory near the opening of the twentieth century. The American nation has been accustomed to geographical expansion. When America reached the continental limits she embarked upon a brief period of overseas imperialism. There are still strong indications that the frontier impetus has not yet run its course, but has simply taken on a new form.

John F. Kennedy capitalized on America's penchant for expansionism when he developed his "New Frontiers" legislative program in 1960. Today it appears that the excitement and romance of the wagon train, of frontier rabble armies grabbing bits and pieces of land, of the various Indian wars, and of the Rough Riders, is being replaced by a new, more sophisticated form of expansionism —into the frontier of space.

This chapter proposes to consider two themes. First of all, it will survey historically the territorial expansionism of the United States. Secondly, it will raise the question as to whether the United States can maintain her internal stability in an

29

age when further territorial expansion, as it has been traditionally viewed, appears to be a waning phenomenon.

The problem is a simple one and it is partially a social problem. For centuries the United States possessed a contiguous, unsettled area where the "mavericks" of civilization could exhaust their excess energy. Those individuals who felt themselves restricted by society had (or felt they had) an opportunity to leave it, and the very type of behavior which might have hampered them in civilized areas, often made them successful on the frontier.

The United States has always had an area where excess steam could be blown off. That area to a large degree no longer exists. True, the frontier of space is a new, exciting, and challenging frontier, but it is not available for anyone who wants to move to it. Rather, it is limited to highly skilled, carefully selected individuals. The average American no longer has a frontier in the nineteenth-century sense. Can he make the adjustment to this new situation without sacrificing some of the dynamism which seemed to be a product of the geographical frontier?

The Expansion of Europe

The story of American expansionism finds its beginnings in late medieval Europe. Passing through the feudal age Europe was essentially a closed entity. But under the leadership of the Italian city-states Europe underwent a period of commercial expansion from about the eleventh century onward. The age of the Crusades and the concomitant planting of European colonies in the Near East over the following two centuries, greatly stimulated further expansion. Additionally, some practical experience in colonization was attained.

As time went on Europeans began to trade more with the Near East. At first they bought eastern goods through Near Eastern middlemen. The Italian city-states, because of their favored geographical position in the Mediterranean, became quite prosperous in the process. It did not take long before other regions of Europe became jealous of Italian wealth, and they began to seek out their own direct routes to the Far East, hoping to cut off both the Near Eastern and Italian middlemen.

The Portuguese, led by Prince Henry the Navigator (1394–1460), yearly pushed further down the African coast, searching for access to the Far East by water. It was a slow process, for all sorts of evil spirits and monsters were reputed to inhabit those unknown waters. But eventually, the Portuguese seaman, Bartholomew Diaz, reached the tip of southern Africa in 1487. And finally, in 1498, Vasco da Gama reached the Far East via the southern tip of the African continent.

The Spanish Empire

While Portugal was making this great progress, however, Spain was not idly sitting by. The joint rulers, Ferdinand and Isabella, had great plans for their newly united nation. An Italian navigator, Christopher Columbus, convinced the Spanish government that the Far East might easily be reached by sailing west (most educated Europeans believed the world was round but greatly underestimated its size). In 1492 Columbus reached the Bahamas, and visited Cuba and Haiti. Convinced that he had landed somewhere in Asia, Columbus called the inhabitants "Indians," after what he thought was the Indian Ocean (which was actually the Caribbean Sea). Columbus made three more voyages to the New World, and when he died in 1506, he was still convinced that he had reached the Far East.

An Expedition Leaves Lisbon for America (Print, 1592)

Other expeditions, however, revealed that the newly discovered land was not Asia. Most navigators, still intent on reaching the fabled East, remained convinced that an opening in the American land mass existed, which would enable them to sail on to their dream. In 1519 an expedition under the leadership of Ferdinand Magellan, seeking such a route, circumnavigated the globe; the voyage required three years to complete. Nonetheless, Magellan's voyage under Spanish auspices did reveal the vastness of the South American continent, thereby aiding the advance of geographical knowledge.

Other explorers, instead of looking for shorter routes to the East, preferred to explore the New World. Hernando Cortes discovered and conquered the wealthy Aztecs of Mexico in 1519. Other conquistadores sought more Indian wealth, but only one was successful. Juan Pizarro, in 1531, conquered the silver-rich Incas of Peru. Subsequently, Spain began to construct numerous colonies in Central and South America, and to some degree in North America. In time her New World colonies made Spain the wealthiest nation in Europe.

The English Challenge

Spain and Portugal, with the assistance of Pope Alexander VI, had divided the new discoveries between themselves in 1493, before they were fully aware of the extent or actual location of what they had discovered. This arrangement between Catholic powers greatly disturbed such seafaring nations as England, who proceeded to ignore it, especially after the Protestant Reformation which began in the early sixteenth century. During the course of the sixteenth century, English seamen of the caliber of John Hawkins, Francis Drake, and Thomas Cavendish, raided and looted Spanish and Portuguese colonies and shipping. This overseas rivalry, coupled with numerous strictly European difficulties, increased the strife between England and Spain.

The ultimate result of the differences was the destruction of the Spanish Armada in 1588 by a combination of English seamanship and natural causes. The demise of the entire Spanish fleet had far-reaching repercussions. Spain was rendered defenseless; her monopoly on the New World was thereby destroyed, and other nations quickly took full advantage. France responded by founding Quebec in 1608. The Dutch sent Henry Hudson on his exploratory voyage of North America in 1609. And in 1638 the Swedes established a temporary colony on the mouth of the Delaware River. But the English were the most successful, and their successes mark the beginning of American expansionism.

The Founding of the American Colonies

The first two English colonial ventures in North America resulted in complete failure. In 1578 Sir Humphrey Gilbert was authorized by the Crown to found a colony. His first expedition was defeated by the Spaniards and his second was wrecked by a storm. Gilbert's half brother, Sir Walter Raleigh, secured a new authorization in 1584, and wasted his fortune on an ill-chosen island off the coast of Virginia.

Jamestown

In 1606 King James I granted a new charter to a group of English merchants. They subdivided into two units: the London Company and the Plymouth Company. The London Company was to establish a colony in southern Virginia, while the Plymouth Company was to plant one to the north. In the spring of 1607 the London Company founded Jamestown with 104 settlers. By fall only thirty-eight were still alive. But the colony survived, mainly through the organizational skills of Captain John Smith, and by 1624 there were some 1,200 people living in Jamestown.

During these years the colony was regarded strictly as a business enterprise, but it was not until 1616, when tobacco curing was discovered, that Virginia began to yield profits. Then the populace began to flourish, mainly through the labor of newly arriving indentured servants and slaves. In 1624 the King revoked the London Company's charter and made Virginia a royal colony, ruled directly by his designated representative. However, he allowed the colonists to keep the representative assembly which had developed during the formative years of their settlement.

The Settling of Plymouth

After Jamestown the next successful English colonial venture occurred at Plymouth, on the coast of Massachusetts. The colony was planted for religious reasons. England was then a Protestant county, but not as thoroughly Protestant as some sects desired. The Puritans for example, felt that there were too many Catholic influences in the Anglican Church and sought to reform it. The Separatists or Pilgrims agreed, but rather than attempt the reform of the existing church, they chose to establish their own. A group of these Separatists set sail for America in 1620 aboard the *Mayflower*. They had organized a trading company, sold stocks, and were financed by a group of wealthy London merchants who hoped to realize a profit from the venture. While still on their ship these Pilgrims drew up the Mayflower Compact which established their governmental system—a pure democracy for recognized church members.

These settlers had actually landed on territory within the jurisdiction of the Plymouth Company, but that company was practically defunct. By 1641 the Pilgrims had gained title to the Plymouth Company's lands and had paid off their London creditors. There they remained as an independent organization until 1691, when King William III annexed them to Massachusetts Bay Colony.

The Growth of New England

The colony of Massachusetts Bay was established by the other dissenting group, the Puritans. In 1629 a Puritan expedition under the direction of John Endicott established the town of Salem. In the following year John Winthrop led a thousand settlers into Massachusetts and established the village of Boston. As religious persecutions continued in England during the Restoration, more and more Puritans migrated to Massachusetts, until, by 1640, approximately 25,000 Puritans lived in the colony. Massachusetts suffered the usual colonial hardships

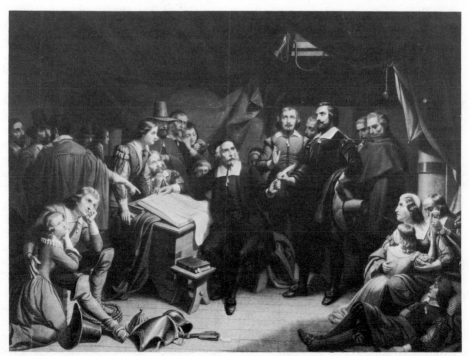

Library of Congress

Signing the Mayflower Compact

but soon developed trade with the mother country in furs, fish, and lumber.

In Massachusetts the church and state were combined; only select adult male church members possessed the right to vote. Laws were passed punishing those who deviated from the Puritan religious code. One Puritan minister, Roger Williams, claimed that the church had no right to punish a person for his personal, private opinions. When the colony banished him in 1635 as a heretic, Williams, with a scant following, founded the settlement of Providence (Rhode Island). Another Puritan, Anne Hutchinson, claimed that some ministers were better than others, thus violating a basic Calvinist doctrine, an especially serious offense for a mere woman. Her exile resulted in her founding the settlement of Portsmouth (also Rhode Island) in 1638. It should be pointed out that in a wilderness environment, banishment could be equivalent to a death sentence.

Religious intolerance had brought about the formation of Massachusetts, and a similar religious intolerance had resulted in the foundation of Rhode Island. In 1644 Parliament, through the efforts of Roger Williams, gave the Rhode Island settlers a right to govern themselves. The various settlements then united to establish a new colony. This new colony upheld freedom of conscience, and church membership was not a qualification for voting. In 1663 King Charles II granted the colony a charter which accepted the principles of representative government and freedom of conscience.

Meanwhile, another colony had developed as an offshoot of Massachusetts Bay. Settlers began pushing into the fertile Connecticut Valley as early as 1635. Three towns, including Hartford, were quickly established. In 1639 representatives from these towns designed a government common to them all. This government was embodied in the Funda-mental Orders of Connecticut, which is widely regarded as the first written constitution in America; the document used the government of Massachusetts as its model. Another colony had been established within the confines of Connecticut by newly arrived English settlers. This was New Haven, which languished in separate existence until 1662, when it was absorbed by Connecticut on the order of King Charles II.

One other colony developed in New England during the early seventeenth century. This was New Hampshire. Originally settled as a series of trading posts as early as 1623, the region was first claimed by Massachusetts Bay Colony. It was not until 1679 that King Charles II recognized New Hampshire as an independent colony.

The Proprietary Colonies—Maryland

All of the colonies which have been mentioned so far were either founded by trading companies or sprang up as offshoots of trading company colonies. The other American colonies developed through the efforts of private individuals known as proprietors. These proprietors were usually noblemen who were owed favors by their king, usually in the form of money due from private loans made to the Crown. The debts were repaid by granting large land tracts in the New World, along with full political jurisdiction over them.

The first successful proprietary colony was Maryland, founded by George Calvert, Lord Baltimore. Long interested in colonial projects he had attempted an ill-fated colonial experiment in Newfoundland in 1623. After this failure he convinced King Charles I to grant him a tract of land in a more suitable area. Calvert died in 1632 and the grant was passed on to his son, Cecilius, also known as Lord Baltimore. Cecilius owned and ruled his land completely, subject only to giving the king one-fifth of the gold and silver mined there each year.

Baltimore was a Catholic and he planned on making his colony a refuge for persecuted Catholics. But since there were not very many English Catholic immigrants, he allowed Protestants to enter his colony. Baltimore's first expedition landed in 1634, and began to flourish almost immediately. The colony recognized representative government. The Maryland colonial assembly in response to the colony's religious structure, passed the revolutionary Toleration Act of 1649. This act granted complete religious toleration to all persons believing in Christ. Non-Christians were still persecuted, but the act was a giant step in the direction of religious toleration.

The Carolinas

The king still held the region of the Carolinas in America. Settlement in North Carolina began around 1654, as settlers sought freedom from the arbitrary rule of Virginia's autocratic Governor Berkeley. The region became known as North Carolina toward the end of the seventeenth century. Meanwhile in 1663 King Charles II had granted the entire area of the Carolinas to a group of nobles who were to rule as joint proprietors. These proprietors, however, were unable to assert themselves over the North Carolina settlers.

But they were not really concerned; they were more interested in the southern part of their territories, where they planned on building up a tropical, plantation system of agriculture. So in 1670 they established the settlement of Charles-Towne. Within ten years the settlement boasted some 1,200 souls. Labor was scarce, despite the large number of indentured servants, so the importation of African slaves progressively increased

with each passing year. The Carolinas grew rapidly and the beginning of a unique economic and social pattern was soon quite evident.

New York and New Jersey

It should be pointed out that the king had originally expected the Carolinas to function as a buffer region to ward off the Spaniards to the south (then in Florida). The Spanish were considered to be a major threat to the security of English holdings in North America. But there was actually a larger threat to England at that time. The Dutch had established a colony on the banks of the Hudson River in 1612, known as New Netherlands. By 1655 this colony numbered some 10,000 people, and the presence of such a number disturbed the English. They were concerned because the Dutch were reaping enormous profits from the fur trade, holding a near monopoly on the business because of the natural advantage of residing along the river. There was also a long-standing, worldwide trade rivalry between the two nations. And finally the Dutch holdings cut the English colonies in half.

In the latter part of the seventeenth century, England and the Netherlands engaged in three bloody wars. On the eve of one of them, in 1664, King Charles II sent a surprise force against New Netherlands, and the totally unprepared Dutch had no choice but to surrender peacefully. The region was granted as a proprietary colony to the King's brother, the Duke of York, who renamed the colony New York. He proceeded to rule the colony with a minimum of political freedom.

The Duke of York subsequently granted part of his holdings to two noblemen who established the colony of New Jersey in 1665. In 1674 one of these two proprietors sold his interest to two Quakers. The colony thus split into East

New Jersey and West New Jersey, and remained in that condition until 1702, when the two parts were reunited under the rule of the king as a royal colony. By that time the combined New Jerseys had a population of 15,000.

Pennsylvania

A young Quaker nobleman named William Penn, who had been associated with the colony of West New Jersey, aspired to found his own colony. It so happened that King Charles II owed him 16,000 pounds, and to cancel this debt the King granted to Penn the territory which became known as the colony of Pennsylvania in 1681. Penn established a very liberal government for his colony and granted religious toleration to all people who accepted the idea of one eternal god.

The colony thus possessed a great deal of appeal for the religiously persecuted of Europe. Consequently, German Lutherans, German Catholics, French and Dutch Huguenots (followers of Calvin), some Anglicans, plus a sprinkling of religious dissidents from practically every European nation settled in Pennsylvania. Within a period of eight years Pennsylvania had a population of 12,000 and soon became the most densely settled and ethnically diversified colony in America. Philadelphia, the capital of Pennsylvania, was the most populated city in the New World, and as a result became the first capital of the United States. A small segment of the inhabitants of Pennsylvania successfully petitioned Penn for autonomous status; and thereby established the colony of Delaware in 1701.

Founding Georgia

There remains only one English colony in North America to discuss. This is the colony of Georgia, the brainchild of James Oglethorpe, a member of the House of Commons. Oglethorpe had two purposes in founding the colony: military and humanitarian. Georgia was a region which was unofficially claimed by both England and Spain. Oglethorpe hoped to preempt the region and erect a powerful border state next to the Spanish holdings in Florida. He also hoped to populate his colony with people who, under existing English law, would have been sent to prison for exceedingly minor infractions, such as not paying a debt on time or "borrowing" a loaf of bread to feed a starving family.

Oglethorpe received his grant from King George II in 1732, and in the following year he founded Savannah with 100 settlers. But the colony did not develop very rapidly. It cost a large amount of money to transport the unfortunates of England to Georgia, and although private individuals and various humanitarian groups contributed toward this end, as well as Oglethorpe himself, the English government refused to become involved. Consequently, by 1760, Georgia counted a free population of approximately 6,000, plus about 3,000 African slaves.

These were not the only colonies founded by the English in the New World. In 1614 the Bermuda Islands became an English colony; in 1627 the British West Indies were added; in 1655 Jamaica came under the Union Jack, not to mention numerous other outposts in Central America and Canada.

By around 1760 the future United States consisted of a chain of settlements clustered along the Atlantic seaboard, stretching from Georgia to New Hampshire. Isolated settlements and individuals could be found in and beyond the Appalachian Mountains, but for all practical purposes these mountains marked the extent of expansion. However, American territory was destined to expand considerably as a result of the Revolutionary War.

Daniel Boone Leading Settlers into the West (1775)

The Movement toward Established National Boundaries

Foreign Intrigue

After the Battle of Saratoga in October, 1777, France agreed to enter the Revolutionary War as an ally of the United States against England. Under the terms of the Family Compact of 1761 France and Spain had combined their mutual destinies in foreign policy matters. But Spain did not desire to become an ally of the United States, even though she sought the downfall of England, because such action might create a bad example for her own American colonies. Nonetheless, France succeeded in coaxing Spain into the war, although not as an ally of the United States. To do so the French promised not to sign a peace treaty until Spain had recaptured Gibraltar. The Americans were unaware of this arrangement, though they had agreed to negotiate for peace jointly with the French. This meant, of course, that the Revolutionary War could not end until Spain had acquired her territorial desires.

Meanwhile the war had been going quite badly for the English. Holland was also fighting, and the Armed Neutrality of the North—an alliance of practically all continental European powers—threatened to declare war on England if she did not alter her high-handed practices on the seas. These additional problems, coupled with their defeat at the Battle of Yorktown in 1782, convinced the English to surrender. The English believed at this point that the American colonies might be reacquired at a later date.

Thus peace negotiations opened in

1782. Spain had been unsuccessful in acquiring Gibraltar, so France promised the trans-Appalachian American West as a substitute. One of the American negotiators, John Jay, heard of this secret arrangement, and the United States regarded France's machinations as justification for opening separate negotiations with the British. Jay, Ben Franklin, and John Adams negotiated the Treaty of Paris, 1783, with the British.

The Yazoo Strip

Boundary settlements in the peace treaty provided some problems for the United States which would not be definitively solved until the 1840's. England and the United States agreed that the Atlantic Ocean and the Mississippi River would form the eastern and western boundaries of the United States. The southern boundary provided a major point of contention. England and Spain

were still at war and consequently, the fate of Florida was not decided. It was agreed that if Spain emerged from the war in possession of Florida, the southern boundary of the United States would be the 31st parallel, but if England owned Florida after the war, the southern boundary would be about 100 miles farther north. (Florida at the time stretched to the Mississippi River.) The area in between, known as the Yazoo Strip, was destined to provide a major dispute with Spain, for Spain owned Florida after the war and pressed for as much territory as possible at the expense of the weak United States. The northern boundary line was left open for discussion and negotiation at a future date. One of the usual premises in the definition of a nation is that it possesses definite geographical boundaries, but such was not the case with the American nation in 1783.

Despite the absence of a well defined northern boundary, the United States pro-

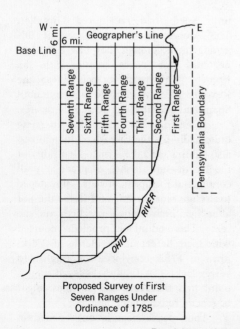

Proposed Survey of First
Seven Ranges Under
Ordinance of 1785

A Township as Numbered
Under Ordinance of 1785

Provisions of the Ordinance of 1785

ceeded to pass the Northwest Ordinance of 1787, which provided procedures for making new states in this undefined area. At the time British troops manned forts scattered throughout much of the region. However, while the United States was busy developing her political stability and strength, many of her citizens were settling the newly acquired western lands.

Under the Articles of Confederation, the government had succeeded in acquiring title to the western lands of the various states which had claimed overlapping territories stretching to the Mississippi River. Technically, the national government was now the sole owner of the public domain, but the initial problem of overlapping claims continued to present itself in a slightly different form.

The Gallipolis Affair

Several private land companies had petitioned Congress to purchase tracts of land beyond the area of settlement, to survey (as authorized in the Ordinance of 1785), and to buy them at below minimum price. Congress usually acquiesced to such demands for two reasons: either it direly needed the money from the land sales to run the government, or individual congressmen were shareholders in the land companies and hoped to realize a huge profit.

One such company was the Scioto Land Company, which held options on western lands, but which did not have the monies to exercise its option. To obtain funds the company decided to sell shares and believed that its marketing chances were much better in Europe than in America. The European agent of the company was the American poet, Joel Barlow, who was quickly taken in by a Frenchman named Playfair. The latter convinced Barlow that he could sell stocks more readily than a foreigner. But Playfair was a rogue and sold not shares in a land company, but actual parcels of land in a

non-existent gleaming white city in the American wilderness—Gallipolis, the City of the French.

Soon, some 600 French settlers set out for their newly purchased homes. When the Scioto officials heard of this they panicked. Hastily borrowing all available funds, they constructed a crude log city and went bankrupt. The disillusioned settlers were given lands by a sympathetic Congress. And Playfair absconded with all the funds. This is a fairly typical story of settlement on the American frontier. Speculators usually obtained land before the settlers could reach it, drove the prices upwards amid fraud and corruption, and proceeded to "take" the settlers as they arrived. These people were often sold non-existent lands, or they were sold a parcel of land which was being sold to dozens of other people. This particular type of land problem was never really solved. It existed as long as the American frontier existed, and is still evidenced by the swamp and desert "vacation home" peddler of the twentieth century.

Jay's and Pinckney's Treaties

The United States made two moves in the direction of solidifying and adding to her boundaries in the mid-1790's. The government paved the way for the eventual realization of a northern boundary by negotiating Jay's Treaty of 1795 with England. The English agreed to evacuate the Northwest forts and kept their promise in 1796. Their main reason for leaving was that the fur trade was beginning to die out in the region and they had hardly any other use for it. The two countries also agreed that a boundary commission would settle the dispute over the northern boundary of Maine (destined to be in heated dispute for some time).

As a result of this treaty with England, Spain was anxious to be friendly with the United States. It was not in

Spain's best interest to see a rapprochement develop between England and the former British colonies. The resultant Treaty of San Lorenzo of 1795, known also as Pinckney's Treaty, was highly favorable toward the United States. Spain gave up all of the disputed Yazoo Strip, even though she had recently claimed that Florida reached as far north as the Ohio River. She also recognized American rights to navigate the Mississippi River freely, thereby giving Americans an avenue of trade, settlement, and exploration. Finally, Spain allowed Americans to have port rights at the mouth of the Mississippi for renewable three-year periods. This latter provision greatly stimulated settlement in the Old Southwest (the general vicinity of Kentucky).

Land Deals, Land Frauds, and War

During Thomas Jefferson's first presidential administration the United States made one of its largest non-military, territorial acquisitions: the Louisiana Purchase of 1803. In 1800 Napoleon had secretly acquired title to the Louisiana Territory from Spain by means of the Treaty of San Ildefonso. In 1801 the United States acquired knowledge of this transfer. Napoleon had probably planned on using the region as a grainery for his European armies. Once victorious in Europe, he would rebuild a French empire in the New World.

Late in 1802 the American right of deposit at New Orleans was withdrawn, and the West clamored for action. Jefferson did not desire a war which would put his country on the same side as England. So he sent Robert Livingston and James Monroe to negotiate with Napoleon for the purchase of the Isle of New Orleans—a tiny triangle of land at the mouth of the Mississippi River, which would presumably have solved the problem of western port facilities. The emissaries were authorized to pay up to $10 million if they could also obtain title to West Florida.

The Louisiana Purchase

In the meantime Napoleon's ventures in neighboring Santo Domingo were failing miserably; he lost 20,000 troops in a single campaign against the ex-slave Toussaint l'Ouverture. His problems were compounded by the fact that a new war was threatening to break out in Europe. And he realized that in such an eventuality, the English Navy would easily seize his New World possessions. Therefore, Napoleon offered the entire Louisiana Territory to the United States for the paltry sum of $15 million. Monroe and Livingston were astounded; they had no authority to agree to such an offer, but their ability to recognize a good bargain overcame any reluctance and they accepted the offer. Napoleon wanted money with which to finance his European military ventures, and may have planned on retaking the region once he was victorious in Europe. The offer did not include Florida, and one-fourth of the sum was payment for American debts owed to France.

Jefferson did not believe that he possessed the constitutional power to purchase the region; but he was able to bypass his doubts in consideration of popular sentiment and the undeniably attractive deal. The Louisiana Territory comprises one-third of the contiguous continental United States and cost the nation 1¼¢ per acre. The purchase doubled the size of the United States and forever solved the Mississippi navigation issue.

The President soon sent Lewis and Clark on their historic expedition (1804–1806) to explore the newly acquired region. Lewis and Clark made the first in a long series of western exploratory ventures; other expeditions were led by such men as Dunbar, Hunter, Pike (who humbly named a certain mountain after himself), and Long. The latter explorer was largely responsible for the credibility given to the myth of the "Great American Desert." Rather than carry through on one of his expeditions, he stopped when he came to a large barren area. Returning to the East he claimed that the American West was one vast desert, unfit for human habitation. His description, which was accepted for over two decades, considerably slowed down trans-Mississippi expansion.

Yazoo Land Fraud

The land fraud issue was very much alive during the Jeffersonian period. In 1789 and again in 1794 the Georgia legislature had sold large portions of the Yazoo Strip to private land companies. In 1794 the Georgia Yazoo Land Company, which consisted of every member of the Georgia legislature except one, bought a huge tract of land with worthless paper money left over from the Revolutionary War. The incident was known as the Yazoo Land Act, and was a case of complete fraud. The legislators bought land at 1½¢ per acre and later sold it at 16¢ per acre.

The fraud was exposed in 1796 and a new Georgia legislature pledged itself to repeal the Yazoo Land Act. But there were several complications. Georgia, North Carolina, South Carolina, and Virginia all claimed parts of the Yazoo Strip. Also, many individuals owned small tracts of land which they had purchased from various land companies. In several cases different land companies had sold the same parcel of land to their respective customers. The result was a legal maze. In an effort to solve the issue, Georgia

formally declared that she owned the entire Yazoo Strip. This caused a wave of protest from the other claimant states.

President Jefferson appointed a three-man commission to negotiate with a committee from Georgia. The end result was a six-point plan in which the federal government took over the entire Yazoo Strip, agreed to buy out all Indian claims, and to pay Georgia $1.25 million for Yazoo land sales. Five million acres were set aside to take care of fraudulent claims. The modern western boundary of Georgia was established, and it was further agreed that Alabama would soon enter the Union as a slave state.

The Yazoo issue was not finally settled until 1810, during the presidency of James Madison. In the Supreme Court case, *Fletcher* v. *Peck,* the main issue was over the legality of the Georgia Repeal Act of 1796. The Court ruled that a land grant is a contract and therefore irrevocable, any fraudulency notwithstanding. The Georgia Repeal Act was declared unconstitutional as an impairment of the inviolability of contract. Significantly, the decision meant that grants by state legislatures to private companies were actually contracts. The ruling set the stage for nineteenth-century business interests to hide behind the federal contract clause, and also supported the concept of laissez-faire (see Chapter Five).

War Spirit in the West

While the Supreme Court was busying itself with the Yazoo issue, land-hungry westerners were busy adding to the national domain. Their appetite during the period prior to the War of 1812 was directed toward Florida and Canada. Interest in Florida was originally caused by a desire for more trade outlets on the Gulf of Mexico. In September, 1810, American settlers who had drifted into West Florida staged a revolt against Spain with the unofficial encouragement and support of President Madison. The rebels sought admission into the Union and Madison accepted them by presidential proclamation in October, 1810. The area comprised one-half of western Florida.

This action only stimulated the appetite of westerners who sought war, particularly with England. Such a war would provide frontiersmen with an opportunity to seize all of Spanish Florida, for Spain was an ally of England against Napoleon. War with England would lead indirectly to war with Spain. But there was an even greater western desire for Canada, primarily because of alleged Indian problems. The Indian Chief Tecumseh and his one-eyed brother, "the Prophet," were attempting to unite all tribes in the West. Disunity had been one of the greatest sources of Indian weakness. At this very time a politician and military leader named William Henry Harrison was in the West cheating Indians out of their land. Harrison employed such techniques as drunkenness, gifts, and threats in exchange for thousands of acres of Indian land. This is exactly what Tecumseh was hoping to stop.

Commencing in 1805, Tecumseh's Indian Confederation was taking definite form by 1808. However, Harrison was still defrauding the Indians, and when they fought back over the next three years, he decisively defeated them at the Battle of Tippecanoe in November, 1811. Tecumseh's project had the blessing of England, which went so far as to provide him with a few supplies, but did not grant official support. The West claimed that England was behind a movement to have the Indians massacre all Americans, for it was common knowledge that Tecumseh had visited a British fort. The West concluded that there was only one way in which to solve this problem permanently: to drive England out of Canada.

Frontier anger would not normally be taken too seriously, but by 1810 the West was acquiring political power and many westerners believed that war with England was both necessary and desirable. During the off-year congressional elections of 1810 the West and South sent some seventy "War Hawks" to Congress. Such men as Henry Clay, John C. Calhoun, and William Crawford were in their number. They did not dominate Congress, but they did capture the balance of power and succeeded in electing one of their number, Henry Clay, to the position of Speaker of the House.

Then came the national elections of 1812. Madison declared himself on the side of the War Hawks. The Peace Republicans nominated DeWitt Clinton (later of Erie Canal fame) and opposed war. New England voted solidly for Clinton; the South and West voted for Madison, and the latter won. War was practically assured.

The War of 1812

Besides emotional fervor the United States did possess some valid complaints against England—unreasonable search and seizure of ships, impressment of American seamen, and some skirmishes on the high seas. But this so-called Second War of Independence need not have been fought. American victories were few; the nation was invaded; Washington was burned. The war ended in December, 1814, with the Treaty of Ghent, which called for the *status quo ante bellum*—a return to conditions as they were before the war began. The United States did not acquire Canada or Florida in its first expansionistic endeavor.

But this nearly useless war did serve a few useful purposes. It stimulated the development of industry in New England as shipping was somewhat curtailed by the English Navy. It did result in a few American victories, notably Andrew

Jackson's success in the Battle of New Orleans, which gave the young nation a new hero. And the Treaty of Ghent did contain provisions whereby conventions would be called to deal with the points of difference between England and the United States. A commercial convention in July, 1815, ended all trade discrimination between the two nations except in the British West Indies. The Rush–Bagot Agreement of 1817 provided for an unprotected boundary between the United States and Canada which still exists. An 1818 convention recognized American rights to fishing off the coast of Newfoundland and authorized shoreline privileges in uninhabited areas. And another 1818 convention extended the Canadian–American boundary to the Rocky Mountains along the 49th parallel. Great Britain and the United States thereupon entered an era of friendship which, although strained on particular issues, still exists.

The Adams–Onis Treaty

In the year following the 1818 conventions, the United States and Spain negotiated the Adams–Onis Treaty, which provided that Spain would cede Florida to the United States. In return the United States agreed to assume all claims of Spaniards living in Florida against their government. Spain was willing to agree to such generous terms because Florida had become almost unmanageable. It was a nest of pirates, thieves, runaway slaves, and Indian renegades, and the Spanish authorities were unable to exercise any firm control. Besides, Florida was little more than a vast swampland. The Spanish Cortes (similar to the American Senate) refused to ratify the treaty, however, hoping for something else in return. But the United States unofficially let it be known that if the treaty was not ratified, the nation would seize Florida by force. This would not have been a difficult task

and Spain realized it. So the treaty was ratified in 1821 and the United States filled out her southern boundary east of the Mississippi River.

The decade which followed is not noted for territorial expansion. Rather, it was an era of consolidation as the nation attempted to bind together its growing land mass by such means as the construction of canals (see Chapter Eleven).

Difficulties and Developments:
North and South

Nor was Andrew Jackson's presidency (1828–1836) noted for expansionism. The nation was preoccupied with the extension of democratic government and with a very serious financial panic which finally struck in 1837. However, Jackson's administration witnessed a development which was destined to create a vast territorial addition to the United States. This change grew out of the American settlement in Spanish, and then Mexican, Texas, and the subsequent Texas independence movement.

The Texas Independence Movement

Texas was long a sparsely settled northern outpost of the Mexican possessions of Spain. By the beginning of the nineteenth century, American settlers were arriving at her borders. The Spaniards decided to solve two problems at once. Texas could be populated and the threat of American pressures would be relieved with one simple measure. Americans would be allowed to enter Texas and receive grants of land if they would accept Catholicism, swear allegiance to Spain, and not introduce slavery to the region. The program appeared to be quite successful on the surface. Some Americans like Sam Houston settled in Texas and took a number of other people with them. The Spanish grants were honored by the Mexicans after their independence was achieved in the early 1820's.

The program had worked because Spain and then Mexico had been lenient or unable to enforce the terms of the land grants. But in the early 1830's this changed, and Americans regarded the provisions, to which they had earlier agreed and now were expected to fulfill, as oppressive. When the Texans began their struggle for independence, the United States was far from neutral. President Jackson allowed men and supplies to cross the border freely into Mexico. What followed is a story well known, including the incident at the Alamo. By 1836 the Texans had obtained their independence from Mexico.

While all this was occurring there was a movement underway in the United States to annex the area. But the rise of the slavery issue delayed the movement, even though most Texans looked favorably on joining the Union. As a result, Texas was forced to content herself with a formal recognition of independence from the United States, on March 1, 1837. Futile annexation efforts in Congress led Texas to withdraw her annexation offer in 1838. She then concentrated on obtaining recognition of her independence in Europe, although she had been entirely unsuccessful in securing an acknowledgement of this fact from Mexico. Treaties were soon signed with France (1839), Holland and Belgium (1840), and Great Britain (1842). The United States became concerned about Texas' diplomatic relationship with Europe, especially with Great Britiain. These fears were increased in mid-1843 when Mexico and Texas arranged a truce through the good offices of France and Great Britain, and Texas informed the United States that she no longer wished to discuss annexation.

The United States was afraid that the Texas Republic might be used by a foreign power which had aggressive designs on the United States or her institutions. The difficulty was further enhanced by the continual threat from Mexico, that she would regard annexation of Texas by the United States as a deliberately unfriendly act. Texas encouraged these fears because she actually desired annexation. Rumors were spread of joint Texan–British action to bring about the abolition of slavery in the United States. This, then, was the situation in Texas on the eve of a new era.

The Webster–Ashburton Treaty

To the north other problems existed, but they were effectively and permanently solved. During John Tyler's presidency (1840–1844) the Secretary of State was the highly capable Daniel Webster, who favorably impressed the British government. The English felt that the time had come for settling some of the issues between the two countries. With this as the goal, the English sent the able Lord Ashburton as representative to the United States.

The two men negotiated the famous Webster–Ashburton Treaty of 1842. The major provisions of this treaty included the settlement of the Maine boundary dispute, with roughly 60 per cent of the territory going to Maine. This in itself was a notable achievement. Two minor boundary adjustments were also made in the Great Lakes region to correct earlier errors. The United States thus rounded out her current boundaries for the eastern two-thirds of the nation—as far west as the Rockies. (Other major provisions of the treaty are not applicable to the subject of expansion and will be considered in Chapter Fourteen.)

A Sketch of the Santa Fe Trail

The Era of Manifest Destiny

Although the United States had already expanded considerably during her brief existence, she had been building up for still another major group of territorial acquisitions for a period of roughly thirty years. The epoch of this new expansion is popularly referred to as the era of Manifest Destiny, and it lasted for the three year period of 1845–1848.

Opening the Far West

For many years most Americans displayed little interest in the Far West. After all, it was nothing but the Great American Desert. The beginning of the Santa Fe trade, in 1821–1822, under the leadership of the St. Louis merchant, William Becknell, helped destroy this myth. He noted that there was much good land along the hundred mile wide "trail" to Santa Fe. Also during the 1820's, Jedediah Smith and his Rocky Mountain Fur Trading Company took wagons overland to the Northwest to set up rendezvous points with the trappers. In the process they opened the Oregon Trail.

The so-called Oregon Territory, stretching from the northern boundary of California to the southern boundary of Alaska, was then held jointly by England and the United States. From 1824 to 1827 the two nations had negotiated unsuccessfully over a means of division. Therefore, they agreed to joint occupation with a twelve-month termination privilege for both countries. For the most part the British controlled the region. They ruled through the medium of the Hudson's Bay Company, a fur trading operation headed by the capable Dr. John McLoughlin. Most of his difficulties came from errant American trappers and missionaries.

California was then a northern province of Mexico, but Mexican control was very tenuous. First the trappers, and then an increasing number of American merchants appeared yearly, spurred on by the promise of huge profits from the hides and tallow, and the China trade business. And finally, the Texans stood ready to do business with the Pacific Coast.

The Annexation of Texas

The situation in independent Texas was the most critical of the times. President Tyler was a southerner, and when he heard repeated rumors of Texas and England combining to end slavery he felt it was time to annex the territory, the threat of war with Mexico notwithstanding. An annexation treaty was signed on April 12, 1844. It stipulated that Texas would enter the Union on equal footing with the other states, would surrender her public lands, but would also pass on her indebtedness (not to exceed $10 million) to the federal government.

Meanwhile the nominations for the general elections of 1844 had been made and the question of Texas was again critical. The Democrats nominated James Polk of Tennessee and came out strongly favoring the annexation of Texas. The Whigs and their candidate, Henry Clay, evaded the question, but the annexation of Texas became a bitter partisan issue because of the slavery expansion argument and the possibility of war with Mexico. The fact that the annexation treaty failed to win approval in Congress helped make it the critical issue in the presidential campaign. Realizing that Texas annexation was popular only in the South, the Democrats sought to make their platform appeal to the North by coming out in favor of occupying the entire Oregon Territory as well.

Polk defeated Clay by a narrow margin, and the Democrats managed to win control of both houses of Congress. President Tyler was still in office as a Lame Duck president. Recognizing the American expansionistic temper and also desiring to add to the pro-slavery Congressional contingent, he hoped to salvage an undistinguished administration by obtaining credit for the annexation of Texas. A treaty with Texas would require a two-thirds majority vote of approval by the Senate, and this would be extremely difficult to obtain, even though Congress, by joint resolution, had already asked the President to renew his negotiations with Texas. Thus, annexation by joint resolution seemed to be the answer; this procedure would only require a simple majority of both houses. Tyler succeeded in pushing his plan through Congress, though the Senate vote was only 27–25 in favor, a minimal margin of victory. The House vote was better, 120–98.

According to the terms of annexation the Lone Star Republic would become a state with a constitution acceptable to Congress. She agreed to a potential subdivision into as many as five states (this would have meant ten slave-state senators instead of two). She would pay her own revolutionary war debt, retain her own public lands, and have slavery protected by the terms of the Missouri Compromise of 1821 (which stipulated that all states carved out of territory south of 36° 30′ north latitude would be slave, while those to the north would be free). The joint resolution was approved and signed by President Tyler three days before he left office. Texas did not officially become a state, however, until December 29, 1845. By this time President Polk was in office, and he had the opportunity to recommend Texas for admission to statehood. Tyler had initiated the measure but he simply did not have enough time left to put it into practice.

War with Mexico

Polk took office with practically half of his territorial program already realized. Mexico had immediately protested the annexation of Texas and broke off diplomatic relations with the United States. But although there had been threats of war over this issue, war was not declared. Actually, war with Mexico arose from a number of different factors, with the Texas situation acting simply as a catalyst. For one thing, the weak Mexican government had repeatedly failed to protect American citizens residing within her borders. For another, very poor trade relations existed between the two countries. And finally, there existed many unpaid claims for damages owed to American citizens by the Mexican government.

But the most significant difficulty of all between the two nations pertained to the southern boundary of Texas. From the days when she was a Mexican province, the southern boundary of Texas had been the Nueces River. But the Texas Republic, backed by the power of the United States, had claimed the Rio Grande as her boundary. President Polk erroneously accepted this Texan claim and ordered General Zachery Taylor to occupy the disputed territory. Apparently Polk came to realize that his position was unsound, because he sent his agent, John Slidell, to Mexico to negotiate for the *purchase* of the disputed region, and also to attempt the purchase of California and the New Mexican territory as well. But the Mexican government, with some justification, refused to treat with Slidell.

With two major armies facing each other in the disputed region it was simply a matter of time before the situation exploded. Skirmishes occurred between the opposing armies, and Polk went before Congress on May 11, 1846, to state that Mexico had invaded American territory, had shed American blood on American soil, and had begun an aggressive war against the United States. At best this was a deliberate falsification. Actually Polk was attempting to justify an already predetermined course of action. Both houses of Congress overwhelmingly endorsed war, but public opinion throughout the country remained divided. This was the occasion, for example, of Henry Thoreau's celebrated refusal to pay his taxes (to support a war of slave expansion).

Mexico had thought that she would win easily, but the United States won every major battle. Even the Mexican capital was captured and some enthusiastic Americans began talking about pushing on to Central America and annexing all of Mexico. It might be pointed out that throughout the nineteenth century there were some people who believed that the United States was destined to embrace the entire North American continent.

The war ended in 1848 with the Treaty of Guadalupe Hidalgo. It is a rather curious treaty because the minister who negotiated it, Nicholas Trist, had been deprived of all authority and ordered to return to the United States by President Polk. But Polk chose to accept the treaty (though he fired Trist) in view of mounting Whig opposition to the war. According to the treaty terms, Mexico recognized the Rio Grande boundary, and ceded California and the New Mexican territory (Nevada, Arizona, New Mexico, and parts of Utah and Colorado) to the United States. In return for such a generous land cession, the United States paid Mexico $15 million. Furthermore, the United States assumed all of the claims of American citizens against the Mexican government, amounting to approximately $3.2 million. The amount of territory acquired in this war constituted one of the largest military land acquisitions ever.

The Oregon Annexation

While the United States was involved militarily with Mexico, she was involved diplomatically with England over the Oregon Territory. The region did not yet seem valuable to most Americans. Geographically, it was partially separated from the rest of the United States by mountain barriers. But a man named Dr. John Floyd had travelled through the region extensively during the 1820's and had begun a "know Oregon" campaign. Already familiar to many fur trappers, the Oregon country soon became a center of missionary activity for such notables as Jason Lee, Marcus Whitman, and Fathers DeSmet and Blanchet.

In 1841 American immigrants began entering the rich farm land of the Willamette Valley. The settlement of these people provided a strong reason for deciding the issue between England and the United States. Finally, in May, 1843, American settlers in Oregon established their own provisional government in keeping with the tradition of the Mayflower Compact. This, coupled with the increased general knowledge of the region, resulted in popular agitation for its possession. Negotiations had been going on for some twenty years, but England had been unwilling to effect a settlement as long as tremendous profits could be realized from the fur trade. Besides, during most of this period, the United States did not really press for a settlement.

But by the mid 1840's the situation had changed for both nations. The fur trade was dying in the Oregon country and England shifted the Hudson's Bay Company operations to Vancouver's Island and centered on the otter and seal industry. At the same time a growing American colony in Oregon was bringing pressure on the government in Washington to settle the issue. On her part England was ready to settle; she had apparently never really thought in terms of permanent colonization.

Polk had been elected partly on a militant "reoccupation of Oregon" platform. One of the popular slogans of the day was "Fifty-four forty or fight!" meaning that the United States should demand the entire Oregon country (up to 54°40′ longitude) and go to war if necessary to obtain it. The President followed through on this threat, or bluff as many historians consider it, in his First Annual Message to Congress. He called for an end to joint occupation and asserted American claims to the entire region. Congress, despite gathering war clouds with Mexico, and fully recognizing the possibility of serious trouble with Great Britain, gave its permission and Polk promptly notified England on May 21, 1846, that joint occupation would be terminated within a year.

Meanwhile negotiations had resumed between the two nations and Polk mellowed considerably when war with Mexico commenced. In June, Great Britain offered to extend the 49th parallel to the sea, exclusive of Vancouver's Island. This would give the United States a little over half of the disputed territory, including the much desired Columbia River basin. Polk sent the offer to the Senate for consideration. The Senate recommended acceptance, and the treaty was formally ratified on July 17, 1846.

By diplomacy the United States had added territories which would eventually make up the states of Washington and Oregon, most of Idaho, and part of Montana. But the peaceful settlement was enacted mainly through a realistic British appraisal of the situation, coupled with a decline in the fur trade in Oregon.

The Settlement at Salt Lake

Another expansionist movement of the 1840's deserves mention. The Church of Jesus Christ of the Latter-Day Saints, founded by Joseph Smith in 1828 in Palmyra, New York, had been gradually moving westward. The Mormons' ideas and practices concerning a theocratic state, communal living, and eventually polygamy, caused them no end of grief. An outraged populace forced them from New York to Ohio, then to Missouri, and back to Illinois, where Smith was hanged by a lynch mob. Brigham Young, their new, practical-minded leader, believed that the only manner by which the Mormons could continue their religion was to move away from civilization.

In 1847 the Mormons began settling around the Great Salt Lake in the northernmost reaches of Mexican territory. Since they cooperated with each other fully, the Mormons were not plagued by many of the problems which most frontier communities experienced. Advanced units set up aid stations along the route to the Salt Lake in preparation for the main migratory body. Cooperation in the utilization of water for irrigation further aided the settlement. The new Mormon settlement provided a convenient half-way rest-and-supply point for the Forty-niners.

The Forty-niners were those thousands of Americans who poured into California in 1849 because of the discovery of gold late in the preceeding year. They brought much wealth to the Mormon community, and they turned a California consisting of isolated, sleepy missions and villages into a thriving, swelling mass of humanity almost overnight.

The decade of the Forties was an era of tremendous territorial growth for the United States. It began with the settlement of the Maine boundary dispute in 1842, and ended with the signing of the Treaty of Guadalupe Hidalgo in 1848. By the end of the decade the United States had achieved, except for the Gadsden Purchase of 1853 (considered below), her present-day contiguous continental bound-aries. This was accomplished mainly in the period 1845–1848—the era of Manifest Destiny—when the nation practically doubled its territory.

Interest in Cuba

Americans, however, did not completely give up the idea of further territorial expansion at the end of the decade. A number of people still expressed interest in acquiring Canada, but with the recent northern boundary settlements and a consolidating Canadian government, this hope was rapidly fading. Likewise to the south there was also a continuing expansionist sentiment. Of particular interest was the island of Cuba. Southern desire for a slave Cuba, during the presidency of Franklin Pierce in the 1850's, helped to increase the tension between North and South which eventually erupted in civil conflict. With the rise in sectional antipathy, American desires for further territorial acquisitions languished until after the Civil War.

Developing the Trans-Mississippi West

The acquisition of such a vast land mass led many Americans to seek some means of transportation to help bind the nation together. A sure solution would be the building of a transcontinental railroad. With this in mind Congress authorized the sending of a survey team through the West to seek out favorable routes for a transcontinental railroad. The survey team reported back that there were four possible routes, but the extreme southern route would have to pass through a small piece of Mexican territory. So in 1853 the United States purchased this tiny triangle of land from Mexico, making possible the fourth railroad route. The transaction is known as the Gadsden Purchase.

Expanding into the Trans-Mississippi West: Crossing the
Eads Bridge at St. Louis, 1874

Expansionism means more than just acquiring a vast territory—especially one which was essentially unsettled. Americans had to populate and develop this new area, and transportation was a crucial factor. In the eastern part of the country the sea and many rivers had long served the purposes of communication and transport, and turnpikes and canals were added in the early decades of the century. There, also, the Indians had posed no serious threat to expansion since there existed an area into which they could retreat or be pushed. But the settlement and development of the Manifest Destiny territories presented different problems to the youthful American nation.

Plains Indian Problems

The post–Civil War West possessed two major problems: Indians and transportation. Americans quickly learned that the Plains Indian was much more adept and much better equipped than his eastern brother. He would fight fiercely to protect his traditional tribal lands. White gold-seekers, farmers, and cattlemen were in constant trouble with the Plains Indians. Many of these incidents took place in the Montana region, home of Chief Red Cloud and part of the Sioux nation, and site of the Black Hills gold country. Red Cloud successfully thwarted the American Calvary and forced the government by treaty to abandon its forts in Indian country. A decade later it was again the Sioux, led by Sitting Bull and Crazy Horse, who were responsible for Custer's Last Stand (1876). To the south the Apache leader Geronimo fought for a dozen years to maintain his tribal lands in the New Mexico region.

It was not until 1890 that the western tribes were finally subdued and herded upon reservations. Even then the Indian had not been defeated militarily. Food, clothing, and shelter for the Plains Indian came primarily from the buffalo; no part of the animal was wasted. In 1870 it is estimated that there were approximately 7 million buffalo roaming the Great Plains. But then America entered upon a buffalo-robe fad and men like William Cody gained immortality (and some wealth) by slaughtering the stupid beasts. Only the hide was taken; the carcass was allowed to rot in the sun. Consequently, by 1883 the buffalo was practically extinct. The near disappearance of the buffalo broke

Indian resistance, and as he retreated, the dirt farmer moved in to try his luck at semi-arid agriculture.

The Sod-House Frontier

Farming on the Great Plains was an extremely difficult proposition. Transportation was a big problem but there were many others. The western farmer had no stands of timber for fencing and building, and little water. The invention of barbed wire solved his fencing problem; the sod house solved his shelter problem; buffalo chips partly solved his heating and cooking problems. Also from time to time the sod-house farmer was plagued with invasions of grasshoppers, which might cover the ground to a depth of several inches. They ate everything except the barbed wire, including the sod-house. There were even reports that emergency crews were called out to shovel grasshoppers off the warm rails of the Union Pacific so the trains could get through.

The Cowboy Frontier

Perhaps the most colorful era of the West was the opening of the cattle country. The period of the "cowboy West" was a rather short one, lasting from the close of the Civil War to roughly 1885 when business-like, fenced-off ranches became the rule. Yet the cowboy West has managed to exert a profound influence on American culture, and judging from movies and television one might gather that the cowboy roamed the West for centuries rather than a few decades.

Meat on the hoof had been driven to local markets since colonial days, usually in the form of droves of swine. Louisville, Cincinnati, Chicago, and St. Louis had all developed as meat packing centers before the Civil War. But their meat came from immediately adjacent areas and was intended primarily for local use. No one planned the raising of meat on the Great Plains for national markets. It happened by accident, after it was discovered near the end of the Civil War that Texas longhorn cattle could survive the bitter winter conditions of the Great Plains without special housing and feed. This discovery coincided with the time when the Union Pacific railroad was pushing across the continent. Also during the Civil War, canned meats had made their initial appearance. At about the same time the refrigerator car was invented. With the transportation and preservation problems so readily solved, ambitious men hit upon the idea of supplying fresh beef to the growing eastern cities.

The entire Great Plains, from Mexico to Canada, and from Kansas to the Rockies, became cow country almost overnight. The new cattlemen bred (or gathered) their stock in Texas and allowed it to wander untended on the Texas plains, with a roundup and branding session every spring. Periodically, the cattle owners would select stock which was ready for market. This is where the cowboy entered the picture. Up to this point the cattle had required little attention, but when ready for market they had a high monetary value and had to be protected. The cowboy was originally an unemployed western wanderer, oftentimes one of the dispossessed veterans of the Civil War. As time went on he developed into a definite type—proud and reckless.

The main characteristic of the cowboy frontier was the Long Drive intiated by an Illinois meat dealer, Joseph McCoy, in 1867. Starting in Texas the cattle would be gently prodded northward over the Great Plains. The destination was the advancing tracks of the Union Pacific. Along this railroad various cowtowns developed, such as Dodge City and Abilene. The towns were wild, especially when the cowboys arrived after months

Destination of the "Long Drive"

on the trail. And although movies greatly romanticize these towns, there is some validity in their portrayal of constant shoot-outs and barroom brawls.

After the Long Drive, cattle were tough and sinewy. Eastern markets preferred tender meat, so the cattlemen developed grazing ranches near the rail centers, where wild Texas Longhorns were interbred with Hereford and Angus bulls, thereby producing quality table meat. Ranches expanded through Colorado and Wyoming by around 1870, and into Montana and the Dakotas before the decade ended.

Originally there was tremendous wealth in the cattle industry. Spurred on by promises of large profits, many adventurers with only a few dollars in their pockets entered the cattle business. As a result there were about 4.5 million beeves on the Great Plains by 1880, compared with an estimated 100,000 wild Texas

Longhorns at the close of the Civil War.

In the process of development the cattleman had over-expanded. He had moved vast numbers of cattle on to grasslands which were suitable only in exceptionally wet years. Also, as the range became more congested, the cattleman had to organize his holdings. This meant the hiring of more hands to protect his cattle from rustlers and the fencing of the range to preserve his claimed grassland. And as the cattleman's costs went up his profits went down.

The winter of 1885 was exceptionally cold. Cattle had survived the cold wintery blasts by drifting, rump to the wind, southward. But now they piled up on the barbed wire fences and tens of thousands were frozen or trampled to death. The survivors were greatly emaciated by spring. That summer it was exceptionally hot and dry and more cattle died. Next, the winter of 1886 was reported to be one of the coldest in American history. Losses forced many cattlemen into bankrupcy. Those cattlemen who survived became modern ranchers. They restricted both their range and their herd size. They began to grow hay to feed their cattle during winter. The cowboy became a menial laborer—digging post holes and mowing hay. The crowning blow came in the late 1880's, when sheepmen and "nesters" moved on to the Great Plains. The cattle frontier had ended.

The Mining Frontier

Another aspect of the post–Civil War West was a mining boom. The 1849 California Gold Rush, and the 1859 mining boom in Colorado were two of the biggest strikes in American history. In addition there was the Black Hills gold rush. For years prospectors had been spreading rumors that gold was to be found in the Black Hills, but the region was Sioux reservation land. Still, a number of prospectors risked discovery by the Sioux in their search for gold. This created quite a job for the Army, whose task it was to keep the prospectors out of Sioux territory. The Army felt that the best way to end its problem was to prove conclusively that gold did not exist in the Black Hills. So in 1874 General George Custer led 1,200 troops and a scientific expedition into Sioux country. The expedition proved, however, that huge quantities of gold were in fact to be found in the region.

Now it was impossible to restrain the prospectors. In 1875 15,000 gold seekers entered Sioux country. And in 1876 the mining community of Deadwood Gulch was founded. Destined to be the last of the rip-roaring western towns, there were probably more murders, brawls, dance-hall girls, and gambling, than in any other town in the history of the West. Deadwood was the dying gasp of a dying way of life, and it also produced vigilante committees and lynchings. But the old West was dead; the remaining critical western problem was transportation (see Chapter Eleven).

The Western Spirit

One of the major contributions of the American frontier, which in many areas was gone by 1890, was the development of an American cultural type. As he reached each new frontier, whether he was a fur trader or farmer, a miner or cattleman, the frontiersman was forced to abandon the ways of organized society and build anew. The basic interests of the frontiersmen were the everyday needs of life. They had not much leisure for theory; they were pragmatists. As a consequence, the frontiersman abandoned many of the class distinctions and aristocratic ways of the settled East. His frontier was almost always more democratic than the more developed region which he had just left. For instance, Wyoming was the first state to grant women the right to vote, and Oregon initiated referendum and recall elections.

The westerner also aided greatly in developing a spirit of American nationalism. Since the frontiersman originally lived beyond the effective jurisdiction of any established state, he could turn only to the federal government for aid—in internal improvements, land policy, and Indian protection. Ironically, many of those individuals who could least withstand the strictures of a highly organized society did much to create one.

The frontiersman was usually an incurable optimist. In his self-confidence, he was convinced that next year would be better than the last, and the following year even more so. His optimism permeated the nation, and until the stock market Crash of 1929, when the spirit of frontier individualism dimmed, this optimism predominated.

Post—Civil War
Expansionism

Before the close of the Civil War the United States had acquired her continental, contiguous boundaries, and she was well on her way toward settling the land within this vast area. The spirit of expansionism had not died, but it did take on a different form. The United States began the acquisition of territories around the world.

Andrew Johnson's Secretary of State, William Seward, was an ardent expansionist, who had dreams of acquiring all of Mexico and Canada. But because of the problems of Reconstruction and the preoccupation with the rise of big business, he was usually forced to concentrate on minor acquisitions which possessed something of value for the nation—small islands located strategically along trade routes.

In the Caribbean Seward negotiated a treaty of annexation with the Dominican Republic but the Senate refused to ratify it. Undaunted, Seward negotiated for the purchase of the Virgin Islands from Denmark, but the Senate also refused to ratify this treaty. At the time geographical expansion was not important to most Americans. The only island which Seward was able to acquire was Midway Island, and this by indirect means. The Navy had long been using the island as a naval base, and Seward claimed it formally on the basis of occupation.

But Seward was not entirely unsuccessful in his endeavors. He did add one very large chunk of territory: Alaska. In 1867 Alaska was owned by Russia, who considered it to be a rather worthless area and sought to avoid both the trouble and the expense of governing it. Furthermore, she believed the region contained nothing of value, except possibly gold, and if such were the case, then either the United States or Canada would take it away from

her. Therefore, Russia was looking for a buyer. At the time, Russian—American relations were quite congenial. Russia had sent her fleet on a "goodwill tour" to the United States during the American Civil War, while the United States was experiencing neutrality problems with other European countries. Russia's probable purpose was to get her fleet out of European waters where it faced potential destruction from Great Britain in a threatened war.

The Russian ambassador, De Stoeckl, offered Alaska to Seward for $7.2 million; he had been instructed to settle for as much as $2 million less. Seward, however, quickly jumped at the first offer and presented a treaty of purchase to the Senate. But the Senate was not anxious to act, claiming that Alaska was too expensive, that it was a worthless territory, and adding a host of technical objections. Seward, amid popular derision ("Seward's Folly," "Seward's Icebox") inaugurated a "know Alaska" campaign at his own personal expense. For one of the few times in his political career he played politics well, and succeeded in obtaining senatorial ratification in April, 1867. The House of Representatives delayed final action for a time by not granting the necessary appropriation, but Alaska soon passed over to the United States. This was enough foreign expansionism to satisfy most Americans. They were more concerned with the rise of big business and with internal improvements.

The Age of American
Imperialism

The 1890's witnessed a change in American attitudes which had been building up over the prior decade. After the Civil War the United States was basically isolationistic in foreign affairs. It was preoccupied with settling and developing its own territories, not with

HARRISON
reason for

acquiring new ones far removed. The frontier had provided a constant arena in which American exuberance and sense of adventure could act itself out. But by 1890 this western reserve had diminished, and American exuberance overflowed in what is known as the era of American Imperialism.

American imperialism was based on a number of factors. One was a desire to prove that the American nation had come of age as a world power. Another factor, related to the first, was a widespread desire to win military glory. Except for the Indian wars, the United States had avoided conflict since the Civil War. An entire generation had grown to manhood without having had the opportunity to experience combat. This disturbed men brought up on the romanticized stories of aging Civil War veterans. An intense and militant nationalism permeated the country.

There was a theory, one which was widely held throughout the late nineteenth century and which has not yet entirely disappeared, that Americans had a duty to spread their civilization to less privileged peoples. This was the Mission Theory, ably expounded and popularized by the historian John Fiske. Another name for it is the "white man's burden," a remarkable rationalization for taking someone else's territories. This, combined with the propaganda put out by Admiral Alfred Thayer Mahan to the effect that world possessions and seapower were essential to American security, culminated in an imperialistic surge of activity. Interest tended to concentrate on two major geographical areas: the Hawaiian Islands and Cuba.

The Annexation of Hawaii

Hawaii had been discussed by people in high governmental circles for some time. During the 1870's several treaties had been negotiated with the Hawaiians which yielded three basic provisions. Hawaii promised not to cede or sell any of her territory to a foreign power. The United States agreed to admit Hawaiian sugar duty-free to American ports. And the American Navy was granted sole use of Pearl Harbor as a fueling station. By 1880 American business interests controlled roughly two-thirds of the island chain. Businessmen had invested heavily because of the cheap labor, cheap land, and no tariff barriers. They exerted even more control over the Hawaiian government than they did at home—which is to say, a great deal.

In 1890 American sugar capitalists pushed through Congress a provision whereby they would receive a bounty on all sugar they produced at home. Thus, they would no longer be competing at a disadvantage with cheaply produced Hawaiian sugar. This obviously ended the favored position of the Hawaiian sugar capitalists, but political developments complicated the problem.

The Americans who had taken power in Hawaii were being resisted by the natives who sought higher taxes and other limitations on the Americans. In 1893 a revolution broke out. The Hawaiian ruler, believing that the United States was preparing to form a protectorate over her kingdom, abdicated. The United States did just that and within two weeks was pressing for formal annexation. Naval interests, business interests, and most expansionists favored the measure. Opposed were many Democrats (because the Republican Harrison was just ending his term and they wanted president-elect Cleveland to receive credit for annexation), and those people who were prejudiced against Hawaii's dark-skinned population.

The result was a delay in ratification of the annexation arrangement. After Cleveland was inaugurated annexation was placed further in doubt. Cleveland had proceeded to appoint a committee to investigate the Hawaiian revolution. His commission indicated that the Hawaiians did not desire American rule. Cleveland then refused to submit the treaty to the Senate. The result was a delay in annexation until 1898. In that year the Spanish–American War displayed the value of Hawaii to most Americans as a permanent naval base. The treaty was then ratified (during the McKinley administration) and the Hawaiian Islands passed over to the United States.

Revolution in Cuba

Americans had long been interested in the future of Cuba, but could never agree on a course of action because of the slavery issue. During the Civil War and for a time afterwards, Americans had taken little interest in the Caribbean island. But in 1895 an insurrection, led by Jose Marti, broke out in Cuba. The reasons for this revolt were two-fold. For one, the nation which owned the island, Spain, had not kept the promises of reform she had made at the close of the Ten Years War (an insurrection lasting from 1868 to 1878). And second, the McKinley Tariff of 1890, which had admitted Cuban sugar duty-free to the United States, was repealed by the Wilson Gorman Tariff of 1894, and a severe economic decline had settled on the island.

Marti's revolution was hardly a full-scaled rebellion. It consisted mostly of part-time insurgents who periodically looted and raided the villages and then hid out in the mountains. Spain, in violation of her customary pattern of relative inactivity, responded to this revolt with vigor. She quickly dispatched 120,000 troops to Cuba, and placed in command General "Bloody Butcher" Weyler, who was so named by a sensationalistic American press.

Weyler inaugurated the *reconcentrado* policy, a system whereby civilians were herded into certain prescribed areas while those outside were shot. He also engaged in the planned destruction of the enemy's source of supply, which just happened to be innocent villages. Both of these actions greatly stimulated American public opinion, even though General Ewing had used a *reconcentrado* technique in Kansas City in April, 1863, and General Sherman had outrivaled Weyler in the destruction of property in his famous march to the sea. But according to the elusive conventions of war, Spain was justified in this action only if she could thereby bring hostilities to a rapid termination. This she was unable to do. Countless tales of Spanish cruelty reached American ears, some real, and some fabricated by a sensationalistic "yellow press" led by Pulitzer's *New York World* and Hearst's *New York Journal*.

Finally, in 1897 Weyler was recalled and the *reconcentrado* policy was ended mainly through American protests. Spain offered limited home rule to the Cubans, but the officer conveying the message, Colonel Ruiz, was hanged by the insurgents. This flagrant act somewhat changed American opinion, and relations between Spain and the United States seemed to improve. As a gesture of goodwill, the United States sent the battleship *Maine* to Havana.

Hostilities with Spain

Circumstances soon changed. In February, 1898, the De Lome incident took place. De Lome was the Spanish minister to the United States who, in a private letter which was intercepted and published in the newspapers, referred to President McKinley as a "spineless politician." De Lome made no attempt to deny the letter, and actually had no real reason to do so, but he hurriedly resigned his post and left the country. The public ignored the fact that a private letter, reflecting an unofficial personal opinion, had been stolen. The entire affair was blamed on the Spanish government, which was accused of deliberately insulting the American presidency.

Then on February 15, 1898, the battleship *Maine* was mysteriously blown up in Havana harbor. Opinion remains divided on the actual cause of the disaster. The United States claimed that Spain was responsible. In a sense this was true, for Spain was responsible for the safety of all foreign ships in her ports. But this does not mean that she caused the explosion. Still, the De Lome incident, the *Maine* disaster, and the reports of the "yellow press," brought the United States to the brink of war. Germany, Austria, Great Britain, France, Italy, Russia, and even the Pope appealed to the United States to avoid war.

The United States insisted that Spain pull her military establishment out of Cuba and initiate solid reforms. On April 9, 1898, Spain agreed to these demands. On April 10, President

McKinley received definite notification of this concession; however, on April 11, he submitted a war message to Congress. He claimed that the United States had to go to war with Spain to defend the cause of humanity, to protect American lives and property in Cuba, to defend American commercial and financial interests in Cuba, to preserve the American system of government, and to avenge the sinking of the *Maine*. Some of McKinley's reasons were ridiculous; none of them had much basis in fact. Spain had ordered the complete cessation of all hostilities, had promised reforms, and had offered to arbitrate the *Maine* incident.

The fact was that the United States wanted a war, both for imperialistic and nationalistic reasons. The defeat of Spain would prove that the United States was a first-rate power. Therefore, by joint resolution on April 19, Congress declared that Cuba was free and independent, demanded Spain's complete withdrawal from the island, directed the President to use the

The Destruction of the Battleship *Maine*

armed forces to secure these ends, and disclaimed any intention of annexing the island (this latter point is known as the Teller Amendment). Interestingly enough, the war declaration was made retroactive to April 21. The United States had fomented an extremely one-sided war and won easily (see Chapter Thirteen).

Acquisitions from the War

Through the good offices of the French ambassador, Spain and the United States agreed to the termination of hostilities on August 12, 1898. Actual peace negotiations opened in Paris on October 1, 1898. One of the problems raised at the peace conference was Spain's desire that the United States annex Cuba and also assume the $400-million indebtedness of the island. The United States was also in a quandary over what to do with the Philippine Islands. Most Americans had never heard of them before Admiral Dewey's victory there, and the government had planned on returning them to Spain. However, to do so would probably have meant more misrule; to render them independent might have placed them at the mercy of other imperialistic powers.

Finally, a peace treaty was signed on December 10, 1898. Puerto Rico and Guam, both former Spanish possessions, were ceded to the United States. Cuba became a free and independent nation. The Philippine Islands were given to the United States, who then paid Spain $20 million for the generous cession. The treaty was one of the most hotly debated in American history. According to its terms the nation would embark on a comparatively new course and become increasingly entangled in the affairs of Europe and Asia. The period of American isolationism would be forever over. A two-thirds vote was required for treaty ratification; an indication of the controversy was the fact that the Senate ratified with only two votes to spare.

American Samoa

The United States made several other territorial acquisitions during the period 1898–1900. One was the islands of Samoa, site of Robert Louis Stevenson's writings. A treaty in 1872 had given the United States rights to a naval station there, and in 1878 the territory became a semi-protectorate. However, because of strong German and British interests in the islands, the United States agreed to a tripartite protectorate in 1889. Amid continuous squabblings the protectorate continued until the United States took a stronger course after the Spanish–American War. Then in 1899, an international agreement between the parties concerned granted the United States complete title to roughly one-half of the total island group. Also in 1899 the Navy took formal possession of Wake Island, basing the claim on prior occupancy.

During the period 1898–1900, the United States had thus acquired the territories of American Samoa, the Hawaiian Islands, the Philippine Islands, Guam, Wake Island, and Puerto Rico; Cuba had been freed but was subject to considerable American influence. Expansionism and the acquisition of territories was not yet at an end. However, the main surge of territorial acquisition was over.

Acquiring the Canal Zone

After the Spanish–American War the United States possessed territories in both major oceans. It was then deemed essential to build an isthmian canal to connect the Atlantic and Pacific fleets. The United States was bound by the terms of the Clayton–Bulwer Treaty with England, which stated that the United States could not build and maintain such a canal unilaterally. Then the two nations signed the Hay–Pauncefote Agreement of 1900 which allowed the United States to build and operate a canal exclusively, but not

to fortify it. The Senate refused to ratify the treaty because of the non-fortification clause. A second Hay–Pauncefote Treaty cleared up this point in 1901. Great Britain then withdrew her fleet from the Caribbean; it was now up to the United States to defend the Americas on her own. The diplomatic paths had been cleared for the building of an isthmian canal.

A new problem arose over where to build the canal: Panama, Nicaragua, or southern Mexico. The latter route was quickly ruled out because of the very high costs involved. McKinley had earlier sent the Walker Commission to Central America to locate usable routes. It had reported in favor of the Panamanian route, but had indicated that a defunct French construction firm, the New Panama Company, had a Colombian franchise on the region (Panama was then a part of Colombia). This company wanted $109 million for its franchise, so the Walker Commission recommended the less favorable Nicaraguan route as being the cheapest.

The House of Representatives approved this route on January 9, 1902, but then the New Panama Company cut its price to $40 million, making the Panamanian route the cheapest. Also, the French engineer, Buneau-Varilla, pointed out that an active volcano posed a potential threat to the Nicaraguan route. As a result, Congress authorized building through Panama on June 2, 1902, if an arrangement could be negotiated with Colombia.

In January, 1903, the Hay–Herran Treaty was negotiated with Colombia, giving the United States a six-mile wide strip of land for $10 million in cash and $250,000 annually thereafter. The Senate immediately ratified the treaty but Colombia did not. The latter nation had sent a communique to her ambassador instructing him not to sign the treaty, but it arrived too late. It seems that the New Panama Company's franchise was due to expire in 1904, and according to the terms of the franchise all equipment would revert to the Colombian government, which could then add another $40 million to the bill. This was not obstructionism; it was simply an attempt on the part of Colombia to strike a better bargain.

President Theodore Roosevelt grew impatient; he wanted the credit for building an isthmian canal. Knowing that many Panamanians did not appreciate their Colombian overlords, he decided to encourage an independence movement. The Panamanians who cooperated made the Waldorf-Astoria Hotel in New York City the headquarters for their revolutionary junta.

On November 3, 1903 a small revolution broke out in Panama. On the preceding evening the American Navy had just happened to arrive and train its guns on the Colombian shore batteries. Then, under the pretext of an 1846 treaty which gave the United States the right to intervene in the affairs of the isthmus to insure unobstructed transportation across it, the American Navy landed and seized all the railroads, holding the trains on the east coast. The Colombian Army was located on the west coast, and had the choice of walking across the isthmus or doing absolutely nothing. Obviously, this naval maneuver aided the Panamanian revolutionaries immensely. On November 4, Panama declared her independence; on November 6, the United States recognized that independence. On November 13, the first Panamanian ambassador to the United States arrived; he was Buneau-Varilla, the French engineer. On November 18, the Hay–Buneau-Varilla Treaty was signed, giving the United States a ten-mile wide strip of land in exchange for $10 million in cash and $250,000 per year afterwards. The treaty was ratified and the canal was built. In the process the United States had picked up the Panama Canal Zone, and added it to her list of possessions.

The Last New Possessions

Now that she was owner of a Latin American territory, the United States continuously involved herself in the affairs of the Latin American republics. Part of this was due to the fact that imperialism took on a commercial rather than a territorial emphasis. It was this interest which led the nation, in 1916, to purchase the Danish West Indies (the Virgin Islands) for the sum of $25 million.

This brought to an end the official acquisition of American territorial possessions. Other territories were acquired by the nation in the decades which followed, but only to govern and not to own. Some of these acquisitions resulted from American participation in international agreements. Others were the result of long-term lease arrangements with friendly powers. A continuing expansionist mood was reflected in the admission of various territories as states—southwestern regions in the early part of this century and Hawaii and Alaska more recently. But this cannot obscure the fact that since 1916 Americans have gone to alien soil as soldiers, builders, and businessmen but not as settlers or governors. Public interest in the homesteaders who migrated to Alaska in the 1950's had the flavor of nostalgia for an era truly lost.

The development of the American character has been strongly influenced by the expansionistic impulse of three centuries' duration. Expansionism, of course, does not necessarily mean that more territories must be added to the national domain. It could pertain to the full development and utilization of the currently held land mass, and it could also involve penetration of the seas and of space.

But the expansionism of the past was often individualistic and unorganized. It did not necessarily require sophisticated equipment and huge capital outlays. Many Americans who were so disposed could become a part of the expansionistic movement as pioneers.

The expansionism of the future will be different. It will be accomplished by individuals who are highly trained. It will be well organized, highly sophisticated, and require huge expenditures of money. It will not be open to any American who simply develops the urge, unless he first undergoes a rigorous training program and a highly selective process. One question raised by this development is whether the American people can any longer identify with expansionism to any considerable degree. And if they cannot, will they lose the dynamic spirit which was largely responsible for developing the wealthiest, most powerful nation on earth?

For Further Reading

Billington, Ray Allen. *Westward Expansion*. New York: Macmillan Company, 1957.

Brebner, John B. *Explorers of North America, 1492–1806*. Garden City: Doubleday and Company, 1955.

Dodd, William E. *Expansion and Conflict*. Boston: Houghton Mifflin, 1915.

Faulkner, William U. *Politics, Reform and Expansion, 1890–1900*. New York: Harper and Row, 1959.

Garrison, George. *Westward Extension, 1841–1850*. New York: Harper and Brothers, 1906.

Graebner, Norman A. *Empire on the Pacific*. New York: Ronald Press, 1955.

Jacobs, Melvin C. *Winning Oregon*. Caldwell, Idaho: Caxton Printers, 1938.

May, Ernest Richard. *Imperial Democracy—The Emergence of America as a Great Power*. New York: Harcourt, Brace, 1961.

Paxson, Frederic L. *History of the American Frontier, 1763–1893*. Boston: Houghton Mifflin, 1924.

Smith, Henry Nash. *Virgin Land: The American West as Symbol and Myth*. Cambridge: Harvard University Press, 1950.

Smith, Justin. *The Annexation of Texas*. New York: Macmillan Company, 1911.

Weinberg, Albert K. *Manifest Destiny*. Baltimore: Johns Hopkins, 1935.

Winther, Oscar O. *The Old Oregon Country*. Stanford: Stanford University Press, 1950.

Chapter Three
The Constitution

Modern Democracy

Since colonial times, Americans have been vitally interested in their rights, political and civil. Today it is practically impossible to scan through newspapers without coming across multitudinous accounts of alleged or real violations of constitutional rights. These same newspapers contain accounts of actual or supposed violations of the rights of state and local governments, of corporations, of institutions, as well as the rights of individual citizens.

There appears to be a rather widespread acceptance of the belief that Americans are protected from encroachment by government upon certain aspects of their behavior, and that government cannot be autocratic. For the government of the United States is a representative democracy, and there is an "American way" of doing things which is held to be sacrosanct. But this raises two very important questions. What is the American way of doing things, and just what

exactly is meant by American representative democracy?

The mass of Americans mouths all the shining shibboleths. Liberals and conservatives, Protestants, Catholics, and Jews, people of all racial and ethnic origins, are in favor of "the American way." But let the reader ask himself a question: what exactly is "the American way"? Do the public speakers know what "the American way" is, and do their audiences? We do not have a clearcut answer because "the American way" is a feeling of individual Americans about what they believe their country stands for. And this feeling depends on individual inclinations, environment, education, and experiences.

This brings to the fore another very critical point, namely: why is it that the American nation cannot formulate a single, concise definition of what it represents? After all, the nation does possess a Constitution which spells out the powers and restrictions of the national government. It has fifty state constitutions which perform a similar function at their level, not to mention thousands of city charters. It would seem that the expression "the American way" should or could have a universal meaning, and that there should be only one exact definition of "democracy." Should not the various constitutions of the American nation spell out the meaning of these words?

American democracy has evolved following no concise plan, and it is headed toward no precisely predetermined goal. Americans believe in rights but these rights are not clearly delineated. Americans believe in freedom but "freedom" is a relative term. Americans believe in majority rule, minority rights, and the theory of self-government, but there exist numerous restrictions on the application of these principles. Americans have been preaching political and social equality for several hundred years, but equality does not exist. America is pluralistic; it consists of countless groups of people who have their own feelings about what America stands for. The ideas of all these groups together comprise the "American way."

Americans began their long road toward democracy in the days of the founding of Jamestown settlement in 1607. Those Englishmen who settled this first permanent outpost some 350 years ago were the product of an already ripened and developed culture. Their task was not only to survive, but to adapt their culture, their previous concepts of government, to a new and alien environment. The result of this adaptation was a new civilization which, although it rested on European foundations, was tempered by the experience of frontier circumstances.

In this chapter the origins, modifications, and evolution of the American governmental system will be considered. We will see how seventeenth-century English government was transplanted and adapted to become the basis of colonial governments. Then, after a long development and a decade of revolution, the experiences and institutions of the colonial governments found expression in the Articles of Confederation. The deficiencies of the Articles of Confederation, in conjunction with colonial experiences and various intellectual influences, gave rise to the formulation of the United States Constitution. And the Constitution itself has undergone radical changes since its inception.

Roots in the European Past

Seventeenth-Century Government

Seventeenth-century English government already embodied the concept of the separation of powers. It consisted of an executive (the Crown), a two-house (bicameral) legislature (Parliament), and a judicial system which was more or less independent. There were a few checks in the system. For instance, either house could block the activities of the other, and the Crown had to sign parliamentary measures for them to become law.

These aspects of English government were destined to be incorporated into the American political system. But a unique American political institution, the judicial review of legislation, is not found in the English system. Judicial review is the ability of a court of law to review any properly passed laws to determine whether or not they are in accordance with the Constitution. This doctrine had been argued in England as early as 1630 (Dr. Bonham's Case), but it had never gained official sanction.

Instead the English used the concept of common law. Common law is synonymous in most cases with custom.

Decisions were rendered by wandering English judges who handed down verdicts based on local customs and past decisions rendered in similar cases (precedents). These precedents gained greater force as time went on and they were increasingly employed. This gave rise to a body of law in England which was unwritten and unofficial, and yet provided the basis for what the English call their constitution, which is not a document but the knowledgeable compilation of common law. Various facets of common law have found their way into the American governmental system, and alleged violations of common law precepts were instrumental in the creation of revolutionary sentiment in the 1760's.

Finally, seventeenth-century Englishmen gave their American cousins the concept of constitutionalism. Arising out of the common-law doctrine, the term "constitution" implied an agreement between the people and their legitimate rulers, which defined the limits and extent of governmental power. The agreement may or may not be written and formalized, but this matters little, for long established custom carries far more weight than newly legislated laws to the contrary.

Theoretical Influences

Besides English institutional contributions to the American governmental system, there were also a number of intellectual influences. The effect of ideas on the affairs of men is sometimes quite difficult to ascertain. During the American colonial era, however, there is considerable evidence that the leaders in the formulation of American independence and constitutionalism were profoundly affected by certain political writers.

One of these writers was John Locke who wrote the famous *Two Treatises on Government*. Locke claimed that government was based on a compact between the people and their rulers, and ultimately resided on the consent of the governed. The people had created a government by giving it a certain well-defined amount of power, and the government was therefore limited as to the measures which it could undertake. Writing in an attempt to justify the English Revolution of 1688, Locke reached the conclusion that the people, retaining ultimate sovereignty, possessed the right of revolution if their government exceeded the limits of its authority. This idea would be used as a partial justification for the American Revolution.

Another prominent political theorist was James Harrington, author of *Oceana*. Harrington believed that there should be a balance between political power and the distribution of property. He postulated that if one man owned all the property in a given society, he would possess all the political power. But if everyone owned something there would be a democracy—a dissemination of power. Those who owned different amounts of property, he believed, should possess corresponding degrees of political power. The views of James Harrington were destined to influence greatly the United States Constitution as it was originally written and interpreted.

The Comte de Montesquieu, a French political thinker, also contributed to American political thought. After observing the English political system, which he admired, Montesquieu formalized the separation-of-powers doctrine. Going one step beyond the existing English system he completely separated the judiciary from the executive and legislative branches of government. And what is more important, he argued that separation of powers was essential as a protection against tyranny.

The Colonial Experience

The colonial experience itself provided Americans with their own theories of government. The Puritans and the Pilgrims, as dissenter groups who were struggling for religious freedom, contributed the tradition of opposition to the Crown. These same settlers also insisted upon written documents, like the Mayflower Compact and the Fundamental Orders of Connecticut, in organizing their governments. These were formal agreements between the people and their rulers defining the powers of government. To a lesser degree this same practice prevailed throughout colonial America. The dissenters also helped spread the idea of representative government. Southern colonies such as Virginia possessed a House of Burgesses, but membership depended on certain property qualifications. In New England membership in the representative bodies belonged to practically everyone—if they met the basic requirement of belonging to the established religion. There is a relatively short step from these measures to a much broader suffrage (the right to vote).

Thus the average colonist in English North America possessed a certain political heritage and he upheld certain other well-defined notions on what government should be. With these basic tools and ideas, he attempted implementation of workable governments in the New World, with varying degrees of success.

Forms of Colonial Government

There were various types of colonial governments. The earliest was initiated in the joint stock company colonies, which were privately owned and financed, and governed with the permission of the Crown. The companies were required to give a percentage of their profits to the Crown, and in exchange, received large grants of governing power. Some, like the Massachusetts Bay Company (chartered in 1618) were practically sovereign—they possessed nearly complete political power. All joint stock companies were profit seeking trade and colonization companies. Eventually, however, three basic types of colonial government developed: proprietary, charter, and royal.

The proprietary colonies were Maryland, New York, New Jersey, Pennsylvania, Delaware, North Carolina, South Carolina, and Georgia. The Crown would grant large tracts of land in America to court favorites, primarily because they were owed large sums of money. These court favorites thereby became proprietors; they were the sole rulers of their lands, and they either moved to them or hired someone to govern in their behalf. Eventually all proprietary colonies were destined to become royal colonies, as the Crown discovered that they were extremely difficult to control under proprietary rule.

Charter colonies were Plymouth (part of Massachusetts), Providence (Rhode Island), Connecticut, and New Haven (united with the latter in 1650). These colonies possessed written agreements granted by the Crown which authorized certain groups to establish their own machinery of government, subject to certain specified limitations. The Fundamental Orders of Connecticut, granted in 1639, was the first written constitution in the New World, and probably the first modern constitution in history. The charter colonies provided a precedent for written compacts, and for the later United States Constitution. Like the proprietary colonies, most charter colonies became royal colonies; but two of them, Rhode Island and Connecticut, were still charter colonies at the time of the American Revolution.

Royal colonies developed around

1700. Control of the colonies was taken by the Crown which then either granted or retained in modification the written charters. All charters provided for a two house (bicameral) colonial legislature, except for Pennsylvania which had one house. All possessed an executive, a colonial governor appointed by the Crown, and independent common-law courts. The upper house of the colonial legislatures was appointed by the Crown, while the lower house was elected by those who possessed certain voting qualifications—no debtor, renter, indentured servant, Negro, non-Protestant, laborer, or female possessed the franchise. Thus, the royal colonies had three distinct branches of government, and this was an established precedent for later American government.

Attempts at Colonial Union

There was another development in colonial times which was significant for later American government. There were various attempts to unite the colonies—or groups of them—and these efforts were quite important for two reasons. For one, the colonies differed greatly from one another. Massachusetts and Georgia, for example, had contrasting needs, interests, and problems; this made the colonies somewhat similar to separate nations. However, the crude efforts to achieve union were uniquely important for the revolutionary era. Secondly, because the colonies tended to regard themselves as separate political entities, attempts at union marked the beginnings of the continuing dispute between federal and state sovereignty.

The most important of all colonial efforts toward union was the Franklin Plan. In 1754 the British government called a meeting of all colonial governors at Albany, New York. They were summoned primarily to discuss measures for dealing with frontier Indian problems, and secondarily to consider means of promoting the common welfare of all the colonies. Benjamin Franklin attended this meeting and proposed a plan calling for a confederation (loose union) of colonies, subject only to Parliament and the Crown. The proposal failed because the Crown felt it would make the colonies too strong. Nevertheless, it was later quite influential in the drafting of the Articles of Confederation.

Union at Last

The Growth of Revolutionary Sentiment

In December of 1763, at the Boston Tea Party, Americans dumped English tea (a government-monopolized commodity) in the harbor rather than pay a slight tax on it. Great Britain soon began a series of legislative measures collectively known as the Intolerable Acts. The Boston Port Act closed the port of Boston until such time as the destroyed tea was paid for. The Massachusetts Government Act suspended all town meetings and the appointive powers of the colonial assembly. The Act for the Impartial Administration of Justice provided that any English official accused of a crime in America would be tried in England. The Quartering Act required colonists to board and support British troops in their homes. Finally, the Quebec Act, which was not intended to punish the colonies but which was passed at the same time as the other measures, extended the boundary of Quebec southward to the Ohio River, recognized French law, and established the Catholic religion throughout the province. This functioned as a block to further colonial expansion, even though it

Die Einwohner von Boston werfen den englisch-ostindischen Thee ins Meer am 18. December 1773.

Contemporary Sketch of the Boston Tea Party

was intended only as a temporary expedient.

Colonial America responded to the Intolerable Acts by calling the First Continental Congress in May, 1774. Every colony except Georgia attended. The Congress issued a Declaration of Rights and Grievances claiming the right of the colonies to legislate for themselves, and calling upon England to guarantee life, liberty, and property. The Congress also set up an instrument known as the Continental Association, an agreement not to trade with England until the Intolerable Acts were repealed. The Congress then split over any further course of action and adjourned.

Throughout the winter of 1775 England enlarged her military forces in America. The result was the calling of the Second Continental Congress in May, 1775. This Congress had two express purposes: to raise an army of defense and to choose a commander-in-chief (George Washington). This revolutionary body was destined to remain in session until 1781, conducting most of the Revolutionary War before it was replaced by a newly organized government.

The Articles of Confederation

One of the early acts of the Second Continental Congress was to appoint a committee to devise a permanent plan of union. The resultant Articles of Confederation created a federal government in which the legislature was supreme. It was a one-house (unicameral) legislature, consisting of no less than two nor more than seven delegates per state, with each state delegation collectively possessing one vote. Salaries would be paid by the states, and binding instructions for voting would be forwarded from the state governments. Hence, delegates were strikingly like modern ambassadors. Delegates could serve only three out of each six years. The purpose of this was to prevent the formation of political power factions. All important bills had to be passed by a two-thirds' majority and all amendments to the Articles required unanimous consent.

The legislature possessed the power to make war and peace, borrow money, make treaties, determine weights and measures, send and receive ambassadors, coin money, and regulate Indian affairs. It possessed an extremely limited taxing power in that it assigned quotas to the states which might or might not be paid. There existed no enforcement powers. The same system prevailed for the militia. No standing army was provided for, but the national government could request the use of state militia. The coinage power was also limited, because the various states could also coin money. As a result the nation was flooded with all types of currency.

The executive branch of the Confederation government was plural, consisting of three co-presidents, each of whom headed a major department. There was a Department of Foreign Affairs, a Department of Finance, and a Department of War, each of which carried out the orders of the legislature. There was no real separation of powers under the Articles; this was further exemplified by the judicial system. The government, though it provided for a national court system, was content to use the state court systems instead.

The Articles government, as far as nationalists were concerned, possessed several very significant weaknesses. It was a loose union of sovereign political entities. The national government had little coercive power over the state governments. Furthermore, it had no power over commerce; states were erecting tariff barriers against one another. There was also a very acute finance problem. The war left a $53-million debt which could not be paid because the government was unable to collect taxes from the states.

This condition was further aggravated by an unstable currency; one of the solutions to the money problem was to print more of it and a wild inflationary spree resulted, on both the state and national levels.

Those Americans who established the government of the Articles of Confederation were partially victims of their own heritage. They feared a strong executive because they identified the office with the Crown and with autocratic colonial governors. They feared a standing army largely because of such measures as the Quartering Act. The states feared giving their power to a central government because of the belief that they might simply be substituting a new tyrant for an old one. The various states put state interests first, believing that freedom was best insured in this manner.

The Constitutional Convention

More and more people were beginning to realize that the Articles government was severely handicapped. The states further began to see that only by giving up some of their sovereignty could an effective national government be created. Thus political opinion began moving toward a new constitution. The preliminary indirect motivation for the forming of a constitution was economic, and the end result was largely tempered by the failures of the Articles government within this sphere.

George Washington was a shrewd businessman. He had a scheme for connecting the Potomac River with the Ohio River by means of a canal. But since the Potomac bordered Virginia and Maryland a meeting had to be arranged to discuss the issue. These two states called the Annapolis Convention of 1786 to consider the entire problem of trade and commerce. There, the participating states petitioned the Articles government to call a meeting of all the states to discuss national problems. The end result was a call to meet at Philadelphia in May, 1787, to consider revising the Articles of Confederation.

Rhode Island did not send a delegate and this created a major problem in that the Articles could not legally be amended except by unanimous vote. New Hampshire and Connecticut also did not send delegates until the convention was half over. Out of the ten states initially attending, seventy-seven delegates were appointed; fifty-five actually attended; thirty-nine eventually signed the document now known as the Constitution.

On May 30, 1787, Edmund Randolph of Virginia proposed a major change in the new convention's procedures. He introduced a resolution calling for the establishment of a national government consisting of three branches, and the rejection of the notion that sovereignty resided with the states. The resolution was voted on and six of the ten attending states concurred. This vote thus constituted a violation of the purpose for calling the convention, and was an attempt to carry out another revolution—the bloodless revolution of 1787. Thus the Constitution was written illegally. But eventually all states ratified the document, thereby honoring the unanimity covenant in the Articles of Confederation.

Proposals for a New Governmental Structure

Three plans were suggested at the convention for the new government. The Virginia Plan (also known as the Randolph or Large State Plan) called for a bicameral legislature. The lower house, elected by the people, would choose an upper house from a list of names submitted by the various state legislatures. The two houses together would then choose an executive. A national court would be established with the power to negate state laws with the concurrence of the national legislation. Representation would be on the sole basis of population, which would have given great political power to the large states.

The smaller states countered with a plan known as the New Jersey Plan (also called the Paterson or Small State Plan). A government of three branches would be created, but the states would retain their sovereignty. There would be a unicameral legislature with equal representation from all the states. The legislature would choose the executive and establish a supreme court to oversee the state courts. The national government would be strengthened because it was stipulated that all acts and treaties would be the supreme law of the land. In actual fact, however, the plan proposed only a slightly improved version of the existing Articles government.

There was also the Hamilton Plan, by which the states would have become mere administrative subdivisions of a supreme national government. This plan was considered to be radical and it was not discussed seriously.

Crucial Compromises

As a result of these plans a series of compromises were worked out, and the end product was the Great Compromise (also known as the Connecticut or Ellsworth Compromise). The lower house would be elected on the basis of population (Virginia Plan), while the upper house would provide equal representation, consisting of two senators from each state (New Jersey Plan). Members of the lower house would be elected by popular vote (democratic); members of the upper house would be elected by the state legislatures (aristocratic). This latter procedure was destined to last until the ratification of the Seventeenth Amendment in 1916.

Another big problem calling for a compromise was how to determine a state's population for taxation and representation purposes. The difficulty was over the presence of slaves. The North wanted to count everyone for taxation purposes, but only whites for purposes of representation since slaves were not citizens. The South took a completely opposite view. The issue was not over the legality of slavery, but simply an attempt on the part of both northern and southern states to further their interests. The issue was solved by an illogical and ridiculous plan: the Three-fifths Compro-

mise. For purposes of both taxation and representation, each Negro would count as three-fifths of a white person. Ridiculous or not, all parties concerned were satisfied with the arrangement.

Another problem arose over the commerce power of the federal government and the slave trade. The North wanted a strong federal commerce power, but the South, as an exporting region, was opposed to this. The South could foresee eventual northern population dominance and had two fears: the North might pass tariff measures favorable only to itself, and it might pass unfavorable legislation on the slave trade. So another compromise was in order. The federal government was given a strong power over commerce subject to three qualifications: (1) there could be no export taxes, (2) there must be uniformity of tariff rates, and (3) there could be no legislation on the slave trade until after 1808, except for a small head-tax (eventually set at $10 per imported slave).

The Test of Ratification

Finally the Constitution was completed. But ahead lay the real test of ratification. The nation was unaware of what had been going on inside Independence Hall. The Convention had decided that when nine states ratified the document, it would be considered as accepted. This came about within the year, but the nine did not include the powerful states of New York and Virginia. It was not believed that the new government would work without the support of these two states. Virginia ratified only after receiving assurances that a federal bill of rights would immediately be added to the document. That New York ratified after a terrific battle was mainly due to the efforts of James Madison, Alexander Hamilton and John Jay, the authors of the *Federalist Papers;* this series of informative essays explained and justified the proposed government.

Constitutional Flexibility

Amending the Constitution

The writers of the Constitution possessed sufficient foresight to recognize that only a flexible instrument of government had any chance of lasting. So they built into the document a means of changing it. Amending the Constitution is a two-stage process. In the initiation stage, a formal proposal of an amendment by the proper authority must be made. The Constitution authorizes two such proper authorities. Two-thirds of both houses of Congress may initiate an amendment, and this is the only method which has ever been successful. However, a request by two-thirds of the state legislatures requires Congress to call a national convention to consider initiating an amendment.

After the amendment has been initiated (and many have), it must be formally ratified by three-fourths of the states before it can become a part of the Constitution. The states have an option in ratifying: the state legislatures may handle the matter, or especially-called state ratifying conventions can do so. Both methods are acceptable and they are interchangeable, but except for the ratification of the anti-prohibition amendment when special conventions were called, the state legislatures have always done the job.

A number of amendments have been initiated which have not been ratified. An example is the child labor amendment, initiated in 1924, which could still be ratified. Usually, however, Congress specifies a time limit for ratification, normally seven years.

Custom in the Governmental Process

The Constitution also grows and develops by means of interpretation. This may be either by custom or by court rulings. Custom of course is not binding, but through long usage, customs sometimes develop greater force than formalized law. And court rulings, although official, may or may not be respected depending on the degree of acceptance by the nation and by the other two branches of government.

The Constitution provides the general framework for the national government; it specifies only what the government may *not* do. The details have been left for Congress to legislate, or for the other two branches of government to interpret. For example, the Constitution provides that the president shall have advisors. Out of this vague statement has grown the cabinet system by legislative enactment. The Constitution states that there shall be a Supreme Court and such inferior courts as Congress deems necessary. The result is federal district courts, circuit courts, customs courts, courts of claims, military courts, etc. The Constitution says nothing concerning committees and permanent regulatory commissions. Yet Congress is organized around a committee structure, and the government establishes special investigating or advisory committees—for instance the Warren Commission to investigate President Kennedy's assassination. And the government has developed a fourth branch: the independent regulatory commission, such as the Securities Exchange Commission, the Federal Trade Commission, and the Federal Reserve Board of Governors. They are perfect illustrations of the evolving constitutional system.

Custom plays a very large role in such developments. The longer a practice is followed the more difficult it is to change or abolish it. George Washington left office claiming that two terms were enough for any man. Every succeeding president honored this admonition except Franklin Roosevelt, who was elected for a fourth term in 1944. The international situation at the time precluded any substantial reaction, but following World War II, Congress initiated a constitutional amendment making the two-term tradition a formal part of the American governmental system.

Judicial decisions in themselves are largely based on custom and precedent. The Supreme Court decides whether or not state and federal laws are in harmony with the Constitution, yet nowhere in the Constitution is the power of judicial review specifically mentioned. Depending on circumstances and the membership of the Court, interpretations of law and the Constitution fluctuate. For example, the Supreme Court is traditionally the champion of free speech. However, during wartime the Court customarily interprets the Constitution in such a manner that free speech may be curtailed for the common good. In the contemporary ideological conflict with Communism, the Court at first took a strict course, then began to mellow as the nation grew accustomed to living in a stress situation.

The Federal System

One of the cornerstones of the American governmental system is its federal structure. A federation is a union of sovereign political entities which give up most of their sovereign power to create a strong central government over them. This form of government is unique because it creates two centers of power: one central national power plus multiple regional powers. The exact limitation of power for these two centers has never been clearly determined and probably never will be. They change according to circumstances.

The legislative and judicial branches of our federal government have rather clearly marked limits of power; the executive does not. However, the power of all three national branches has grown over the years, particularly in the twentieth century. This resulted primarily from an on-going reinterpretation of the Constitution in response to constantly changing national situations.

State versus Federal Power

The various states, according to the Tenth Amendment, possess all powers not specifically delegated to the federal government. But what these unenumerated powers are has never been clearly defined. The national government and the various state governments are, however, supreme within their respective areas of authority. For instance, states may pass divorce and marriage laws, and no matter how much the federal government might disagree with them and desire uniformity, it can do nothing unless a state law violates a right of federal citizenship.

Within its sphere of activity, the federal government is superior to all state governments. Article VI, Section 2 of the Constitution states that no state law may conflict with a national law or treaty. The agency which decides if there is a conflict is the Supreme Court, utilizing the doctrine of judicial review. Thus, a branch of the federal government passes on the limitations of federal power. Furthermore, the federal government is the only agency which can create and admit new states into the Union.

The Constitution grants Congress the power to admit new states subject only to two restrictions. No state may be formed from existing states without state permission, and no state may be formed by a union of all or parts of existing states without agreement from all parties concerned. Thus, the boundaries of a state are inviolate and the federal government is pledged to protect them.

The Northwest Ordinance

A majority of American states have entered the Union by passing through the territorial stage. The only exceptions are the original thirteen plus West Virginia, which was formed from part of seceded Virginia during the Civil War, and Texas, which entered the Union from the status of a free and independent nation. The procedure authorized by Congress in 1787 has been followed to the present; the Northwest Ordinance was one of the few lasting accomplishments of the Articles government.

The Ordinance authorized Congress to set the boundaries of a territory and appoint a governor, a secretary, and three judges to maintain order. When the adult white male population of the territory reached 5,000, the people could elect the lower house of a territorial legislature. This lower house would submit a list of ten names to the national Congress which would pick five for a territorial upper house. The appointed officials would remain during this stage, but a non-voting representative to Congress would be elected. When the total free population of the territory reached 60,000, the territory could petition for statehood. Congress would then authorize the calling of a territorial constitutional convention to draw up a state constitution. If this was acceptable to Congress, the territory could enter the Union on full equality with the older states.

Special conditions can be imposed on a petitioning territory by Congress. The territory must either comply or be delayed in attaining statehood. It was this sort of situation which caused the delay in Missouri's statehood petition in 1819 until the Missouri Compromise of 1821 ironed out the difficulties. The most recent special conditions imposed had to do with Alaska in 1958. The territory had to agree to federal regulation of its wildlife resources until such time as the Secretary of the Interior felt that Alaska could properly police herself. Alaska was forced to concur.

As the founder of the several states,

the federal government has several important obligations toward them. It must respect their boundaries. It must protect them from foreign invasion and domestic rebellion if requested by the state governor or by the state legislature in his absence. Otherwise, the federal government cannot enter a state unless there is a federal issue at stake. And the federal government must insure that every state has a democratic form of government.

Constitutional Delineation of State Powers

In turn, there are a number of restrictions on the states. They are not allowed to make any treaties with foreign nations, nor can they enter into agreements with other states without the permission of Congress. No state may maintain a standing army except for such forces as are necessary to preserve domestic tranquility. The states have no power over interstate commerce and may pass no law violating a contract. Under the terms of the Fourteenth Amendment no state can pass a law which violates the rights of national citizenship.

Two state powers are somewhat limited. One of these is the taxing power. There can be no state export or import taxes. There must be equality of taxation and taxes cannot impair a contract. Finally, the states are prohibited from taxing any federal lands or property. In turn the federal government refrains from taxing state property by free choice. This is the so-called "inter-governmental immunities" doctrine espoused by the Supreme Court in *McCulloch* v. *Maryland* (1819). State governments cannot coin or print money, but they can charter banks which can issue a form of currency —the check or bank note, not considered legal tender. State governments utilized this technique to get around the constitutional prohibition on coining money during much of the nineteenth century.

State governments also have certain obligations to each other. All acts and laws of one state must be respected by all other states. If one state has exceedingly lax divorce and marriage laws, other states must still recognize the validity of such marriages and divorces. Similarly, states may impose residence requirements for voting, or various health laws, but they cannot otherwise discriminate against the citizens of other states. The Constitution also provides that people who are charged with a crime in one state and flee to another state must be returned on proper demand. This is known as rendition. And finally, if states have a disagreement with one another, and are unable to find satisfaction, the Supreme Court will settle the issue, and its decision is binding on all disputants.

The Expansion of Federal Control— Implied Powers

The relationship between the federal and state governments is constantly changing. Generally, the powers of the federal government have been growing over the years at the expense of state autonomy and control. This growth is caused by a number of related factors. Perhaps the most important cause has been the development of nationwide economic and industrial institutions— railroads, labor unions, manufacturing corporations, banks. Since no one state can effectively regulate the behavior of such large and powerful entities, federal legislation has been required. This development is justified on the basis of the Constitutional delegation of power over interstate commerce to Congress. The nature of modern warfare has occasionally made necessary the federal regulation of nearly all aspects of personal life. Even political opinion has been included among these aspects by some, and the Cold War ideological conflict has heightened this tendency.

The reasons why the United States government has been able to expand its powers to meet these new and changing circumstances are found in the doctrine of Constitutionally implied powers, advocated by the Supreme Court in *McCulloch* v. *Maryland*; decided in 1819, this case tested the ability of the federal government to charter a national bank. The reasoning of the Court in this historic case deserves attention.

Chief Justice John Marshall ruled that since the federal government is supreme in the sphere of its specific enumerated powers, it must also possess the means of putting these powers into effect. The Court ruled that "if the end be legitimate, if it be within the scope of the Constitution, then any means consistent with that end, if not expressly forbidden by the Constitution, are allowable." Thus, if the federal government has the power to coin money, then following this line of reasoning it has the power to establish mints, build vaults, and perhaps enter the business of mining gold and silver. Whether one agrees or disagrees with the decision, it is the legal basis for the growth of federal power.

The implied powers doctrine has been used to justify the so-called grant-in-aid system, whereby the federal government finances certain state and local activities. According to this system, Congress will grant monies to the states subject to a series of special conditions. One is that the states use the money for the exact purpose indicated. Another is that the state will use a certain portion of its own money for the specified purpose. Still another requires the state to set up a competent agency to administer the project in conjunction with the federal government. And finally, in return for federal monetary assistance the state must recognize the federal right to control and regulate the particular activity which it aids. A good example of the grant-in-aid program is the interstate highway program.

The grant-in-aid system has enabled the federal government to obtain more power in former state spheres of activity. The states do not have to accept the program, but if they refuse they lose an opportunity to use tax dollars which their citizenry contributed. In effect, participation in the grant-in-aid program makes the state an administrative subdivision of the federal government for certain purposes.

There are definite advantages to the grant-in-aid system. It enables the states to undertake programs which they normally could not afford. It sets up minimum national standards for those projects financed. It divides the cost of such projects according to the ability to pay—in the tradition of American progressivism. Finally, it is apparently the only way to handle certain national problems.

There is a contention that the federal government will eventually abolish the states, and that the states are now unable to perform adequately the functions originally assigned to them. However, while the power of the federal government has grown over the years, state powers have grown also, albeit not nearly as much. The ultimate future of the state governments as originally established is somewhat dubious, but regardless of the growing complexity of American civilization, they continue to provide certain noteworthy services. They provide an ideal training ground for national politicians and serve as a laboratory for new ideas. Furthermore, no matter what form the governmental structure may take in the future, the state and local levels will still permit closer contact between citizens and elected officials than will the national level.

The Legislative Branch

The legislative branch of government, established as a bicameral system, was set up as a compromise measure. The lower house was designed to provide participation in the government by the mass of people, and the upper house was to function as a citadel for vested interests.

The Senate, or upper house, consists of two members elected from each state for a six-year term. Thus, representation is based on geography, not population. The populous states of New York and California have no more representation in the Senate than sparsely populated Montana and New Mexico. The six-year terms are staggered so that only one-third of the Senate must stand for re-election every two years. This probably tends to make the upper house somewhat more conservative than the lower chamber.

A state's representation in the House of Representatives, the lower house, depends on its population. There are now 435 seats in the House and they are apportioned on the basis of state population figures. All states are required by federal fiat to divide their territory into districts from which representatives are elected. These districts must be approximately equal in population. Elections for the House occur every two years, when the entire membership of the House is up for re-election. The elections are held so that they correspond to the time when one-third of the Senate is elected.

Congress has a number of functions to perform. Both houses of Congress possess the power to discipline their members, but the power is rarely exercised. On very few occasions have members been officially censured, and most of these occurred during the Civil War and Reconstruction era.

The Impeachment Process

Congress also possesses the power of impeachment and legislative trial. Under this power Congress can bring charges against, and remove from office, any civil official of the federal government. In modern America there is an unofficial rule that only the gravest violations of law and propriety are grounds for impeachment although such was not always the case.

There are two steps involved in the process. First comes the initiation of impeachment proceedings. Any member or group within the House may prefer charges against a government official. These charges are then studied by the House Judiciary Committee or by a specially appointed investigating committee. The committee decides whether or not there is sufficient validity to the charges. If a simple majority of the House concurs with the charges, the individual is impeached. Impeachment is nothing more than the formal bringing of charges by the proper authority against a public official.

The second step of the impeachment process involves the Senate. Acting as a trial court the Senate must decide if the impeached person should be removed from office. The procedures are those followed in a regular trial, and the House appoints a committee which acts as public prosecutors. Witnesses are called and the defendant is allowed counsel. After the trial the Senate conducts a secret vote to determine removal. If a two-thirds' majority of Senators concurs with the charges, the individual is removed from office. The presidential power of pardon does not apply to impeachment proceedings.

Only one president has been impeached in American history. He was President Andrew Johnson and the action was taken in 1867. Johnson was impeached for strictly partisan reasons; he was unsuccessfully attempting to stop radical reconstructionists from inflicting severe punishment on ex-Confederate states. The Senate vote was only one short for removal and Johnson remained in office. In 1804, Supreme Court Justice Samuel Chase was impeached for drinking at parties and arriving late at court. The Senate refused to remove him. These are

exceptions to the usual conduct of impeachment proceedings. The general guideline is that the offensive conduct should make the accused individual subject to prosecution in a civil or criminal court after removal.

Other Non-Legislative Powers

Another important function of Congress is to supervise the various administrative agencies of government. Such agencies as the Interstate Commerce Commission are set up by congressional enactment under the executive branch. But Congress establishes the rules and operating procedures, provides the finances, and requires periodic reports on the conduct of these agencies.

One of the most important powers of Congress, probably second only to the passage of legislation itself, is the power of investigation. The purpose of the investigative power is to enable Congress to acquire the necessary information to determine what types of legislation are needed. This power is occasionally abused. Some investigating committees have been less concerned with obtaining information than with exposing and discrediting private individuals. The Un-American Activities Committee under Senator Joseph McCarthy was a classic example. Public opinion was brought to bear on individuals who might have belonged to a Communist Party in the 1930's but who left it as soon as they ascertained its aims. In the semi-hysteria of the Korean War era, an appearance before McCarthy's committee was sometimes worse than a lifetime jail sentence.

The difficulty is compounded by the fact that investigating committees are not bound by the rules which govern courts. A committee is free to accept evidence which would be thrown out of a regular court—even hearsay evidence. Committees defend themselves by claiming that they are not conducting trials, but this is only technically true. The results may be more damaging than those of a regular trial.

In an age when television cameras enter an investigation chamber, some politicians have established their public images through their conducting of congressional investigations. For example, Senator Estes Kefauver obtained his national reputation through his Crime Committee hearings in the early 1950's. Before their occurrence he was relatively unknown nationally; afterwards, he was a presidential candidate.

Limits on Congressional Power

The Congress of the United States may legislate only according to powers either expressly granted or implied in the Constitution. This points to two problem areas: emergency legislative power and the delegation of legislative power. During time of war or other severe national emergency Congress has claimed emergency powers—authority beyond the normal scope of the Constitution—to deal with extraordinary circumstances. The Supreme Court has repeatedly ruled that there is no emergency power, but Congress continues to use it. The Court has always invalidated wartime emergency legislation after peace was achieved and the issue had become less imperative. It invalidated emergency legislation passed during the Depression of the 1930's, but became involved in a serious political squabble in the process (Roosevelt's Court fight). Legally, no emergency legislative power exists in the Constitution; while under certain circumstances it may be supported by common sense and fact. It is probably because this emergency legislative power could be abused that the Supreme Court has never seen fit to accept it officially.

The other difficulty concerns the delegation of legislative authority. Under certain circumstances it is legal. Congress does have the power to set up agencies or assign prescribed legislative actions to the executive. But the Supreme Court has repeatedly held that a delegation must contain very well defined limits. For example, Congress alone possesses the constitutional power to levy tariffs, yet it can authorize the president to raise or lower tariff rates on his own authority if it sets limits and conditions on his actions. This has been the case since the Reciprocal Trade Act of 1934.

Most problems over the delegation of legislative power arise from the development of the unofficial "fourth branch" of the federal government, the independent regulatory commissions. With the growing complexities of government, Congress has been setting up commissions to handle specific tasks since 1887.

Congressional Organization and Procedure

The organization of both houses of Congress is a complex matter. Both houses are empowered by the Constitution to elect their own officers and to determine their own rules and procedures. The Congress as it exists today is the product of long-standing custom and legislative enactment.

In both houses one candidate from each of the major parties is nominated for the top position—Speaker of the House or President *pro tempore* of the Senate. Nominees are selected by party caucus and everyone in the party is expected (almost required) to vote for his party's nominee. Hence, there is usually no debate and no surprising voting results. Both houses then determine their respective rules. With the Senate this is a relatively simple task. The Senate is regarded as a continuing body because only one-third of its membership is up for re-election at one time, so there is seldom any controversy. Each Senate adopts the rules of the preceding Senate, usually with very minor adjustments. But such is not always the case in the House of Representatives. Each House is considered to be a completely new assembly, and consequently must adopt its own rules. In practice, the House tends to accept the rules of the preceding one, but occasionally, a violent scene erupts.

The actual governance of Congress is something which has grown up outside of the Constitution; it is not unconstitutional but it is extraconstitutional. Caucuses of the major parties, meeting throughout each session of Congress, determine what action will be taken during the session, and are responsible for the various appointments to committees within the Congress. In the Senate the principle governing agencies are the Democratic Policy Committee and the Republican Policy Committee. In the House of Representatives the counterparts are the Democratic Steering Committee and the Republican Steering Committee. These committees attempt to put their programs into practice through floor leaders, called majority floor leaders if the party controls that house, and minority floor leaders if it does not. These floor leaders are aided by assistant floor leaders known as party whips.

One of the most controversial instruments in Congress is the congressional committee. Modern government is an extremely complex affair, necessitating control by experts if it is to function properly. Since no single member of Congress can become expert on all legislative matters, soon after the birth of the new government Congress began setting up specialized committees.

A committee is nothing more than a small group of congressmen who are assigned to particular governmental activities within the scope of the legislative branch. Both houses have many standing (permanent) committees, the members of which are supposed to know more about their special areas of government than anyone else. These committees have been devised to cover the major areas of normal governmental operation. From time to time special temporary committees are appointed to deal with unique problems of government.

Both houses have evolved strong unwritten procedures to govern the selection of committee appointments. As matters now stand the major criterion for committee selection is seniority—the length of continuous service in a particular house of Congress. The longer a member serves in his house the better will be his committee appointments. In addition, the longer he serves on a particular committee, the higher will be his ranking, until finally, when he has more committee seniority than anyone else, he will probably be named chairman of the committee if his party controls his house. A chairmanship is thus based on seniority and party control.

There are some major criticisms of the seniority system. A repeatedly re-elected congressman oftentimes comes from a very safe constituency, and in the process, he sometimes loses touch with the temper of the nation. Also, length of service does not necessarily make a man the best choice for a particular job. Finally, the seniority system results in the oldest members of Congress holding on to the most important positions, occasionally when their mental powers and energy are no longer at their peak.

A Bill Becomes a Law

The exact means by which a bill (proposed law) finds its way into the statute books is a highly complex process. Both houses of Congress must pass an identical version of a bill in order for it to become law. In both houses when a bill is introduced, it is assigned to an appropriate committee for study and, if released from the committee, placed on a calendar (a schedule for debating and voting). If accepted by a majority vote in one house, it passes on to the other house, where an identical process takes place. If there are problems in passing an identical bill—if both houses pass slightly different versions of the same bill —a conference committee is established, which consists of the principal supporters of the bill in both houses. Their task is to iron out the differences.

Either house of Congress may initiate a bill and pass it on to the other house. However, in some respects the two houses have different roles to play in the legislative process. For instance, all revenue bills must originate in the House of Representatives. And only the Senate can confirm executive appointments or ratify treaties. But it is to be noted that the Senate must agree to House revenue bills for them to become law, and the House can block any senatorial confirmation or treaty ratification by withholding the money needed to pay salaries or implement arrangements. So the two houses can and often do check each other.

However, even if both houses of Congress agree on a proposed law, revenue measure, or treaty, none of these measures actually become law until the president signs them. And the president possesses a veto power which Congress can override only with a two-thirds majority vote of both houses.

The Chief Executive

Separate Branches of Government

The checks-and-balances concept of the colonial period found ready application in the relationship between the president and his Congress. The president is elected for a four-year term, and regardless of the changing makeup of the legislature, he remains president for that period. This can lead to serious problems, as when the president belongs to one party while a majority of the Congress belongs to the opposition party. Theoretically at least, this could lead to a stalemate. Often it does lead to a lack of cooperation between the two branches of government. The Truman and Hoover administrations are both examples of this development. Congress has no way of forcing the president to do its bidding, and the contrary is equally true.

This aspect of American government is unique among all democratic governments in the world. Democratic parliamentary governments choose their executive and his principal advisors from the majority party in the parliamentary assembly. If and when that party loses its majority a new ministry is chosen. The outstanding advantage of this system is that it precludes the possibility of a governmental stalemate from lack of cooperation between the two branches of government (of course, they are not really separate). A major disadvantage is that the parliamentary system lends itself to instability; during periods of stress several ministries could come and go within the span of a single year. In the American system, elected officials usually realize that they are stuck with each other, and like it or not they tend to cooperate in the interest of the nation. Occasionally this cooperation is not forthcoming, but there are ways of getting around it which will be discussed below.

A Changing Presidential Role

The role of the president with his Congress is today far different from what the Founding Fathers intended. They had hoped that the president would be removed from the legislature and intervene primarily to act as an umpire in cases of conflict. Two developments changed this: the rise of the two-party system, and the emergence of the popular vote in selecting their president. As the party system developed, the president became firmly identified with his fellow party members in Congress to the degree that, if he failed to follow party philosophy, he might be ousted from his party, as was the case with John Tyler and the Whig party.

Ever since the people obtained a greater voice in selecting their chief executive, they have rightly believed they possess some right to evaluate his work. He was blamed or praised for whatever legislation was passed during his administration. Even in the present one often hears people asking why the president does not pass a certain law. He often fails because only the Congress may pass a law. In the minds of many voters the president directs and controls all legislation, but this hardly conforms to the hallowed principle of the separation of powers.

However, since presidents traditionally want to be re-elected or to retire from office with a strong public image, they have made many attempts during the last century to gain leadership over legislative action. One strong nineteenth-century president was Abraham Lincoln. But many historians say that the modern presidency began with Theodore Roosevelt and currently culminates in Lyndon Johnson. In this century, with dynamic men in the White House—notably Theodore Roosevelt, Woodrow Wilson, and Franklin Roosevelt, and to some extent Kennedy and Johnson—the presidency has gained the initiative to a considerable degree.

Checks and Balances

The strong president often opens himself to charges of attempting to establish a dictatorship. Such charges are mainly nonsense. Traditionally, when one branch of the federal government gets a little too powerful, the other two branches restrain it. The actual powers of the presidency, grounded in the nebulous statement in the Constitution that the president "possesses all executive power," have no well-defined limits. Presidential power depends greatly on the ambitions, ability, and personality of each individual executive. The general trend, however, has been rather clearly toward a greater executive dominance over Congress.

Some of the presidential power is constitutionally granted, but a great portion of it has come about through custom and tradition. Constitutionally, the president has the power to call Congress into special session, to inform Congress periodically of the state of the nation, to recommend legislation, and to veto acts of Congress. The calling of a special session creates an aura of urgency which a strong executive may capitalize on. A presidential message for a nation-wide television audience can be quite influential.

The president's veto power is a direct control over Congress. Originally it was intended that the president would veto congressional acts only for the gravest of reasons. But from Andrew Jackson's presidency (1828–1836), presidents also began vetoing legislation for personal reasons. Thus, the modern president often uses the threat of a veto to convince congressional leaders to embody his thinking in their legislation. The veto power has far more significance than usually meets the eye.

The executive also controls his Congress through the power of patronage. The president has the authority to fill literally thousands of federal jobs by executive appointment. Quite naturally, successful congressmen would like to have some of these positions filled by their key supporters. The president is aware of this and many times offers a patronage job in exchange for support on a certain piece of legislation. Once the appointment has been made, some of the presidential advantage is obviously lost. However, the Supreme Court has ruled that although the president appoints with the advice and consent of the Senate, he can remove most appointees at his own discretion. To exercise this perogative could be politically inexpedient, so the president usually is content with the use of threat to maintain some control over congressmen.

Also, presidential control over executive agencies can make things difficult for a recalcitrant congressman. A cooperative congressman will usually find a great deal of executive help in obtaining information and services while an unfriendly one will not be so fortunate. Presidential cooperation may extend to the point of endorsing an issue which is of concern only to the people in a friendly congressman's home district.

Finally, the executive resorts to personal conferences with individual congressmen, usually party leaders and committee chairmen. At these conferences he makes his desires known and uses many devices to convince these leaders to adopt his viewpoint. Bargains may be made, threats may be employed, and favors may be granted. If a president has a strong and forceful personality he often gets what he wants.

A president's biggest weapon against Congress, however, is his personal influence with the American people. To the mass of Americans he is the United States government. And whether they like him or not they usually respect him. Knowing this, a president works hard to obtain public backing for his views. He attempts to convince the people, in order to have the people convince their congressmen to pursue his program.

This influencing is accomplished in a number of ways. The president holds private meetings with and attempts to gain the support of various influential people throughout the country; such as heads of pressure groups, influential organizations, or noted private citizens. On occasion he goes on nationwide television to explain why a particular action should be taken, in order to elicit the support of the people. Kennedy's famous speech on the Cuban missile crisis of 1962 is one example of the effects of such a maneuver.

The Emergence of the Modern Presidency

The presidency really began to move for public support of its policies with Theodore Roosevelt, who introduced the technique of going directly to the people in order to create a public clamor over a particular piece of legislation. This is mainly how he obtained the passage of the Pure Food and Drug Act, an entirely new type of legislation which Congress had earlier rejected. His successor, William Howard Taft, did little to further presidential influence. But Woodrow Wilson revived the personally delivered State of the Union message (it had been passed on to Congress in written form since the second president, John Adams), and also initiated the press conference as a method of making his views known to the nation.

The presidency throughout the 1920's was fairly inactive. It appears that the American people were temporarily tired of the reform and idealism of Wilson's era. They wanted no great political movement and therefore elected presidents who would respect their conservatism. Hence, Harding, Coolidge, and Hoover did little to enhance the power of the presidency. But all three men did make use of the speaking tour to enhance their personal influence with the people.

The unrivaled master at mustering public opinion was Franklin Delano Roosevelt. His regular informal radio broadcasts to the American people, the so-called "fireside chats," had a tremendous influence on the American people.

He also used the press conference as a sounding board for his policies. Roosevelt cajoled, threatened, bargained, and bullied acceptance for his legislative program. Truman, although desirous of being a strong executive, was plagued with a hostile Congress and a public which generally refused to acknowledge the momentuous issues facing it. Eisenhower, the hero of World War II, had less need of active campaigning for public support. Head of a political party and executive leader of a nation, he was at the same time almost above factional politics. Kennedy, it seems, attempted to follow in Roosevelt's footsteps and developed a very effective public image, but his Congress was not sufficiently controlled. Johnson, a master at congressional manipulations, is suffering from the handicaps of an unpopular war and charges of a lack of candor.

Presidential Power and the Supreme Court

Like the Congress the American presidency often operates under the implied powers doctrine. In *Cunningham* v. *Neagle* (1890), the Supreme Court held that the president could act in the public interest even in the absence of constitutional or statutory power. Although the Court has recognized the right of the president to stretch his powers under certain circumstances, it has never defined this power. At times the Court has limited the exercise of such power. A notable recent example was Truman's seizure of the steel mills in 1952. He did so to avoid a massive strike which probably would have resulted in serious shortages of critical materials during the Korean War. The Supreme Court overruled his action, stating that no national emergency existed since the United States was not at war, but was merely engaged in a police action.

A few observations on the role of the Supreme Court in American politics should be made. The Court is the overseer of the areas in the Constitution in which authority is not spelled out. In effect the Court must arbitrate between Congress and the executive. It will often side with one branch against the other, but the alliance is always of a temporary nature. The Court rarely rules against one of the other branches if that branch is exceptionally strong; rather, it tends to do battle with a weak executive or a weak Congress.

For example, after the Civil War Congress was supreme. Some of the reconstruction measures which it passed were held to be unconstitutional. But the Court refused to rule against these measures for a very good reason: the Congress was powerful enough to impeach President Andrew Johnson, and might also impeach a few Supreme Court members. In later years, but only after the nation had elected a less radical legislative body, the Court did rule many of these measures unconstitutional.

Only once did the Court attack a strong executive: Franklin Roosevelt. A Depression era leader, Roosevelt had developed a far-reaching program of relief, recovery, and reform measures to solve the economic plight of the nation. Practically all of these measures required an expansion of federal power. Alarmed by this development the Court declared many of the New Deal measures to be unconstitutional. Roosevelt took this as a challenge and proposed a measure whereby the Court would have its membership increased by six, giving Roosevelt six new appointments to the Court. While a tremendous legislative battle raged over Roosevelt's Judiciary Reorganization Bill, the Supreme Court changed its approach. Roosevelt did not obtain the passage of his bill due to strong legislative opposition, but he seemed to succeed in frightening

By Seibel In The RICHMOND TIMES-DISPATCH
**The Separation of Powers,
Roosevelt Style**

the Court into a more liberal frame of mind.

The Court is able to limit the power of weak executives. It limited Eisenhower's removal power because it knew that he probably would not protest. It limited Truman in the aforementioned steel seizure incident because the Court knew that it had the backing of a Republican Congress. The power of the executive thus depends on the personal strength of the man in the White House, and what is just as important, the political condition of the nation during his presidency.

Consequently, executive power is in a state of flux; it has no definite limits. The doctrine of implied powers applies to the presidency, but the Supreme Court has refused to define it. This position of the Court has allowed the executive the elasticity required to meet various new situations. Each new presidential assertion of power is usually judged on its own peculiar merits.

The Powers of the Presidency—Enforcement

The presidency has several powers specifically granted in the Constitution. They include the pardoning power, appointment and removal, command of the military, the enforcement power, and the leadership in foreign affairs. The pardoning power gives the president the opportunity to cancel, reduce, or delay the sentence of any individual convicted of a federal crime. Treason and impeachment are the only exceptions.

Under the enforcement power the president is given the obligation to enforce all laws and treaties. And he is given the equipment with which to fulfill this obligation. He has at his disposal the Department of Justice, the Federal Bureau of Investigation, the Coast Guard, and a host of regulatory and investigatory agencies. He may also make use of the Armed Forces, and, at his discretion, the various national guard units.

A constitutional prohibition limits the president's ability to enter the states to enforce the law. He can do this only at the request of the proper state authority or if a federal law is being violated. However, this gives the executive a fair degree of flexibility. Any number of reasons can be used to justify executive disregard of state restrictions: obstruction of the mails, violation of the rights of federal citizenship, or interference with interstate commerce. The extent of the executive enforcement power today has been illustrated by Eisenhower's use of troops in Little Rock, Arkansas, and Kennedy's use of troops in Oxford, Mississippi. In both cases state failure to obey federal court orders was involved, and in both cases the executive was constitutionally justified.

The Supreme Court has gone so far as to recognize the right of the president to contravene express laws of Congress. In *U.S.* v. *Midwest Oil,* the Court held

that the president could withdraw oil bearing lands from public use even though
Congress had opened them to the public.
In this case Theodore Roosevelt claimed
the lands were needed to support a mechanized navy. The Court held that he was
acting in the public interest and was in a
better position to know day-to-day
developments than was his Congress.

Approximately 100 executive orders
have established Indian reservations, 50
have established wildlife reserves, and
around 150 have withdrawn lands for
military use—all in the absence of or
opposed to congressional enactment.
This does not mean that the president may
violate any law at will, but does stress that
each presidential action is judged on its
own merits.

The Appointment Power

The Constitution grants the president
the authority to appoint all federal judges,
ambassadors, consuls, and other public
officials with the advice and consent of
the Senate. Along with this power is the
right to remove appointed officials from
office. The presidential power of appointment and removal, has been a fairly
controversial issue in American constitutional history. The first great case
before the Supreme Court, *Marbury* v.
Madison (1803), was concerned with the
appointment of federal judges. Also the
impeachment of Andrew Johnson was
based on his removal of a Cabinet official
from office in face of what later proved
to be an unconstitutional congressional
law to the contrary.

Although the powers of the government are growing in practically all areas,
the presidential appointment power is a
notable exception. In 1883 Congress
passed the Pendleton Act which established the Civil Service system. It
authorized government employment based
on merit for employees who were in

low level, non–policy-making jobs. Each
succeeding presidential administration
expanded the number of jobs under
Civil Service, usually for strictly partisan reasons, until by the mid-twentieth
century, some 2.3 million jobs were under
Civil Service. However, the presidential
appointment power was limited to 25,000
positions. The only appointive government officeholders remaining are those in
strictly policy-making positions.

The Removal Power

The only check on this authority is
the necessity of obtaining approval or confirmation from the Senate. This is strictly
a matter of politics. However, the presidential removal power is a far more
complex affair, mainly because the Constitution is silent on it. A general theory
on the subject was formulated by James
Madison, one of the principal authors of
the Constitution. He claimed, and most
statesmen agreed, that the president had
the authority to remove appointed
officials. Madison held that the president
possessed a right to expect loyal and
efficient service from his subordinates, and
if they blocked his program or were dere-
lict in their duties, he could remove them.
But Madison also suggested that Congress
might establish some appointive positions,
not completely executive in character,
and set up specific removal procedures for
them. This position was widely held until
the time of Johnson's impeachment.

In 1866 the radical Reconstruction
Congress passed the Tenure of Office Act,
which stated that the president could not
remove any appointed official, who had
been confirmed by the Senate, without
prior permission of the Senate. The act
was aimed at maintaining Edwin Stanton,
in his position as Secretary of War.
Nevertheless, Johnson removed the disloyal Stanton hoping to obtain a test case
before the Supreme Court. His impeach-

ment followed instead and this particular law was never tested in the courts. But much later, President Wilson removed a postmaster under similar circumstances, and in *Myers* v. *U.S.* (1926) the Court held that he had acted within his authority. Thus he has the power to remove, and without the Senate's consent, any appointed official with purely executive duties.

Appointed officials whose duties are not purely executive are members of the various regulatory commissions which are technically under the executive branch, but which have legislative and judicial functions as well. The president cannot remove such officials on his own authority. This position has been maintained by the Court in *Humphrey's Executor* v. *U.S.* (1935). The real criterion for removal then, is the nature of the office held. Each case is usually decided on its merits according to the political situation at the time. In *Morgan* v. *T.V.A.* (1940) the Court upheld Roosevelt's removal of the chairman of the Tennessee Valley Authority, claiming that the agency was strictly executive. But in *Wiener* v. *U.S.* (1958) the Court held that Eisenhower's removal of a member of the War Claims Commission was illegal. Of course, Roosevelt had recently done battle with the Court, and Eisenhower was an outgoing executive who was not in the best of health.

The Military Power

One of the broadest powers of the presidency is the military power—the presidential role as commander-in-chief. The major wartime presidents, throughout American history, have expanded the powers of the presidency far more than all other presidents combined: these were Lincoln, Wilson, and Franklin Roosevelt. The president constitutionally possesses the power to wage war, and this is con-

strued to mean the power to wage war successfully. In the words of Chief Justice Hughes, the American Constitution is a "fighting constitution"; during wartime the powers of the presidency are practically unlimited.

In the twentieth century the Court has been gradually extending the meaning of the word "war" to encompass almost any national emergency. The Court has ruled and Congress has agreed, that the declaration of a national emergency is strictly up to the judgment of the president. Therefore the office of the presidency is one of limited constitutional powers during peacetime, while it is allowed to approach dictatorial limits during severe wartime conditions. This great elasticity is largely responsible for the permanence of the American governmental system.

The Power over Foreign Affairs

Related to the presidential military power is the authority over foreign affairs. Statutes are made by Congress, subject to a presidential veto which can be overridden. Treaties are made by the president subject to a two-thirds agreement by the Senate. Nonetheless, a treaty is a sort of presidential law, and the president holds the primary voice in this type of national policy making. The Constitution provides no real limitations on the scope of the treaty making power, and thus, the authority to negotiate treaties is a major source of presidential strength.

The supremacy clause in the Constitution states that all statutes made under the Constitution shall be the law of the land. But it also states that all treaties made *under the authority* of the government shall be the law of the land as well. This suggests that the president may establish by treaty a policy which might be unconstitutional by statute, and this is exactly what has happened.

In *Missouri* v. *Holland* the Court up-held a treaty between the United States and Canada regulating the killing of migratory birds. Before the treaty a federal law regulating the killing of migratory birds was held unconstitutional as an infringement on the rights of the states. The Court held that the treaty-making power is superior to legislation. After the treaty Congress again passed a law regulating the killing of migratory birds and it was upheld. This means that the president is often capable of creating national policy, subject only to the restriction of the Senate's concurrence.

The Cabinet

The heads of the major departments of the executive branch of government comprise the Cabinet. This body evolved by custom, not by law, for the Constitution states nothing concerning a Cabinet. It was originally intended that the Senate would act as an advisory body to the executive. However, legislative enactments in 1789 created four departments: State, Treasury, War, and Attorney General, and President Washington chose to regard these department heads as his intimate advisors. The actual term "Cabinet" was first used in 1793, and the system is now an intimate part of the American governmental system.

Every president meets with his Cabinet on a regular basis, but its importance has varied with each administration. Meetings are secret, votes are rarely taken, and the entire procedure is completely beyond the control of Congress. Beneath each Cabinet position there are anywhere from a couple of hundred to several thousand appointive positions. All of these positions are filled with an eye toward enhancing the power and prestige of the chief executive.

There appears to be a traditional method of choosing a Cabinet. The secretary of state, for instance, is usually one of the leading political figures within his party. The secretary of commerce and the secretary of the treasury are usually easterners who command the respect of the business community. The positions of secretary of the interior and secretary of agriculture invariably go to westerners. The presidential campaign manager often becomes postmaster general. A major effort is made to represent all sections and interest groups in the country. All major religious faiths are represented, and since Franklin Roosevelt's administrations there has been a woman in the Cabinet. The basic aim of the president is to represent the entire country and thereby solidify his administration.

The Vice-Presidency

Some mention should be made of the vice-presidency. Up to the days of Roosevelt the vice-president occupied a dead-end position. He had two duties: to preside over the Senate and to take over the presidency if the president died or resigned. Therefore, he was chosen for political reasons with little or no heed paid to his abilities. The main consideration in his selection was usually his ability to balance the ticket. For this reason, leading party "mavericks" were often nominated for purposes of obliterating their political careers. Theodore Roosevelt was one such personality; he was thought to be a reformer at a time when his party reflected vested interests and conservatism. He was also quite popular. His selection balanced the ticket with conservative William McKinley and he was supposedly withdrawn from public life. But McKinley was assassinated and Roosevelt became the chief executive. So the maneuver can backfire.

In contemporary America the vice-president plays a more important role. He is still chosen politically, but he is assigned an increasing number of tasks. He is becoming a presidential trouble shooter and general public relations man for his government. However, he is still the subject of many jokes centering around his traditional obscurity.

The Federal Judiciary

The Constitution states that there shall be a Supreme Court and such inferior courts as Congress may establish. Federal judges are appointed for life (to remove them from political pressure), and the Supreme Court is to have original jurisdiction (try cases for the first time as contrasted with appeals cases) in all cases involving ambassadors, consuls, other public federal officials, and all matters in which a state is a party. This is the sum total of constitutional statements concerning the federal judiciary. The rest of the court system was set up by statute, along with the jurisdictions of the various court levels (what cases would be heard by a particular type of court). The basis of the federal court system was laid down in the Judiciary Act of 1789, and has not changed substantively.

The Lower Federal Courts

The district court is the lowest level federal court. Its number has grown from an original thirteen (one for each state) to a total of ninety-five. With very few technical exceptions, all civil and criminal cases arising out of federal law are first tried in this court. Next come the circuit or appeals courts. Originally there were three such courts; now there are eleven. The appeals court has two primary functions. One is to hear appeals from district court decisions and to sift out cases on their way to the Supreme Court. The other is to enforce the decisions of national regulatory agencies. Also, certain technical major federal violations are heard initially in the appeals courts rather than the federal district courts.

The Supreme Court

The Supreme Court, besides the original jurisdiction specified in the Constitution, hears appeals from federal appeals courts and from the various state supreme courts if there is a federal question or interpretation involved. Finally, the Supreme Court is the sole judge of which cases it is required to or should hear.

The Supreme Court is probably more violently attacked than any other governmental institution. It is viewed as the "cult of the robe" by some, who liken it to the aristocratic English House of Lords. One twentieth-century senator has called the Court a modern version of radical reconstruction. Another group claims it is dominated by Communists. It has been charged with being un-American, favoring criminals, discriminating against whites, and legislating for the nation.

Why so much criticism? The Supreme Court is vilified because it is furthest removed from popular control of all three branches of the federal government. Justices hold office for life subject to good behavior. They cannot be removed except by impeachment and as such, they tend to act independently, and probably sometimes in opposition to what the people or the Congress or the executive might desire. The criticism and the controversy prove the power of the Supreme Court.

For all the power that a Supreme Court justice wields, there exist no official requirements for the position, but every justice except one has practiced law before assuming the bench. Appointments are made primarily on political grounds. They may cross party lines because presidents appoint men to the Court who they feel will represent their particular political philosophy. A sometimes serious problem with the Court is the issue of old age. Holding office for life, some justices have taken this provision quite literally, and have held on to their positions when they were incapable of functioning properly because of poor health or senility. A member of the federal judiciary cannot be impeached only because he is old.

Politics on the Court

The Supreme Court must be careful to preserve its prestige, for it has no enforcement powers of its own but relies on the executive for implementation. As such, it will never anticipate an issue in deciding a case and will back off from certain types of cases, claiming that other governmental agencies are better qualified to render decisions. Also, it will not assert itself strongly unless it can count on the support of either the president or the Congress or both of them.

There is a widespread popular belief that the Supreme Court is above politics and the law is unchanging. This is hardly the case. The Court is deeply involved in politics and justices are appointed to the bench for political reasons. Law changes as circumstances change, and the decisions of the Supreme Court change correspondingly. There have been many instances throughout the nation's history when the Court has overruled itself and failed to honor its own precedents.

Law in its crude stages is simply formalized custom. Governmental structure is set up by a society mainly to preserve its customs and laws. The American form of government will continue to evolve, as it has in the past. And it will do so in the direction of greater power for the federal government as the nation moves towards a welfare-state approach to its problems.

For Further Reading

Beard, Charles A. *An Economic Interpretation of the Constitution of the United States.*
New York: Macmillan Company, 1913.

Berman, Daniel M. *In Congress Assembled: The Legislative Process in National Government.* New York: Macmillan Company, 1964.

Brown, Stuart G. *The American Presidency: Leadership, Partisanship, and Popularity.*
New York: Macmillan Company, 1966.

Elazar, Daniel. *American Federalism.* New York: Crowell, 1966.

Farrand, Max. *The Framing of the Constitution of the United States.* New Haven:
Yale University Press, 1940.

Holcombe, Arthur N. *Our More Perfect Union.* Cambridge: Harvard University
Press, 1950.

Jennings, M. Kent, and Zeigler, L. Harmon, (eds.). *The Electoral Process.* Englewood
Cliffs: Prentice-Hall, 1966.

Mayers, Lewis. *The American Legal System.* 2d ed. New York: Harper and Row,
1964.

Montross, Lynn. Reluctant Rebels: *The Story of the Continental Congress.* New
York: Harper, 1950.

Rossiter, Clinton. *Seedtime of the Republic.* New York: Harcourt, Brace, 1952.

Rourke, Francis E. (ed.). *Bureaucratic Power in National Politics.* Boston: Little,
Brown, 1965.

Snider, Clyde F. *Local Government in Rural America.* New York: Appleton-Century-
Crofts, 1957.

Sutherland, Arthur E. *Constitutionalism in America: Origins and Evolution of Its
Fundamental Ideas.* New York: Blaisdell, 1965.

Chapter Four
Politics: American Style

A sometimes confusing situation in modern America arises out of the nation's political party system. Americans have traditionally formed into groups to accomplish their political aims more effectively. Very early in the American experience the people learned the effectiveness of political groupings. They could praise individualism, but from a practical viewpoint uniqueness did not produce political results. People of like interests had to pool their strength and talents. They did this in forming colonies and settlements. They did this, as in the case of the Mayflower Compact, by forming a group even for migratory purposes. Americans are known as joiners, especially when they want to get something done in the political realm.

Conflicting viewpoints on what direction the American governmental system should take, led very early in the nation's history to the formation of political parties. Originally, these political parties rested on well-defined philosophical bases. When an individual said he was a Federalist or a Republican, people knew exactly what he stood for. But the current traditional party labels of "Democrat" and "Republican" are practically devoid of such clarity. The people are no longer sure what ideology or philosophy is at the basis of a particular political party.

Instead, the American public constantly hears such terminology as "liberal" and "conservative," "radical" or "moderate," "left" and "right," and even "extremist," used to describe political viewpoints, and often these labels only confuse. It is sometimes exceedingly difficult to distinguish between a liberal Republican and a liberal Democrat; such individuals are supposedly members of opposing political organizations, but what they stand for is unclear. This has created a serious difficulty for the American party system.

Accepted as a sacrosanct part of the American political structure, the American party system has evolved outside of the written Constitution, primarily as a matter of expediency. Through long-standing usage it has become very much a part of what is commonly referred to as American democracy in action.

A consideration of the evolution of this party system, in conjunction with the various schools of political thought involved in its formation, will serve as an aid to understanding modern political parties. It will also serve to buttress one of the key points emphasized in Chapter Three, namely, the evolutionary nature of the constitutional process.

Americans are well known for their persistent readiness to criticize their government. And criticism, if properly tendered, can have a very good effect. But this presupposes that people first understand the political "rules of the game." The Constitution on paper is not entirely the constitution in actual practice. An understanding of the actual practice of politics is equally important if criticism is to have any constructive effect and the American governmental system is to make sense.

Types of Political Organizations

Americans have hit upon two types of organizations to make their political demands felt, one for specific purposes of limited scope, and the other for more general, long-range purposes. Those organizations developed for specific purposes are called pressure groups. Those organized for general purposes are known as political parties.

There is a definite series of distinctions between the American pressure group and the political party. The pressure group is organized to attain specific goals of direct personal benefit only to the members of the group. It has a specific purpose and it cannot compromise this purpose. A political party, on the other hand, is organized solely with the intent of capturing political power. It has a program; it has a set of goals to be attained, but these are really secondary. They are willingly sacrificed if necessary in order to capture political power.

A political party is a very loose-knit organization. There are no dues which must be paid; there is no official membership process (some states, however, require voters to list a party affiliation in order to vote in a primary election). And there are no official set rules of conduct. This is in contrast with the pressure group which has an official membership roster, which charges dues, and which demands unswerving loyalty to the express purposes of the group.

However, political parties have one strong similarity with the pressure groups. They have a strong core of active leaders and a majority of more or less inactive members who do little else but vote. This hard core consists of party officers, workers, contributors, and political office holders. They also have a group of drifters, people who are not really committed, except in a temporary sense. With respect to the political party, this drifter group consists of approximately 20 per cent of the total electorate. They are the people who pick and choose candidates for voting purposes and accept no particular stated party philosophy. Their allegiance is hardly ever counted on; it is an illusive and transitory thing.

The loose-knit organizational structure that would be a definite handicap to the pressure group is a definite boon to the political party. For in the latter case the political party acts as a harmonizing agent for the various pressure groups. Additionally, and obviously, the candidates of the political parties very strongly desire to be elected to, and maintained in, office; therefore, they pay considerable heed to the wishes of their constituency. The professional career politician never ignores those who keep him in office.

Origins of the Party System

At the time of the formulation of the Constitution a single-party system was anticipated. This fact is brought out by the original procedure established for the choosing of the president and vice-president. The candidate who received the highest number of electoral votes, if a majority, was elected president, while the candidate with the second highest number of votes was named vice-president. Candidates did not run for a specific office, nor did they run on a particular ticket. If this procedure were still in effect, Goldwater would have been Johnson's vice-president, and Nixon would have been Kennedy's. The hopeless impasse which would result from this, especially in an era when the vice-president is given progressively more responsibility by the president, should be quite obvious.

Conflicting Notions of Government

Even before the time of the constitutional convention at Philadelphia, the rudiments of a two-party system existed. The Continental Congress had split into two groups. One of these groups was the confederalists, also known as radicals, because they favored a weak national government as it was eventually established in the Articles of Confederation. The other group was the nationalists, or conservatives, who wanted a strong, national governing system.

A note of explanation is in order. A word like "conservative" is relative. Strong government was traditional in the British system. The conservatives, in effect, wanted a continuance of the strong-government principle. In the mid–twentieth century a conservative is opposed to the concept of a strong federal government. He supposedly prefers the so-called laissez faire government of earlier decades. A partial definition of conservative, then, is one who favors little or no change from the pre-existing order. On the other hand the radical or the liberal usually wants a considerable change from the preceding order. It may be in the direction of strong or weak government; it depends on what form of government preceded it. The liberals of the revolutionary period wanted weak government; in the contemporary world they favor a highly complex and involved governmental structure.

However, the two groups, confederalists and nationalists, remained fairly constant and quiet until the beginning of George Washington's second administration in 1793. Washington's secretary of state was Thomas Jefferson, the brilliant Virginian who had penned the Declaration of Independence. His secretary of the treasury was Alexander Hamilton, a self-made financial genius. The different political philosophies of these two Cabinet members provided the ideological bases for the nation's first two major political parties.

Hamiltonianism

As the major premise of Alexander Hamilton's political philosophy was based on a very high regard for the rights of property, he favored a strong central government as the best method to preserve property from the attacks of the impoverished masses. Being in favor of property rights, Hamilton espoused measures which enhanced the accumulation of property by those who already possessed it.

Hence, Hamilton desired the development of an urban, industrialized nation to provide investment opportunities. He favored protective tariffs and internal improvements as methods of aiding the propertied class. He wanted the nation's economy to function in the manner of a modern corporation: issuing bonds, entering into long range indebtedness, and investing heavily in the present in order to increase the potential of the future. Governmental credit ratings were high on his list of priorities. Alexander Hamilton favored an aristocracy based on birth and wealth. He favored the traditional privileged class and apparently had little faith in the abilities or attitudes of the common man. The name of the political organization which he helped form was the Federalist Party.

Jeffersonianism

The key tenet of Thomas Jefferson's political philosophy was the idea of equal opportunity. The Enlightenment concept of the rights and dignity of the common man were an integral part of his thinking. Jefferson regarded strong government as being potentially tyrannical. Hence, he favored weak national government, believing that the rights of the individual would best be preserved by the various state governments. He was one of the nation's first great champions of state's rights. Jefferson did not share Hamilton's views on the future course of the American nation. The idea of a sprawling industrial megalopolis probably would have appalled him. He favored a nation consisting of individual small farmers as the one most likely to preserve the dignity of each individual.

Additionally, it follows that he would be opposed to such concepts as protective tariffs and internal improvements; these were essential only to an industrialized society. Concerning governmental financial indebtedness, Jefferson was opposed to the concept. He believed that it unfairly passed on to future generations the financial obligations of the present. And while Hamilton admired the contemporary English form of government, Jefferson was a great admirer of the French Revolution and what it ideologically represented.

Jefferson also favored an aristocracy. He seemingly believed that complete equality was an impossibility. The most virtuous and the most talented, he felt, should occupy the primary positions in society. But no man should be honored simply because he possessed more wealth than the next man, or because he inherited money and position. Hence, Jefferson was one of the nation's first promoters of a well formulated system of mass education. He believed in a qualified democracy and had faith in the ruling abilities of the common man, but he maintained that only through education could the democratic system hope to achieve success.

George Washington was basically a Federalist, and on most issues sided with Hamilton. Finally Jefferson quit the Cabinet in disgust and devoted his energies to the development of his political party, which became known as the Jeffersonian Republican Party. The two-party system had developed.

At the very basis of the controversy between Hamilton and Jefferson was a philosophical issue, stemming back to two Old World philosophers: Thomas Hobbes and John Locke. Hobbes held that man was naturally depraved and could not be trusted to handle power. Therefore, Hobbes concluded that the only way to control man was through fear and government needed sufficient power to enforce its dictates. This is the ideological basis of Hamilton's view on government. Locke, on the other hand, believed that man was naturally good and capable of considerable improvement. This comprised the basis for Jefferson's views, and helps to explain his emphasis on education.

Historical Development of the American Party System

Washington's presidential successor, John Adams, was a complete Federalist.

The Federalists, during his administration, succeeded in alienating all but the aristocracy, always a very small part of the population. They did so by passing many laws designed to aid the wealthy: the National Bank Act, the Land Law of 1796, the strong show of force in suppressing the Whiskey Rebellion, and the infamous Alien and Sedition Acts of 1798.

The Election of 1800

So in 1800 Thomas Jefferson was able to capture the presidency. He had been vice-president under John Adams during the preceding four years. The election of 1800 was unique in that Thomas Jefferson and Aaron Burr both received the same number of votes. Burr was supposed to be the vice-president but the ballots were not marked by office. Burr, therefore, saw an opportunity to possibly capture the presidency. There followed a drawn out political battle which culminated in Jefferson's victory and the ratification of the Twelfth Amendment.

This amendment constitutionally provided for a party system. It stipulated that the presidential and vice-presidential candidates would run for specific offices by separate ballot. It further provided that in the event no candidate received a majority of the electoral vote, the House of Representatives would choose as president one of the top three candidates. (The Constitution had originally allowed selection from among the top five candidates.)

Collapse of the Federalist Party

The Jeffersonian Republicans remained in power while the Federalist Party gradually deteriorated. By the end of the War of 1812, the nation had, in fact, a one-party system. However, the Republicans had been gradually changing their political ideology, becoming more like the Federalists both in belief and action. The War of 1812, and the spirit of nationalism which it inculcated, was to a large extent responsible for this change. During the two administrations of President James Monroe (1816–1824), the party became known as the National Republican Party.

The Election of 1824

The election of 1824 witnessed the reappearance of the two-party system. Andrew Jackson easily carried the popular vote in that election, but since there were four leading contenders for the presidency, no candidate received a majority of the electoral vote. The election went to the House of Representatives which was required to choose one of the top three contenders for the presidency. The fourth highest candidate was Henry Clay, who was also speaker of the house. He threw his influence to the candidate closest to his own political views, John Quincy Adams, who subsequently was chosen president. Clay was immediately rewarded for his efforts by being appointed secretary of state.

Andrew Jackson had been one of the nation's few legitimately unwilling candidates. However, losing the election in the House, after winning a plurality, caused him to believe that he had been cheated. A new political party began to form around Jackson which was known as the Jacksonian Democratic Party. This party was the child of the original Jeffersonian Republican Party in terms of political ideology. The National Republican Party, meanwhile, was in the process of becoming known as the Whig Party, tracing its ideology back to the original Federalist Party.

Effect of Slavery on the Party System

This was basically the political framework until the closing years of the 1840's when a significant domestic issue split the party system apart: the extension of slavery. The Democratic Party split into northern and southern wings, while the Whig Party lost its prestige and leadership. The appeal of the Whig Party was strictly in the industrially developing North. But it was forced to share the area with northern Democrats and a growing number of third-party movements. The southland possessed a one party system; almost all were members of the southern wing of the Democratic Party although there were a number of southern Whigs who were different in name only and moved into the Democratic Party in the 1850's.

In 1854 the North came up with its answer to the southern one-party system. The new Republican Party was a northern party consisting of a coalition of ex-Whigs, third-party movements, and some northern Democrats. Southern Democrats traced their lineage back to Jeffersonian Republicanism. Northern Republicans, especially after the Civil War, maintained a somewhat tenuous resemblance to the original Federalists. Their real unity during the 1850's was based on a position calling for no further extension of the slavery system. With the passage of time they added various other policies to make their party acceptable to more people. By the end of the Civil War, the Republican Party would be strongly reminiscent of the Federalists.

Dominance of the Republican Party

During the Civil War itself, the Republicans temporarily adopted the name "Union Party," to create the illusion that politics was suspended until after the crisis. Following the war there was again a one-party system in American politics as a reconstruction Congress, consisting of a solid Republican majority, attempted to prevent the re-establishment of the Democratic Party in the South. But as interest in reconstruction began to

dwindle, the Democratic Party gradually began to re-emerge. It became the sole party in the South by 1876 and the nation witnessed the beginning of the "solid South" phenomenon. Still, from the pre Civil War era up to the election of Woodrow Wilson in 1912, the nation experienced only one Democratic president, Grover Cleveland, elected on two separate occasions (1885–1889 and 1893–1897).

In 1893 there was a temporary split and realignment of the two major parties. The issue was over whether or not American currency should be backed by gold or silver, and it crossed traditional party lines. But by 1897 the issue ceased to be critical, and the party organizations returned to their normal pattern until 1912.

Election of 1912

A very interesting situation developed in that year. Theodore Roosevelt had left the White House in 1909 and had successfully put forth William Howard Taft as his handpicked successor. But over the next four years the two men separated after a series of misunderstandings, and Roosevelt decided to seek the Republican presidential nomination in 1912. However, he began his move far too late and Taft was able to capture the nomination. Roosevelt thereupon bolted the nominating convention and was selected by a faction of the Republican Party known as the Progressive Republican Party or the Bull Moose Party.

This split in the Republican vote assured victory for the Democratic Party candidate, Woodrow Wilson, who polled far fewer popular votes than the combined Republican vote. The really unique aspect of this election was that Theodore Roosevelt, a third-party candidate, finished ahead of Taft. This marked the only time in American political history when a third-party candidate had achieved such success. The Progressive Party, incidentally, died out by 1920.

The Parties After World War I

After World War I the two traditional parties, Democratic and Republican, were stabilized. The Republicans were generally satisfied with what they had accomplished over the last half century of dominance, and became the party of retrenchment and the status quo. The party tended to attract a high percentage of people who were conservatives, although there was a highly vocal liberal minority within the party. The Democratic Party, for obvious reasons, was not satisfied. It sought a more active government and tended to attract a higher percentage of liberals, including some ex-Republican progressives who were dissatisfied with the limited scope of their party's reform program.

By the 1920's, neither of the two major parties could be traced back directly to one of the two original parties. The post–World War I Republican Party was satisfied with the status quo and it sought a curb on government initiative. This was in accordance with Jeffersonian principles. But the Republicans were satisfied with a political system which had been erected through the use of Federalist principles during the big business era of the nineteenth century, to which Thomas Jefferson would have been violently opposed. At the same time the Democratic Party, after having once been identified with southern slavery and an aristocratic society, was beginning to champion the rights of the common man, and resurrecting its roots from the Jacksonian era. But the Democrats did so by advocating further action, power, and involvement by the federal government, and this, of course, was Hamiltonian in

viewpoint. The two major parties had become a mixture of the philosophies which had distinguished the two original schools of American politics.

The Modern Political Party

Traditional Appeal of the Parties

To attempt a comparison of the political ideologies of the two major parties in the contemporary era is difficult. This is mainly because the parties themselves are split into liberal, conservative, and moderate wings. The difficulty is enhanced because the major parties were given misleading and incorrect stereotypes—the Democratic Party is called the party of the poor, while the Republicans are supposed to favor the rich. There are rich and poor in both parties, in the rank and file and in elected office.

An American can hardly pick up a newspaper or watch a news report without coming across such terms as "left," "right," and "moderate." What these terms mean, however, is not always clear. The terms originated to some extent in English parliamentary practice. His Majesty's Loyal Opposition, the liberal Whig Party, was seated on the left side of the assembly chamber, and his conservative supporters, the Tories, were seated on the right side of the chamber. In the United States "right" is synonymous with "conservative," and "left" is synonymous with "liberal." In addition, however, there is a far left, which consists of socialists and communists, and a far right, which consists of such organizations as the John Birch Society and the Ku Klux Klan. There is also a much larger moderate group composed of the people who are neither liberal nor conservative, but rather a combination of the two positions, depending on particular issues.

"Conservative" versus "Liberal"

"Conservative" primarily means to favor the status quo and to be reluctant to change. The classical American conservative in the contemporary era is thinking in terms of the pre–New Deal era, although most conservatives support one-time progressive measures such as social security. "Liberal" usually means to favor most changes in the direction of more governmental services. The liberal is more committed to experimentation and change than the conservative.

Except for the ultras at both ends of the political spectrum, all of these views are well within the American political tradition. And the differences in opinion are very healthy for the nation. The liberals help to keep the governmental structure from falling behind the times, while the conservatives try to restrain the liberals from pushing too far too fast. The fringe areas of politics also serve a useful purpose, although sometimes in a negative sense. The militancy of the far right, for instance, has caused many Americans to seriously analyze the purposes for which their country is supposed to stand. Additionally, the far left has brought out a traditional defense mechanism, the end result of which is a strong (though sometimes misguided) patriotism.

Crossing Party Lines

Neither the Democrats nor the Republicans succeed in passing congressional legislation by a strictly partisan vote. Individual congressmen normally vote according to their own personal ideology on a particular issue, unless party leaders feel it is of extreme importance to the party. Liberal Democrats and liberal Republicans normally vote together; conservative Democrats and Republicans do likewise. The moderate center tends to split over bills sponsored by their respective parties, but possesses no deep-seated party loyalties.

There are hardly any hundred-percent liberals or conservatives. A politician may be liberal on some measures and quite conservative on others. And this tends to be the general practice rather than the exception. A politician who is branded as a liberal may be extremely conservative on Negro voting rights but highly receptive to a welfare-state program. On the other hand, a politician branded as a conservative may be staunchly opposed to welfare programs, but just as staunchly champion the civil rights of minority groups. In sum, the contemporary party labels of Democratic and Republican are nearly devoid of meaning. Terms such as "liberal" and "conservative" are usually far more intelligible to the voters, even though they too are somewhat confusing. Definitive party labels no longer exist, nor do ideologically opposed parties.

The Organization of a Political Party

The Precinct

Political parties are organized like giant pyramids, with the precincts at the base and the national committees at the apex. The key job, the one which determines the success of the party at the polls, is that of precinct leader. The size of a precinct depends on the density of population; it may comprise one city block or it may consist of a number of blocks. The primary job of the precinct leader is to get the people in his area to the polls on election day.

The Ward

The next level of organization is the ward, which consists of several precincts. A ward is an administrative subdivision within a large city, usually corresponding to the boundaries within which an alderman is elected. The ward chairman coordinates the activities of the precincts within his area and serves on his party's central city committee. This committee selects candidates for local offices, handles the patronage, and in general, coordinates all party activities at the local level.

In rural areas there are rarely precincts or wards. There is, however, a county organization which is very similar to the central city committee. It performs similar tasks on a county-wide basis, and is composed of the political leaders of the various communities within the county.

The next level of party structure is an elusive, temporary, district organization. It corresponds geographically to the areas from which federal and state congressmen are elected. It exists solely to aid candidates running for these offices. Unlike the city and county organizations which are permanent, it generally disappears between election years.

State Central Committee

Over all of these structures stands the state central committee. It has a number of important functions: it selects candidates at the state level, coordinates the party activities for the entire state, and cooperates with the national committees. The leader of the state party system is either a United States senator, the governor, or some third person agreed upon by these individuals. This third person could well be a ranking congressman or influential businessman. The real backbone of the American political party system is found within the state.

National Committees

There is also a national level of party organization which exists to coordinate the various state organizations during national elections. Both houses of the Congress have Republican and Democratic committees to aid in re-electing their partisans to Congress. There is also a national committee whose primary purpose is to call and organize the national party nominating conventions. In nonelection years it is not very active, functioning only to create a favorable image for the party.

The Need for Money

Besides votes a political party needs money more than anything else. A major political party spends millions of dollars each year, and during presidential elections the figure is much higher. Under the provisions of the Hatch Acts (1940–1941), Congress stipulated that a party may spend no more than $3 million per year. But there is no real way of knowing exactly how much money is used to get a candidate into office.

The money comes from a number of sources, and not without some degree of pressure. Candidates, office holders, their relatives and friends, and holders of patronage jobs are all expected to contribute. Pressure groups contribute heavily to whichever party or candidate they believe will push their special interests. Wealthy individuals make large contributions, perhaps hoping to obtain some appointment to enhance their prestige, or perhaps out of a spirit of civic-mindedness. Finally, there are the fund raising dinners which add considerably to the party treasury.

Because of this great dependence on money for political success, there is the considerable possibility of corruption. Therefore, every state has some sort of "corrupt practices" act to regulate election procedures. These laws cover bribery, intimidation, manipulation of voters, and the size of contributions. The real merit of these laws depends on the sincerity of each state in enforcing them. They are, however, rarely enforced to the full extent of the law.

The Hatch Acts

In addition, the federal government also has legislation designed to regulate conduct in federal elections. This legislation (mentioned above) is the Hatch Acts of 1940 and 1941. No federal employees other than those in policy-making positions, no corporation, and no labor union can make contributions to a political party. Also, individual contributions are limited to $5000 per year per candidate or committee. Then there are various limits on the amount which a candidate himself can spend in seeking office. These financial limitations do not include money used for travel, stationery and postage, telephone bills, and printing costs. This allows a tremendous degree of latitude for campaign spending. The intent of the law is to keep highly financed candidates from "buying" votes through specially created jobs, etc.

Periodically, there have been unsuccessful attempts to have the federal government absorb the campaign expenses for candidates. President Johnson himself, has suggested such a procedure. All candidates for a particular office would be authorized to spend a prescribed amount of money for their campaigns, and the federal government would pick up the tab. A major advantage of this system would be the termination of pressures for financial resources which could be corrupting. But at the same time, a highly popular, widely backed candidate would be placed on equal financial footing with rivals who might not command

much support with the people. The issue is consequently not yet decided.

Third-Party Movements

The Nature of Third Parties

In addition to the two major political parties there have often been third-party movements in the United States. These parties usually are nothing more than glorified pressure groups, although some of them have attained more broadly based organizations. Most often they appear during periods of national stress, capture a small percentage of votes, and disappear shortly afterwards. They have experienced little electoral success on the national scene. Most of their achievements have been obtained in municipal and state campaigns.

Perhaps the most successful of all third-party movements involved the activities of the Grangers in the 1870's, and their more influential successor the Populist Party which significantly affected the nation (see Chapter Six). The Free Soil Party of the late 1840's which was formed to prevent the expansion of slavery in the federal territories, achieved some success before fading into the new Republican Party. The Quids comprised an early third-party movement. Led by John Randolph of Virginia, they claimed to remain true to the original Jeffersonian ideals, even after Jefferson himself was accused of violating them as president. An Anti-Masonic Party was formed partly to protest against Andrew Jackson (he was a Mason), and went on to oppose Catholics as well. The Know-Nothing Party was formed in the South in the 1850's because dissident southerners felt alienated from the traditional parties. Then there have been Loco-focos, Barnburners, Greenbackers, Unionists, Laborites, etc., at various periods in the nation's

Historical Pictures Service, Chicago

A Poster Depicting Granger–Populist Ideals

history. And the nation has always had such organizations as the Anti-Prohibition Party. The specific goals of most of these parties indicate that they were more like pressure groups than political parties.

In the twentieth century there exist the Socialist and Communist party candi-dates, who usually poll something in the order of 25,000 votes in a national election year. Of course, the number of votes captured by these parties depends on the political complexion of the country at the time, and the appeal of particular candi-dates.

For instance, the Socialist candidate, Eugene Debs, polled close to a million votes in the presidential election of 1920, while he was serving a sentence in a federal prison which had arisen out of the hysteria of the World War I era. He polled a similar vote in 1912. The Socialist Party is one of the more successful third parties in American political history, and has strongly influenced progressive legislation (see Chapter Twelve). The Communist Party, on the other hand, has had little influence. Then there are always a few more ephemeral candidates. For instance, a self-appointed Ruler of the Universe polled close to 25,000 popular votes in the presidential election of 1960.

Why Third Parties are Weak

But all things considered, the American political structure is such that it is practically impossible for a third party to attain any lasting degree of success. There are two basic reasons for this. For one, the United States possesses a basic political unit known as the single member district. Under this system the candidate who gets the most votes in a certain geographical area wins the election, regardless of how many other candidates there are and what their vote might be. In most European countries, however, candidates are entitled to fractional seats, while the losing candidate in the United States gets nothing. Again in Europe, if the losing candidate polls 25 per cent of the vote in his area, his party is entitled to one-fourth of a seat. This system encourages third parties, of which there are many in Europe.

Second, there exists one major office in the United States which is filled by a nationwide vote—the office of the presidency (of course, the office of the vice-presidency is in the same category). The candidate must obtain a majority of the electoral vote in order to win. There-

fore, to elect a president the people must combine into major groups often disregarding sectional, economic, and personal interests. In European countries these various factions form temporary coalitions to select an executive, who may be removed if the composition of the coalition changes even slightly.

The Nominating System

The strength of the political party organization in America is best exemplified in the nomination process. If the membership of a given political party could not agree on a particular candidate for office, the vote would be fragmented and defeat probably assured. This party selection is known as the nomination process.

However, one does not have to be nominated by a political party in order to run for public office. One can file for office by submitting a petition signed by a specified number of voters. This number varies from state to state. One then runs as an Independent, or whatever else one wants to be called. A person can also be elected to public office by doing absolutely nothing. Almost every ballot or voting machine provides for a write-in vote; the voter may cast his ballot for anyone he desires, even if the name does not appear on the official ballot, simply by writing it in.

But with very few exceptions, and these are on the local level, the only manner by which a candidate can be elected to public office is through the nomination of a major party organization. Historically, three types of nominating procedures have been used: the party caucus, the party convention, and the nominating primary.

The Caucus System

The caucus system was used from pre-revolutionary days to the presidency of Andrew Jackson. The party caucus was nothing more than an informal meeting of political and civic leaders, who agreed on a candidate to support for election. The populace, in this procedure, possessed absolutely no voice in the selection of political candidates. As time went on the caucus became more structured, and included representation from as many areas and factions as was reasonably possible, in order to obtain a broader support for the candidates.

At the same time there existed state and national legislative caucuses. Party members holding elective office in the state legislatures would meet and decide on candidates for various state executive offices, while partisans holding seats in the national Congress would decide on the candidate for the presidency.

The caucus was a closed system. It was a vestige of aristocracy in a nation which was becoming more and more democratic. Throughout the 1820's, with the admission of a number of new liberal western states, the franchise was broadening. More people were acquiring the right to vote, as long standing property and religious qualifications were being eliminated. With the candidacy of Andrew Jackson the people presumably acquired the will to use their new political power. They seemingly had a people's champion whom they desired to put into the White House. So the caucus system was attacked and faltered during the 1820's. By the 1830's it was practically non-existent.

The Party Convention

Arising to take its place was a more specialized, representative form of the caucus system, the party convention. An elaborately devised system of choosing delegates from all levels of the party organization was initiated. These delegates, it was hoped, would reflect all shades of party opinion. Theoretically,

a candidate would be chosen who would reflect the wishes of the maximum possible number of party members.

Although the convention system was an improvement over the caucus, it still possessed certain drawbacks. Local delegates were usually selected through the offices of the local political boss. The people themselves were still far removed from having a significant voice. However, the convention system is still in existence in contemporary America on the national level, while a few states also use it. Except for the highly colorful national presidential nominating convention (and in a few states), the system has been giving way, since 1900, to a new method which allows for direct voter participation in nominations.

The Nominating Primary

The nominating primary election is nothing more than an election of party candidates for office by the members of the party themselves, following normal election procedures. Any person can have his name placed on the primary ballot simply by filing a petition with the signatures of a specified number of voters. This number varies from state to state, and ranges anywhere from 10 per cent to 50 per cent of the registered voters. The candidate who wins the most votes in the primary election captures the nomination. He need not obtain a majority of the votes cast except in a few southern states. In those states, if no one obtains a majority the election is held again and again until someone, hopefully, does.

The primary is normally a partisan affair. Both Democrats and Republicans use it in an attempt to obtain the strongest possible candidates for particular offices. But there is also a non-partisan primary, where candidates for certain offices, usually judgeships, are chosen without reference to political affiliation. In this case the two candidates who win the most votes in the primary election run against each other in the regular election.

There are two types of partisan primary: the open and the closed. The closed primary limits the vote for party candidates to members of that particular party. The purpose is to prevent the opposing party from electing the presumed weakest candidate to oppose their party's theoretically stronger candidate. Two systems are employed to prevent this. Some states require voters, upon registering, to signify an affiliation with a particular party. On the day of the primary election the voter's name is checked against his registration card and he is given a primary ballot for that party. This system works fairly well. The other system is extremely weak. Voters are ask to declare their party allegiance, past and future, at the primary polls. This is, obviously, a much poorer method.

In the open-primary states, voters are given a ballot which lists all candidates for the two major parties in separate columns. The voter may select names in either column, but not in both. A split ticket cannot be voted in a primary election.

The Presidential Election Process

The biggest and hardest nominating job is that for the office of the presidency. During a presidential election year every technique in American politics operates at peak performance. The caucus, the convention, and the primary are all used. Organizations spring up which are not casts, and speeches inundate the nation.

The method by which a president is chosen is one of the most misunderstood and complicated processes in America. The Constitution states the president and vice-president shall be elected for a four year term. Each state shall choose a group equal to the total number of federal senators and representatives from the state. This group will then meet and cast its votes for the president and vice-president on specifically marked ballots. The ballots are sealed and sent to the president of the United States Senate who opens them before a joint session of Congress. The candidate who receives a majority of these so-called electoral votes is declared president. If no candidate receives a majority, the House of Representatives, with each state delegation having one vote for this purpose, will choose one of the top three candidates for the office. All states must cast their ballots on the same day.

This is the entire procedure except for the Twenty-second Amendment which limits a president to two terms and less than two years of an unexpired term, the total not to exceed ten years, and the Twenty-third Amendment which gives electoral votes (three) to the District of Columbia.

Nominating a President

The Constitution says nothing concerning how a president shall be nominated. The political parties themselves devised the techniques for nominating candidates for the presidential office. Party delegates to nominating conventions are chosen by a variety of methods. Some are elected at primary elections; some are appointed by party committees within the state; others are chosen through the medium of a state delegate nominating convention, plus various combinations of these methods. But regardless of the method of selection, the majority of delegates to the national convention are professional politicians.

What the average American witnesses at a presidential nominating convention is usually window dressing. The real work at a convention is done not on the floor of the convention hall, but primarily in private meetings at which bargains and compromises are mostly responsible for the voting results of the following day. Still, the exciting activities of the convention, capture the imagination of the nation.

Conducting the Campaign

Having nominated a presidential and vice-presidential candidate, the party is ready to begin its campaign in earnest. Various national sub-committees are organized and the state party committees are mobilized to conduct and coordinate the election effort under the direction of the national committee. Campaign slogans, buttons, and posters are devised and disseminated. Arrangements are made for television and radio announcements to "advertise" the candidate to the public.

Campaign strategy, obviously, depends on circumstances. Party leaders attempt to gauge public opinion to ascertain the type of man desired as a national leader. Then they try to endow their candidate with these popular characteristics. Politicians have learned over the years that the public votes mainly for personalities rather than on issues. There is a great deal of Hollywood star-building and Madison Avenue advertising involved in a presidential campaign.

Obtaining Public Support

Party leaders and campaign strategists must then determine the issues which appeal to most voters. In 1916 Wilson campaigned on the slogan "he kept us out of war" because the public wanted to avoid intervention in the European war. Wilson had, in certain respects, already challenged Germany, and in 1917 the United States was at war, but the slogan helped win the election for him. In 1920 Harding called for a return to "normalcy," capitalizing on the disillusionment in the nation caused by World War

I and the intense reform movement. It succeeded for him just as the prosperity image worked for Coolidge and Hoover.

In 1932 Franklin Roosevelt campaigned on a platform calling for bold, persistent experimentation to solve the nation's economic problems. This is exactly what Depression America wanted to hear. In 1936 he campaigned on his past performance. In 1940, with war in Europe, and the position of the United States in some jeopardy, he campaigned on the theme that it was not expedient to change horses in midstream. In 1960 after eight years of the aging Dwight Eisenhower, John F. Kennedy campaigned on the idea of youth and the New Frontier. His appeal was centered on challenge, dynamism, and responsibility— and the nation was apparently ready for it. The successful candidate is invariably the one who correctly ascertains what the public wants to hear and then says it.

Another point which receives very serious consideration is whether or not to overtly attack the opposition. For instance, Kennedy could not attack Eisenhower because Eisenhower held a place of high esteem in the minds of most Americans. So he avoided the issue. Roosevelt, on the other hand, gained considerably by attacking the unpopular Herbert Hoover. James Blaine and Grover Cleveland conducted one of the "best" mudslinging campaigns in American political history in 1884. Cleveland was charged with immorality; Blaine was charged with corruption. Both charges were true.

The Electoral College

Regardless of the type of campaign, the end result is what happens on election day. However, the president of the United States is not really elected by the votes cast by the tens of millions in the polling booths, but rather by the electoral college—those electors chosen within each state, equalling in number the members in the national Congress from that state. Technically, the votes cast in the polling booths for a particular candidate elect a slate of electors pledged to cast their votes for that candidate. But the electors are not legally bound to vote according to the wishes of the people. Theoretically, they could elect someone else, although it has never happened.

A curious situation has sometimes occurred in the electoral system, in which a candidate has won the popular vote and then been defeated in the electoral college. When Grover Cleveland was elected in 1884 he won office by a majority of 25,000 popular votes. However, he lost the election in 1888 although he won the popular vote by 100,000. Woodrow Wilson captured the presidency in 1912 with roughly 9 million popular votes, but his two Republican opponents combined polled approximately 16 million votes. In fact if a candidate carries the twelve most populous states by one popular vote each, and loses the rest by overwhelming margins, he is still the winner.

Consistently in Congress, amendments are proposed to either abolish or modify the electoral college. They all fail either because certain states, usually the large ones, block them, or because of opposition from strong vested interests in local political machines. The control of the electoral vote is potentially a powerful weapon for a state. For example, in the election of 1960, if Nixon (instead of Kennedy) had carried New York state, the eight votes which Mississippi refused to cast for either major party candidate would have prevented either of them from obtaining a majority of the electoral vote, and the election would have gone into the House of Representatives. In a close election, one state could seriously disrupt the electoral process under the present system, and states desire to keep this power for bargaining purposes.

Pressure Groups and American Pluralism

Most Americans have heard the statement that America is a pluralistic society. The validity of this statement is partially evidenced by the large number of pressure groups operating in the country. In the American social structure, great emphasis is placed on the integrity and respect of the individual—at least theoretically. But in a nation close to the two hundred million mark in population, it is exceedingly difficult for the private citizen to stand up and make himself heard in governmental circles.

Therefore, Americans have traditionally formed into groups. These groups may be economic, such as the Chamber of Commerce, or they may be social, religious, or fraternal. The collective voice of hundreds or thousands of people carries far more weight than any individual. America is most certainly a pluralistic society; composed of many groups each seeking certain goals, and often working against one another. It is the group rather than the individual which is the basic motivating force in the United States.

One particular type of group is the political interest group, better known as the pressure group. They are largely responsible for much of the dynamism in the American political system. One of the functions of government in a democratic society is to regulate these various groups and to somehow provide for the best interests of the majority.

The Scope of Pressure Groups

There are literally tens of thousands of pressure groups operating in America. They range from impressive, well financed national groups which maintain large professional staffs in the nation's capital, to much smaller local groups. All pressure groups are concerned with bringing about some changes in the system which would be to their particular benefit. A pressure group is held together by motives of self-interest.

The magnitude and scope of pressure groups can best be illustrated by briefly considering some of the more significant ones. The two outstanding business pressure groups are the Chamber of Commerce and the National Association of Manufacturers. The Chamber of Commerce is concerned primarily with curbing governmental regulation of prices and wages, and with encouraging the government to increase its internal improvements program. The National Association of Manufacturers primarily works at counteracting the strength of organized labor, but it also encourages federal measures which aid business. Both groups lobby for low corporate taxes and both spend considerable sums of money to maintain powerful, professional lobbies.

It should be pointed out that pressure groups are often inconsistent. They will be against the concept of big government if a particular expansion of governmental power is detrimental to their special interests, but they will favor enhanced governmental power if it aids their cause.

A very powerful pressure group for labor is the AFL-CIO. It seeks higher minimum wage laws, more governmental regulation of business, and various programs which appeal to the lower income groups, such as public housing and improved social security benefits. The union lobby in Washington is one of the most powerful in the nation. Union leaders exercise a considerable influence over the voting behavior of literally millions of people through their union newspapers. Unions also exercise tremendous power due to their wealth. In contemporary America the larger unions possess ample funds to maintain powerful professional lobbies.

Farmers, too, have their national pressure groups. The American Farm Bureau Federation, composed of the large and wealthy farming interests, represents their special interests in Washington. The National Grange and the National Farmers Union represent the middle-income and poorer farmers. The National Grange draws most of its strength from the New England area, while the National Farmers Union is primarily a Plains states organization. All farmer pressure groups favor less government regulation of production. All of them favor increased parity; all favor lower taxes on real property.

Then there are various other special interest groups. The National Association for the Advancement of Colored People, for example, is principally concerned with the enforcement of civil and voting rights for Negroes. It is without a doubt one of the strongest pressure groups operating on the contemporary American scene. Its numbers are less than organized labor, but in terms of organization and enthusiasm it is unparalleled.

While most other pressure groups are concerned primarily with lobbying efforts in Congress, the NAACP also expends considerable energies to elicit support from the federal court system to accomplish its aims. The NAACP is one of the most controversial pressure groups in America, mainly because many people associate their personal biases and prejudices with it. Partly this is because the Negro possesses tremendous voting strength in the nation's large cities. In the past this strength has been ineffectual, but with recent successful attempts to organize it, politicians are now being forced to pay attention to the swelling urban Negro population. This is evidenced by the election of Negro mayors in large urban areas during the 1967 local elections.

The Techniques of Success

These groups and many others are highly successful because they are well organized. They are all endowed by small individual contributors, plus some much larger sums donated by wealthy supporters who usually prefer to remain anonymous. They all maintain professional lobbies in Washington. Lobbies consist of groups of people whose prime purpose is to visit various congressmen most congressmen, usually with an eye toward the next election, conduct themselves accordingly.

Pressure groups also make their influence felt on political parties. For instance, Democratic Party success in recent years has depended mainly on the support of the large city vote. The two largest voting blocks in the cities are the unions and the Negroes. Therefore, the successful party must pay attention to these two groups when it comes time to select candidates and adopt a platform. Consequently, the Republican Party has made some limited attempts during the past few years aimed at also capturing these votes. This is a difficult task, since the Republicans must first change the image, held by many, that it is the party of the rich. Nonetheless, both parties recognize the desirability of controlling, or at least obtaining the support of, certain pressure groups if they are going to capture political power.

Political pressure groups do not act only on the national level. Some are organized strictly as state or local groups, but their intent, based of course on local circumstances, is quite similar. When a group of housewives picket a busy thoroughfare because of the absence of a crossing light they are acting as a spontaneous pressure group. They are organized in an attempt to force the city authorities to perform an action which is only of special interest to themselves. Similarly, when a citizens group is formed to promote a new city park it is operating as a pressure group. Whenever a group of people attempt to enforce their particular interests on the majority, they are acting as a pressure group.

The Trouble with Pressure Groups

Although these groups exert a large influence on all levels of government, they have certain limitations. For instance, it sometimes happens that people who belong to pressure groups belong to several of them concurrently, and occasionally, they belong to different groups which have conflicting purposes. Consequently, each pressure group consists of a minority uniquely committed to obtaining certain results, and a large number of people who are less dedicated and less militant. This means that pressure groups do not always have the strength which their membership rolls indicate. However, the greater the number of people belonging to a particular pressure group, the larger should be the dedicated minority.

Segments of pressure groups are sometimes quite diversified in aims and tactics. For example, the Chamber of Commerce seeks government-granted benefits for businessmen. But segments within the Chamber of Commerce propose different measures for accomplishing this goal, or seek other kinds of benefits. Therefore, it is sometimes difficult for a large pressure group to determine a set policy which will receive the backing of its entire membership. The upper echelons of a pressure group often endorse measures which are opposed by the rank and file, who then demonstrate their disapproval at the polls. Consequently, the professional politician spends considerable time studying pressure groups. A group which does not have the support of its membership is very rarely given consideration. But a group which is united can damage the politician, and so he pays attention to its demands.

Measuring Public Opinion

The countless millions of disinterested Americans who never become members of pressure groups or political organizations traditionally become very active when some action is attempted which is not in accordance with the nebulous American rules of the game. An excellent example of this occurred shortly after Franklin Roosevelt's impressive re-election in 1936. He was at the crest of his popularity, having carried forty-six of the forty-eight states in the election. Most Americans loved or respected him for his various far-reaching attempts to curb the Depression, and they allowed him an unprecedented latitude for experimentation.

However, Roosevelt's experimental legislation was being invalidated consistently by a rather conservative Supreme Court. Therefore he introduced a legislative measure to revamp the Court. The nation, in response, was greatly alarmed. As much as Roosevelt was admired, he was held to be tampering with something basic to American government: the separation of powers doctrine. As a consequence, he suffered his greatest legislative defeat. Such is the strength of American public opinion when it is sufficiently aroused. Recognizing this force, pressure groups and governmental officials exert considerable effort to obtain the support of public opinion.

The Difficulty of the Problem

The political party has the difficult task of determining how to solicit the support of pressure groups and private individuals. On the surface this may appear to be relatively simple. The party first determines what the pressure groups and individual Americans want, and then attempts to give them as much as possible. But the methods employed in determining what is wanted are quite complex and never really certain. Public opinion is an extremely difficult item to ascertain correctly.

Public opinion is nothing more than the collective attitudes, ideas, prejudices, desires, habits, of the people. Any one of literally thousands of factors can form a person's attitudes: home, church, school, television, newspapers, a sign board, a casual remark—anything. These attitudes can and do change radically overnight. Politicians rely on a number of different techniques for measuring public opinion.

Two of these sources of public opinion have already been mentioned. One is the pressure group, and the other is voting behavior. Who gets elected, and on what issues, gives the politician a general idea as to what is desired by the people. However, this type of information is sometimes a couple of years old, and hence can be unreliable.

Another method of determining public opinion is the mailbag. A number of people regularly write, call, or visit their elected officials to make known their opinions. Politicians tend to pay a considerable amount of attention to this type of contact. It is often grassroots opinion and tends to reflect what the average housewife or laborer is thinking. Politicians sometimes pay more attention to these individual expressions of opinion than they do to organized pressure groups, which many times reflect only the opinions of a single segment of American society.

The Mass Media

Still another possible aid to the politician is the newspaper. People generally buy newspapers whose editorial policies are in agreement with their own views. At least, this is an assumption made by politicians. However, there is also a large portion of the public which buys a particular paper because it has better sports coverage, or hits the street on their way to or from work. Most people do not read editorials. So again, newspapers do not give the politician a completely reliable picture of public opinion.

Newspapers possess other drawbacks. The journalist is supposed to report the news accurately, quickly, and objectively. However, newspapers are commercial enterprises. They are, therefore, greatly concerned with circulation and have been known to distort the facts in order to obtain increased circulation. Of course the classic example of this occurred in the last century: the "yellow press" of the Spanish–American War era. The nature of newspaper reporting itself creates some problems. Newspapers

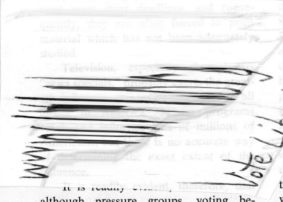

although pressure groups, voting behavior, the mailbag, the newspaper, and television tend to reflect public opinion, its character is still unclear. Politicians and political parties have consequently invested considerable time and money in an attempt to develop an accurate method of measuring public opinion. The best technique which has been developed is the political poll. Politicians have been conducting their own informal polls for decades, but in recent years the poll has become something of a science, employing the techniques of the advertising industry.

Professional Polling Methods

The idea is to poll a sampling of the population which is expected to reflect the attitudes of the entire nation. The method employed is to obtain the private opinions of a few people in every professional, economic, and social bracket, in all voting age groups, and geographical areas. This supposedly gives a cross section of thinking on a particular subject. However, the poll's accuracy depends mainly on the size and selection of the sample. The completely accurate poll would, obviously, be one which surveys every individual American.

An interesting example of an improperly conducted sampling poll occurred in 1936, when the technique was still in its infancy. In that year the *Literary Digest* conducted a poll to discover who would be elected president in ... Landon or Franklin Delano ... To obtain its data the *Literary Digest* called every tenth person in ... one directory in every city and ... America. The results of the ... indicated a landslide victory for Alf ... n, but the election results could not ... been more to the contrary.

There was a major error in the ...mpling technique. In the year 1936, ...he midst of the Great Depression, the telephone was still a luxury item. Only well-to-do people owned a household telephone and they generally were not at all happy with Roosevelt's New Deal. The poll results were accurate for the people sampled, but the sampling technique did not approach a true cross section of public opinion.

Most of the contemporary political polls are conducted in a more thorough manner. The Gallup Poll, one of the better known, is a case in point. It goes to considerable pains to interview as many segments of the population as it can. But even a scientifically conducted poll can be mistaken. In 1948 the Gallup Poll picked the Republican, Thomas Dewey, to capture the presidency, but instead he lost to Harry Truman. An embarrassed Chicago newspaper headlined a Dewey victory on the morning after election day.

Drawbacks of Political Polls

There are a number of very critical difficulties associated with the conducting of an accurate poll. It is very difficult to obtain a cross section of every group in America because of time and expense. Additionally, the poll cannot account for last minute shifts of opinions (this was part of the problem with the Gallup Poll in 1948). Opinions can be completely accurate at the time taken, but completely irrelevant on election day.

An example of how a last minute development by the parties or the candidates can drastically alter public opinion occurred in 1884. In this election Grover Cleveland was the presidential underdog. There had not been a Democratic president since before the Civil War, and the party had to contend with the "bloody shirt" issue—the South had seceded under Democratic Party rule and, therefore, the Democratic Party was associated with treason. The Republican presidential candidate, Benjamin Harrison, was far out in front.

But on election eve two incidents occurred which changed the election results. A Republican partisan, Reverend Buchard, gave an impromptu speech at a train station in New York during which he referred to the Democratic Party as the party of "Rum, Romanism, and Rebellion." The reference to rum was an oblique condemnation of the immigrant poor. "Rebellion" referred to the old bloody shirt issue. "Romanism" was a direct appeal to religious prejudice against Catholics, and here lay Buchard's most serious mistake. It so happened that New York contained a heavy concentration of Irish Catholic immigrants, most of whom were Republicans. They crossed over to the Democratic column on election day and Cleveland carried populous New York state by 1100 votes. Also the Republicans held a gala dinner at the Waldorf Astoria on election eve.

Only multi-millionaire supporters were invited to attend. The Democrats tellingly claimed that these were the only people the Republicans really cared about.

The accuracy of a political poll often depends on the manner in which the questions are phrased. A negative or awkward question can confuse the person being polled. People tend to give more definite answers about candidates than about issues, and to become bored with long questionnaires. However, polls do provide a noteworthy service for the politician. And although they are not completely foolproof, they are still more accurate than any other means of measuring day-to-day public opinion. They tend to give politicians a better insight as to the desires of their constituents.

As the density of the American population continues to increase it will become even more necessary for individuals to influence government through group efforts. And as Americans acquire more leisure they will have more time to participate actively in pressure groups and political parties. The party structure itself is also undergoing a transition, because of the ideological weaknesses of both major parties. Whether the present system will evolve into a liberal and conservative party structure is not known, but this would make more sense than the present system.

However, because democracy functions best in a small group, size brings an increasing number of problems. The American nation is faced with the serious difficulty of allowing for individual expression, yet at the same time controlling and regulating an increasingly complex society. Technology and education will aid in finding solutions to these problems, but they will also bring new ones. A more sophisticated, well educated population, possessed of sufficient leisure to study political issues, will be more opinionated and demand greater receptiveness from political leaders. And finally, because of the mass media, the politician will be functioning under the microscope of public scrutiny. The people and the politics of the United States will be facing serious challenges to their contemporary mode of operation for years to come.

For Further Reading

Chambers, William N. *The Democrats, 1789–1964: A Short History of a Popular Party*. Princeton: D. Van Nostrand, 1964.

Eldersveld, Samuel J. *Political Parties: A Behavioral Analysis*. Chicago: Rand McNally, 1964.

Fenton, John D. *People and Parties in Politics*. Glenview, Illinois: Scott Foresman, 1966.

Hesseltine, William B. *Third Party Movements in the United States*. Princeton: D. Van Nostrand, 1962.

Holtzman, Abraham. *Interest Groups and Lobbying*. New York: Macmillan Company, 1966.

Jacob, Herbert, and Vines, Kenneth, (eds.). *Politics in the American States*. Boston: Little, Brown, 1965.

Jones, Charles O. *The Republican Party*. New York: Macmillan Company, 1965.

Key, V. O., Jr. *Politics, Parties, and Pressure Groups*. 5th ed. New York: Crowell, 1964.

Kornhauser, William. *The Politics of Mass Society*. New York: The Free Press, 1961.

Lippmann, Walter. *Public Opinion*. New York: MacMillan Company, 1953.

Lockard, Duane. *The Politics of State and Local Government*. New York: Macmillan Company, 1963.

Seasholes, Bradbury. *Voting, Interest Groups, and Parties*. Glenview, Illinois: Scott Foresman, 1967.

Ziegler, Harmon. *Interest Groups in American Society*. Englewood Cliffs: Prentice-Hall, 1964.

Part Two
The Modes Of Production
In A Democratic Society

Chapter Five
American Economic Policies

The fiscal policies of the United States government have changed considerably over the years. In contemporary America they provide one of the most controversial issues on the public scene. The government has become deeply involved in regulating the economy through the expansion and contraction of credit, revising the tax structure, the issuance of large contracts to private corporations, minimum wage laws, price ceilings, tariff policies, and manipulation of the value of the currency.

Americans are particularly concerned over what the government does in these areas, because it is where they feel themselves most directly affected by government: in the purse or the wallet. Income-tax time is one of the most dreaded times of the year for many Americans, and it is in many cases their only direct contact with government. Americans are most heated in their convictions on governmental fiscal and economic policies, for they are personal issues.

There is also great concern about another governmental economic matter:

the soaring national debt. All sorts of theories have been devised and advanced concerning this debt, its ceiling, its possible retirement, and even whether there should be a debt at all. At one point in American history it was widely held that economics and politics should be kept separate. This is the so-called laissez-faire doctrine, which propounded that while government might provide aid for business, it should not regulate it.

The present chapter is a survey of the development of the role of the federal government in the field of economics, and an explanation of the temper of the nation as each new attempt at governmental regulation was being initiated. Earlier in this book the evolving nature of the American constitutional system was emphasized. This evolution is intimately related to the development of economic policy.

The original Constitution made no provisions for a federal income tax. It did not and could not foresee the day when government defense spending would become a major prop for the American economy. It could not have foreseen the tremendous growth of industry and commerce which necessitated many regulations. Nor could it have foreseen the time when American tariff policy and the value of our currency would be crucial in world affairs.

Today, the government of the United States is the nation's largest single employer, the largest single customer of the business community, and the greatest debtor in the entire economy. Government itself has become big business.

Economics in the Founding of the American Colonies

The American colonies were originally settled for economic reasons. North and South America were accidentally discovered during a search for better trade routes to the East. And the developing theory of mercantilism played a major role in actual settlement.

Salutary Neglect

Nationalism in the modern sense was a new phenomenon at the time of the discovery of America. Nationalism at that time generally took the form of military rivalry among the various developing nation-states of Europe, but an economic dimension was being added. As was indicated in Chapter Two, mercantilist theory demanded the establishment of colonies to act as sources of raw materials and as a market area for surplus goods produced by the mother country. Many individuals who settled in America were motivated by personal economic considerations. Trading companies were responsible for some settlements. Payment of debts in land placed others in the position of New World landlords. And many individuals, rich and poor, were attracted by the prospect of free land and enhanced economic opportunities in a virgin environment. Of course, factors

other than economic ones were partially responsible for the settlement of America.

Unfortunately, from the English point of view, England was unable to put her mercantilistic theory into practice until after the colonies had grown quite accustomed to doing without any serious political or economic control by the mother country. During the course of the seventeenth, and roughly the first half of the eighteenth century, Americans were left pretty much to themselves, mainly because England was preoccupied with other pressing matters. This era of inadvertent but beneficial ("salutary") neglect lasted until the close of the French and Indian War in 1763.

The Salutary Neglect was the result of a number of factors. England was plagued by considerable internal difficulty for a large portion of the period. In 1649 the English Revolution erupted and King Charles I was beheaded. Civil war followed, as Cavaliers (supporters of the monarchy) fought Roundheads (supporters of parliamentary supremacy). The monarchy, somewhat weakened, was restored in 1688, and in view of immediate past history chose not to push the royal prerogative. Also during most of the period England was either preparing, fighting, or recovering from wars with France. There were four major wars against the French King Louis XIV. Finally, England possessed little experience in governing colonies. She was operating under a vague philosophy of allowing the colonies to govern themselves to some extent, believing that voluntary cooperation could be achieved.

During this period of Salutary Neglect, then, the colonies learned to live without stringent English regulation. However, there were some English attempts at colonial legislation. A committee known as either the Lords of Trade, or the Board of Trade and Plantations, was established to make recommendations concerning colonial legislation in 1660.

This committee fully adopted the prevailing notion of mercantilism. It recommended that the colonists should sell only to England, buy only from England; and England alone should produce their manufactured goods.

The Navigation Acts

The committee's recommendations resulted in the First Navigation Act passed in 1660. The act stipulated that only English ships, or colonial-owned ships captained by Englishmen, could trade with the colonies. These ships could be built only in England or the colonies. The act also contained a list of "enumerated articles,"—goods which colonists could sell only to England or to other English colonies. The list included sugar, cotton, wool, indigo, dye-woods, ginger, and tobacco. Because tobacco could not be grown in England or purchased from any foreign country, the American colonies held a worldwide monopoly and could name their own price to England. Most colonists accepted the fact that the act was intended to protect the interests of the entire British imperial system.

The Second Navigation Act, passed in 1663, affected the colonists more seriously. This act provided that colonial purchases from any European country had to pass through England. The law was designed to prevent colonial trade with other nations, and to stimulate the profits of English merchants. Import and export duties were charged on such goods by the English government, though a system of rebates enabled the American colonists to purchase their goods through England about as cheaply as if they had purchased them directly. Still, there was a considerable amount of red tape involved, and this was not appreciated by the colonists.

A Third Navigation Act went into effect in 1673. Because they had been ignoring the enumerated lists, colonial shippers were now bound to pay an import duty equal to the English import duty on their inter-colonial trade, unless they were willing to swear officially that a particular cargo was bound only for England. Shippers had been using false bills of lading to engage in illicit trade activities. A number of English customs officials were sent to America to enforce the act. The Americans did everything possible to avoid cooperating with them.

Disturbed by this colonial waywardness, England appointed Sir Edmund Andros to oversee all of the New England colonies, since they were undoubtedly the worse offenders. From 1684 to 1688 these colonies were brought together, called the Dominion of New England, and subjected to arbitrary British rule. When King James II was removed from the English throne in 1688, the colonists imprisoned Andros and reasserted their former political power. Only in New York did arbitrary rule continue, as Andros' lieutenant, Jacob Leisler, managed to set up a temporary dictatorship. The new English monarchs of the following year, William and Mary, were a little unsure of their royal powers, and they made no attempt to reestablish the Dominion of New England. However, New Hampshire, Massachusetts, Pennsylvania, Maryland, and New Jersey quickly became royal colonies. In New York, Leisler was hanged by the citizenry and a royal governor replaced him.

A new navigation act was passed in 1696. Parliament had gained supremacy in England, but Americans found no corresponding increase in their political powers. In fact, with the establishment of royal colonies, the way was paved for greater control by England. The latest navigation act was indicative of this. It was designed to enforce the three earlier acts, to which no one had paid much attention. All colonial governors were made personally liable for the strict enforcement of the acts. They were subjected to the threat of heavy fine and removal from office for failure to perform their duties rigidly. New English-controlled customs courts were set up in America, and more customs officials were appointed.

During the years that followed England gradually expanded her list of enumerated articles. The most hated expansion concerned molasses. The Molasses Act of 1733 prohibited the American colonies from trading with non-English colonies in the West Indies. This was ill-advised legislation. English markets in that area could not begin to absorb American trade, and most of the money in the American colonies came from trade with non-English colonies. But the Molasses Act worked little appreciable harm on the American economy because, like other pieces of British imperial legislation, it was cheerfully and almost completely ignored by most colonials. And in general, despite her great show of concern, England made no serious attempt to enforce the acts. She apparently realized that prosperous colonies were more useful to her than economically dependent ones. As long as this condition prevailed, Americans were fairly content. However, England possessed the legislation should she ever choose to enforce it. This eventually happened, but only after Americans had become thoroughly accustomed to pursuing their own course of action.

The real significance of these developments is that, because of economic factors coupled with geography, Americans had avoided English laws. England should have known better; she had ample evidence of what to expect. The Parson's Cause, for example, was a clear indication that colonials were far more interested in making money than they were in supporting English laws and traditions. In addition, some Americans were beginning to develop a rationale for their behavior. In 1750 Patrick Henry made his first documented appearance in Amer-

ica and blasted parliamentary legislation for the colonies, claiming that it was a violation of the "superior law"—the natural rights of life, liberty, and property as found in the writings of John Locke. In 1761 another colonist, James Otis, used similar reasoning in arguing against writs of assistance—arbitrary search warrants which were being issued in the colonies, ostensibly to search for smuggled goods. Americans were ideologically well prepared to do battle with England should the latter choose to press for serious enforcement of mercantilistic legislation.

Revolutionary Sentiment and Economic Affairs

The Sugar and Currency Acts

Following the passage of the Proclamation of 1763 after the French and Indian War (see Chapter Two), England proceeded to pass a series of legislative measures designed to enforce her mercantilistic policies. The Sugar Act of 1764 lowered the old import–export taxes on sugar, but rigidly enforced the lowered rates. The act made considerable inroads on the highly prosperous triangular trade, with a resultant drain of money from New England. It greatly angered and embittered the merchant class.

The Currency Act of 1764 outlawed the printing of paper money in the colonies. The act was intended to curb the inflationary aspects of uncontrolled paper-money printing. However, England ignored the fact that the colonies possessed an inadequate supply of hard money. Now every kind of currency became scarce in the colonies. The measure greatly alienated the lower economic classes, who, in this case, found common cause with the merchants. The two classes had formerly been opposed to each other; their union was created by a common hostility to English parliamentary legislation detrimental to their economic activities.

In 1764 it was also decided by Parliament to permanently station 10,000 British regular troops in America. The colonists were required to pay one-third of the cost directly; the rest would be paid from the revenues obtained by the Sugar Act and from a Stamp Act. This was considered by England to be a very fair measure since the troops would be used for the defense of the colonies. But the colonists wondered about whom they would be defended against, now that the French had been removed. The colonists also did not like having a defense measure forced on them and they protested.

The Stamp Act

The Stamp Act was also passed in 1764. It provided for a small tax on every newspaper sold and on every legal document issued in the colonies. All of the hostilities which had been building up against parliamentary legislation for the colonies erupted over this measure. Arguments of "taxation without representation" were advanced. Most colonists still admitted the right of England to tax them— but only their foreign commerce.

Nine colonies met in the Stamp Act Congress to protest formally against taxation without representation. Stamp agents were terrorized and colonists refused to purchase the stamps. But what created the greatest pressures on England were the various non-importation agreements, whereby colonial merchants agreed not to purchase any goods from England until the Stamp Act was repealed. This action had a greater effect on Parliament (because of political pressure brought to bear by English merchants) than the burning down of government warehouses in the colonies which contained the hated stamps.

The increasing pressure from the English merchant class, moved Parliament to repeal the Stamp Act in 1766. At the same time, however, Parliament passed the Declaratory Act which stipulated that Parliament did indeed possess the power to pass legislation encompassing all colonial matters. In other words, England had not accepted the colonial arguments but was bowing to economic pressures. The colonists, however, were unconcerned with abstractions. England could claim any powers she desired—like the earlier navigation acts—as long as she did not attempt to enforce them.

The period of strife was temporarily over. Unfortunately, King George III, at this time, attempted to reassert former kingly prerogatives by gaining control over the parliamentary mechanism. He did manage to enhance royal power at the expense of English parliamentarians, with a decidedly detrimental result for the American colonies. George III was almost totally ignorant of American problems, and his chancellor of the exchequer, Charles Townshend, was openly hostile to colonials. Over a minor issue, New York's refusal to honor script pledges for requisitions by British troops (they wanted cash), Townshend suspended the colony's legislature, authorized scores of writs of assistance, and reinforced the navigation acts in the colony.

Townshend was also responsible for the passage of the Townshend Duties in 1767, which placed an import tax on tea, glass, paper, and paint. By so doing, he was deferring to the colonial protests against internal taxation, and accepting the colonial recognition of the British right to tax foreign commerce of the colonies. But Americans again protested, this time assuming a more extreme position. Still arguing against taxation without representation, the colonists now claimed that taxation of foreign commerce for revenue-raising purposes was subject to the same objections as internal taxation. Additionally some of the more radical colonists claimed that all taxation and all legislation by Parliament was tyrannical because Americans were not represented in that body.

One of the leading instigators of the more radical protest was Sam Adams. He initiated the practice of sending letters throughout the colonies describing grievances, in an attempt to solidify colonial dissent. Adams succeeded in creating a loose-knit association of protest which provided the nucleus for future colonial action. Non-importation agreements were again entered into and once more were successful. Economic pressures forced Parliament to repeal the duties (except for the tea tax) which maintained their right of taxation. The tea tax served the same symbolic purpose as the Declaratory Act of three years before.

For the next few years relations between England and her colonies were fairly peaceful, as England passed no further legislation. The only hostile incident was the Boston Massacre, which was a highly exaggerated affair. During this period, however, a solid group of radicals, led by Sam Adams of Massachusetts and Thomas Jefferson, Patrick Henry, and Richard Henry Lee, all of Virginia, organized Committees of Correspondence. These committees, consisting entirely of radicals, appeared in every colony and maintained revolutionary sentiment at a time when the mass of the people were mostly uninterested.

Tea Act

Then came the Tea Act, one of the most important immediate causes of the American Revolution. The East India Company (an English trading company with an official monopoly on tea) could sell tea only at auction in London. Americans who acquired legal tea were thus required to pay an export tax from England,

an import tax into America, plus handling charges, transportation costs, and profit margins for the Company. In addition, the English wholesaler, the American wholesaler, and the American retailer all helped to increase the consumer's price. This made for rather expensive tea.

In 1773, however, the East India Company had a 17-million-pound surplus of tea. In true mercantilistic fashion, the government desired to aid the company, and allowed it to sell this surplus directly to the American retailer, subject only to the American import tax. By eliminating various middlemen, plus the English export tax, the price of the Company's tea in America declined. Besides American tea merchants plagued by the British monopoly, the only other Americans who were really opposed to the Act were smugglers. Now legal tea could be purchased more cheaply than smuggled tea. Therefore, disguised as Indians, such smugglers as Sam Adams and John Hancock staged the Boston Tea Party, dumping the Company's tea in Boston harbor.

England was justifiably outraged and passed a series of punitive measures known as the Intolerable Acts. The colonies responded to this by calling the First Continental Congress. Representatives from all the colonies met to determine a course of action against England, and decided on two activities. One was the issuance of a violent protest against infringement of the rights of Englishmen, called the Declaration of Rights and Grievances. The other was the formation of the Continental Association, a colony-wide non-importation agreement enforced by vigilante action to pressure England into rescinding her legislation for the third time. The Convention then disbanded, leaving an important precedent for the future. A Second Continental Congress would be called the following year; it was destined to conduct most of the Revolutionary War.

A number of economic issues loomed

large in the American independence movement. The issue of taxation without representation was one of them. The lack of an adequate colonial currency was another. And the heavy indebtedness to England is yet a third. England's decision to collect revenues from her American colonies stemmed from the failure of Americans to contribute much to the prosecution of the French and Indian War. Independence, however, did not bring a ready solution to most of these economic problems.

The Economics of Establishing a National Government

Of all the difficulties besetting the Articles of Confederation government, financial ones were probably the most serious. Because of the harsh experience with England, Americans were fearful of large concentrations of governmental power and therefore refused to give their own national government sufficient powers for ordinary affairs. Only when no other course of action seemed available did many Americans finally accept the fact that government should have some coercive power in the financial realm. But this was a long-evolving process.

Chaos and Crisis

When the Articles of Confederation went into effect, the national debt stood at approximately $72 million. Of this sum $11.7 million was owed to Spain, France, and Holland; $18 million comprised state debts contracted in behalf of the war; the other $42.5 million consisted of money owed by the national government to its citizens in bond repayments. The interest on the national debt amounted to approximately $3 million per year, while the operating expenses for government amounted to some $500,000 per year. These sums are small by modern standards, but the total revenues of the national government in 1784, for example, amounted to only $371,000.

A special committee was appointed by Congress to study the various problems in the nation's financial structure. Headed by Robert Morris, the committee reported that there was only one practical way for the government to raise money— by taxation. But the Articles of Confederation government possessed no enforcement powers. As a result, Morris eliminated the idea of direct taxation and concentrated on import taxes.

Morris and Alexander Hamilton jointly presented a finance bill to the government. It called for state monetary contributions on the basis of population, a 5 per cent duty on all imports, and specific higher duties on salt, rum, wine, brandy, and tea. The bill failed to pass. Rhode Island claimed it was a violation of state sovereignty (this was the first time this particular argument was officially used). New York, already taxing imports, also opposed it.

In 1786 however, the 5 per cent import tax measure passed, but the various states made no attempt at enforcement. The debt continued to grow and the national government continued to be without adequate operating funds. In fact, 1786 proved also to be a crisis year for the currency issue as well. Two illustrations will bear this out: Shay's Rebellion, and *Trevett v. Weeden.*

Massachusetts had passed a land tax in 1781. Specie (gold and silver coin) was declared the legal tender of the state and the land tax had to be paid in specie. Shay, a farmer who resided in the western portion of the state then considered the frontier, had plenty of produce but no money. In fact, very few people in Massachusetts had any specie; they operated on a barter economy. Still, the state government insisted that the tax be paid in specie. Shay was willing to pay, but since he possessed no hard money, he offered to pay in kind (produce). When this was refused, Shay and his fellow farmers led a revolt against the state government. The revolt was put down only when the national government mobilized the state militias.

Neighboring Rhode Island took a different position. There everyone was required to accept the state's paper currency as legal payment for all debts. But since it was backed by nothing the paper was worth nothing. This condition led to a significant court case, *Trevett* v. *Weeden*. Weeden was a butcher from whom Trevett bought large quantities of meat and then attempted to pay with worthless state money. Weeden refused to accept the valueless paper. The state court ruled that Weeden had no choice but to accept the money. The result was that practically every business operating in the state of Rhode Island closed its doors.

Establishing a Strong Government

The predictable solution to the financial problems besetting the nation was the creation of a strong central government which would have the exclusive power to tax and to issue a regulatory currency. The states would have to be denied powers which would hinder the effectiveness of the national government in this realm. The situation indeed worsened when states began levying tariffs on one another as if they were foreign nations. Also, each state had its own postage stamps which practically prohibited the sending of letters out of state. The financial structure of the nation was in a critical condition.

The merchant class desired stronger government because with a stable economy they would be able to enlarge their profits. Those with something to lose tend to be more conservative than those with nothing to lose. The merchant class wanted a strong national government which was similar to the political structure of England. They desired little change from the pre-existing colonial order, and may be considered conservative nationalists.

The impetus for a federal constitution arose out of a proposed business scheme. George Washington wanted to build a canal from the Potomac River to the Ohio River. Such a canal would involve the water rights of Virginia, Maryland, and Pennsylvania. The result was the Annapolis Convention of 1786 which decided that all the states should meet and discuss problems of trade and commerce. Consequently, a call was made for all the states to meet at Philadelphia on May 14, 1787, to discuss means by which the Articles might be rendered more effective.

The delegates chosen to attend this convention represented mainly upper-class opinions and commercial interests. Out of the fifty-five delegates who actually attended the constitutional convention, forty owned large quantities of government bonds, and fourteen speculated heavily in western lands. The bonds and the land would be far more valuable if a strong, solvent government were established. Thus practically every delegate possessed personal, and usually economic, reasons for desiring a strong government. The resultant constitutional system, outlined in Chapter Three, well reflected their wishes.

The problem of finance continued to be a major issue under the Constitution, but now the machinery and power existed to solve it. The new nation quickly passed a revenue act which called for a 5 per cent tax on all imports, a 15 per cent tax on luxury imports, and an elaborate system of port taxes computed at 6¢ per ton on all American built and operated ships, 30¢ per ton on all American-built but foreign-operated ships, and 50¢ per ton on all foreign-built and -operated ships. This rather simple measure, sponsored by James Madison, paid the entire cost of running the government at that time. It did not, however, provide funds for the reduction of the national debt.

Hamiltonian Fiscal Policy

At this point the financial acumen of Alexander Hamilton began to dominate. As the first Secretary of the Treasury, Hamilton probably did more than any other individual to build a strong national government. The philosophy which gave substance to his fiscal policy is still quite in vogue. According to Hamilton a nation had to pay its indebtedness if it wanted to establish a strong international credit rating. In the final analysis, he felt that this would determine the success or failure of the revolution. With this in mind Hamilton presented a complete financial program in 1790, which was enacted into law. He personally computed the total national debt to be $54,124,464.56 in 1790. Approximately $12 million of this amount was owed to Europe; the rest was the domestic debt.

Hamilton wanted to pay off the entire foreign debt with full accrued interest, and Congress readily agreed. But he also wanted to pay off the domestic debt, and on this point Congress balked. Hamilton wanted to pay the face value of government bonds, dollar for dollar. The problem was that as the bonds had depreciated many holders had panicked and sold them to avoid further losses. As a result a small number of individuals held large quantities of depreciated bonds which they had bought at considerably below face value. After a bitter congressional battle, and aided by the fact that many congressmen were the holders of these bonds, the measure was passed.

Thus the national debt was funded—the government officially recognized the existence of the debt and promised to pay it. Old bonds were traded in for new ones, including all accrued interest, at better interest rates. This raised the national debt to $70 million, but it estab-lished public credit, which is simply confidence in the determination of the government to meet its financial obligations. There was still the chance, however that the bonds might depreciate again.

Hamilton precluded this possibility very ingeniously. He established a sinking fund of $150,000 to stabilize the value of the new bonds. This money was used by government agents to buy bonds secretly at prices equal to or even above their face value. This curbed the inclination to sell in a falling market. The sinking fund, incidentally, was the cause of the nation's first congressional investigation, initiated by Thomas Jefferson. The fund was declared illegal in 1796 (as it should have been), but by that time public credit was already firmly established.

Although it cost only $600,000 per year to run the government during the Washington administration, the annual interest on the national debt was approximately $2.2 million. Therefore, if the government was to be financially stable, it required roughly $2.8 million in revenues each year. Unlike Jefferson, Hamilton was not in the least concerned with paying off the national debt. But he held that the government should meet its interest payments, and perhaps pay a token amount on the principal. According to Hamilton, the best method of insuring against future revolutions was to have the government owe money to its citizens. As a consequence, the people would be very much concerned about the welfare of that government.

Jefferson was an influential and tenacious critic of Hamilton's financial policies. When Hamilton decided that the federal government should assume all state debts contracted in behalf of the Revolution, Jefferson vehemently protested. The sum involved was approximately $20 million, and Hamilton hoped both to strengthen public credit and to further subordinate the states to the federal government. He obtained his state-debt-assumption proposal by working out a compromise with Jefferson.

Jefferson agreed to back Hamilton's debt plan if Hamilton would support Jefferson's desire to locate the American capital in Virginia. The deal was struck and after ten years in Philadelphia the national capital moved to the shores of the Potomac, on land donated by Virginia and Maryland. Jefferson believed the move would enhance the domination of the national government by the Virginia aristocracy. Hamilton, with ideas of an industrialized society, and consequent transportation improvements, was not concerned about location. Years later, Jefferson admitted that he had gotten the worst of the bargain.

The Whiskey Rebellion

Hamilton collected his necessary revenues from the tariff, an excise tax, the sale of public lands, the postal system (it used to operate at a profit), and a whiskey tax. His whiskey tax had a threefold purpose. It would bring in considerable revenues—approximately $700,000 per year. It would fall heavily on the people of the back country who were not avid supporters of strong government, while at the same time avoiding the wealthy individuals upon whom Hamilton relied for support. And the enforcement of this tax —Hamilton knew it would be unpopular —would prove the power of the federal government.

Westerners had been distilling their grain because of transportation difficulties. It was easier to send a few gallons of whiskey to the East than to send an equivalent value of grain, which would be much larger in volume and therefore more difficult to transport. Also, the profits were much better. Hamilton's tax had to be paid in cash, of which the westerners had little. He realized that a revolt was in the making, but he welcomed it. The re-

bellion began in the back country of Pennsylvania in 1794. At Hamilton's suggestion, Washington federalized 15,000 militia from Virginia, Maryland, and Pennsylvania, and easily subdued the rebels. The leaders were arrested, convicted of rebellion, and then pardoned. The government proved that it could enforce the collection of a tax, even if unpopular. However, the strong show of force on the part of the Federalists convinced many people to support Thomas Jefferson's new Republican Party.

The National Bank

Another Hamiltonian financial policy was the establishment of the First National Bank. He argued that such a bank would create a uniform currency, make capital available for internal improvements, attract foreign capital, provide a safe depository for government funds, collect taxes, disburse funds, act as a restraining agent on inflation and the overexpansion of credit, and obtain necessary loans for the government. The Bank, established in 1791, was closely modelled after the Bank of England. Chartered for twenty years, the bank issued $10 million in capital stock, one-fifth of which was purchased by the federal government, and the rest by private investors. All government money was placed in the bank.

There were more protests over the bank charter than there were over the debt-assumption issue. The main criticism was that the bank was monopolistic. This was true but it was argued that a monopolistic system was needed. In addition, though the Constitution prohibited states from issuing currency, state-chartered banks could issue a form of currency—the bank note, thus alleviating monopolistic control. A more cogent argument was that four-fifths of the stock subscribers were private citizens who were drawing 8.5 per cent interest from their government investment. Still, the bank was quite successful and did almost all that Hamilton hoped it would.

Hamilton also favored a protective tariff. He felt that such a tariff acted in the best interests of both the farmers and the manufacturers. He wanted both duties and bounties, plus a prohibition on the exportation of raw materials. The revenue aspects of his tariff became law; the protective features did not (until 1816). This was the only Hamiltonian finance measure which failed to become law. Still, Hamilton provided the basis for American tariff legislation during the nineteenth century.

Hamilton's fiscal policies were antithetical to the Republican Party's philosophy. Therefore, when Thomas Jefferson captured the presidency in 1800 there were some attempts at change. Jefferson especially sought to pay off the national debt by 1816. This meant that $7.5 million would have to be paid on the principal each year, and Jefferson made a concerted effort to do so. He dismissed the American ambassadors to Russia, Prussia, Portugal, and Holland as an economy measure, claiming that they were not really needed in any case, and reduced the already meager salaries of customs officials. But he did not tamper with Hamilton's basic financial structure. In fact, in order to pay for the Louisiana Purchase, Jefferson borrowed the money from the First National Bank.

The War of 1812 and Economic Nationalism

In the years that followed the American economy moved forward very slowly. Americans discovered that there had been certain advantages in being part of the British trade empire. The nation had little industry but was able to engage in trade and commerce. What brought about a series of rapid changes was the War of 1812. In some measure the causes of this war were economic. Additionally the spirit of nationalism engendered by the conflict helped create some notable financial developments after its conclusion.

Western Recession and War

It was mentioned in Chapter Two that the main impetus for the War of 1812 was found in the American West. A major cause for this western militancy was economic. The West had been unable to keep its economy moving forward at a steady pace. It experienced either "boom" or "bust" conditions, and the period 1807–1812 happened to be a "bust" era.

This western recession was brought on by five basic factors, four of which were almost strictly internal. For one thing, there was a basic unsoundness in the agricultural economy. The size of the crop was always an uncertainty as well as the price it would bring. Secondly, there was a great deal of overproduction. Farmers have traditionally attempted to produce as much as possible, completely ignoring supply and demand principles. Third, there was a high degree of speculation in land. Farmers bought land at inflated prices, not to raise crops on but to sell at a later date at a good profit. This remained a common practice until the stock market Crash of 1929. Finally, the West was plagued by poor transportation. An inadequate transportation system raised costs tremendously, and also lessened profits. These four points alone were sufficient to have caued a recession. But it is the fifth, an external factor, upon which westerners concentrated and which led to a war with England.

The Napoleonic wars were then raging in Europe. In 1800 the British Admiralty Court had ruled that neutral nations could trade with belligerents in noncontraband goods during wartime. If trade goods were actually imported into neutral nations by neutral ships, regard-

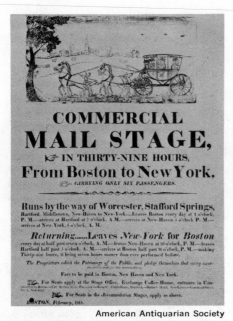

American Antiquarian Society

Early Transportation, 1815
Advertisement

less of where they were obtained, they became neutral and could be sold to belligerents.

This decision meant millions to American shippers who were making a great deal of money at England's expense by engaging in the French West Indies Trade. If a French ship was transporting goods from the West Indies to France, it was liable to capture by England, whereas an American vessel was not. And Americans were trading surplus western farm goods for West Indies products.

In 1805 England crushed Napoleon's navy at the Battle of Trafalgar, thus attaining supremacy on the high seas. Consequently she altered her policy. In the Essex decision, she recognized American rights to trade with the French West Indies. However, the United States had to show intent of leaving such goods in America rather than exporting them to France. This could be done in two ways: either by paying the full tariff duty on

such imported goods, or by unloading and leaving them in America for a reasonable length of time. Both procedures seriously cut into American profit margins.

England believed that the United States had taken advantage of the military situation, and to a large extent this was true. The Essex decision thus provided the major maritime cause for the War of 1812. For although few Americans were actually involved in the French West Indies trade, that trade did help create western prosperity, because it provided a proximate outlet for surplus western crops. The Essex decision curtailed American trade, thereby depressing western prices. And it was the West which eventually led the nation into war with England. Westerners blamed all of their financial problems on England, and almost completely ignored their internal problems.

Economic Nationalism

The American nation emerged from the War of 1812 in an intensely nationalistic mood, ready to grant government extensive powers. This was readily accomplished because in this Era of Good Feelings, there was a near total lack of political strife. There was only one political party at that time, and no organized opposition. Outstanding political developments which bolstered nationalism included John Marshall's Supreme Court decisions and Henry Clay's American System, a comprehensive approach to national development. There were also a number of significant laws passed in the fiscal realm.

A Second National Bank was created. The first bank bill had expired in 1811 and Congress had failed to renew it. After 1811 state "wildcat" banks (banks without adequate reserves to back up their loans) and various kinds of unstable currency suddenly appeared. With approximately $15 million in gold reserves these wildcat banks issued $175 million in paper money. The situation was well out of hand, and it had placed the nation in difficult financial straits during the War of 1812. Without an adequate banking or currency system, the government was forced to borrow the entire amount needed to pay for the war—$200 million—by issuing interest-bearing bonds.

The new national bank destroyed the wildcat banks and their currency. Government currency was placed only in sound banks. The government also bought up just enough of the insolvent banks' currency to exceed their reserves, and then demanded payment. The banks had no choice but to close their doors.

The National Bank Act of 1816 was supported by President Madison and his secretary of the treasury, A. J. Dallas, and introduced in Congress by John C. Calhoun. The bank was chartered for a twenty-year period and capitalized with $85 million, one-fifth to come from the government, and four-fifths from private investors. A twenty-five man board of directors was established, with five appointed by the government and twenty elected by the stockholders. Private investors were required to pay the government the sum of $1.5 million for the privilege of not being taxed; they had invested in the only tax-exempt bank in America. The secretary of the treasury was given the authority to withdraw government funds from the bank whenever he deemed it appropriate, and could also check the bank's books whenever he desired. The national bank was authorized to create branch banks if deemed necessary.

Madison's administration also used the old Hamiltonian arguments to favor a high tariff. John Randolph of Virginia and his Quids (a third-party movement) claimed the tariff was an immense tax on one portion of the community to put money in the pockets of a minority. The South disagreed with him, but within ten years when cotton became king, it had changed its mind. The Tariff of 1816 was passed easily by a large majority. It was the first truly protective tariff in the peacetime history of the United States. Its rates were high enough to discourage the importation of such items as cotton, wool, and cloth. The tariff contained three distinctive features: the minimum value principle, classification, and the sliding scale.

According to the minimum-value principle a product was considered to have a set cost which corresponded to the cost of producing and selling that good at a reasonable profit in the United States. Though the actual market price of the foreign item might be far less than a similar American-produced good, the tariff rate would be applied to the assumed American cost. Consequently, it was theoretically possible for the tariff charge to exceed the actual cost of the foreign good.

Goods were classified into categories, and Secretary Dallas established the guidelines. In Class I were placed all goods which were being produced in the United States in sufficient quantities to supply the domestic needs of the country. A 20–25 per cent tariff, strictly a protective tariff, was levied on comparable foreign goods. In Class III were placed all goods which American industry could not or would not supply for the American market. On these goods a small tax, usually 1–2 per cent was placed, strictly for revenue purposes. No effort was made to keep Class III goods out of the country.

Class II contained all goods which were being produced in the United States in quantities that might someday increase enough to meet American needs. This is where the sliding scale was used. Everything in Class II was taxed somewhere between the 1 per cent and 25 per cent limits established for the other two classes, depending on exactly how much American industry was producing. The secretary of the treasury was empowered to raise or lower rates within these limits as production changed. In so doing he was not required to apply to Congress for each adjustment.

Henry Clay and John Marshall

Henry Clay's American System proposed a centralized role for the government in economic affairs. It sought a consolidation of various governmental functions and institutions. The System was not formulated by Clay as a complete treatise on government; rather, it was developed by degrees over a period of years. It marked an attempt to make all portions of the nation dependent upon one another through the medium of commercial intercourse and called for a planned economy.

The American System looked inward and therefore was isolationistic. According to Clay, American trade should be strictly internal, not international. Nothing should be purchased from abroad and only the national surplus should be exported, with cash being the only acceptable mode of payment. This aspect of the American System is strongly reminiscent of the old mercantilist concept of a favorable balance of trade.

Government, Clay added, should work to raise the standard of living, cut unemployment, diversify and nationalize the economy—basically a Hamiltonian position. Clay's planned economic system required a strong federal government, possessed of exclusive power to regulate the economy. Clay would probably have supported laws on excess profits and minimum wages had they been thought of at the time. Some of Clay's ideas were accepted during his lifetime, but many of them had to await the New Deal before they were widely accepted and implemented. By that time few people identified them with Henry Clay.

Many of the Supreme Court rulings of Chief Justice John Marshall were also quite important for the future economic development of the United States. In *Dartmouth College* v. *Woodward,* a case decided in 1819, Marshall broadly interpreted the federal Constitution's contract clause. The state of New Hampshire had attempted to amend a college charter which had been issued to Dartmouth in 1769, and reconfirmed by the revolutionary state government. The original charter had rendered the college tax-exempt as a private charitable institution. New Hampshire sought to revoke the tax exemption and the state court upheld the action. Marshall ruled that the contract clause applied in this case: a state had no power to impair a contract once issued. Not only did the decision further enhance the power of the Supreme Court and the Constitution at the expense of the states, but more importantly, by emphasizing the sanctity of contracts, it provided a legal bolster for the development of big business later in the century.

In *Gibbons* v. *Ogden* (1824), Marshall expanded and clarified the federal interstate commerce power. The state of New York had granted a monopoly to two men, Livingston and Fulton, to operate steamboats on the Hudson River. From these gentlemen another man named Ogden bought the right to operate steamboats on the river himself. And still another man named Gibbons purchased a federal trade license and proceeded to operate steamboats on the river, disregarding the monopoly. Ogden sued Gibbons in the state court and was upheld. Gibbons thereupon carried an appeal to the United States Supreme Court. Marshall ruled that New York could not legally grant a monopoly on the Hudson River because New York possessed no jurisdiction over the river. He ruled that all rivers and all interstate commerce were under the exclusive control of the federal government. In his reasoning, Marshall defined interstate commerce as "any intercourse" crossing a state boundary. In the process, Marshall laid the groundwork for future governmental regulation of such unforseen facilities as the telephone, radio, and television.

The final presidential administration in the Era of Good Feelings was that of John Quincy Adams. His election in 1824 had been decided in the House of Representatives after a famous controversy. Adam's Secretary of State was Henry Clay, and the two men agreed on the American System. But Adams lacked the popular support needed to implement it; he had a cold personality and was confronted by growing opposition from the developing political organization of Andrew Jackson.

The Tariff Controversy

Sectional Conflict

The one big issue during the Adams administration was the tariff. As has already been indicated, the Tariff of 1816 had passed easily. A new tariff with higher rates was passed in 1824, but by a rather narrow margin. The reason for this was that during the preceding eight years the South had moved to a predominantly cotton economy. It sold cotton to Europe and received manufactured goods in exchange. But these goods became quite expensive because of the high tariff barriers. Therefore, the South claimed that the tariff cut into its profit margin—which it did in terms of buying power.

Outside of the cotton South, particular interests favored the tariff. For instance, Louisiana sugar cane interests supported the tariff to eliminate cheap Caribbean sugar. Kentuckians supported it to keep out cheap rum. Western sheepmen favored a high tariff on wool—and they succeeded in obtaining one in 1824. The North favored a tariff to protect its own products. But cotton required no protection; it had no competition on the world market. (The modern answer to the southern problem would probably be gov-

ernment price support.) The South, then, was really being hurt by the tariff. And it would be hurt more as it increased cotton production. Although some northern merchants opposed the tariff, claiming that it curtailed international trade, the principal and strongest opposition came from the southern cotton interests.

The tariff issue resulted in a strange series of events in 1828. During the off-year congressional elections of 1826, the anti-administration forces had greatly increased their strength. They realized that tariff supporters desired even higher tariffs. They decided to take advantage of this situation to insure the election of Jackson in 1828. They realized that for Jackson to be elected he required the support of the pro-tariff North and the anti-tariff South. So they introduced an enormously high tariff and accepted no downward revisions. It was believed that by making the tariff ridiculously high, even the northerners would vote against it, and the tariff would be defeated. Then the Jacksonians could claim the support of the North by running on the record of favoring high tariffs, while announcing to the South that they had defeated the high tariff proposal and thereby win that section also.

They were, however, incorrect in thinking that the North would not favor such a high tariff. In fact, the North regarded it as much better than the existing tariff. The tariff measure passed—the so-called Tariff of Abominations. Fortunately for the political career of Jackson, the South blamed the high tariff on the Adams administration. The Tariff of 1828 helped create a president, but it was also responsible for the Exposition of 1828, John C. Calhoun's succinct statement of the southern political philosophy (See Chapter Nine).

During Jackson's presidency the government had an abundance of money. It appeared the national debt would be completely paid off by 1835, and this was an item of considerable concern. The nation was acquiring progressively increased revenues due to high tariffs and land sales. The Treasury was accumulating a surplus of money and because of the deleterious effects of capital accumulation, it had to be halted.

Various sections of the country came forth with solutions. The West sought to either use the surplus money for internal improvements or to avoid the surplus by giving away land instead of selling it. The South preferred to end the tariff. The North wanted increased internal improvements, but no end to the tariff and no free land. Clay, not wanting to end the tariff, suggested distribution: a plan to divide the surplus money among the states and allow them to use it for their own purposes. The distribution idea was hotly debated, but nothing was done because the surplus disappeared in the Panic of 1837. However, the issue had succeeded in polarizing the various sections of the nation, and Jackson's new Democratic Party was seriously threatened by open schism. The Webster–Hayne debates, the controversy over Jackson's invasion of Florida back in 1818, the Peggy Eaton affair, and the crisis at the Jefferson Day dinner in 1830, all combined to increase the strife between the northern and southern wings of the Democratic Party.

Tariff legislation during this time really brought the issue of sectionalism to a head. Since the government had been accumulating a surplus of money, Jackson asked Congress in December, 1831, to consider revisions in the tariff. The result was the Tariff of 1832 which somewhat lowered the 1828 Tariff of Abomination rates. However, the South was still incensed because it felt the reduction was only minimal.

Nullification and the Tariff

In the state elections of 1832 a major campaign issue in South Carolina was the nullification of the tariff. By a vote of 136–26 South Carolina passed an Ordinance of Nullification, which stated that the Tariffs of 1828 and 1832 were null and void in South Carolina, as of February 1, 1833. The Ordinance prohibited appeals to federal courts from any legal issue arising out of nullification. Also, the federal government was warned that if it attempted to use force to collect tariff duties in South Carolina, the state would have no choice but to secede from the union.

On November 27, 1832, the South Carolina legislature authorized the Governor to raise an army. The South had supported Jackson because it believed he would lower or eliminate the tariff. But by 1832 the South had apparently lost faith. The 1832 tariff, it seems, had only reduced rates on raw materials, not on manufactured goods, and it was with manufactured goods that the South was most directly concerned.

Jackson stationed federal troops around the borders of South Carolina, and suggested to Congress that it might be wise to consider lowering the tariff. In December, 1832, he issued a proclamation to South Carolina, stating that nullification was incompatible with the Union and would not be allowed. South Carolina's Governor Hayne (of debate fame) issued a counter-proclamation reiterating his position. John C. Calhoun resigned as vice-president of the United States, completely broke with Jackson, and became a federal Senator from South Carolina.

In March, 1833, Congress passed the Force Bill, giving the president authority to forcibly prevent nullification. Both Jackson and South Carolina realized that in the event of war, South Carolina would be annihilated. Jackson realized that violence would not only hurt his popularity but might also encourage the rest of the South to join openly with South Carolina. Then in 1833 a new tariff measure was passed which provided for a gradual reduction of the tariff rates over a ten-year period to a maximum rate of 20 per cent. South Carolina responded by rescinding her Ordinance of Nullification, however, she then "nullified" the Force Bill. Both sides claimed a victory; actually it was a truce. South Carolina was momentarily appeased, but the issue was not settled.

The election of 1832 was a landslide victory for Jackson. He received 219 electoral votes compared to 49 votes for his nearest competitor, Henry Clay. The new vice-president was Martin Van Buren of New York. There were two major issues in this presidential election, both of which were economic. The tariff issue and the proposed rechartering of the Second National Bank.

The Bank War and the
Panic of 1837

The National Bank was due to expire in 1836. Headed by Nicolas Biddle, the bank had been well managed and generally accepted by both North and South. However, the West hated it for a number of reasons, and Jackson was a westerner. One important reason was that the bank controlled state banks, and thereby prohibited wildcat banking practices. The West wanted loose money which was now unavailable. The National Bank had also been involved in foreclosing on some westerners. In addition people who had been hurt by unsound banks, believed that the entire banking industry was essentially dishonest. It was further argued by some that the banking business was privileged. These four arguments, however, carried little weight.

But there was a fifth argument which rendered the bank quite vulnerable. The bank had become deeply involved in politics. Seeking to insure the rechartering of the bank, Biddle had loaned large sums of money to individual congressmen

and newspaper chains. Additionally, he retained Daniel Webster as the chief attorney for the bank, and Webster was then a member of Congress.

Both Webster and Clay convinced Biddle to seek the recharter of the bank before the national elections of 1832, even though it was not due to expire until 1836. The idea was to make the bank a major issue in the campaign, believing that Congress would pass the recharter measure and Jackson would not interfere. They were only half-right. Congress did recharter the bank but Jackson vetoed the measure, claiming that it was unconstitutional, despite the fact that the Supreme Court, in *McCulloch* v. *Maryland* (1819), had apparently accepted the constitutionality of the bank. Jackson, however, held that the bank was controlled by foreigners and only a handful of wealthy Americans. Therefore, it was undemocratic; it granted a monopoly to the privileged class.

Jackson and the National Bank

By stressing the undemocratic features of the bank, Jackson succeeded in eliciting mass support for his position, and the strategy of the bank proponents backfired. Thus, Jackson interpreted his re-election as public approval of his bank policy. Jackson next determined to remove all government money from the bank in an attempt to destroy it. This was a legal procedure, authorized by the initial bank proposal which stated that the secretary of the treasury—a presidential appointee—could remove federal money at will. Secretary McLane, however, refused and was "kicked upstairs" by Jackson to the position of secretary of state. The new secretary of the treasury, Duane, also refused to withdraw the money and was dismissed. Finally, a third secretary of the treasury, Roger B. Taney, agreed and the money was removed. Taney was rewarded for his action by being appointed chief justice of the Supreme Court to succeed Marshall, and in 1857 rendered the historic Dred Scott decision.

Jackson had Taney place the government money in favored banks located mostly in the West. He thereby drained money from the commercialized East and placed it in the hands of the westerners. Also by curbing the power of the National Bank, speculation in land and currency once more increased. The result was tremendous money and credit inflation in the West, with land prices rising some 500 per cent between 1834 and 1836. Increased land prices further stuffed the federal treasury, and these additional funds were also placed in the speculating banks, which further expanded the credit, and the cycle repeated itself.

Finally, Jackson, who reportedly was far from an expert on financial matters, realized that the situation had to cease. He issued his Specie Circular in July, 1836, stating that all further land payments had to be made in gold or silver. However, the treasury surplus was still growing. Finally, the Distribution Act stipulated that all money in the treasury in excess of $5 million would be distributed to the states as pseudo-loans effective January 1, 1837. It was understood that the loans were not to be repaid. Most states were already spending heavily on internal improvements. Buying most of their equipment from England, they had created an unfavorable balance of trade. International payments are normally made in specie. But in this period of tremendous inflation there was not a sufficient supply of hard money in the banks.

Also, the Distribution Act required that the favored state banks return the federal funds, placed there after removal from the National Bank, to the government so that they might be distributed to the states. Overextended, these banks were unable to comply; bank failures followed in rapid succession. The procedure

soon spread to England where overextended merchants also fell into bankruptcy. When the economic recession struck England, the South lost her best customer for cotton, and subsequently also fell upon hard times. The plight of the West and the South had a naturally detrimental effect on northern markets. As a result, the United States entered a complete economic depression. This was the Panic of 1837.

Van Buren and Panic

Before the depression had become a reality, however, the presidential election took place. Martin Van Buren was Jackson's handpicked successor. Van Buren took office in time to bear the full force of the panic while Jackson escaped all blame. It is important to note that the United States would probably have had a major depression without Jackson's famous bank battle, but it might not have been as serious. Jackson's destruction of the Second National Bank was one of the prime causes for the severity of the panic. It created the atmosphere for western land speculation and greatly aggravated the impetus for internal improvements and the increasing unfavorable trade balance. By destroying the bank no matter how monopolistic and undemocratic it was, Jackson had destroyed the only regulatory agency in the American economic structure.

The voters, for the most part, never blamed Jackson for the depression. He helped create it, but Van Buren had to cope with it. Van Buren was inaugurated in March, 1837. In May the New York banks suspended specie payment, and by the end of the month, every other bank in the country had followed suit. Van Buren was President when this occurred; therefore, reasoned many Americans, he caused the panic and the depression.

Van Buren was the product of a political philosophy which lasted at least through the Hoover administration. This philosophy maintained that the national government should concern itself primarily with political matters. Thus economic problems, would be principally handled by the states and localities. There is, therefore, an ideological parallel between Van Buren and Hoover. Both men were the victims of an unfortunate political viewpoint, and both had to face depressions not of their own making.

Van Buren called Congress into Special Session in September, 1837. He sought and obtained the repeal of the Distribution Act. He proposed a new plan for handling government funds—the Sub-Treasury System. He wanted all government funds to be placed in storage vaults, completely divorced from the banking business. Government funds would always be immediately available for governmental use, and speculation with funds by favored banks would be eliminated. This proposal further split the Democratic Party, and many of its wealthier members moved into the Whig Party. However, the Sub-Treasury System did become law in 1840.

Meanwhile, several other developments were taking place. Most states were establishing solid regulations for their banking establishments. For example, some state laws required that banks be bonded; others set up reserve requirements which had to be met in order to obtain a banking license. In addition, having been severely burned by their devotion to internal improvements, most states decided to leave such future ventures in the hands of private enterprise. The result was the development of the corporation with limited liability. Finally, most states repudiated their indebtedness incurred during this period. This was a heavy blow to American credit abroad (Europeans could not distinguish between federal and state governments), yet it did enable the states to remove an overwhelming financial burden.

Continuing Problems with the South

The depression was the largest issue during the Van Buren presidency. During those years of economic stagnation, the Whig Party—the original anti-Jackson party—found its power increasing. It captured both houses of Congress in the off-year elections of 1838, and won the presidency in 1840, with the ticket of William Harrison and John Tyler. The Whigs also held several other key political posts. Daniel Webster was secretary of state, and Henry Clay was majority leader in the Senate. A month after the inauguration Harrison died and Tyler became the first vice-president to succeed to the presidency under such circumstances. Unsure of his position, he allowed Clay to dominate him.

He supported the Pre-emption Act of 1841, which legalized squatter's rights. He supported the Bankruptcy Act of 1841, which allowed the filing of bankruptcy to repudiate payment of debts. Also, he supported the Tariff of 1842 which raised the prevailing duties. Finally, he agreed to the repeal of the Sub-treasury System, but then began to follow his own convictions. On two occasions Tyler vetoed a Clay-sponsored Third National Bank bill. The second bank measure had been specifically designed to overcome Tyler's initial objections. The remainder of the Tyler administration was marked by an almost complete legislative standstill.

Party Realignment

But the presidency of John Tyler did mark an important development in the nation's pre–Civil War history. American parties and politicians unconsciously began to align themselves on increasingly hostile sides. In 1828 Van Buren and Calhoun had both been members of the Democratic Party. Calhoun next moved into the Whig Party after his split with

Jackson. Other southerners followed, leaving the Democratic Party a northern party as of 1830. The rise of the Whig Party to power brought about some changes. Primarily because of the bank issue, wealthy northerners joined the Whigs, and the Whig Party gradually adopted Hamiltonian philosophy. With this development, southern Whigs like Calhoun, Tyler, and Polk, moved back into the Democratic Party in the early 1840's.

The reason for this was that the Panic of 1837 had sensitized the conservative elements of both Whigs and Democrats and they merged. The liberal wings of both parties also merged. The result was a northern liberal Whig Party and a southern conservative Democratic Party. Thus, after 1844, the Whigs had some sort of ideological unity. And this unity, under the leadership of John Q. Adams, Webster, and Clay was embodied in the American System. Democratic fidelity, in contrast, was largely based on the original political philosophy of Thomas Jefferson. The issues which brought about this new political regimentation development were primarily economic. Strictly sectional party systems had developed therefore, before slavery became the predominant issue.

Slavery and Economics

When slavery did become an issue, it was a political–economic one. Almost all southern wealth was tied up in land and slaves. As the cotton economy expanded slave prices rose, and cotton prices tended to level off. Thus, it was costing more to produce the same quantity of cotton. This forced many small slave holders to sell out, thereby increasing the power of the large plantation owners. The southern planter was in a position of having little choice but to live with his system. He had tied up his money in slaves and cotton to the point where there was no way of profitably

getting out. For him to give up his slaves was tantamount to giving up both prestige and power. As an economic system, the slave–plantation economy was inflexible and often unprofitable. The diversified northern system was much stronger. This was of momentous political and economic significance as the Civil War era approached.

For the time being, however, the South was reasonably quiescent. During the Polk administration the Walker Tariff was passed (1846). This measure lowered the rates of the existing 1842 tariff considerably, and satisfied southerners. Also in 1846 Polk obtained from Congress legislation which re-established the Subtreasury System. This, basically, would remain the banking policy of the federal government until the Federal Reserve Act of 1913, except for a brief period during the Civil War.

The decade of the 1850's was one of increasing strife between North and South. One of the most significant events was the development of the newly formed Republican Party. Strictly a northern party, it drew a great deal of support from ex-Whigs, and almost fully reflected the old Hamiltonian philosophy. Of course, this ran counter to southern interests. The party came out in favor of the protective tariff, a new national bank, an elaborate system of internal improvements, and a Homestead Act which would provide free land in the West. The South was convinced that it was emphatically not in its interest to live under a Republican government. It officially expressed this attitude when Lincoln ran for the presidency in 1860.

In 1857 the Dred Scott case was heard by the Supreme Court. Dred Scott had been a slave whose owner had taken him to free territory. He sued in the courts claiming that he was a free man since he had resided on free soil. Chief Justice Taney ruled that Scott could not sue in a court because he was not a citizen. This could have ended the case but Taney in a vain attempt to settle the slavery issue for all time went on to consider whether or not Congress had the authority to exclude slavery anywhere. Taney reasoned that Congress had the power to legislate for the territories for the free and equal benefit of all American citizens. This included protection of property rights, and slaves were property. Therefore, the Missouri Compromise was unconstitutional because it deprived American citizens of their property rights. Taney's decision pushed the slavery extension argument to its extreme. And in so doing, he further increased the strife between North and South.

Also in 1857 the nation experienced another financial panic. The reasons for this comparatively mild economic dislocation were the same as earlier ones. The North sought relief through an increased protective tariff and banking reforms. But the South, due to a continually rising demand for cotton, hardly felt the panic and opposed the federal legislation. Northerners were quick to point out that the South was not interested in the national welfare. The incident measurably increased the hostility between the sections.

Resources for War

Finally, civil conflict came and the North had certain material advantages. Twenty-three states remained in the Union, compared to eleven who joined the Confederacy. Northern population stood at 22 million, whereas the South had only 9 million, including 3.5 million slaves who could hardly be considered a military asset (besides, it was against the law to arm a slave). Much more money was in the North, as well as banks and European financial ties. Added to this, the North possessed far greater taxable property and more efficient tax laws. The South was simply on a credit economy and had hardly any resources for financing a war.

The North possessed an established currency, while the Confederacy, as a new nation, was forced to create one rapidly.

Two types of materials are necessary for the successful prosecution of a war: primary military equipment and subsistence materials. The North had both a developing industrial economy and a varied subsistence crop economy. The South had mainly limited herself to cotton, and consequently, was not independent in the production of foodstuffs. The North had a decided advantage. Only in the category of morale did the South possess an advantage over the North.

Important developments occurred in the North during the course of the Civil War. Industry was rapidly developing; there were various banking improvements. Also, as the Republicans unequivocally favored protective tariffs, there were several upward tariff revisions.

In both North and South consideration had to be given to finance measures. The South experienced considerable difficulty. It repeatedly issued paper money which by 1865, shortly before the war ended, was worth less than 2¢ on the dollar. The North issued $450 million in paper greenbacks which held their value after the war. Both sides also issued bonds to finance their respective causes. Northern bonds did well because investment money was abundant and resources were well established. Southern bonds fared poorly and after the war they were worthless.

The Free Silver Issue

In post–Civil War America tariffs continued to be a major economic issue, but there was a still more important one. This was the currency issue. The paper money of the Civil War era, the greenbacks, had been declared legal by the Supreme Court, but President Rutherford B. Hayes (1876–1880) hoped to put the nation's currency back on the gold standard.

Steamboats—Symbol of the West's Rising Importance

He therefore ordered the accumulation of gold by the government. As the gold was collected the value of paper money appreciated. Finally, in 1878, a paper dollar was actually worth 100¢.

Soft Money and a High Tariff

The farmers who held mortgages on their farms were greatly disturbed by this. They had borrowed dollars worth considerably less than 100¢, and were being required to repay those dollars with more expensive ones. The cry went up for soft money—paper or anything else less valuable than gold. Prosperity, however, quickly ended the demands for paper, and the debtor class turned to free silver for a cheaper form of money.

Traditionally, the value of gold and silver rested on the market price of these metals. This meant that gold was worth about sixteen times more than the same amount of silver. Quite naturally, since both gold and silver coin were used, Americans spent the silver and hoarded the gold (Gresham's law), because the value of gold was greater. To curb this practice, Congress in 1873, had authorized the dropping of silver as currency, and ended the legal ratio of 16:1 for gold and silver. Few people were concerned at the time, but later, this action became known as the Crime of '73.

As more and more silver lodes were discovered in the West, its value in relation to gold dropped. With the development, silver miners began clamoring for the re-establishment of silver currency at the old 16:1 ratio, for this would drive up the price of silver. And those people who wanted a more flexible currency added to the demand.

The result of this demand was the passage of the Bland–Allison Act in 1878, which authorized the Secretary of the Treasury to buy $2–4 million in silver, at market price, and coin it at a ratio of 16:1.

However, since coinage would be limited, and since the circulating value of silver was based on the value of gold, the law neither drove up the price of silver, nor did it satisfy debtor demands. Still, silver miners and farmers believed it was a step in the right direction, and were momentarily appeased.

In 1888 the nation witnessed the first presidential election since the Civil War in which the main campaign issue was the tariff. The Republicans nominated Benjamin Harrison and came out in favor of a high protective tariff. The Democrats renominated Grover Cleveland and avoided taking a definite stand on the tariff. Since the tariff was considered to be quite important by big business, the business community poured significant sums of money into Republican campaign chests. The Republicans then initiated an elaborate nationwide "tariff education" movement. The Democrats lacked the funds to combat this development.

The end result was the passage of the McKinley Tariff of 1890. This tariff carried the highest peacetime rates in the history of the nation up till then. The rates were so high that they almost immediately caused a noticeable increase in the price of consumer goods. The high cost of living was justifiably blamed on the Republicans, who, as a result, lost control of both houses of Congress in the off-year elections of 1890.

Another important financial measure, this one dealing with the currency, was also passed in 1890. The Sherman Silver Purchase Act authorized the federal government to purchase $4–8 million in silver each month ($4.5 million was the actual figure as this was the nation's total monthly production), and to issue a new paper currency based on silver reserves. At this point the federal government possessed nearly double the amount considered to be the essential minimum gold reserve. But the Sherman Act drained gold from the Treasury in order to pay for

the silver, while at the same time, the McKinley Tariff cut revenues since it was too high to allow goods into the country. By early 1893 there was barely the essential minimum of gold left. Over one-half of the nation's gold reserves had been expended within a two-year period.

This deteriorating situation was apparent at the time of the 1892 presidential election. Harrison ran again for the Republicans, and Cleveland ran for the third consecutive time for the Democrats. The nation was clearly dissatisfied, being in the early stages of the brewing Panic of 1893, and Cleveland easily won the election.

The Panic of 1893

The panic which Cleveland had to face was caused by a number of clearly delineated factors. One cause was the European depression which drastically cut into American foreign markets. Another factor was the general agricultural depression which began in the 1880's. Also, the United States had been on a long speculative spree (this had caused a brief panic in 1873); there had been a general overexpansion, and by the 1890's a slowdown was in progress. And finally, the Silver Act and a dwindling gold reserve were decisive factors in triggering the panic.

Cleveland immediately called Congress into Special Session and had it repeal the Sherman Silver Purchase Act. This action cost him western support, but was successful because most eastern Republican backed him. He then attempted to build up gold reserves by purchasing huge quantities of gold. This was very difficult to do, for no one wanted to release their gold. Cleveland, in an effort to stabilize gold reserves, made a deal with the financeer, J. P. Morgan and a select group of financeers. They were permitted to buy $62 million in government bonds, drawing 4.5 per cent interest, at $104.50 a share, instead of the current market price

of $111.00 a share. This gave the group a
rather tidy profit. In return, Morgan and
associates agreed to obtain at least one-
half of the needed gold from foreign
sources, and to use their influence to stabilize the national currency. This was accomplished and the economy was stabilized. Cleveland, however, was violently
criticized for "selling out to Wall Street,"
and became an exceedingly unpopular
president.

The currency issue sprang to life again
in the 1890's, but then was strongly connected with the farmer protest movement
and will be dealt with in Chapter Six.
Aside from this later protest, there was
little substantive political change. The
Republicans remained in power from
Cleveland to Wilson—a period of sixteen
years. Also, American involvement in
imperialistic ventures during most of this
period tended to take attention away from
domestic financial manners. Then, in
1913 a Democratic candidate captured the
presidency. Woodrow Wilson was only
the second Democrat to do so since before the Civil War.

Woodrow Wilson to Herbert Hoover

In his first message to Congress Wilson called for reform. He sought a significant reduction in the tariff. This was
accomplished in the Underwood–Simmons
Act, which not only reduced the rates but
lessened the number of items taxed. An
income tax provision was added to the
tariff bill to make up for lost revenues.
Known as the Hull Bill, it called for a
straight 1 per cent tax on all incomes over
$3000 for single persons and $4000 for
married persons. The tax, in keeping
with the authorization of the as yet unused
Sixteenth Amendment, was graduated to
a maximum rate of 7 per cent on incomes
in excess of $500,000. Since the tax was
slight, and since only a small number of
people were affected by it, it was readily
accepted.

Also in 1913 the Glass–Owens Banking Act was passed, which set up the Federal Reserve System. Designed to establish a government-controlled banking and
currency system, the act set up twelve federal reserve banks, privately controlled
but regulated by a new government agency
—the Federal Reserve Board. The original board did not have all the powers it
possesses today. It could not set discount
rates, but it could veto any changes in
existing rates. The Federal Reserve Act,
however, was probably the outstanding
legislative achievement of the Wilson
presidency.

Financing World War I

World War I, which began in 1914 in
Europe, and eventually involved America
by 1917, turned American financial developments into new channels. Initially,
finance was concerned with underwriting
the Entente's costly efforts. When, in
1917, America became a true belligerent,
the problems of paying for the war became more critical.

In financing a war there are only two
possible courses of action—pay now or
pay later—and usually both are employed. To pay "now" meant much
higher taxes and the United States by the
Revenue Act of 1917 raised taxes to 2
percent on a $1000 exemption, with rates
scaled upward to 67 per cent. The Revenue Act of 1918 raised rates to 6 per cent
on a $1000 exemption, increasing to a
77 per cent maximum. Not only were the
tax rates increased, but a number of new
taxes were introduced: various luxury and
excise taxes, excess profits taxes, and a
"victory surtax."

To pay later meant to borrow, and this
was done by issuing government bonds
known as Liberty Loans during the war,
and as Victory Loans afterwards. There
was no difficulty at all in selling the bonds.
Total war expenses for the nation
amounted to roughly $33 billion: $11 bil-

lion was obtained by increased taxes, and the remainder came from bond subscriptions. Before the war the total national debt was slightly over $1 billion. After the war it was approaching $24 billion, and the nation was on its way to contemporary fiscal indebtedness.

The American people accepted the financial burdens quite willingly, as the sacrifices were relatively mild and of short duration. But after the war, there was a problem concerning the repayment of money advanced by the United States to her allies. This foreign indebtedness comprised a large portion of the American national debt, and American taxpayers were not pleased by the prospect of paying the debts owed by the taxpayers of other nations. (See Chapter Fourteen for further discussion.)

The Post-War Situation

In the post-war era the Republicans were once again in power. They attempted to re-establish the policies followed in the late nineteenth century, the most important of which was the high tariff. The existing tariff was the rather moderate Underwood–Simmons Act of 1913. However, the American people apparently desired a high tariff again for two reasons. First, it was argued that the nation had grown strong under the old protective tariff principle. The second argument advanced was that new post-war European factories were beginning to compete with the United States and were underselling American goods in certain areas.

As a result, farmers and laborers joined business in pushing for high tariff rates. The government responded by enacting the Fordney–McCumber Tariff of 1922, which drastically raised the rates. It was the highest peacetime American tariff to date, and it produced some dire effects which helped bring on the Great Depression. It curtailed the free flow of goods on the international market, and it forced some American capital out of the country to overcome retaliatory European high tariffs. This had an adverse effect on the American labor market, although at the time it was hardly noticeable.

There was one very worthwhile accomplishment during the Harding administration (1920–1923). This was the Budget and Accounting Act which revamped and rendered more efficient the accounting practices of the federal government. But what was more important, it reformed budgetary practices. Formerly, each government agency separately appeared before Congress seeking its annual appropriation. This practice possessed several serious drawbacks: it involved a considerable amount of wasted congressional time; it resulted in a great deal of duplication; it opened itself to fraud since the agency, regardless of its national importance, received money only in proportion to the strength of its lobby. The new law required that all agency requests for funds should be submitted to the executive, where they would be checked and consolidated. Then, the executive would formulate and present a single budget bill to Congress for its consideration. This was a noteworthy improvement, but was regarded at the time as being highly controversial.

Throughout the Harding, Coolidge, and Hoover administrations, the economic philosophy of Secretary of the Treasury Andrew Mellon predominated. And in view of the impending depression his assumptions have become quite controversial. There was a radical new economic theory in existence—the Hansen thesis—with which Mellon was in complete disagreement. It called for high taxes during periods of prosperity, and low taxes during depressed periods. Mellon's views called for keeping taxes low, and government expenditures even lower, at all times. He favored low taxes for everyone, with the very wealthy obtaining the most substantial cuts. His policies allowed the people to retain too much capital, and this resulted in vast inflation and speculation. Mellon ignored the prosperity of the decade, which could have easily supported higher taxes.

The Gathering Storm

Herbert Hoover took office in March, 1929, just in time to become the symbol of hard times to the American people. A few months after his inauguration, without his help or hindrance, the stock market crashed (October, 1929), and the nation entered the most serious depression in its history. The multitudinous reasons for the Crash had been developing throughout the entire decade.

The plight of the farmer was a contributory factor. Unable to adjust from his period of overexpansion during the war years, and faced with dwindling markets, the farmer became a major drag on the American economy. His low income had far-reaching consequences. Lowered farm income slowed the demand for manufactured goods. This reduced the number of people required in industry, and many workers were laid off. This gave the industrial workers as a group, less money with which to purchase foodstuffs and manufactured goods. This further lowered farm income, and the cycle kept repeating itself. There was a downward-moving economic spiral throughout the decade, and it was compounded by the appearance of the technologically unemployed—for instance blacksmiths, some carriage-makers, and some brewers and distillers. Also, the apparent prosperity of the decade was uneven. Besides agriculture, construction and various other industries did not share fully in the economic upswing.

Also, a new marketing procedure was introduced during the decade: installment buying. This was primarily what kept industry going until the crash. People bought on credit, thus tending to keep up the demand for goods. Manufacturers and bankers encouraged this practice as they were getting rich; credit was very easy to obtain. And in this era of loose credit, few people concerned themselves with the actual cost of goods; only monthly payments seemed important. As a result, most goods were overpriced. In addition the Federal Reserve Board made no attempt to control the loose credit situation.

Also, during this decade, personal savings were disastrously low. Speculation, both in real estate and in stocks, seemed to provide more promise than the more staid savings account. It was considered to be a patriotic act of faith in the future betterment of the nation. Land speculation dates back to the colonial period. During the Twenties, real estate prices were forced extremely high, particularly in the Florida land boom. Land speculation peaked out by the middle of the decade primarily because of the hurricanes in Florida. Speculation then turned almost exclusively to the stock market.

Returns on stocks are normally based on two factors: yield (dividends) and appreciation. People completely ignored yield and concentrated on potential appreciation of market value. This forced the price of stocks higher and higher. A $100 share of stock might be forced as high as $400–500 in market price during the decade. Brokers and bankers backed this speculation; they were making high commissions and earning high interest rates. They began to put these profits in the market themselves, along with other funds which they held in trust. Many Americans who bought stocks considered themselves to be experts on the market. Actually, an overwhelming majority of these people had only gained their first acquaintance with investments by buying war bonds during the First World War.

Crash and Depression

The market began to slide in early 1929. It recovered slightly but then be-

WORST STOCK CRASH STEMMED BY BANKS; 12,894,650-SHARE DAY SWAMPS MARKET; LEADERS CONFER, FIND CONDITIONS SOUND

FINANCIERS EASE TENSION

Five Wall Street Bankers Hold Two Meetings at Morgan Office.

Wall Street Optimistic After Stormy Day; Clerical Work May Force Holiday Tomorrow

Confidence in the soundness of the stock market structure, notwithstanding the upheaval of the last few days, was voiced last night by bankers and other financial leaders. Sentiment as expressed by the heads of some of the largest banking institutions and by industrial executives as well was distinctly cheerful and the feeling was general that the worst had been seen. Wall Street ended the day in an optimistic frame of mind.

LOSSES RECOVERED IN PART

Upward Trend Start• With 200,000-Share Order for Steel.

From "The New York Times," October 25, 1929.

STOCK PRICES SLUMP $14,000,000,000 IN NATION-WIDE STAMPEDE TO UNLOAD; BANKERS TO SUPPORT MARKET TODAY

Sixteen Leading Issues Down $2,893,520,108; Tel. & Tel. and Steel Among Heaviest Losers

PREMIER ISSUES HARD HIT

From "The New York Times," October 29, 1929.

STOCKS COLLAPSE IN 16,410,030-SHARE DAY, BUT RALLY AT CLOSE CHEERS BROKERS; BANKERS OPTIMISTIC, TO CONTINUE AID

LEADERS SEE FEAR WANING

Point to 'Lifting Spells' in Trading as Sign of Buying Activity.

GROUP MEETS TWICE IN DAY

240 Issues Lose $15,894,818,894 in Month; Slump in Full Exchange List Vastly Larger

The drastic effects of Wall Street's October bear market is shown by valuation tables prepared last night by THE NEW YORK TIMES, which place the decline in the market value of 240 representative issues on the New York Stock Exchange at $15,894,818,894 during the period from Oct. 1 to yesterday's closing. Since there are 1,279 issues listed on the New York Stock Exchange, the total depreciation for the month is estimated at between two and three times the loss for the 240 issues covered by THE TIMES table.

Among the losses of the various groups comprising the 240 stocks in THE TIMES valuation table were the following:

CLOSING RALLY VIGOROUS

Leading Issues Regain From 4 to 14 Points in 15 Minutes.

INVESTMENT TRUSTS BUY

From "The New York Times," October 30, 1929.

Historical Pictures Service, Chicago

The Crash on Wall Street, 1929

gan to slide again, down and down, until finally came ultimate disaster. But the end of the fantastic market speculation need not have caused a complete financial collapse. The labor force, factories, raw materials, and markets still remained, and, therefore, portions of the economy seemed to be salvageable. But there was a portentous psychological factor involved. People had regarded the stock market as the barometer of prosperity, and with its fall also went the confidence necessary to sustain new growth. Despair was increased by the fact that the Depression was worldwide. Many people believed that capitalism had run its course.

The downward economic spiral rapidly increased after the stock market Crash. Between 12 and 15 million people lost their jobs, and those fortunate enough to remain employed received wage and hour reductions. It was the Hoover administration's unenviable misfortune to be faced with this catastrophe.

A competent and honest man, Hoover was the victim both of circumstances and an outmoded, yet widely held financial theory and political philosophy. However, he did inaugurate a Depression program. The Agricultural Marketing Act of 1929 set up the Federal Farm Board, financed by a $500 million revolving fund. Its purpose was to loan money to self-established farmer cooperatives. Then the Hawley–Smoot Tariff was passed, raising the previous Fordney–McCumber rates from 33 to 40 per cent. (Its record-high rates brought immediate retaliation from many foreign countries.) Agricultural rates were raised even more. Hoover got the nation's leading industrialists and labor leaders to agree to a truce and the bargain was generally kept. He increased public works to stimulate the economy and provide jobs. And immigration was further reduced. He set up the President's Committee for Unemployment Relief in 1930. But Hoover believed that relief should be handled primarily by vari-

ous private agencies. This was one of his biggest mistakes, as they were utterly unable to perform this task.

Hoover believed in the essential soundness of the American economy, ignoring, for the most part, the psychological problem of confidence, and the structural flaws in the system. Still, he did attempt to restore confidence by setting up the National Credit Association in 1931, which rediscounted bank assets in an effort to stabilize the economy. When this accomplished nothing, he established the Reconstruction Finance Corporation to stimulate business. Financed with $3 billion the RFC loaned money at low rates to key industries, hoping that these industries would be stimulated to rehire and expand into their former markets. This measure, which was adapted as part of the future New Deal recovery program, was extremely unpopular. It appeared to be relief for the rich instead of for the poor. Its great failure hinged on the long and inevitable time lag before the project began to accomplish what was intended. Also, the sum of $3 billion was far too small to do the job. While theoretically sound, the RFC had little but adverse effects.

Hoover's policies did not begin to solve the depression, which in fact became increasingly severe. In the off-year congressional elections of 1930 the Democrats made considerable gains. Then, in 1932, Franklin Roosevelt easily defeated Hoover for the presidency, and promised a "new deal" for the American people.

Enter the New Deal

As Depression-era dollars became scarce, they became quite expensive. President Roosevelt wanted controlled inflation; this was an important part of bringing the nation back to a healthy economic state. The Emergency Banking Act of 1933 halted all transactions, exports, and hoarding of gold. The Federal Re-

The Depths of Depression

serve System began issuing notes against assets, and for all practical purposes, the nation was taken off the gold standard. A conservative measure, it was widely supported by the business community and did stabilize the nation's banking institutions.

Roosevelt then began devaluating the dollar. He commenced the purchase of gold to drive up the price of the metal, while cutting the amount of gold backing up each dollar. The Silver Purchase Act of 1934 was designed for a similar purpose. Also early in 1934, Congress stabilized the gold dollar at 59.6 per cent of its pre-Depression value. The federal government had begun the formal manipulation of the currency for purposes of creating a healthy economic climate.

There were three basic categories of New Deal Legislation: relief, recovery, and reform. Relief was the biggest immediate problem, and the federal government under Roosevelt quickly acted. The Federal Emergency Relief Act of 1933 was designed to strengthen Hoover's RFC and to provide direct federal relief for the needy. Government money and surplus commodities would be given over to the states for distribution. But the idea of direct charity was viewed with alarm, so in 1935 the Works Progress Administration took over the relief program. It had three basic aims: to provide work rather than charity; to be administered by local authorities since they supposedly best understood local problems; and to furnish labor costs by the federal government and material and equipment costs by local government. The WPA was subjected to much criticism, some of it justified, but it kept people from starving and placed some money in circulation. These same results were accomplished by other New Deal creations such as the Civilian Conservation Corps.

Under recovery there were two basic enactments. The Agricultural Adjustment Administration, created in May, 1933, and the National Recovery Administration, set up in June, 1933. The former was designed for agricultural recovery, and the latter to bring about industrial recovery. The AAA (see Chapter Six) attempted to regulate agricultural production and thereby to produce temporary artificial shortages in order to force up prices. The government would pay farmers to limit production of certain basic crops like corn, hogs, wheat, and cotton. The basic idea behind NRA, (see Chapters Seven and Eight), was for government and the various industries to draw up fair codes of labor practices, which were to have the force of law. These codes established maximum work weeks, forbade child labor, and set up minimum wage laws. Jobs and income would thereby be created. The only real problem concerned enforcement. Every industry entered into an agreement, but few kept their word. Their failure to do so, in many cases, was caused by regulatory problems rather than arbitrary evasion.

The government apparently understood and subsequently attempted to remove some of the pressure by creating a demand for goods and services. The Public Works Administration was established under NRA for large-scale, long-range government building projects. It was financed with $3.3 billion in federal funds. The Tennessee Valley Authority was enacted authorizing federal use, conservation, and development of the natural resources of the Tennessee river system. Both acts stimulated the industrial system while injecting money into the economy of the nation.

Reform measures constituted a difficult legal maze, encompassing literally hundreds of individual laws. In 1933 the Glass–Steagall Banking Act created the Federal Deposit Insurance Corporation— the FDIC. Private banks would pay a slight fee to the federal government which, in turn, would guarantee individual bank deposits up to $2500 (changed to $10,000 in 1950). An FDIC bank had to be a member of the Federal Reserve System, and the Federal Reserve Board was empowered to control the availability of money. Commercial banks, under another provision of the act, were denied the right to maintain securities outlets or to engage in investment banking, practices which had greatly aided in creating the Depression.

The Securities Exchange Commission also was set up in 1934, to prevent stock market frauds. All corporations with stocks listed on the market had to register with the SEC, and give it accurate information on their securities. The act established marginal requirements and controlled broker's loans, two of the characteristics of the 1920's bull market.

The year 1934 marked a new approach to tariff legislation. The Reciprocal Trade Agreements Act authorized the president to lower tariffs by as much as 50 per cent with individual nations, depending on what reductions these nations would make for American goods. Three-year agreements were negotiated with various nations, and senatorial concurrence was not necessary. The act was renewed in 1937. By 1939, Secretary of State Hull had negotiated agreements with twenty-one nations, with an overall tariff reduction approximating 29 per cent. Traditional protectionist policy was gradually discarded.

A host of other measures were passed, including the Wagner–Connery National Labor Relations Act, the Social Security Act, the Federal Communications Act, the Federal Power Commission Act, and the Rural Electrification Act. Most of these measures will be alluded to below, especially in those chapters dealing with agriculture, labor, business, and welfare-statism.

World War II and After

The World War II era brought new economic problems to the United States, which were quite opposite from depression. The economy was booming. Wages and prices were increasing so rapidly that

Roosevelt ordered a "freeze" on both in 1943. Still, labor managed to emerge from the war with 50 per cent salary increases, while real income rose approximately 33 per cent.

Financing the war was a difficult problem. It cost more than $320 billion, more than twice the total expenditures of the nation from its founding through 1941. Taxes paid roughly 40 per cent of the bill. A $500 exemption was allowed with a $1200 family exemption. The basic rate was 6 per cent. Incomes over $2000 carried a 13 per cent rate which rose progressively to 82 per cent on incomes over $200,000. Everyone paid a 5 per cent victory tax on their gross income. Corporate taxes averaged 40 per cent with a 90 per cent excess profits tax. The Revenue Act of 1943 authorized payroll deductions and post-war business tax credits. In addition, there were countless luxury taxes, most of which still exist.

The other 60 per cent of the war cost was obtained by issuing bonds, which raised the national debt to $260 billion by the close of the war. Americans cooperated willingly; people at last were making money and practically everyone had a relative or close friend fighting somewhere. The biggest citizen gripe in America was not about taxes but rationing.

Post-war Europe was in a ravaged state. With the beginning of the Cold War, the United States and Great Britain deemed it essential to rebuild the German economy, to facilitate a general European recovery. According to the American viewpoint, western Europe had to be stabilized economically before it could be politically durable, and thus ward off the threat of communism. This became the basic aim of American foreign policy from 1947 onward. The Truman Doctrine of 1947 was established to aid Greece and Turkey economically. In requesting aid President Truman indicated that "the seeds of totalitarian regimes are nurtured by misery and want." The Marshall Plan

developed this notion for the total reconstruction of western Europe. Hence, economics again was at the base of American foreign policy (see Chapter Fourteen).

World War II had created a critical inflationary spiral in wartime America, which led to the establishment of the Office of Price Administration. Tremendous pressures existed after the war to prematurely remove wage, rent, and price controls. Truman resisted but to no avail, and the result was a 25 per cent increase in prices the first half-month after controls were ended. Prices continued to move upward at a rate as high as 30 per cent per month, and were followed by wage increases, followed by price increases again. The inflationary spiral was only checked by the reintroduction of some wartime economic controls during the Korean War era.

The Eisenhower presidency (1952–1960) was very much concerned about the detrimental economic effects which might result at the end of the war, from the reduction of large military expenditures (a huge backlog of consumer demands had avoided this after World War II). A recession in the economy did occur however, and both Democrats and Republicans argued over what the government should do about it. Both parties assumed that the government had the legitimate function of providing a healthy economic climate for the nation.

The solution devised called for a loosening of credit to stimulate purchasing, a tax cut to pour money into the economy, and an increase in various government benefits: for instance unemployment compensation and retirement benefits, to increase spending power. These measures were destined to become standard devices for economic control. A sharp upswing in the economy followed, and the Federal Reserve Board tightened credit to prevent a new inflationary spiral. The loosening and tightening of credit by this agency has become a standard regulatory practice.

When a recession hit again at the close of 1957, the now standard formula was reapplied: an easing of credit, more government expenditures, and an extension of government benefits. Recovery followed but slacked off again in 1960—an election year.

Part of John Kennedy's campaign called attention to the unstable, slumping economy of the later Eisenhower years. But he also utilized, as president, the devices of tax cuts, increased government spending and benefits, and control of interest rates to stimulate the economy. This is also the strategy which President Johnson is employing in his espousal of tax increases and a curtailment of government spending, due to an inflationary spiral. The system can work both ways.

The old and unworkable notion of laissez faire has given way to direct government involvement in economic affairs. And there is no discernible trend to indicate any change in the foreseeable future. The "new economics" has achieved a firm hold on both political parties, although the method of implementation, and the exact blending of these various regulatory devices, varies somewhat. The contemporary presidency is seeking authorization to raise or lower tax rates within prescribed congressional limits, to more exactly and immediately control the economy. Considered quite revolutionary for the time being, it will most probably be enacted in the not too distant future. This means that Americans are learning to better control their own environment. The government is making a concerted effort to prevent both depression and wild inflation—to smooth out the economic climate of the nation.

For Further Reading

Bernstein, Marver H. *Regulating Business by Independent Commission.* Princeton: Princeton University Press, 1955.

Crockett, J. P. *Federal Tax System of the United States.* New York: Columbia University Press, 1955.

Faulkner, Harold U. *American Economic History.* New York: Harpers, 1943.

——. *The Decline of Laissez Faire, 1897–1917.* New York: Rinehart, 1951.

Friedman, Milton, and Schwartz, Anna. *A Monetary History of the United States.* Princeton: Princeton University Press, 1963.

Harris, Seymour E. (ed.). *The New Economics: Keynes' Influence on Theory and Public Policy.* New York: Knopf, 1947.

Heilbroner, Robert, and Bernstein, Peter L. *A Primer on Government Spending.* New York: Random House, 1963.

Johnson, Arthur M. *Government-Business Relations: A Pragmatic Approach to the American Experience.* Columbus, Ohio: Merrill, 1965.

Redford, Emmette S. *American Government and the Economy.* New York: Macmillan Company, 1965.

Robertson, Ross M. *History of the American Economy.* 2d ed. New York: Harcourt, Brace, 1964.

Smithies, Arthur. *Budgetary Process in the United States.* New York: McGraw-Hill, 1955.

Soule, George. *Prosperity Decade: From War to Depression, 1917–1929.* New York: Rinehart, 1947.

Steiner, George A. *Government's Role in Economic Life.* New York: McGraw-Hill, 1953.

Taussig, Frank W. *Tariff History of the United States.* 8th ed. New York: Putnam, 1931.

Watson, Donald S. *Economic Policy: Business and Government.* Boston: Houghton Mifflin, 1960.

Chapter Six
American Agrarianism

Farming in America has undergone a profound change over the past several decades, and it is still in a state of transition. From a position of almost complete economic self-sufficiency the farmer has moved to a role wherein he is subsidized by the federal government. From a position of considerable political power he has witnessed a diminution of that influence as his numbers decrease. And at the same time his cultural and social milieu, which at one point was quite distinct from that of his urban cousin, has become less and less unique.

Technology has played a major role in this transition, particularly in the areas of transportation, communications, and the devices and techniques of mass production. A network of superhighways has ended the farmer's isolation from urban centers, and at the same time, suburbia is slowly encroaching on his domain, eagerly converting once fertile farmland into shopping centers and housing tracts. Through television, radio, and periodical publications, the farmer is subjected to many of the influences and pressures that the city-dweller experiences.

The devices of mass production have perhaps exerted the most profound changes on the American farmer. At one point in the nation's history, his productivity was limited to his personal, individualized, physical labor. No longer is this true. One modern machine can accomplish the work of scores of men, which means that one farmer with modern machinery is capable of producing far more than dozens of farmers a half-century ago. But this is an expensive proposition, and it points to the heart of the farm problem.

The American farmer is capable of producing far more than his society requires. A surplus of foodstuffs results in a lowering of the price of these foodstuffs. But the cost involved in the purchase and operation of expensive equipment, the use of sophisticated fertilizers, and the application of the techniques of scientific farming, require that farming be performed on a large scale if it is to be profitable. So the modern farmer is caught in a dilemma. His situation demands that he produce as much as possible (to utilize his investment efficiently), but to do so lowers his profits by glutting the market with unnecessary goods.

One result of this development is that many farmers have migrated to urban areas, thereby becoming a minority element in contemporary society. But this very minority element, if unaided and uncontrolled, is capable of wreaking havoc on the entire American economy; farming is a necessary, integral part of the American economy.

It took the farmer a long time to realize that he had been transformed from an independent, self-sufficient operator to a modern capitalistic businessman. However it took even longer for the federal government to realize this fact, and also to recognize the critical role which the farmer plays in the national economy. But now that the realization has been made the farmer finds himself being subsidized and controlled by the federal government. He finds that he is often not allowed to farm as diligently as he might like. To accept the fact that he can make more money by working less has often required a difficult psychological adjustment. It is especially difficult because many traditional beliefs have for years been grounded in the notion that a man gets ahead by working harder than the next man.

Early Status of the Farmer

Farming was the principal pursuit of an overwhelming majority of the settlers who came to America during the colonial period. As was mentioned in Chapter One, the opportunity to own land was an important motivating factor for many of these people. The colonies were established in part to provide food for the tables of Englishmen. And even in New England, with her developing tradition of trade and commerce, small-scale farming

was the economic mainstay throughout much of the colonial period. The middle and southern colonies possessed the climate and soil whereby an agricultural surplus could be produced for export. The rocky, barren soil of New England could not, and this was a principal reason why many New Englanders took up other endeavors to supplement their subsistence agriculture.

The farmer was accorded considerable respect and prestige by Thomas Jefferson. His *Notes on Virginia* state: "Those who labor in the earth are the chosen people of God, if ever He had a Chosen people, whose breasts He has made His peculiar deposit for substantial and genuine virtue." Jefferson held that the closer a man was to the soil and nature, the closer he was to his God. Therefore, the farmer was the most virtuous of people. Conversely the city was evil because it was not close to nature. This was the main ideological reason why Jefferson espoused an American nation consisting of small farmers. For Jefferson deduced that democracy could function only with a virtuous population, and a virtuous population was possible only through a close identification with nature.

Thematically, the tension between urban and rural interests became the struggle between a bucolic life and an industrial system. The Jeffersonian theme ran counter to the political philosophy of the Federalist Party which was in power until 1801. This was evidenced by the Federalist-inspired Land Law of 1796. It set the price of surveyed public lands at $2 per acre. The minimum purchase was one section (640 acres), with 50 per cent down. This meant that the least one could spend to acquire a homestead was $640, a large sum of money for those days. The Land Law rather effectively prevented all but the very wealthy from purchasing lands from the national domain.

This situation changed after Jefferson gained the presidency. The land law was liberalized. In 1800, the new law allowed half-sections to be purchased at $2 per acre, with 25 per cent down and four years to pay. This was still expensive, but its revision had to wait until the Republicans had a firmer control of the government. Finally, in 1804, a land law allowed the purchase of quarter-sections of land at $2 per acre, with 25 per cent down and four years to pay. For $80 down a man could now purchase a 160-acre farm. This finally put land legally within the reach of most of the poor. Of course, all along people had been settling beyond the limits of surveyed public lands. They paid nothing for their farms, but by the same token they did not hold legal title. This gave rise to an increasing demand for squatter's rights, so that the original settler would have first opportunity to gain title to these lands whenever they were opened for purchase.

The Heyday of the American Farmer

By the close of the War of 1812 significant agricultural development was beginning to take place in America. It had been curtailed during the colonial and revolutionary periods because of inadequate transportation. The Louisiana Purchase (1803) had opened the Old Southwest to agricultural development by providing the Mississippi River waterway. The internal improvements boom of the 1820's and 1830's also helped the transport of goods, especially with the building of the Erie Canal, which provided access to the Northwest Territory. These developments, coupled with road-building programs and various canal projects, opened the Mississippi Valley to large-scale agricultural pursuits.

Interestingly enough, as the farmer's frontier pushed into the eastern Mississippi Valley, it passed around the plains area of central Indiana and Illinois, which contained some of the most fertile land in the country. Traditionally, farmers judged the richness of the soil by the density of trees growing on it. They were unable to recognize that the prairie soil was so rich that thick prairie grass prevented trees from taking root. Hilly wooded areas were settled first, leaving the best for last. As a consequence, it was not until the 1850's that the grasslands were fully settled, after having been avoided for roughly two decades.

In both the Gulf area and the Great Lakes region the small individual farmer came first. After he had cleared the land, wealthier farmers from the East would attempt to buy him out. This was particularly true in the Gulf region where the small farms were rapidly consolidated into large plantations. The dispossessed farmer would then usually move further west and repeat the entire process.

The pattern of agriculture thus differed from North to South. Initially, however, the agricultural frontier was more homogeneous. First loyalty was given to the West, and only secondarily to the Northeast or South. This was largely caused by the common problems faced by all frontier farmers. But more importantly, the trans-Appalachian West was bound together by the Mississippi River, the main artery of transportation and communication. With the coming of the steamboat, Gulf-area and Great-Lakes-region farmers were less isolated from each other than they were from eastern cities only several hundred miles away. When the railroad age commenced in the 1840's, however, this situation changed because railroads were primarily built east to west, across the old north–south lines of communication.

A Central Role in Art and Politics

During this period of enormous agricultural expansioin, the farmer was also gaining political power. The farmer ultimately triumphed with the election of Andrew Jackson in 1828. This was the period when American authors began to exploit the theme of rural innocence versus

The Prairie Farmer

urban iniquity. Writers almost invariably reached the same conclusions: that life in primitive nature was always superior to civilization.

This was the message found in the novels of James Fenimore Cooper. In *The Deerslayer* (1841), for instance, the hero representing natural virtue struggles to avoid the corruption of civilization. In utilizing this favored theme, Cooper made an attempt to re-establish the primacy of natural law. His heroes were always the embodiment of perfection, their primitiveness being only the natural distillation of divinity. The so-called civilized man, in his novels, had lost his association with nature, and consequently had fallen from grace. The same theme was later to appear in the work of Herman Melville and Mark Twain, but in a more somber mode:

the ultimate defeat of the natural, naive hero seemed inevitable.

This burgeoning primitivism corresponded to the ethos of Jacksonian democracy, which emphasized the simple dignity and importance of the common man and pointed a condemning finger at the type of civilization conceived by Alexander Hamilton. But this attitude did not reside strictly within the ideological realm. The farmer was proving his ability to determine the course of American events in a practical sense. It was he who had prompted the moves which culminated in the Louisiana Purchase; it was he who was mainly responsible for the War of 1812. Finally it was he who dispossessed the Indians of their tribal lands. During the years following the War of 1812, a swelling western population made new demands on the federal government. The nation had experienced a rather mild panic in 1819, and the West clamored for governmental action.

One result of these demands was the passage of the Land Law of 1820 which authorized the sale of public lands in parcels as small as eighty acres at a price of $1.25 per acre. This meant that a small farm site now could be purchased for only $100. Another result of frontier demands was the Relief Act of 1821, designed to aid the western farmer who was in arrears on the money owed the government for his farm. The law provided him with three options. He could pay off his total debt immediately by returning a proportionate amount of his lands to the federal government. He could pay off his total debt immediately at a 38 per cent discount if he could locate the funds. Or, he could keep all of his lands and pay them off over an eight-year period at no interest whatsoever. Very advantageous to farmers, these laws exemplified their ability to initiate change by the national government.

During the Jacksonian presidency two new ideas concerning land distribution were officially formulated. One of these, *graduation,* held that the government should sell as much land as possible at the highest possible price, then gradually reduce the price on unsold land until it was all either sold or finally given away. The other idea, *pre-emption,* called for giving those people who first settled upon unsurveyed lands the initial opportunity to buy them when they were offered for sale. Synonymous with this concept was the term *squatter's rights.* Neither of these notions became law during Jackson's presidency; sectional interests prevented him from implementing them. As a westerner he personally favored liberal land laws, but northern manufacturers feared their enactment would drain away their labor supply to the West. Also, southern planters did not desire competition from small operators in buying western lands. Both sections worried about lowering eastern property values. As the national leader Jackson did not press the issue.

Remaining at the base of the western land problem was the inability of the average farmer to obtain lands at a cost which he could afford. A large part of the problem was caused by speculators and developers who bought at public auction huge tracts of land and then sold parcels to working farmers at a considerable profit.

One solution to speculation was to "squat" on the land, and then demand the right to buy it at the minimum legal price. This became a widespread practice; it is estimated that over a half of all the settlers on new lands were initially squatters. But even so, squatters experienced a serious problem. When their lands were eventually opened for sale, someone might easily buy their farms out from under them.

When Martin Van Buren became president, he attempted to gain some support for his unpopular administration by passing a pre-emption law. As a result, a Pre-emption Act passed Congress in 1838, which allowed squatters to purchase land at minimum price. A more permanent

Pre-emption Act was passed in 1841, early in the John Tyler administration. It allowed any adult male to pre-empt 160 acres of surveyed land simply by making improvements on it. The land could later be purchased at the minimum price.

But even this did not really satisfy the demands of the farmer. When it came time to purchase his land, he still had critical problems. Forced to borrow money, he was at the mercy of lenders who usually required him to pay extremely high interest. The only obvious solution, from the farmer's viewpoint, was for the government to give land away. This idea was first introduced in Congress in 1846, but at the time it was overshadowed by the rising slavery issue.

Regional Competition

From the Jacksonian era forward, there were three key domestic issues contested between the sections: tariff policy, internal improvements, and land policy. The South, because of its plantations and European trade, was opposed to tariffs, opposed to federal internal improvements, and in favor of high-priced land. The Northeast, because of its manufacturing and marketing interests, favored high tariffs, wanted federal internal improvements, and desired high-priced land. The West, seeking protection and accessible markets, favored tariffs and internal improvements, but wanted cheap land. With increasing European immigration to the Northeast, that section eventually gave up its opposition to cheap land, since there appeared to be an abundant and continuing labor supply. Thus, the Northeast was ready to form an alliance with the West against the South. As the Gulf region converted to plantations it adopted the prevailing southern attitudes.

In the years that followed, the agricultural frontier continued to advance. In 1841 American farmers quickly passing over the Great Plains began their push into the fertile Oregon country, settling in the Columbia River Basin. Some farmers began pushing into the still-fertile, eastern

A Sod House in Nebraska

portions of the trans-Mississippi West, opening the sod-house frontier mentioned in Chapter Two. In this same period the Mormons settled the harsh Great Basin area later known as Utah.

During the 1850's the westward movement of the frontier became thoroughly enmeshed in the rising slavery issue. The settlement of new lands led to the formation of the Kansas and Nebraska territories in 1854. But the legislative measure which organized these territories, the Kansas–Nebraska Act, also espoused popular sovereignty which contradicted the geographical limitations in the Missouri Compromise (see Chapter Two). *Popular sovereignty* meant that the people of a given territory would decide for themselves whether to enact a free or slave state. Proponents of both views poured into Kansas, hoping to influence the election results. What resulted, however, was a bloody civil conflict that gave the territory its name of "bleeding Kansas." This conflict was not entirely a result of those problems which ultimately caused the Civil War. To some extent strife was caused by conflicting local land claims; thousands of settlers in a concentrated area were staking out government land years before sales began (in mid-1856).

During the Civil War era, both northern and western farmers enjoyed an increasing prosperity. Army food contracts greatly stimulated the demand for agricultural goods. At the same time foreign markets opened up because of the increase in European industrialization. Also, considerable aid was forthcoming from the federal government in making farm land available to settlers. In May, 1862, the Homestead Act was passed. Under its provisions, the government gave 160 acres of land to anyone who would live on and farm it for five years.

The amount of land allowed each individual under the terms of the Homestead Act was unrealistic. Western farmers, unless they were engaged in ir-

rigation farming, needed many more acres to support themselves than farmers in more fertile areas. And if they did irrigate, 160 acres of land was far more than they could handle. In the years that followed, changes to increase western land holdings were made in various land acts. The Timber Culture Act of 1873 gave a homesteader an additional 160 acres if he planted at least 40 acres of trees within a four-year period. The Desert Land Act of 1877 allowed the acquisition of 640 acres in the desert Southwest for 25¢ per acre, with an additional $1 per acre and proof of some irrigation within three years. And the Timber and Stone Act of 1878 authorized the purchase of 160 acres of valuable timber- or stone-bearing lands at $2.50 per acre to any citizen or alien who had initiated naturalization proceedings. Unfortunately, there was a great deal of fraud involved in the administration of these various acts. And, as matters turned out, millions of acres of the public domain went to speculators and investors rather than to individual farmers. During this same period of agricultural expansion, other segments of the United States were developing a vast industrial complex.

Agriculture during the Age of Big Business

Farmer Discontent

The age of big business in America was only superficially roseate. Beneath its optimism there was dissent, and much of it came from the farmer. Throughout the age of big business the farmer was engaged in a continuing protest. This protest was a two-stage affair. First came the Grange movement, followed, after a brief interlude, by the Populist revolt. Both movements stemmed from the same basic farmer complaints, though their approaches were different.

One of the biggest complaints was directed against the railroads. The farmer had originally favored railroads as the solution to marketing problems, but gradually turned against them, claiming that their rates were both too high and discriminatory. An elaborate rebate system had been devised which was forcing farmers to pay higher rates than manufacturers for shipping the same quantity of goods. The railroads claimed rates had to be higher because of the bulky nature of farm goods. However, the primary reason rates were high was that usually only one railroad serviced a given area; there was no competition.

The farmer also had a complaint against the middleman. This was the individual who handled agricultural goods before they reached the retailer; he was the warehouseman or grain elevator operator, and later the processor. The farmer claimed that the middleman's profits were higher than his own, and generally this was true. The farmer was at a disadvantage in that he had to store a perishable crop and therefore the middleman was able to charge exorbitant prices.

The farmer claimed that manufacturers overcharged him on his purchases. This, too, was a legitimate complaint. The manufacturer was aided by a protective tariff, whereas the farmer was not. The farmer bought in a protected market, thus paying more than the original price for an item, but he sold his produce in an unprotected market. A double standard was being employed, with the farmer on the short end.

Another major farmer complaint was directed against the credit system. The farmer was usually in debt and was forced to obtain his money from commercial sources. He claimed that the interest rates, like railroad rates, were both high and discriminatory. The discrimination charge was valid; bankers generally viewed the farmer as a poor credit risk. All he usually had for collateral was farmland, and with plenty of free land still available, his loan security was quite limited. How-

ever, while discrimination in loans was evident, the contention that rates were too high must be tempered. The farmer usually paid 8 to 10 per cent interest, whereas given industrialists sometimes were forced to pay as high as 25 per cent for their use of money.

In addition the currency situation did not satisfy the farmer. During this period the farmer was generally unsophisticated concerning technical economic matters. He knew that he did not have enough money; therefore, he desired inflation and he backed almost any movement which might possibly create an inflated currency like greenbacks or Free Silver. This would raise agricultural prices while lowering the real value of his mortgage payments. His real income would not necessarily be increased, but he would be paying off his debts with progressively cheaper dollars.

The farmer also claimed that taxes were too high and once again discriminatory. They were high because of two factors. Government corruption resulted in a system wherein as much as two-thirds of each tax dollar disappeared in graft. The farmer was justifiably incensed over this. But high taxes also resulted from a widespread demand for the government to provide more public services, which it did. On this latter point the farmer, who also desired these new services, had little cause for complaint. However, concerning discrimination the farmer was entirely correct. During the age of big business there were no such things as corporate taxes and personal-income taxes. The man who earned a million dollars a year in dividends paid no tax on them. But the farmer, whose cash income was usually quite meager, was forced to pay a tax on his land. The average farmer on the sod-house frontier sometimes paid more taxes than the millionaire capitalist.

The farmer was also dissatisfied with agricultural prices. He was no longer a self-sufficient individual. He had become a small businessman, but he did not yet realize this fact. He grew a cash crop, then bought all of the items he and his family had formerly made for themselves. If he had a bad year he operated at a deficit. If he had an exceptionally good year, so probably did all the other farmers in his area, and the market price for his goods would often drop because of a crop surplus. Thus, whether he had a good year or a bad year, the end result was all too often the same. In addition, commodity prices were generally dropping during the period, because of three principal factors: more efficient farm production, a large number of new farms created by the demands of the Civil War era, and competition from newly opened farmlands in South America and Canada.

The farmer also had a political complaint. He had once been an important political element in his society, but the new city political machines were encroaching on his former power. He believed that he was no longer properly represented in his government and this was partially true. However, not only the farmer but other of the nation's working groups shared the same valid complaint. He claimed that the politicians were purposefully deceiving him and this too was partially true. But the farmer was generally ignorant of political matters, primarily because his economic status did not permit him the time to study political issues. Also, his numbers were scattered and thus he was usually unable to express his discontent with an organized collective voice.

Finally, the farmer complained about being isolated from the rest of the world. He was removed from concentrated society and in his isolation continually criticized that society for being evil. However, it was really up to the farmer to devise a solution for this social complaint.

The Grange

The farmer thus possessed a large number of serious and justifiable complaints. With these basic grievances the first formal protest movement began. This was the Grange movement, officially known as the Patrons of Husbandry, which dates from 1868.

The man who organized this first movement was Oliver Hudson Kelley, a minor political figure who had been sent south by the federal government during the early Reconstruction period. Kelley was impressed by the general agricultural backwardness of the South in particular, and of the entire nation in general. He believed that an organization of farmers was necessary to alleviate this unfortunate situation. With this in mind, he formed in 1868, a semi-secretive society which he called the Patrons of Husbandry. Local chapters of this organization were called Granges, and the name was quickly applied to the entire movement. In 1873, the year of the panic, there were more than ten thousand Granges in the Midwest, plus a sizeable number in the South, and a scattering of others throughout the rest of the nation. The peak year was 1875 when the Grange counted some 800,000 individual memberships. This meant that one out of every eight farmers was a member.

The Grangers favored economy in government, political and social equality, and better educational opportunities, along with a correction of the farmer complaints listed above. They were opposed primarily to the railroads and the credit system. The Grange was not designed as a political organization; it marked an attempt at forming a pressure group. The original idea of the Grange movement was to develop a mutual self-help organization. The general plan called for holding regular local meetings to discuss and seek solutions to practical farmer complaints. The meetings would then be followed by a social hour (this helped solve the farmers' feeling of social isolation).

The Grangers decided to establish cooperatives to help solve the economic problems plaguing them, both in the buying of manufactured goods and the selling of agricultural produce. A collective marketing scheme was utilized for selling, whereby the farmers would agree to hold back a portion of their crop, in order to drive up the price to a certain prescribed level before selling. Collective large-quantity buying was employed to obtain cheaper rates for manufactured goods. Theoretically, this was a good idea, but it did not work in actual practice. Manufacturers and retailers recognized what the farmers were attempting to do, so they collectively agreed to maintain their prices. Some enterprising individuals, however, took advantage of the situation and established such cooperative mail-order houses as Sears and Roebuck and Montgomery Ward. The cooperative system in general was a failing venture, primarily because of poor administration.

The Grangers also entered the political field. The Grange itself was not a political organization, but individual Grangers joined or formed various independent political organizations. The political movement flourished for about five years in the Midwest while only slightly affecting other parts of the country. The Grangers were generally quite successful in the county, and displayed some success on the state level. Nationally it was very limited, for a high degree of success entailed a thorough knowledge of both political issues and the proper candidates for certain offices, not to mention very large sums of money for campaigning. Only areas with high concentrations of farmers elected Grangers to public office.

Illinois, Iowa, Kansas, Missouri, and particularly Wisconsin elected considerable numbers of Grangers to their state legislatures. These representatives obtained the balance of power in their legislatures, and sided with whichever of the major parties agreed to support their programs. Thus, the major parties began to cater to the farm group for support, and individual Democrats and Republicans were elected to office with the support of Granger organizations. As a result, a number of laws were passed, most of which revolved around regulation of the railroads and the middleman.

Railroad regulation, however, was a national, not a state problem, because of its intrinsic interstate character. Granger-controlled state legislatures prescribed railroad rates and initiated various investigations, but very little was actually accomplished. The laws were usually poorly drafted and the courts were generally unsympathetic, declaring them unconstitutional for any one of three basic reasons. One reason was that the laws attempted to regulate activities which went beyond the boundaries of a state, and this was a generally correct interpretation. Another was that some of the laws were so badly worded that the courts declared them inoperative; this was occasionally valid. And finally, the courts were biased in favor of the railroads, since judges were usually appointed by governors who were involved with big business interests. Legislation pertaining to the middleman usually suffered a similar fate.

The most famous of all Grange-adopted laws was one passed in Illinois in 1871, which provided for a state warehouse commission to fix rates for operators. The law was eventually tested in the United States Supreme Court in 1873, in the case of *Munn* v. *Illinois*. Munn was a member of a Chicago firm which refused to comply with the state regulations. He sued the state but received an adverse decision in the state courts, and then appealed the decision to the Supreme Court. The Supreme Court ruled that if a business affected a sizeable portion of the public interest, the state could regulate it, because it directly affected the public interest. The case dealt only with warehouses, but it provided an important precedent for later cases involving similar issues. Also, it laid down the basic principle, now widely used, for the setting of public utility rates.

Beginning in 1875 the Grange movement began to decline. The reasons for

Library of Congress

A Granger Meeting

this were manifold. Because of their political victories, which proved to be deceptively futile, many people believed that all farmer problems had been legislated out of existence. Therefore, they dropped out of the movement. Others believed that the establishment of the cooperatives would solve their problems. So when the cooperatives began to fail, they not only dropped out of them, but they dropped out of the whole Grange movement as well. And finally, the farmer protest movement was unable to fight prosperity. The period from 1876 to 1881 witnessed a noticeable increase in agricultural prices. Thus the criticism of the farmers began to mellow somewhat as they began to make more money.

Successors to the Grange

The social and educational aspects (the original non-political purposes) of the Grange movement remained. Through-

out the late 1870's and the early 1880's, the Grange had stimulated farmer discussion groups and the idea of such organizations remained. As a consequence, other farmer organizations developed. The most important of these were the National Farmers Alliance, a midwestern and northern farmer group, and the National Farmers Alliance and Industrial Union, a southern group.

Both of these groups had the same basic complaints and organization as the earlier Grange. Both developed during the late 1870's and grew in the 1880's when the decline of the Grange became pronounced. Since their regional differences appeared very slight, they decided to attempt consolidation. A joint convention was held in St. Louis, in 1889, but the attempt was fraught with difficulties from the outset. The leaders of both organizations wanted to be the leaders of the combined organization—there was a clash of personalities. And it was quickly discovered that northern and southern farm problems were not identical. The northern farm problem centered around railroad regulation, while the southern problem centered around a fixed rate for a staple commodity—cotton. Diversified agriculture, as an adjunct to economic reconstruction, was only beginning in the South. Also, there was a question as to how political matters would be handled. The North tended to vote according to the promises of the individual candidates, whereas the South voted a straight Democratic Party ticket, regardless of candidates and issues, because of anti-Negro and anti-Yankee feelings. And finally, both organizations favored an expansion of the currency, but were unable to agree on the amount or the method of implementation.

Thus there was no merger, and the northern group began to disintegrate while the other maintained a rather shaky existence. However, after 1890 there was a noticeable reinvigoration of the merger concept. Old southern notions of Democratic Party supremacy were beginning to be replaced by renewed political activity. The catalyst developed in Kansas, where a new third-party movement, the Populist Party, was in its formative stages.

The Populist Movement

The party's name was derived from *vox populi*, "the voice of the people." The party consisted of remnants of the Grange, some labor organizations, and a sprinkling of reformers. In some degree it was an alliance of northern and southern farm groups. The Populists concentrated on elections on the state level where they were quite successful. They soon captured state offices and even elected representatives to the national Congress. Populism was a very colorful political movement, possessed of heavy overtones of the religious camp-meeting revival.

The party also possessed some extremely competent and colorful leaders.

One of the more important of these was Ignatius Donnelly, a very able eccentric from Minnesota, who had taken part in almost every reform movement of his day. His oratory was of the rough-and-tumble, fire-and-brimstone variety. Another leader was Jerome Simpson, better known as "sockless Jerry," because he never wore socks. Simpson acted like a stereotyped "hick," but he was actually very well educated and a veteran of third-party politics. His oratory stressed economic problems, on which he was an expert. The farmers loved him. Mary Elizabeth Lease, a Kansas farm woman who became the first female lawyer in her state, was another important Populist. Inclined to brash oratory like her male colleagues, she shocked many audiences. Her fame rested primarily on her famous statement: "What you farmers need to do is to raise more hell and less corn." She was the chief travelling orator of the movement. Finally there was General James Weaver, a well educated Iowan lawyer and Civil War veteran. Relatively conservative and fairly moderate in his oratory, Weaver had been the presidential candidate for the short-lived Greenback Party.

In 1890 the southern Populists were not interested in an independent third party movement. With fair success they managed to capture local and state units of the Democratic Party from within. In the process three new prominent southern leaders developed: Ben Tilden, a young congressman from South Carolina, Tom Watson of Georgia, and Leonides Polk. But few Populists won federal office in this election and they found they could not attack their problems as Democrats at the state level. To bring about Populist reforms of transportation, prices, currency, and credit, a national party would have to be organized.

The Populists took steps in this direction in 1892, when a national convention was held. It was an open convention and the South sent the largest contingent. The convention decided that a national organization should be formed and agreed to meet later in the year to choose national candidates and draw up a party platform. This was done in Omaha, Nebraska, on July 4, 1892.

General Weaver was nominated for the presidency, and a man named Fields, an ex-Confederate officer, was picked as his running mate. The detailed party platform called for regulation of the railroads and communications, establishment of a government commission to regulate monopolies, expansion of the currency (although no specific method was advocated), efficiency in government and further expansion of the civil service system, female suffrage, the direct election of federal senators, and a graduated income tax. The platform was far-reaching and in some cases revolutionary. Most of it was destined to be adopted later in the form of constitutional amendments. Basically, the Populist Party claimed a twofold purpose: to provide direct financial benefits for farmers, and to create a more democratic and efficient governmental system.

There were certain problems within the Populist movement. It possessed little financial backing and no real national organization, since most support came from midwestern farmers. As matters turned out, the South failed to support the movement as promised. One reason for this was that the presidential candidate was an ex–Union general. And Mary Lease, who had campaigned throughout the South in behalf of the candidates, probably lost more votes than she gained; most voters thought women should stay quietly at home.

The movement was quite successful in the Midwest, however. The strategy was excellent on the state level, where the Populists usually combined strength with one of the two major parties if it was sympathetic to the Populist cause. On the national scene, even though Weaver did

poll twenty-two electoral votes—a fair showing for a first attempt—the movement faltered. Ten Populists were elected to the House of Representatives, and perhaps some fifty more were elected under different party labels. However, these victories were insufficient to accomplish much of importance.

The 1892 election marked an end to the attempt to unite North and South. The party thereafter was primarily a midwestern party. But it was still quite optimistic concerning the 1896 presidential election. Weaver had made a good showing in 1892, considering that it was the party's first attempt at capturing high office. The Panic of 1893 had caused farm prices to drop considerably, and had also increased unemployment. Hence, farmers and industrial workers were both restless, and Cleveland was not a very popular president. His repeal of the Sherman Silver Purchase Act and his deal with J. P. Morgan had alienated the large debtor class. His conduct in the Chicago Pullman strike had alienated much of the working class. The Populists believed that 1896 was their big chance for success.

Free Silver and Bryan

There was another movement, however, which had been building between 1894 and 1896. It was a movement in favor of the free and unlimited coinage of silver at a ratio of 16:1 (see Chapter Five). Principle advocates were the silver miners (who had financial resources) and the farmers (who had numbers); between the two a powerful combination could be established. The Republicans favored remaining on the gold standard, while the Democrats were fairly evenly split. The Populist Party decided to hold its convention after those of the two major parties. The Republicans met and adopted a plank opposed to free silver and to reform measures. They nominated the conservative William McKinley, who was considered

In Favor of Free Silver

the candidate of big business. The Democrats met and nominated the relatively unknown William Jennings Bryan. He captured the nomination because of his superlative oratory, particularly his famous "Cross of Gold" speech. Bryan was violently opposed to the gold standard, and primarily because of him the Democrats decided to endorse free silver.

The Populists had expected both major parties to advocate the gold standard. They would then hold their convention, endorse free silver, and in the process, pick up a large segment of silver supporters from the Democratic Party plus a sprinkling of dissident Republicans. But the plan backfired, placing the Populists in an awkward position. They could either endorse free silver, nominate their own candidates, and compete with the Democrats (thereby splitting the silver vote), or they could endorse free silver, nominate Bryan, and in the process be swallowed by the Democratic Party.

They decided on a half-way measure. The Populists endorsed free silver and nominated the Democratic Party nominee, Bryan, as their presidential candidate. But they disagreed with the Democratic Party's choice of Arthur Sowell for vice-president, and instead nominated Tom Watson, a southern Populist, as Bryan's running mate. The semi-combined parties worked poorly together. There was considerable voter confusion over the two vice-presidential candidates. As a consequence, the Democrats lost three farm states, the East, and even three border states. The Republican, William McKinley, won the popular vote by a half-million and carried the electoral vote by a margin of 271 to 176.

The Populist Party died in 1896 and so did the silver issue shortly afterwards. The disappearance of the silver issue was caused mainly by a marked increase in the world's gold supply, brought on by huge new gold strikes in the Klondike and in Australia. The old once-natural ratio of silver to gold (16:1) was thereby re-established. Also, the organized farm movement began to fade away as prosperity again began to mellow criticism.

A Period of Prosperity:
Roosevelt to Wilson

In the years that followed the farmer was somewhat appeased because reforming presidents were in office. Some reform legislation beneficial to the farmer was enacted into law. One of these laws was the Hepburn Act of 1906 which strengthened the ineffectual Interstate Commerce Act of 1887. Under the original act the government was required to prove in courts that its suggested rates for railroads were proper, and it rarely could do so. The new measure authorized the government to fix definite rates, and it was up to the carriers to prove that the rates were improper. Naturally, the measure was bitterly opposed by the railroads. President Theodore Roosevelt managed to obtain passage by using the threat of public ownership of the railroads if the measure was not enacted. The probable bluff apparently worked. The Pure Food and Drug Act, also of 1906, regulated the middleman-processor of the food industry. It established minimal standards for preparing foods, required reasonably honest labeling, and provided for the federal inspection of all meat in interstate commerce.

Indirectly, the Roosevelt administration performed other considerable services for the agricultural community. The Newlands Act provided that the proceeds from all future sales of public lands would be used expressly for the irrigation of arid regions, thus reclaiming large tracts of wasted land. Sluice miners and lumber barons were destroying literally millions of acres of tillable soil with their reckless procedures. Roosevelt was unable to override certain vested interests, and could not regulate miners and lumberers, but he did appoint a National Conservation Committee which studied all phases of the nation's natural resources. The result would be positive action at a later date.

As World War I approached and finally engulfed Europe, the American farmer was prospering. Competition was no longer a problem. He was selling to both sides in the European war. The farmer was spurred on to an even larger expansion by the Hollis–Bulkley Act of 1916, which created twelve federal farm loan banks and capitalized each of them with one-half million dollars. This so-called rural credits bill made currency more available for increasing farm productivity.

When the United States became involved in the war in April, 1917, the American farmer, for the first time, had no problem selling everything he could produce. He found himself feeding not only the entire American nation, including 5 million American troops who had ceased to be producers, but also the armies of America's European allies, plus their civilian populations.

Because of this unprecedented demand for American agricultural goods, the Federal Food Administration was established in 1917. Headed by Herbert Hoover, the agency attempted to utilize American food supplies in the most efficient manner. Hoover made a plea for voluntary cooperation which did not completely override the public's hoarding instinct. Still, the United States experienced "breadless" Mondays and "porkless" Thursdays. He also encouraged farmers to produce more food, and placed controls on food wholesalers by means of licensing.

Lean Years for the American Farmer

The Growth of the Farm Bloc

The end of the war brought with it a brief period of economic dislocation which created a general falling-off of American prosperity. Industry and commerce quickly recovered, because of the official Republican Party philosophy which called for aiding business as much as possible. But the neglected farmer watched his profits decline. The result of this was the formation of an unofficial group of congressmen from the agricultural states who were known as the Farm Bloc. Although Republicans, these congressmen could not accept their party's primary concern with the wealthy commercial class. They felt, in view of slumping agricultural prices, that major governmental attention should be directed to the farm problem.

It was through their efforts that the Fordney–McCumber Tariff (1923) contained high protective features for certain agricultural products for the first time in tariff history. They pushed through a $1 billion appropriation for the War Finance Corporation to finance and improve the transportation of agricultural goods in 1921. Also passed in 1921 was the Packers and Stockyard Act, which gave increased federal power over the meat packing industry and lessened the control of that industry over the producers—regulation of the middleman. The group was additionally responsible for the passage of a Futures Trading Act which attempted to control speculation in the grain market, thereby helping to stabilize farm prices. And in 1922 they maneuvered through Congress the Capper–Volstead Act, which authorized the setting up of farmer cooperatives under federal supervision. However, none of these measures actually solved the farm problem.

Everyone was better off in the 1920's, it appeared—everyone except the farmer. He had once again some very serious problems. During the war he had expanded his production enormously, moving out on submarginal lands to do so. Nevertheless he had been able to produce more with less labor and poorer soil, because of improved labor-saving machines, new methods of enriching the soil, and the utilization of irrigation. Many American farmers had transformed themselves from small operators into large businessmen during the war years. The new agricultural techniques required large-scale farming operations. Like the industrialist, the farmer could not allow his expensive machinery to stand idle, or his high-priced fields to lie fallow; tremendous sums of money were tied up in land and machinery.

During the war era most farmers had been unconcerned about increasing expenditures and high interest payments, because agricultural produce was in great demand at high prices in both Europe and America. But after the war the demand for farm goods dropped, and as the demand lessened, so too did prices. Still remaining, however, were the huge capital investments and the high interest payments.

Immigration restriction had a detrimental effect on the demand for farm goods. For decades European immigrants had been swelling the population of eastern cities, thereby increasing the demand for foodstuffs. The immigration measures of the 1920's reduced these numbers by almost two-thirds, and thereby cut deeply into what formerly had been a constantly expanding market for the farmer. The rate of population growth was suddenly and rapidly dropping off.

Change in diet was another factor. In the prosperous Twenties the slender look became quite fashionable. The demand that women be capable of strenuous physical labor no longer held; the large physique was no longer admired or needed. If 25 million women—roughly half the female population of the decade—switched to black coffee and dry toast instead of the traditional hearty breakfast, one can well imagine the vast curtailment of the farm market. Perhaps 50 million fewer eggs a day were consumed and 5 million fewer pounds of butter.

Skimpier clothes were also quite fashionable during the Twenties. Short skirts replaced the once numerous ankle-length petticoats and bustles. There was probably several yards less of cloth in a flapper dress than in a Gay Nineties dress. Multiply this figure by the number of dresses sold in the nation, and one can well imagine the curtailment of demand in the cotton and wool industries.

The birth rate also dwindled in the Twenties. Rising prosperity and a preoccupation with fun during the decade changed the family values of America, particularly in the upper and middle classes. An increasing involvement outside the home caused many to decide against the restrictions imposed by having a large family. The lower economic class continued to experience a high birth rate, but these people could not add significantly to the farm market; they lacked the requisite cash income.

New industries, particularly the automobile manufacturers, were helping to make various agricultural products obsolete. For instance, the synthetic fibers developed during the war hurt wool and cotton as much as new fashions did. New synthetic dyes competed with southern indigo. And the automobile practically killed the giant horse and feed industry. Prohibition, too, had a detrimental effect on agricultural products, especially the grain industry: barley, malt, and hops, not to mention various fruit juice extracts. The average American cheated quite a bit on prohibition, but most of the illegal alcohol entered the United States by way of Canada or the Caribbean, and American agricultural production was not utilized to any great extent.

In addition to this the American farmer was beginning to face new competition from exceptionally rich farmlands in Argentina, Canada, and Australia. As a result of all of these factors, farm mortgages grew while farm income kept dropping. To curb this trend the aforementioned Farm Bloc had been established. But it accomplished very little of significance even with the various legislative measures of 1921–1922 .

Legislative Attempts to Aid the Farmer

Eventually, the Farm Bloc devised the Peek–Johnson plan to aid the farmer. George Peek ran the Moline Illinois Plow Company, and General Hugh Johnson was one of his associates. Together they worked out a plan to place agriculture on an equal footing with industry. It called for a two-price system: a high American price for agricultural goods, and a low foreign price for the surplus. In this manner, the American farmer could make high profits from a domestic market which was protected by high tariffs and dump his surplus (even at a sizeable loss if necessary) on the European market. By using 1914 prices as a proposed base rate, the proposal contained the nucleus of the future parity system.

Senator Charles McNary of Oregon, and Representative Gilbert Haugen of Iowa, attempted to push the Peek–Johnson plan through Congress. Passage of the McNary–Haugen bills (four of them) was hotly contended throughout the decade. The first attempt occurred in 1924. The measure called for the creation of an Agricultural Export Corporation, a federal agency which would buy up all domestic surplus at a rate to be determined by an average of the 1905–1914 prices, and then to sell the surplus in Europe for whatever could be obtained. Easterners and southern Democrats combined to defeat the measure on two different occasions.

A 1927 bill proposed a Federal Farm Board to administer and direct the sale of surplus commodities abroad through farm cooperatives. The government itself would not buy the surplus, but its sale would be cushioned by a stabilization fund which would be used to bolster foreign prices. This measure passed both houses of Congress but was vetoed by President Coolidge, who regarded it as class legislation. A slightly amended version of the 1927 bill was vetoed by the president in 1928, and congressional sentiment was not sufficiently strong to override his veto.

During the 1928 presidential campaign, the proponents of the McNary–Haugen bills sought unsuccessfully to have their proposals placed in either one of the major party platforms. The Republicans wanted no part of it; they preferred to favor industrial interests. The Democrats were apparently content to straddle the fence. They had just healed the 1924 rift between urban and rural forces in the party, and had no intention of splitting the party again.

After Herbert Hoover took office in March, 1929, he asked Congress to provide some help for the farmer. The result of this request was the Agricultural Marketing Act of 1929. It established a nine-man Federal Farm Board, capitalized with a $500-million fund. The farmers themselves were to establish "stabilizing cooperatives"—organizations pertaining to a specific crop, which had as their primary purpose the profitable disposal of that crop. These stabilizing cooperatives would work directly with the Federal Farm Board. They would decide what to do with their own product for purposes of surplus control: buy, store, destroy, etc. They would do this under the guidance of the Federal Farm Board, aided in their task with temporary loans from the $500-million fund.

The Federal Farm Board kept setting up cooperatives throughout 1929 and 1930. These cooperatives had exhausted all of their funds by early 1932 in an effort to bolster continually sagging prices, and the Federal Farm Board admitted defeat. The agency stopped lending money to the cooperatives, allowed prices to seek their own level, and worked on a new plan. The farm problem, it was decided, was caused mainly by overproduction. If the farmer would cut back on the amount he was producing, prices would naturally rise. The Federal Farm Board began encouraging farmers to cut back, but was unable to offer any really strong inducement to implement a reduction.

However, the federal government had

come around to a recognition of the basic farm problem, and had also assumed some responsibility for solving it. Therefore, the stage was set for Franklin Roosevelt, who would implement the Federal Farm Board's recommendations within his New Deal program.

The New Deal Agricultural Program

When Roosevelt took office the nation was in dire need of relief, especially the farmer. Many farmers were suffering the forced sales of their farms because of delinquent mortgage payments. The Farm Credit Association was established to refinance roughly one-fifth of existing farm mortgages. Debtors were still responsible for the interest and penalty payments, but the federal government proved to be a more understanding lender than commercial sources.

At almost the same time (1933), the Agricultural Adjustment Act was passed. Since the many political and farm factions could not agree on a single course of action, various plans were incorporated into the bill, making it an omnibus law. One alternative was acreage restriction, another was crop destruction, and still another called for dumping any surplus in Europe. In general, the farmers were opposed to any measure which would result in limitations on the amount they could produce.

Still, it was fairly obvious to objective observers that the farm problem was caused mainly by overproduction. The only manner in which to drive up farm prices was to reduce the quantity of farm goods available. Therefore, the government would have to regulate farm production in order to drive prices upward.

The AAA was passed too late in 1933 to arrange for crop curtailment that year, and farm recovery was postponed for at least another year. However, there was one possible immediate solution, and Secretary of Agriculture Henry Wallace was given the task of implementing it. Crops already in production would have to be destroyed. Wallace was able to convince southern farmers to plow up their cotton, and gave them millions of dollars for doing so. The hog market was glutted and the farmers themselves came up with the solution. The result was the slaughtering of 6 million shoats and 200,000 pregnant sows, with the federal government underwriting the entire cost.

This destruction brought on tremendous public protest. People were angry because the government was destroying food while millions were going hungry. Therefore about one-tenth of the slaughter was salvaged and passed on through relief programs, to needy individuals. The destruction of surpluses was also applied to wheat and corn—the basic commodities of agricultural production—against more protest over such radical methods.

Various farm groups were initially quite violent, but Roosevelt had shrewdly appointed George Peek as director of the program. By the winter of 1933–1934, the farmers' criticism was beginning to subside, as the government poured out money for their use. The Commodity Credit Corporation was established to lend money to farmers in excess of the market price of their goods. And the Frazier–Lemke Bankruptcy Act allowed farmers to re-buy foreclosed farm properties at the new Depression appraisal prices, with federal loans carrying 1 per cent interest. Farmers were beginning to feel that perhaps their way of life was still salvageable.

Such measures, however, were costing the government tremendous sums of money. The revenues needed to finance the farm aid program were to be obtained by levying a "processing tax" on those manufacturers who prepared farm goods for public consumption—canners, packers, and butchers. This was destined to become a very important and contentious point.

The theory behind the AAA was quite sound. Farm production would be curtailed until prices reached their normal levels. At that point the government would be able to end benefit payments, because the entire economy (it was hoped) would have recovered to the point where individuals could afford to purchase farm goods at normal prices.

Overproduction also found a natural barrier during the Depression. In his expansion the farmer had moved to submarginal lands, which normally could not support agricultural pursuits. In 1934 came the Dust Bowl—drought and high winds to blow away the topsoil of Oklahoma and Arkansas. One result was a greater curtailment of farm production than AAA could possibly have achieved. The next two years proved the validity of the AAA. Farm prices rose approximately 50 per cent during Roosevelt's first administration, including, of course, the government payments which were artificially bolstering prices. The AAA was thus quite successful in its original purpose of aiding the farmer.

AAA was operating on a dangerous premise, however. Farm prices were rising not because of normal market improvement, but as a result of government aid. And the program, which had been based on voluntary cooperation, was beginning to break down. As prices rose, a growing number of farmers were retreating to their former ways—they would produce more to make more. Also, the ultimate success of the farm program rested on the ability of the government to solve the unemployment problem and in this, the NRA (National Recovery Administration) was experiencing considerable difficulty. And finally, various cases were working their way through the federal courts, with the ultimate aim of testing the constitutionality of the Agricultural Adjustment Act.

The constitutional test finally came in January, 1936, in the case of *United States* v. *Butler*. In that decision the Supreme Court held that AAA was unconstitutional by a 6–3 vote. The majority ruled that a tax levied on the processors of food, and then given to farmers to persuade them to pursue a certain course of action, was inconsistent with the Constitution. The decision also stated that the farm problem was strictly a local affair, and thus not the legitimate concern of the federal government. The minority opinion referred to this decision as based on a "tortured construction" of the Constitution. Nonetheless, AAA was no more.

A second AAA was created in 1938. In this new program the federal government would establish the amount of produce which any given farmer should prepare for market, allowing for a reasonable reserve. Farmers complying with government-prescribed limits would be eligible for price adjustment. The standard of adjustment was parity with 1909–1914 industrial prices. The Commodity Credit Corporation was authorized to lend anywhere from 52 to 75 per cent of parity to deserving, cooperating farmers. The second AAA was financed entirely by congressional appropriation, thus amounting to a direct federal subsidization of the farmer. There were many precedents for this type of governmental activity, and the constitutionality of the new measure was upheld.

Another measure, minor when compared with the AAA, was passed in 1937. The Farm Security Administration Act provided for federal financing for any new farmer who would accept Department of Agriculture guidance. The purpose of the act was to encourage people to try their skills at running a successful small farm.

The Contemporary Farmer: World War II and After

War in Europe and then American involvement brought boom conditions to every aspect of the American economy. As in the World War I era the farmer found a ready market for everything he could possibly produce. An elaborate system of food rationing was developed.

A ration stamp was necessary to purchase certain commodities, and a black market for agricultural and other goods appeared. By this time, the American farmer had expanded to his maximum productive capacity.

The post-war nation, however, again witnessed the American farmer producing far more than required, with resultant sagging agricultural prices. Initially, this was overcome as the United States pumped billions of dollars worth of goods and services into war-torn Europe. A large portion of the surplus agricultural product of the nation was thereby absorbed, with the farmer receiving heavy subsidization from the federal government. But Europe eventually recovered and American farm goods were no longer in such demand.

The problem for post-war America was to find the best method of implementing New Deal solutions to overproduction and the declining rural purchasing power. The Agricultural Act of 1948 provided for flexible price supports ranging from 60 to 90 per cent of parity. But President Truman was a firm adherent of rigid, rather than flexible price supports, and pushed for a straight 90 per cent support system.

Thus, he obtained the vote of the farmer in his bid for election in 1948, and in the following year the battle over a farm program began. Truman's secretary of agriculture initiated a program called the Brannon Plan. It allowed farm prices to find their own natural level, thereby providing considerable material benefits for the average consumer. The government would simply make up the difference to the farmer. However, this approach was too open for some congressmen. The resultant Agriculture Act of 1949 established a 90 per cent support program for commodities which met government-prescribed production and marketing quotas—the rigid-support concept. This remained the basic policy until the Eisenhower administration.

The Agricultural Research Service was created in 1953. It attempted to aid the farmer through government research in agricultural production. The agency also performed market research, and disseminated its findings to the farmers. But Eisenhower's secretary of agriculture, Ezra Taft Benson, opposed rigid price supports, and the Agriculture Act of 1954 adopted a flexible policy. In 1956 the soil-bank idea was incorporated into his program. This ingenious device stipulated that farm land would be withdrawn from production and cooperating farmers would be paid by the federal government.

The various legislative enactments of the post-war era were not entirely successful. Subsidizing the small farmer apparently did not really enable him to keep up with the rest of the economy. Only the large-scale farmer was aided measurably. As a result, during the first two decades following the war, the number of working farmers were cut in half. The small farmers are rapidly selling out, leaving huge industrialized farms to replace them. As the exodus from the farm continues, the percentage of the population actually involved in agriculture grows smaller.

However, by the mid-1960's it appeared as if some balance between prices and production was beginning to be achieved. The Food Stamp Plan of 1964 was an aid in this respect. So was Lyndon Johnson's Food for Freedom Pact, which provided for the stepping up of some agricultural productivity in order to maintain minimal national reserves. Also, the Wilderness Act of 1964 provided a giant reservoir of virgin land either for the future, when a vastly increased population will need progressively more agriculture, or immediately, for recreational use. This measure withdrew from possible commercial exploitation some 9 million acres of forested lands, and authorized the addition of another 5.5 million acres at some future date.

Even in a highly regulated agricultural economy, there still remain price difficulties. The profits of the middleman and the retailer more often than not continue to be higher than those of the actual producers of agricultural goods. The net result has been strikes by various farming groups, and increased federal regulation of the entire farming industry, from field to retail counter. In time perhaps the farm problem will be solved by the population explosion. And thus the American farmer's social position will have run full circle— from one of prestige to a loss of status and then back again.

For Further Reading

Black, John D. *Agricultural Reform in the United States.* New York: McGraw-Hill, 1929.

Buck, Solon J. *The Agrarian Crusade.* New Haven: Yale University Press, 1920.

———. *The Granger Movement.* Cambridge: Harvard University Press, 1913.

Cochrane, Willard W. *The City Man's Guide to the Farm Problem.* Minneapolis: University of Minnesota Press, 1965.

Dick, Everett. *The Sod-House Frontier, 1854–1890.* New York: Appleton-Century-Crofts, 1939.

Hardin, Charles M. *The Politics of Agriculture.* New York: The Free Press, 1952.

Hathaway, Dale. *Problems of Progress in the Agricultural Economy.* Glenview, Illinois: Scott Foresman, 1964.

Heady, Earl O. *et al. Roots of the Farm Problem.* Ames, Iowa: Iowa State University Press, 1965.

Hicks, John D. *The Populist Revolt.* Minneapolis: University of Minnesota Press, 1955.

Higbee, Edward. *Farms and Farmers in an Urban Age.* New York: Twentieth Century Fund, 1963.

Shannon, Fred A. *American Farmer's Movements.* Princeton: D. Van Nostrand, 1957.

———. *The Farmer's Last Frontier: Agriculture, 1860–1897.* New York: Farrar and Rinehart, 1945.

Shepherd, Geoffrey. *Farm Policy: New Directions.* Ames, Iowa: Iowa State University Press, 1964.

Chapter Seven
American Industrialism

When the American colonies were established they were not intended to be producers of manufactured goods. Their function was to provide raw materials to the mother country and to buy manufactured goods in return. At the time when the American colonies were developing revolutionary sentiment, the industrial revolution was beginning in England. By 1800, England was an industrial power while the United States was still an almost entirely rural nation. Yet during the span of the next century the United States overcame this formidable gap to become the industrial leader of the world. She continued to develop industrially to a level beyond serious competition from almost any other nation.

Of course, this rapid development caused a considerable number of growing pains for the young American nation. The classic unbridled free-enterprise system, as it existed during the latter third of the nineteenth century, may have created a world industrial leader, but it also created a number of serious problems which

have lasted into the contemporary era. The giant corporations, political entities in themselves, are viewed with fear and distrust by many Americans. Any top-ranking American corporation has more wealth and power than most national governments throughout the world. And highly concentrated power is often viewed with alarm, since ready evidence of its potential abuse can easily be found.

The industrial revolution came to America approximately a century after it appeared in Europe. And here the events and developments of a century were telescoped into a single generation. A mighty industrialized nation was created, but the price was extremely high in terms of the blood and sweat of millions of impoverished industrial workers.

The result of this unbridled economic power was a modification of the free-enterprise system. Pure capitalism no longer exists in the United States, and if blame must be placed for the change, then industry itself is the culprit. For big business in America aptly demonstrated that it needed to be regulated. The conduct of the big-business community less than a century ago materially aided the growth of federal power.

Industry and Commerce:
The Rural Period

America was founded by businessmen. Jamestown was established by the London Company, an English trading company which hoped to make a profit out of the venture. In fact one of the principal reasons for English expansion throughout the world was the desire to find new outlets for surplus English capital. Even the Puritans who settled at Plymouth Rock had organized a trading company, had sold stocks, and were financed by a group of wealthy English merchants who hoped to realize a profit. It was only after the initial mercantile impulse, and then in close conjunction with it, that the quest for political and religious freedom entered the picture.

Early Industrialism

The southern planters, with their large self-sustaining plantations, were in effect small capitalists. New England, characterized by small farms, also exhibited some commerce and ship-building beginning in the early colonial days. The middle colonies also produced some early manufacturing. Containing large concentrations of middle-class German tradesmen and Quaker merchants, these colonies produced iron, paper, textiles, and glass.

By the time of the American Revolution a class of businessmen had developed. Those who were engaged in small-scale manufacturing, equally as much as those engaged in smuggling activities, were guilty of violating the English Navigation Acts. It was these people who created the atmosphere in which patriotic sentiment prospered. Such men as Samuel Adams and John Hancock were smugglers

first and patriots next. Their primary motivation toward revolution was economic. It was this same group of men which later pushed for a strong national government and was concerned over the lack of an adequate currency, the credit system, the postal system, and a national commerce power. The mass of the people were relatively indifferent or hostile to these notions, and tended to prefer a weak national government. But business interests exerted their power to establish a constitutional system which placed considerable emphasis on property rights and commerce.

Still, the United States did not develop into an industrial nation overnight. It remained an overwhelmingly agrarian country for decades. Indeed the United States remained quite primitive, hardly beyond the pioneering stage, except for a slender chain of "civilized" settlements along the Atlantic seaboard. It was the War of 1812 that created a nationalistic demand for government to aid in the internal development of resources. The war was also responsible for the beginning of industrial development. In the latter part of the War of 1812, England had seen fit to blockade American shipping. Merchants were placed in a position of possessing capital but being unable to do anything with it. The solution decided upon was to begin small-scale industry. If trade was temporarily impossible, then the nation would manufacture those goods which had formerly been acquired by trade. This was a significant event in the development of industry.

Following years saw the establishment of the rudimentary ingredients necessary to support an industrialized economy. There were notable improvements in the transportation system. The rise of the railroad, commencing in the 1830's, was a decided boon, both for enhancing manufacturing and for creating a national market (see Chapter Eleven). Henry Clay's American System sought the establishment of the protective-tariff principle and

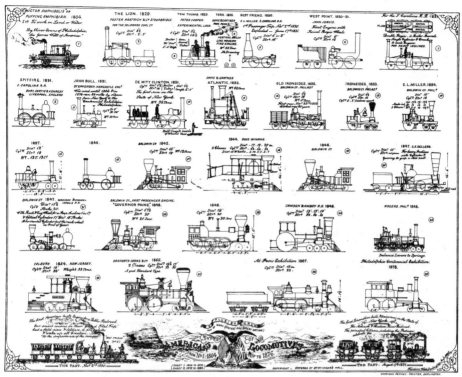

Early Railroad Engines—Symbol of the Relation
Between Transportation and Industry

emphasized domestic development at the expense of foreign trade. The federal government assumed broader powers in the area of interstate commerce, and upheld the sanctity of contracts. Small industries, usually run by a single family, began to dot the nation. This provided an impetus for the growth of towns, and rendered a certain small portion of the population dependent on others for raw materials and foodstuff. The United States still was not an industrialized nation, but it had developed some industry and laid the foundation for much more.

Civil War Expansion

The Civil War made major demands on the nascent American industrial complex. Before the war manufacturing was primarily done through the "farming-out" system. Enterprising individuals would purchase raw materials for a given product, and carry them from home craftsman to home craftsman, where various stages or all of the work were performed. The completed manufactured product would then be sold. The more successful of these individuals would gather a group together under one roof, in a crude facsimile of the modern factory system. Wartime demands, however, forced a more efficient system.

These demands produced many new developments and inventions during the war years. Illustrative inventions include canned foods, the sewing machine, and the shoemaking machine. Naturally the armament industry boomed, with a corresponding increase in the demand for iron, which had already been stimulated by the railroads. These activities produced an inflationary rise during the war years. Also, there was an overabundant supply of labor and this gave rise to unofficial wage freezes. In addition women began entering industry—e.g. the northern textile mills—to raise the family income, and the net result was a general lowering of the wage scale. The United States emerged from the war with hostility increasing between labor and management.

The Ingredients of Industrial Growth

The pattern had been set; big business was beginning a real factory system. It was developing better machinery; it was raising the standard of living; it was creating employer–employee problems. This was mainly a post–Civil War development, but the war itself was a major catalyst. Five basic ingredients are necessary for a large-scale productive economy: natural resources, an adequate labor supply, sufficient capital, the entrepreneur or organizer, and adequate markets. All of these were present long before the American Civil War, and they had been partially developed, but they were present in superabundance after the war because of the vast expansion that the war created.

Natural Resources

Natural resources refers not only to national mineral wealth, but to agricultural capability as well. The Civil War had provided a great stimulus for agricultural development. The Homestead Act was also a great boon, as well as the opening of the Great Plains by the railroads. Many labor-saving machines were invented, with the end result that the nation's agricultural productivity was sufficient to support the large urban populations necessary for a factory system.

Some of the world's richest repositories of timber, coal, iron, and petroleum are located in America. Most of the basic minerals needed for an industrialized economy are concentrated in fairly accessible areas. Furthermore, during the Civil War years these areas had been tied together by the expansion of the railroad network.

Labor Supply

The labor supply in the United States grew phenomenally in the immediate postwar years. A number of unrelated factors contributed to this change. For several reasons many farm boys emigrated from rural areas. Some had been replaced by the new machinery; others had gained their first acquaintance with city life while in the military and decided it was more exciting than country life; and still others (predominantly southerners or ex–Confederate sympathizers) had lost their farms during the course of the war. These displaced farmers helped swell the growing urban population.

The labor supply was also increased by the freeing of the slaves. The Negro was generally unskilled and conditioned for routine backbreaking work. His desire to flee the South with its racial prejudice made him readily available to the northern factory operator.

Immigration was a final factor contributing to the labor supply. In the 1840's many Irish had arrived and gone to work on the railroads. Following the war a new flood of immigration, characterized by the influx of people from southern and eastern Europe, was just beginning. For the most part they, too, were unskilled and thus available for routine factory work. Employers encouraged this immigration because these people would accept extremely low wages.

This burgeoning labor supply was not, however, perfectly distributed. There were more unskilled workers available than were needed, and this tended to keep wages low. Also, there was an inadequate number of skilled workers available to run the new and complicated machinery.

Capital

Capital was required to operate the industrial economy. Money had to be provided to purchase machinery and raw materials, pay salaries until profits were realized, and provide for the marketing of products. Part of this money came from Europe where surplus funds were available, but most of it came from within the United States. This was a significant achievement, since a century before there had often been insufficient funds for normal daily functions. There were a number of sources from which this money came.

One of these developed out of the Civil War. The war had been highly profitable for many northern businessmen who, aided by government contracts, greatly expanded their meager facilities. And to pay manufacturers, the government had greatly increased the supply of money during the war through the issuance of $450 million in greenbacks and the sale of bonds. Most of this money was earned legally, but there were many cases of fraudulent war contracts which contributed to the swelling profits. All wartime profits were available after the civil conflict for investment purposes.

Large fortunes had also been realized from other sources. The California gold strike of 1849, the silver strikes of 1859, and the 1876 Black Hills strike, all contributed. Coupled with this were fortunes made before the war in industries that were now dead or dying—like the fur trade, the whaling industry, and California hides-and-tallow (see Chapter Two).

And finally, many average people had managed to save some money during the war. Some factory workers and farmers had a little money. Many widows had some money from the fairly new insurance industry. Also, a number of soldiers had not had the opportunity to spend their military pay during the war years. Very few of these people possessed enough capital to begin business enterprises, but collectively there existed a large pool of wealth to be tapped. Somebody simply had to devise a plausible way of doing it.

Organization

The entrepreneur, or organizer, became the agent of synthesis. Many of the new entrepreneurs had been military officers, and had gained considerable experience in managerial activities. Troop movements, logistics, and the disbursal of funds were problems not too unlike the handling of natural resources, labor supply, and capital expenditures in business. Others among the new organizers had gained their experience as civilians. James Pierpont Morgan, for example, had obtained his start by selling government war bonds. He went on to become one of the greatest financiers in the history of the nation.

These entrepreneurs possessed no set background. Some were educated, others were not. Some came from wealthy families, others from abject poverty. Some were long-standing Americans and others were fresh immigrants. Some knew something about the business world, and others operated through the apparent use of native ability. But all were clever, ruthless, efficient, patient, and visionary. They generally possessed little technical knowledge of the industries which they represented, which implies that they could have been successful in any type or business endeavor.

Markets

Markets were the final necessary factor in industrial growth. A demand for manufactured goods was present and ever-growing, because of the constantly expanding population. And the Constitution forbade trade restrictions between the states, thus allowing a truly national market. This continental domestic market was assured American manufacturers by protective tariffs, and was readily accessible because of the expanded transportation systems.

There were also a number of miscellaneous factors which collectively aided the rise of big business. The United States possessed a patent system, whereas most European nations did not. Thus, Americans could readily "borrow" European ideas and enjoy government protection of their own inventions. In 1863, 1864, 1865, and 1866 laws were passed to regulate banking operations. They provided greater security for bank deposits and reduced the number of different bank notes in existence. They sought one basic standard of value (in 1863 there were over seven thousand different types of bank notes in circulation). Most state bank notes were driven out of existence by placing a 10 per cent federal tax on them. This technique soon brought about the initiation of a new type of banking procedure —the checking account—and another aspect of modern business practice was achieved.

The Corporation

A new form of business organization was also initiated; it was the corporation, which had its native origin in the older English joint stock trading company. The corporation had both a positive and a negative aspect. Positively, it enabled the "little man" to invest his small savings and become part-owner of a giant operation, and enabled the organizer to acquire capital for business development. Negatively, the system harbored a degree of irresponsibility. It limited a bankrupt corporation's liability to the extent of its assets. The stockholders might lose their investments, but no more than that. In privately owned business, on the other hand, the individual is responsible to the extent of his personal property holdings for the entire indebtedness; obviously, he

would tend to be more conservative in his business operations.

The Age of Big Business

The Effects of Growth

Conditions were ready for a booming industrial economy. Most of the new prosperity was quickly siphoned off by the captains of industry. In general, the average American paid more for his manufactured goods, while still receiving comparatively low wages. The protective tariff and the mode of business practice were determining factors in this situation.

The so-called big three in the rise of industrial America were the railroads, iron and steel, and the petroleum industries. The railroads were the most colorful and probably the most crucial. They quickly transported raw materials, sometimes at reasonable cost, distributed the finished products to the national market, and transported people to the growing industrial centers. They were also the largest customers of the steel industry, which employed millions and in turn served as one of the bases for all other industrial development. The petroleum industry was a comparatively slow starter, but became exceedingly important before the end of the century.

The rise of big business significantly affected all Americans. The factory system, which gathered machinery, labor, and raw materials together, created the wage-slave. It destroyed the old farming-out process, and introduced both the division of labor and the assembly-line technique. These innovations eradicated the older sense of community the pre-industrial workers had often shared with their employers and allowed them little pride in their handiwork.

Subsequently the factory town developed, in which health and safety factors were at an absolute minimum. Transportation did not grow in proportion to population density, and slums and crowded tenements were the result. The workers had the unpleasant choice of either quitting their jobs and moving out (economically unfeasible), or holding their jobs and living in slums.

However, for the American consumer there was a greater variety of goods available on the market. Big business was increasing the volume of commodities available, and lowering the per-unit production cost with the new technology. But very little of this production saving was passed on to the consumers. As a result, the profit margin of the industrialist increased, and was bolstered by the presence of a high protective tariff.

The Climate of Corruption

The businessman had turned to politics at a very early stage as a means of increasing and protecting his profits. His main concern was to remove local laws which increased his operating expenses for things like smoke-control systems or safety devices around his machinery. He was usually highly successful; and even if health and safety laws were passed, he soon discovered that a few well placed dollars discouraged their enforcement. His next concern was on the national level where he sought federal laws designed to aid business, such as higher tariffs. He contributed to campaigns and financed the elections of carefully selected candidates, and was often rewarded with plush government contracts and favorable legislation. Consequently, the highest principles often were lacking in government, and there was probably more graft and corruption in the late nineteenth century than in any other period in American history.

Politicians during the era of big business were generally mediocre in ability; there were no outstanding political leaders and no critical political issues. Since

everyone else appeared to be making money, many politicians decided they should make money out of politics. Therefore, many began to capitalize on their political authority and sold "favors." The public at large was generally uninterested. The public had had its fill of political problems during the long years of Reconstruction; a period of reaction had set in. The average person was preoccupied with making money, and there were many rags-to-riches tales around to encourage this attitude.

At the base of them was a myth fostered by Horatio Alger, a contemporary author of numerous "success stories." The myth held that any hard working individual, if he lived frugally, could eventually become wealthy. There were a number of examples. Andrew Carnegie once a penniless immigrant newspaper boy, rose to command millions. If Carnegie could do it, reasoned many Americans, so could they. What many people failed to consider was that although some individuals did acquire great fortunes, they constituted the exception rather than the rule.

There was a third possible reason for the political immorality so prevalent during the big-business era. There was generally a one-party system in the North, commanded by the Republicans. Such a situation tended to hide political issues, and what made matters worse was the presidency of Ulysses S. Grant (1868–1876).

Grant's Presidency

Grant had become president on the basis of his military reputation, not because of any political qualifications. The Republicans believed he would make a popular, weak, and manageable president. His Democratic opponent in 1868, Horatio Seymour, was an extremely poor candidate and few people doubted Grant's ability to win. His 1872 opponent, Horace Greeley, was not much of a threat either. It was expected that the Grant administrations would be ineffectual, and they were. The professional politicians handled matters. Then, beginning in 1870, many cases of fraud and corruption began to be uncovered.

One of the first scandals concerned the Whiskey Ring. Distillers had avoided paying the federal liquor tax in St. Louis through an arrangement with the local tax collector's office. The fraud involved the head of the St. Louis Internal Revenue Office and the Assistant Secretary of the Treasury.

Another fraud stemmed from the government's attempts to collect delinquent taxes from the Civil War era. Since these taxes were extremely difficult to collect, it was decided that specially appointed individuals would collect them on a percentage basis, which was fixed at a very high 50 per cent. A man named Sanborn was one of the collectors. Through an arrangement with the Secretary of the Treasury, Sanborn also illegally collected current taxes and retained the 50 per cent "collection fee" in doing so.

Another scandal involved the Secretary of War, who was legally empowered to manage the Indian reservations. This included such duties as the setting up of trading posts. He gave all the contracts to his wife, who then acted as a "front man" and reissued them to various traders on condition that they split their profits with her. When this practice became known the Secretary of War was impeached. He was acquitted because he chose to resign his office while proceedings were being initiated against him.

Another interesting incident involved one of Grant's ex-army cronies, General Shank. Although he possessed absolutely no qualifications for the post, Shank was appointed Ambassador to Great Britain, strictly because he was Grant's friend. Shank was quite popular in England, since he taught poker to the diplomatic corps. But when he began to peddle worthless

stocks in a non-existent western mine, he exceeded the limits of propriety. Discovering this deception, the British demanded Shank's recall.

The biggest scandal of the Grant administration, however, involved the Credit Mobilier Construction Company and the Union Pacific Railroad. The railroad had received large land grants and sizeable loans from the federal government to help defray construction expenses. It also sold stocks but decided that the dividends being paid to the bulk of stockholders were too large. In order to solve their problems the men who controlled the Union Pacific founded the Credit Mobilier Construction Company. They gave all construction contracts to their own construction company at costs which equalled the profits of the Union Pacific. Consequently, the Credit Mobilier reaped tremendous profits while the Union Pacific showed none. The stockholders received nothing while a handful of "operators" became extremely wealthy.

These promoters feared a possible congressional investigation since they were manipulating federal funds. To guard against this possibility they decided to make Credit Mobilier stock available to select congressmen. The market price of the Credit Mobilier Company had rapidly risen, yet the owners sold the stock to government officials at its original subscription price, and on 100 per cent credit (it being understood that no recipient would be pressured to pay for his stock). When the scandal broke, approximately forty congressmen were implicated, including one future president, James Garfield.

In March, 1873, Congress raised the salaries of its members from $5000 to $7500 per year, making the increase retroactive for two years. In effect Congress thereby voted to pay each member $5000 from tax funds, plus a 50 per cent raise if he was re-elected. On this occasion, however, the politicians had gone too far for even a complacent public. Americans

William W. Belknap

protested violently, and the act—the "Salary Grab Act"—was repealed at the next session of Congress.

The final major scandal of the Grant era was the gold conspiracy. The federal government controlled large quantities of gold, and from time to time the Secretary of the Treasury released some of it for use in international trade. Two financial manipulators, Jay Gould and Jim Fiske, also controlled large quantities of gold. They reasoned that if the federal government would stop releasing gold, its market price would rise, and they could sell their gold at a great profit.

Jay Gould met Grant, took him on a lengthy holiday on his private railroad train, and easily maneuvered the President into supporting his plan. Grant was convinced that the farmer would reap great benefits if the government would cease its gold issues. Gould and Fiske then bought every ounce of gold they could get their hands on. As the gold supply constricted, prices began to rise and business panicked. In view of this the Secretary of the Treasury also panicked and released gold in violation of Grant's instructions. Gould and Fiske were almost caught, but they managed to net an estimated $3 million profit from their scheme. Although Grant had clean hands, he did display a stunning artlessness.

Despite all these scandals there is no evidence to indicate that Grant was dishonest. He was simply politically naive and highly susceptible to flattery. Also, he harbored a deep sense of loyalty to his ex-army friends. He freely appointed them to government positions, and they just as freely proceeded to loot the federal treasury.

From Hayes to Cleveland

Grant's presidential successor, Rutherford B. Hayes, was a comparatively honest and efficient man, but not an astute politician. Throughout the big-business era the most able candidates failed to win the nominations. The Republican Party was split between the Old Guard and the new reformers. Neither group was strong enough to control the other, so the result was usually a compromise candidate. This situation would change only after the Democrats had rebuilt a strong competitive party in the North.

The greatest political mistake of Hayes' career was his seeking of honesty and efficiency in government. These were hardly objectives for a successful politician during this period. When he fired a fellow Republican, Chester Arthur, Collector of the Port of New York City, for inefficiency and possible dishonesty, he lost much party support, especially from the big-city machines. Then his role in the silver issue cost him rural votes, and finally his strike-breaking actions alienated labor.

His successor, James Garfield, was another compromise candidate. His running mate was the recently fired Chester A. Arthur. Garfield himself had been implicated in the Credit Mobilier Scandal. Of course the Democrats' candidates were not much better. Winfield Scott Hancock was the presidential nominee; his chief qualification was that he had been a Civil War general, and his running mate, William English, was an even greater nonentity. There were no substantive issues and Garfield won.

Garfield began a weak investigation of the Grant scandals which was unforgiveable to a majority of Republicans. But before he could make any other "mistakes," he was shot by a disappointed office seeker (July, 1881) and died shortly afterwards. Arthur became president and surprised everyone by obtaining the passage of the Civil Service Act and unsuccessfully attempting other reform measures.

In 1884, Grover Cleveland became the first Democrat to win the presidency since Buchanan in 1856. Cleveland initiated the first attempt to regulate business activities. The Interstate Commerce Act of 1887 was passed ostensibly to regulate the railroads. In the process it created a precedent for all future regulatory commissions, and the establishment of the "fourth branch" of American government. A five-man commission was appointed by the President for staggered six-year terms. This commission possessed the power to issue cease-and-desist orders; it could suggest rates; it could agree to company-proposed rates; it could disallow rates. But it could not set rates itself. Normally, the railroads went along with commission-suggested rates, but there were problems of enforcement, as well as unsympathetic courts. As a result, the original commission was rather ineffectual. Still, it marked the beginning of legislation in an entirely new area, and the commission would be considerably strengthened by Theodore Roosevelt.

Cleveland was narrowly deafeated in the 1888 election by Benjamin Harrison. A Republican was again president and the party acted as if Harrison had won by a landslide, expecting a return to the permissiveness of the Grant regime. But the Grant days were a thing of the past; Harrison would have no part of them. In fact, a major reform measure was passed during his administration.

Federal Anti-Trust Action

The Sherman Anti-Trust Act of 1890 passed both houses of Congress by overwhelming votes. The Senate voted 52–1 in favor of the measure, and the House recorderd a phenomenal 242–0 vote. There were two principal reasons for the passage of the bill. First, elections were coming and the people were clamoring for reform; they had gone full cycle and were becoming interested in politics again. Second, the bill involved legislation in a totally new area. Even those congressmen who were on the payroll of big business were not opposed to voting for the measure since the law would have to be interpreted by the big-business–dominated federal court system.

The original act set up no regulatory commission. Rather, the attorney general and the Justice Department were charged with its enforcement. The bill provided that every contract in restraint of trade was illegal, and that anyone who attempted to create a monopoly was guilty of a federal misdemeanor. Furthermore, various proceedings were authorized to enforce the act. Criminal action could be undertaken—indictments for violation of the law in a criminal court. Equity proceedings could be undertaken—measures designed to prevent a certain action from taking place, such as an injunction. And finally, civil damages could be initiated: injured parties were permitted to sue violators at triple the damages they actually suffered. The Sherman Anti-Trust Act thus provided the basis for the eventual regulation of business by the federal government.

Progress and Innovation

So far only a bleak picture of the big-business era has been presented. However, there were a number of worthwhile achievements during the period. While it is true that many of the processes and machinery used in American industry were "borrowed" from Europe, and especially England, American men of science were quite creative. The United States was making significant strides in the field of technology.

The rapid expansion of the railroad system was fostered by many important inventions. Steel rails appeared in the 1870's, quickly replacing the older wooden rails with iron straps running along the tops. George Pullman built the first sleeping car in 1864. George Westinghouse invented the air brake in 1868, rendering rail travel much safer. Huge steel bridges were built, beginning with the Brooklyn Bridge in 1873.

There was a veritable revolution in the field of communications. The first major breakthrough had preceded the big-business era: Samuel F. B. Morse's telegraph of the 1840's. But Cyrus Field successfully laid a transatlantic cable in 1866 and Alexander Graham Bell introduced the telephone ten years later. The government greatly extended and improved mail facilities, taking full advantage of the railroads.

All of these developments immeasurably aided the rise of an industrial America, but other discoveries were equally important. The typewriter was invented by Lathan Scholes in 1867, providing a major area of business employment for women. Commercial electricity made its appearance in the 1870's. Charles Brush perfected the arc light and the dynamo during the time when Thomas Edison was developing the phonograph and the electric lightbulb. In 1882 Edison successfully lighted New York's Wall Street with electricity. Literally thouands of inventions, from improved milling processes to better methods of making steel, annually improved the technology of the nation. All of these discoveries are considered commonplace in contemporary America, but without them the extent of the American industrial revolution could never have been realized.

There was a justifying ideology predominant during the age of big business and the first decade of the twentieth century. It was known as the Gospel of Wealth. The gospel was based on the old Protestant idea that material success in life was a sign of divine favor. The more a man was able to accumulate the greater the likelihood that he would find eternal salvation. Such a doctrine neatly buttressed the philosophy of the big-business era. (See Chapter Fifteen.) The doctrine was widely accepted in America by not only the mass of people, but by educators and clergymen as well. Most industrialists encouraged this notion by behaving like—and often believing they were—men of honest goodwill. They were admired and emulated as often as they were condemned, therefore. Their power made them attractive until its misuse began to attract attention.

An Era of Reform

The immediate impetus for the reform fervor that developed soon after 1900 came from such magazines as *Collier's, Munsey's, McClure's, Cosmopolitan,* the *Ladies' Home Journal,* and the *Arena.* These were different from most nineteenth-century magazines in being cheaper, designed for the mass audience now provided by the educational system and the growth of the great cities.

The Muckrakers

These magazines took it upon themselves to inform the public of major developments in local and national politics and industry. Especially between 1902 and 1907 their circulation was increased by public interest in a new kind of article which exposed outrageous political corruption, terrible social conditions, and the power of the great trusts. The articles were written by people who came to be called muckrakers because they assiduously sought out information that many wanted to hide.

The muckrakers tended to be young people with good education, a knack for writing, and often a sense of mission. These men and women presented detailed and accurate accounts of what was wrong with America. They were splendid informative reporters, not unlike first-rate detectives. There were some libel suits but never any convictions. Intent on arousing the public conscience, the muckrakers rarely offered solutions to prob-

The Effects of Industrialization: A Slum Tenement

lems, which they left to the concerned public. Those few muckrakers who did offer solutions commonly advocated socialism as one answer.

Lincoln Steffens was the leading muckraker on graft and corruption in state and local government. In his best work, *Shame of the Cities,* he showed that the political bosses in many major cities were affiliated with racketeers in an effort to defraud government of its revenues. He also discovered that services which should have been provided to the citizenry were either inadequate or absent. Whether Democrats or Republicans were in power was irrelevant—graft was still present. He also claimed that every single state government was corrupt, and backed up his claim with documented evidence.

National government received little criticism at the hands of the muckrakers. However, David Philip, in an article entitled "Treason in the Senate," pointed out exactly who elected senators. Philip demonstrated that 75 per cent of all United States senators were on the payrolls of corporations.

Muckraker critics of the economic system were many. Ida Tarbell spent five long years gathering sufficient information to uncover the monopolistic practices of the Standard Oil Company. Thomas Lawson was an ex-stockbroker who analyzed fraudulent manipulations in the market. Ray Stannard Baker wrote on labor and railroad rate problems. And Samuel Hopkins Adams revealed the tremendous frauds of the patent medicine industry.

The muckrakers also wrote books. Gustavus Meyers, for instance, wrote an enlightening three-volume *History of the Great American Fortunes.* The most influential book was Upton Sinclair's *The Jungle.* Written as a novel, the work concerned itself with the revolting social conditions, evil practices, and financial manipulations of the meat-packing industry. Sinclair offered a solution: government operation of the industry. His work was a best-seller in 1906 and was eventually translated into seventeen languages. It so influenced Theodore Roosevelt that the ultimate result was the passage of the Pure Food and Drug Act.

The muckrakers attacked almost all abuses and hypocrisies—the evils of drink, long working hours, child labor, irreligious churches, etc. They did not revolutionize American society. Generally, they approved of both capitalism and democracy and sought to show the gap between American ideals and practices, thus displaying the need for reform. They affected many Americans by causing them to doubt supposed American superiority and innocence, by awakening their collective conscience.

The muckrakers were largely responsible for a public demand that the major parties initiate some reform. Some politicians became convinced that reform was necessary, while others backed measures because they were popular and desired re-election. Still others opposed to reform felt that they could best blunt the effectiveness of the movement from within, so they joined. Of course, there were those who were openly opposed to reform because it ran counter to vested interests or because they feared it would get out of hand.

Theodore Roosevelt and Industrial Regulation

The influence of the muckrakers was obvious in Teddy Roosevelt's presidential administration. The governmental regulation of big business was the major issue during his tenure (1901–1909). There were then three basic views on the subject. One held that government should not concern itself with regulation of business at all; this was a reiteration of the old laissez-faire idea. Another view, usually advanced by socialists, maintained that either the state or the workers should control industrial enterprises. This group was very small around 1900, but it steadily grew until World War I.

There was a third view, the majority view, which held that there was something wrong with monopolies. This group was split, however, between those who felt that all monopolies were essentially bad, and those who distinguished between good and bad ones. This latter group would not regulate good monopolies, but would regulate those which misbehaved. This was essentially Roosevelt's viewpoint. When he first took office the business interests feared him. There was a fairly substantial drop in the stock market, and party leaders urged him to make some sort of conciliatory statement.

In December, 1901, Roosevelt did make a statement. But because Roosevelt had not quite made up his mind on how to proceed, it was both rambling and obscure. He suggested only the creation of a Department of Commerce as a Cabinet post. Actually, nothing more should have been expected. Roosevelt's party had traditionally received its strength from the business interests, and since the Democrats had long been clamoring for reform, Roosevelt could not very well adopt their attitude.

But Roosevelt did favor federal checks on big business. His first action came in February, 1902. Business had already grown complacent as a result of his ambiguous statement of the previous December. Then, Attorney General Knox issued a press release wherein he stated that Roosevelt had asked him for an opinion on a recent business merger. Knox stated that he thought it was illegal, and the government would initiate legal action to dissolve it. The company was the Northern Securities Company, headed by J. P. Morgan, the top financier in the country. Roosevelt's popularity with business and the stock market now once

again dropped. Morgan issued a statement quite similar to that of a foreign state department, offering to negotiate the dispute. It marked an excellent example of big business complacency and power.

In court, the government stressed the amount of control exercised by this holding organization (it had exchanged stocks with various railroads in order to coordinate and control their efforts), and charged that it was a combination in restraint of trade in the transportation industry. Basing its power of prosecution upon the little-enforced Sherman Anti-Trust Act of 1890, the government won the case by a slim 5–4 vote in the Supreme Court in 1904.

Undaunted, Morgan immediately formed a new organization with an interlocking directorship to accomplish the same ends. In this case all the railroads just happened to elect identical boards of directors. Still, Roosevelt had brought charges against the very symbol of big business power and had won, at least superficially. This encouraged reformers, reassured the general public as to Roosevelt's inclinations, and forced big business to adopt more subtle schemes of monopoly. Roosevelt followed this prosecution with others, most of which were successful. But his success was only in the eyes of Roosevelt and an admiring public; actual business practices remained essentially untouched.

In 1887 the Interstate Commerce Act had been passed to regulate the public carriers of goods and people, but it had not given the government the power to set definite rates. Furthermore, the courts were generally sympathetic to business interests. Roosevelt attacked the indiscriminate rate system unsuccessfully through the Elkins Act of 1903, but when this failed to solve the problem the Hepburn Act was passed in 1906. It changed only one provision of the Interstate Commerce Act: the government could now fix rates, and it was up to the carriers to prove their objections valid. In the interim the government rates stood.

The Hepburn Act was strongly opposed by big business. But Roosevelt had managed to obtain passage with two techniques. He threatened public ownership of the railroads, a bluff which apparently worked. Also, he appealed directly to the people, demanding that they force their congressmen to support the measure. As such, Roosevelt was one of the first presidents who did not leave legislation strictly in the hands of Congress, but used his influence to force favored legislation. Hence, some contend he was the first truly modern president.

One of Roosevelt's greatest struggles erupted after he read Upton Sinclair's *The Jungle*. In December, 1905, there was a bill in Congress to regulate the food-preparation industry, but it was bottled up in committee. A Dr. Wiley had prepared a scientific report for Congress in which he damned the food industry but it was being kept from the public. Meanwhile Roosevelt had demanded proof of Sinclair's accusations from the publisher and had received it. He decided that the industry needed regulating and he obtained it exactly the way he obtained the Hepburn Act—by going to the people. The result was the Pure Food and Drug Act of 1906. It set up the Pure Food and Drug Administration to control the preparation and advertising of goods prepared for human consumption. The original measure was not extremely effective, but eventually, various amendments strengthened it.

This was the last new regulatory measure for a time. The provisions of the various regulatory enactments were ably enforced by Roosevelt and by his hand-picked successor, William Howard Taft. In fact, more trusts were disbanded by Taft in his four year presidency than by Roosevelt in almost eight years, only with-out the fanfare (Roosevelt was his own best press agent). However, most anti-trust legislation was still not very effective.

Wilson and the Clayton Act

In 1912, Woodrow Wilson, a Democrat, won the presidency. A definite liberal, Wilson sought to make the Sherman Act effective. To obtain anti-trust legislation he personally appeared before Congress to elicit support. The forces of vested interests fought bitterly, but in the end the Clayton Anti-Trust Act of 1914 was passed. The bill struck specifically at the intent of business organizations, particularly the interlocking directorship which had replaced the older holding company. Also, it weakly hinted that the law was not intended for labor union regulation (the Sherman Act had often been applied against unions as combinations in restraint of trade rather than against monopolies). A separate law established a Federal Trade Commission in 1915, and still another further strengthened the Interstate Commerce Commission.

Wilson did not regard himself as a trust-buster. Holding out the olive branch, he suggested to business that the government would be willing to review organizational structures and advise on what did or did not comply with the new law. However, he did insist that government should make certain that free competition was not subverted. Several large corporations requested this review, and voluntarily accepted governmental advice. With this development the nation was beginning to formulate the contemporary policy of regulation, cooperation, and aid which now characterizes the federal government's dealings with big business.

None of the government regulations seemed to slow down American industrial development; they simply corrected or lessened some of the more apparent abuses. The nation was rapidly accumulating a surplus of capital and goods and was transforming itself into a world creditor. Because of this it began to look elsewhere for economic opportunities. This was evidenced in the Pan-Americanism of 1889 forward, in the growth of imperialistic ventures, and in the Dollar Diplomacy of the early twentieth century. The United States also developed economic interests in Europe, and these became a critical issue as World War I errupted.

Industrialism from World War I to the Depression

The United States was the only country in the world with sufficient capital to buy European war bonds. And quite naturally, the viability of these bonds depended on the fate of the countries issuing them. American financiers bought the bonds of all warring nations, but their overwhelming investment was with the Western powers; geographical proximity and long standing financial ties were principal factors.

Prior to the outbreak of the European war there had been a worldwide trade rivalry between England, Germany, and the United States. But with the advent of war, England and Germany were forced to absorb their surpluses in the war effort. This gave the United States their world markets. Ultimately, the United States began selling civilian goods, both manufactured and agricultural, to her former trade rivals. The result was prosperity in America; huge profits were being made and wages were rising. Scarcely an American was not better off economically as a result of the European conflict. For obvious reasons Americans tended to favor the side which was the nation's biggest customer: the Allies, especially England. This does not mean that Americans wanted to become involved in the war; they most definitely did not.

As the war progressed both Central and Western powers began to lose the ability to pay cash for American goods. This created a dilemma for American business and government. The nation could either stop selling all together or start selling on credit. Either alternative was a risky proposition. To stop selling would throw a damper on American prosperity, and neither government nor business wanted this to happen. To sell on credit meant the possibility of a deepening involvement in the fate of Europe. The business community was willing to take this risk, whereas most other Americans were not.

Industrial Mobilization

War, however, did come to America in 1917. Economic considerations turned out to be only one of many precipitating factors. With war came the first real national mobilization and control of American industrial resources. Measures unthinkable in peacetime were readily justified by the war effort. Many of these measures, although designed to last only for the duration of the war, remained to provide the foundation-stones for both Depression and World War II regulation.

There were a number of good reasons advanced to support the position that American business and industry needed regulating during World War I. It was felt that the economy was being violently disrupted, and this could easily result in runaway inflation. It was also held that civilians might panic and begin to stock up on essential goods required by the military, thereby creating an artificial shortage. There was also the distinct possibility that some businessmen, eyeing potentially enormous profits, might compete in such a manner as to act against the national interest. Finally, it was believed by the government that absolute coordination of the American industrial machine was required to supply the Army and the Allies with necessary wartime goods.

The basis for wartime legislation of

this nature was the Military Appropriations Act of 1916. The act authorized the creation of a Council of National Defense, consisting of the Secretaries of War, Navy, Agriculture, Commerce, Labor, and Interior, plus leading industrialists and financiers who served as dollar-per-year advisors. These advisors included Walter Gifford of American Telephone and Telegraph, Samuel Gompers of the AFL, Bernard Baruch (a leading entreprenuer), Daniel Willard of the Baltimore and Ohio Railroad, and many others. Most of these advisors were active supporters of the Republican party, but they cooperated fully with the Democrat, Woodrow Wilson.

The task charged to the Council was to coordinate the natural and industrial resources of the nation for purposes of national security. A number of sub-boards were authorized for specific economic areas, headed by salaried individuals possessed of nearly dictatorial powers, and responsible directly to Wilson. With the exception of the Shipping Board of September, 1916, all of these boards were established after American intervention in the war, and all were given progressively increased powers.

The most powerful of the wartime boards was the War Industries Board, created during the summer of 1917. Besides supervising the other bodies, the War Industries Board had as its primary purpose convincing American industry to produce only essential goods. Industry cooperated because the head of the Board, Bernard Baruch, had the power to establish priority lists on essential materials. The recalcitrant manufacturer soon discovered that raw materials became unavailable to him. Baruch standardized American production and prices, and in effect created a planned national economy.

A Railroads War Board was established late in 1917, and was headed by Secretary of the Treasury William McAdoo. Its purpose was to promote the efficient use of the nation's transportation system for military supplies and troop movements. McAdoo consolidated all railroads into one vast system. Equipment, trackage, rates, rolling stock, and services were standardized. Any notion of profits for stockholders was ignored; the railroads existed strictly for the national interest.

The Shipping Board which had been established prior to American entrance in the war was capitalized initially with $2 billion, for the purpose of buying, building, chartering, and operating merchant vessels. By the end of the war the Board was responsible for the building of roughly 150 ships per month, and had increased the total tonnage of American shipping tenfold within the span of a year and a half. The Board was further charged with the task of transporting troops and supplies to Europe and did an excellent job.

The Return to Peace

Thus did the United States convert herself into an efficient war machine. Wilson possessed more unbridled power than any previous president. And all this was justified strictly on utilitarian grounds, though not without some congressional opposition.

Immediately after the war the transportation and utilities industries were subject to further legislation. The Esch–Cummings Act of 1920 returned the railroads and express companies to private ownership, but subjected them to greater federal control than existed in the pre-war period. The Interstate Commerce Commission was empowered to allow and encourage railroad consolidation, which would be made exempt from anti-trust prosecution. The Commission was also granted unequivocal power to establish rates. The policy established called for a 6 per cent profit rate based on the property value of the industry. In recognition of the plight of the railroads (they had depreciated under government operation), Congress set up a $300-million revolving fund to aid in the financing of capital improvements. The railroads became a subsidized industry, fighting a battle for continued existence with the new modes of transportation: the automobile and later the airplane.

A similar procedure was utilized for the merchant marine. The government emerged from the war owning a very large merchant fleet. This was turned back to private ownership, but again, with increased federal controls. The Merchant Marine Act of 1920 (the Jones Act) made the Shipping Board a permanent body and ordered the government to sell its merchant fleet. The control aspects of the measure were commendable (for instance trade rates and routes) but the disposal of the fleet aroused much justifiable criticism. Ships were sold at 10¢ on the dollar. There was corruption and profiteering— the only demonstrable case of profiteering in the war. The law set up a $25-million revolving fund to aid in financing government ship sales. And before the decade ended, the government, under the provisions of the Merchant Marine Act of 1928, was also subsidizing the shipping industry.

During the war, the government had engaged in the manufacture of nitrates (explosive chemical compounds) at the Muscle Shoals Dam on the Tennessee River. With the termination of hostilities, the hydroelectric power was no longer needed to produce explosives. Therefore, the government sold the power to a private concern, the Alabama Power Company, which sold it at a profit to its customers. This created demands for government control over utilities operations. But the nation apparently was not quite ready for this major progressive step until the era of Franklin Roosevelt, despite the persistent efforts of Senator George Norris.

A policy was established with the Water Power Act of 1920 which created the Federal Power Commission. The Commission was empowered to license private firms to utilize public power sites, and subject such firms to rate control. The licenses were to be granted for a fifty-year period only, and few investors were willing to accept these conditions. The hydroelectric issue was not equitably settled until the 1930's.

It should be pointed out that Wilson had nothing to do with the passage of this post-war legislation. (He had suffered a severe stroke in October, 1919, and was virtually incapacitated until his death in 1921.) It was the handiwork of a Republican Congress which had been elected in 1918. And except for the above, all federal wartime controls on industry were simply halted. Wartime agencies were completely disbanded and regulatory laws were repealed. No federal provisions were made for re-tooling. War contracts were cancelled with absolutely no advance notice. There was no planning; industry was handled arbitrarily and suffered some critical setbacks. The American economy survived mainly because of the resourcefulness of the American businessman who, forced to absorb these government-inflicted loses, then passed them on to the American consumer throughout the 1920's.

The Twenties

Business during the Twenties employed a double standard. It sought from the government a continuation of war era supports and aids, but without wartime regulation. And business was not disappointed as the Republicans under Harding, Coolidge, and Hoover, aided it through a judicious selection of business sympathizers to fill various regulatory posts.

Advances in industrial technology created far reaching changes in American life during the 1920's. Of particular significance was the development of the automobile. The new automobile industry employed 5 million persons and gave rise to or made possible many subsidiary industries: motels, drive-ins, repair shops, filling stations, an expanded tourist trade, and the roadhouse. In 1920 the entire nation produced 1.9 million cars; by 1929 the annual rate of production had risen to 4.8 million. The rapid expansion of automobile ownership, coupled with the new need for highways, greatly boosted the economy. By the end of the decade, Ford, Chrysler, and General Motors had successfully eliminated scores of competitors, and had assumed what appeared to be a permanent niche in the American economy.

Another significant technological development was the motion picture industry. From 1919 with the formation of United Artist Corporation, the new art form grew in popularity throughout the decade until, by the time of the Depression, 100 million Americans were attending the movies weekly. A new multi-million-dollar business had been established.

There was another major technological advance which also created a new industry. This was radio. In November, 1920, a station in Pittsburg, Pennsylvania, began regular broadcasts for the first time. In 1921 the radio industry did a retail business of $10 million in crystal sets and earphones. By 1929 this figure had risen to $400 million, marking a phenomenal growth for the new industry.

And there was still another business which probably made more money than the automobile, cinema, and radio industries combined. The nation's "noble experiment" with prohibition was responsible for making crime a big business. From the very beginning officials realized that they were charged with the task of enforcing an unenforceable law. Many Americans resented what they considered to be an invasion of their privacy. Drinkers kept on drinking, and many nondrinkers took up the pastime for excitement. Incidentally, many enterprising Americans had already gained considerable experience in the art of bootlegging—supplying illegal booze—because twenty-six states had passed prohibition laws before the Eighteenth Amendment went into effect in 1920.

It took but a short time for some individuals to realize that bootlegging, though illegal, was an extremely profitable business. The risks involved were originally slight, because many law-enforcers and law-makers disapproved of prohibition. But eventually the more resourceful of the bootleggers, in the nineteenth-century tradition of unrestrained capitalism, destroyed their competition—often violently. Big-time crime had come to America. With the tremendous wealth realized from the illicit booze, the bootlegger soon moved into other areas of crime: prostitution, narcotics, and gambling.

There was another side to the surface prosperity of the 1920's. The causes for the Great Depression, in large measure, were to be found in the industrial development of this preceding decade. The single most important ingredient was the firm establishment of mass-production technique (with the division of labor on an assembly line). Output in manufactured goods was increasing yearly. This necessitated a high yearly increase in individual purchasing power in order to maintain a healthy economy. For a number of years there was no real problem; various new markets existed and real income (what a given quantity of money will actually buy) was increasing substantially. But the economic system eventually became unbalanced. Economists estimate that industrial productivity increased three times as fast as real income during the latter two-thirds of the decade. Hence, the domestic market was incapable of absorbing what American industry was producing. And the surplus could not be dumped on Europe because of high tariff barriers.

Depression and Attempts at Recovery

The Depression came, and with the collapse of the stock market, bank failures, and individual failures, industry began to close its doors. Some of this was the re-

sult of irrational panic. Some of it was
actually necessary since industry had been
producing too much all along. Moving
into the 1930's, American industry was
critically weak.

The NIRA

Roosevelt attempted to solve the
plight of the farmer with the Agricultural
Adjustment Administration (see Chapter
Six). His solution for industrial recovery
was the National Industrial Recovery Act
of 1933. The implementation of both
measures was to depend on the voluntary
cooperation of all parties involved. There
was a great deal of precedent for this in
World War I legislation and the activities
of some industries during the Twenties.
Also, a number of theorists, labor leaders,
and industrialists had been pushing for the
government to take the lead in reviving
business. The man charged with coming
up with a concrete proposal was Raymond
Moley, and he believed in voluntary cooperation. The resultant legislation was
essentially what industry had been seeking, except for certain provisions favorable to labor.

The National Industrial Recovery Act
contained two basic sections. The first
created the National Recovery Administration and dealt with the problems of
industry: production, unemployment,
prices, etc. The second created the Public Works Administration (see Chapter
Eleven). The basic idea of the NRA was
for government representatives to sit
down with representatives from various
industries and work out codes of fair price
and labor practices. It was specified that
when a majority of the companies engaged
in a particular industry had reached an
agreement with the government, that
agreement would be binding on the entire
industry and would have the force of law.
And if the representatives of a particular
industry did not cooperate, the president
was empowered to draw up his own code

By Darling, NEW YORK HERALD TRIBUNE

Business, an Unwilling Groom

for that industry; this too would have the
force of law.

Separate and unique codes were
established for each of the many industries
in the country. They all reflected a
marked change in the concept of government business regulation. The Sherman
and Clayton Acts had been aimed at halting monopolies, price fixing, and infringe-
ments on free competition. The trend under NRA was in the direction of price
fixing. If the companies in a given industry could agree on what NRA considered
to be a fair price for a particular product,
that industry would be exempted from
anti-trust prosecution. The idea was to
avoid ruthless competition, which was believed to have been partially responsible
for the Depression, but at the same time
to insure fair prices for the consumer. All
of the codes established minimum wages
and maximum hours, and forbade child
labor. Also, every code recognized the
right of collective bargaining (explained
in Chapter Eight).

The NRA would create new jobs by shortening the work week, and would increase spending-power by setting minimum wages. As a consequence the demand for both manufactured and agricultural goods would increase, and recovery would begin. Employers who voluntarily accepted the codes were authorized to display "Blue Eagle" decals on their windows as an indication of their patriotism. Some 2 million American employers proudly displayed these stickers, all bearing the slogan: "We Do Our Part."

However, it was one thing to put up stickers, and quite another to put into practice what they represented. Few employers sincerely abided by the codes, primarily because higher wages and more employees raised the expenses of the employer, but did not immediately present him with any additional profits. The codes were exceedingly difficult to enforce. To keep a close check on every employer would have added tremendously to an already swelling government bureaucracy. And Roosevelt was reluctant to increase the federal budget any further. Voluntary cooperation was an impossible premise. Blue Eagles covered the land, while stacks of impressive codes gave the workers the things they had been striving for—on paper. Individual employers cheated on code provisions, and individual workers, in their desperate situation, were forced to accept the situation.

PWA and TVA

The government fully recognized the hardships imposed on business by the NRA codes. It was acknowledged that the employers required something concrete and more immediate. This was the reason for the creation of the Public Works Administration.

The PWA was set up to administer large-scale, long-range government building projects, for which the government initially appropriated $3.3 billion. Heavy construction projects would result in orders for structural steel, concrete, glass, etc., and this would stimulate industries to re-hire workers. Of course, the construction industry, which was one of the major drags on the economy during the 1920's, would receive direct stimulus.

Partially to buttress industrial recovery and partially to implement the conservation of natural resources, Congress, in the spring of 1933, passed a measure creating the Tennessee Valley Authority. TVA climaxed a long battle over the fate of the World War I Muscle Shoals project. Senator George Norris of Nebraska had unsuccessfully pursued the TVA idea throughout the 1920's. But his allegiance to Franklin Roosevelt (he was a Republican turned Independent) finally helped bring the idea to reality.

The act authorized federal use, conservation, and development of the natural resources of the Tennessee River system. This necessitated a large amount of heavy construction for dams and hydroelectric plants. The measure brought to fruition one of the fondest dreams of the early progressives: the federal government had moved into the world of business and was competing with private industry in the generating and selling of electricity. There was a tremendous amount of protest and criticism concerning TVA, but the government claimed that by operating its own hydroelectric plants it could obtain very accurate guideposts for determining the fairness of rates charged by private producers. The constitutionality of this measure was eventually upheld by the Supreme Court in *Ashwander* v. *TVA*.

Despite all the New Deal measures to stimulate industry, the results were extremely limited. The unemployment rates of 1933 and 1939 were essentially the same, even though there had been some increase in the size of the working force. Nonetheless, though the New Deal recovery program did not lift the nation from the depths of the Depression, it halted the downward trend. What succeeded in releasing the United States from the Depression were the economic demands created by World War II.

The Emergence of Opulence

During World War II, the mobilization of the nation's industrial resources approximated the pattern created in World War I. A Council of National Defense was established in 1940. Originally an advisory group, the Council quickly became a branch of the War Department, and was charged with coordinating the civilian production effort.

Transportation was left in the hands of private industry, but was thoroughly regulated by the Office of Defense Transportation. Depression-era developments had both aided and hindered the transportation system. It was helped by the many roads and bridges constructed as part of the relief and recovery programs. It was hindered because the Depression years left much transportation equipment in very poor condition.

A War Shipping Board was established to coordinate and facilitate the construction and operation of an enormous merchant marine. The problems of transporting men and equipment during World War I began to look like child's play in retrospect. Millions of American fighting men and their equipment scattered over the globe, making the problem of supply increasingly difficult. Allies also required supplies and equipment, and shipments always faced the dangers of submarines and a new war device, the ship-based airplane. But the United States utilized the assembly-line technique for ship-building, and by the end of the war, ships which had once taken almost a year to construct were being turned out in two weeks.

A War Production Board was established, partially to aid industry in retooling for war, but primarily to control

the use of raw materials. A system of priorities was used as in World War I, but shortages still occurred, particularly in rubber and aluminum. The rubber shortage was due to Japanese control of the rubber plantations of Southeast Asia. But the United States had stockpiled the commodity before hostilities began, and with a tight rationing system and the development of synthetic rubber the problem was controlled. The aluminum shortage was caused by different factors. Plenty of aluminum was available, but the industry was still in its infancy. The government solved this problem by entering the bauxite mining business.

The work of the War Production Board was unwittingly aided by Depression-era conditions. Millions of Americans had received training through various federal Depression projects, and the TVA stood ready to gear itself to full-scale production. Also, an estimated 5.5 million individuals were eagerly awaiting jobs; many had already been hired before Pearl Harbor, when the government began building its defenses.

An Industrial Giant

In seeking reasons why the United States and her allies were able to win World War II, one factor stands out above all others: American industrial supremacy. By mid-1942 the United States was producing more than all of her allies combined. By the end of the war American industrial production had assumed worldwide dominance. Of course, some domestic shortages were experienced because of the duration and severity of the conflict. However, the technology of the war years left a rich legacy for the post-war world: jets, rockets, nuclear fission, television, and a highly developed industrial machine, to name only a part.

Since the close of World War II the general trend has become unmistakable. The American economy continues to boom. Installment sales have increased over 500 per cent since World War II, constituting roughly one-fourth of expendable income. There was a slight inflationary spiral in the 1940's caused by the dislocation brought on by demobilization, a brief recession in the late 1950's, and periods of instability in the market. Today there are some indications that a constantly depreciating dollar and soaring prices may threaten the economic well-being of the nation.

Contemporary America exhibits a new type of corporation. It is much larger, more diversified, and much more sophisticated than earlier business organizations. The classic entrepreneur has been replaced by highly trained and specialized corporate bureaucrats and administrators. These corporations control vast sums of wealth, and, with the aid of computers, expend it into highly technical production lines for a waiting market which has already been identified through market surveys and government census reports. The government provided a boon to industry by creating, in 1966, the Cabinet-level Department of Transportation to regulate and render more efficient the entire communications system of the nation.

New multi-million-dollar businesses have appeared on the American scene. About sixty corporations regularly produce gross annual sales of over $1 billion. An industry which has had a profound effect on society is television. Developed in crude form in 1939, the device was on the commercial market less than a decade later. Jet aircraft, first produced by Germany early in World War II, have now been widely accepted in commercial air traffic. The vast electronics industry also received its impetus from the war. Nuclear power has been harnessed and is used in the generation of electricity, in naval vessels, and is being considered for spacecraft. Rocketry has landed spacecraft on the moon and neighboring planets. And to guarantee this trend, an increasing percentage of business capital is being funneled into basic technological research.

There is another significant economic development in the contemporary era. The federal government has become the greatest customer of industry. Because of the Cold War, American defense spending has increased tremendously. The American military budget for the Vietnamese War would bankrupt most other nations. Besides defense, the government pours billions of dollars into space, internal improvements, and poverty-aid programs. A question worthy of consideration is what would happen to the economy if all government defense spending, along with the space program, and various other high-cost federal programs were halted? The economy is strong, but federal spending is largely responsible for its well-being.

For Further Reading

Chamberlain, John. *The Enterprising Americans: A Business History of the United States*. New York: Harper and Row, 1967.

Cochran, Thomas C. *Basic History of American Business*. Princeton: D. Van Nostrand, 1959.

Degler, Carl N. *The Age of the Economic Revolution, 1876–1901*. Glenview, Illinois: Scott Foresman, 1967.

Edwards, George W. *The Evolution of Finance Capitalism*. New York: Longmans Green, 1938.

Fite, Gilbert, and Reese, Jim. *An Economic History of the United States*. 2d ed. Boston: Houghton Mifflin, 1965.

Galbraith, John K. *American Capitalism*. Boston: Houghton Mifflin, 1956.

Hacker, Louis M. *American Capitalism: Its Promise and Accomplishment*. Princeton: D. Van Nostrand, 1957.

Josephson, Matthew. *The Robber Barons*. New York: Harcourt, Brace, 1934.

McCloskey, Robert Green. *American Conservatism in the Age of Enterprise, 1865–1910*. New York: Harper and Row, 1964.

Monsen, R. Joseph. *Modern American Capitalism: Ideologies and Issues*. Boston: Houghton Mifflin, 1963.

Moody, John. *The Truth about Trusts*. New York: Moody, 1904.

Oliver, John W. *History of American Technology*. New York: Ronald Press, 1956.

Ripley, William Z. (ed.). *Trusts, Pools, and Corporations*. Boston: Ginn, 1916.

Chapter Eight
American Labor

One of the dominant forces in modern American life is the highly developed labor organization—the union. Almost all industrial workers, craftsmen, and many clerical and retail-sales employees belong to some type of a labor organization. In recent years the organized labor movement has made considerable inroads in the professional and semi-professional areas, which were once considered to be beyond the pale of union activities.

Organized labor, through its various trust funds, strike funds, and operating budgets, controls a large portion of the American economy. In the preceding chapter the political and monetary power of the giant corporations was indicated. Unionism was developed to counteract this corporate power and the concomitant abuses and injustices experienced by workers.

The organized labor movement has fought a long and sometimes violent uphill battle. Initially, big business, the government and a majority of the population were opposed to unions. There was an ideological argument which, in effect, created a double standard. The concept of laissez faire upheld the free enterprise system in theory, but in actual practice, the government was expected to aid business with such devices as protective tariffs and land grants.

It was additionally believed that, since organized labor was a threat to big business interests, government should prevent it from achieving success. Thus the provisions of the Sherman Anti-Trust Act were at first employed not against the corporations but against unions. It was commonplace for injunctions to be issued freely to hinder union activities.

There is a partial explanation for this practice. Early American unionism was identified with European radicalism. The former, however, had no intention of overthrowing capitalism; it sought merely to capture and enjoy some of the fruits of capitalism. But the latter often utilized violence and sought radical changes in government and economics. This type of unionism was not viewed as being compatible with American traditions.

The Condition of Early Laborers

The settlers who first came to colonial America brought with them some of the germ seeds for future unionism. Their European heritage included the medieval guild system, a union-type of organization (its terminology of apprentice and craftsman still remains), which regulated the prices, profits, and workmanship for individual crafts. Further, it handled burial benefits, survivors' aid, and loan funds for its membership. It was not unionism in the modern sense, but modern industry had not yet developed. This aspect of the European heritage had no immediate application. Except for indentured servants and slaves, most people worked for themselves. As long as the American economy was essentially agricultural, unionism could not become a pressing issue.

There was some manufacturing during the colonial period, and by the end of the War of 1812, small factories were beginning to appear. Most of these new enterprises were family-owned affairs, employing very few people. Some of the employees were working only until they could accumulate enough money to move to the West. Others were farmers who worked on a seasonal basis.

Some industries began developing along more modern industrial lines. As competition increased, wages were cut and less skilled workers were hired to replace craftsmen. This gave rise to an early union movement. Most large cities developed city-wide craft unions, beginning in the 1830's. In Philadelphia an American Working Men's Party was established to promote a ten-hour day. The factory town of Lowell, Massachusetts, which directed its efforts toward hiring young women to work in the textile mills,

experienced a strike in 1834, over a 15 per cent wage cut. The strikers were defeated but a rash of strikes plagued employers for the next several years. National union membership during the 1830's is estimated to have been as high as 300,-000. But the Panic of 1837 destroyed the early union movement. While a number of unions continued to exist, they were not effective.

The only tangible success for unions during the period occurred in 1842. In that year the legitimacy of labor organizations was upheld in *Commonwealth* v. *Hunt*. But workers were insufficiently organized; the number of industrial workers was still very small, and the problems they faced had not yet become overly oppressive to a large enough group. This situation began to change during the Civil War. Northern industry boomed during the war period, and the economy was generally quite prosperous, except for the industrial workers. Wartime inflation hit them hard, especially since their wages were not rising and living costs were. The reason was that there was an overabundant supply of labor, partly swelled by the increasing immigration rate. Industry responded to this with wage freezes. Also, women were beginning to enter industry in increasing numbers, and this encouraged a relative lowering of the wage scale. Labor was the one large exception to northern prosperity during the war, and the seeds of the post–Civil War union movement were sown during this period.

Working Conditions during the Big-Business Era

At the end of the Civil War, great industrial development was taking place. The huge manufacturing enterprises were taking definite form, and along with them, the number of people employed as industrial workers had markedly increased. With these developments, conditions were ripe for the beginning of a concerted union movement. The industrial worker possessed three major and very legitimate grievances against his employer: low wages, long working hours, and poor working conditions.

There was no question that wages were much too low. There was a great disparity between the worker's wages and the compensation of his employer. Incomes were generally going up, but most of the increase went to the very wealthy. The gap was widening and a deep class cleavage along economic lines was becoming apparent. The employer claimed that he had to pay low wages for two basic reasons. He argued that he had invested in expensive machinery, which enabled the worker to work less. He also claimed that his own superior ingenuity entitled him to receive more than his workers. Labor did possess a legitimate complaint on the question of wages.

Another area of considerable controversy concerned the length of working hours. Most industrial workers put in a six-day week, and some even worked the full seven. In addition most of them worked ten to twelve hours per day, but fourteen hours was not uncommon. The worker desired a radical change. His ultimate goal was a five and one-half to six day work week at eight hours per day. Employers countered by claiming that working hours must be long; machinery had to be utilized as much as possible because of the tremendous capital investment in it.

Employers failed to realize that long hours prevented their employees from having sufficient time for healthy leisure. The physical and emotional strain placed on the workers lowered both morale and efficiency. But the employer's usual response to inefficiency was replacement. Employers further failed to realize that shorter hours and higher wages would give the people more time to spend and enjoy their wages, thus expanding markets. Henry Ford recognized this in the early twentieth century.

The other chief worker grievance was poor working conditions. At best working conditions were shocking. Sanitation was almost wholly inadequate in the factories. Ventilation equipment rarely existed even in dusty flour mills. Safety equipment was practically non-existent. Protective screening around moving machinery cost money, and so, reasoned many employers, did not add to the profits. It was considered unwise to expend capital for non-productive purposes, even though it might prevent workers from being seriously injured. Again, most workers could easily be replaced, so the average employer was not really worried about injuries to his employees. Nothing resembling workmen's compensation or accident insurance existed for the laboring man.

There were many other worker's grievances, depending on locality and type of industry. They had probably always been present, even before the factory system was fully developed, but after the Civil War they became intensified. This was due to increased, centralized mechanization under the new factory system and radically changed employer–employee relationships. The new system was cold and impersonal. Business had organized a very formal and complex hierarchy, with the individual worker far removed from any contact with the "big boss," whom in all probability he had never met or even seen. The personal relationships which characterized some of the small factories of the pre–Civil War era were gone forever. The usual employer was at best indifferent to his employees. A workman could no longer complain to his boss. He had only a foreman who was out to make himself look as good as possible to his superiors. This was true at every management level throughout the corporate organization. The average worker was practically powerless.

The worker would therefore have to develop an equally powerful organization to counteract the new impersonal business structure if he hoped to deal with his employer from a position which commanded strength and respect. It was necessary to turn to the formation of unions to gain collective strength. This is how the corporation had attained its power: through the collective economic wealth gathered from individual stockholders.

The Move to Unionization

The National Labor Union

The first important national labor movement was organized in 1866. In that year the National Labor Union was established by William H. Sylvis. It was destined for failure but the reasons for its failure served as examples to future unions on what they should avoid. As such, the National Labor Union does have some significance.

The union was made up of anyone willing to join it; different types of workers, including farmers, both skilled and unskilled labor, people of both sexes, all races and ethnic groups, some sympathetic businessmen, and an occasional corporation "spy." The membership even included some individuals who were totally unsympathetic to the very idea of unionism. For example, farmers generally believed that wages for industrial workers were already quite satisfactory, but they wanted higher prices for agricultural goods. Factory workers believed that farm prices were already too high, but that wages were too low.

There were obviously, too many conflicting viewpoints. Unskilled workers claimed that time on the job alone should determine the rate of compensation. Skilled workers claimed that not only time on the job but the skill involved in the work being performed should determine

the rate of pay. Under such circumstances, it was impossible to develop a truly united front.

The union was also sadly lacking in finances. Dues amounted to only 25¢ per year. As a result, a number of workers felt that the union was too cheap to be worthwhile, and that joining it would be a waste of time. The union had no money with which to develop a strong professional lobby in Washington, or a substantial strike fund.

Also, the union became interested in many types of reform, including a number of causes which had little to do with basic labor grievances. For example it campaigned for prohibition and female suffrage. As a consequence, the union spread its energies over too wide an area and accomplished very little.

The union also entered politics. It organized its own Labor Party and nominated national candidates in 1872, but succeeded in polling only 25,000 votes nationwide. This lack of union strength, was primarily caused by the reticence of experienced politicians to commit themselves to such an untried organization. This widespread lack of support brought an end to the Labor Party in 1872, and to the National Labor Union as well.

Birth of the Knights of Labor

As the National Labor Union died, another national labor movement was rising to take its place. It was the Knights of Labor, founded by Uriah Stephens in 1869. Stephens believed that a labor union could both solve the problems of the industrial worker and serve as a purifying force on American society. Actually, Stephens became so idealistic that he oftentimes overlooked the essentials of modern unionism. When Stephens died shortly after getting his union established, he was replaced by Terrence Powderly, who held essentially identical views. The union grew slowly and by 1883 its mem-

A Knights of Labor Meeting: Early Integrated Unionism

bership had reached 52,000. Before its collapse it numbered close to one million. It was the first union which represented a large number of workers.

The Knights of Labor followed the same basic policies as the National Labor Union with few exceptions. The union did not enter the field of politics, and it did not allow lawyers and prohibitionists to join. Otherwise, it had the same low dues and broad membership as its predecessor. Hence, it suffered from the same major drawback: it had no real unity of purpose. The overall results, then, were almost identical to those of the National Labor Union.

The Strike

There was, however, a large difference in tactics between the Knights and the earlier National Labor Union. The Knights became involved in many strikes. Actually it was involved in far more strikes than it desired. It acknowledged responsibility for those strikes which it actually endorsed and supported nationally; but it was also blamed for unendorsed strikes by local unions which held membership in the national organization, and for strikes called by unions which were in no way affiliated with it. The Knights of Labor was held responsible for practically every strike and every act of labor violence in the country. The organization's membership was comprehensive enough to be representative of the entire labor movement, and therefore most Americans identified all labor activities with it.

Most of the labor strikes occurred in the mid-1880's, and practically all of them were failures. These strikes had certain basic similarities, some of which lasted well into the present century. They were all vigorously conducted and supported by the local membership. They antagonized an anti-union public which traditionally blamed strikes and the resultant consumer inconvenience solely on the strikers, totally ignoring the circumstances which were responsible for the strike. Also, the national headquarters consistently failed to give the strikers vigorous support and encouragement.

Every strike was short on financial resources. The workers had no strike fund and no personal savings with which to maintain themselves. Business leaders, on the other hand, possessed ample reserves and could easily outwait the workers, forcing them into submission. In fact, many strikes were quickly converted into lockouts; employers refused to allow their employees to work for a time, and then would allow them to return only at a reduction in pay or an increase in working hours. This practice was quite common and successful during the big business era.

The Knights of Labor had a negative public image and poor leadership. Powderly was unable to make firm, immediate decisions about which strikes to support. The same was true of most union leaders during the period; this was the experimental stage for unionism. Hence, local strikes were often broken before the national leadership could make up its mind what to do. The union had also entered the cooperative field just as the Patrons of Husbandry had done (see Chapter Six). And it failed for identical reasons. This failure had important ramifications for Knights of Labor membership rolls: lack of continued support and the rise of indifference.

The Haymarket Riot

An event known as the Haymarket Riot brought about the downfall of the Knights of Labor. Local unions in Illinois, had proclaimed a one-day general strike in Chicago on May 1, 1886. The purpose was to demonstrate in favor of an eight-hour work day, and to indicate the economic paralysis which would result if all workers in the city refused to work. The one-day strike was carried off without incident. But when the workers returned to their jobs on the following day, they found themselves locked out. It seemed that while the strikers were conducting their demonstration strike, the owners had gotten together and agreed on a collective lockout.

It so happened that over the preceding decade, Chicago had become a center for European anarchists who sought by violent means to destroy all government. The group was headed by August Spies, who published a German-language newspaper, and repeatedly denounced the American political system and advocated anarchy. On May 3, Spies gave a speech to the locked-out workers who were milling about outside the McCormick Reaper plant. He attempted to incite the workers to violence but they remained peaceful throughout his speech. There was no violence. But suddenly, the police arrived and broke up the meeting; in the process, several workers were killed. The situation was promising from the anarchistic point of view, for blood had been shed and perhaps the workers would now listen.

That night Spies issued a call to arms to all Chicago workers. He proposed that a mass meeting be held in Haymarket Square on the following day, May 4, to determine what to do with a criminal government and a criminal business operation. The city granted a permit authorizing the meeting. It was very well attended and was conducted in an orderly manner. A number of speakers, mostly anarchists, talked to the crowd, but the crowd did not become unruly. All of a sudden, the police arrived again, and began to break up the meeting. Someone tossed a home-made bomb into the crowd and a general riot ensued. By the time the riot ended, seven policemen were dead and seventy more were wounded. Four workers were killed and approximately fifty others were wounded. Public opinion immediately blamed the workers.

Spies and seven other anarchists were indicted on the charge of "inciting to murder." There was absolutely no real evidence against them. But Spies had once drawn a diagram on how to construct a homemade bomb, and all eight indicted men were known anarchists. Therefore, they were presumed guilty. The judge who heard the trial was Albert Garvey, a noted Chicago industrialist, who was not expected to support organized labor.

There were three possible explanations for the bombing. A unionist or an

Library of Congress

An Artist's Version of the Haymarket Riot, 1886

anarchist could have thrown the bomb to initiate the riot. Or a big-business henchman could have tossed it, hoping thereby to discredit the workers. There is no real evidence to support any one of these possible explanations. But the riot did occur and it had some significant after-effects.

All eight anarchists were convicted. One received a fifteen-year prison term and the other seven were sentenced to death. Of this seven, four were actually hanged; one committed suicide rather than face the gallows, and two had their sentences commuted to life imprisonment and were later pardoned by the courageous governor of Illinois, John Altgeld. The Knights of Labor was in no way involved in the Chicago strike. But during the course of the trials, it did petition for clemency for the accused anarchists. The mass of Americans jumped to the conclusion that the Knights had instigated the riot because it was now openly sympathizing with the anarchists. Workers themselves, knowing that the union had completely failed to support the strike effort, turned against the Knights, and the union began to disintegrate.

Samuel Gompers and the AFL

A successor union was already in the process of developing. In 1881 the American Federation of Labor was founded by the extremely capable and experienced Samuel Gompers, who was destined to be the president of the union for all but one of the next forty years. During the half-decade immediately preceeding the Haymarket Riot, Gompers had effectively organized his new labor group, and was ready to take over the national leadership of the labor movement.

Gompers organized his union mainly because he was dissatisfied with the structure and operation of other union groups. The American Federation of Labor stipulated that, with very few exceptions, membership would be limited to skilled industrial workers. By this significant stipulation Gompers began with a common bond among the membership. And these skilled workers were in a much better bargaining position than their unskilled counterparts, simply because they could not be replaced so easily. They knew this and so did their employers.

The AFL was a federation of local, specialized unions. Individual crafts would form individual unions, and then collectively elect officers for a single national board to represent all craft unions. This national board was supposed to handle lobbying, exert pressure on congressmen, and disseminate propaganda to elicit public support. It acted as a general buttressing agent for all the individual craft unions. The individual unions were allowed to handle their own problems— those peculiar to their craft. All common problems were to be handled by the national board.

The common unskilled industrial worker did not fit into the AFL scheme of things. If he had been allowed membership, he would easily have outnumbered the skilled workers and weakened their advantageous bargaining position. Also, at this stage of union development, it would have been impossible to organize every unskilled worker into a single nationwide union.

The American Federation of Labor possessed three distinctive characteristics. One of these pertained to dues. The union insisted on high initiation fees and annual dues. There were several reasons for this. First of all a stronger psychological commitment might stem from making a larger contribution. Skilled workers, moreover, could generally afford to pay higher dues than other workers because they commanded higher salaries. Finally, the union insisted on building up a huge treasury to provide ample funds for lobbying, organizational work, and the establishment of a large strike fund. This seemed the only way in which to counteract the advantageous position of the wealthy corporations.

The general strategy of the AFL called for winning public support. Initially, this was more important than gaining higher salaries or shorter hours. The union established a speakers' bureau, an agency consisting of polished, well-informed orators, who were prepared to speak anywhere, anytime, to whomever would listen. These speakers were quite a contrast to the anarchists whom a large percentage of the American public identified as typical labor leaders. Unlike the preceding Knights of Labor, which intended to alter the capitalistic structure, Gompers wanted to become an integral part of that structure.

And Gompers was quite cunning in his bargaining strategy. His long-range goal was to raise wages and cut working hours. Other unions would demand exorbitant wage increases and sizeable reductions in the work week. But what usually happened was that employers refused to even consider such demands, believing that these union leaders were probably lunatics. Gompers took a different approach. He would ask for minimal increases in pay, and perhaps a one- or two-hour reduction in the work week. This tended to place him in a more favorable position with the employers.

His demands were realistic; they were small enough so that the companies would actually spend far less by going along with them than they would have spent (through lost profits) in breaking the workers with a lengthy lockout. So Gompers would often obtain his small demands while other unions usually got nothing. Then, too, Gompers would insist on contracts; these were usually short-term agreements which stipulated the wages and hours of the workers. This practice was viewed quite favorably by the employers; it was businesslike and it guaranteed no labor problems for a specified period of time. As soon as the contract expired, Gompers would ask for another minimal increase, along with another one-hour reduction in the work week. And employers often agreed because Gompers was extremely faithful in keeping his part of the bargain. A peaceful labor situation for a period of six months or so was well worth a few extra dollars in wages to the employer. In the long run, with considerable patience, Gompers realized his original goals.

A third unique characteristic of the American Federation of Labor was its strict business goals. It was organized for specific purposes: higher wages, shorter hours, and better working conditions. No outside interests were allowed to enter into union activities and dissipate their strength. Within its own organizational framework, the AFL did provide certain services for its membership: loan funds, educational funds, death benefits. But these were merely secondary activities and were never allowed to interfere with the primary functions of the union.

As a result, the AFL gained in prestige and strength. Its policy, which it successfully followed, called for a peaceful nonstrike settlement whenever possible. It strove to avoid any controversy which might place it in an unfavorable position before the public eye. By 1900 the AFL had attained a position of respectability in the United States. It was approved in some quarters, tolerated in others, and fought bitterly only by isolated small groups of employers.

Other union movements were going on during the period, but they did not achieve the importance or success of the AFL. For the most part they were local, wildcat organizations, like the Molly Maguires of the 1870's, which tended to tear down part of the favorable image created by the AFL. Some of the other union attempts eventually succeeded, such as the Brotherhood of Railway Workers, but this success did not rival Gompers' efforts. And the ineffectual Knights of Labor continued to exist as a rallying-

New England Factory Life About 1900

point for unskilled industrial workers, including some Negroes. By around the turn of the century, however, only about a tenth of all industrial workers were unionized. The highly selective practices of the AFL were destined to create serious problems for the future.

Radicalism, Reform, and Reversal

The successful establishment of a single national union, consisting only of skilled workers, could hardly solve the plight of most industrial laborers. The year 1900 was no magic date for unionism. A long uphill battle remained, and real success would not be achieved until Franklin Roosevelt was serving his second term as president.

A massive steel strike took place in 1892 at Andrew Carnegie's Homestead plant. Carnegie was often in Scotland, and his lieutenant, Henry Frick, was in charge of the steel works. Frick had no intention of negotiating with the strikers. His answer was to destroy the strike by bringing in some 300 armed strike-breakers. The strikers armed themselves, and a full-scale riot ensued. Troops eventually restored order, and the company hired "scabs," (individuals who took over the jobs of the strikers) and destroyed the union.

In 1894 there occurred the huge Pullman Railroad strike. The Pullman factory in Chicago had constructed a model town and rented the houses to its employees (no others were available). Further, all groceries were purchased at a company-owned store, children attended company-operated schools, and people worshiped in company-built churches. In this manner almost all the wages of the workers quickly returned to the employer. In 1894 the company lowered wages, claiming poor profits; there was no corresponding cut in rent or food costs. This created a tremendous protest.

In the strike that followed there was some violence, most of it along the railroad lines away from Chicago. The governor of Illinois, John Altgeld, was pro-labor, and he refused to break up the strike through the use of injunctions and troops (both common practices during the period). He specifically disavowed the use of federal troops to break the strike. President Cleveland sent them nonetheless, claiming that the United States mail was being interfered with. The strike was forcibly broken up at bayonet point.

This was a fairly common practice. If federal troops were not used, big businessmen would employ professional strikebreakers to do the job. So-called "detective agencies" became very lucrative businesses. Their function was to destroy any semblance of union success. Murder and violence were not uncommon. Labor leaders were occasionally murdered on their front porches. Men were burned out of their homes or refused jobs unless they disclaimed any intention of joining a union (yellow dog contracts). A blacklist was employed to make certain that a union man would never obtain another industrial job. Some strike attempts resulted in several days of pitched battle, with both sides suffering serious casualties.

However, there was another side to the labor picture. Beginning with the twentieth century, with more enlightened presidents and with the difficulties of the big-business era beginning to settle, a more conciliatory viewpoint was being developed with respect to unionism. It was well reflected by Theodore Roosevelt during the coal strike of 1902.

Theodore Roosevelt and the Coal Strike

Roosevelt could not be termed pro-labor, but he was much more sympathetic than any of his presidential predecessors. The 1902 coal strike, conducted by John Mitchell, was actually a resurrection of an earlier totally unsuccessful strike in 1900. The strikers sought a 20 per cent pay increase, an eight-hour working day, and recognition of the United Mine Workers as their union. The strike was called in May, 1902, and involved approximately 150,000 miners, many from the "captive mines" of Pennsylvania. (Captive mines were those owned by companies which were primarily involved in other industries that had a great need for coal, e.g., railroads which required coal to operate locomotives.) Conditions in the captive mines were considerably worse than they were in other mines.

In this case the mines were owned by railroads, and the greatest offender was the Reading Railroad, headed by George Baer, a Carnegie associate who refused to meet with union representatives and would not consider arbitration. Baer wrote a public letter in which he made known his views on the proper position of the working man. He indicated that the captains of industry were possessed of a divine Christian right of ownership. Labor should willingly and unquestioningly follow their leadership in order to avoid evil ways. Baer's letter, published in many newspapers, was the very epitome of the Gospel of Wealth. It caused many people who were normally anti-union to become sympathetic to the strikers.

Previous strikes in the coal fields had been characterized by a high incidence of violence and the destruction of property by both strikers and strikebreakers, the use of federal and state troops to break up the strikes, court-issued injunctions prohibiting the conducting of a strike; and a public opinion which was usually overwhelmingly on the side of the mine operators. But these conditions were not present in the 1902 strike. It was conducted in a peaceful manner. Troops were present, but only to preserve order and not to break the strike. There was no court interference and the public did not take sides.

However, by September, 1902, there was an acute coal shortage. This aroused public opinion against miners, owners, politicians—everybody—because nothing was being done. And in November, 1902, the off-year congressional elections would be held.

The Republican administration had to do something. However, there existed no federal machinery to handle such a problem, and business would not willingly cooperate with Roosevelt's attempt at mediation. The offer was unequivocally refused by Baer, whereas Mitchell had agreed with some qualifications. Roosevelt released both replies to the press, and this caused public opinion to turn mainly against the mine owners.

A master at spreading rumors, Roosevelt caused information to reach J. P. Morgan that he planned on seizing the entire railroad industry and socializing it. Because of his financial involvement in the railroads, Morgan decided to pressure Baer into accepting a settlement, fearing that Roosevelt might just be rash enough to carry out his threat. So Baer agreed to mediation. Roosevelt appointed a commission including Baer, a union sympathizer named E. E. Clark, and himself to settle the dispute. The workers obtained a 10 per cent salary increase and a nine-hour day, but no recognition for their union. The results of the strike settlement were not in themselves significant. But the role which the federal government played in forcing a settlement was highly indicative of future policy.

In the eyes of many labor leaders, the only answer to corporate anti-union activities was radicalism. With this in mind, the Industrial Workers of the World was established in 1905, and launched a drive to organize all non-union industrial workers, both skilled and unskilled. The union never succeeded in attracting a very large membership, but it did involve itself in a series of violent labor disputes. The Wobblies were linked, over the next half dozen years, to a number of activities which horrified both the general public and many union leaders. But the IWW was not alone; even more conservative unions were occasionally involved in acts of violence. It was a symptom of the growing frustration of the working class.

Wilson and Labor

Labor received its first major legislative breakthrough during the presidency of Woodrow Wilson. The Clayton Anti-Trust Act of 1914 was briefly considered by labor to be their Magna Charta, because it weakly hinted that union activities were exempt from anti-trust prosecution. This had been a favorite tool of business in its attempt to destroy unionism under the terms of the older Sherman Anti-Trust Act. Furthermore, in 1916, Wilson pushed through Congress the Kern–McGillicuddy workman's compensation law, which rendered the employer liable for injuries suffered by employees while performing their duties. And at almost the same time, the Keating–Owen child labor law was passed (later held to be unconstitutional).

But the most significant measure favoring labor was the Adamson Act of 1916. During the summer of 1916 the nation was threatened with a massive railroad strike which would have tied up over 90 per cent of the nation's railroad system. The potential strikers wanted an eight-hour day and time-and-a-half for overtime. Wilson realized that a serious strike during the period immediately before the presidential election, would not help his candidacy, so he attempted to arbitrate. He convinced the railroad unions to drop their overtime demand. In return Wilson claimed that an eight-hour working day was just. But the railroad leaders refused to accept the compromise offer. President Wilson pleaded and threatened but nothing happened.

Wilson then went to Congress, and the

resultant Adamson Act decreed an eight-hour day for the transportation industry under the authority of the interstate commerce power (marking a significant expansion of this power). This averted a strike. Quite naturally, the railroads protested this radical new measure, but the Supreme Court, in January, 1917, upheld the constitutionality of the law. This legislative enactment marked a major breakthrough in recognition of the rights of the working man.

Wilson's Republican opponent in 1916, Charles Evans Hughes, attempted to make a campaign issue out of the Adamson Act. He argued that Wilson was giving in to pressures from the working class, thereby creating a dangerous precedent and betraying the business community. Wilson countered by defending the eight-hour day as a basic right of the working man. He lost part of the business vote, but he readily captured the labor and socialist vote.

The World War I era witnessed additional measures which, in the long run, were beneficial to labor. In April, 1918, the National War Labor Board was established to prevent strikes, but not to side with business against the workers. In the booming wartime economy wages were rising, but the economic gap between employer and employee was widening. Business wanted a "freeze" on wages for the duration. Moderate union leaders like Samuel Gompers wanted reasonable increases to reflect the improvement of the economy; in return, they would pledge no strikes. Wilson accepted this latter position.

The purpose of the board was twofold. It sought to prevent strikes by federal mediation; and it attempted to utilize the labor force as efficiently as possible for the war effort. For the former task a sub-board, the War Labor Policies Board, was set up and headed by Felix Frankfurter. It proved to be the crude forerunner of the National Labor Relations Board still two decades in the future. Efficiency of labor allocation was accomplished in conjunction with local draft boards. If a worker left a job in an essential industry for a non-essential job, he was immediately drafted. This effectively solved the problem. In general, the two boards applied the eight-hour-day provisions of the Adamson Act to all workers, supported equal pay for women (who were beginning to enter industry in large numbers), recognized the right of collective bargaining, and in effect promoted the cause of moderate unionism.

Post-War Labor Problems

The end of the war, however, brought with it a rash of labor problems. As soon as hostilities ceased a wave of strikes occurred as workers sought to obtain a larger piece of corporate profits. For the most part these strikes resulted in dismal failure. The public again blamed the strikers for consumer inconveniences and became openly hostile. In addition, the Red Scare, a period of post-war hysteria and reaction, convinced most Americans that any attempt to alter the economic structure in any way was subversive.

There was a steel strike in 1919 which involved approximately 300,000 workers. The strikers were seeking an eight-hour day, a six-day week, an end to the twenty-four-hour work shift, and recognition of their union as bargaining agent. The strike was drawn out but ended in complete failure.

There was also a police "strike" in Boston in 1919. The policemen belonged to a local social organization known as the Boston Social Club. Very much underpaid, they announced their intention of converting the organization into a union. The city authorities ordered them not to unionize under penalty of suspension. But the policemen went ahead and were subsequently suspended. Technically there was no strike; the police were locked out for organizing themselves. In the absence of a law-enforcement agency, crime rapidly increased. The governor of Massachusetts, Calvin Coolidge, called out the National Guard to maintain order. The suspended policemen, incidentally, were never called back to work; new police were hired to replace them.

Also in 1919, a massive coal strike was called by John L. Lewis, the tenacious president of the United Mine Workers. But it failed to last very long. The miners had been too hasty, and had gone on strike before wartime legislation against strikes had terminated. Attorney General Palmer utilized this legislation to force the miners back to work, and government arbitration was then effected. The union obtained a very limited victory, but this was an exception to the general pattern.

In 1920 the Republican, Warren Harding, defeated the Democratic candidate, James Cox, for the presidency. The election ushered in an era which was both conservative and retrogressive. The Republicans, in the 1920's, sought to reinvigorate their alliance with big business, which had been characteristic of the latter part of the nineteenth century. And the reforming spirit of the Wilson years disappeared into the disillusionment of the post-war decade.

There was only one obstacle to the re-establishment of the nineteenth century brand of capitalism: organized labor. The union worker, according to many businessmen, was an extremely ignorant and selfish creature who existed only to destroy and subvert solid business practices. And this worker had the audacity to seek to preserve his limited wartime gains. This position the businessmen could not accept. In fact, there were many attempts, particularly early in the decade, to cut wages and to lengthen working hours. And the government, as had once been traditional, was expected to aid in these attempts.

Initially, Harding chose to stay clear of employer–employee problems. When approximately 90,000 New England textile workers walked off the job early in 1922 and remained on strike for a period of six months, he did nothing. The textile workers had been offered a 20 per cent wage cut, having already accepted a 22.5 per cent reduction in salary the previous year. The new company proposal would give the workers $14 for a fifty-four-hour work week. With no goverment intervention the strike was settled; the wages were not cut.

The situation was somewhat different in the coal mines. Again, the employers wanted to reduce wages, and they did—by as much as 47 per cent. But rather than lengthen the work week, as was the general practice, they sought to shorten it. The mines had increased production during World War I, and with the termination of hostilities this was no longer necessary. So at best, the average miner worked only one to four days each week, depending on the season. Recognizing that it was unrealistic to seek an extended work week, the miners asked for steady employment instead. They wanted a guaranteed thirty-hour week all year.

The employers saw only one possible solution to the plight of the mines, and that was to cut labor costs to a bare minimum. When the 47 per cent pay cut was announced in April, 1922, a massive coal strike, involving roughly 700,000 miners began. The strike issue went far deeper than mere wage cuts; the miner was reconciled to these within reason. The strike was primarily viewed as a life-and-death struggle for the very survival of unions in the coal fields.

For two months the strike proceeded with no appreciable violence. Then a company superintendent from southern Illinois, C. K. McDowell, employed strikebreakers to end the walkout. The strikers refused to submit passively to this situation. A vicious wave of violence followed, in which strikebreakers and McDowell lost their lives. A local coroner's jury, made up of miners who were naturally pro-labor, claimed that McDowell himself had started the entire melee by killing a striker; therefore, his death was justifiable homicide. No one was convicted of anything. At this point Harding decided to intervene.

The President forced a reopening of the mines on the basis of the old wage agreement. The operators were willing, but the strikers were not. The result was the patrolling of the mines by state and federal troops, and very little work. John L. Lewis finally agreed to send his men back to work if the federal government would agree to investigate the coal industry thoroughly. A bargain was struck and the miners returned to work. In September, 1922, Congress created the federal Coal Commission, headed by the highly competent John Hammond.

The Coal Commission eventually submitted a lengthy report which called for many reforms favorable to the mine workers. This report was totally ignored by a complacent Congress. The government had not really kept its word. The plight of the coal miner remained a very serious problem throughout the decade, and was a contributory factor in the impending Depression.

The nation was simultaneously experiencing a massive railroad strike. Railroad workers received a 12 per cent wage cut in the spring of 1922, and they walked off the job. Within a short period of time all the railroad workers, except for the shopmen, were back on the job. For an additional two months they remained out, and this seriously affected the continued operation of the railroads. Attorney General Dougherty asked Federal District Judge James Wilkerson, of Chicago, to issue an injunction ordering the strikers back to work. The resultant injunction was the most sweeping in American history. It forbade the union to encourage its workers to strike, either by letter, or circular, or even word of mouth. The injunction rendered the union totally powerless.

The labor situation went from bad to worse. Most Americans were aware of the existence of child labor in the mines and mills, and they were opposed to it. But the Supreme Court in 1922, as it had done in 1918, declared a congressional enactment forbidding child labor to be unconstitutional. A child labor amendment to the federal Constitution was proposed and, for all practical purposes, defeated in 1924. Efforts to legislate on the length of working hours for women was also blocked. In 1923 the Supreme Court declared a Washington, D. C. minimum-wage law for women unconstitutional. The reasoning of the Court was that it violated the right to enter freely into a contract. Clearly, labor's situation was still perilous.

The anti-labor impulse was further increased by the many lower-court decisions against the right to picket. To walk a picket line was an extremely controversial activity in the 1920's. To some people it was actually subversive. Yellow dog contracts (which stipulated as a condition of employment the worker's promise never to join a union) continued to be used widely. As late as 1917 the Supreme Court had ruled that such contracts were constitutional, again citing the right to enter freely into a contract.

As a consequence of these developments and attitudes, the organized labor movement suffered serious setbacks during the Twenties. Union membership dropped off considerably, and most of the gains of the war years were obliterated. Both major parties, aware of the plight of the working man, promised some sort of aid during the presidential campaign of 1924; but none was forthcoming. The Republican platform of 1928 tended to sympathize unconstructively with labor.

The Democratic platform took a stronger stand: it demanded the strict regulation of business and supported the concept of collective bargaining. However, the Democrats lost the election.

Labor Advances under the New Deal Banner

By the end of the 1920's the industrial worker was probably in worse condition than ever before. What was true in the Twenties concerning wage and hour cuts, mushroomed with the onslaught of the Great Depression. An estimated 12 to 15 million workers lost their jobs. The worker had to await the presidency of Franklin Roosevelt for any relief. Roosevelt campaigned in 1932 on a platform calling for relief of the working man and reform of the economic system.

Roosevelt attempted to carry out his promise through the passage of the National Industrial Recovery Act of 1933. This measure has already been considered in the previous chapter, except for its labor provisions. Certain aspects of the codes established under the authority of the act deserve further amplification.

Labor Codes

All of the codes established maximum work weeks. These varied from industry to industry, but in general the new average was around forty-four hours per week. Some industries were working their employees as many as seventy or eighty hours per week during the Depression, while millions were unemployed. By establishing a maximum work week, new jobs would be created for the unemployed.

All of the codes established minimum wages. Again, this varied from industry to industry, but the average was roughly 40¢ per hour, a substantial increase for many workers. The Depression trend had been to lay off men and hire women at lower wages and longer hours for the same

jobs. This practice would be ended under the code provisions, and the individual wage earner would have a greater purchasing power to aid in restoring a normal economy.

All of the codes forbade child labor. The Depression had witnessed a resurgence of child labor because a child could be gotten to work longer than an adult for considerably less salary. In the process the head of a family could be replaced by an eight-year-old.

It is to be emphasized that all of these code provisions were to have the force of law, according to the terms of the National Recovery Act. So in effect, the government was telling industry to pay adequate salaries and schedule reasonable hours for their employees. These were the conditions that unions had been striving to obtain for decades.

The most controversial point of the labor measures was Section 7(a) of the act. According to its provisions the federal government recognized the right of labor to engage in collective bargaining. The only qualification was that a majority of the workers in a given industry had to agree on a bargaining agent. This particular measure was bitterly opposed by the industrialists, although there was little probability of strikes for higher wages during a depression period.

As matters turned out the codes were not successful, because industry did not abide by them and federal officials found them almost impossible to enforce. And in 1935 the NIRA was declared unconstitutional by the Supreme Court. But the measure was significant in marking the acceptance by the federal government of its responsibility to guarantee certain basic rights for the working man.

The long-standing conflict between skilled and unskilled industrial workers had never ended. The AFL had continued its policy of discriminating against the unskilled. It began to weaken late in 1935 when the Committee for Industrial Organization, within the framework of the

By Kirby, NEW YORK WORLD-TELEGRAM

Picketing (1937)

AFL, commenced a drive to unionize all workers, regardless of degree of skill, on an industry-wide basis.

Employers resisted this unionizing attempt. Finally, violence erupted in 1937 in the automobile plants. This visibly disturbed the conservative leaders of the AFL. An effort was made to control and subdue the Committee for Industrial Organization by the parent organization. When this happened the CIO split away from the AFL, and under the leadership of John L. Lewis, formed a separate union in 1938. The CIO avoided the selectivity of the AFL and commenced a long and bloody battle to unionize unskilled workers. The two unions went their separate ways until 1955 when they finally declared a shaky truce and rejoined forces. In the interim many unskilled workers had been unionized.

NLRA

In 1935 the government came up with a new measure to replace the National Industrial Recovery Act. The measure was known as either the Wagner–Connery Act or the National Labor Relations Act, and was aimed at restating and strengthening Section 7(a) of the unconstitutional NIRA. The measure established an independent National Labor Relations Board, consisting of three members, to interpret and enforce the rights of collective bargaining.

There were five basic points to the new law. No business organization was allowed to interfere with the establishment of a union. Businessmen were prohibited from discriminating against union members in their hiring practices. Businessmen were prohibited from exercising any financial controls over unions. An employer was not allowed to fire an employee who had filed charges against him before the National Labor Relations Board. And finally, business was required to bargain with duly authorized union representatives.

In effect the old yellow dog contract was prohibited and Section 7(a) was strengthened immeasurably. Besides filling a void left by the invalidation of the NIRA, the National Labor Relations Act was aimed quite pointedly at company-sponsored unions, of which Henry Ford's "welfare capitalism" union was the most well known.

Thus the machinery was established. But the board (NLRB) was still faced with serious problems. For example, which union was to be recognized if two or more groups claimed the allegiance of a given working force; should one union or several unions represent the workers in a given industry? This was a problem which had to be dealt with as organized labor began to put its own house in order, and it is still not completely solved. There was also the problem of gaining widespread acceptance for NLRB rulings. The board was largely handicapped during its first few years of operation because many New Dealers were opposed to taking a militant stand on the labor issue. In their opinion, national recovery was far more important than labor advancement, which could be postponed to a more opportune time. So the National Labor Relations Board had an uphill battle. The National Labor Relations Act only replaced one of the provisions of the defunct NIRA. The provisions dealing with maximum hours, minimum wages, and child labor were not incorporated. These deficiencies were remedied in the Fair Labor Standards Act of 1938. The new measure had nothing to do with codes. It simply replaced what the codes had contained with a federal statute. Hence, there was no delegation of legislative power to the executive which could be declared unconstitutional.

The law established a 25¢-per-hour minimum wage for industrial workers, and provided for its gradual increase to 40¢ per hour by 1945. It established a maximum work week of forty-four hours, with provisions for its future reduction to forty hours. Time-and-a-half for overtime was prescribed. Child labor was forbidden in industry; this meant that persons had to be eighteen to work in heavy industry and sixteen for light jobs. The act was passed under the federal commerce power, and its constitutionality was upheld. This measure entailed a broad expansion of the federal commerce power.

These New Deal measures provided some aid to the working man, but did not nearly solve all his problems. The concept of responsible unionism had gained governmental acceptance, but one of the key problems plaguing the industrial worker remained: the unemployment problem. The potential American involvement in the spreading conflict which culminated in World War II, served to aid the industrial worker in temporarily solving the unemployment problem.

Labor in Contemporary America

In the late summer of 1940 Roosevelt asked Congress for funds to build up the nation's defense system. Congress re-sponded by appropriating $18 billion for the fiscal year 1940–1941, more than twice the money spent in any year during World War I when the nation was an actual combatant. This appropriation resulted in numerous war contracts for the building of tanks, guns, and aircraft. The happy result for labor was more jobs. At the same time Congress passed the Burke–Wadsworth Selective Service Act which created the nation's first peacetime draft. The act increased the size of the army by roughly 1.1 million men, thus removing many men from the unemployment rolls.

Labor in World War II

When war actually came, American labor experienced one of its most prosperous eras. Some 16 million Americans were drafted or enlisted into the Armed Forces, leaving no serious unemployment problem during the war. Wartime demands required a degree of industrial productivity unparalleled in human history. Many workers found themselves working sixteen-hour shifts on a regular basis, but there were still some unemployed. Figures vary slightly, but they indicate that between 600,000 and 700,000 people never found employment, even in a booming wartime economy. These were the hardcore unemployables, either totally illiterate or untrainable.

The mobilization of the nation's economic resources followed a pattern similar to that of World War I. But problems of regulation were compounded by the length and severity of the conflict. One of these problems was a runaway economy, and the resultant wartime inflation. This was equally true with respect to wages.

The standard no-strike pledges by labor and the no-lockout pledges by businessmen were made at the very beginning of the conflict. But a serious problem developed when prices rose some 61 per cent from 1940 through 1942. Labor justly expected that wages should correspond to price inflation. A National War Labor Board was established to prevent work stoppages and to stabilize wages. The board adopted the general policy of a 15 per cent wage increase to cover the rising costs of the first year of war. But with costs mounting so rapidly, a wage agreement was obsolete within a few weeks after it had been negotiated, and thus labor was quite restless. When John L. Lewis threatened a nationwide miners' strike in 1943, President Roosevelt responded promptly by seizing the mines. Prior to this crisis over 3,000 strikes had occurred during the early war years, creating a very critical labor situation.

It appeared rather obvious that drastic measures would have to be taken. Higher taxes were authorized; Roosevelt issued a "freeze" order on all prices and wages in April, 1943, and installment buying was drastically curtailed. When these measures failed to solve the problem completely, a measure was enacted which, although hailed by the anti-union stalwarts, was justified only in conjunction with serious international exigencies. This was the Smith–Connally War Labor Disputes Act, which was passed over Roosevelt's veto.

This law required all unions to give a thirty-day notice prior to taking a strike vote. If a strike vote was taken (and ostensibly the thirty-day period would be used to discourage it), the vote had to be conducted under the supervision of the National Labor Relations Board. If the president regarded the industry as essential to the war effort, he could seize it for the duration of the war. And it was made a federal criminal offense to strike against a government-operated industry. In other words, strikes would only be tolerated in industries which were not connected with the war effort.

Incidents continued to occur, and various industries were seized by the federal government. Finally prices became more or less stabilized (through the Office of Price Adjustment) and the cost of living settled down to a 1 per cent per year growth rate for the duration. However, this did not happen until the end of 1943, when the war was half over. Meanwhile, in view of continued labor unrest and critical shortages, it was proposed to draft civilians into essential industries, and to pay them according to the military pay scale. This would not only solve the wage problem, but it would also wipe out any possibility of strikes. The measure passed the House of Representatives in December, 1944, but Germany collapsed before the Senate could vote on the measure, so it was abandoned. The United States had come close to 100 per cent mobilization during the war.

Before the famous freeze order of mid-1943, wages and prices had been skyrocketing. Still, unions managed to emerge from the war years with average increases approximating some 50 per cent. Since industry was operating on a cost-plus basis (the government paid all production expenses plus a reasonable profit), it was usually quite willing to grant pay increases. The strike problem arose in non–cost-plus industries—the ones not essential to the war effort. But ultimately, the federal government payed the bill for these wage increases, and this affected the value of money. Real income, however, is estimated to have risen approximately 33 per cent during the war years.

Post-War Chaos

The years following World War II were quite chaotic on the labor scene. Strikes were rampant in 1946, partly brought on by rising prices as wartime controls were removed, and by the staunch determination of union leaders to make up for wartime freezes. But the labor issue went beyond inflation and union determination. Fear of communist infiltration of organized labor helped create a 1940's version of the old Red Scare. The number of strikes was a factor also. Close to 5 million workers went on strike during 1946, tying up many different industries.

The federal government took an active role in the labor disputes. In April, 1946, Truman seized the coal mines when John L. Lewis ordered 400,000 miners on strike. Truman mediated a settlement with the union, but the owners would not accept it. Lewis called his miners out again, without stopping to consider that the government was still operating the industry, and that he was striking against the federal government. A federal district court found Lewis in contempt, fined him personally $10,000, and fined his union the staggering sum of $3.5 million. A Supreme Court review upheld the lower court's action, including the government mine seizure and subsequent negotiation of a contract, but reduced the fine against the union to $700,000. During 1946 Truman also seized the railroads in the face of a 250,000-man strike, and successfully mediated a settlement. Still, unlike the post–World War I era, labor did make some significant gains. The new problem was one of ever-increasing prosperity and how to control it.

The Taft–Hartley Act

The Wagner–Connery Act of 1935 had been passed in the belief that big business possessed an unfair advantage over labor. By 1947, in view of constant and serious work stoppages, this attitude had changed considerably. It was widely felt that if unions were powerful enough to disrupt the economy in such a devastating manner, it was time to check them. The result of this changed attitude was the Taft–Hartley Act of 1947.

Passed by a large majority in both houses of Congress over President Truman's ringing veto, the measure restricted unions in a number of ways. Unions were required to file their complete financial records with the Department of Labor. If a union called a strike, the government, under the provisions of the Taft–Hartley Act, could delay it for a sixty-day period, during which time it was hoped that a settlement would be negotiated. Some of the powers of the National Labor Relations Board were given to a newly appointed government attorney, who was assigned only one task: to oversee labor disputes. All union officials were required to swear their loyalty to the American governmental system. The closed shop, which employs only union members, was forbidden. Workers were free to either join or reject a union. And the federal government was authorized to take over an industry and settle any strike which occurred during a national emergency. The Taft–Hartley Act, instead of settling the labor issue, ushered in a period of extreme discontent.

President Truman attempted to push through Congress a legislative program known as the Fair Deal. Among the measures which he espoused were a full and fair employment practices bill and a boost in the minimum-wage law. This was partly tied in with the civil rights issue, since Negroes were often barred from union membership (see Chapter Nine). He did not obtain his full employment bill, but Congress did authorize government research into the problems of unemployment in the Maximum Employment Act of 1946. In the 1948 presidential campaign, Truman called for the repeal of Taft–Hartley and the enactment of higher minimum wages. He was successful in pushing the minimum wage from 40¢ to 75¢ per hour, but he did not succeed in having the Taft–Hartley Act repealed. This was partially his own fault. Congress did agree to amend the act to remove some of its more objectionable features, but the President would accept nothing but complete repeal.

The labor situation changed again with the advent of the Korean War. A

limited wartime economy was reintro-
duced, and there were difficulties over
strikes, labor shortages, and soaring prices.
A new Selective Service Act partially took
care of the nation's unemployment problem. It was during the Korean conflict
that Truman performed his celebrated
seizure of the steel mills, in 1952, using his
power as commander-in-chief for justification. The steel companies obtained a
court injunction against the President, and
the Supreme Court upheld the injunction,
claiming that the nation was not at war;
therefore, there were no appropriate emergency measures authorized. The Korean
War, according to the Court, was merely a
police action. As a result, 650,000 steel
workers walked off the job, forcing a partial shutdown of the armament industry.
Truman, however, eventually did mediate
a settlement of the labor dispute.

In 1952 the Democratic presidential
candidate, Adlai Stevenson, favored the
repeal of the Taft–Hartley Act. The Republicans, under the leadership of Dwight
Eisenhower, did not. Yet President Eisenhower appointed the chief executive of
the Plumbers Union, Martin Durkin, as
his Secretary of Labor. Durkin prepared
a lengthy list of proposed changes in the
Taft–Hartley law, got nowhere with the
President, and quickly resigned. The incident embittered many labor leaders who
felt that Durkin and labor had been sold
out to traditional Republicanism. Still,
the Eisenhower presidency witnessed an
increase in the legal minimum wage to $1
per hour in 1956 (this pertained only to
those industries covered by the interstate
commerce clause). The national economy generally experienced rising wages,
and this tended to keep labor resentment
somewhat mollified.

However, a crisis was developing,
caused by the mounting unemployment
during the Eisenhower years. In large
measure this was owing to a growing technology which was putting millions out of
work. A number of strikes occurred.

Unions were accused of "feather-bed-
ding," i.e., insisting that certain jobs be
filled even though they had become obsolete and unnecessary. Business was accused of doubling its profits every time it
raised workers' wages, and with justifying
its position by claiming that increased
labor costs were the major ill of the entire
economy. But what really affected labor
most was the public's belief that the unions
were beset by gangsterism.

In 1957 a Senate investigation in-
quired into union operations and discovered that strongarm activities, graft,
and corruption existed. Dave Beck, president of the powerful Teamsters Union,
invoked the Fifth Amendment, refusing to
testify because of possible self-incrimination, over 200 times in his testimony before the Senate committee. He was
eventually convicted of embezzling union
funds. His successor, James Hoffa, was
also a highly controversial character, and
upon his election, the American Federation of Labor broke all ties with the Teamsters Union. A lengthy battle then began
in the courts over Hoffa's leadership and
practices, which finally led to his imprisonment in the late 1960's.

As a reaction to the controversial type
of union leadership characterized by Beck
and Hoffa, the Landrum–Griffin Act was
passed in 1959. The measure, which repealed most of the Taft–Hartley Act, was
designed primarily to make union organizations more responsive to their membership. The law required democratic elections of union officials, and rendered these
union officials liable for the manner in
which they handled union funds.
Furthermore, the use of strongarm tactics
was outlawed, plus a host of minor reforms.

Labor had gone full circle. Originally, unions had been established to
counteract the uncontrolled power of the
giant corporations during the age of big
business. Gains came very slowly, since
government tended to side with business

against the claimed "labor menace." But
the gains eventually came, although not
without considerable blood and tears, and
the government gave unions legal protection, under the leadership of progressive,
liberal-minded presidents.

Unions, thereupon, grew quite strong.
And when thousands of crippling strikes
plagued the nation from the 1940's forward, it became apparent to many Americans that perhaps they were too powerful.
Unions could exert a very detrimental ef-

fect on the economy if they desired to do
so. And there was already ample precedent for regulating powerful organizations; business enterprises had been regulated for some decades because of their
vast economic power. Finally, when
gangsters were linked to powerful organized labor, the die was fully cast. The
industrial worker had gone full circle. He
had become an integral, but fully regulated
peer on the American economic scene.

For Further Reading

Brissenden, Paul F. *The I.W.W.: A Study of American Syndicalism.* New York: Columbia University Press, 1919.

Brooks, Thomas R. *Toil and Trouble: A History of American Labor.* Boston: Dell
Publishing, 1967.

Committee on Economic Development. *Union Powers and Union Functions: Toward a
Better Balance.* New York: Committee on Economic Development, 1964.

Dulles, Foster. *Labor in America.* New York: Crowell, 1949.

Ely, Richard T. *The Labor Movement in the United States.* New York: Crowell, 1886.

Kerr, Clark. *Unions and Union Leaders of Their Own Choosing.* New York: Fund for
the Republic, 1958.

McAdams, Alan K. *Power and Politics in Labor Legislation.* New York: Columbia
University Press, 1964.

Maher, John E. *Labor and the Economy.* Boston: Allyn and Bacon, 1965.

Marshall, F. Ray. *Labor in the South.* Cambridge: Harvard University Press, 1967.

Mills, C. Wright. *The New Men of Power: America's Labor Leaders.* New York:
Harcourt, Brace, 1945.

Perlman, Selig, and Taft, Philip. *History of Labor in the United States, 1896–1932.*
New York: Macmillan Company, 1935.

Walsh, J. Raymond. *C.I.O., Industrial Unionism in America.* New York: Norton,
1937.

Part Three
Guarantees And Benefits
For The American People

Chapter Nine
Civil Rights

Undoubtedly one of the most difficult and controversial problems in America today is that of minority rights. The Poor People's campaign and the Black Power movement of today had their beginnings in peaceful demonstrations and boycotts over clear-cut civil rights issues in the Fifties. But as the focus on constitutional rights seemed to accomplish little, the leaders of minority groups in the Sixties have broadened their concerns to include the attainment of economic and political power; legal equality now seems less important to them than social equality, and they are less inclined toward nonviolence. This radicalization has been paralleled by the increasing frequency of riots in most of our cities' ghettoes, which cause great destruction of life and property. As a result the impatience of many minority leaders is matched by increasing hostility among members of the white majority; fear, frustration, and misunderstanding often seem to predominate over compassion, justice, and reason.

The Constitution, which was written some 180 years ago, appeared to guarantee certain basic rights to every American citizen. Unfortunately, not everyone born in America was allowed full-fledged citizenship, and constitutional guarantees were often applied only to a rather select group of individuals. It is not only the Negro descendants of slaves whose civil rights have thus been impaired. The United States has a long history of violating the civil rights of many minorities. People of Latin descent and people of "undesirable" European origin have been subjected to prejudice and persecution. The Jews, the Puerto Ricans, the Orientals of California, and the Indians and Mexicans of the Southwest, have all shared common grievances with the American Negro.

The civil rights problem also extends beyond racial or ethnic groups. It applies to the federal Bill of Rights, and as such, includes the rights of religious and political minorities. The present chapter will first consider civil rights in the broadest context, and then present a chronological view of civil rights and minority issues throughout American history.

The Rights of Americans

Civil rights may be divided into three broad categories. There are those dealing with personal liberty: the right of individuals to perform certain actions without being hindered by government. There are those dealing with governmental procedures: the methods by which government may enforce itself on the individual without unduly infringing on individual rights. And there are those dealing with property rights.

The Thirteenth Amendment

The civil rights dealing with personal liberty comprise a large and amorphous area, subject to constant examination and interpretation by judicial bodies. For example, the Thirteenth Amendment guarantees a right to personal security. This has been interpreted as stating that no person may legally be enslaved by individuals or government. But this right is subject to various qualifications. An individual can not sign himself into slavery, but he may enter into contracts to perform certain services and be required by law to carry out his contract's terms. A person may also be required to serve jury duty. Some individuals have unsuccessfully claimed that this comprises involuntary servitude, in that government is forcing them to do something against their will. The courts have repeatedly ruled, however, that compulsory jury duty is legal. Some Americans have sued in the federal courts, claiming that their constitutional guarantee against involuntary servitude was being violated by the military draft. The Supreme Court has ruled that such service is a responsibility of citizenship, with the self-preservation of the American nation taking precedence over individual rights.

The Thirteenth Amendment also guarantees freedom from mob violence and intimidation. However, the problem of keeping the peace (which is what the right involves) is mainly a state governmental function which is not always carried out properly. This points to a peculiarity in the American governmental system. There are no federal crimes against persons, such as murder. Protection and prosecution are left to the states' police powers. When President Kennedy was assassinated in 1963, the federal government could not indict on a charge of murder; only the state of Texas had the legal authority. The refusal of states to prosecute lynch mobs has been fairly common in America. And the federal government, unable to prosecute for murder, has had to indict those concerned on lesser charges which carry considerably smaller penalties.

Over the past few years there have been moves in the direction of greater federal involvement in cases where state governments have been uncooperative. An excellent example was the protection of a citizen in Oxford, Mississippi, by federalized troops. But this was enforcement, not prosecution, which is an entirely different matter.

The First Amendment

In the First Amendment there is a guarantee of religious freedom. The abuse of this concept has been an integral part of Western civilization for centuries. It was sometimes made a crime punishable by death or exile to hold religious beliefs contrary to an official state religion; there are also instances of religious dissenters being denied the civil rights of official worshippers. The First Amendment in America maintains that an individual may chose his own religion and practice it without help or hindrance from the government as long as he does not violate criminal law. Thus a religious sect which practised human sacrifice as a part of its ceremonies, could legally be suppressed by the government.

There are some difficult problems involved in the guarantee of religious freedom. These include conscientious objection to military service, the status of parochial schools, religious instruction in public schools, and the activities of various non-conformist sects. The government has usually allowed a fairly wide degree of latitude in such matters, the general rule being that most practices may be allowed if no harm is inflicted on anyone.

The legitimate conscientious objector may face difficulties in adhering to his beliefs. Local draft boards interpret what proof of sincerity is or is not acceptable. Consequently, some sincere war objectors have been placed in prison. The acknowledged conscientious objector may be drafted, but for non-combatant jobs. Usually, such people work in the medical corps, and recently, a pacifist corpsman received the Congressional Medal of Honor for heroism. To be a pacifist does not imply cowardice; and some conscientious objectors have performed admirable service for their country.

The government recognizes rights of religious groups to establish and conduct their own private schools, subject to state educational requirements. A major contemporary issue concerns whether these schools are entitled to tax support. Those who hold that taxes should go to the support of church-affiliated schools claim that now they are paying taxes for public education, plus expenditures for other schools as well. They claim further that they are keeping general taxes lower for other people by not using the public schools. Opponents claim that public schools exist for everyone, and individuals are free to use or not use them. The Supreme Court's view maintains that parochial schools are entitled to fire and police protection (both tax-supported), and that the states can aid private schools if they desire, provided only that they are

not discriminatory. Therefore, some states like New Jersey provide public bus transportation for parochial school students. In addition, the federal government, in its educational aid programs, advances funds to public, private, and parochial institutions on a non-discriminatory basis.

The Supreme Court has taken a strong position on religious instruction in public schools. Under no circumstances can a particular religious creed be taught, but a survey of all religions may be offered. Students may be released from school for religious instruction by their own ministers at some place other than the school premises. The guiding principle is that government should remain neutral in religious matters.

In the recent controversial prayer decision by the Court, it was held that a non-sectarian prayer was contrary to freedom of religion. The stated objection of the Court was that the prayer had been written by a state legislature, which violated the principle of separation of church and state.

The government experiences most of its religious problems with non-conformist sects. In 1940, for example, children who belonged to the Jehovah Witnesses refused to salute the flag and recite the Pledge of Allegiance in the classroom, because this was considered to be worshipping a false god. The Court eventually ruled that such non-conformist attitudes, unless they caused social and political havoc, could be tolerated in a nation which upholds individuality. Each case, therefore, would be decided on its own merits.

The First Amendment also guarantees the right of free speech and freedom of the press. These are extremely controversial and complicated civil rights. The national government has placed restrictions on both these rights in time of war and according to the international situation. In most instances the courts have agreed with these procedures.

Again, national self-preservation is held superior to individual civil rights.

In restricting freedom of speech, it has been generally accepted that whenever speech constitutes a "clear and present danger" to the United States government, it can be curtailed. The contemporary concern with the teaching of communism in American schools originally reached the Supreme Court in 1919. *Schenck* v. *United States* ruled that communism may be taught as an abstract doctrine. But it cannot be taught in such a manner as to advocate the violent overthrow of the American system.

There is a related question of loyalty oaths. Many schools, for instance, require that teachers take an oath of loyalty to the Constitution as a condition for employment. Many teachers view these oaths as an affront to their patriotism, especially since other people in responsible positions are not required to swear allegiance. Presumably, a true revolutionary would falsely swear such an oath.

Censorship poses another problem. Newspapers are governed by the doctrine of "no prior censorship," meaning that a newspaper cannot be stopped from printing an article until after it has already been printed. Then its distribution can be halted or the company may be sued. With this sort of threat, newspapers are usually quite careful to censor their own stories.

Movies and magazines are granted a fairly high degree of leniency. The federal government has invalidated many state censorship laws, claiming that they violated freedom of the press. Movies and magazines must be obviously prurient in order to be censored, but there still remains the question of what is obscene. The answer depends largely on the background and interests of the person viewing or reading the material.

The federal government exercises a general censorship over printed material through its control of the mails, and also indirectly regulates radio broadcasts through the Federal Communications Commission. The government exercises considerable censorship over information about its own activities. It is becoming progressively more circumspect in its releases to news media concerning matters deemed "secret." A serious question pertains to how secret many of these government activities really should be. Government, under its present policy, is capable of hiding its mistakes from the electorate, thus contradicting democratic theory.

Under the provisions of the First Amendment Americans possess the right to peaceful assembly and petition. Local government may deny meetings only for reasons of public health and safety, not because it disagrees with the nature of the meeting or its participants. A communist meeting is entitled to as much protection as a meeting of the Boy Scouts, as long as the violent overthrow of the government is not advocated. People have a right to voice unpopular views collectively.

According to the Second Amendment the people have the right to bear arms. The "arms" referred to are military weapons; state militia systems and local police forces are thus guaranteed. In medieval England, none but a nobleman was permitted to carry a sword. The intent was to keep the mass of people from having any power to rise against the government. Early in American history if was felt necessary for citizens to retain the ability to defend themselves against government should it become tyrannical. This resulted in placing police powers outside of federal authority. As for private weapons, they are subject to government regulation for purposes of safety and order. The prohibition of the carrying of concealed weapons such as switch-blade knives has been held constitutional. Constitutionally, the government could declare ownership of any weapon by a private individual to be illegal, but it could not abolish local or state police forces.

The Fourteenth Amendment

One of the most important of all constitutional amendments is the Fourteenth Amendment. Initially, it was felt that the state governments would guarantee a "bill of rights" to their citizens. It was the federal government which was feared. However, the period prior to the Civil War demonstrated that state governments, rather than the federal government, most often condoned the violation of basic civil rights. Hence in the Reconstruction era the Fourteenth Amendment was ratified (1867). Basically, this amendment applied the federal Bill of Rights to state governments by stating that the privileges and immunities of federal citizenship cannot be denied by any other governmental unit. It guarantees the right of equal protection before the law of all persons. And as it has been interpreted through numerous court decisions this guarantee today is applied mainly to racial discrimination in the general categories of housing, employment, education, and access to public facilities.

The residential right holds that a person cannot be denied housing because of race, color, or creed. It does not apply, however, to the actions of private individuals, provided they do not involve any governmental agency or an institution which deals with the general public. To get around this constitutional guarantee of fair housing the "restrictive covenant" was devised. This was a scheme whereby a piece of property was sold on condition that it never be sold thereafter to Negroes, Jews, or other specified groups. These restrictions were made a part of the sale contract. However, the seller had no recourse against the buyer if the latter decided to ignore the restrictive covenant, because enforcement meant involving an agency of government. The Supreme Court since 1948 has declared restrictive covenants unconstitutional, holding that every citizen has a right to live where he desires, providing he has sufficient resources to substantiate his desire. Even so, this guarantee is still being violated through more subtle measures: harassment, undue red tape, and occasional threat and violence.

The constitutional prohibition in the area of employment states that no citizen, all other things being equal, can be denied a job because of race or creed. The sole criterion for employment should be the ability of the applicant to do the job. The principal violators of this right are unions and individual (non-corporate) employers. Again, this is a very difficult right to enforce because it is sometimes impossible to prove discrimination. However, there can be no discrimination in the Armed Forces, civil service, or in private industries receiving government contracts or aid. Some states and a number of localities have laws prohibiting employment discrimination. It is still practiced, but not to the extent it once was.

The right to education many consider the most critical. Its proper enforcement often determines the rights of residence and employment, for a highly trained individual is almost always in demand. In 1896 the Supreme Court, in *Plessy* v. *Ferguson,* ruled that segregation in public schools was constitutional, providing that facilities were equal. The "separate but equal" doctrine was continually expanded to include other areas such as public transportation and public accommodations. But there was never anything remotely approaching equal facilities for the races. The doctrine was nothing but a sham promoted to institutionalize prejudice.

Finally in 1950 in the case, *Sweatt* v. *Painter,* a group of Texas law students claimed that separated schools could not be equal. The Supreme Court agreed: in faculty, prestige, facilities—by the very fact that children were forcibly separated —they could not be equal. The stage was set for the historic *Brown* v. *Board of Education* case in 1954.

The Court specifically overturned its half-century–old ruling of "separate but equal" facilities, and further stated that all citizens have the right to attend the school of their choice. States were ordered to desegregate with all reasonable haste, and the lower federal courts were instructed to enforce the ruling. The order still has not been carried out completely, although considerable progress has been made. Students now have the right, backed by the full power of the federal government, to attend the institution of their choice, subject only to entrance requirements common to all applicants.

The fourth category of civil rights guaranteed by the Fourteenth Amendment concerns public facilities. All people, regardless of race, color, or creed, are entitled to the equal use of public facilities such as transportation, restaurants, and places of entertainment. The federal government is able to act in this area through its power over interstate commerce; much, however, remains to be done.

Procedural and Property-Right Guarantees

The second broad category of civil rights encompasses guarantees of fairness in governmental procedures. This means that government must proceed in a certain prescribed manner in enforcing the law. These procedures are spelled out in basic form in certain of the first ten amendments (the Bill of Rights).

The Fifth Amendment is probably the best known. It guarantees the right to indictment by grand jury. No person may be detained for an alleged crime against the national government unless a federal grand jury decides that there is sufficient evidence for trying him for that crime. The public prosecutor presents evidence to the grand jury which then decides whether the accused should be tried on the charges specified. If so, the person is tried before a trial jury. This constitutional provision does not apply completely to state criminal systems. A person must still be accused formally of a crime, but there are two methods of accomplishing this. Some states use the grand jury system, others use the equally valid "information" process, whereby the district attorney, as an elected official of the people, formally brings charges against the accused (informs against him), who subsequently faces a trial jury.

The Constitution also provides the right to a writ of *habeas corpus*. This means that a person cannot be arbitrarily charged with a crime or imprisoned. There must be sufficient evidence for confinement, and the charges must be specified. The American colonists who came from Europe sought to avoid the Old World practices of unlimited detention for unspecified reasons.

There is a constitutional guarantee of a speedy public trial by jury. This applies to any infraction which carries a significant penalty with conviction. The accused must be given a jury trial, although in most states he has the option of waiving a jury and having the judge determine his guilt. In some instances he could possibly obtain more leniency in this manner, especially if public opinion is highly aroused against him. A jury consists of twelve persons who must decide guilt by a unanimous decision. Under such a system the guilty go free more often than the innocent are convicted; unanimity is quite difficult to obtain.

Due Process

There also exists a right to "due process of law." This encompasses such items as a right to legal counsel, the right to present evidence or counter-evidence, trial by a proper court, the right to call witnesses, rights of appeal, and others. This is a very broad field and one that has never been fully defined. It is known as procedural due process.

But there is also something called substantive due process. This primarily means that a person must not only be tried according to certain prescribed procedures, but he must also be tried according to reasonable laws. Even though a law is not technically unconstitutional, the Supreme Court can invalidate it, if it decides that the law is unreasonable. It may be considerably out-of-date, having been passed centuries earlier. It may be foolish or inapplicable. Whatever the reasons may be, substantive due process provides another broad area for federal action. The implication is that anything which is reasonable (for instance the economic legislation of the New Deal era) may be legal and desirable, even though the Constitution is completely silent on the matter.

There are a few other procedural rights which deserve mention. Cruel and unusual punishment is forbidden. A person cannot be maimed as punishment for a crime (at one time in England a petty thief had his hands cut off for a second offense, and branding was quite common). He cannot be tortured, and if he is sentenced to death the execution must be as brief and painless as possible.

There can be no double jeopardy: a person cannot be tried twice by the same court for the same crime. This requires some explanation. An individual may commit a criminal act which is a violation of both federal and state law. Both levels of government may try the offender, but normally the federal government yields to the state, unless it later becomes dissatisfied with the results of the trial. The right to no double jeopardy also means that the trial must be completely fair and observe procedural due process. Otherwise, it is not a proper trial and may be held repeatedly until correct.

Illegally obtained evidence is inadmissable in the courts. There are elaborate rules on what is and is not proper evidence. One of the important contemporary problems concerns evidence obtained from wiretapping. The federal government no longer uses such evidence in court, seeking to avoid invasion of the right to privacy. However, some states still use it to obtain convictions, which often stand unless the defendant appeals his case on constitutional grounds to the federal courts.

One of the best known procedural rights is that pertaining to self-incrimination. A person cannot be compelled to testify against himself in a federal court. Invoking the Fifth Amendment is often an admission that one has something to hide; it does not necessarily mean that he is guilty of a crime. The Supreme Court only applied the Fifth Amendment self-incrimination clause to the state judicial systems in 1964. Before that time, in some states individuals could be compelled to testify against themselves under penalty of a contempt-of-court citation.

Property Rights

The third broad category of civil rights pertains to property. Although property rights reside largely within the purview of the individual states, the vast bulk of all legislation, state and federal, is concerned with the regulation of property. The Constitution upholds the right and almost the sacrosanctity of private property. The federal government is constitutionally bound to define, protect, and regulate the use of private property. The government also possesses the superficially contradictory power of being able to take for public use, if considered to be sufficiently in the public interest, any private property.

All levels of government possess the right of eminent domain. Private property rights are not absolute, and if it is in the best interests of the majority that certain private property should be made public, this can be done. There is only one restriction on government in the exercise of eminent domain. Property owners must be given a fair market price for their property, plus a nominal amount to compensate for the inconvenience of selling against their wishes. Furthermore, private property cannot be used solely at the discretion of the property owner. He may be required to allow access or the use of certain unique features, or be forced to conform to certain regulations on how he may use his property.

Civil rights applies to certain fundamental human rights which cannot be transgressed by the various levels of government. The concept does not apply directly to the opinions or actions of people as private individuals. The various levels of government have no authority or power over what an individual may think about a certain race, creed, or ethnic group. Prejudice, bias, and personal interest probably cannot be legislated out of existence, although they may be lessened by education.

On the individual level, respect for the dignity of one's fellow man is a moral, not a political question. The federal government has made one concerted attempt in the area of moral legislation: Prohibition. It was a miserable failure. No law can overcome simple prejudice, and no law can force a man to befriend another. But with the probable advent of civil and political equality, social mobility and interchange will gradually evolve and discrimination may gradually disappear.

Finally, civil rights are not absolute rights; they are relative to time and circumstances. The right to free speech does not allow slander. The right to life does not mean that government cannot require men to fight and perhaps die for their country. The right to liberty does not mean that a criminal cannot be imprisoned. Also, some of these rights are quite flexible. They may be limited in wartime because national self-preservation takes precedence over all other rights. They may even be limited during periods of domestic unrest to lessen the possibility of open civil disorder. But many Americans proudly uphold their civil rights, even though they have never been completely defined.

Historic Origins of Civil Rights

English colonists brought the basis of the Bill of Rights with them when they migrated to America. The English governmental system had already given Englishmen certain protections before the law. Unfortunately, this protection was afforded primarily along class lines. And although the average lower-class Englishman believed in his "rights," in actual practice they were consistently violated.

In assessing the reasons why Englishmen came to America, it is evident that many of them came seeking various types of freedom. Freedom from an established church was one motivating factor. A seeking for real equality before the law was yet another. The acquisition of property was high on the list. The ideas of the European Enlightenment, with their emphasis on the rights and dignity of man, and the insistence that human beings could exert some controlling effect on their environment were motivating factors. Early American colonists were conditioned to believe that there were rights to which each man was entitled,

Effects of the Fugitive Slave Law

and which every government was bound to guarantee and respect.

The Limits of an Ideal

But in actual practice Americans, from the earliest colonial days, did not follow what they preached. Within twelve years of the founding of Jamestown, slavery was introduced. It was assumed that Africans were not entitled to the rights which the colonists claimed for themselves; they were inferior creatures. This claimed inferiority between peoples went beyond a simple racial issue and was incorporated within another English tradition which was also contradictory to egalitarian ideals.

This was the tradition of an aristocratic or privileged class. Southern planters developed this concept in trying to place themselves in the position of great feudal lords. To some extent other colonists upheld the same basic idea. In

New England and several of the middle colonies, there existed class divisions based on both wealth and religion. So although American colonists talked about certain basic human rights, it commonly remained talk. The contradiction between theory and practice found in the Constitution dates from pre-Revolutionary times.

Nonetheless, the period of the Enlightment in Europe did emphasize the dignity of the individual. And many Englishmen, after spending time in America, began to accept its implications. They already possessed certain basic rights such as assembly and trial by jury. Besides, John Locke, the apologist for the English Revolution of 1688, claimed that government should protect and safeguard life, liberty, and property. This was the doctrine of a superior natural law which superseded any state law. As time went on this concept had an active effect on American settlers. They were aided by the fact that England was three months away by round trip, and this gave them the opportunity to experiment.

The events of the pre-Revolutionary era helped to crystallize American public opinion. Primarily for economic reasons (England was attempting to enforce her mercantilistic legislation after 1763), Americans quickly discovered all sorts of "rights" which were being denied. Taxation without representation was only one of them. The Declaration of Rights and Grievances, issued by the First Continental Congress in 1774, reiterated what Americans thought were their basic rights as Englishmen.

The men who authored the United States Constitution had certain conceptions of what government should do. A basic belief was that government existed to promote limited objectives, namely to protect life, liberty, and property. Further, the framework of government and the powers given to it should be spelled out carefully on paper, in order to avoid any misunderstanding.

Most opposition to ratification of the Constitution arose out of a fear that the new government might usurp the prerogatives of the people and the states, and rather than being a protector of basic rights, the government might become the oppressor. Hence, a number of states, and in particular Virginia, ratified the document only on the condition that certain amplifications of citizens' rights be added. The result was the initiation of twelve proposed amendments, and the eventual ratification of ten of them during the opening months of Washington's presidency. These first ten amendments became known as the Bill of Rights. This removed much criticism of the new government, and the states emerged for a time as the champions of civil rights.

The Alien and Sedition Acts

Still, the original government was very suspicious of democracy, and was somewhat aristocratic in form and interpretation. Adherence to basic human rights was, as it had been during the colonial period, mostly rhetorical. A historic case in point was the passage of the Alien and Sedition Acts in 1798, under the presidency of John Adams. These were included in a series of four separate laws.

A Naturalization Law raised the period of residence for citizenship from five to fourteen years. This act involved no violation of constitutional rights, although it was quite unrealistic. An Alien Friends Act authorized the president to order any alien out of the country if the president personally considered him dangerous. A three-year prison term was authorized for failure to comply, and any alien who had been ordered out of the country and then returned, could be imprisoned indefinitely. An Alien Enemies Act gave the president the authority to imprison any alien from an enemy nation for whatever reasons he chose. A Sedition Act stated that any conspiracy against the government, or any verbal or written attack on the president or Congress, was a high misdemeanor. Conviction of the conspiracy charge carried a $5000 fine and/or a five-year prison term. Conviction of criticizing the president or Congress was punishable by a $2000 fine and/or a two-year prison term. These Alien and Sedition Acts were among the most repressive measures in American history.

These high-handed measures prompted strong protests against the new government. The Kentucky–Virginia Resolutions, authored primarily by Thomas Jefferson, claimed the measures were unconstitutional, and as such, were null and void. This marked the first official use of the not yet fully formulated doctrine of nullification and interposition. According to this theory the state has the right to guarantee its citizens from violations by the federal government, in place of the Supreme Court.

Later popularized by John C. Calhoun in his Exposition and Protest (1828), the viewpoint is still held by some contemporary Americans.

An Era of Open Contradiction

The first real breakdown of aristocratic traditions had its origins in the latter part of the Era of Good Feelings. In 1824 there was only one political party in the country; all were called Jeffersonian Republicans, and ostensibly supported a strong nationalistic approach to government (contrary to Jefferson's early views on sovereignty). But the unity of this party was beginning to break down because of sectional differences. The presidential election of 1824 bore this out.

It is to be recalled that Andrew Jackson was greatly irritated over his failure to be chosen president in 1824. Jackson claimed that he, rather than John Quincy Adams, should have been chosen by the House because he received the most popular votes, not to mention electoral votes. Actually, this had no valid Constitutional basis but Jackson felt that the people had been cheated and he determined to do something about it. The result was the formation of a new national party, the Jacksonian Democratic Party, which drew its principal strength from Americans opposed to rule by a supposed aristocracy.

The climax came in the election of 1828, which Jackson won handsomely. There were a number of factors contributing to his victory over the incumbent Adams in that year. Jackson had to some degree successfully labelled Adams as corrupt. Furthermore, the contest was one of personalities. It was the freedom-loving Jackson, who was "one of the boys" and a military hero, versus the aristocratic, mild-mannered, and aloof Adams.

There was also an important series of extra-personal developments taking place, which were significant by 1828. A broadening suffrage had been evolving, especially prevalent in the new western states which had recently entered the union and possessed no property qualifications for voting. The frontiersmen possessed the right to vote and desired to elect a fellow westerner, Andrew Jackson, to the presidency. Also, suffrage in the East was extended when property qualifications were generally lowered. In many instances eastern factory workers allied with western farmers. Finally, and perhaps most important, by 1828 all but two states chose their presidential electors by popular vote.

A more democratic system had elected Jackson to the presidency, generally with the belief that he would best reflect the will of the people. But the Jacksonian presidency witnessed some major curtailments of civil liberties. One of these had to do with Jackson's Indian policy, which was quite popular at the time.

Jackson's Indian Policy

Initially, the American Indian had not suffered too greatly at the hands of the settlers. This was mainly because there was a large area into which he could retreat, thereby lessening constant contact with the European. But as settlement crossed the Appalachians into the Ohio Valley additional problems began to arise. The general view of the Indian maintained that he must stay out of the white man's way, and allow his lands to be expropriated. Some Indians fought back and others retreated.

The white man claimed that the Indian deserved to be removed because he was uncivilized. If this was the real problem then harmony would be achieved through adaptation. At least, so reasoned the Cherokee. This Indian tribe had completely accepted the white man's civilization. It had reduced its language to a written form and had its own newspaper. It had taken up ranching and farming, and had built schools and homes. It even petitioned Congress for statehood. But southerners wanted Cherokee lands.

The facade of rationalization crumbled. The desire for land linked with an omnipresent racism were the reality. Jackson removed the Cherokee from their lands. Forced to abandon their homes in the dead of winter, they were marched on foot to Oklahoma, over the infamous Trail of Tears. Many other tribes, now knowing what to expect, chose to resist the settler's encroachement. Two Indian wars came in the wake of the Cherokee removal. The Fox and Sauk tribes of northern Illinois were not moving as ordered, and the result was the Black Hawk War. A similar war occured with the Seminole in Florida. Jackson's policy called for removing Indians forcibly and without any moral consideration, because whites wanted their lands. There was little criticism and much elation over his course of action.

In the election of 1832 the nation witnessed the first real political party founded on prejudice. The Anti-Masonic Party appeared primarily to oppose Andrew Jackson (he was a Mason), but also secured a large portion of anti-Catholic sentiment to boot. Its candidate for the presidency was William Wirt of Virginia, who failed to capture a single electoral vote. From this time forward, there existed organized opposition to minority groups and beliefs.

Aspects of American Racism

A dominant theme running throughout pre–Civil War history was the alleged supremacy of Anglo-Saxons. Studying history, some individuals came up with

A Southern Slave Auction

the unfounded and absurd conclusion that the Anglo-Saxons were a superior "race." After all, was not England the trade and commerce capital of the world? And was not the American branch of that race in the process of taming an entire continent? There were then 40 million Anglo-Saxons in the world, and they controlled over half of the world's population. The conclusion was that America was inevitably destined for greatness.

These same racist theories were invoked by Americans at the time of the Mexican War to justify the grabbing of land from Mexico. The reasoning was that Mexicans were inferior, wretched creatures, who were incapable of using their territories properly. Only Americans could fully utilize Mexican territories and resources; therefore, Americans were entitled to them. The pseudo-logic bears strong resemblance to the later theories of the social Darwinists (see Chapter Fifteen).

A growing number of Americans were beginning to question this thinking, especially as it applied to slavery. In a nation which espoused democracy and the dignity of the individual, the existence of slavery was an enigma. It should be pointed out that many people who were opposed to slavery did not advocate racial equality. Others felt that in time the Negro could eventually earn full civil rights, while still others believed that he was entitled to them immediately.

In 1848 the Free Soil Party was formed as a coalition of abolitionists and those who wanted no further spread of slavery and would choke it off by limiting it to its present size. The party did well in the election, sending thirteen delegates to Congress. The dissenting views on slavery in America could no longer be ignored. And when Chief Justice Taney ruled in the Dred Scott case that Negroes were not meant for citizenship, this only further incensed those who felt that slavery was morally wrong.

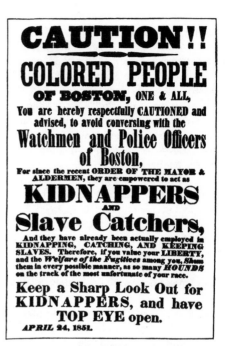

Warning to Freedmen of Their Tenuous Status

The climax came with the presidential election of 1860. Even before the Democratic nominating convention met, the southern states drew up a manifesto stating their position if a Republican was elected to the presidency. Called the Alabama Platform, the manifesto indicated that the South would not submit to the election of the candidate of a "foul sectional party," meaning of course, the Republican Party, which had come out against the further territorial extension of slavery.

Civil Rights in Civil War and Reconstruction

The Republican Abraham Lincoln won and the South seceded even before he was inaugurated. With the firing on the federal post in Charleston Harbor, Fort Sumter, on April 12, 1861, the Civil

War began. At the time few people were talking about ending slavery. In Lincoln's own words, the war was being fought to preserve the Union. But the "peculiar institution" of the South could not be ignored. As the war progressed Union forces were capturing slaves, and the question arose as to what to do with them. In late 1861 a congressional joint resolution called for the emancipation of all slaves held by owners who were hostile to the United States government. In late 1862 Lincoln decided on compensated emancipation and used it in loyal Delaware. The owners received $400 per slave by the government as payment for their erstwhile property.

The Emancipation Proclamation

Because of the growing number of confiscated slaves, and various diplomatic considerations, Lincoln decided to inject a humanitarian motive into the conflict. This was not mere political expediency, although it helped politically; it reflected Lincoln's personal views. In July, 1862, Lincoln drafted the Emancipation Proclamation, then waited for the dubious victory at Antietam before issuing it.

The Proclamation stated that all slaves in areas which were in a state of rebellion against the federal government were free as of January 1, 1863. The measure did not apply to non-secession slave states, nor did it apply to secessionist areas which had already been reconquered. In reality the Proclamation, at the exact time when it was issued, freed not a single slave. The federal government "freed" slaves only in those areas over which it exercised no control. Slavery continued to exist in the United States, and general abolition did not come about until individual states abolished it, or constitutional amendments were ratified after the war.

West Virginia, which had seceded from Virginia and joined the Union when Virginia joined the Confederacy, passed a statute calling for gradual emancipation in 1863. Both Missouri and Maryland abolished slavery early in 1865 while the war was still in progress. The almost immediately reconquered Confederate state of Tennessee (which had managed to escape the provisions of the Emancipation Proclamation by not being in a state of rebellion at the time) did likewise. At the close of the war both Delaware and Kentucky still condoned slavery. And its non-existence in other states rested entirely on state preference and action. So the Civil War itself did not bring an end to slavery in America.

Reconstruction

After the war ended the South had to be reconstructed. It had been socially, economically, and politically devastated. The plantation system based on slave labor had to be replaced. A new class structure which included the newly freed Negroes, a white aristocratic group which had lost much of its former power, and the poorer whites who were then in open competition with the Negro on the labor market, had to be developed. Prior to the Civil War all three groups lived within well defined boundaries. All were aware of their social limits. But after the war no single group knew exactly what its relationships were to the other two. White supremacy was temporarily ended in the South; the southern social system entered upon a stormy, chaotic, and fluid period —which is not yet entirely over.

Lincoln had proposed a reconstruction plan in December, 1863. It simply called for the taking of oaths of future loyalty to the government by 10 per cent of the voters in the 1860 election. The plan contained no civil rights measures, and no proposed constitutional amendments; it was actually quite lenient and sympathetic toward the South.

Congress responded with the Wade–

Davis bill of 1864 which was not at all lenient. It called for loyalty oaths from a majority of all adult white males, and barred all Confederate office holders, state and national, and all who had voluntarily borne arms against the Union, from voting eligibility. Among other measures, states were required to abolish slavery by state constitutional amendment. A conflict immediately developed between the two plans.

Lincoln had sought rapid reunion by utilizing a loyal southern minority and calling for the abolition of slavery. Had he lived he most probably would have allowed most ex-Confederates to re-enter public life and would have given some Negroes the right to vote. But Lincoln was assassinated before he had a chance to put his ideas into effect. His successor, Andrew Johnson, was a weak president, dominated by a Congress which was bent on punishing the South for having caused the war. Johnson, incidentally, believed in the abolition of slavery, but not in civil rights for the Negro. However, Congress and not the president ultimately governed reconstruction policy. In December, 1865, the first of the three reconstruction amendments was ratified. The Thirteenth Amendment prohibited slavery or involuntary servitude.

The Freedman's Bureau

Congress, in response to southern intransigence established a form of aid for the "disadvantaged." Southern states had enacted Black Codes, a series of legislative measures designed to regulate the Negro's role and activities in society. Some regulation was probably needed, but the type enacted was harsh and discriminatory. The congressional answer was the creation of the Freedman's Bureau. First established in March, 1865, for a one-year period, the measure basically called for federal rather than state supervision of Negro problems of re-

adjustment. A new, more stringent Bureau was established in March, 1866. Created for an indefinite period, the new Bureau provided that all court cases involving Negroes would be handled by military rather than state courts.

The new Bureau was supposed to be impartial, educational, and rehabilitative. It sent teachers to prepare Negroes for independence and citizenship. However, these teachers more often than not regarded themselves as missionaries for the radical sentiment. They caused some Negroes who were then completely ignorant of American government (to educate a slave was a crime in some states) to be elected to state and federal offices, where they understandably performed quite poorly. Modern segregationists pointed accusingly at this brief period of Negro rule, although actually most Negro office-holders were being manipulated by vindictive northerners. The general theory behind the Freedman's Bureau was quite good; in practice many contend, however, that it was slightly less than horrible.

Some reconstructionists felt that the Freedman's Bureau did not go far enough, so Congress passed the comprehensive Civil Rights Act of 1866, over President Johnson's veto. The Civil Rights Act applied the federal Bill of Rights to state governments. But Congress had doubts about the constitutionality of this measure (it was clearly unconstitutional), therefore the Fourteenth Amendment was proposed to correct this drawback.

The Amendment prohibited the states from violating the privileges and immunities of federal citizenship, and the deprivation of life, liberty, and property without recourse to due process of law. Another provision abrogated the Three-Fifths Compromise and provided that if a state denied anyone his voting rights without just cause, the state's representation in Congress would be reduced accordingly. Also included were clauses declaring the

Confederate debt null and void, and barring ex-Confederates from ever holding federal or state offices without the approval of two-thirds of both houses of Congress.

Southern Resistance

By March, 1867, this proposed amendment was defeated. There were then thirty-seven states in the Union, and twenty-eight ratifications were needed for adoption (three-fourths of all states). But ten states had already rejected the amendment, seven of which were ex-Confederate states plus three loyal slave states. Congress was greatly disturbed by this turn of events. The result was the passage of a new and more radical Reconstruction Act, in March, 1867.

Congress declared that no legal government existed in any southern state except Tennessee. If the South wanted to regain statehood, it would have to follow a new plan. The South was divided into five military districts, each governed by a general who ruled with martial law. The states were to draft new constitutions which had to include Negro suffrage, disenfranchisement of ex-Confederates, and ratification of the Thirteenth and Fourteenth Amendments. Once a sufficient number of states had ratified the amendments to make them operative, the states could petition for readmittance into the Union. Interestingly enough, Congress was demanding that the southern states perform a legitimate act of a state (ratification) as a condition for becoming a state.

Up to this point many southerners had in some measure cooperated with reconstruction, but they balked at the Fourteenth Amendment. There was a possible out for recalcitrant southerners: the act did not establish procedures or time limits. Therefore, southerners reasoned they could either do nothing and remain under martial law, or follow the

new plan and place themselves under the rule of Negroes, carpetbaggers (northerners who went to the South primarily for material gain), and scalawags (southerners who sympathized with northern attitudes). They did nothing. Congress simply passed another Reconstruction Act, which authorized the military governors to force individuals to form new state constitutions.

In 1869 the last of the reconstruction amendments, the Fifteenth, was proposed. It declared that no person shall be deprived of the right to vote because of race, color, or creed. It was made an integral part of the reconstruction program and ratified in 1870. The South accepted it peaceably because the section was tired of fighting, and because the amendment was worded negatively, thus subject to reinterpretation by the courts at a later date.

However, individual southerners soon began to react to the continued reconstruction measures. They began to protest through such organizations as the Knights of the White Camelia and the Ku Klux Klan. Originally, these were fraternal organizations, consisting of ex-aristocrats who got together to reminisce about the "good old days." But eventually the Klansmen began to play on Negro superstitutions. It was soon discovered that such efforts bore amazing results in keeping Negroes away from the polls. The idea caught on; lower-class whites who intensely hated the Negro joined in, and eventually, serious acts of violence became commonplace. The leadership of the Klan passed over to lower-class southern whites, who most hated and feared the Negro, in part because of economic considerations.

The result of this development was the passage of a series of three congressional measures collectively known as the Force Acts. These measures were aimed primarily at protecting voting rights and at breaking up secret armed organizations. Federal troops were utilized to enforce them. As a result, by 1871 the Klan was practically destroyed and in 1880 was extinct (it would be resurrected by different people in 1915).

Civil Rights Issues through World War I

Taming the "Savages"

While the American Negro was in limbo owing to his semi-free status, the American Indian was faring no better. The old policy of pushing the Indian westward continued until settlement reached the trans-Mississippi West. The western Indian had nowhere to retreat, and he was aware of how eastern tribes had been treated by the white man. Added to this, the Plains Indian was a skilled hunter and horseman, and an especially fierce fighter when aroused. He refused to be pushed, and would use every ounce of his strength to preserve his dwindling freedom.

The pre–Civil War period had witnessed scores of broken treaties and bloody battles; clashes between whites and Indians had never really abated. Beginning in 1867 the government pursued in earnest a policy of placing all Indians on reservations. The governmental attitude was well explained when a high ranking official claimed that no honor was involved when dealing with savages. The tribes were gradually pushed onto reservations, but decades of bloody war followed before the Indian was reconciled or subdued.

In 1884 Congress passed the Dawes Act. This measure was designed to break up the tribal system, and emphasized individual land ownership. Each Indian family was given a quarter section of land, and if they behaved satisfactorily, provisions were made to grant them citizenship after a twenty-five–year period. As matters turned out citizenship was granted

to all Indians only in 1924; prior to that time they were merely wards of the national government, living a pauperized life on worthless western reservations. American Indians acquired basic civil rights with their citizenship, but these were very often violated. In 1934 Congress passed the Indian Reorganization Act, restoring the old tribal system, which gave the Indians some incentive for self-improvement. But many American Indians, even in our prosperous age, live a life of abject poverty. A group whose dignity has been destroyed over a period of centuries cannot be expected to regain it within a couple of generations.

The ugly image of prejudice reared its head again in the 1890's. American theories of Anglo-Saxon racial superiority took on the complexion of the "mission theory." The underlying assumption was that Anglo-Saxon Americans were far superior to everyone else, and in their magnanimity recognized some duty to uplift the primitives of the world. This was one of the assumptions implicit in the rising American imperialism. Yet it was contradictory. With the annexation of both Hawaii and the Philippines major opposition arose over the fact that the natives, primarily non-white, could use their new citizenship as a means of entering the United States. The attitude succeeded in delaying Hawaiian annexation for a time and also complicated the Philippine issue.

Racism and the Far East

The conclusion of the Russo-Japanese War at the Portsmouth Conference of 1905, called through the efforts of Teddy Roosevelt, brought to a head another controversy. Japan had not obtained the war indemnity she desired, and since her resources had been severely strained by the war effort, depression and unemployment resulted. Japanese workers came to the West Coast seeking employment (there were already numbers of Chinese in California dating from the period when the transcontinental railroads were built). Many Californians resented the presence of the Japanese; it was another plain case of racial prejudice. In October, 1906, the San Francisco Board of Education ordered all Orientals (there were ninety-three) to attend segregated schools, giving as the reason that they were crowding the white children out. Japan considered the action to be an insult to her honor and her people; she was right on both counts.

President Roosevelt was stymied. He had no control over the local school board, but that board had created an international controversy. Roosevelt diplomatically effected a compromise solution. San Francisco would rescind the segregation order if Roosevelt would halt further Japanese immigration. Japan refused to comply with such a discriminatory immigration policy, but she did agree to halt the issuance of passports temporarily. This Gentlemen's Agreement solved the immediate problem. However, other problems continued to crop up between the two nations, tending to make the Japanese increasingly resentful and belligerent.

During the Wilson years the issue with Japan became more serious. An attempt was being made to pass a law in the California state legislature which would deny Japanese-Americans the right to own land. Wilson did not object; he asked simply that the law not be worded directly so as to arouse Japanese hostility. Wilson was a racist and Californians knew it. The President had issued new segregation orders for the federal civil service which set back Negro gains by at least twenty years. Therefore they worded the law directly in spite of his suggestion, and Japan was further incensed with the United States.

War and Civil Liberties

During World War I most civil rights were curtailed. There were a few individuals who actively resisted the war effort, and there were some cases of espionage and sabotage. The Industrial Workers of the World, a radical union branded the war as a capitalistic plot. Socialists in general were also opposed, though they were usually law-abiding. But after the Bolshevik revolution in Russia, some sympathizers became quite vociferous. And in their attempt to further spread the supposedly inevitable revolution of the proletariat, the American Communist Party found its obscure beginnings. Both the Revolution and its supporters helped cause a wave of hysteria and fear, out of which developed the Red Scare of 1919–1920.

Actually this response was far out of proportion to the alleged danger. It resulted in the passage of a number of federal laws designed to eliminate and punish the disloyal. For the second time in American history the nation witnessed a severe curtailment of basic constitutional privileges.

The Espionage Act of 1917 provided a maximum fine of $10,000 and/or twenty years imprisonment for the obstruction or attempted obstruction of the military. The law was aimed initially at pacifist and later at communist groups which were encouraging young men to avoid the draft. Compare the severity of this law with what Americans are allowed to do today while protesting the Vietnam conflict.

The Trade with the Enemy Act of 1917 created the office of Alien Property Custodian and established federal controls over international trade. The Alien Property Custodian was empowered to seize and control the personal property of aliens and enemy nationals residing in the United States for the duration of the war. As it turned out some of these people did not regain their property after the war, and the office was the center of a serious scandal in the 1920's.

A series of minor laws gave the Post Office Department various wartime powers. One such law authorized the strict censorship of the American foreign-language press. Another empowered the postmaster general to ban from the mail anything which he considered disloyal literature. And still another authorized the strict censorship of all mail leaving the country.

The Sabotage Act of 1918 made it a federal crime to destroy any private property having anything to do with the war effort. This particular act pertained primarily to any mode of transportation and to any equipment used, or which could possibly be used, for war production. It covered almost everything.

And last, but definitely not the least serious, was the Sedition Act of 1918 which was undoubtedly the most repressive piece of wartime legislation in the nation's history. The act made it a federal crime to utter a disloyal statement. Exceedingly vague, the law was enforced indiscriminately. Two classic examples bear this out.

A Socialist, Mrs. Rose Stokes, was sentenced to a ten-year prison term for the following statement: "I am for the people, and the government is for the profiteers." Yet most loyal progressives would have agreed with her statement. (Her conviction was eventually reversed.) Eugene Debs, another leading Socialist, received a ten-year jail sentence for referring to the war as "the supreme curse of capitalism." After serving some three years of his sentence he was pardoned by President Harding.

The behavior of the super-patriots was considerably more distasteful than that of anti-war groups. Various "do-gooders" were encouraged to report the "suspicious" behavior of their neighbors. Every German-American allegedly was a spy for the Kaiser's war machine. There were many persecutions of loyal German-Americans, simply because Germany had been the land of their birth. Homes of German-Americans were burned by "patriots"; their businesses were destroyed; occasionally, there were lynchings. Anyone who listened to a composition by Wagner or Beethoven was committing a disloyal act. There were numerous public burnings of German-authored books and art objects. The teaching of the German language in schools was discontinued. The wild anti-German frenzy created a new parlance . Hamburger became "swiss steak"; dachshunds became "liberty pups"; the frankfurter became the "hot dog"; sauerkraut became "liberty cabbage"; German measles became "liberty measles", etc.

Although public behavior cannot be condoned, it can be explained. In 1917 the population of the United States was roughly 100 million. Of this number 8 million had been born in Germany, and 500,000 were technically members of the German reserve army. Obviously, they ignored and repudiated their reserve status upon becoming American citizens. However, the Attorney General still publicly suggested that the use of 500,000 lamp posts would remove this threat to American security. The fact that 8 per cent of the population had originated in the enemy's land quite naturally had an unnerving effect, but it did not excuse what transpired. The most loyal German-American suffered acutely. There was little room for non-conformity in wartime America. In 1916 Wilson had expressed the fear that unbridled hatred might descend on the American people if they became involved in a major war. It

turned out to be a highly accurate pre-
diction.

Women's Suffrage

The end of the war witnessed both
advance and retrogression on the issue of
civil rights. In 1919 the Nineteenth
Amendment was ratified, giving women
the right to vote. Although voting is a
political rather than a civil right, the
acquisition of the power of the ballot
placed women in a position whereby they
could effectively bring to an end their
second-class civil status. The hopes of a
century of protest, demonstration, and
struggle had finally been realized.

The Red Scare

However, in contradiction to this
notable advance, 1919 also witnessed the
beginning of the Red Scare. Fear of Bol-
sheviks, European disorder, plotting
anarchists, bomb rumors, and the under-
mining of the government by subversives,
brought the American people to a semi-
hysterical state. In many eyes anyone
critical of the traditional American system
was suspected of being a radical. Therefore, pacifists, reformers, labor leaders,
and socialists were all highly suspect.

There had been a violent reaction
to people not fully behind the war effort,
and now this was transferred to all who
were thought to favor a leftist view of
society. In 1919 this emotionalism was
further compounded by an exaggerated
and primarily irrational fear of the
Soviets. Some prominent government
officials were in the vanguard of this mass
hysterical movement. Attorney General
Palmer, with an eye toward the presidential nomination in 1920, was one of
them. Seven of the nine members of the
Supreme Court supported such feelings
and upheld laws designed to implement
them (Justices Holmes and Brandeis were
the only defenders of constitutional

rights). Wilson himself appeared to have
become totally intolerant of any pacifist,
anarchist, or socialist. And the newly
formed American Legion performed real
yeoman service in vitalizing and perpetu-
ating the current hysteria.

The Red Scare reached its zenith in
early 1920 with the Palmer Raids, initiated
by the Attorney General. In late December, 1919, he had rounded up 249
Russian aliens and forcibly deported
them to the Soviet Union. The idea
mushroomed; in January, 1920, in a
nationwide Palmer Raid, approximately
4,000 suspected radicals were arbitrarily
thrown in jail, in total disregard for constitutional rights. The hysteria was so
serious that when a New York Socialist
named Berger was elected to Congress, he
was denied his seat. In a special election
he was re-elected but again denied his seat.
In a second special election he won again
by an even greater majority, and this time
Congress went along with the wishes of
his constituency.

The unquestionable illegality of the
Palmer Raids and their flouting of constitutional rights created a counter-move
toward more sane conduct. A standing
attempt to continue the wartime anti-
sedition legislation was defeated. Responsible Americans were able to point
out that the Palmerites were really the
ones who constituted a threat to American democracy.

A Growing Impetus for
Full Civil Rights

Violations of civil rights during the
1920's stemmed mainly from a movement
known as fundamentalism. A struggle
within Protestant ranks over the prevailing national temper (materialistic, hedonistic, and scientific) had resulted in
a temporary victory for conservative
religious leaders. Based in a Calvinist
theology espoused mainly by a group of

religious extremists, this so-called fundamentalism of the Twenties gave no quarter to the modern thinker. No credence was paid to technological discoveries or intellectual theorizing. All truth was supposed to be derived from literal interpretations of the Bible. A fundamentalist did not question a literal reading of the Book of Genesis. Geologists who claimed otherwise were obviously the agents of the devil. And above all, the hardly new theory of evolution was held to be downright immoral.

Fundamentalism resulted in the historic Scopes case (Monkey Trial) in Dayton, Tennessee, held in the summer of 1925. It seems that the political strength of the fundamentalists was such that various state legislatures passed laws supporting and buttressing their beliefs. To teach evolution in the schools was not only a crime against fundamentalist religious beliefs; it was made a crime against the state as well.

The Ku Klux Klan, which had been re-established in 1915 was, and still is, primarily a fundamentalist group. It marked an attempt to establish by force what was not being accomplished by law. To a certain extent, religious fundamentalism led to an unholy alliance of the Klan, the American Legion, the Daughters of the American Revolution, the American First Foundation, and such industrial notables as Henry Ford, which attacked whatever was not considered to be traditionally American. It was in part a reaction to post-war problems and the progressive measures which had preceded it. This reaction included careful scrutiny of all textbooks and public library acquisitions. It involved a considerable amount of anti-Jewish and to a lesser degree, anti-Catholic sentiment. It did not weaken until the events of the Depression gave people other things with which to concern themselves.

All along the groundwork was being established for the Negro civil rights movement. The South had re-established a semi-slave system with the close of reconstruction. Negroes realized that their few civil rights were rapidly being denied them; Jim Crow laws, southern segregationist legislation, had taken them away. The Supreme Court case of *Plessy* v. *Ferguson* (1896) had given legal sanction to segregation. Also, various state laws were enacted in the latter nineteenth century to maintain the Negro in an inferior position. But the majority of the nation was uninterested. The National Association for the Advancement of Colored People, established in 1909 in an attempt to assert basic rights for Negroes, was initially unsuccessful. Other early developments occurred during World War I, with the exodus of Negroes to northern cities, and the establishment of Negro combat units. The Negro "problem" was rapidly taking on the form of a national dilemma. The emergence of the Klan, of bitter fundamentalism, and of widespread prejudice kept any advances from being made for a time. It was actually during and after the presidency of Franklin Roosevelt that the civil rights guaranteed in the Constitution began to be applied to all peoples. The struggle is not nearly over.

The Effect of the Second World War

The World War II era again witnessed the eruption of wartime hysteria and the concomitant trampling of basic constitutional rights. However, the American people did not reach the repressive extreme experienced during the First World War. This was probably because there was not as much dissent over the war effort. Socialists and communists tended to support the war very strongly because they were extremely interested in aiding the threatened Soviet Union.

Most wartime problems arose from fascist organizations operating in the United States. Members of some groups were engaged in sabotage and espionage activities; the German American Bund was one of these. The Federal Bureau of Investigation proceeded quite effectively against these subversives, who were usually tried in military courts and sometimes given the death sentence. General rabble-rousers were tried in civilian courts and were normally locked up for the duration. Some were simply forced into positions which rendered them ineffectual, but were allowed to remain free.

The activities against subversives and dissenters by the government was usually fair. However, there was one area in which the government performed in a most uncommendable manner. This concerned the action taken against American citizens of Japanese ancestry. It was decided to relocate approximately 110,-000 Japanese-Americans from the West Coast. Roughly 75,000 of them were native-born American citizens. The government claimed that there was a sufficiently high level of disloyalty among these people to justify the action. These charges were later proven to be entirely groundless. However, not unlike the Cherokees a century earlier, the Japanese were abruptly moved to relocation camps in the interior of the nation. The move wreaked havoc on their personal and financial lives; no doubt racism was a significant factor in the decision.

During the course of the war the nation experienced other stresses and strains. The population was exceedingly mobile as needs developed for large concentrations of workers at various locations to handle wartime production schedules. The population shift was responsible for creating new racial tensions, particularly with respect to the Negro-Americans who left the rural South in ever-increasing numbers to work in northern industrial centers.

The influx spread beyond the traditional Negro sections of town, and clashes occurred with white groups. Minor race riots became commonplace. The riot in Detroit, in June, 1943, was one of the worst in American history. Racial strife was given additional impetus by two conflicting notions. Whites tended to regard every Negro as an inferior, bumbling person. Negroes, on the other hand, were beginning to acquire a new, more positive identity. In some factories they had jobs equal to those held by whites. And perhaps more significant in forming this new self-image was the performance of Negro troops overseas.

Beginning of Integration

In face of mounting pressure several notable breakthroughs occurred. An executive order forbade racial discrimination in defense plants. A Fair Employment Practices Committee was established to implement this order. The Army began commissioning Negro officers during the latter part of the war, and eventually some 8,000 Negroes held commissions. It was a fairly crude beginning, but World War II provided the impetus for a growing clamor for equality, which was destined to culminate in the contemporary civil rights movement.

During the war, however, most conditions were quite bad. Whites would often call wildcat strikes if a Negro happened to get a better job than a white man. The Red Cross Blood Bank segregated Negro-donated blood. Needless to state, those countries which the United States was then fighting made tremendous propaganda capital out of these incidents, just as contemporary adversaries exploit America's current domestic turmoil.

The 1944 presidential election pointed clearly to future political alignments. Franklin Roosevelt earlier had gained the support of the laboring forces and Negroes who crowded the northern cities. They were one of the main sources of his political power. Therefore, when he decided to run for an unprecedented fourth term in 1944, it stood to reason that his stand on Negro rights would play an important role in the campaign. The Republican platform as well made a bid for Negro support when it called for anti-lynching legislation and the abolishment of the poll tax.

The Democratic Party was far from unified in 1944. Southern Democrats were opposed to the President's general desegregation attitude, and they were violently opposed to Vice-President Henry Wallace's stand on the abolition of the poll tax. There were some threats and rumors that the southern Democrats would bolt the party. Therefore Wallace was replaced by a compromise vice-presidential candidate, Senator Harry S. Truman, of Missouri. The Democrats maintained Negro allegiance and won the election. But the political stage had been set for the appearance of the Dixiecrats in 1948.

The Civil Rights Movement

In the Democratic national convention of 1948, Truman was easily nominated. His civil-rights plank was adopted exactly as he desired, mainly through the efforts of Hubert Humphrey. When this happened thirty-five southern delegates walked off the convention floor. Southern Democrats (Dixiecrats) organized the States' Rights Party which polled 1,170,-000 popular votes in the election, carrying four states and thirty-nine electoral votes. But Harry Truman still won the election and his party captured control of both houses of Congress.

Moderately successful with his Fair Deal domestic program, Truman's major setback concerned his civil rights program. The President had appointed a Committee on Civil Rights back in 1946. This group had made a number of recom-

mendations, such as the abolition of the poll tax, federal anti-lynching legislation, and federal instead of state enforcement of already existing civil rights legislation. Truman annually submitted his request to Congress, and Congress annually turned it down, thanks to a solid coalition of southern Democrats and their threat of a filibuster. But the President did succeed in putting a few dents in the walls of inequality.

He was the first president to appoint a Negro to the federal judiciary. He invited leading Negroes to his inauguration. He ended segregation in the Armed Forces by executive order in 1948. He wiped out some of the segregation in government offices. Considering the fact that the United States was experiencing a period of prosperity, and considering that unrest was definitely not widespread, Truman accomplished a great deal. The nation was not in a reforming mood.

Education and Civil Rights

In the 1952 presidential election the Republicans endorsed the "principle" of civil rights. The Democrats, however, again called for a full civil rights program. But the election was not really concerned with domestic issues. The Korean War took precedence over all other problems, and Eisenhower won in large part because of his promise to end the war. Still, the Eisenhower years witnessed the first monumental government action on the civil rights issue. The historic *Brown* v. *Board of Education* Supreme Court case in 1954, overruled segregation in the public schools. Overturning the half-century –old "separate but equal" doctrine, the decision set the stage for the desegregation of many public activities and facilities. Partial elimination of employment discrimination was achieved in companies handling government contracts. And after one unsuccessful attempt, Eisenhower obtained the passage of the Civil

'It's Just A Matter Of Time Now, Before It Falls'

WALL OF SEGREGATION

U. S. SUPREME COURT

Historical Pictures Service, Chicago

Rights Act of 1957. Vice-President Richard Nixon and Democratic Senate majority leader Lyndon Johnson were instrumental in its passage. However, the Act was considerably weaker than what Harry Truman had originally proposed. The law established a Civil Rights Commission, authorized federal court injunctions against denial of voting rights in federal elections, established uniform standards for jury selection, and appointed an assistant attorney general to handle civil-rights issues.

In one area of the civil-rights struggle Eisenhower was forcefully challenged. Governor Orval Faubus, of Arkansas, attempted to obstruct the carrying out of public school desegregation in his state. After an eruption of violence, President Eisenhower sent in paratroopers and federalized the Arkansas National Guard. The full force of the federal government was finally being utilized to enforce the desegregation order.

The civil-rights issues was not, by any means, settled. Similar confrontations occurred in Alabama and Mississippi during the Kennedy administration. Two rather stringent civil-rights acts were passed in the early 1960's. The Civil Rights Act of 1960 required states and localities to maintain accurate voting records, and authorized the Attorney General to investigate these records. Where voting violations were discovered, federal courts could appoint "referees" who, in conjunction with the courts, could enforce compliance.

A more complete Civil Rights Act was passed in 1964. It barred racial discrimination in public accomodations, and strengthened the enforcement of voting rights and the carrying out of school desegregation rulings. The machinery and a timetable was established to end employment discrimination, and an Equal Employment Opportunity Commission was set up. Additionally, discrimination in any federal program or activity was expressly forbidden. A Voting Rights Act in 1965 further strengthened the enforcement of voting rights provisions.

Problems within the Movement

But the advances in the realm of civil rights are being marred by murders, violations of basic human rights by some local authorities, lawlessness on the part of some civil rights demonstrators, and a wave of race riots originating in such urban areas as Watts and Harlem. The concept of nonviolence as developed by Martin Luther King, Jr. for his Southern Christian Leadership Conference in 1957, has somewhat fallen by the wayside, and some Negro leaders are openly threatening violence if significant advances are not made.

The original strategy of nonviolence enjoyed some success, especially in the static South and in influencing the federal government to take more positive action. But it did not provide the degree of accomplishment desired by many civil-rights advocates. As a result the civil-rights movement began to fragment. It now lacks unity of purpose. The momentum which it created continues, although its future remains uncertain in view of the murder of Martin Luther King in 1968. In the aftermath of King's assassination, Congress responded with the Civil Rights Act of 1968, a monumental attempt to outlaw all aspects of segregation and inequality in American society.

Minority groups have gained most of their political rights, as well as the recognition and partial implementation of their social rights; the main problem remaining is poverty, which prevents many people from enjoying and making use of their rights. Poverty breeds on itself and must be eradicated if civil and political equality are to be attained. This comprises a fundamental part of the goals of the federal government in the 1960's.

For Further Reading

Barth, Alan. *The Loyalty of Free Men.* New York: The Viking Press, 1951.

———. *The Price of Liberty.* New York: The Viking Press, 1961.

Berger, Morroe. *Equality by Statute: The Revolution in Civil Rights.* Garden City: Doubleday and Company, 1967.

Brant, Irving. *The Bill of Rights: Its Origin and Meaning.* Indianapolis: Bobbs-Merrill, 1965.

Brophy, William A., and Aberle, Sophie D. (comp.). *The Indian: America's Unfinished Business.* Norman: University of Oklahoma Press, 1966.

Emerson, Thomas I., and Haber, David. *Political and Civil Rights in the United States.* 2 volumes, rev. ed. Buffalo, New York: Dennis and Company, 1964.

Ferguson, Clarence C. *Desegregation and the Law.* New Brunswick: Rutgers University Press, 1957.

Handlin, Oscar and Mary. *The Dimensions of Liberty.* Cambridge: Harvard University Press, 1961.

Longaker, Richard P. *The Presidency and Individual Liberties.* Ithaca: Cornell University Press, 1961.

Parker, Donald, O'Neil, Robert, and Nicholas, Econopouly. *Civil Liberties: Case Studies and the Law.* Boston: Houghton Mifflin, 1965.

Chapter Ten
American Education

The ideology of the American Revolution in part grew out of the European Enlightenment in an age when men were freely investigating and inquiring into the fundamental nature of things. The powers of the human intellect were being emphasized, and men once again postulated that they could influence their environment. The dynamic assumptions of the European Enlightenment often found popular expression among the pioneers of the New World.

Democracy has at its very core the assumption that people are capable of governing themselves. However this assumption depends on the intellectual ability of the people to understand the problems of an increasingly complex world. There is quite an obvious difference between having a capability and actually utilizing that capability. Hence, many of the theoreticians and founders of the American republic continually emphasized the necessity for proper education in order to insure the success of the American nation.

Thomas Jefferson deserves credit for doing much to popularize the value and need of education. He claimed that democracy could not succeed without an intelligent electorate. Benjamin Franklin, Noah Webster, and Benjamin Rush were not far behind in advocating the same basic idea.

A discussion of the development and role of education is especially significant because the educational system exerts a strong effect on the entire American structure. There were about 2.5 million teachers in the United States in the fall of 1967. Taking into account administrative personnel, office help, and maintenance people, this number could be increased to approximately 3.25 million people directly employed by educational institutions. This means approximately $26 billion in direct salaries per year, not to mention the outlay for buildings, equipment, and supplies. A number of auxiliary industries, such as publishing houses, laboratory suppliers, and of course, the construction industry itself, would compound these figures to a great degree. Education is an integral part of the American economy; it is big business.

Also, by sheer force of numbers, those people involved in education are potentially a major political force. Of course, educators as a group suffer from the same drawback as other large groups, namely, lack of unanimity in political goals. Still, the politician cannot really afford to alienate them, and there has developed over recent decades a fairly close tie between higher education and government defense and research programs. Top ranking professors, particularly in science, international relations, and business, have become consultants to the government. Also, the federal government is financing expensive research projects on college campuses across the nation.

There is another and perhaps more significant aspect to education. The professional educator influences opinions, values, and attitudes. Thomas Jefferson was quite correct when he wrote of the value of education for the success of a democracy. An estimated 55 million people, over one-fourth of the nation's total population, are attending schools, and confronting ideas which will affect their attitudes, beliefs, and values, either consciously or subconsciously.

The importance of education, as society becomes more complex, will vastly increase. More wealth and more power have been gained in the past decade than during any other comparable period in American history.

Colonial Educational Developments

Early in the colonial period Americans began to establish an educational system, particularly in the New England and the middle colonies. In the southern colonies, because of their aristocratic nature, there was nothing which remotely approached democratic education. There existed no formal education for any but members of this elite, which employed tutors to instruct their young. Upon completion of tutoring, they would continue their education either in Europe, or at the new American college, William and Mary, founded in 1693.

New Englanders, in contrast, were deeply concerned about education for everyone. Every town had its public school, and many laws were passed obligating parents to provide a prescribed number of years of formal education for their children. However, the subject matter of New England's public schools was primarily religious. Very little attention was given to secular subjects. Nonetheless, regardless of the motivation, the tradition of a public school education for everyone was being established. New England established a number of colleges during the colonial period, primarily to train and educate future ministers. These include Harvard founded in 1636, Yale founded in 1701, Brown founded in 1764, and Dartmouth founded in 1769. Gradually, these divinity schools added various secular subjects and evolved into contemporary universities with widely diverse programs.

Public schools also appeared at quite an early date in the Middle Colonies, but they did not receive the same emphasis as in New England. Responsibility for education rested primarily with the various religious groups, and the number of strictly public institutions was quite limited. Education was derived mainly from the reading of religious works. And all institutions of higher learning originated as training schools for future clergymen. The Anglicans established King's College (the future Columbia) in 1754. The Presbyterians founded Princeton in 1746, and the Dutch Reformed Church established Rutgers in 1766. Benjamin Franklin sponsored a secular academy in

Philadelphia in 1751, which was destined forty years later to provide the basis for the University of Pennsylvania.

Throughout the settlement period in America, schools were either sparse or entirely lacking on the frontier. The people possessed neither the time nor the leisure for educational activities. Also, they were not sufficiently concentrated to justify a school economically; transportation was exceedingly difficult.

Notable progress was made in colonial America in the field of higher education. Unfortunately, the same was not true for the lower levels of education. Long before the American Revolution the New England town school was beginning to deteriorate. There were two reasons for this. One was the debilitating effect of the European Enlightenment on American religion, especially significant as New England schools were religiously oriented. The other was the growing instability of New England towns; younger people often abandoned them seeking better opportunities, and the towns began to wither away. In an attempt to fill the gap, various prominent New Englanders began to establish and finance private academies.

Little change occurred in the South's educational system up to the revolutionary period, but there were some developments in the middle colonies. Public education continued to exist, but the colonists also established private academies, similar to those in New England. Additionally, because of the existence of large numbers of non–English-speaking peoples in the middle colonies, particularly Germans, private ethnic schools were established.

But for most people, colonial American education was acquired either in an informal manner or through a fairly well developed apprentice system. The written word was widely disseminated in colonial America, and since many colonists came from the European middle class, they knew how to write and read. The first printing press in the colonies was set up in Massachusetts in 1639. Several other New England colonies established printing presses before the close of the seventeenth century. During the course of the eighteenth century, newspapers (broadsides) and magazines spread rapidly. There were forty-three newspapers being published in America by 1765. These newspapers were unlike modern ones because they were devoted in large measure to the publication of literary essays.

Most original literary work was imported from Europe; some colonists accumulated large book collections. Intellectual historians contend that ideas from these private libraries were transferred to the more widely read newspapers, and in that manner filtered down to the populace. New England clergymen and southern planters generally appeared to be the most avid collectors and readers.

Because of the great expense involved in purchasing books, attempts were made to establish public libraries. Again, this was primarily a middle and New England colonial development. Boston established the first colonial public library in 1656. More widely in vogue during the pre-revolutionary period were the subscription libraries, championed by Benjamin Franklin. These were open to the general public for in-house use; only those who paid substantial annual dues could borrow any books.

The Developmental Stage of American Education

During the Revolutionary era, Thomas Jefferson established the most complete theory concerning American education. His entire political philosophy, influenced largely by Plato's *Republic,* rested on the proper education of the citizenry. If all men would be taught virtue, he reasoned, there would be no need for strong government. Jefferson was an important advocate of the value of education, and also of the responsibility of government in making education possible.

The status of higher education changed little over the next half century, but some developments did occur on the lower educational levels. Education remained largely a private matter, but there was a move, especially during the Jacksonian period, in the direction of free universal public education.

The Bible remained the basic textbook but new educational "texts" were being developed. Especially popular were William McGuffey's *Eclectic Readers* and Peter Parley's textbooks. Most education ended with grade school. By 1840 for every hundred grade school graduates there were ten who eventually completed high school and one who completed college. However, most people never graduated from grade school; two or three years was probably the average time spent in school. Women were still generally excluded from higher education. The first woman to receive a college degree graduated from Oberlin College in 1841.

On the lower educational levels, major emphasis was on reading, writing, and numbers. Education in public schools was extremely practical. In private academies the emphasis was different: the goal was to prepare people for college, and consequently different subject areas were introduced, mainly the liberal arts. College students followed an exacting curriculum devoted to classical languages, philosophy, literature, and music. There was little room for deviation because the elective system did not exist. This produced graduates who were well-equipped to be polished gentlemen, but who were

often unequipped for gainful employment. However, there were several noteworthy developments: the establishment of a number of state normal schools and various church-related colleges in the Mississippi Valley.

Medical education was very poor. Little scientific knowledge was possessed by most Americans, and the common remedy for illness was blood-letting, a practice based on the erroneous assumption that illness was caused by blood. The most significant medical achievement of the period was the discovery of smallpox vaccination (it had been discovered by the Chinese in the fourth century but was unknown to the Western World). Most operations, including major amputations, were performed with the patient either conscious or in a drunken stupor. Anesthetics did not appear until the 1840's. Also, there was a general tendency for barbers to double as physicians. Most Americans, particularly frontiersmen, used home remedies for illnesses and performed their own surgical operations.

Dentistry was just as bad. The most common remedy for a toothache was a well-applied set of pliers, usually handled by the local blacksmith. Occasionally, teeth were "saved" temporarily by means of a hand drill, and slivers of hard wood being driven into the cavity to act as filling. Some people had false teeth, and initially these were made out of wood.

For both the dentist and the physician, a couple of correspondence courses and a not too thorough examination usually bought a title. Strict state licensing requirements did not exist. But these professions were not really different from most others. To become a lawyer, for instance, meant to apprentice oneself to a practicing attorney for a time, then begin practice whenever it was felt sufficient knowledge had been acquired. Formal schooling was not a requirement. Some notable impetus for the development of formal education resulted from the pas-

Medicine in the Civil War

sage of the Morrill Land Grant Act of 1862. Under its provisions the federal government gave the states 30,000 acres of land for each electoral vote possessed by the state. The proceeds from this land had to be used to finance the building and operation of agricultural and mechanical colleges. The precedent for this Act was the Ordinance of 1785, which had established the survey system used throughout the development of the country, and had reserved Section Sixteen of each township for the support of public education. The Morrill Act laid the foundation for many of the major state universities.

Education during the Age of Big Business

The age of big business which followed the termination of the Civil War had a somewhat deadening effect on the American cultural scene. One of the bright spots was in the realm of public education. However, the potential of popular education was really a regional experience. The southern educational system, what little there was, had been obliterated by the war. It was not rebuilt and southern education lagged far behind the systems established in other parts of the country.

In the North there was a definite trend in the direction of universal free public education through the secondary level. Seven million children were enrolled in the nation's public schools in 1870; by 1900 this figure had increased to 15 million. The entire nation spent $63 million on public education in 1870; by 1900 the figure was well over $1 billion, much of which, however, was in the form of construction of school buildings.

On the college level the trend was away from the humanities and toward more practical courses of study. The traditional study of liberal arts was being replaced by such subjects as bookkeeping, engineering, and management. The elective system so familiar to contemporary American college students was being developed.

The entire scope of education was changing. But this was not a sudden development. During the course of the nineteenth century, well over 10,000 American students acquired university training in Germany. While there, they learned German educational techniques. These included minute specialization of subject matter, the conducting of monographic studies, and the scientific laboratory approach. These techniques were brought back to America where university training was still quite primitive.

Development of Graduate Studies

Advanced, or postgraduate studies did not really begin in the United States until the 1870's, with the introduction of the German seminar method. The postgraduate research degree was the German Doctor of Philosophy. The Ph.D. came into its own around 1880, even though Yale had granted the nation's first Ph.D. in 1861. Real impetus for advanced graduate education appeared with the founding of Johns Hopkins University in 1876 by Daniel Gilman. Harvard, the University of Chicago, and Columbia quickly developed graduate programs. Such disciplines as economics, political science, and history were given autonomy, and degrees were awarded in these subjects. Formerly, literature or philosophy embraced all of these disciplines.

Various professional organizations were founded. Examples include the American Historical Association, the American Psychological Association, the Mississippi Valley Historical Association, the American Philosophical Association, and the American Bar Association. All

told, approximately 250 different learned societies were organized during the last three decades of the nineteenth century.

Generally, however, professional schools were rather poor. Passing marks in a few courses still usually earned a Bachelor of Medicine degree, and the recipient was technically a physician. Most people continued to frequent the local blacksmith rather than the dentist. But the nation was at the beginning of a period of tremendous progress in the medical profession, and improvements were being made constantly. This was partly owing to the availability of large sums of money for educational purposes, plus the fact that the United States was developing scientifically and culturally as a nation.

There was also a considerable growth of private institutions of higher learning, which were founded and financed by individual industrialists. Leland Stanford of railroad fame endowed Stanford University. Commodore Vanderbilt, shipping and railroad magnate, established Vanderbilt University. John Rockefeller, oil entrepreneur, endowed the University of Chicago. And people such as Andrew Carnegie were busy constructing public libraries across the land. Also, many new state colleges were developing, primarily as a result of the heavy endowment authorized under the terms of the Morrill Act passed during Lincoln's administration.

There existed a general trend to conduct private schools along the lines of business organizations. Instead of successful teachers, businessmen were beginning to administer colleges. The new administrators emphasized budgetary control and expansion programs, the very techniques of business organizations. In addition, these men effected some substantial changes in the educational curriculum. They wanted the practical brainpower needed to run large corporations, and since most schools were

Conducting Exams at Princeton College

supported by big-business donations, they tended to accept the new directives. Engineering, physics, commerce and finance, and the practical arts were greatly emphasized. Even in the state educational systems, where the state legislatures ultimately controlled the colleges, the results were the same. For the legislatures were also controlled by big-business.

Bringing Knowledge down to Earth

Helping to justify these developments was the American philosophy popularly known as pragmatism. One of the key tenets of pragmatism held that philosophy should concern itself with contemporary social problems, rather than traditional metaphysics. John Dewey claimed that both the new philosophy and the educational system should avoid abstract ideas, and deal with concrete, realistic problems of everyday life.

Dewey, like Jefferson, steadfastly expounded on the role of a proper education. He maintained that it was in the field of education where the practical-minded philosopher could best demonstrate his effectiveness and influence. Dewey was intimately involved in restructuring traditional American educational processes. He emphasized group activities and more practically oriented studies. He saw the social sciences as being perhaps the most important of all studies, because they were practical disciplines, devoted to the betterment of social living.

One of the most marked developments in the general field of education during the latter nineteenth century, was the popularization of knowledge. In all societies and in all ages there has existed a wide gap between an educated class and the so-called common man. But a peculiarity of the American social structure is that this gap has been fairly narrow. It is the contention of many intellectual historians that the United

States has made greater progress in creating an articulation between scholars and the popular mind than almost any other nation. This reconciliation was effected largely during the age of big business, and a number of factors were responsible.

The work of Edward Youmans in popularizing science was one very important factor. As all students are aware, there are often both simple and difficult ways of handling the same subject. Rather than write about abstract theories in the field of science, Youmans wrote some easily understandable scientific textbooks, which had practical application in the popular mind. Besides this, Youmans developed the *Popular Science Monthly* into a magazine which was widely read.

What also had an important effect on the popularization of knowledge was the major movement for adult education. In 1874 a man named Henry Leipziger inaugurated a series of evening lectures at the New York City Young Men's Hebrew Association. During the 1880's the Young Men's Christian Association organized evening adult education courses across the nation.

Also in 1874, Lewis Miller, a wealthy industrialist, organized the Chautauqua Assembly, not too unlike the Lyceum movement established by Josiah Holbrook in the 1820's. It was Miller's contention (and Holbrook's before him) that people from all walks of life should occasionally meet in intellectual discourse. The theorist should be aware of his effect on the artisan and vice versa. This he believed was only accomplished by interaction among the various intellectual subgroups. Out of this thinking came the commercial Chautauqua movement. These lecture agencies sent scholars on tours throughout the entire nation, including rural areas, bringing famous speakers before the people. The Chautauqua meetings were not only well attended, but they made money for promoter and speaker alike (so did the earlier Lyceum).

A Summer Y.M.C.A. Encampment at Chautauqua Lake

Individual speakers received payment for their services based on the size of the audience they could attract. Hence, a speaker would go out of his way to make sure he developed a talk which would be well received. Often, the commercial value of the movement led to an emphasis on entertainment rather than scholarship.

Enterprising people were quick to take advantage of the growing incomes of American families and their interest in education. As a result, many commercialized correspondence schools were established throughout the country. By the beginning of World War I over 300 private correspondence schools, enrolling well over a million Americans, were in operation. Some of these schools were quite professional, however many were simply "diploma mills."

Other contributing factors in the popularization of knowledge include the growth of free public libraries, and the application of mass-production techniques to the book publishing industry, which made possible cheaply priced books. Fictional works were priced anywhere between 10¢ and 25¢ per volume, well within the reach of most American wage earners. A new editorial policy in newspaper publishing was another contributory factor. With an eye toward increased circulation, men such as Joseph Pulitzer and William Randolph Hearst, wrote for the supposed average reader, and tended to emphasize sensationalism and emotionalism. They were extremely successful.

Cheaply priced popular magazines also appeared. Again, the motivation was primarily commercial, but Americans still became adept at reading in the process. The new *Lady's Home Journal,* for instance, sold for 10¢ a copy and contained torrid fiction and articles on new techniques in dishwashing, woven ingeniously together. Another magazine, *McClure's,* appealed to the popular mind by concentrating on exposé-type stories. The rash of magazines which appeared during the 1880's and 1890's was destined to provide a vehicle for the publication of muckraker writing in the early twentieth century. The reform movement which followed provided ample proof that Americans read these magazines avidly, and that they were greatly influenced by them.

The illiteracy rate in the United States in 1880 was estimated at 17 per cent. As a result of all these educational developments it was down to 11 per cent by 1900, and it should be emphasized that during this twenty-year period, hundreds

of thousands of uneducated and usually illiterate immigrants had entered the country. Perhaps the quality of American education was not the best, but most Americans could read and write. The opportunity for formal schooling was improving, and most Americans took advantage of it if their financial circumstances permitted. In 1880 the average number of years of formal schooling in the nation was less than four. By 1900 the average had risen to five. And just prior to World War I it had risen to slightly over six.

Education in the Early Twentieth Century

During the first decades of the twentieth century, American education was heavily influenced by John Dewey. Calling for a "problem-solving" approach to instruction, Dewey's ideas had been introduced in a number of private, progressive schools. By the World War I era his theories were finding their way into state normal (teachers) colleges. By the 1920's they were entering public school systems. Dewey had placed almost complete faith in the value of education for solving national problems. Many Americans shared his faith in improved schooling as the preventive for social disintegration.

Some figures will adequately describe what was happening. Between the time of the Spanish–American War and American entrance into World War I, the number of students attending elementary schools increased from 16 million to 20 million. College enrollments more than doubled. The South was beginning to establish a modern educational system, and most of the enrollment increase took place in that part of the country. A significant new trend was in the direction of vocational education (see below), made possible by World War I–era legislation.

The American educational structure was developing so rapidly that some people decided it was time to take a sober look at the system. It was soon discovered that huge donors were unduly influencing what was being taught in the schools. Academic freedom was becoming a very serious problem. There were instances of college professors being fired because they espoused views which were not considered appropriate by their school's largest donors. This condition, coupled with the growing numerical ranks of the teaching profession, led to the formation of the American Association of University Professors in 1914.

In the post–World War I era, with increased wealth and leisure being enjoyed by many Americans, there was a marked increase in reading. By the end of the decade more than 100,000 Americans belonged to the Book-of-the-Month Club, and other similar bookselling organizations were established.

More phenomenal, however, was the growth of the newspaper industry. The trend was in the direction of newspaper syndicates. Large-scale mass production, nationally syndicated columns, mass advertising, and mass distribution were utilized. The net result was a drop in the price of newspapers, with little improvement in the quality of what was being produced. Americans continued to be addicted to sensationalistic stories, and more people bought newspapers because of crossword puzzles (quite a fad at the time) than for editorial policy. However, one out of every three Americans bought a newspaper every day by the end of the 1920's. Magazine circulation continued to rise, but its general quality dropped off considerably. In the false prosperity of the disillusioned post-war era, most Americans were not concerned with intellectual essays or exposés of government. They wanted escapism and the publishers gave them the *True Confessions* type of magazine which was immensely popular.

Universal Secondary Education

Probably the main advance of the 1920's was to make high school education a distinct possibility for almost every young American. In 1900 there were approximately 520,000 children enrolled in the nation's public high schools. In 1910 the number had risen to 915,000. In 1920 it was up to 2.2 million, and in 1930 the figure stood at 4.4 million. Enrollment was practically doubling every ten years—a staggering rate of growth.

At this point a unique aspect of the American educational structure came into play. With the democratizing of education the system necessarily became less selective. Standards were based on the average, and as the base grew, the average was lowered. With less selectivity, the nature of the various curricula had to change. Many of the new students were not qualified to handle traditional subjects. So such courses as Latin and algebra were for some replaced by courses in bookkeeping, shorthand, typing, the industrial arts, and vocational training.

Vast improvements in the nation's transportation system made possible advances in the educational realm. The standard rural structure was the one-room ungraded school house, hardly efficient by modern standards. A rural area could not support a graded school system. With the advent of the automobile, the consolidated school district made its appearance on the American scene. In a further effort to improve the instructional program, the junior high school was inaugurated during the Twenties.

College enrollment figures also exhibited a marked increase. In 1900 there were approximately 170,000 students in American colleges. In 1910 the number had risen to roughly 270,000; in 1920 to

520,000 thousand; and in 1930 to 1.1 million. This rapid growth led some educators to think in terms of two year colleges, and the number of junior colleges practically tripled during the first decade after World War I. At the same time that junior colleges were being rapidly established, there was another trend toward postgraduate professional training. As a result, the number of doctoral degrees, both M.D.'s and Ph.D.'s, increased annually. A large part of this increase was caused by the growing demand for college professors, while another part was caused by industry's developing demand for high-level specialists, especially in the sciences.

Government Aid to Education

The prosperity of the Twenties was sufficiently strong to enable various levels of government to expend increasing sums of money on the expansion of educational facilities. The federal government had provided major impetus for educational growth when it passed two wartime-era measures. Both measures legalized the dollar-matching principle according to which the federal government would contribute revenues comparable with the amount expended by other governmental levels for specific activities. The Smith–Lever Act of 1914 authorized this technique for agricultural education, and the Smith–Hughes Act of 1917 did the same for vocational education. Once the postwar recession era had passed, various local governments increasingly took advantage of these two statutes.

There was another factor concerning education during this period. Free elementary public education had supposedly been achieved by the close of the First World War. With this goal behind them, many of the advocates of public education turned their attention to secondary and higher education. With the general approval of its citizens, most states passed laws making it compulsory for children to stay in school, usually until their sixteenth

birthday. On the college level enrollments were increasing at a rate of roughly 50,000 per year. By 1929 approximately one out of every seven Americans of college age was attending some institution of higher learning.

Government and Education Begin to Join Hands

With the Crash of 1929 and the Depression years which immediately followed, American education suffered some temporary reverses. However, the role of the academician in public affairs became entrenched in the public mind. When Franklin Roosevelt entered the White House he established what was known as his Brain Trust. The term applied to several of Roosevelt's intimate advisors, who developed many of the basic ideas and details of his New Deal legislative program. This group was unofficially headed by Raymond Moley, who was aided in recruitment by the Dean of the Harvard Law School, Felix Frankfurter, later a member of the Supreme Court.

All of these men were experts in various disciplines, particularly economics and law. Roosevelt had begun the practice of consulting with such men while serving as governor of New York, and he had put together an organization of these intellectuals during his campaign to capture the Democratic presidential nomination in 1932. He constantly kept a nucleus of academic advisors throughout his long presidency.

Outside of this innovative development, education experienced several disruptive movements. The severe economic dislocation forced a vast number of individuals to drop out of school, not only from colleges, but from elementary and high schools as well. Teachers themselves tended to hold their jobs, but with substantial cuts in salary and far fewer students.

The government was fully cognizant

of this situation. Part of the relief program, it was hoped, would enable children to continue their education. Various government projects were established to enable children to remain in school. The most notable was the National Youth Administration which employed over two million young people, mainly in the summer months. Also, under the supervision of the Works Progress Administration, programs such as the Federal Arts Project, the Federal Writers Project, and the Federal Theatre Project were established. The result was the creation of some literary and artistic work, and the codifying of federal documents and historical collections.

The World War II years witnessed a tremendous demand for college-trained personnel, and college facilities were used by the military to instruct their people. Better billets in the military were available to those who possessed certain educational credentials, perhaps a high school or college diploma, but often just a service school certificate. With American forces fighting around the world, there was a heavy demand for skills in foreign languages. Wartime technology created a great need for scientists and engineers. There were not enough trained people available, so the military sent promising individuals to college, usually for short term courses. The military was thus responsible for providing a number of Americans with the beginning of a college education, and many hoped to continue their studies after the cessation of hostilities. Also, in the various service schools, many technical skills were taught to members of the Armed Forces.

The G.I. Bill

The educational hopes of many returning service men were realized when the government passed the G.I. Bill, which provided for partial government financing of the educational pursuits of the veterans. Partly designed to prevent a huge surplus on the labor market with the discharge of millions of troops, the measure was primarily intended to upgrade the general level of skills in the country and to aid the veteran in adjusting to a gainful civilian life. Within six months after the close of the war, every college in the country was overflowing with ex-soldiers. Whereas total college enrollments stood at 1.4 million shortly before the war, by 1949 there were 2.4 million students enrolled in the nation's colleges and universities. But not all of the emphasis was on college education. Under the provisions of the G.I. Bill, veterans could also complete high school, attend vocational school, or take advantage of various job training programs. As a result, some 7.8 million American veterans were aided in some manner by the G.I. Bill. The measure was later extended to cover Korean War veterans, thus adding another 1.5 million individuals to this number.

The general educational trends of the twentieth century continued, but at an accelerated pace. The Korean War was responsible for reducing college enrollments for a time, but by 1955 total enrollments had reached 2.7 million. By the end of the war there was a veritable explosion in the American birth rate. This meant that there would be huge demands on higher education in the 1960's. Secondary-school education for all had been fairly well achieved. Proponents of universal education set their sights on new goals.

The Economics of Education

Of serious consequence in post-war American society was the economic status of educators. Teaching salaries were not keeping up with advances in income levels for other professional people or even with blue-collar workers. The school janitor more often than not received a higher salary than the trained classroom teacher. College professors discovered that they could abandon teaching and go into industry where much higher salaries and better working conditions awaited them. At the very time when additional teachers were needed to meet rising demands, teaching ranks were being depleted because of insufficient income. An interesting contradiction running throughout much of American history has been an intense desire for a good universal educational program, but a general reluctance to pay for it.

Educational officials attempted to rectify this development in a number of ways. Tuition rates were increased, but not enough to compensate for inflationary losses. Wealthy alumni were solicited for contributions to establish funds to finance higher faculty salaries, and some contributed quite generously. Legislative agencies were pressured into authorizing tax increases to bring in more funds. However, there still remained a general reluctance to pay the teacher a salary appropriate to his training, ability, and responsibility. The Ford Foundation took the initiative in 1955 with a grant of $500 million which was specifically given for the purpose of raising faculty salaries in medical schools. But the problem of compensation was not solved in the 1950's.

New Trends in the Pursuit of Knowledge

The influx of new students into the nation's schools created a seemingly wild array of new course offerings. The common core of courses often became hard to distinguish; even such basic course requirements as mathematics or composition might be waived. Some educators felt that this was necessary to take care of the vast, diversified number of people entering higher education. However, other educators viewed the situation with considerable alarm, believing that the entire educational structure had been destroyed. They proposed a rigid, non-elective, liberal

arts curriculum. Such a concept, however, was outdated, and few educators took their proposals seriously. A compromise program, calling for certain basic courses during the first two years of college followed by two years of specialized courses of the student's own choosing, was achieved. Flexibility became the key descriptive word for contemporary education, and conversely, traditionalism was often viewed with disdain.

The newspaper trends noted in the Twenties continued in the post–World War II society. The influence and prestige of the syndicated columns increased while their numbers expanded. In one sense, American newspapers improved considerably. Events between the late Thirties and the mid-Forties made the American people more concerned about world affairs. Therefore newspaper coverage in the postwar world devoted much more attention to covering international news. It was uncommon for a good newspaper not to have correspondents stationed around the world gathering news on foreign developments. Numerous magazines devoted to current events were established.

Also coming into their own as informative devices were radio and television. The new media devoted an increasing portion of time to reporting the news, aired various "special" informative programs, and provided some educational television channels as well.

Education and the Supreme Court

The mid-Fifties witnessed a tremendous and violent controversy in the field of education. In a series of decisions the Supreme Court began to question whether or not the required equality in educational facilities was being achieved. It had become standard practice for southern states to send Negroes in law, medical, and graduate studies out of state and pay their tuition, rather than construct separate facilities for small numbers. The Court ruled that this was not the intent of the separate but equal doctrine, since white students were being allowed to attend such schools in their own states. This meant that states desiring segregation would be required to duplicate extremely expensive facilities.

The Supreme Court had proceeded slowly and carefully, testing public opinion with a number of minor desegregation rulings. The state was finally set for the historic case, *Brown* v. *Board of Education of Topeka,* in 1954. The Supreme Court unanimously ruled that so-called separate but equal facilities were inherently unequal. The Court specifically overruled the separate but equal doctrine as it had been promulgated in *Plessy* v. *Ferguson* in 1896. In one single sweeping decision the Court completely obliterated a legal system and procedure which had been officially sanctioned for over half a century, and thereby revolutionized the educational structure of the nation.

Opposition to Equality

A year after the decision the Court ruled that desegregation should proceed with all reasonable haste. However, the manner in which the various states responded varied considerably. Washington, D.C., integrated its school system immediately. The border states of Delaware, Kentucky, Maryland, Missouri, and Oklahoma soon began gradual integration, and accomplished it with a minimum of strife. Arkansas, Tennessee, North Carolina, and Texas made a weak start in this direction. And the deep South developed an obstructionist attitude. Years after the decision was rendered, no integration had taken place in some of the southern states. The more recalcitrant ones went so far as to disband their public school districts rather than comply. It became apparent that deep-seated customs usually carried more weight than judicial decisions.

The federal government made no con-certed attempt to implement the Supreme Court ruling. Most public officials tended to maintain a quiet neutrality, which served to encourage obstructionists. The lack of commitment was underscored in the presidential election of 1956, when integration was still not an important campaign issue.

The situation changed during the following year. Governor Orval Faubus of Arkansas, called out his state's National Guard to forcibly prevent the court-ordered integration of a handful of Negro students in Little Rock High School. Faced with a direct affront to the Court, President Eisenhower acted. He sent in paratroopers, federalized the Arkansas National Guard, and enforced compliance with the federal ruling. Nonetheless, more subtle attempts at non-compliance continued, and by the end of the Eisenhower presidency, integration was only one-tenth achieved.

President Kennedy had strong personal feelings on integration, but proceeded cautiously because of political considerations. However, when Governor Ross Barnett of Mississippi, refused to admit a Negro, James Meredith, to the state university in 1962, Kennedy forced the issue. Some violence ensued and Kennedy subsequently asked Congress for stronger civil rights legislation.

President Johnson was able to obtain the Kennedy request from Congress. The 1964 Civil Rights Act contained sections designed to implement the desegregation of public schools. And the clause prohibiting the use of federal funds in any program or agency which practiced discrimination, has been a powerful weapon, especially in view of a burgeoning federal aid to education program.

A New Era in Education

Federal aid to education is not new or unique to the contemporary United States. The first federal act giving aid to education was passed in 1785, under the Articles of Confederation. The Ordinance of 1785 donated one section of land out of each township (approximately thirty-six square miles) for the support of local schools. A similar measure was passed in 1862. The Morrill Land Grant Act, previously mentioned, applied to agricultural and mechanical schools. The Smith–Lever Act and the Smith–Hughes Act passed during World War I provided grants-in-aid for agricultural and vocational education. Various grants and aids were authorized during the Depression era to keep schools in operation and to provide a modicum of relief.

When the National Defense Education Act was passed in 1958, right after the launching of Sputnik I by the Soviets, federal aid to education became a controversial domestic issue. The 1958 act provided huge grants for the states to aid them in financing courses and programs in the sciences, mathematics, and foreign languages—subjects deemed to be essential to the security of the United States. The aid was welcomed but there was some protest over its giving. These protests shall be considered momentarily.

The 1960 Republican Party platform contained a plank calling for federal aid in the construction of educational facilities. The Democratic Party platform called for federal aid for school construction, and also for federal aid in improving teacher salaries. In 1961, because of increasing unemployment primarily brought on by a lack of proper training a federal aid to education measure was passed. It provided funds for the training and retraining of unemployed youths and adults. This measure was expanded during the Johnson administration to become part of the War on Poverty program. Higher education received aid in the form of long-term construction loans, and some dollar matching grant funds.

In 1965 the Higher Education Act was passed. This measure established a na-

tional teachers corps, instituted a program of graduate fellowships to further prepare elementary and secondary school teachers, and provided grants and contracts to improve teacher training programs. The purpose of the enactment was to improve the quality of education and to help meet critical shortages of adequately trained teaching personnel. The measure was further expanded in 1967 under the terms of the Education Professions Act. This law created a National Advisory Council on Education to review and coordinate all federal programs having anything to do with aid to education. The Teachers Corp provision of the previous act was extended for another three years. Graduate fellowships were broadened to include students who were preparing for adult and vocational teaching careers, as well as the elementary and secondary careers listed in the 1965 act.

However, the federal government, under both Republican and Democratic administrations, has run into considerable opposition in getting education aid measures approved. Only when national security appeared to be threatened following Soviet scientific achievements was a majority of legislators willing to accept the program with a minimum of controversy.

In addition to the somewhat new role assumed by the federal government in the field of education, various private foundations, such as Ford and Carnegie, have performed a genuine and important service to the nation's educational system with large grants and research projects. In addition there are the tens of thousands of alumni who contribute, sometimes lavishly, to their alma mater.

The Community College

Throughout this chapter various educational goals have been chronologically presented. First came the demand for universal public elementary education. And when it was basically achieved attention was centered on universal public secondary education. Now that this goal has been fairly well realized, there is a new demand being made by many educators, and it too, appears to be making considerable headway.

The current demand is for at least two years of free public education beyond secondary school. The term "college" is deliberately not used, because advocates do not necessarily believe that everyone can profit from two years of college for various reasons, but could benefit from one or two years of some kind of education beyond the high school level. This is where the comprehensive community college enters the picture. In the mid-1960's one of these institutions is being founded every week somewhere in the nation. And stories of brand new institutions reaching an enrollment of ten thousand students within a period of five years have become commonplace.

Not all states have, as yet, formalized community college systems. However, state after state is passing so-called "junior college laws," establishing post-high school educational systems for their citizens. And there are some people and states who, viewing the California system, desire that community colleges be free public institutions.

This new community college marks a rather complete synthesis of various educational theories and objectives. Traditional college-level work is offered, but so is technical and occupational study as well. Emphasis is placed on developmental work for under-achievers and adult education programs for those people who have no degree or certificate objectives. The new institutions are also concerned with social and civic problems. In years to come people will be experiencing a serious new problem: what to do with their leisure time. The teaching of skills and hobbies, the cultivating of an interest in theatre or sports, or simply the inculcating of a desire to learn for the sake of under-standing, may become the salvation for members of a future leisure class.

In recent years the educational profession has begun to more easily acquire and retain the necessary personnel. This is mainly because teaching salaries are most definitely on the upswing. It would appear that the material rewards to be obtained in the field of education will continue to increase. Many of the young men and women who leave college have a sense of dedication and responsibility, but this does not mean that they would willingly accept the role of a second-class citizen as teachers.

The federal government will continue to expand its activities in the field of education, and it will be encouraged to do so by a majority of people in the field. At the very basis of this development is the necessity for money. Many school districts are prohibited by law from operating at a deficit; the federal government, obviously, is not. Money is needed if a meaningful educational system is to keep pace with the demands of a complex, industrialized, technological society.

The number of Americans who go to some sort of a college will continue to increase substantially. According to Office of Education figures, there were 6,963,687 students enrolled in the nation's colleges and universities in the fall of 1967. It would not be far afield to state that by the end of the century the latest goal will be realized, and students will have the opportunity for two years of free education beyond high school.

The American university has also experienced rapid expansion and developing complexity. Universities expand in order to keep pace with society. Additional campuses must be built; schools must be added; expensive equipment must be acquired; new programs must be developed.

The system will become more costly as time goes on, as it becomes more complex. However, this raises another very serious problem, the solution to which is not readily evident. These vast universities will experience severe strains in attempting to coordinate their activities; there is already evidence of this occurring. In addition they will have to develop a high degree of coordination with state four-year colleges, the community college systems, and to some extent with secondary school systems.

The ultimate success or failure of the American educational system may well rest on whether or not the educators will be able to streamline and coordinate their activities in order to avoid duplication of efforts with other levels of education. Additionally more and more institutions will be seeking progressively larger revenues from the same financial sources. Although the United States is a wealthy nation these sources are limited, and efficiency and economy must be utilized.

The Future of Private Education

The field of private and parochial education is faced with continuing and serious problems. Two possible alternates appear to exist. Either the federal government will begin a massive program of aid to all private and parochial schools, although this seems unlikely, or these schools will probably have to close their doors or seriously curtail their efforts. It is a dilemma, and most private schools, unless they are among those few heavily-endowed, long-standing institutions, are in dire financial straits.

On the secondary level there has been a significant slowdown in private and parochial school construction. Also, there is a shortage of teachers willing to teach for the lower salaries offered by such institutions, and physical facilities are rarely even close to those of the public institutions. Elementary schools are already overcrowded, and as new churches which traditionally maintained their own schools are constructed in the sprawling American suburbs, many of them are not

By Messner, ROCHESTER TIMES-UNION

The Camel and the Needle's Eye

even bothering with the initiation of a school.

Private education will not cease in the United States. It will remain solidly entrenched at the college level, although its numbers will be somewhat depleted as the less financially sound schools fall by the wayside. Private secondary and elementary schools will limp along, as there will probably always be people who prefer to send their children to such schools regardless of the cost involved.

One thing is quite certain. In the years and decades to come, American education will undergo some almost fantastic changes. And those people who are making their careers in education will enjoy increased benefits, better salaries, enhanced prestige, and above all, stimulation and satisfaction. It is absolutely essential that the United States produce the brainpower needed to run her complex society, and it is the formidable task of education to provide the personnel.

For Further Reading

Bestor, Arthur E., Jr. *Educational Wastelands.* Urbana: University of Illinois Press, 1953.

Curti, Merle. *The Social Ideas of American Educators.* New York: Charles Scribners, 1935.

Good, H. G. *A History of American Education.* New York: Macmillan Company, 1956.

Hillway, Tyrus. *Education in American Society.* Boston: Houghton Mifflin, 1961.

Hutchins, Robert M. *The Conflict of Education in a Democratic Society.* New York: Harper and Row, 1953.

Karier, Clarence J. *Man, Society, and Education: A History of American Educational Ideas.* Glenview, Illinois: Scott Foresman, 1967.

Knight, Douglas M. *et al. Federal Government and Higher Education.* Englewood Cliffs: Prentice-Hall, 1960.

Maritain, Jacques. *Education at the Crossroads.* New Haven: Yale University Press, 1943.

Meyer, Adolph. *The Development of Education in the Twentieth Century.* New York: Prentice-Hall, 1939.

Ortans, Harold. *Effects of Federal Programs on Higher Education.* Washington: Brookings Institution, 1962.

Rivlin, Alice M. *The Role of the Federal Government in Financing Higher Education.* Washington: Brookings Institution, 1961.

Rugg, Harold. *Culture and Education in America.* New York: Harcourt, Brace, 1931.

Chapter Eleven
Internal Improvements

The term *internal improvements* encompasses the construction of roads, highways, harbors and seaways, dams, etc., by various governmental agencies. Such projects improve the physical resources of the country to provide faster and more efficient movement of people and goods, and promote use of and accessibility to remote, unspoiled regions. Any level of government may embark upon internal improvement projects—municipal, state, or federal.

An investigation of the internal improvement issue reveals one of the more important and colorful developments in American history. The issue has travelled from a position of extreme controversy to its current standing as an assumed part of government activity. Early in the nation's history there was a widespread belief that only states and localities should involve themselves in internal improvement projects. However, few provisions were made for those westerners who lived beyond state boundaries, in territories governed by the national Congress. Be-

cause of their demands, coupled with similar requests from business interests, the federal government progressively entered the field.

The internal improvements issue in part exemplifies the evolving nature of the American governmental process. Nothing in the Constitution explicitly states that the federal government should build road systems, aid railroads in their expansion, construct dams, and so forth. But the federal government does all of these things. Rising construction costs and popular demands, coupled with the very real need for such activities, were responsible for this change.

Internal improvements are similar to the educational system in the sense that they constitute a tremendous national force in the economic sphere. The building of a massive interstate highway system, or the development of a river system such as that handled by the Tennessee Valley Authority, involves staggering sums of money. The amount required usually surpasses the ability of all but the federal government to pay it. Such an expenditure provides orders for basic industry and employment for construction companies.

Necessity has been used to justify this development. Various nationwide internal improvements have been needed in different historical eras. Therefore, the federal government developed the power to undertake them. Constitutional justification has come from two sources: the implied powers doctrine and a very broad interpretation of the interstate commerce power. Not to be overlooked is the general welfare clause, often cited as authority for whatever the government intends.

Government has occasionally used internal improvement programs for two simultaneous purposes. In addition to the primary functions already discussed, internal improvement projects provide an ideal vehicle for relief during periods of national economic stress. Such was particularly the case from the New Deal era forward.

The present chapter will trace the development of internal improvements in the United States, placing emphasis on major pieces of legislation and public attitudes which either aided or hindered this development.

Colonial Internal Improvements

In colonial America internal improvement projects were practically nonexistent. Some harbor facilities were constructed, but roads were usually exceedingly primitive; dusty paths in dry weather and a sea of mire in wet weather. It was very difficult to move about the colonies. The best approach was to travel by sea along the coastline, then go either by horseback or bone-jarring coach for the remainder of the journey. The lack of many basic transportation facilities exerted a significant influence on the early development of the American colonies.

For one thing, the lack of ready transportation forced the colonists to concentrate on the eastern seaboard below the fall line of the streams; the point where the streams ceased to be navigable and rapids and waterfalls began. This was usually beneficial in that it prevented the colonies from expanding too rapidly, thereby allowing them to consolidate their strength before pushing into the interior. Of course, there was a major drawback to this which was destined to create problems at a later date. While English colonists were avoiding the trans-Appalachian regions, French explorers readily laid claim to them. Thus, when American colonists crossed over the Appalachians they experienced an immediate conflict with the French.

Transportation and Isolation

There was yet another point which was destined to be of more lasting significance. The American colonies did not engage in a great deal of interchange with each other. They tended to develop in semi-isolated pockets, and as such, they evolved differing forms of government and social systems. Hence, it is probably valid, after 1700, to consider the American colonies in terms of the classic four basic sections: southern, middle, New England, and frontier. The centripetal force for a future nation had not been created, and the United States would be plagued with sectionalism for at least the first 100 years of her existence. What began during the colonial period culminated at Appomattox a century and a half later.

However, there was a positive side to this lack of cohesiveness from the American viewpoint. Since settlements were some distance apart, and were not well connected with a good road system, it was practically impossible to defeat the colonies in battle. Even though the American colonists were vastly overmatched, they probably could have carried on the Revolutionary War with England for decades without being decisively defeated. The land area was far too large and impenetrable for even a powerful nation such as England to subdue without a significantly larger effort, and the English taxpayers would not and probably could not support such an extended enterprise.

Throughout the colonial period, internal improvement projects resided strictly within the hands of local governing bodies. The parish, town, or township handled the building of bridges and roads, and the construction of harbors and piers in their respective areas. Some work was done by the various colonial governments, but it was minimal. Actually, there was little need for such projects since most settlements were located purposely on navigable waterways.

Quite by accident, during the French and Indian War, Americans acquired an access route beyond the Appalachians. In 1755 the English sent General Braddock and a contingent of professional troops to support the colonists. He slowly advanced to within ten miles of the French stronghold of Fort Duquesne, in the Ohio Valley, where he was defeated. But in the process he had constructed a road which was destined to become an important avenue for future western settlement.

It should be pointed out that during this period of American history the terrain was exceedingly rugged. The eastern seaboard was covered thickly with trees and brush and had to be cleared in order to get a wagon through even in good weather. Also, there were many swamps and marshes which have long since been removed. It is quite difficult to comprehend the frontiersman's problems when the entire land was totally undeveloped.

Political Effects of the Frontier

This condition meant that people who initially lived in the westernmost reaches of their states were almost completely isolated from their government, while those residing beyond the Appalachians were totally isolated. Hence, during the period of the Articles of Confederation government, various western communities were clamoring for statehood. There were a number of valid complaints stemming from their physical isolation. One was the inaccessibility to the courts by westerners. Another was their general inability to get to the seat of government without taking off weeks from their work. Conversely, the lack of any governmental services on the frontier, particularly some sort of a policing agency, was considered to be a serious deficiency. It was primarily because of this western unrest, brought on to a large extent by the lack of an adequate internal improvement program, that pressures were created which resulted in the passage of the Northwest Ordinance of 1787. The Ordinance established the procedures for the admission of new states into the Union. Westerners were agitating for the establishment of their own governments. Some frontiersmen intrigued with Spain, France, and England for this purpose. Loyalty to a national government hardly existed.

Problems during the Foundation Period

The problem of the lack of internal improvements continued to plague the government for decades. In 1789 Congress passed a Judiciary Act which established the federal court system. One provision of this act required that Supreme Court Justices be assigned to each of three circuit courts for a period of six months out of every year. This meant that for half a year, the members of the Supreme Court actually rode from town to town on horseback or by coach, to hear cases then before the circuit court. Since travel was both quite difficult and extremely strenuous, many good justices resigned their posts, leaving mediocre personalities to staff the bench.

The internal improvement issue was

one of the significant areas of conflict between Thomas Jefferson and Alexander Hamilton. Their controversy led to the formation of the nation's first two major political parties during the Washington administration. Hamilton, who envisioned an urbanized, industrialized nation, naturally supported federally sponsored internal improvement projects. Jefferson, who desired a more rural nation with a decentralized national government, held that internal improvements should be handled by the state and local governments only. Hence, the Federalist Party, as a proponent of strong central government, would uphold internal improvements as being a legitimate function of government, while the Republican Party would not. New Englanders and especially westerners were destined to support the Hamiltonian position. Southerners, with a preponderant agricultural system and navigable rivers, would support Jefferson.

This difference between the two political thinkers was not immediately critical, since the government was financially unable to do anything. However, the battlelines for the internal improvement issue were drawn for the future.

It was primarily the lack of an adequate transportation system which led to the Whiskey Rebellion in 1795. Westerners were in the habit of converting their grain products into alcohol. The primary reason for this was that bulky grains were exceedingly difficult to transport over the mountains to eastern markets. The alcohol, in a much more concentrated form, brought higher profits, and was considerably easier to handle.

Probably another reason why the internal improvement issue was not pressed early in the nation's history was that the populated land mass was relatively small; most people were concentrated on the eastern seaboard and thus had water transportation readily available. However from the time of the Louisiana Purchase forward conditions changed. Henceforth, the United States was a larger, more sprawling nation, and if an adequate transportation system was not established, the nation would tend to fragment because of inadequate communication and interchange.

It was for this reason that a number of early American statesmen argued that the Mississippi River should be the "natural" western boundary of the nation. To go farther west was ridiculous, they argued, because a nation could not become that large and be governed effectively. After the Louisiana Purchase the Rocky Mountains became the western boundary of the nation; it was a natural barrier. With this large increase in territorial size (the Louisiana Purchase doubled the land mass), something had to be done quickly, as an issue developed which pointedly indicated this.

It is to be recalled from Chapter Two that the West experienced a severe recession during the period 1807–1812. One of the factors causing this recession and all other future western economic dislocations was poor transportation, which raised costs tremendously and lessened profits accordingly. The American farmer was destined to be continually plagued with transportation problems until well into the twentieth century.

The westerner now proved that his numbers were sufficiently large and his political power sufficiently strong to force his demands on the established East. After all, western agitation had in part forced the War of 1812 on the nation. It was time to pay more attention to his demands following the abortive "Second War of Independence." Nationalism predominated and federally sponsored internal improvement projects were well-received.

The First Internal Improvements Boom

The Era of Good Feelings following the War of 1812 equated the physical development and growth of the nation with the success of democracy. Attempts were made to avoid localism and particularism in politics, and the national government began to assume many new powers. The West played a significant role in the growth and development of this nationalism. The West had peculiar problems; it was very nationalistic because, lacking state governments in the territories, it was forced to look toward the federal government for aid. Hence, the Era of Good Feelings was marked by an attempt to improve transportation and communications. This demand, primarily western, increased the spirit of nationalism which was then permeating the nation.

The American System

Henry Clay's American System, another product of the Era of Good Feelings, presented an extremely nationalistic type of government. It marked an attempt to make all portions of the country dependent upon one another through the medium of commercial intercourse. Clay, an isolationist, called for strictly internal trade; the various sections of the country would be required to buy and sell everything to each other. Only the national surplus should be exported, and only cash should be received for it. Nothing would be purchased from abroad; American industry would be expected to produce all needed goods.

It follows from this that Clay would emphasize the need for internal improvements, and he did. Clay made internal improvements a pressing national political issue. However, he favored only those improvements which were national in character, such as harbors, waterways, and roads. There had always been some local internal improvements, so he was not concerned with them. But he would support measures in New England, the deep South, or the West, if he felt that all Americans would benefit to some extent by their development. Clay wanted a planned na-

tional economy, and a vast internal improvements program by the federal government necessarily followed.

The Erie Canal and Aftermath

The administration of John Quincy Adams experienced one of the first concerted internal improvement movements in the nation's history. In 1825 the Erie Canal, a 363-mile waterway, which connected the Hudson River with Lake Erie, was completed after eight long years of backbreaking work. The project had been the dream of the governor of New York, DeWitt Clinton. The canal, although highly controversial during its planning and constructing stages, was an instantaneous financial success. It greatly reduced both the cost and the time required to transport goods to and from the interior and the eastern seaboard. The canal opened the northwest country to settlement. To some extent it was responsible for making New York City a great commercial center of the modern world, and for the founding of a lake-trading post known as Chicago. At the time the canal was opened, it was the only direct route to the interior from an eastern city.

Other eastern port cities quickly rose to challenge New York's leadership, and they also attempted to connect with the West by means of canals. Unfortunately, no other eastern port city possessed the natural advantages enjoyed by New York. The low-lying Appalachian Mountains were at their backs, whereas New York was blessed with a long navigable river slightly to the north of the mountain chain. Still, Yankee ingenuity found the means of partly overcoming this handicap.

Philadelphia came up with the most ingenious system. It inaugurated the so-called "Pennsylvania System," a series of canals and portages connecting the city with the Ohio River. Canals were constructed along the level portions of the route. Crossing the mountains was handled by constructing a series of inclined

Locks on the Erie Canal

The James River Canal in Virginia

planes complete with cables to pull the specially designed barges on rails across the passes. The system was very expensive, especially since these portages were some thirty-six miles in length. But surprisingly enough, and this underlined the need for improvements, the canal was a financial success. However, it never seriously rivalled the more economical Erie Canal.

Other towns could not believe what had happened. If Philadelphia could make a success of a canal under such unfavorable conditions, so, many other communities felt, could they. A wild and extravagant canal craze struck the nation. It appeared that almost every other American town wanted to connect to the nearest adjacent town, or the West, or a major river, by means of a canal. Some dug ditches hoping rain water would fill them. Others built canals which trailed off to nowhere—often the site of a new town which never materialized. Some communities began projects only to run out of funds halfway along the line. Many of these partially completed canals remain today as remnants of an earlier optimism. Most of these projects were simply absurd, although a few did relieve the pressure on an inadequate transportation system.

However, there was an aftermath. Some communities, spurred on by the hope for huge profits, had vastly overextended their financial resources and were forced into bankruptcy. These failures were destined to be contributory factors in the Panic of 1837.

Slightly preceeding the canal age, but with developments which carried into the period, was a federally sponsored internal improvement project. President James Madison, who had been a most significant contributor at the constitutional convention, had desired a program of federal internal improvements. But he thought a constitutional amendment would be necessary to bring this about. However, his nationalistic Congress was more than will-

ing to enact such a program, regardless of his constitutional scruples. A Cumberland Road, designed to connect East and West along the old colonial Braddock route, had been initiated in 1811, but practically nothing had been accomplished. By 1818 the road went only as far as Wheeling, Virginia (now West Virginia). Annually, Congress had been appropriating only nominal funds for the construction of the road. The constitutional conflict between the executive and the legislative had temporarily blocked a program.

John C. Calhoun proposed in 1816 that the Second National Bank pay a "bonus" of $1.5 million to the federal government which would be used for internal improvement projects. This bonus idea, with some objections, passed through both houses of Congress. President Madison, however, vetoed the proposal. The new National Republicans, still intent on internal improvements, mistakenly agreed on nominating James Monroe for the presidency in 1816. Monroe was a strong adherent of the original political philosophy of Thomas Jefferson, and therefore could not accept the constitutionality of the vast federal internal improvement program which his Congress proposed. He did, however, allow the Cumberland Road to be completed since it had already been initiated. But when a proposal was made by Congress in 1822 to repair the road, erect toll gates on it, and collect tolls for financing future road maintenance, Monroe vetoed it. He claimed that internal improvements, if properly controlled, were desirable; but a constitutional amendment would be necessary for the government to exercise the proposed power.

His presidential successor, John Quincy Adams, did not possess such constitutional inhibitions, but he was not a highly popular leader with his Congress. Before leaving office, Monroe had agreed to federally sponsored surveys of possible transportation routes, and Adams attempted to use this as a lever for the construction of a complete system of national roads. A great deal of surveying was done during his administration, but there was only one tangible result. Beginning in 1825 the Cumberland Road was extended westward with Jefferson City, Missouri, as its ultimate destination. The construction eventually reached Vandalia, Illinois, a dozen years later, but was then abandoned owing to the economic distress evidenced by the Panic of 1837, and more significantly because of the rise of a new and better form of transportation, the railroad.

However, Adams did spend more money during his administration on roads and harbors than all of his predecessors combined. Ports were improved, some canal projects were undertaken, and navigable streams were dredged. The American nation was moving toward a fairly good system of internal improvements, sponsored mainly by the federal government.

The Jacksonian Era and Retrenchment

A check on internal improvement programs came during the presidency of Andrew Jackson. There were significant regional differences over the issue. The West still wanted them, believing that a great deal remained to be done. The South was generally opposed because such projects cost a great deal of money and this meant higher taxes. New England was definitely in favor of any measures which would render markets more accessible. Hence, internal improvements had become one of the major political issues of the era.

Jackson had been elected to the presidency through the combined support of both North and South, and for a time attempted to placate both sections. Thus, on internal improvements, he was publicly ambivalent, but his personal inclinations

were discernible by his conduct in 1830.

Congress had appropriated the sum of $150,000 for the construction of a road from Lexington, Kentucky, to Maysville, Kentucky. This particular road was planned as a section of a national road running north and south. It was planned to hook up with the east-west National Road at Zanesville, Ohio, and eventually connect with Natchez, Mississippi. Jackson regarded the road as a strictly local measure. He either failed or refused to recognize its eventual national character, and he vetoed it. He claimed that for the federal government to construct a purely intrastate road was clearly an unconstitutional act. He further suggested that a constitutional amendment was necessary if the federal government was going to continue its activities in this field.

The veto served to halt internal improvement projects for a few years, and this was probably beneficial. Jackson was not opposed to all internal improvements as such. He did agree to projects dealing with harbors and navigable streams (which he regarded as completely and clearly constitutional). He also favored and supported a number of internal improvement measures in the federal territories. Where he did become quite orthodox was on road projects strictly within the boundaries of a given state. A truly national road he would not and did not interfere with. He left unhampered the continuing construction of the National Road, most of which was being carried on during his presidency.

Jackson's stand on internal improvements was probably prudent. However, he lost both political advantage and consistency owing to his stand on another, somewhat related issue. During the latter half of his presidency, the government had been accumulating surplus funds, which was not considered economically unsound. The various sections came forth with solutions. The West sought to use the surplus for additional internal improvements. As an alternative, the surplus could be avoided by giving away land (land sales and tariffs were then the principal sources of federal revenues). The South preferred to end the tariff; this would solve one of that section's major problems. New England wanted increased internal improvements, but no free land and no end to the tariff. Henry Clay had a solution for the dilemma. Divide the surplus among the states and allow them to do what they wanted with the money. It could be used for rebates on tariffs in the South, rebates on land sales and financing of internal improvements in the West, and internal improvement projects in New England.

The Distribution Act was finally legislated into existence in 1836. It provided that all money in the treasury in excess of $5 million would be distributed to the states as "loans," effective January 1, 1837. It was further understood that the loans would not be repaid. Most states were already investing fortunes in internal improvements. Buying much of their equipment from England, the states faced a very unfavorable balance of trade. Credit was extremely loose in the West, and in the period of rapid inflation which followed, there was insufficient hard money to meet international payments. The result was the Panic of 1837, and internal improvement projects played a major role in initiating it.

There was an important aftermath to the Panic. Having been burned seriously by their internal improvement ventures, most states decided to give up such projects, and leave them in the hands of private enterprise. The result was the development of the corporation with limited liability. Instead of building roads and canals themselves, states would contract limited liability corporations to handle them. Private enterprise would be considerably aided and supported in these efforts, but the state would not leave itself financially vulnerable.

New Modes of Transportation and Communication

Both the canal craze and the government's role in road building projects would have waned without a panic or Jackson's veto. Because while these two internal improvements were being developed, the railroad was going through its experimental stages. In the 1830's various local railroad lines were constructed.

The Railroad

These early railroads were scarcely akin to later roads. Trains, at first, were drawn by horses or driven by huge sails. Even when the switch was made to the steam engine, wood was initially used as fuel. During the 1830's, however, quite a bit of knowledge was gained on grade requirements, curvages, design of rolling stock, preparation of trackage, etc., all of which provided the foundation for a new transportation mania.

During the 1840's the railroad became the most popular, speedy, and efficient mode of land transportation. Very few states participated directly in the building or operation of railroads, but most gave the railroad promoters as much help and encouragement as was possible. Individual states would lend money for railroad construction, or would buy large quantities of railroad stocks. They would grant various legal benefits to the lines, such as a partial or complete tax exemption for a specified number of years. If the state had any lands of its own, these lands were often deeded over to the railroads to help defray construction and initial operation expenses.

In addition, the various localities were encouraged by the railroaders to bid for a proposed line to pass through their areas. This could be done by granting money to the railroad, lending it considerable sums, buying huge blocks of railroad stocks, or guaranteeing a certain amount of business each year. Beginning in 1850, the federal government moved into the picture. In that year, Senator Stephen Douglas of Illinois, convinced Congress to grant federal lands within his state to the state, so that they might then be given to the Illinois Central Railroad to help defray construction expenses.

Other land grants quickly followed, and soon it became a customary method of aiding the railroads. In the decade immediately prior to the Civil War, some 20 million acres of the public domain were given to railroads. With this type of aid, railroad expansion proceeded at an ever increasing rate. The nation counted 32 miles of trackage in 1830. In 1840 the figure exceeded 2,800 miles; by 1850 it was over 9,000 miles; and by 1860 it was well beyond 30,000 miles. Most of the railroad construction occurred in the concentrated Northeast; the South, although it did engage in some railroad building, preferred to rely on its many navigable rivers for transportation. Meanwhile, the Northeast was being very effectively linked to the West by rail, and the South tended to become more isolated from the rest of the country. This would develop into a major factor in the brewing civil conflict.

As the railroads slowly pushed westward they came into contact with the river steamboat. This transportation device had earlier tied the West with the South—down the natural highway provided by the Mississippi River system. These steamboats were both large and swift. They helped make possible the development of the West before the railroads came, and continued to be of benefit for decades to follow. However, the steamboat possessed one very serious and obvious drawback. Its use was limited strictly to navigable rivers, of which there were very few in the trans-Mississippi West. Also, they did not solve the transportation problems of those westerners who lived some distance from the rivers. In order to foster a stronger sense of nationalism and a greater degree of economic cohesiveness, it was held to be necessary to develop a rapid transportation and communications system between the West and the states in the East.

Need for Rapid Communication

With this in mind, the federal government contracted with private concerns for a mail delivery between New York City and San Francisco twice each month. Mail was shipped by sea from New York to the Isthmus of Panama, unloaded and transported to the Pacific Ocean overland, then reloaded and shipped up the West Coast by ocean again. The time required for such a trip was roughly thirty days, and the cost was generally prohibitive.

The Post Office Appropriations Act of 1857 authorized an overland mail service. Bids would be accepted from private concerns, with the winner required to provide weekly mail service from St. Louis to San Francisco, and to complete each trip within a twenty-five day period. The firm selected would be granted a federal subsidy of $600,000 per year. A New York company headed by John Butterfield and William Fargo obtained the contract, and a year later, the Butterfield Overland Express was in business.

The firm introduced the Concord Coach, a massive, gaudily-painted structure which held up to nine passengers. The journey was far from pleasant and the $200 fee for the trip was very expensive (higher than the annual income of most Americans at the time), but the Express prospered. Soon other routes were authorized by the government: the Kansas and Stockton Express, and the San Antonio Express covered them. All acted as carriers of United States mail.

Some other individuals in the field of transportation were convinced that a route directly across the central United States

Library of Congress

The Pony Express

would be faster. But they felt that the government would not subsidize any other routes unless a superior approach could first be demonstrated. The firm of Russell, Majors, and Waddell organized a freighting operation on their own initiative to service the mountain state area. With the large profits realized from this venture, they underwrote an experiment —the Pony Express, to provide rapid cross-country mail service. Young riders on swift horses dashed across the country. The chain stretched from St. Joseph, Missouri, to San Francisco. The system was exhorbitantly expensive, but a trip could be made in under eleven days. However, the operation could only survive with a government subsidy, and it was not forthcoming.

The government was more interested in financing another newer mode of communication between East and West. Congress had promised a $40,000 annual subsidy to any firm constructing an operative telegraph system across the country. The telegraph was completed in 1861 and the Pony Express, for all its romance and color, became a thing of the past. And with the coming of the railroad into the West, the staging and freighting lines began a long decline.

The Age of the Railroads

During the Civil War era railroad development expanded tremendously; some 5,000 miles of new trackage was put down in the North. But at the same time southern railroads were being obliterated by northern military forces. However, wartime demands did improve northern transportation.

By the close of the Civil War a substantial network of railroads existed as far west as the first tier of states on the western bank of the Mississippi River. These railroads had expanded mainly through the receipt of land grants given to them by the federal government. Also, various states had granted credit and lands, and the population and commerce of local towns and settlements promised profits in the foreseeable future.

Building railroads on the Great Plains, however, was an entirely different matter. No states existed to grant lands, credits, or loans. No towns existed to promise future profits. And few settlers wanted to buy railroad lands in the middle of nowhere. Besides this, there were plenty of new problems facing the railroad builders: lack of timber for construction, a food and water shortage, and hostile Indians. Everything needed for constructing the railroad—including equipment, manpower, and protection—had to be transported from the East. The cost, then, would be staggering, and the sparse settlement of the western areas precluded, for a long time, any desire on the part of private enterprise to build a transcontinental railroad.

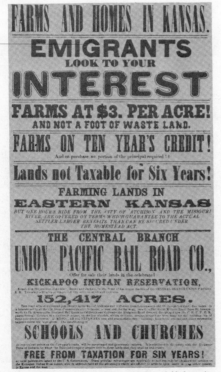

Baker Library, Harvard University

Railroad Land Grants for Sale,
an Advertisement (1867)

The Transcontinental Railroad

The idea of a transcontinental railroad had been discussed since before the 1850's. Congress had authorized a survey of possible routes, and it was reported that there were four locations along which a railroad could be built. One of these cut through a tiny corner of northern Mexico, which the Gadsden Purchase quickly acquired for the nation. But this was the extent of Congressional action as the legislative branch became embroiled in an increasingly acrimonious debate over which route should be chosen.

At the heart of the controversy was the strife and rivalry existing between North and South. Southerners wanted a southern route, while northerners desired the opposite. Neither side was apparently willing to compromise. Stephen Douglas championed the Kansas–Nebraska Act of 1854, which upheld the concept of popular sovereignty, hoping to elicit southern support for a transcontinental railroad to run through Chicago, where he held extensive real estate investments. All he accomplished at the time was the compounding of the slavery expansion issue.

The Republican Party platform of 1860 endorsed the building of a transcontinental railroad. Then with the secession of the southern states in 1860 and 1861, there was no problem choosing a route. Without the southerners being represented, Congress speedily chose the northern route (actually the second most northern of the four proposed routes). The building of a transcontinental railroad was authorized in 1862.

Two private companies were selected to begin construction on the road in order to expedite its completion. The Central Pacific began building from the San Francisco area eastward, while the Union Pacific began building from the 100th meridian (in the general vicinity of Omaha, Nebraska) westward. Chinese coolies (unskilled laborers) were brought in to perform much of the backbreaking work on the Central Pacific, and Irish immigrants handled the same task for the Union Pacific.

Governmental Involvement

The federal government aided the project significantly. The railroad was granted a 400-foot right-of-way along its route. In addition, it received ten alternate sections of public land for each mile of track it put down. The railroad could then sell the land, which rose in value since it was adjacent to the railroad, and help recoup its expenses. Added to this, the federal government loaned the companies $16,000 for each mile of track laid on level ground, $32,000 for each mile in hilly terrain, and $48,000 for each mile constructed through mountainous regions. Graft, corruption, and undue generosity prevailed. For instance, the Central Pacific received mountain loans while building across the desert. Much money found its way into the vaults of the railroad promoters. The actual cost of building the railroad was estimated to have been around $50 million, but somehow or other $300 million was "spent" on the project.

The two railroads were building toward each other, and quite naturally they built as rapidly as possible in order to capture the major share of the government benefits. As such, the road was not built to last, and shortly after its completion, much of the trackage had to be relaid. Also, Congress had established no point where the railroads were to meet. Consequently, the roads passed each other in surveying and bed preparation. Congress hastily corrected the situation by establishing a point near Ogden, Utah, where the

Library of Congress

Completing the First Transcontinental Railroad
Near Ogden, Utah, 1869

two lines would connect. There, in May, 1869, with great pomp, the first transcontinental railroad was completed.

The federal government also chartered private companies to build three other transcontinental roads. These later transcontinentals did not receive loans from the federal government, but they did receive very generous land grants. They acquired twenty sections of land for each mile of track laid within the boundaries of a state, and forty sections of land for each mile of track put down in the federal territories.

The first of these later lines to be chartered by Congress was the Northern Pacific in 1864. Begun originally to connect Lake Superior with Portland, Oregon, the road experienced considerable financial difficulties. Eventually though, a railroad genius, James Hill, took over the operation and completed the road in 1883. This railroad brought the solution for the transportation problems experienced by Great Plains farmers.

In 1866 Congress granted a charter to the Atlantic and Pacific Railroad to construct a southwestern route to California. The company went bankrupt and was soon taken over by the Atchison, Topeka and Santa Fe Railroad, which had received a state grant to build across Kansas and proceeded to build to the California border. At that juncture it was forced to lease trackage owned by Leland Stanford, Charles Crocker, Mark Hopkins, and Collis Huntington, the developers of the Central Pacific and the Southern Pacific railroads. These men had effectively gained political power in California, and would not allow any outside railroad to infringe on their empire. Still, with the lease arrangement, another transcontinental railroad was completed in 1883.

The last charter authorized by the federal government was granted in 1871. Congress authorized the Texas and Pacific Railroad to construct a line far to the south. However, the group of Stanford, Crocker, Hopkins, and Huntington preempted the right-of-way and obtained territorial charters to build eastward toward this line. It did not take this wealthy group long to completely absorb the Texas and Pacific, and the line was completed in 1882. This was the transcontinental road of the Southern Pacific.

The building of the four transcontinentals captured the imagination of much of the American nation. But these four lines alone did not solve the nation's transportation problems. Numerous spur lines had to be constructed in order to make the railroads accessible to more people. In the western states there was a continuation of state and federal aid. In addition, new spur lines were constructed in the East, while the South completely rebuilt its railroad system, connecting it with the rest of the country. Private capital was willing to take care of eastern and southern expansion, because of the presence of established communities which promised immediate profits.

By the close of the Civil War there were 35,000 miles of railroads in the United States. By 1870 this figure had risen to 52,000 miles; by 1880 it was up to 93,000 miles, and by 1890 it had jumped to 163,000 miles. This last date has traditionally marked the close of the railroad age. Additional trackage continued to be laid, and railroads consolidated and improved their service. But for all practical purposes the basic railroad structure of the United States had been completed.

A better postal system followed railroad construction. Also, the communications network of the country was further enhanced by the successful laying of a trans-Atlantic cable in 1866 (an unsuccessful attempt had been made in 1858). In the 1870's Alexander Graham Bell introduced the telephone, and by 1890 approximately four hundred and fifty thousand were in service. Communications and transportation had been developed to the extent that industrialism became possible on a major scale, and the provincialism which had marked the country before the Civil War was on the decline. In light of existing technology the United States possessed an effective transportation system.

The Building of the Panama Canal

The next notable transportational improvement on the part of the government was the building of the Panama Canal. Although much of this story lies within the realm of diplomatic history, it will be considered, because of its direct effect on transportation, in the present chapter.

The United States had long been interested in and had made use of the Isthmus of Panama. An 1846 treaty with Colombia had given the United States the right to intervene in the affairs of the isthmus in order to insure unfettered transportation across it. After the Spanish–American War the United States, possessing territories on both the Atlantic and Pacific Oceans, deemed it essential to build an isthmian canal to connect her two naval fleets. However, back in the 1850's, the nation had ratified the Clayton–Bulwer Treaty with England which stipulated that the United States would never build such a canal unilaterally.

In 1898 the United States began negotiations with England on the subject, but they were not strongly pursued. However, an impatient Congress introduced a bill calling for the building of a canal in 1900, whether there was a restrictive treaty in existence or not. In addition, President McKinley had already sent a survey team, the Walker Commission, to seek out possible routes for a canal through Central America.

Conditions were quite friendly between the United States and England at this time, and the two nations rather quickly signed the Hay–Pauncefote Treaty of 1900, which allowed the United States to build an isthmian canal by herself. The Senate refused to ratify the treaty since it did not allow for the building of fortifications to protect what would be a sizeable American investment. A second Hay–Pauncefote Treaty cleared up this point in 1901. Great Britain subsequently withdrew her naval forces from the western hemisphere. The diplomatic paths had been cleared for construction.

A new problem, that of acquiring a location for the proposed canal, next took precedence. The Walker Commission had reported that there were three possible routes: one through Panama, one through Nicaraugua, and one through southern Mexico. The lengthy Mexican route was immediately ruled out because of its great cost. The Walker Commission proposed the Panamanian route as the best, but there were complications.

A defunct French company, the New Panama Company, already held a franchise from Colombia (Panama was then a province of Colombia) to build a canal. The company wanted an exorbitant $109 million for its franchise, which was actually almost worthless. Therefore, the Walker Commission recommended the Nicaraugan route. The House of Representatives approved their choice on January 9, 1902, and in consequence the New Panama Company immediately reduced its asking price to $40 million.

This new development made the Panama route cheaper than any other; it was already the most desirable one for several reasons. Earlier the French engineer on the defunct Panama project, Buneau-Varilla, pointed out that there was an active volcano along the Nicaraugan route, and went so far as to place a postage stamp depicting an erupting volcano in the hands of each United States Senator. As a result, Congress authorized the Panamanian route on June 2, 1902, provided an arrangement could be negotiated with Colombia.

In January, 1903, the Hay–Herran Treaty was negotiated with Colombia, giving the United States a six-mile strip of land across the isthmus in exchange for $10 million cash and $250,000 per year afterwards. The Senate immediately ratified the treaty, but Colombia did not. That nation had sent a communiqué to Herran ordering him not to sign, but it arrived too late. Colombia was not opposed to an agreement with the United States, but saw an opportunity to obtain more money. It so happened that the New Panama Company's franchise was due to expire in 1904, and according to its terms, all equipment would automatically revert to the Colombian government. Therefore, another $40 million could be added to the American bill.

President Theodore Roosevelt, an impatient man, apparently wanted the credit for building an isthmian canal. Knowing that the Panamanians desired to break away from their Colombian overlords, he collaborated in staging an independence movement (see Chapter Two). Following independence, the United States, under the terms of the Hay–Buneau-Varilla Treaty, obtained a ten-mile wide strip of land in exchange for $10 million in cash and $250,000 annually thereafter. All legal paths were cleared for construction of the canal.

The engineering problems involved in canal construction were phenomenal. All along it was thought that a sea level canal could be constructed, but it was quickly discovered that locks were needed to compensate for differences in the water levels of the Atlantic and Pacific Oceans. Also, the region was infested with malaria and other tropical diseases, and sanitation was

Library of Congress

A Sketch of the Panama Canal under Construction

a major problem. The federal government underwrote the entire cost of the project which amounted to $388 million, including the desired fortifications. Bonds were issued to cover the construction costs.

The original intention was that toll charges would eventually pay for the construction costs, and as matters turned out, this was accurate. Within fifteen years after the canal opened in the late summer of 1914, it had paid all of the costs on the issued bonds. Earlier, Congress had become involved in an international and domestic controversy. In 1912, long before the canal opened, Congress exempted American ships from paying tolls for use of the canal. Great Britain protested because this constituted a violation of the terms of the Hay–Pauncefote Treaty, which stipulated that the canal would be open to all the ships of the world on completely equal terms. She did not oppose government rebates to American shippers, but she was dissatisfied with the prospect of foreign nations paying for the use of the canal, while American shippers paid nothing. American railroad interests, incidentally, seconded England's protests; they did not enjoy the prospect of increased competition from the shipping industry. President Wilson obtained the repeal of the provision just two months before the canal was opened, primarily to placate England.

Expanding Federal Internal Improvements Projects

In 1916 the federal government became involved in another massive internal improvement program. Automobiles had existed, although mainly in the experimental stage, for roughly twenty years. This new transportation device suffered from one very serious drawback. It could not operate successfully on the type of roads used by horses and carriages. One of the greatest inconveniences suffered by auto enthusiasts was the constant tendency

to get stuck in the mud somewhere. Opponents of the new horseless carriages, on the other hand, pointed out that automobiles were destroying the nation's roads. State and local authorities were totally unable to cope with the new and expensive problem.

The Federal Highways Act of 1916 established the dollar-matching principle for road building projects. The federal government would contribute a dollar for every dollar spent by the state. Congress appropriated $5 million for this purpose in 1916, the first appropriation for the apparently bottomless pit of highway construction.

Government Aid to Public Transportation

Throughout America's past the federal government has aided private enterprise in the construction of internal improvements which were deemed essential. According to Chief Justice John Marshall's dictum that "the power to create is the power to preserve," the government, largely responsible for creating these systems, assumed the responsibility for their future welfare. Following World War I the federal government began subsidizing various modes of public transportation in order to insure their continued operation.

First came the Esch–Cummings Act of 1920. In addition to returning the railroads to private hands following wartime controls, the federal government established a $300 million revolving fund to aid the railroads in financing capital improvements. Besides this, the federal government continued to purchase railroad space for United States mail which acted as a boon for the railroad industry. The railroad had become a subsidized industry, buttressed financially by the federal government. In short, it probably could not have continued without federal support. Conditions, however, would worsen with the appearance of the automobile, and eventually, the airplane.

The Jones Merchant Marine Act of 1920 dealt with another aspect of the nation's transportation system. The act authorized the disposal of the huge merchant fleet acquired by the federal government during World War I. But it did so by setting up a congressional appropriation of $25 million to create a revolving fund. The money was to be used to help finance these ships by private investors who purchased them from the government at a fraction of their original cost. The Jones–White Act of 1928 went one step further. Through the medium of mail contracts, which had little to do with the actual volume of mail, the merchant marine was given money by the federal government. The scheme amounted to direct subsidization of the shipping industry by the federal government.

Meanwhile the automobile developed at an extremely rapid pace throughout the 1920's. Governor Al Smith of New York, recognizing the potentiality of the automobile built the nation's "first scenic highway," the Hutchinson River Parkway. Chicago was busy grappling with a novel problem, heavy traffic, and partially solved

Problems with the Horseless Carriage

it by constructing Lakefront Drive, the nation's first city expressway. In 1920 the nation produced 1.9 million automobiles; in 1929 it produced 4.8 million. The total number of vehicles registered in the country in that year exceeded 26 million. Obviously, 26 million automobiles required a tremendous amount of highway building. All levels of government combined, local, state, and federal, spent approximately $10 billion on highway construction during the 1920's.

The Airplane

The federal government also became involved with another new mode of transportation during the Twenties; this was the airplane. Still in its infancy during the World War I era, and largely used for stunt activities during the Twenties, the airplane rapidly assumed major significance. The government provided aid for the new airplane industry through the traditional device of plush mail contracts. This subsidy kept airplanes in operation during the decade. Very few private individuals travelled by plane, and few planes were large enough to make air freight service feasible. The space-per-mile principle of contract rates was inaugurated in 1929, with the government claiming that encouraging private enterprise to construct larger planes was not only important for carrying the mail, but it might also serve a very useful national purpose in wartime.

There was a distinct tendency on the part of the government to grant mail subsidies to the better financed and operated airlines. As a result many smaller companies quickly went out of business. In 1934, owing to protests from these struggling small operators, the government cancelled all air mail contracts, and gave the job to army pilots. A quick succession of fatal crashes followed, and Congress rapidly gave the mail contracts back to private companies. The Mead–McKellar

Air Mail Act of 1935 allowed for a sliding scale of government mail payments to the airlines, and subsidies tended to dwindle as the airplane became better established. Finally, federal subsidies were no longer needed; passenger and air freight business easily replaced them.

A New Dimension Is Added

Internal improvements under the administration of Franklin Roosevelt took on a different character. Previously, the term applied only to government participation or support in projects which would benefit the nation's transportation facilities. This aspect of internal improvements was maintained under Roosevelt, but a new dimension was added. Roosevelt utilized internal improvement projects as a vehicle for carrying out New Deal relief programs.

The WPA

The Federal Relief Appropriations Act of 1935 set up guidelines for the spending of $5 billion on a limited federal relief program. The implementing agency established was the Works Progress Administration, known as the WPA. There were three basic concepts found in the act. One was that the unemployed would be given relief, not by direct charity, but by being given some sort of work to earn a wage—and the salary would be a little less than the prevailing average in order to discourage people from remaining on relief. Another provision called for the money grants to be spent strictly on wages. The money would go for furnishing the manpower for projects, not the materials, equipment, and initial planning. This led directly to the third concept. It was stipulated that local authorities, since they supposedly understood their needs better than anyone else, would administer the details of the program. They would create the

ideas and furnish all equipment and materials needed for the projects.

This, however, allowed an undetermined amount of waste to infiltrate the program. In some instances a vast reservoir of paid labor was wasted. Local officials usually saw to it that absolutely no materials or equipment were required for their projects. The cliché that a WPA worker dug a hole one day only to fill it the next, and dig it out again on the third day, was not entirely without foundation. One of the favored projects was cutting weeds, both summer and winter. Some of the more enterprising communities, if they possessed sufficient financial resources, did use the paid federal labor for worthwhile purposes. A favorite constructive device was to build brick streets. Used brick was very cheap but the task was extremely time-consuming. At the termination of these projects there was at least something tangible.

Despite abuses, the agency was responsible for furnishing the labor which built 13,000 playgrounds, 1,000 airports, 6,000 school buildings, and 2,500 hospitals. A large part of the work entailed building streets and improving country roads. Some of it was also used in the building of earthen dams, levees, and small bridges. The intent was to create work for people in order to avoid a direct public dole. In the process miscellaneous internal improvements were undertaken.

The PWA

The Public Works Administration, known as the PWA, was primarily a recovery measure of the New Deal. Its major function was to place money into the industrial economy in order to stimulate business to re-hire and re-establish purchasing power. In the years of its existence, PWA spent close to $6 billion on projects which concentrated on waterways, harbor improvements, dam construction, and federal highway programs.

In these programs, the government paid for the materials required, by contracting with private business to have the work done. Workers were paid their regular salaries by the various contractors who hired them, but ultimately, the government provided the money.

The Merchant Marine Act of 1936 continued the subsidization of ocean-going merchant vessels. But instead of using mail contracts for this purpose, a new system was developed. Basically, the government paid the shippers the difference in construction and operating costs for a foreign ship compared to the cost for an American ship. In 1939 Congress initiated a ship trade-in program, whereby a private shipper could grant an old vessel to the government in exchange for a very generous allowance toward a new one.

The TVA

One of the most massive and significant of all internal improvement projects was the establishment of the Tennessee Valley Authority in 1933. The measure was the climax of a long battle concerning the fate of the World War I era Muscle Shoals project. At that time the government had begun the production of nitrates, used for explosives, at a generating site on the Tennessee River. But before the government had completed construction on its plant the war had ended. Using this development as a lever, such liberals as George Norris pushed for government construction and operation of dams throughout the country. However, following World War I all that was accomplished was the passage of the Federal Water Power Act of 1920. This measure gave the newly created Water Power Commission the authorization to control water power sites by issuing licenses for a period of fifty years. The relatively short time limit discouraged most private investors, since the capital investment in a hydroelectric plant was extremely large.

Norris, meanwhile, kept agitating for government involvement in the area, and did so to the extent that he actively supported a member of the opposition, the Democrat Franklin Roosevelt, for the presidency. He was not disappointed. The New Deal, using conservation of natural resources, the use of public utilities for the best interests of the people, and the general control and operation of the entire field of water power sites as basic arguments, decided to enter the area on an experimental basis. The geographical region selected was the Tennessee Valley, within which the old Muscle Shoals project had been located. In addition, the measure would further stimulate the recovery of the nation because of the huge demands by the construction industry in building dams and generating plants.

TVA was given a number of tasks to perform. These included the construction of dams for the improvement of navigation and flood control, the building and operation of hydroelectric plants and the subsequent selling of the power generated, and the production of fertilizers for agricultural use (a nitrate plant can produce either explosives or fertilizers). With Muscle Shoals as a beginning, TVA proceeded to construct six major dams with revenues provided from the Public Works Administration.

The TVA was extremely controversial, but its constitutionality was upheld by the Supreme Court. The federal government then proceeded to embark upon other large dam-building projects in this new area of internal improvements. Dams were constructed along the Columbia, the Colorado and the Missouri Rivers. Ultimately, more than forty such dams, including the famous Kentucky and Hoover Dams were constructed.

A Multi–Billion-Dollar Enterprise

In 1954 a major federal internal improvement project was launched. This program was unique as it involved joint action with America's northern neighbor, Canada. Every president beginning with Herbert Hoover had pressed Congress to authorize the building of a St. Lawrence Seaway. The project called for connecting the Atlantic Ocean with the Great Lakes by means of a waterway suitable for ocean-going vessels. Most of the route was suitable for such purpose, but there were a few major obstructions which had to be cleared. Canada had been in favor of the project all along, and was growing impatient with a vacillating United States Congress.

Canadian threats to build the project unaided, coupled with an increasing need for transportation facilities to the industrial centers surrounding the Great Lakes, led President Eisenhower to strongly press Congress for agreement. A government corporation was established to handle the American part of the project. This corporation financed its activities by selling well over $100 million in bonds to the United States Treasury. Hydroelectric installations on the American side of the route were to be handled by the State of New York at its own expense, and by Ontario on its side. The seaway was finally completed and opened to ocean craft in 1959. Eisenhower regarded this Seaway as one of his proudest achievements as president.

Today and Tomorrow

During Eisenhower's administration another major segment of internal improvement legislation was passed. The Federal Highway Act of 1956 significantly extended the grant-in-aid program for highway building. With the idea of developing a nationwide interstate highway system of uniform construction, the federal government authorized the construction of over 42 million miles of highway over a sixteen-year period. The states would handle the actual construction, subject to federal standards and coordination.

Pushing the dollar-matching principle to new limits, the federal government agreed to pay 90 per cent of the total cost; the states had only to contribute the remaining 10 per cent.

Various levels of government continue to engage in internal improvement projects. An attempt to keep the nation's highway system adequate for the rapidly growing number of automobiles is a tremendous task. Also, there are discussions of federally sponsored mass transit systems in the major cities. The government is actually spending more money each year on strictly routine highway, bridge, and dam construction than it spent on all the major projects of the last century. In addition special projects cost billions more, as the $33.5 billion initially authorized for construction of the interstate highway system indicates.

For a nation of its immense size, the United States has developed its transportation and communications systems to an extremely sophisticated level. Internal improvement projects have created a whole new way of life for many Americans. The building of huge dams created reservoirs which have become, in some instances, beautiful recreational areas where many Americans vacation. This was not a prime function of internal improvement construction, but the aftermath of these projects has played an important role on the contemporary American scene.

Internal improvements have displayed viable working arrangements between private enterprise and governmental agencies. They have altered the federal system, as the evolving nature of American society has given progressively more power to the national government under the authority of the general-welfare clause. Most Americans no longer question the authority of the federal government to engage in highway building. In fact, state governments are constantly asking for more help in meeting the straining needs of a sound transportation system. And there is yet another aspect worthy of consideration.

Internal improvements cost money—a great deal of money. Only the federal government has the financial resources necessary for most projects. But the federal government, although it spends billions of dollars per year on internal improvements, receives a considerable return on its investments. Part of the great prosperity of the United States is caused by the stimulating effect of these various programs. Part of the expansion and prosperity of the construction industry rests on the money spent by the government. The additional people who are hired to work on these projects significantly add to the Gross National Product of the nation. And individuals and corporations alike return a large portion of this money to the federal government in the form of taxes.

Not to be discounted is the effect on the farmer, the manufacturer, and other Americans of having a government sensitive to internal improvement needs. The United States could not possibly have the highly industrialized, urbanized economy which it does, were it not for the existence of the communications system within which it operates. One might consider the tremendous detrimental effects on the nation if the government should suddenly halt all its spending on internal improvements. No other agency exists which has the financial resources available to meet these essential needs.

For Further Reading

Billington, Ray Allen. *Westward Expansion.* New York: Macmillan Company, 1957.

Burch, Philip H., Jr. *Highway Revenue and Expenditure Policy in the United States.* New Brunswick: Rutgers University Press, 1962.

Clawson, Marion, and Held, Burnell. *The Federal Lands: Their Use and Management.* Baltimore: Johns Hopkins, 1957.

Goodrich, Carter. *Government Promotion of American Canals and Railroads.* New York: Columbia University Press, 1960.

Hibbard, Banjamin H. *A History of the Public Land Policies.* Madison: University of Wisconsin Press, 1965.

Maas, Arthur, *et al. Design of Water-Resource Systems.* Cambridge: Harvard University Press, 1962.

Moody, John. *The Railroad Builders.* New Haven: Harvard University Press, 1919.

Mott, George Fox (ed.). *Transportation Century.* Baton Rouge: Louisiana State University Press, 1967.

Riegel, Robert E. *The Story of the Western Railroads.* New York: Macmillan Company, 1926.

Sampson, Roy, and Farris, Martin. *Domestic Transportation: Practice, Theory and Policy.* Boston: Houghton Mifflin, 1966.

Taylor, George Rogers. *The Transportation Revolution, 1815–1860.* New York: Harpers, 1968.

Thayer, Frederick C., Jr. *Air Transport Policy and National Security.* Chapel Hill: University of North Carolina Press, 1965.

Chapter Twelve
The Welfare State in America

The phrase "general Welfare" occurs twice in the Constitution of the United States: once in the Preamble, and once in Section 8 of Article I, where the powers of Congress are enumerated. But although the framers of the Constitution clearly intended to "promote" and "provide for" the general welfare, they did very little to define it. The phrase seems almost an afterthought, inserted to cover anything that might have been left out accidentally. Thus, if all those powers clearly authorized under "the Common Defence" are subtracted from Section 8, most of the remaining items deal with matters of economic organization—regulating commerce, coining money, and establishing post offices. Even the promotion of science and the arts (certainly part of the general welfare by eighteenth-century thinking) is closely tied to providing for the registration of patents and copyright; there is no hint that the Congress is to act as a kind of universal patron. This is not to criticize the Constitution—the powers granted to Congress were remarkable compared with those still exercised by most European monarchs—but only to note how little of it depended *explicitly* upon the notion of the "general Welfare." The same appears to be true of the Declaration of Independence and the first ten amendments to the Constitution: these mention laws of nature, unalienable rights, and the pursuit of happiness, but not the "general Welfare." Nevertheless, the Constitution does succeed in leaving the impression that the general welfare is something the government should do what it can to promote, by exercising the powers specifically granted to it.

The Founding Fathers' concern, in the name of the general welfare, with such matters as coinage and post offices is in strong contrast to Lyndon Johnson's 1964 Great Society program for ending poverty and racial injustice. Implicit in that domestic platform was a promise to use all the powers of the federal government for the declared purpose of improving the entire quality of American life, without limit.

Critics of this type of legislative program and attitude have often deplored what they call the trend toward the welfare state. And yet the Great Society program is only the latest product of an ideology that can be traced at least as far back as the turn of the century. Use of the term "welfare state," on the other hand, did not become common in the United States until several years after World War II. English and Scandinavian versions of the welfare state owe their creation to the efforts of political parties firmly identified with socialist ideology. But the American laws and government agencies identified as "socialistic" by their native critics were not, in fact, the work of socialists, although socialist demands and theories undoubtedly played some part in their formation. In short, if there is a welfare state in America, or if America is moving in the direction of building one, it is a wholly American phenomenon, with deep roots in the American past.

Defining the Welfare State

The point is an important one, since American critics of welfare-statism frequently treat it as if it were something wholly alien to the American tradition. This alone, they think, is sufficient grounds for rejecting it. Of course, as earlier chapters have repeatedly indicated, there is no one American tradition in any narrow political sense, but rather a succession of competing traditions. But even if it is admitted that welfare-statism is nothing new on the American scene, historical inquiry is still impeded by various semantic difficulties with the term itself. Only when these difficulties, many of them compounded by political controversy, have been cleared up, can the road that leads from the "general Welfare" phrase in the Constitution to the Great Society be traced.

Whose Welfare?

For the contemporary reader, the strongest associations of the term "welfare" are with programs of charity for the poor and helpless. Clearly, this is not *identical* with the general welfare, though caring for a part of the population might be called a contribution to the welfare of the whole. All societies recognize the need for welfare in this sense; that is what anthropologists mean when they speak of social organization having a universal welfare function. But societies differ in the means through which the welfare function is fulfilled.

As a general rule, the smaller the society and the lower its level of technology, the more likely it is that the family, in the broadest sense of the term, will be wholly responsible for the welfare of its own members. However, even primitive societies have welfare problems —orphans, the insane, the maimed. In all such cases, some higher authority than the family will have to step in if the welfare of these disadvantaged groups is to be preserved. As societies grow larger, more complex, and more mobile, traditional patterns of welfare are disrupted. Generally, there is less and less that the unaided family can do. This is particularly the case if technological change is altering the status of the family as an economic unit. This was true of America in the post–Civil War years, and it is true today, for rather similar reasons. Welfare problems do not occur in a social or economic vacuum; they are symptomatic of larger social problems, such as urbanization and industrialization.

If the welfare function is universal, why is the term "welfare state" surrounded by controversy? The answer is that the controversy has very little to do with the welfare function as such, and far more to do with the function of the state. In addition, when proponents of the welfare state speak of welfare, they mean something much closer to "the general well-being" than the welfare function.

"The State" as an Enemy

The very term "state" has an alien, unfriendly sound to American ears. The truth is that the state, considered as an all-embracing, all-powerful entity that governs the lives of its citizens in a benevolent but impersonal way, is a European concept that has never succeeded in becoming naturalized. It is not something Americans have had much experience with, and it is something they would rather not have experience with if they can help it. When Americans hear the term "welfare state" they feel a monster breathing down their necks.

Government, on the other hand, is admitted by most Americans to be a necessary institution. Like other institutions, it may perform well or badly and is capable of being improved. Moreover, it is not omnipotent or all-embracing as the state tends to be, but traditionally exists on at least three separate levels: local, state, and federal. One important aspect of the welfare state controversy is over which level of government shall take care of the welfare function.

The use of "welfare" in the sense of "the general well-being" seems at first sight to be as innocuous and neutral as the "general Welfare" of the Constitution. But attempts to *define* this broader kind of welfare nearly always emphasize the role of the federal government at the expense of local and state government. After all, what could be more logical than that the well-being of the whole society should be taken care of by the government of all the people? Thus welfare becomes an area in which the federal government, just because it *is* the federal government, has a greater stake than government of any other kind.

Of course, there is more to welfare-statism than this. Welfare in its American

context has strong historical associations with the doctrine of natural rights, and hence with the notion of equality. Proponents of the welfare state argue that if all men have an equal right to the "pursuit of Happiness," a system that both creates and perpetuates economic inequities violates that right. To this thinkers of a more conservative frame of mind often reply that the argument is logical enough, but that there is a limit to the amount of logic that can be applied directly to human affairs. Besides, they argue, economic freedom is the basis of all other freedoms, and constant federal intervention to redress inequities in the economic sphere will end by abolishing any "happiness" worth pursuing in other spheres.

It is not the purpose of this chapter to examine the entire history of the conflict in American politics between the positive and negative conceptions of government. The conflict can be traced back as far as Hamilton and Jefferson, and each generation of American political thinkers has rediscovered and reinterpreted it in the light of contemporary experience. It should be noted, however, that there is a certain artificiality in tracing the roots of American welfare-statism back beyond the period of industrialization that followed the Civil War.

It is not merely that the problems of the modern welfare state, to a very great extent, are the problems of industrialization. Nor is it sufficient to point out that nearly all federal regulation of the economic system between the end of the Civil War and the New Deal was carried out in the name of repairing and revitalizing the free enterprise system. The meager social legislation of that period accepted as an inevitable fact of life that the system would produce its casualties. Growing dissatisfaction with laissez faire did not imply an immediate demand for the welfare state.

It could not possibly have done so.

Until the American people entered World War I, they had received no demonstration of what a modern government could do to mobilize and allocate a nation's resources; and in wartime even American governments had always been given extraordinary powers. It took the experience of the Great Depression to prove that in peacetime too there were social emergencies so serious and so widespread that only the federal government could even attempt to deal with them. Many of the attempts ended in failure; it is still being debated whether any single measure undertaken by the Roosevelt administration, including the much-heralded Tennessee Valley Authority, was wholly a success. But it was as a result of the New Deal that it finally became meaningful to talk of welfare-statism in an American context.

Welfare Institutions before 1930

The English Inheritance

Care for the poor and helpless during the colonial period was governed directly by the British Poor Law of 1603. Although this law explicitly provided for government-sponsored welfare, it also assumed that families and charitable individuals would still have some part to play. Indeed, the Law of Charitable Uses, also passed in 1603, was carefully designed to regulate the public uses of private philanthropy, and to encourage the making of charitable bequests in the public interest. Both laws remained in force without major changes for over three hundred years; in the eighteenth century, George Washington was only one of many wealthy Americans who followed the Law of Charitable Uses in letter, if not in spirit.

Elizabethan welfare legislation had teeth in it; as early as 1572, contributions to the upkeep of the indigent poor (voluntary until then) were made compulsory and arrangements instituted to collect them. The law of 1601 established a regular taxation system, with some guidelines as to who was to receive what kind of care. The needy were classified into those who were irremediably helpless and lacking in necessities (the aged, chronically ill, or severely handicapped), and those, including dependent children, who were capable of becoming self-supporting. These latter were to be found work, or have work created for them; children were to be indentured as apprentices.

Although this welfare system was uniformly established throughout England and the colonies, it was still intended to be administered on a local basis. In fact, the Poor Law of 1601 was a codification of what had been the best of customary local practice. It was a system that aimed to do little more than prevent starvation, but it was not necessarily inhumane. Churches and voluntary associations were still expected to perform a charitable role; so were private individuals, under the Law of Charitable Uses. If the care provided was meager, at least it was not impersonal. The "poor of the parish" were individuals known to the community, not abstract "problem cases," and many of them were provided for in private homes by individuals, often only slightly less poor than they, who had contracted to take care of them for a fee that came from the Poor Law taxes. The more wealthy communities might construct almshouses and make sure that orphans really were taught useful trades.

The least that could be said for the system was that it recognized the needy and dependent as a group with legitimate claims on society. The main disadvantage of it was that, since the law envisaged only local administration, the quality of care a needy or dependent individual might receive depended entirely on the economic level of the community in which he resided and on the conscientiousness of its leading citizens. But, on the whole, the system appears to have been adequate for the welfare needs of a stable pre-industrial society.

Industrialism Creates Problems

The beginnings of industrialism during the last quarter of the eighteenth century brought the Poor Law system under severe strain in both England and America. People moved from the country to the town in search of work, and from one town to another. The stability of the family, hitherto the main guardian of the welfare function, was seriously affected. In addition, the population was growing; there were more poor in need of public assistance, and purely local resources were no longer adequate.

By the early nineteenth century, demands for Poor Law reform were widespread. Investigations were made, with a view to fresh legislation—in England by the central government, in America by the states. The result was a new philosophy of welfare that called for bigger and better poorhouses and poor farms. The final triumph of the Protestant ethic had coincided with the first appearance of industrial unemployment as a social problem, and the consequent increase in the number of "able-bodied poor." Since, according to the Protestant ethic, a man's moral worth could and should be judged mainly by his material attainments, the assumption easily arose that the poor were poor through their own fault.

Added to this prejudice against the poor were the principles of the English philosopher and jurist Jeremy Bentham (1748–1832). Bentham's political philosophy, humane though its intentions were, tended to be used throughout the early Victorian period as justification for the manipulation of rewards and punishments in the interests of a social efficiency held to represent the greatest happiness of the greatest number. If for "greatest number" we read "monied classes," it must be conceded that the British Poor Law Re-

form Act of 1834 was thoroughly Benthamite in spirit. No single piece of welfare legislation in America during this period corresponded in scope to the act, even at the state level.

Both the British and the American poor law reformers were agreed, however, that the old, haphazard system of care in private homes had to go. It would be more efficient if all the poor, sick, and helpless of each community were grouped together into one institution, which could then be inspected from time to time—in England, by the central government, in America by the state authorities. This general pattern of care was followed, with some modifications, until the early twentieth century. The new poor-houses soon acquired a bad name as dreary, unhealthy places presided over by unfriendly and occasionally sadistic officials. This fitted well with the purpose of the reformers, who had imagined that if the standard of public welfare were too far removed from utter poverty, personal initiative would be destroyed. Since the depravity of the poor seemed to have no limit, attempts were made to put a ceiling on public welfare expenditures by the imposition of strict residence requirements. Indeed, under the laws of some states, it became possible to live in a city for years without ever qualifying for welfare assistance.

The States Begin to Help

Humanitarian reaction against the new system and the spirit that inspired it began in the 1830's, and continued for the rest of the century. But the success it achieved was limited, as were its goals. Important among these was recognition of the special needs of certain groups—children, the deaf, the blind, the mentally disturbed or deficient—too often classified with the aged and indigent and too often mistreated because they had trouble looking after themselves.

Dorothea Dix (1802–1887), a former

schoolteacher and author of books for children, began a highly effective one-woman campaign to interest state governments in establishing separate institutions for these classes of dependent individuals, especially the insane. She was persistent, sincere, and had remarkable skill as a lobbyist (she preferred to approach influential persons in private, and, having converted them to her cause, leave the public speaking to them). Thanks largely to her efforts, most states had asylums by the 1860's, and a variety of other special services by the end of the century.

Recognition by the states that certain welfare functions were too expensive or difficult for local authorities to fulfill adequately was accompanied by the beginnings of state welfare administration. Appropriately enough, Massachusetts, where Dorothea Dix had started her crusade, was the first in the field when it established a Board of State Charities in 1863. Most other states slowly came to follow Massachusetts' example, though as late as World War I there were still ten that had not. But there were still severe limitations, most of which have persisted till the present day, on the amount of authority these boards could exercise over local welfare programs.

The constitutional doctrine of states' rights prevented Congress from getting help for the states from the federal government when the executive branch did not want to give it. This became clear in 1854, when President Franklin Pierce vetoed a bill that would have authorized grants of public land for state mental hospitals—a measure strongly urged by Dorothea Dix. President Pierce declared himself opposed to the whole philosophy of centralized welfare aid, and his verdict was allowed to stand until the 1930's.

It should be remembered that there were plenty of other worthy causes to engage the attention of American reformers during the Jacksonian era and the years that led up to the Civil War. The Temperance movement was gaining strength throughout the period, and issued in much state legislation during the 1850's. Free public education, as we saw in an earlier chapter, was already an issue in the 1820's. As time went on, the issue of abolition bulked so much larger than any other that other areas of reform were neglected for it, and the abolitionists seemed to have very little energy left once this supreme object had been gained.

Welfare Measures in the Era of Laissez Faire

Thus it was that the period of rapid economic and social expansion after the Civil War found the country entirely lacking in a central authority to fulfill or oversee performance of the welfare function. Between 1830 and 1870 the number of people living in cities had increased from just over 1 million to nearly 10 million. Immigration, too, was on the increase; by 1870 no less than 42 per cent of the population in the middle Atlantic states was either foreign-born or of foreign-born parentage. The Negro had been freed, but was now in process of being disfranchised in a different way. The Homestead Act of 1862 ended in the land speculation it had been designed to prevent, and the western frontier, by the 1890's, was ceasing to be the land of opportunity. Supported by powerful political machines that exploited the immigrant vote, the governments of the great eastern cities had become bywords for corruption. In 1873 there was a serious economic depression, and a still more serious one twenty years later. Farm prices fell as investment in manufacturing rose. The carefree, self-reliant farmer of American popular tradition became embittered and insecure. Contemporary satirists labeled this period of unprecedented individual wealth "the Gilded Age"; the glitter was all on the surface.

None of these social dislocations inspired a feeling of responsibility in the only institution with the power and resources to apply effective remedies: the federal government. The state governments were not much better, but even they sometimes wanted the federal governments to do more. Thus in 1876 Congress was forced to undertake the regulation of immigration, hitherto largely a state function, because of a ruling by the Supreme Court. Emergency legislation of this kind resulted in the creation of such distinctly federal welfare institutions as the U.S. Public Health Service. Understaffed, short of funds, and strictly limited in their functions, they nevertheless remained in existence, and could be expanded and given new functions when the right legislative occasion finally arose.

Meanwhile, the atmosphere for welfare legislation could not have been more unfavorable. The dominant social philosophy during the 1880's and 1890's was Social Darwinism, a sociological adaptation of Charles Darwin's biological evolutionism (see Chapter Fifteen). Since the new breed of American industrial tycoons and financiers had clearly "survived," they, and those who depended on them or admired them, were enchanted with a doctrine that looked on the "survival of the fittest" as the order of nature, and therefore something no government should interfere with. It was not callousness but a sincere belief in the Darwinian nature of the economic order that led President Grover Cleveland in 1893 to veto a modest appropriation for the distribution of seed to Texan farmers who had been ruined by drought.

Early Federal Help for Working Children

Opposition to this state of affairs took the form of appeals to regulate the economic system in such a manner that a greater number of people could enrich themselves. Nevertheless, the Protestant conscience of the growing middle class had been awakened to the condition of the poor, and gradually began to concern itself with such issues as child labor and the improvement of working conditions for women.

Progress was very slow; at first, even the basic facts were lacking since no government agency, state or federal, had seen any need to collect them. Manufacturers were opposed to any welfare measures that might increase labor costs. Cheap labor, after all, had been the rationale for unlimited immigration. In 1906 over 1.7 million children under fifteen (of both sexes) were employed in agricultural and industrial labor, many of them at night, and the majority for ten or eleven hours a day. The conditions under which they worked condemned many to die before reaching adulthood. Several of the northern states had recently passed legislation banning certain types of labor for children under sixteen. But the law seemed easy enough to evade, and in the South the trend toward child labor was actually increasing.

Not until the first White House Conference of 1909 did any American president dare to flout the forces of big business so far as to play host to the "child labor people," as the reformers were called. The result was the creation, three years later, of the U.S. Children's Bureau, to investigate and report on the problem. Even so, a bill regulating child labor failed to pass the Senate—the "millionaires club" —in 1914. There was no federal child or maternal welfare legislation until the 1920's, and still child labor was not abolished. All this took place, or rather failed to take place, after the so-called triumph of Progressivism, a political movement that some scholars have seen as a forerunner of welfare-statism.

Public Health Measures

Federal public health programs were even slower to develop; in fact, it can be said that, compared with the services provided in many industrialized countries, they were only getting under way in the 1960's. A promising start had been made in the colonial period when Benjamin Franklin, among other public-spirited citizens, secured the founding of the Pennsylvania Hospital in 1750. Benjamin Rush, physician and social reformer, was years ahead of his time when he had a wing for the insane added to that hospital in 1796. But local and state governments generally lagged far behind the example of Pennsylvania. Unreliable water, poor drainage, and recurring epidemics were conditions that most city governments preferred to ignore until the mid-nineteenth century.

Finally, the year 1866 saw the establishment of the New York Metropolitan Board of Health. Ten states followed suit in the next eleven years, though many large cities held out for another decade. Discovery of the causes of infection dramatically reduced mortality from epidemics, and vigorous programs of public education in hygiene and basic health facts were carried out by the voluntary health associations that have remained a vital feature of the American scene. However, the doctrine of local responsibility for health services remained firmly entrenched, and it was not until 1953, with the establishment of the Department of Health, Education, and Welfare, that the health care of all citizens was explicitly recognized as an object of federal action.

Welfare Philosophy and Economic Policy

Laissez Faire and the American Dream

The preceding sketch of how a developing American society dealt with its welfare function has largely ignored governmental promotion of the general welfare. Since the historical associations of this latter kind of welfare activity have been with federal subsidization and regulation of private economic interests, its relevance to the origins of American welfare-statism may be doubted. However, the main target of the welfare state's American critics has always been "big government," by which they generally mean some form of federal interference with the allegedly sacrosanct status of private property. To this they add that the freedom to accumulate and enjoy property is the basis for all other freedoms.

Advocates of increased governmental regulation reply that there is nothing new about "big government" in favor of monied interests. One has only to remember Hamilton's writings, the early creation of a protective tariff, and the government sales of public land to wealthy speculators at low rates. Moreover, the most impressive form taken by private property, at least since the days of John Marshall, has been the large business corporation which so excited public indignation in the late nineteenth century.

The whole controversy has long been bedeviled by the terms used to argue it. Opponents of "big government," who like to think of themselves as constitutional purists, tend to invoke the doctrine of laissez faire, while actually favoring some variation of mercantilism. The last precedent these Hamiltonians will invoke is Alexander Hamilton himself. Jeffersonians, on the other hand, invoke strong government in the name of weak. It is as if a perpetual battle is going on in American politics to prove who is *really* in favor of laissez faire. All this greatly complicates any search for the origins of American welfare-statism. Bare description of how American society at various periods has dealt with the welfare function tends not only to leave out much legislation which later became highly relevant to that function, but also to give a quite misleading impression of continuity. The truth is that whole decades went by in the history of American social legislation during which things were simply allowed to drift. Programs that in other countries would take at least a decade to plan and implement were then rushed through in a few weeks or months, creating intense conservative opposition by their very speed and novelty. Writing the history of some of these programs is like mapping a river that continually changes its course.

If, on the other hand, we concentrate not on actual programs and measures but on the evolution of American ideas about welfare, we are faced with the confusing fact that national political programs in the United States are nearly always phrased in terms of the general welfare. However, the ideologies of various native reform movements can be shown to contain elements that, when actually applied during the New Deal, were often attacked as alien to the American tradition. A discussion of the most important of them and their relation to the doctrine of laissez faire can show how very far from "socialistic" were the actual attempts at governmental regulation of the economy between the establishment of the Interstate Commerce Commission in 1887 and the entry of the United States into World War I in 1917.

Jacksonian Reform

The Jacksonian democrats, as has often been pointed out, were the first generation of American reformers to face the consequences of the new industrialism. They weighed the value of political equality under the Constitution as interpreted by Chief Justice Marshall, and found it wanting. If the Constitution really meant what it said about natural rights, they argued, then it applied not only to the rural freeholder but to the industrial proletariat. It was precisely experience of conditions in the eastern cities that gave rise to the Jacksonian reform movement known as locofocoism. Amer-

ica, like Disraeli's England, was becoming split into "two societies": the poor and the rich, or (some Jacksonians said) the producers and the non-producers. It was distrust of the latter that, in 1832, led Jackson himself to veto the re-charter of the Second Bank of the United States—an action viewed by the newly-formed Whig Party as a direct attack upon private property as an institution.

Jacksonian democracy was anything but a philosophy of "big government." The Jacksonians favored government action against monopoly, but only in order to restore laissez faire. Nevertheless, they encouraged state legislation in such areas as public education, the law of debt, and even conditions of labor. However, state-financed attempts at programs of internal improvement were not a success, and after the Civil War the Hamiltonian philosophy resumed its sway. Thus the United States entered the period of increased urbanization with little or no conception of the positive role that government could play in guiding social and economic change.

The Rise of Business Power

After the Civil War the leading companies in many industries took steps to minimize competition by forming trusts. Exposure of the trusts during the 1880's, and of the monopolistic practices of the railroads, led at first to weak state legislation, and finally, in 1887, to the federal Interstate Commerce Commission. (See Chapter Five.) The ICC was followed in 1890 by the Sherman Anti-Trust Act. This was hardly a socialistic measure, since its ostensible purpose—touchingly naive in the world of Rockefeller, Carnegie, and Morgan—was to restore something like the pre–Civil War pattern of laissez faire. Actually, its creation was primarily a sop to public opinion; few suits were brought under it, and the Supreme Court soon ruled that it could not be applied to manufacturing industries anyway, since these were not "interstate." The act has led a somewhat more active life in the twentieth century, but its political reputation can be judged from the fact that during the first years of the New Deal it was immediately set aside in favor of NRA (see Chapter Eight). Among those urging its return to favor were some of the heads of the very trusts it was supposed to intimidate.

The businessmen of the 1890's still talked of laissez faire, but they looked to Congress for favors. The same Congress that passed the Sherman Antitrust Act also pursued a protectionist tariff policy, and gave away millions in the form of steamship subsidies, programs of internal improvement, and state tax rebates. From the early 1870's onwards, the voice of reform was seldom absent from American life.

The farmers, as has already been pointed out, were suffering from the fall in farm prices and the changing nature of the American economy. Their main targets were the banks and railroads and the get-rich-quick spirit with which the expansion of commerce seemed to be poisoning the well-springs of rural virtue. Their view of history was backward-looking and conspiratorial. The conspiracy was of the rich against the working man. The early farmers' association known as the Grange, which was at its strongest in the mid-1870's, claimed to be nonpolitical; basically, it aimed to regulate the profits of the transportation and distribution businesses on which the farmer depended, or to bypass them through co-operatives. Since this policy, pursued at state level, failed to raise farm prices, regional associations were formed, but still on an ostensibly nonpartisan basis. However, in 1890 a People's or "Populist" Party, recruited mainly from the farmers' associations, was formed in Kansas, and other western states soon followed. Two years later, a national People's Party was calling for, among other things, govern-

ment ownership of railroads and communications, and a graduated income tax.

The Populists were the first effective American political movement since the birth of industrialism to insist that the federal government had any real responsibility for the common welfare. As a political party, their fate was that of all American third party movements: in order to remain a national political force, they had to sacrifice at least part of their identity to one of the two major parties. As ideologists, however, they were remarkably successful. It became a permanent feature of Democratic party policy that, where farmers were concerned, somehow the classic principles of laissez faire did not apply.

Protestant Protest

It was not, however, the farm bloc that was to supply a dominant American ethos of reform for the twentieth century. This was the achievement of the urban, white, mainly Protestant middle class, which grew from about a million in the early 1870's to nearly 6 million in 1900. The eventual triumph of this group's values accounts for much in American welfare-statism that often puzzles European political analysts—the relative lack of violence accompanying major social upheavals, the pragmatic administrative spirit, the apparent lack of ideology, and the curious insensitivity to the psychological aspects of racism.

The middle classes who voted for reform did not feel the need for a Marx or a Lenin to tell them what they should believe or how they should view their society. Certainly, they had some awareness of economic factors, of the role of special interests in politics. Under the American system it was hard not to acquire such awareness if one read the newspapers, and those who were slow to acquire it had it rammed into them by the talented muckraking journalists of 1902–1906. But the nature of their concern with social questions was essentially that of an economically privileged but morally enlightened class wishing to share its enlightenment but not its privileges. All would be well with society, they thought, if only the rich and powerful would have the decency to play the social game as they did, and join in the righteous enterprise of uplifting the poor. Even when the Great Depression removed for many the economic basis of this lofty approach, it was not revolution that they called for but a morally respectable version of the old status quo.

The rank-and-file spirit of the reform movement that became known as Progressivism should not be confused with that of its leaders, who were usually far more radical. Theodore Roosevelt sometimes appeared to condemn capitalism altogether, and mentioned the dreaded word "revolution." But the ideological roots of Progressivism are to be found not in Socialism or Communism but in Protestantism; the Progressive mind was a Protestant mind.

These Protestants were well-educated, often prosperous men, with a stake in society; they were not interested in starting or joining mass movements, which they distrusted. Such were the Mugwumps, an intellectual but economically conservative group of urban reformers who flourished in the large eastern cities during the late 1870's and early 1880's. The chief goal of the Mugwumps was civil service reform; their favorite theme was the decline of public responsibility among the upper classes. As a political movement they were of only passing importance, but the Mugwump spirit lived on in the ideals of such distinguished later reformers as Woodrow Wilson.

The other immediate ancestor of Progressivism was the Social Gospel movement, which can be traced back to the 1860's, but which found its first spokesman in Washington Gladden, a Congregationalist minister. In a book published in 1876, Gladden advocated a more Christian spirit in labor relations, and was the harbinger of an intellectual movement that soon headed in the direction of socialism. He himself was not hostile to private enterprise, only to the spirit in which it was currently pursued. But his concern for the disadvantaged led him to recommend social reforms that would have meant abandoning negative government completely. "Applied Christianity," the title of one of Gladden's books, became a slogan of the day in middle-class Protestant circles. Far more radical was another Congregationalist minister, George D. Herron, who throughout the 1890's condemned the existing order unequivocally, calling it the survival of the unfit. Christianity has never charged its adherents with a duty to love the rich. To Herron, and others like him, the Sermon on the Mount was a direct call to social justice—a call that the government should be the first to heed.

Other Social Gospelers formed their own socialist organizations—the longest-lived was the Society of Christian Socialists, founded in 1889 by the Episcopalian W. D. P. Bliss. But Christian Socialism retained the middle-class dislike of mass movements, and in spite of the impressive activities of individuals like Bliss it was always more of an intellectual than a political force. In spite of such worthy offshoots of independent allies of the Social Gospelers as the settlement house movement, it is probably true that the Social Gospelers' criticism of American capitalism was destructive rather than constructive. It helped to destroy faith in laissez faire as a morally respectable political philosophy. The history of Progressivism—and of liberal politics after that—was to be the history of a search for a faith to replace the one that had been lost.

Little mention has been made here of the various American Socialist parties because, in spite of some local successes, they never became a power on the national scene comparable to the Progressives. In two presidential elections, those of 1912 and 1920, the Socialist candidate Eugene V. Debs (see Chapter Four), did receive nearly a million votes. But the Socialists never won their way into the electoral college, whereas the Progressives did this twice: once in 1912, with Theodore Roosevelt, and once in 1924, with Robert M. La Follette. A few socialist writers, especially Edward Bellamy, whose utopia *Looking Backward* was a bestseller from its first appearance in 1888, exerted an influence on the more thoughtful portion of the middle classes comparable to that of the Social Gospelers. Some historians have called the years between 1880 and 1917 the "golden age" of American Socialism. But it was less of a golden age than a false dawn.

The Progressive Movement

A good case could be made for the thesis that the only real leader the Progressive movement ever had was Robert M. La Follette. Certainly, the year 1924, when La Follette ran as Progressive candidate for President and lost, is a convenient date to choose for the end of the Progressive era. The period of reaction that followed does not make the achievements of Progressivism appear very lasting ones, either in the sphere of promoting the general welfare or in that of safeguarding the welfare of particular groups in the interest of social justice. A few states with Progressive legislatures—notably, La Follette's own Wisconsin—had made strides toward welfare-statism that were not to be matched on the national scene until the New Deal. But, given the fact that regulatory legislation is worth only as much as Congress appropriates to administer it and can proceed only as far as the courts will let it, the various Progressive measures passed under Theodore Roosevelt, Taft, and Wilson seem at first sight like minor battles in bygone wars.

But this viewpoint ignores two major factors. In the first place, a genuine social movement cannot be equated with the political party that represents it or the individuals who speak in its name. The People's Party died an unheroic death in 1908; Populism went marching on, until it established itself in the Department of Agriculture. Nobody reads the works of the Social Gospelers today, but Americans have become accustomed to hearing the clergy take controversial positions on social matters.

In the second place Americans tend to view history too much with the eyes of hindsight. An event that looks like a rather mild foretaste of things to come may, because of its novelty, affect contemporaries like a whole revolution. Such was the case in 1902 with Theodore Roosevelt's antitrust proceeding against J. P. Morgan's Northern Securities Company (see Chapter Seven). The Progressives, and the country as a whole, suddenly realized what a president could do if he were so minded. It must be remembered that this was the height of the muckraking period in Progressive journalism; to the Progressive conscience, the country was full of abuses that needed to be remedied immediately. It must also be remembered that Roosevelt was a Republican, albeit a Progressive Republican who had been nominated vice president in order to render him harmless in the eyes of party conservatives. Roosevelt's impulsiveness frightened his own party, but they were even more frightened of the Democrats.

Roosevelt's major legislative achievements, such as they were, all belong to the first two years of his second term; the Republican majority in Congress saw to that. Roosevelt did make progress in the areas of conservation and the regulation of business in the interest of public health. Much as he loved the wide open spaces, Roosevelt did not invent the philosophy of conservation; this was the work of others.

But he made conservation—including conservation of the area that was to become the Tennessee Valley—a political fact, and he used the position of the presidency to boost the philosophy.

Nor did he write *The Jungle,* a terrifying account by Upton Sinclair, an acknowledged socialist, of the meat-packing industry; the important thing was that Roosevelt read it, and admitted to having read it. The symbolic importance of this to the Progressive movement was far greater than the legislative importance of the Meat Inspection Amendment to the Agriculture Appropriations Act of 1906, or the Pure Food and Drug Act of the same year. The notion that politics could, after all, have something to do with the movement of ideas—was not simply a matter of influence, corruption, and big business—was a revelation to middle-class intellectuals. Suddenly, the gap between reform and power seemed to have been closed—or, at least, to have become capable of being bridged. Earnest Protestant intellectuals could not forget this.

Once the power of the presidency had been demonstrated in such matters as conservation, the reformers were still more unwilling to let federal regulation of the welfare function remain uncharted territory. Roosevelt himself, chafing under the frustrations of his last two years in office, moved toward the conclusion that the selfishness of the trusts was a social menace that would have to be dealt with once and for all. His principal solution was still federal regulation, though when he seceded from the Republican Party in 1912 to form the Progressive Party he endorsed the principles of unionism. The bulk of the Progressives, however, were not ready to follow him in this; the middle-class prejudice against the combination of working men was too strong.

The principal contribution of the Progressive movement to American welfare-statism was its demonstration that reform was a popular cause. Passage of Progressive legislation (including the Sixteenth Amendment which authorized an income tax) under the Republican William Howard Taft could not conceal the fact that the Republicans were not a reform party. And yet the New Freedom of Woodrow Wilson, which triumphed in the election of 1912, involved a return to states' rights—so much so that Wilson could not even find it in himself to support federal child welfare legislation. Wilson's Federal Reserve Act of 1913 was an important step in freeing the government from dependence on Wall Street. The Federal Trade Commission Act of 1914 was also an antitrust measure, consistent with the more active conception of the presidency pioneered by Theodore Roosevelt.

But more important than either for the future of welfare-statism was his appointment, in 1916, of Louis Brandeis to the Supreme Court. This was yet another illustration of the way in which the advancement of equalitarianism in America has depended not so much on mass movements as on individuals acting in the knowledge of mass movements. By 1916, the place of equalitarianism in the American Dream was so firmly established that the two major parties were quarreling however reluctantly about means rather than ends on the road to reform.

Toward a General-Welfare State: The New Deal

The New Deal and Economic Rights

From Woodrow Wilson onwards, a kind of continuity in the development of welfare institutions is supplied by one underlying theme: the growth of federal power. The question of whether there was also a steady growth of welfare-statism may be reduced to the question of what this power was used for—in other words, whose welfare was being promoted. There is also the closely related question of whose welfare successive presidents and sessions of Congress *thought* they were promoting, and in the name of what political philosophy. No brand of Americanism has ever claimed to be less than the only original and authentic one. This does not mean that the labels, slogans, and platforms have no importance. What American society eventually decides to recognize as the true image of itself, for which it is always searching, will depend to a great extent on what it has decided it wants to resemble. This latter decision is not yet in, though perhaps its outlines can already be discerned.

It is true that, in the history of American welfare-statism, the New Deal, especially the Social Security Act of 1935, marks a turning point. So does the election—and overwhelming re-election—of Franklin Delano Roosevelt, as unequivocal an expression of the popular will as has ever taken place in American politics. But was it an ideological turning point, as well as a political one?

In 1932, a year in which there were over 12 million unemployed, after more than 2,300 banks had failed the previous year, and industrial production had fallen by better than 50 per cent since 1929, the *popular* vote for Hoover was nearly 16 million, or about 7 million less than that for Roosevelt himself. Whether one regards this as a large difference or a small one depends on his interpretation of the New Deal as a whole. A vote for Roosevelt in 1932 was not necessarily a vote against what most people understood by laissez faire, however.

Considered in isolation, the Social Security Act seems like a sudden and revolutionary assumption by the federal government of welfare functions hitherto reserved to the states. But there was nothing sudden about it; the industrial depression was already six years old, and depression on the farm had lasted longer

than that. Nor can the act be called revolutionary, except as an invitation to do better. In fact, it was a compromise from a constitutional point of view, since it was designed to supplement existing programs. The United States, after all, was the only advanced industrial country to enter the Great Depression without a national social security program of some kind, and it was only after the inadequacy of both state and private resources had been demonstrated that the government was able to enact even this measure of reform. The need for relief and recovery in 1932 was clear to all; the need for reform was not.

What the majority voted for when they elected Roosevelt over Hoover was a different style of getting things done—a style they thought would bring relief sooner to those who needed it most. Hoover, after all, had nearly three years in which to plan and carry out a relief program. By the end of that period the average unemployed American, rightly or wrongly, thought of Hoover mainly as someone who met the emergency by loaning large sums of money to businessmen (through the Reconstruction Finance Corporation). He was also the man who had refused to see the Bonus Expeditionary Force, a small army of veterans who had marched on Washington and then encamped there to lobby for the immediate payment of a post-war bonus to which they were legally entitled (see Chapter Thirteen). Meanwhile Franklin Roosevelt, a popular reform governor of New York, had been making speeches about the "forgotten man at the bottom of the economic pyramid," and urging a more adventurous approach to solving the nation's crisis—a program of "bold, persistent experimentation."

Influences on New Deal Thinking

Roosevelt had not mistaken the temper of the country; he understood that it was prepared for experiment, but that revolution in the name of class interests was not the American way. It was hard to apply formulae derived from the Marxist theory of class warfare in a country where the ordinary industrial worker, if he thought in class terms at all, aspired mainly to join the bourgeoisie. In 1932, the U.S. Communist Party's able presidential candidate, William Z. Foster, received only about 100,000 votes, or nearly eight times fewer than Norman Thomas, the highly respectable Socialist whose beliefs had more to do with the Social Gospel movement than with Marx or Lenin. Communists had been sent to organize the Washington bonus marchers, but they had made little headway. They had somewhat more success in organizing labor strikes and boycotts, to which their methods were more suited; they also won over some leading intellectuals, for a time. But although there was much loose talk of revolution in the years immediately following the Great Crash, observers with experience of actual revolutions in Europe and elsewhere were amazed at the continuing faith of the American people in their system, and at their reluctance to press their demands by violence.

If the voters did not feel the need to follow European examples, neither did Roosevelt and his advisers. The experience of both Populism and Progressivism had provided them with a grab bag of administrative and ideological precedents. So had World War I, with government control of railroads and government construction of the merchant fleet that was the "bridge to France." There was no single favorite constitutional device, like the office of dictator in the late Roman republic, to which the nation could resort in the emergency. If there had been, it seems unlikely that American democracy would have survived in its present form.

Instead, the New Dealers were in a position to recall a whole welter of reform measures, including regulatory statutes, independent regulatory commissions, tariff legislation, grants-in-aid to states and private organizations, wartime bonds drawn from both government and industry, price controls, government-financed loan companies, presidential orders, and plain moral suasion by the president himself. Theodore Roosevelt's New Nationalism of 1910 remained an inspiring example of political concern for the purely human aspects of welfare. Some states had long ago enacted some types of social legislation under Progressive administrations. Forty states and territories had workmen's compensation laws by 1917; the first state old-age pension law was passed in Arizona three years earlier (it was soon ruled unconstitutional). Special state pensions for mothers of dependent children were available in Missouri and Illinois as early as 1911.

At least two prominent New Dealers, Harry Hopkins and Henry Wallace, had been deeply influenced by the Social Gospel movement. If the Progressives' conviction that trust-busting was the reformer's first duty was not much in evidence during the New Deal's early years, F.D.R. himself affected an almost Populist horror of financiers. La Follette, running for president on the Progressive Party ticket in 1924 with strong rural support, had advocated (among other measures) federal recognition of the workers' right to collective bargaining, a federal child labor law, and—of course—federal aid to farmers. He got nearly 5 million votes. The Eighteenth Amendment (Prohibition) had given evidence of how a determined group of reformers could change the entire pattern of national life; so had the Nineteenth Amendment, by which women obtained the right to vote, hitherto granted only by individual states and territories.

Another potent influence was Woodrow Wilson, whose faith that that something called fair competition could be legislated into existence proceeded from a perhaps unconscious nostalgia for a less complex and presumably happier America. More significant for the New Deal than his Clayton Anti-Trust Act or his Federal Trade Commission was his success in establishing the Federal Reserve System, and so taking control of bank rates and money supply at least partly out of private hands. Wilson had called his program "the New Freedom," and had done his best to attract the Progressive vote through labor legislation and the extension of government credit to farmers. But his foreign policy—he had promised during the election campaign of 1916 to keep America out of the war—brought about an electoral repudiation of reform that lasted until the Great Depression.

Curiously enough, it was not a reform measure at all (not even the Revenue Act of 1916, which greatly increased the federal power to tax incomes) that provided the most impressive demonstration of "big government" under Wilson, but a measure originally intended as a concession to business. La Follette's Seaman's Act of 1915, which rescued American seamen from a status that had amounted to involuntary servitude, antagonized the shipowners, whose business had been declining since the early 1860's. For years, congressional intentions had hovered between regulation and subsidy; finally in 1916 a bill was passed that provided both, under the aegis of an independent regulatory commission called the Shipping Board.

The regulatory powers of the Board were similar to those of the ICC with respect to railroads, but it differed from the ICC in being authorized to set up a corporation with a capitalization of $50 million in federal funds for the actual purchase of ships, which were to be sold later to private interests. The reason was the war; shipping goods to Europe had suddenly become very profitable, and the country lacked the merchant ships to take advantage of this. With American entry into the war, the Board was granted special powers and a greatly increased budget (it eventually passed three billion dollars) to build a "bridge to Europe." The ships were built by private firms, but the Board appears to have regarded itself during these years simply as the agent of the president. The result was that when peace was declared the federal government found itself the owner and operator of a huge merchant fleet. (See Chapter Eleven.)

It is possible to make too much of the similarities between the New Deal and Progressivism. Many of the basic ideals were the same, but the circumstances were entirely different. The virtual collapse of the economic system and the resultant unemployment and hardship, together with the bankruptcy of the states, compelled the New Dealers to find some way of involving the federal government heavily in social legislation. The government's interest in the labor market could no longer be a purely humanitarian one, as it had been in the first two decades of the century. Clearly, it was no use to improve working conditions if there was no work. Roosevelt's immediate response was to make the government itself an employer on a large scale. The concept of federal government as the actual organizer of the free enterprise labor market—a concept already adopted in Great Britain with the Labour Exchange Act of 1903 and the institution of unemployment insurance through Lloyd George's National Insurance Act of 1911—evolved only slowly, and was not formally recognized by Congress until after the New Deal was over.

New Deal Welfare Measures

Franklin Roosevelt's first concern, as he had promised in his campaign speeches, was to "get the country moving again." During his famous Hundred Days, between early March and mid-June 1933, the Congress passed fifteen major pieces of legislation. The most important of these were concerned exclusively with relief and recovery. The Federal Emergency Relief Act set up a national relief system. The Agricultural Adjustment Act offered farmers a subsidy for *not* planting a certain proportion of their acreage—a System Act, with modifications, has been used to maintain farm prices to this day (see Chapter Six). The Emergency Farm Mortgage Act saved many farmers from losing their farms, and the Tennessee Valley Authority Act set up a government corporation to bring electrical power and scientific agriculture to the Tennessee Valley. The Truth in Securities Act prevented the issue of "watered stock," and the Home Owners Loan Act did for the rest of the nation what the Emergency Farm Mortgage Act had done for the farmers. But the most interesting and controversial of all these early pieces of legislation was the National Industrial Recovery Act (NIRA), an attempt to give private industry a chance to regulate itself under federal supervision, combined with a public works program for which the Congress appropriated $3.3 billion. (See Chapter Eight.)

The year 1935 is generally considered a turning point in the history of the New Deal. Conservative business and financial interests were by now thoroughly aroused in opposition to the Securities Act of 1933 and the Securities Exchange Act of 1934, which made the sale of listed stocks and bonds subject to regulation by the Securities and Exchange Commission. Since the worst of the economic crisis appeared, to those who still had jobs or businesses, to be over, many wanted a return to business as usual. A group calling itself the American Liberty League, which included a number of leading Democrats who had broken with Roosevelt and obtained support from several major business corporations, began to demand a return to laissez faire. The group received a setback when

Herbert Hoover refused to join it, and it soon became known in New Deal circles as the "I Can't Take It Club."

Since the Democrats increased their majority in both houses during the congressional elections of 1934, Roosevelt could for the time being laugh off this kind of opposition. In 1935 the Congress appropriated nearly $5 billion for emergency relief—the largest single appropriation in American history—and gave Roosevelt a virtually free hand in spending it. There is still much controversy among historians over the use he made of this mandate. On the one hand, with the passage of such measures as the National Labor Relations Act of 1935 and the Fair Labor Standards Act of 1938 (see Chapter Eight), he appeared to be giving up the attempt at obtaining cooperation from business and courting the labor vote in a way he had not done before. On the other hand, he incurred criticism from some leading New Dealers for relying increasingly on the federal government's power to tax in order to create incentives for local participation in the federal recovery programs.

But by far the largest portion of the emergency relief appropriation went to the Works Progress Administration which embarked on a vast public works program that, despite the low wages, soon became known with some justification as a boondoggle. Roosevelt, however, in this and in other measures, was attempting to redistribute purchasing power in a manner conducive to stability. In 1919, as his economists told him, the top 5 per cent of persons in the income pyramid had received over 24 per cent of all disposable income, and this share had increased to over 33 per cent in 1929. Facts like this made the Republicans' talk of old-fashioned American virtues sound a little hollow—and the general public was beginning to be aware of the facts. With the passage of the Social Security Act of

1935 and the Railroad Retirement Acts of 1934 and 1935, it began to be clear what the New Deal was all about: it would spend its best efforts on making life better for ordinary people.

The Social Security Act was certainly drawn up in this spirit. What outraged the conservatives—and still does outrage them—was that the tax for retirement benefits under the act was compulsory. Nothing else about the act can be called revolutionary, or even particularly conducive to social security, except by comparison with what had gone before. The unemployment insurance provisions, for instance, fell far short of the standard already attained in Britain, and was tied to state administrations by the matching-funds device, as was federal aid for children, the handicapped, and the chronically dependent. Federal efforts in the housing field were still more modest; they consisted mainly in lending money, first to private construction interests and then to state and local authorities. The results were generally admitted to be a failure. There was no program of federal aid for medical care. Nevertheless, all this legislation set powerful precedents, and broke through political barriers that before 1933 had seemed impenetrable.

By 1938 the New Deal's most vital legislative work was completed, though economic recovery remained slow. Roosevelt himself had intended to seek a mandate for still more social legislation after the war was over. In his State of the Union message in 1944—a message that turned out to be his political testament—he spoke of the "second Bill of Rights" which he thought the New Deal had established for the American people. This included the rights to an adequate standard of living, a decent home, medical care and the chance for good health, insurance against accident, old age, and unemployment, and a good education. All these things together, he concluded, were what he meant by security. He was far from

By Bishop in the ST. LOUIS STAR-TIMES

F.D.R. Bringing the Prodigal Home

claiming that these rights had all become realities under his administration, but he thought that they were rights that could and should be secured through federal legislation.

Welfare since the New Deal

President Truman's Fair Deal continued this emphasis on the economic security of the individual, and established a cabinet-level Council of Economic Advisers. But his only substantial accomplishment in the field of welfare legislation was the Employment Act of 1946. Although this act formally committed the federal government "to maintain as a matter of continuing policy a full, bountiful and growing economy," and coupled this with an explicit rejection of laissez faire as an economic philosophy, it instituted no administrative measures toward this end. Nevertheless, it was a historic declaration, and a fitting epitaph to the Great Depression. If some detected the influence of the English economist John Maynard Keynes in all this, it could not have worried the majority of congressmen, for they had undoubtedly never heard of him. Besides, there were plenty of economists in the government now; perhaps that, after all, was the New Deal's most lasting achievement.

Another measure of the Truman administration was the National Mental Health Act of 1947, which at last admitted the federal government into the very area of responsibility from which President Franklin Pierce had banned it through his veto of 1854. It should be noted, too, that Truman did propose a federal medical insurance program, the forerunner of Medicare, which was defeated amidst talk of "socialized medicine." He was more successful in another area: the Federal Housing Act of 1949 provided for low-rent public housing projects subsidized by the national government.

The development of American welfare-statism since 1947 displays a number of marked features, but has not yet given definitive evidence of its ultimate direction. On the political level, there seems to be—or at least there was, until the war in Vietnam became an overriding American commitment—an area of agreement between the two major parties that has been aptly labeled the "welfare consensus." This consensus managed to survive the Korean War in much better shape than Woodrow Wilson's version of Progressivism survived World War I. Thus both the Republican Congress of 1954 and the Democratic Congress of 1956 passed extensions to the Social Security Act, and increases in social security benefits were promised by both major presidential candidates in their campaigns of 1968. It was Dwight D. Eisenhower, a Republican, who created the post of the first federal Secretary of Health, Education, and Welfare; and though he was opposed to any further expansion of TVA, he did sign the Housing Act of 1954, a measure designed to increase the number of home-owners.

Another important development has been the immense increase in American scholarly writing and thinking about the nature of the welfare state, and the rise of something resembling an intellectual consensus in this area. It is generally agreed that whatever else it may be, a welfare state is at least one that actively pursues programs to raise worker income, aid the disabled and unemployed, and institute reforms that, it is hoped, will serve the interests of social justice and improve the general quality of social life. Programs to raise worker income include the expansion of such public services as education, low-cost housing, and free recreational facilities; they are financed by progressive tax systems. Labor's economic interests are also served by legislation to insure minimum wages and the right to collective bargaining, and to protect the consumer from misleading advertising and substandard merchandise.

The traditional welfare function, aid to the disabled, becomes increasingly diversified as the needs of different groups are recognized and met with appropriate social services. Aid to the unemployed is complemented by measures to eliminate unemployment for all those capable of productive work. Economic exploitation of the natural environment must not be grossly contrary to the public interest; the arts and sciences are supported as national assets.

The United States now has federal programs in all these areas, including government aid for certain categories of medical care since 1965. But thinking about what the welfare state is capable of providing has stimulated research into what the needs of American society actually are. And, of course, existing welfare programs, judged by the standards of Roosevelt's "second Bill of Rights," have been found inadequate to those needs. Americans are becoming increasingly aware that the existence of far too many citizens—

especially black Americans—is one of poverty in the midst of plenty.

Coupled with this, however, has been a more optimistic strain of thinking along the lines that, since America is now rich and powerful enough to eliminate poverty altogether, American welfare-statism should now aim higher than its previous, merely economic goals. This note was present in both President Kennedy's New Frontier program and President Johnson's Great Society, which otherwise have essentially been continuations of the New Deal. One New Deal feature, though, is either absent or muted: the Progressive insistence on trust-busting. Instead, the federal government now prefers to initiate specific legislation, such as the Truth-in-Lending Act, to protect the needs of the private consumer, and to safeguard what it takes to be the general economic welfare by using its own immense power as a purchaser of almost every kind of industrial and agricultural product. The president may also attempt moral suasion, in true Progressive style. But he is not likely to call immediately for yet another regulatory commission.

In the late 1960's, the debate over welfare seemed to be about means, rather than ends, with wide discussion of such possible substitutes for traditional welfare relief as a guaranteed annual income. The War on Poverty, defined by President Johnson's message to Congress on the Economic Opportunity Act of 1964, was acknowledged by both parties to be necessary in some form. As usual, the Democrats wanted more spending and more federal power, and the Republicans wanted less. The Republicans were more likely to speak of welfare as destroying incentive and initiative, and the Democrats of equality of opportunity. But as it became increasingly evident that the economic problem of welfare was also a racial problem, it was problematic how long either party could afford to remain frozen in these traditional attitudes.

For Further Reading

Altmeyer, Arthur. *The Formative Years of Social Security*. Madison: University of Wisconsin Press, 1966.

Bornet, Vaugan O. *Welfare Services Surveyed*. Norman: University of Oklahoma Press, 1961.

Boskin, Joseph. *Opposition Politics: the Anti–New Deal Tradition*. Beverly Hills: Glencoe Press, 1968.

Childs, Marquis W. and Douglass Cater. *Ethics in a Business Society*. New York: Harper and Row, 1954.

Creating the Great Society. Washington, D.C.: The New Republic, 1965.

Crosland, C. A. R. *The Future of Socialism*. New York: Schocken Books, 1963.

Cushman, Robert E. *The Independent Regulatory Commissions*. New York: Oxford University Press, 1941.

Fine, Sidney. *Laissez Faire and the General-Welfare State*. Ann Arbor: University of Michigan Press, 1956.

Friedman, Lawrence M. *Government and Slum Housing: A Century of Frustration*. Chicago: Rand McNally, 1968.

Friedman, Milton. *Capitalism and Freedom*. Chicago: University of Chicago Press, 1962.

Galbraith, John Kenneth. *The Affluent Society*. Boston: Houghton Mifflin Company, 1958.

Hall, M. Penelope. *The Social Services of Modern England*. London: Routledge, 1965.

Harrington, Michael. *The Other America*. New York: Macmillan Company, 1962.

Hofstadter, Richard. *The Age of Reform: From Bryan to F.D.R.* New York: Alfred A. Knopf, 1955.

Kipnis, Ira. *The American Socialist Movement, 1897–1912*. New York: Columbia University Press, 1952.

Knowles, John H. *Hospitals, Doctors, and the Public Interest*. Cambridge: Harvard University Press, 1965.

Krinsky, Fred and Joseph Boskin. *The Welfare State: Who is My Brother's Keeper?* Beverly Hills: Glencoe Press, 1968.

May, Edgar. *The Wasted Americans.* New York: Harper and Row, 1964.

Miller, Herman P. *Rich Man Poor Man.* New York: Thomas Y. Crowell Company, 1964.

Musolf, Lloyd D. *Government and the Economy.* Glenview, Ill.: Scott, Foresman and Co., 1965.

Reagan, Michael D. *Politics, Economics, and the General Welfare.* Glenview, Ill.: Scott, Foresman and Company, 1965.

Report of the National Advisory Commission on Civil Disorders. Washington, D.C.: U.S. Government Printing Office, 1968.

Schlesinger, Arthur M., Sr. *The American as Reformer.* Cambridge: Harvard University Press, 1955.

Schlesinger, Arthur M., Jr. *The Coming of the New Deal.* Boston: Houghton Mifflin Company, 1959.

Schoor, Alvin L. *Slums and Social Insecurity.* Washington, D.C.: U.S. Government Printing Office, 1963.

Seligman, Ben B. (ed.). *Poverty as a Public Issue.* New York: The Free Press, 1965.

Steiner, Gilbert Y. *Social Insecurity: The Politics of Welfare.* Chicago: Rand McNally, 1966.

Theobald, Robert. *Social Policies for America in the Seventies.* Garden City, N.Y.: Doubleday and Company, 1968.

Part Four
Preserving And Defining
American Traditions

Chapter Thirteen
The Military in American History

A standing military force is something of an enigma in a democratic society. The American nation began its existence quite fearful of the military. Experience with British troops had alerted Americans to the dangers of a strong and permanent military arm. As a consequence, for a large part of the nation's history, its military forces consisted primarily of undisciplined state militias. Even when the nation overcame its initial fears and authorized a standing army, it was relatively small and ineffectual. However, the continental isolation of the nation, coupled with the weakness of our immediate neighbors, made the existence of a large, permanent army unnecessary —at least for a time.

Conscription was first used during the Civil War but it was not effectively or rigidly enforced. Except for the Civil War, volunteers fought all our wars until America became involved in World War I. But the huge military machine then established did not cause a great deal of concern, since it was only in existence for a short period. After World War I, the draft was ended and the military forces were allowed to languish.

From 1940 onward, the military became a major and apparently permanent part of American life. In that year the first peacetime draft was authorized, and a large military establishment has existed ever since. The armed forces were cut back tremendously after World War II, but the nation still retained a large force used for occupation purposes, and for fulfilling its new international commitments. The Korean War re-established the draft and a new expansion of the military began.

Many Americans are opposed to the draft; some are opposed to all military service. But most Americans accept that which they don't like as a matter of duty— or necessity. A small minority actively resists induction into military service for

315

a variety of reasons, some of which are based on traditional American principles. Since this resistance usually results in a prison sentence or self-imposed exile, it is not lightly undertaken.

The American Constitution guarantees individual rights, freedom of choice, and the right to dissent. However, a military organization, by its very nature, cannot allow its members these rights. The individual must necessarily be submerged in such a group; his actions must be limited to carrying out orders which must not be questioned. In effect, military personnel are not free in the same sense their civilian counterparts are.

The present chapter will survey American military history in broad outline— how the United States has raised armies and fought wars. Necessarily, the discussion will touch upon such related issues as disarmament, dissent, and draft riots.

Colonial Experiences with the Military

Throughout the colonial period American colonists had become accustomed to living in the company of British troops. Originally, these troops came to America for two reasons: one was to fight against France, England's European and colonial rival; the other was to control and occasionally to fight Indians. Some colonial support was expected, but usually in the form of honoring requisitions from British forces. Frontiersmen did take an active part in fighting Indians because they were personally involved, but France appeared to be no great menace to them personally since British troops were present.

However, no serious problems were encountered with the military for the simple reason that England did not have a large contingent of troops in the New World. English military theory called for a small professional army, buttressed in time of emergency by a colonial militia.

Technically, all free men belonged to the militia and could be called upon for service, but in actuality, such demands were not always honored.

At times these colonial militiamen showed considerable prowess as Indian fighters, though it must be remembered that most of the eastern Indians were not effectively organized. Even so, the colonials could take on the best of professional troops if they developed a sincere desire to do so. Americans have commonly made good fighting men when they have been convinced of the urgency of the situation. One example will serve to illustrate this characteristic.

Bacon's Rebellion

In 1642 Sir John Berkeley was appointed royal governor of Virginia by Charles I, then King of England. But in 1649, after several civil wars, the Roundheads, supporters of Parliament who were led by Oliver Cromwell, took power and beheaded the King. They retained power until 1660 when Charles II regained the throne. During this period Berkeley remained as inconspicuous as possible, fearing for his governorship. He ignored demands of the Virginia settlers for protection from the Indians, reasoning that "men of quality" did not live on the frontier and that the settlers were unworthy of protection. Besides, he was personally involved in trading with the Indians and was unwilling to antagonize them. In 1676 a young settler, Nathaniel Bacon, raised his own army and defeated the Indians. With this victory Bacon gained some influence in the Virginia Assembly and was given further responsibility for the protection of the settlers. Berkeley began to fear Bacon's popularity and made plans to destroy him. When Bacon returned from one of his expeditions against the Indians, he found Berkeley's troops blocking the road to Jamestown. Bacon overran the British troops, burned Jamestown and chased Berkeley out of the colony.

Bacon died shortly afterwards and Berkeley returned to the colony. Immediately, he began hanging Bacon's leaderless followers, and King Charles II recalled him in disgrace for his excesses, pointing out that Berkeley had hanged more colonials over the incident than Charles had for the beheading of his father. Bacon's Rebellion of 1677 is important for two reasons. It manifested the same spirit which triggered the American Revolution a century later, and it showed that colonials could be good fighting men when they got their "dander" up.

The French and Indian War

In the last of the military conflicts between England and France fought in the New World, there were significant developments. The French and Indian War originated in America in 1754 and spread to Europe two years later. It started in 1749 by the establishment of an English settlement in the vicinity of present-day southwestern Pennsylvania. France viewed this action as being detrimental to her fur trading interests. In 1752 the French governor of Canada, the Marquis Duquesne de Menneville, encouraged pro-French Indians to attack the settlement and he began constructing forts throughout the region.

England authorized her colonists to defend their settlement against the French and Governor Dinwiddie of Virginia sent a young aristocrat named George Washington to warn the French not to interfere with the English outpost. The French politely sent the twenty-year-old Washington home. Dinwiddie, incensed, raised a military force, placed it under the command of Washington, and sent him back into the interior. In the interim, a partially completed fort which was being constructed by the English to protect their settlement was attacked, captured, and

completed by the French. In May, 1754, French and English forces clashed; Washington was defeated at his base, Fort Necessity, and the French and Indian War had begun.

At first hostilities were confined to the New World, but both sides gradually expanded the scope of the war. In 1755 the English sent General Braddock with a contingent of professional troops to fight the French. He was decisively defeated at the French Fort Duquesne, leaving the English militarily powerless in the back country.

In the beginning of 1756, France and England were engaged in open warfare on several fronts, with France maintaining the upper hand in America. It was woefully apparent that the British commanders knew very little about frontier fighting. There was also a notable lack of colonial cooperation. Americans would fight Indians, but they felt that it was up to England to fight the French. Only those colonies which were in immediate danger of a French attack would allow their militias to fight.

In the meantime, Prime Minister William Pitt, attempting to respond to the situation, ruthlessly replaced officers until he found men who could fight under conditions found in the New World. James Wolfe was one of these capable commanders. He met the brilliant French commander, Montcalm, at the decisive battle of Quebec in September, 1759. Both leaders were killed, but England was considered the victor because Montcalm had been killed. In the following year, another competent English commander, Jeffrey Amherst, captured Montreal. England had, in effect, won Canada from the French. Fighting continued, however, in other parts of the world until France decided to give up in 1763. The resultant Treaty of Paris removed French influence from the North American continent.

American colonists had played a

fairly valuable supporting role in driving the French out of America but actually did far less than they could have done. Colonial militias refused to cooperate with British regulars; the colonies refused to unite for their own common defense. New England smugglers, in utter defiance of British orders to the contrary, traded with the French and prolonged the war in the process. It was not viewed as an American war.

Conduct by colonials in the war was responsible for a change in thinking on the part of England. It was decided to permanently station 10,000 British troops in America. The colonists would be required to pay one-third of the cost directly and the other two-thirds would be paid from revenues accruing from the Sugar Act and the Stamp Act, both of which were passed in 1764. This meant, of course, that Americans would be paying the entire cost of an unwanted defense force. England considered this to be a fair measure since the troops would be used to defend the colonists. The colonists wondered from whom they would be defended, since France was out of the picture. Since they didn't like the idea of having a defense measure imposed upon them, they protested against it. American fear and distrust of a regular military force had begun to develop.

The Boston Massacre

A revolutionary movement was beginning to form in America, and one of the incidents which aided it was the Boston Massacre. In 1770 two regiments of British regulars in Boston were jeered by a mob; some threw rocks and bottles at the marching troops. One soldier fired in the air; someone else yelled "fire," and a general riot ensued, during which five colonists were killed. The fault seems to have been entirely on the side of the colonists for this incident, but the story spread differently throughout the colonies.

Armed British troops had maliciously fired upon innocent women and children, and killed scores of them. Henceforth, military troops were scarcely better than murderers in the eyes of many unthinking Americans. Three years later, shortly after the Boston Tea Party, England passed a series of legislative measures designed to punish the colonies for dumping British tea into the sea. One of these was the Quartering Act, which required colonials who possessed sufficient space to provide room and board for British regulars in their homes. It should be pointed out that at the time enlisted military men were generally not of the best character. The act involved a gross invasion of privacy and gave the colonists another reason to hate the military.

The colonies were ready for revolution. The British commander in America, General Gage, did nothing to ease the situation since he had no orders. Prime Minister Pitt, on the other hand, offered to end all parliamentary taxation in America if the colonists themselves would assume the responsibility for raising sufficient revenues. But the colonists were not in a conciliatory mood. It seems that whenever they pressured England with a non-importation agreement, England backed down. This was taken as a sign of weakness which could be exploited.

The Revolutionary War and the Foundation Period

In April, 1775, General Gage led a military detachment in search of the rabble-rousing John Hancock and Samuel Adams. Colonial militiamen drew up to oppose Gage but were badly disorganized. Someone fired a shot, and the Revolutionary War had begun. The British regulars easily crushed the farmer–soldiers at this, the Battle of Lexington, and then went on to Concord where they destroyed some supply dumps so that they

TO ALL BRAVE, HEALTHY, ABLE BODIED, AND WELL
DISPOSED YOUNG MEN,
IN THIS NEIGHBOURHOOD, WHO HAVE ANY INCLINATION TO JOIN THE TROOPS,
NOW RAISING UNDER
GENERAL WASHINGTON,
FOR THE DEFENCE OF THE
LIBERTIES AND INDEPENDENCE
OF THE UNITED STATES,
Against the hostile designs of foreign enemies,

TAKE NOTICE,

Historical Pictures Service, Chicago

Recruiting Poster for the Continental Army

wouldn't fall into the hands of the revolutionaries. It was then that Paul Revere made the ride which gained him immortality thanks to Longfellow. The British return to Boston turned into a rout, as militiamen, emotionally geared for battle, harried the regulars with sniper fire.

In May, Virginia issued a call for the Second Continental Congress (the first had met one year earlier to protest the "Intolerable Acts"). It concerned itself with raising a citizen army and chose George Washington as its commander-in-chief. Washington took his fresh troops to Bunker Hill and engaged the British in June, but was driven off by General Gage after three attempts. This greatly disturbed the British who wondered why it

was so difficult for professional troops to disband a disorganized mob. So Gage was dismissed and General Howe, who was sympathetic to the American cause—an excellent gentleman but a terrible soldier—assumed command. He allowed Washington to train his force in full view of his headquarters, optimistically hoping that the colonials would get tired of marching and go home.

While this was going on, Benedict Arnold, Ethan Allen, and the Green Mountain boys had gained control of the upstate New York region. Geographically, the area was strategic in that it connected Canada by means of a portage system through Lake Champlain and the Hudson River. The two English forts guarding the portage, Crown Point and Fort Ticonderoga, were taken and the captured British cannon were sent to Washington, who trained them on Howe's headquarters. Howe decided his headquarters were insecure so he evacuated Boston. Nothing else of significance happened for some time.

In early 1777, England formulated plans for a full-scale invasion of the hotbed of radicalism, New England. A three-pronged attack was planned. "Gentleman" Johnny Burgoyne was to move southward from Canada through the Lake Champlain region, General Howe was to move northward and General St. Leger was to move eastward from Ontario. The three forces were to converge on Albany, taking New York and all of New England out of the war. A blockade of the coastline completed the plan.

Unfortunately for the English, St. Leger got bogged down by the terrain and was turned back by Arnold. Howe experienced temporary difficulties in locating his objective. Burgoyne and his 5,800 troops were decisively defeated at the Battle of Saratoga in October, 1777. This was one of the two decisive battles of the war. England was forced to prepare for a lengthy war, and the victory enabled the thirteen united states of North America to obtain a military alliance with England's arch-enemy, France.

Valley Forge—and Yorktown

Washington retired to Valley Forge where he spent a bitter winter. Most of his troops deserted, and for the next three years interest in the war waned on both sides. Plagued with European conflict and domestic problems, England's prosecution of the American war became inept. The American army morale was very low for reasons of boredom and insufficient funds for soldiers' pay. The situation worsened from April, 1778, through April, 1779. A group of plotters headed by Conway, an Irish officer in Washington's command, attempted to have Washington relieved for inefficiency. And hardly had this incident blown over when the Benedict Arnold betrayal occurred (1780). An early hero in the revolutionary army, Arnold found himself in financial trouble and began selling minor bits of information to the British. For political reasons he was only reprimanded for this. He then received command of West Point (actually a demotion) and immediately opened negotiations to turn it over to the British. The incident had a very bad effect on faltering American morale. Americans simply were no longer excited about their war.

Against this background General Clinton (he had replaced Howe after Saratoga), hoping to capitalize on American disillusionment, decided to attempt to trap Washington by drawing him into a major battle and defeating him, thereby completely breaking colonial resistance. Lord Charles Cornwallis, under his command, was ordered to rest his troops on the Yorktown peninsula (in Virginia) in preparation for battle. It was poor strategy to move troops into an area where they could themselves be trapped, but the English fleet *was* anchored at his rear. Washington, however, appeared to scent the trap and deceptively moved toward New York. Cornwallis, believing that the plan had failed, relaxed his guard. It was at this point that the French fleet under Admiral de Grasse executed one of the most brilliant maneuvers of the war: they coaxed the English into chasing them, leaving Cornwallis unprotected. Washington, supported by 8,000 French troops, then backtracked and attacked. Realizing the hopelessness of his position, Cornwallis surrendered at Yorktown in October, 1781.

Following the defeat of Cornwallis, England gave up the war. She still held the major cities of America, controlled the St. Lawrence and Hudson Rivers, and had 30,000 troops in the colonies—a total which the American forces never approached. But she was tired and wanted to end the war. The reasons were many. She was fighting France, Spain, and Holland. Victory in America would have required an effort which the strained treasury could not afford and the English people would not tolerate. Americans seemed to have luck on their side. They had not outfought the British, but they had outmaneuvered them. Finally, England still held the notion that her American colonies would eventually return to the British imperial system.

The Military in the New Nation

The Treaty of Paris, signed in 1783, formally ended the war and substantiated the legal existence of the new nation. But the new government under the Articles of Confederation was given no authority to raise a national army. This presented very serious difficulties. Although many diplomatic issues were still to be resolved with Great Britain and Spain at the close of the war, neither of the European powers took American negotiators seriously; they knew full well that the United States could do nothing without an army. On the domestic scene as well, an army could have helped matters considerably, not only in putting down local rebellions, but in handling the Indian problems which were constantly occurring.

But since Americans identified armies with autocratic government and had not fought to obtain freedom from one tyrant in order to lose it to a new one, the government was forced to rely upon the state militias to handle problems as they arose. The state militias were both weak and ineffective, and what is more significant, they refused to answer the call of their national government. Americans were not ready yet to sanction a national army.

The new Constitution, adopted in 1787, did not specifically forbid the estab-

lishment of a national standing army, but the government still chose to follow the practice of using state militia systems to handle military matters. The new document did permit the president to press the state militias into federal service. This meant that the nation could have an army anytime it desired.

Alexander Hamilton wanted to test the power of the new government; when the Whiskey Rebellion broke out in the back country of Pennsylvania in 1794, he advised President Washington to mobilize the militia and put down the rebellion. Washington accepted this advice and requisitioned 15,000 militia troops from Pennsylvania, Maryland, and Virginia. This massive force easily overpowered the rebels and the revolt was put down without bloodshed. However, the people who had feared the establishment of the military from the beginning, now had an issue to rally around. The government had just proven that it could enforce an unpopular law through the use of military force. This was just what all the hullaballoo with England had been about. This strong show of force was a contributing factor in the downfall of the Federalist Party.

In spite of its early success, the militia system was quickly proved ineffectual. Encouraged by English fur traders who knew that settlement in the Old Northwest would bring to an end the lucrative fur trade, the Indian tribes there were on the verge of open warfare. Expeditions were sent out in 1790 under General Hamar and in 1791 under Governor St. Clair of the Northwest Territory. Both were miserable failures. President Washington then directed "Mad Anthony" Wayne to pacify the Indians. General Wayne avoided the mistakes of the two earlier expeditions by training his troops thoroughly and insisting upon strict discipline; this meant that the commander had to physically defeat the loudest troublemakers in his unit. The result was the formation of an efficient army which defeated the Indians at the Battle of Fallen Timbers. In the Treaty of Fort Grenville, the Indians ceded all of Ohio and eastern Indiana to the United States.

The XYZ Affair

In 1793 the French, represented by the enthusiastic Citizen Genêt called upon the United States to honor the Treaty of Alliance—which we had entered into during the Revolutionary War—by fighting the British. At this time the French Revolution was in progress, along with a general European war in which England and France were the main antagonists. The United States refused to become involved, in effect repudiating the Treaty when Washington issued the Neutrality Proclamation in 1793. The French, bitter at what they regarded as a betrayal, refused to accept the United States' foreign minister to France, C. C. Pinckney, and ordered him out of the country. Realizing that the new Republican Party led by Jefferson was pro-French, they campaigned actively on his behalf in 1796 and thereby contributed to his defeat.

After the election in 1796 President Adams attempted to smooth the diplomatic turmoil by sending a three-man diplomatic team to France, but the new deputation had no greater success than Pinckney; three French ministers met them and demanded a huge bribe in return for the privilege of negotiating with Talleyrand, the French foreign minister. The Americans refused to pay and the anonymous Frenchmen became known as X, Y, and Z. The treatment of our emissaries had an immediate unifying effect on the country, enabling Adams to secure appropriations for the military and to begin to build a navy. Since the French were at this time seizing our merchant ships, the navy was sorely needed.

When Jefferson became president in 1800, he immediately mothballed the Navy as an economy move. Then, be-

cause the United States became involved in the Tripolitan War (1801–1804), he quickly restored it. The pirate rulers on the North African coast were demanding and receiving tribute from all nations in return for safe passage of their vessels. Even England, with her large navy, was paying the tribute. But the United States refused to pay the tribute demanded by the Pasha of Tripoli, and a three-year naval war followed. War continued intermittently in North Africa until the last pirate state, Tunisia, finally came to terms in 1816. The United States never paid any tribute.

The Era of the War of 1812

Trying to Remain Neutral

During the Napoleonic Wars a new conflict evolved between England and the United States; American ships carrying goods from the French West Indies to France were being halted and searched by the English for contraband and seamen were being taken off the ships to be impressed into English naval service. In an attempt to end these transgressions Congress passed the Jefferson-sponsored Nicholson Non-Importation Agreement in 1806. There would be no further importation of English goods when such goods could be obtained elsewhere (the same weapon had been used during the colonial period). Jefferson then sent William Pinkney and James Monroe to negotiate a trade agreement, but the resulting treaty was so unfavorable that it was never adopted.

In the meantime, the British ship *Leander* fired upon an American vessel, killing one American seaman; the American public became quite hostile toward England. Then, in June of 1807, the English *Leopard* fired on the American *Chesapeake,* killing three, wounding eighteen, and impressing four seamen; this further aroused the American public. Jefferson demanded an unofficial apology but the British government did not respond. In consequence, Jefferson asked Congress for an embargo act. The resultant measure, passed in December, 1807, restricted all ships to port except those that were empty and those American ships that were engaged only in coastal trading. Also, $1.25 million was appropriated to build the Navy. The objective was to eliminate trade with England and Europe, thereby preventing further incidents. But the legislation proved unsuccessful for two reasons: western farmers lost important markets for their surplus, and eastern shippers were critically hurt. Jefferson claimed that England would be hurt more than we if the policy were continued, but Americans wanted no part of it; the legislation was repealed in 1808.

In 1809 the Force Act was passed, putting the state militias at the disposal of the federal government in time of emergency—a redundancy, since the Constitution already authorized this. But Massachusetts and Connecticut jointly issued the Connecticut Resolution, in which they claimed the measure was unconstitutional and stated that they would refuse to abide by it. A law was then passed closing American ports to England and France only. This was also unsuccessful, since 80 per cent of all American foreign trade was with England and it was sorely needed by the American economy. The unauthorized Erskine Treaty of 1809 would have solved the problems with England by rescinding the British Orders in Council, but some American ships set sail only to discover that the agreement had been repudiated. England allowed these particular ships to pass unmolested but a considerable amount of embarrassment was felt by both governments.

In 1810 the United States passed Macon's Bill No. 2, which re-opened American ports to trade from England and France but stated that as soon as a satisfactory agreement was negotiated with one of these countries, trade would be discontinued with the other. The United States thereby hoped to force an agreement with at least one country. Napoleon quickly took advantage of the measure. He had his foreign minister, Cadore, issue a statement, known as the Cadore Letter, according to which France would end her Continental System on November 1, 1810, if England would rescind her Orders in Council and the United States would enforce respect for her "neutral rights" on the high seas—two enormous qualifications. The letter, in effect, promised nothing. President Madison ill-advisedly accepted Napoleon's offer, and, ignoring the conditions it imposed, closed off trade with England.

In an effort to improve the poor relations between the two countries, England sent a minister named Foster to negotiate a settlement for the *Chesapeake.* But while Foster was en route, the American warship, *President,* captured the English ship, *Little Belt.* Although the *Little Belt* was one-third the size of the *President,* the American people were elated; the *Chesapeake* had been avenged. Consequently, the United States was no longer interested in negotiations. In 1811 the English ambassador was recalled and not replaced. Madison responded by recalling the American ambassador, thereby completing the diplomatic break.

During the off-year congressional elections of 1810, the West had elected a number of "War Hawks," including Henry Clay, John Calhoun, and William Crawford. They were ardent expansionists and nationalists who favored war with England for several reasons: the desire to annex Spanish Florida and British Canada (Spain was England's ally against France), the Indian unrest (which was blamed on England but was in fact due to the greed and aggression of the frontier settlers), and various economic problems. (See Chapter Five.) They spoke eloquently about the evils of search and seizure and the impressment of seamen, and became great champions of "American honor." The New Englanders who were most affected by those issues did not favor war, however; England was their best customer.

President Madison, a Republican, was forced to take a stand on the war issue; the party was divided into two opposing factions, those favoring the war (the Hawks) and those opposed to it (the Doves of the day). In June, 1812, after he had been nominated but before the election, Madison asked Congress for a declaration of war and received it. Madison's opponent in the election was De Witt Clinton, a Federalist, who was strongly supported in New England and New York. Although Madison won, the election was very close, demonstrating the deep split over the war issue.

The Course of the Fighting

The country in 1812 was not financially prepared for war: Congress had allowed Hamilton's National Bank to collapse, no tariff measures had been passed, and tax bills were being neglected. The war cost over $200 million and it was financed largely by interest-bearing government bonds. The nation had few military leaders, and no more than 30,000 troops were under arms at any given time. Recruits were hard to get, ill-trained, and usually undisciplined. There was no conscription, and if a person got upset with military life, he simply went home. The situation in the Navy was not much better.

At the onset of the war Washington military strategists concocted a grand but extremely impractical plan for winning the war and achieving the objectives of the various war proponents. Canada had first priority and was to be subjected to a three-pronged attack issuing from Detroit, Fort Niagara and Lake Champlain. The force

from Lake Champlain was to capture Montreal, the very important Canadian stronghold on the St. Lawrence River. The attack was a complete fiasco; not only did the army fail to capture its assigned targets through terrible mismanagement —it came perilously close to losing New York. In the South and West the plan was to subdue the Indians and eventually capture Spanish Florida. Jackson did manage to defeat the Indians, but the war was over before he could turn to Florida.

The British, on the other hand, crippled the country financially with a devastatingly effective blockade with which the United States Navy was never able to cope. They also landed an invasion force at Chesapeake Bay and eventually burned Washington, an insult long remembered by anti-British patriots. Clearly, the United States would have lost the war had not England been too busy with France to devote sufficient attention to America.

Although the war was badly fought by the United States and the nation was generally on the defensive, there were some significant American victories. In September, 1813, Captain Oliver Hazard Perry decisively defeated a British naval squadron on Lake Erie. In 1814 Captain Thomas MacDonough accomplished a similar feat on Lake Champlain. Though these were more skirmishes than battles and were fought by American privateers and Navy sloops, their psychological value was great. England, surprised by American naval ability, tended to show more respect for the American fleet after the war.

In October of 1813 General William Henry Harrison won the Battle of the Thames River (Ontario, Canada) and in the process recaptured much of the American territory that had been invaded by the British. It was in this battle that the brilliant Indian leader, Tecumseh, then a general in the British Army, was killed.

General Andrew Jackson, with a haphazard frontier army made up of miscellaneous sailors, militiamen, and settlers (including some Negroes) fought two major battles. In the first, at Horseshoe Bend, Alabama, he defeated the Creek Indians and permanently ended their power east of the Mississippi, though minor battles were still to be fought. In the second he defeated an experienced English army fresh from victories in the Napoleonic Wars. Jackson's victory in this case was due mainly to British disrespect for American fighting ability and their ignorance of frontier fighting techniques. The Battle of New Orleans, in which 2,000 British were killed, was fought two weeks after the war had officially ended.

There was no American unity of purpose about the war; frontiersmen were ardent proponents but New Englanders openly opposed it. At the Hartford Convention in 1814, attended by delegates from five New England states, there was talk of secession and much bitterness resulted. Though neither side really won the war, it did serve one useful purpose: nationalism grew at the expense of sectionalism as Americans demanded the federal legislation needed to prosecute the war.

The Era of Good Feelings which followed the war was a period in which there were major changes in American thinking about the military; unpreparedness in the war had caused a considerable amount of alarm. President Madison and Secretary of State Monroe both urged that a permanent peacetime army be created and in 1815, Congress responded by creating a 10,000-man army and appropriating eight million dollars for the Navy. National defense had become a must and the old colonial fears of a standing army had begun to fade somewhat. Another change was also necessary. Massachusetts and Connecticut had refused to relinquish control of their state militias during the war, and the participation of several other states had been somewhat erratic. This sort of situation could not be tolerated if the United States was to be the great power which many of its citizens thought it should be.

The Mexican War

In two bloody and costly major battles, Texas gained her independence: the battle of the Alamo, which the Texans lost, and the battle of San Jacinto, which they won under Sam Houston. Both came in the spring of 1836. Texas independence posed several problems for the United States and greatly increased tensions between the United States and Mexico. At the heart of the difficulty was the proposed annexation of Texas by the United States, which Mexico vehemently opposed, realizing full well that she had little chance of retaining her territory in the Southwest and California if Texas belonged to the Union. Slavery also reared its ugly head with the question of whether or not Texas would be a slave state. After much political maneuvering, Texas was admitted to the Union (as a slave state) in 1846; two years later President Polk provoked Mexico into a war which would add California and the Southwest to the United States.

The Texans claimed the Rio Grande as their southern boundary in spite of the fact that the boundary had been the Nueces River (somewhat to the north) when Texas was a Mexican province. President Polk, however, supported the Texas claim and ordered General Zachary Taylor to position his troops in the disputed territory, hoping to create an incident. Then John Slidell was sent to Mexico with authorization to purchase the disputed territory, the rest of New Mexico, and California as well. Slidell was not received very amiably by the Mexicans (who were insulted by a very meager offer), so Polk ordered Taylor to arrange his forces throughout the entire disputed area.

When hostilities broke out between Mexican and American forces in the region, Polk officially regarded this as an act of war by Mexico even though he had already been in the process of drafting a war message; now he could blame the entire affair on the Mexicans. In May, 1846, both houses of Congress overwhelmingly endorsed a war declaration, since "American blood" had been "shed on American soil." The nation remained divided, however, over the issue of slavery expansion which would become critical when California was annexed.

The Campaign in Mexico

Congress appropriated $10 million for the war and authorized a 50,000-man volunteer army; in actuality there were three major United States forces engaged in the war. General Zachary Taylor started from Corpus Christi (in the disputed area of Texas) in 1846 and moved south along the coast to Palo Alto where a major battle was fought; he then moved inland to Monterrey. Colonel Alexander Doniphan left Santa Fe in August of 1846 and moved south to reach the Sacramento River in February of 1847 where he won a major battle fifteen miles outside the Mexican town of Chihuahua. He then moved eastward to join Taylor at Buena Vista, where Taylor had just completed one of the most decisive battles of the war. At the battle of Buena Vista (February 22–23), 1,800 Mexicans under General Santa Anna were killed as against approximately 700 Americans.

The third force under the colorful General Winfield Scott embarked from New Orleans and made an amphibious landing at Veracruz in March of 1847. Although he met little resistance there, he fought six difficult battles on his way to Mexico City, 250 miles to the west. Strategically, the most important was the battle of Cerro Gordo during which Scott's 8,000-man army met a force of over 12,000 Mexican troops under the command of General Santa Anna. Again, Mexican casualties were more than double

that of the Americans: 1,000 versus 400. After Cerro Gordo, Scott pushed on toward Mexico City. Only one major obstacle remained in his path: the heavily fortified castle at Chapultepec. In this battle, which occupies a unique spot in Mexican history, the fighting was unbelievably fierce. The Americans finally won, using scaling ladders and cannon, but the Mexicans fought to the last man. The castle had been employed as a military academy for boys and even the cadets (the youngest of whom was thirteen) fought in the pitched battle. It was reported that the last six boys threw themselves from the roof of the castle rather than be captured and today there is a large monument in Mexico City dedicated to the boy heroes of Chapultepec.

Mexico City was captured in a twenty-four-hour battle in September of 1847, ending the military phase of the war. It was a war in which the Mexicans never really had a chance; although they outnumbered the Americans in almost every battle, their weapons (smooth-bore muskets, for the most part) were so poor that time after time they were annihilated before they ever got within effective firing range. The cost of the war in lives was a mute tribute to their bravery. In many ways it was one of the most vicious wars ever fought; both sides suffered from disease and lack of medical supplies; atrocities again on both sides, but particularly by the Texans, were the order of the day; American soldiers looted Mexico City and were in turn killed from ambush; desertions from both armies ran as high as 20 per cent. On the other side, General Winfield Scott's march from the sea to the "halls of Montezuma" is widely regarded as a classic military operation.

California

Mexico was only one arena of the war. Colonel Stephen Kearny took Santa Fe in August, 1846, with practically no resistance, and claimed all of New Mexico for the United States. He then left with part of his command for California, leaving the remaining troops with Colonel Doniphan, who was ordered to advance into Mexico and join up with Taylor. In California there had been rumors of war and annexation for some time. The Bear Flag Revolt occurred in June, 1846, as Americans asked John C. Fremont to lead them against the Mexicans. When Fremont heard that war had been declared by the United States he did so, and wound up becoming military governor of California before Kearny arrived. Kearny arrested Fremont for exceeding his authority, and the latter was court-martialed and convicted. However, since he had been secretly acting under orders, President Polk had him released at once.

The American army at this time suffered from a number of deficiencies. There was a considerable lack of coordination and communication. Individual officers indiscriminately violated orders, and many of them got away with it. The military was permeated with politics and personality conflicts. Scott and Taylor, for instance, hated each other and both sought to use the Mexican campaign as a stepping stone to the presidency. Discipline was something talked about but rarely enforced.

From the close of the Mexican War up to the beginning of the Civil War, the military was occupied almost exclusively with the protection of settlers and miners who had settled on Indian land. For the most part this amounted to garrison duty in such western forts as Fort Kearny and Fort Laramie. Occasional skirmishes with Indians did occur, but major battles with the Indians were not fought until the close of the Civil War.

America's First Modern War: The Civil War

Before the Republican nominating convention convened in 1860, southern Democrats indicated that they would not submit to the election of the candidate of a "foul sectional party." Therefore, after Lincoln was elected but before his inauguration, the secessionists, intending to present the new president with an accomplished fact when he took office, worked at building the Confederacy. It was widely believed that the current president, Buchanan, would do nothing, and this was correct. It was further felt that Lincoln would not take action against secession either—this was very wrong.

Although Lincoln was president, the Democrats (southerners made up the largest contingent in the party) still controlled Congress, and Lincoln's program, whatever it might be, could have been blocked. The South actually had nothing to fear. Nevertheless, Alabama, Mississippi, and South Carolina took the lead in secession. South Carolina passed her Ordinance of Secession on December 20, 1860. She severed all bonds with the Union, offered to pay her share of the national debt, sought her share of national properties and territories, and urged other southern states to join her. South Carolina viewed secession as a peaceful and orderly severance.

Other slave states began calling conventions, most of which were to meet in January, 1861. Florida seceded on January 9, Alabama on January 13, Mississippi on January 15, Georgia on January 17, Louisiana on January 26, and Texas on January 31. Other southern states either planned to secede or were awaiting a Union compromise effort, but the federal government did nothing in this regard.

A situation developed which considerably hastened the war. There were three federal forts in Charleston Harbor (South Carolina), Fort Moultrie, Castle Pinckney, and Fort Sumter. The commander of the forts, Major Robert Anderson, moved all of his forces to Fort Sumter on December 26, 1860, for defense and supply purposes. South Carolina immediately occupied the evacuated forts. On

January 5, 1861, President Buchanan attempted to send additional supplies to Fort Sumter. The merchant vessel he sent was fired upon by the Confederates and withdrew. Buchanan made no further attempt to supply the fort.

Lincoln's Options

This was the situation when Lincoln took office in March. His Inaugural Address was conciliatory toward the South, but he faced two critical and immediate problems: one was what to do with Fort Sumter and the other was how to prevent the secession of the remaining southern states. He decided to defend Sumter at any cost. Meanwhile, the Confederate General Beauregard had demanded the surrender of the fort by April 11. Major Anderson agreed to do so if he was not supplied, but on the 15th, not the 11th; he indicated that as a commanding officer he could not do otherwise. Beauregard was impatient; rather than wait the three extra days for a possible bloodless surrender, he bombarded Fort Sumter on April 12.

With this development Lincoln gave up all hope for compromise. He issued a call for 75,000 militia troops. The northern states cooperated but the South, for obvious reasons, did not. Virginia considered the militia call to be coercion and seceded on April 17. Arkansas followed on May 6, North Carolina on May 20, and Tennessee on June 4. This ended most of Lincoln's worries concerning the secession of the upper South. He did manage, however, to maintain the technical allegiance of Kentucky, Maryland, Delaware, and

Library of Congress

Firing on Fort Sumter (1861)

Missouri, where northern and southern sentiment was fairly evenly divided.

Resources and Strategy

A total of eleven states joined the Confederacy, leaving twenty-three states in the Union. A comparison of the resources of North and South at the beginning of the war is valuable in that it makes possible an understanding of various tactical moves which, on the surface, appear incomprehensible. Union population amounted to 22 million, whereas Confederate population was 9 million, including 3.5 million slaves who could not be counted for military purposes. Most of the money was in the North, as well as the important European banking connections. The North possessed an established currency, whereas the South had to create one. The North possessed a diversified agriculture plus industrial centers; it could support a military machine. The South had limited itself to the production of cotton, and would thus experience considerable difficulties.

Only in morale did the South hold an advantage. To the southerner this was a war of independence, and the result was a crusading zeal. Possessing a cause, the South presented a more united front than the northerners, who held varying viewpoints on the secession issue. The southern military machine, though small, was much more efficient than the northern one because many southern gentlemen had adopted military careers. Southern militia units, usually in better condition than their northern counterparts, were replete with excellent riflemen; in their basically rural society, southerners had maintained their outdoor skills. The existence of a rigid class structure, such as existed in the South, pre-conditioned certain segments of the society for military life. Finally, the southerner, fighting on his own soil with short supply lines and better knowledge of the terrain, was not as subject to loss of morale as the northern soldier who was far from home. The southerner was fighting to defend his home from the northern invader.

The North possessed great advantages; fully aware of this, the South hoped in vain to elicit the support of the border and western states. When it became apparent that this support was not forthcoming the South felt that its only remaining realistic chance for success was to defeat the North decisively in key engagements early in the war, thus discouraging the northerners and destroying their will to continue.

Men for the two armies came from a variety of sources. The regular United States Army was, of course, a primary source. At the outbreak of the war the nation possessed a 16,000-man Army and a Navy of roughly 9,000 men. Practically all enlisted men remained loyal to the Union, but approximately one-fourth of the officers resigned their commissions to join the Confederate forces. (Robert E. Lee was one of these officers.) The men who resigned were generally better military men than those who remained and consequently, throughout the war, the South displayed better military leadership than the North. The state militia systems, another source of manpower, were usually loyal to their state government.

Both sides made use of volunteer units. Volunteers would join as groups, elect their own officers, choose their own uniforms, and become distinct units within the regular army. In most instances, both northern and southern "enlistments" were supposed to last for twelve months. The government had always used this system of raising an army, and though its demands for troops were not generally met, there were sufficient enlistments to maintain a war effort. Now for the first time there was an insufficient number of troops on both sides, and a new method of raising men was needed; the conscription system was the result.

Recruiting and Logistics

Both sides had counted on a relatively short war, so when the war was almost a year old they faced a serious problem; enlistments were due to expire. In March, 1862, the Confederacy "froze" all enlistments for a three-year total period of service and began to draft all white males between the ages of 18 and 35. Shortly thereafter the limit was raised to 45. In February, 1864, age limits were extended to cover the 17–50 age group. In March, 1865, the Confederacy authorized freedom for slaves who would enlist, but this came too late for any appreciable results. The North, however, had sought the enlistment of Negroes since 1862 and over 200,000 Afro-Americans had responded; of these, 125,000 were ex-slaves who had broken away from their southern owners to fight on the side of the Union. In addition, some 200,000 Negro civilians were employed by the army as cooks, construction workers, teamsters, and spies.

Because of its greater source of manpower, the North was not compelled to draft individuals until March, 1863. The system then authorized the draft for a given district only when it failed to attract sufficient enlistments. All males between 20 and 45 years of age were liable, but the system was designed primarily to encourage enlistments and worked quite well. An elaborate system of bounties was used, with some men receiving up to $1000, to garner enlistments. At first a draftee could hire a substitute or pay the government $300 to avoid service, but this practice was abolished owing to widespread criticism.

There was resistance to the draft in North and South alike. In the North there were draft riots in several cities during the summer of 1863. Some individuals in the South and some state governments refused to cooperate with the conscription system. Protest over Selective Service in the 1960's is nothing new. Many of those people who did enter the armies, deserted; both sides were continually plagued by this problem. The North suffered about 200,000 desertions from an army of 1.5 million. Southern desertions numbered approximately 100,000 from an army of a million.

The war brought with it some other serious military problems, one of which was poor discipline. Though neither side was a model of discipline, the South, with its class structure was generally better off. Lack of food was not a problem in the North, though there were some initial transportation difficulties. In the South this was a serious problem from the beginning and was never completely solved. Armaments were another problem; southern arms were obtained from the state militias, from captured federal arsenals and from abandoned battlefields. In the North industry was capable of producing whatever was needed, but there was considerable graft and corruption. Both sides used muzzle-loading rifles although they were outdated. The North developed and used twenty-inch guns with an eight-mile range, machine guns, telescopic sights, and a balloon corps (for observation). The South used these weapons only when they could be captured from the North but did have one sophisticated weapon of its own; the submarine, *Hunley*, which sank the U.S.S. *Housatonic*.

Since it was on the offensive, the North determined war strategy while the South fought a holding action, engaging the North only when conditions were favorable and hoping to stay in the war until the North grew tired of it. Northern naval strategy called for blockading the South to prevent the sale of cotton and the purchase of food and weapons. Because the South had no navy and was unable to acquire one, the blockade was successful. The Union Navy, on the other hand, improved tremendously during the course of the war, mainly through the efforts of Naval Secretary Giddeon Wells. Those few southern ships that did evade the northern blockade were tiny craft capable of outrunning Union warships.

A Game of Chess

Land strategy was akin to a chess game; the key pieces were the capitals at Richmond and Washington, where tremendous resources were tied up in defense. The two defending armies were effectively immobilized throughout the war, as each side maneuvered to frighten the other side into deploying more troops around its capital.

The two-part northern land strategy called first for maintaining a secure area around the capital. Then the Confederacy was to be split into east and west by gaining control of the Mississippi River. This would take the war away from the border states, and physically separate Arkansas, Texas, and part of Louisiana from the Confederacy, thus blocking the passage of vital troops and provisions. The Navy moved up the Mississippi from the Gulf of Mexico and the Army moved southward from Cairo, Illinois to converge, on July 4, 1863, at Vicksburg, where one of the bloodiest battles of the war was fought.

This being accomplished, the next plan called for further weakening the Confederacy by splitting it into upper and lower South. This goal was ultimately realized by Sherman's march from Chattanooga to Atlanta during the summer of 1864. According to the plan, the Union army in Atlanta would then move northward, the army in defense of Washington would move southward, and the Confederate forces would be bottled up around Richmond and forced to surrender.

Things did not work out quite this smoothly. Grant succeeded in defeating Lee, who surrendered at Appomattox, but General Sherman, who had been moving north, was slowed down by General Johnston's Confederate army which was not defeated until after Lee's surrender.

The vanquished Confederate armies were accorded generous terms; officers kept their sidearms, all cavalrymen retained their horses, all military personnel were paroled. Lee surrendered on April 9, 1865, six days before Abraham Lincoln's assassination. Johnston did not surrender until April 26. By May 4, all Confederate armies in the East had disbanded. Finally on May 26, the western Confederate army, located in Texas, surrendered without ever having fought a major battle, thus ending the Civil War.

There had been a few flaws in the northern strategy; the planners did not expect the important Battle of Gettysburg which took place in mid-1863. The South, briefly invading the North, could not mount a sustained action but the move nearly threw the Union into a state of panic—as was intended. Following a drawn battle, the Confederates retired to the South, but more northern troops had to be deployed around Washington as a result of the attack. The most important setback to northern strategy was the southern refusal to lose; although vastly outnumbered, the Confederates continually won battles which slowed down the North —battles like Bull Run, Fredricksburg, Chancellorsville, and Murfreesboro.

The Price of Victory

The North turned out to be its own great enemy. The military is subordinate to civilian authority in the United States —a power Lincoln took quite literally. He ruthlessly replaced commanders until he found men who could win, no matter the method. He replaced General Mc-

Clellan, an excellent organizer, with General Grant when McClellan refused to risk his army in battle; Grant won by wearing down the enemy whenever possible, regardless of the cost. He would trade lives and casualties with the Confederates, knowing that the result would eventually be victory.

Accurate records were not kept during the Civil War, but it was extremely costly. Union losses amounted to an estimated 360,000 men, and Confederate losses were 260,000, not to mention hundreds of thousands of maimed and

Library of Congress

The Price of War

wounded men. In addition, the war left feelings of hate and bitterness which have not been entirely erased now, a century later.

While fighting the war, Union forces also engaged various western Indian tribes; this sporadic conflict was to last for decades. The Sioux turned out to be the most formidable foe, but the Apache were also quite able fighters.

"A Splendid Little War" and Its Aftermath

When the Spanish-American War began in April of 1898, the principal national asset was enthusiasm. As before, the United States was unprepared militarily; its small, ill-equipped army was experienced only in Indian warfare, the militia system existed in name only, and the military leaders were generally inept. Most of them had never fought an engagement or planned strategy. The nation did have the nucleus of a modern navy, largely through the persistent efforts of Assistant Naval Secretary Theodore Roosevelt. What helped the United States immeasurably was the fact that the Spanish military was in even worse shape than the United States Army and the Spanish navy still consisted primarily of out-moded wooden ships.

When it was announced that the Spanish had dispatched a fleet, mass hysteria gripped the East Coast; it was thought that this was an invasion force. In fact, it was a wretchedly poor fleet of four warships and three small torpedo boats that was sailing (under protest) to protect Cuba from the expected American invasion. In response to the public clamor, Commodore Schley was ordered to protect the East Coast and given a motley collection of small craft, old Civil War vessels, and tugboats with which to do it. Fortunately this "flying squadron" never had to perform. At this time Commodore George Dewey was commanding the Pacific fleet while Captain William Sampson was in charge of the main Atlantic fleet. Army operations were in the inexperienced hands of General William Shafter.

It was decided that a regular Army of less than 30,000 officers and men was somewhat insufficient, so it was increased to roughly 62,000; to this was added a volunteer army of 125,000. The volunteer forces came mainly from the state militias, but Congress did authorize the president to accept for service three independent calvary units. One of these was the Rough Riders, commanded by Colonel Leonard Wood and assisted by Lieutenant Colonel Theodore Roosevelt, who resigned his naval post in order to get in on the action. The Rough Riders consisted of college boys, professional athletes, cowboys, and adventurers, none of whom possessed real military qualifications. The nation did not yet emphasize professionalism in its military operations.

The first major battle occurred in Manila Bay in the Philippines. Dewey bottled the Spanish fleet in the bay and destroyed it at his leisure. No Americans were killed in the battle, but over 400 Spaniards lost their lives. It was a major naval victory and it made Dewey a national hero, but nothing further transpired until army personnel arrived. Eleven hundred troops captured Manila with the loss of eighteen lives, and the Pacific phase of the Spanish-American War had ended.

In the Caribbean things were a little different. A Spanish fleet commanded by Admiral Pascual Cervera was steaming toward Cuba. Both Sampson and Schley knew of its coming, but somehow the ships managed to slip into Santiago Bay. It was then quite easy to keep the Spanish fleet in the narrow bay, but Sampson decided to make certain that it could not escape. A young naval lieutenant, Hobson, was ordered to sink an old collier in the channel; he sank the ship in the wrong place (leaving the channel open) and was then captured by the Spaniards. He became the second "hero" of the war. Sampson would not enter the bay because he lacked maneuvering room and feared non-existent Spanish shore batteries; Cervera would not leave because he faced almost certain destruction. It was a stalemate.

Sampson called for troops. However, the entire American Army (except for the troops sent to Manila) was piled up at Tampa, Florida, which had inadequate port facilities; most of the Army had arrived there with inadequate supplies and equipment. Finally, 17,000 troops, including the Rough Riders, were transported to Cuba. The troops proceeded overland toward Santiago. (This is when the legendary charge up San Juan Hill took place.) As the Army advanced, the fall of Santiago became imminent, which jeopardized Cervera's fleet in the bay.

Cervera was ordered to attempt to escape—an order which he strongly protested. His fleet was destroyed on July 3, after he had barely managed to break out into open water. Five hundred Spaniards were killed as their wooden-decked ships were burned in this grossly unequal battle. Only one American was killed.

Another stalemate ensued; Sampson still refused to enter the bay, fearing the non-existent shore batteries. But the city was starving and surrendered to the Army on condition that the Navy transport Spanish forces back to Spain. The surrender took place on July 16. (The Navy, incidentally, was not immediately informed of the surrender provisions.)

On July 21 the United States invaded Puerto Rico.

The American army, which had avoided battle casualties, was dying from disease. Winter uniforms in tropical Cuba, coupled with spoiled food, polluted water, and a general lack of sanitation, caused epidemics of dysentery, typhoid, and malaria. Had the war dragged on, the United States would have been in most unfortunate circumstances, but as matters turned out Spain soon asked for a termination of all hostilities; this occurred on August 12, 1898.

As was typical of the American military, the volunteer army was disbanded after the end of hostilities. But two events soon caused the nation to depart from its tradition. The United States acquired the Philippines as part of the settlement of the Spanish-American War. The Filipinos, however, expected independence, and when the United States took over, a revolution broke out. The Americans were eventually required to send 70,000 troops over a two-year period to the Philippines to suppress the revolution. Unlike the Cuban situation, the Philippine fight for freedom turned into a vicious, brutal war with heavy casualties on both sides. The Filipinos, having no army, fought a guerrilla action in the thick jungles of their home. There were many atrocities which shocked Americans at home and caused anti-war sentiment to skyrocket. The revolution failed in 1901, when the leader Emilio Aguinaldo was captured, but the resistance movement continued until 1946, when the Filipinos were granted their independence.

The other policy-changing event was the Boxer Rebellion in China. The Boxers were an organization of nationalistic Chinese who deeply resented the economic control of China exercised by many European interests. In 1900, they launched a terrorist campaign to drive the foreigners out of China, but were stopped in their efforts by an international army composed of British, French, German, American, Russian, and Japanese forces. Over 200 civilians were killed and several diplomats were beseiged by the Boxers before the rebellion was smashed. For the first time in American history, during a period when the nation was officially at peace, American troops were fighting an international battle on foreign soil.

The Era of the First World War

Two significant events happened in the summer of 1914 which were eventually to involve United States military forces. War erupted in Europe following the assassination of Archduke Franz Ferdinand, heir to the Austrian throne. In July, President Huerta of Mexico was forced to resign by his rival, Venustiano Carranza. No sooner had Carranza taken power in Mexico, than a new rival arose to challenge him—the flamboyant Francisco (Pancho) Villa—revolutionary, patriot, and bandit. Villa made several attempts to wrest power from Carranza, but since he did not have the people's support he was unsuccessful. He even captured and held Mexico City for a brief period. Unable to depose Carranza by himself, he then attempted to produce hostilities between the United States and Mexico in the hope that U.S. troops would accomplish what he had been unable to do. He killed American citizens in San Ysabel, held up trains, and finally attacked the New Mexican town of Columbus, killing seventeen Americans. Villa almost achieved his purpose when General John Pershing followed him deep into Mexico and fought several times with Carranza's forces. However Pershing withdrew before war broke out—without capturing the wily Francisco Villa.

Raising an Army for Europe

A major factor in Pershing's withdrawal was the war in Europe; though the United States maintained official neutrality, by 1916 everyone realized that America would soon be involved. A fight with Mexico would have been very inconvenient. Pershing's army had grown to 200,000 men. When war was declared the nation's National Guard was called up, producing 900,000 additional troops with some military experience. But this army, now totaling 1.1 million men, was not nearly sufficient.

It had been expected that Americans would not be required to engage in much European fighting; America would be mainly a producer and transporter of war goods and services. The Allies, however, quickly informed the United States of their vast manpower needs. General Pershing, who was placed in charge of American Expeditionary Forces in Europe, soon asked for a million trained troops by the spring of 1918. Obviously the United States would require a much larger army.

The troops came from two sources; there were volunteers, but they never amounted to more than a trickle. It was therefore decided that a draft system had to be re-established; in true democratic spirit, it was named the Selective Service

Attention!

ALL MALES between the ages of 21 and 30 years, both inclusive, must personally appear at the polling place in the Election District in which they reside, on

TUESDAY, JUNE 5th, 1917

between the hours of 7 A.M. and 9 P. M. and

Register

in accordance with the President's Proclamation.

Any male person, between these ages, who fails to register on June 5th, 1917, will be subject to imprisonment in jail or other penal institution for a term of one year

NO EXCUSE FOR FAILURE TO REGISTER WILL BE ACCEPTED

NON-RESIDENTS must apply personally for registration, at the office of the County Clerk, at Kingston, N. Y., AT ONCE, in order that their registration cards may be in the hands of the Registration Board of their home district before June 5, 1917

Employers of males between these ages are earnestly requested to assist in the enforcement of the President's Proclamation.

Signed,

BOARD OF REGISTRATION
of Ulster County
E. T. SHULTIS, Sheriff
C. K. LOUGHRAN, County Clerk
Dr. FRANK JOHNSTON, Medical Officer

Historical Pictures Service, Chicago

World War I Draft Registration Poster

Act of 1917. The theory implied was that every male was liable for military service, but that many could best serve their country in their civilian occupations. An elaborate system of deferments was set up on this premise.

The Selective Service Act, which required all males between the ages of 21 and 31 to register by June 5, 1917, applied to 10 million men. The registration information was turned over to civilian-controlled local draft boards—there were 10,500 of them across the nation. Selec-

tion was accomplished by drawing from a fishbowl, taking into account various deferments. On July 20, 1917, Secretary of War Baker, completely blindfolded, ceremoniously drew the first number (258) from the fishbowl. The holder of that number in every one of the nation's draft boards was thereby selected—unless he was able to arrange a deferment.

By December, 1917, a half million draftees were ready for service. By July, 1918, just eighteen months later, the United States had a million trained troops in Europe. But even this was now insufficient. Therefore in August, 1918, the draft act was revised, extending the registration age limits to 18 and 45; this raised the total number of registrants to 24 million, of which 6 million were considered acceptable for service. Ultimately, the nation raised a total military force of 5 million men; 2 million of these were sent to Europe.

Teddy Roosevelt, now nearing 60 and half blind, offered to raise a new unit of Rough Riders with himself in command. President Wilson turned him down, and both General Pershing and General Peyton March, who was commanding general of the entire Army, breathed a sigh of relief. Roosevelt took the refusal personally.

Neither the Navy nor the Marine Corps utilized the draft; the Selective Service Act stimulated enough enlistments for these services. They possessed more esprit de corps, since their membership was composed of volunteer professionals, and hence were much better prepared for war in 1917 than their land counterparts. Also, in August of 1916 Congress had authorized a naval construction program which was past the blueprint stage by the time war began. Major emphasis was placed on building destroyers to combat German submarines; as a result the Navy greatly aided the British by initiating the convoy system. The Navy counted some brilliant young officers on its rolls: Chester

World War I Draftees Marching to Induction

Nimitz and William Halsey were among them.

There were few complaints in the country over the draft. This was due mainly to the broad exemptions authorized under the Selective Service Act, and the fact that most Americans viewed the war as a short crusade to "make the world safe for democracy." Some ethnic groups, socialists, and strong progressives, were opposed to the war effort, though they possessed little influence. The nation on the whole supported American participation in the war.

Entering an Old War

The United States entered a military conflict which had been going on for approximately three years. And for all but the first weeks of this war, the contending forces had been engaged in a bitter stalemate along the French front. Heavy artillery, machine guns, and trenches kept the opponents well balanced. This should have meant an easy allied victory once the United States disrupted the balance, but such was not the case.

The summer of 1917 was disastrous for the allies. Prompted by visions of American aid, the French launched an abortive and costly offensive in April. England did likewise in July. The result was some 750,000 casualties for allied armies and no ground gained. In the fall Italy suffered similar defeats, and Russia moved into the Bolshevik phase of her revolution, which culminated in her withdrawal from the war in March, 1918, via the Treaty of Brest Litovsk. The Germans then transferred all their forces to the western front. With each passing month the need for American forces grew greater.

Allied commanders sought to absorb American troops as replacements for their decimated ranks. Pershing refused, arguing that European armies had lost their morale, were tired, and were used to defensive warfare. He claimed that a fresh, spirited army with offensive warfare as its goal was the only hope for turning the tide.

Americans first gained battle experience after Germany launched her final major offensive in March, 1918. Up to this point, American troops in France were either occupying quiet sectors of the front or they were continuing their hasty stateside training. These troops were placed at the disposal of the newly created commander-in-chief of allied armies, Ferdinand Foch. As yet there was no organized American army in Europe; there were various divisions and regiments of troops. Major American accomplishments against the German offensive included the Second Division's victories at Chateau-Thierry and Belleau Wood. The Soissons counteroffensive of mid-July was spearheaded by American troops and was the turning point of the war.

After the destruction of the German offensive in July, Pershing set himself to the task of organizing a full-scale army. This was accomplished in August, 1918, when the First American Army, commanded by Pershing, became one of the component armies of the allied military machine. This First Army played a significant role in the allied offensive of early fall, 1918, primarily on the St. Mihiel and Meuse–Argonne sectors. One of the principles in the Argonne phase was Colonel George Marshall, who was destined to play a major role in World War II.

The Return to Peace

In October the Second American Army was established, but the war was almost over. The only significant development at the time was the introduction of the airplane as an offensive weapon. Planes had been used for reconnaissance previously, and had been involved in some "dog fights;" but in October, Colonel Wil-liam Mitchell led bombing runs on the German homeland, foreboding great changes in military tactics. By the beginning of November the allied momentum overwhelmingly indicated victory, and on November 11 the armistice was signed.

American troops had fought well and they fought bravely in their first real foreign war. They appeared at a time when the war balance was shaky and the allies were on the verge of collapse. Both sides were tired and depleted, and although American fighting ability was noteworthy the greatest American contribution to the war was a psychological contribution. The thought of millions of fresh American troops pouring into the trenches stimulated the allies to renewed effort and discouraged the Central Powers. But America suffered heavy casualties in the war, considering the duration of participation. Some 50,000 Americans were killed and about 250,000 were wounded.

As in the nation's earlier wars troops were discharged as quickly as possible. The sheer size of the disbanding army created havoc on the labor market and raised serious problems of dislocation. This gave rise to the Bonus Bill issue during the 1920's. Veterans argued that they were entitled to a federal bonus for having served. They used several basic arguments to support their demand: the hardships of readjustment to civilian life, and the fact that while they had risked their lives at low pay, civilians at home had been drawing high wartime wages. Their position was defensible, and the newly formed American Legion became their champion.

What brought the bonus issue to a head was the slight recession of 1920. Congress was quite sympathetic to bonus demands. After all, a potential 5 million voter–family groups were involved. The idea of a bonus ran counter to the official Republican financial policy of low expenditures; the main objection to the bonus was the vast amount of money required to implement it. Nonetheless, by 1921 the Senate had agreed to adopt some sort of bonus measure (it was not decided whether it should be a cash payment or a paid-up insurance policy). Harding was quite upset, and for the only time during his presidency he effectively utilized his powers. Personally appearing before the Senate, he temporarily blocked action on the bonus proposal.

But the bonus impulse was too great to be squelched. In mid-1922 with congressional elections coming up, Congress passed a bonus bill which utilized the paid-up insurance idea. Harding again vetoed it, but the veterans did not give up the fight. In the spring of 1924, after Harding's death, Congress passed the Adjusted Compensation Act. President Coolidge vetoed it, but Congress overrode his veto. The act gave each veteran a twenty-year policy, the size of which was determined by duration and location of his service. The veteran was given $1 worth of insurance for each day served in the United States, and $1.50 for each day served overseas, which put a theoretical limit of about $800 on maximum policy size. The policy itself could be cashed only after twenty years, but veterans could borrow up to 22.5 per cent of its face value. This satisfied them temporarily.

With the advent of the Depression at the end of the decade, the bonus issue created a domestic crisis. In response to a renewed demand, Congress authorized veterans to borrow up to 50 per cent of the face value of their policies, over the veto of President Hoover. This cost the government roughly $1.8 billion. Within a short time the veterans were again demanding more, and in the early spring of 1932 the Bonus Expeditionary Force was organized. Approximately 11,000 people marched on Washington, where they set up a camp town (called Hooverville). The President had them forcibly evicted and their shanties burned. A sympathetic Congress afterward voted funds for their homeward journeys. The incident did not add to Hoover's dwindling popularity.

Historical Pictures Service, Chicago

Federal Troops Evicting the Bonus Army from "Hooverville"

World War II

Mobilization

The various attempts America made to avoid involvement in World War II, and the diplomatic machinations of Roosevelt to aid western Europe, will be considered in Chapter Fourteen. But on the pre-war domestic scene there were legislative enactments which implemented the gradual change in policy from appeasement to military preparedness.

In response to his requests to Congress for appropriations to build up the military, President Roosevelt received close to $18 billion for the fiscal year 1940–1941. This was more than the nation had spent for a comparable period during World War I, when the nation was actually engaged in fighting. And Congress was not content with providing only for the building of tanks, ships, and aircraft.

September, 1940 witnessed the passage of the first peacetime military conscription law in American history. The Burke–Wadsworth Selective Service and Training Act required all males between the ages of 21 and 35 to register for the draft. This provided a pool of 16 million men. Draftees were liable for one year of service, but as it turned out initial draftees were destined for a good five years of military life. The size of the Army was increased from 265,000 to 1.4 million—a large peacetime army, but the nation was expecting war.

As the nation moved toward war, the one-year draft act was approaching its expiration date, September, 1941. Roosevelt wanted to renew it; Congress and the nation, though they sympathized with the allies, were reluctant to take that step. A measure authorizing a six-month extension, with a $10-per-month pay raise after one year of service, finally passed Congress by a narrow margin. A switch of a half-dozen votes could have left the nation nearly powerless on Pearl Harbor day.

The events of December 7, 1941, ended any hesitation on the part of the nation. With the Japanese attack, defense became absolutely imperative. The nation united behind the war effort to a degree never before witnessed in America, and the military man was generally glorified. One of the most immediate concerns facing the nation was to raise an army. The Burke–Wadsworth Act was again amended to extend service to the duration of hostilities plus six months. In February, 1942, the age limits were broadened to include the 20–44 age group. A further amendment of April, 1942, authorized the drafting of individuals between 45 and 65 years old for critical industries. And in June, 1942, the age limits for those liable for military service were extended to cover the 18–44 age group.

Headed by General Lewis B. Hershey, the Selective Service System was managed with minimal difficulty. Exemptions were authorized, but because of great manpower needs they were not as broad as during World War I. The best grounds for a deferment was employment in a critical industry. Roughly 10 million Americans were drafted into service. This, coupled with activated National Guard and Reserve units plus both male and female enlistees, raised the American military to nearly 16 million. This was four times the combined strength of Union and Confederate armies at their peak. It was more than three times larger than the World War I military.

In addition to the military there was a domestic volunteer force of 5 million Civilian Defense workers who served as air raid wardens and medical aids. All were somewhat involved in the war effort; the nation was almost totally mobilized. There was even a move to draft people into industry, which failed to materialize only because the war ended before it could be enacted.

The chief factors which had contributed to repeated German military victories were a highly centralized command, a large, well trained and experienced army, superiority of equipment, and possession of the initiative. If the Allies were to be successful they had to counteract these factors. In January, 1942, twenty-six nations warring against the Axis signed a document embodying the basic principles of the Atlantic Charter (see Chapter Fourteen) and became the United Nations. Their foremost purpose was to develop a unity of command to counteract German might. At the same conferences, a general strategy for the European theatre was laid out: the invasion of North Africa, the jump to Sicily and then Italy, and the opening of a second western front against Germany. Since Japan was not considered to be an immediate threat, it was decided to concentrate on Europe for the time being, and meet Japan with a holding action in the Pacific.

The War in Europe

The European situation in the first half of 1942 was disheartening. The Soviet Union was being overrun by the Germans. General Erwin Rommel, in command of Axis armies in Egypt, was at the peak of his performance. He had pushed to within seventy miles of Alexandria against the British—the last stop before the Suez Canal. Had Rommel completed his thrust, Germany would have linked up with Japan and the results could have been disastrous for the Allies. Furthermore, before men and materiel could be positioned for an invasion of Europe the Mediterranean Sea had to be brought under Allied control, and North Africa was the key to the Mediterranean. A massive invasion of North Africa began in November of 1942, while Field Marshall Montgomery turned the Germans back at El Alamein. An English, American, and French force under General Eisenhower

worked its way through Morocco and Algeria, and the Axis armies were forced back into Tunisia. By May, 1943, North Africa was cleared of the enemy.

At the Casablanca Conference in January of 1943, Roosevelt and Prime Minister Winston Churchill had agreed to strike at the "soft underbelly" of Europe by knocking Italy out of the war. This became the prime Allied objective of 1943. Stalin demanded the opening of a second European front, but the two western statesmen felt that Italy was more important. It would further clear the Mediterranean, ease the shipment of supplies to Russia, and remove some pressure from Russia by tying up German troops in Italy.

Meanwhile, Germany had already lost the initiative in the Soviet Union when her occupying forces were routed at Stalingrad in November, 1942. Russia had simply repeated the strategy used against Napoleon in 1812. She bought time by retreating into her land mass, meanwhile collecting her forces and amassing stockpiles of American equipment. When German supply lines were vastly extended (an important factor in a mechanized ground war) and the harsh winter was setting in, she launched her counterattack. The loss in Russian lives was staggering but the initiative was won, and as the Italian campaign was progressing in the west, the Soviet Army developed a sustained drive which, by January, 1944, had carried into Poland.

In July, 1943, Sicily was invaded. Montgomery hit from the east; Canadians attacked the center; General George Patton struck from the west. Sicily crumbled almost immediately. Morale in Italy was already quite low, and Mussolini was overthrown on July 25. The Italian mainland was bombed, and a secret armistice was arranged between Eisenhower and Italian Marshall Badoglio. For all practical purposes, an Italian defeat was a foregone conclusion by mid-August. But six weeks of bloody fighting remained, and more was to come later in northern Italy against German forces. On September 3, Badoglio signed an armistice that put Italy on the side of the United Nations as a co-belligerent.

General Mark Clark then led an invasion of Italy designed to drive out the German troops which were pouring into the country. The situation was critical at first, but on October 1, 1943, Naples was taken and Italy declared war on Germany. The Allies had succeeded in freeing the Mediterranean. They had tied up a number of German divisions, preventing their use on the eastern front. They had gained control of most of the Italian navy. And most important, they had acquired valuable airstrips in southern Italy, from which to bomb Germany. A stalemate ensued in Italy along the Gustav Line, running roughly thirty miles north of Naples, but the defenses were breached in May, 1944; by early August, the Allies had advanced through Florence into northern Italy. Another brief stalemate occurred next, but in June Rome fell and Italy established a democratic government.

The Italian campaign and the Russian counteroffensive kept Germany very busy during 1943 and early 1944. This bought time for the western Allies. Britain and the United States had been amassing supplies for the opening of a second front. Throughout 1942, and increasingly in 1943, Allied airmen had been "softening up" Germany and destroying her industrial centers by saturation bombing. The culmination was the Normandy invasion of June 6, 1944.

Some 3,200 craft landed 250,000 troops on that date. Over the next three months 2.5 million troops, 500,000 vehicles, and 17 million tons of supplies were unloaded at prefabricated ports along the Normandy beachhead. Eight thousand airplanes and constant barrages from battleships curtailed enemy operations. The foothold was soon established

and the battle for the liberation of France got under way.

A smaller invasion force was landed in southern France to sap German strength, and Paris was liberated on August 25. Americans bridged the impregnable Siegfried Line in October, while British and Canadian troops pushed through Belgium and Holland. At the same time Russia succeeded in taking Bulgaria. Allied armies advanced on all fronts.

Still, General von Rundstedt launched a suicidal counteroffensive to break Allied momentum. Near Ardennes, fifteen German divisions broke through on December 16, 1944, in the bloody Battle of the Bulge. Allied forces were driven out of the Rhineland, and losses were heavy, but Germany had poured the last of her dwindling reserves into the attack. The move was only temporarily successful, and probably lengthened the European war by only about six weeks. By the end of January, 1945, the Allies had regained what had been lost, and German reserves were gone. Also by this time, Russia was in control of most of Germany's eastern satellites. In the early spring of 1945, the Allies opened a concerted drive on three fronts in an attempt to bring the European war to an end.

Russia had launched a late-winter offensive and by March, 1945, was in eastern Germany, having driven 2 million Nazis before her. On March 7 western armies reached and crossed the Rhine River, gaining control of the rich Saar Valley. In mid-April a concerted push was made northward through Italy, and on April 29 the German armies in Italy surrendered. Italian partisans "liberated" Mussolini from the Germans and brought him to an ignominious end. Germany was now fighting the Allies on her own soil on all fronts. The forces of the Third Reich could no longer retreat; instead, they collapsed.

On May 7, 1945, Germany surrendered. Fighting officially ended on the following day. Ten million troops had been killed in the European theatre; approximately 160,000 of the dead were American. The European war is estimated to have cost in excess of $1 trillion, not counting civilian property damage. But the war was not yet over for the United States.

The War with Japan

On December 7, 1941, the Americans had suffered 3,000 casualties and the loss of eight battleships and many other ships and airplanes at Pearl Harbor. During the months that followed, the Japanese appeared invincible. They possessed superiority over the United States in both sea and air power. The attack on Pearl had been followed on the same day with an attack on the Philippines which wiped out American air forces in that area. Within the following six months, Japan captured Guam, Wake Island, and Hong Kong. She occupied Indo-China and Thailand, and conquered the supposedly impregnable English naval base at Singapore. The Japanese cut the Burma Road, seized nearly every strategic point in the Netherlands East Indies, and destroyed organized resistance in the Philippines. They had also seized several of the islands in the Aleutian chain off the coast of Alaska.

By April, 1942, Allied morale in the Pacific was extremely low. The only bright spot had been Major James Doolittle's carrier-based bomber raid over Tokyo. Its military significance was negligible, but it did have a psychological effect on the Japanese. The Allies feared that India and Australia would soon fall to the men of Nippon; they did not realize that Japan had strained to her limits, and the tide was ready to turn.

In May, 1942, American carrier-based planes inflicted very heavy losses on the Japanese fleet in the Battle of Coral Sea, Japan's first defeat. The victory was followed by an equally impressive one in June, 1942; Admiral Chester Nimitz had intercepted a Japanese message calling for an attack on Midway Island as a preliminary to an invasion of the Hawaiian Islands, and American planes again attacked successfully in the Battle of Midway. These two major victories took the initiative from Japan, greatly curtailed her naval power, and put the United States in the position of determining Pacific strategy. Japan was checked and America began the slow and painful road to victory.

The Pacific strategy called for the capture of Japan's Outer Defense Area: Wake Island, the Marshalls, the Gilberts, and the Solomons. These islands would provide air bases for raids on Japan's Secondary Defense Area: the Carolines, the Marianas, the Philippines, Thailand, Indo-China, and the Netherlands Indies. A penetration of these areas would permit the United States to raid Japan's Inner Defense Area: the home islands, Korea, and parts of China.

The reduction of Japan's Outer Defense Area began with an attack on Guadalcanal in the Solomons, in August of 1942. By the end of the month, Americans had captured the Henderson Field airstrip. Then followed a checking operation as the United States prepared herself for renewed battle. In November, 1943, Tarawa, with its excellent airfield was taken after a costly battle. Then the bombing of the Marshall Islands was begun. At the same time American and Australian troops were engaging in a bloody but eventually successful campaign in New Guinea. By April, 1944, the Marshalls were essentially under American control.

The United States had effectively destroyed the Outer Defense Area. Pockets still remained (Guam was not recaptured until mid-July), but the United States was ready to begin a penetration of the Secondary Defense Area. In mid-June an attack was launched on the Marianas at Saipan. While Marines were engaged in this painfully slow and bloody reduction of Japan's far-flung possessions, General Douglas MacArthur was laying the groundwork for fulfilling his promise to return to the Philippines. In the fall of 1943, the United States had gained naval and air superiority in the Southwest Pacific. By mid-1944 MacArthur was ready to move with ground forces.

On October 20, 1944, a massive landing was made at Leyte Gulf in the Philippines. Since this move threatened Japanese control over the Philippines, and ultimately over the Netherlands East Indies, the Japanese fleet engaged the American fleet in a major naval battle, the four-day Battle of Leyte Gulf. The results were crippling for Japanese naval power. By the end of 1944, the United States had control over Leyte and began bombing Japanese installations throughout the rest of the Philippines. February 27, 1945, ended the campaign for the Philippines.

All along, American B-29's had been bombing Japan from bases in China. But supply lines were weak and the number of missions flown was limited. The bombings had more of a nuisance value than a strategic one. But while engaged in the Philippine campaign, American forces were planning to establish airstrips from which to launch major bombing assaults on Japan. To do so, more proximate airstrips were needed. The result was Iwo Jima and Okinawa, two of the bloodiest battles of the war. Only 700 miles from Tokyo, Iwo Jima was a highly strategic point. Both Japan and the United States realized this, and the Japanese fought bitterly. An American invasionary force of 115,000 men was required to establish a beachhead. The United States suffered 20,000 casualties at Iwo Jima. Okinawa was worse: 200,000 troops were used in the invasion, and there were 49,000 American casualties. In the two campaigns an estimated 130,000 Japanese were killed. At Okinawa Japan introduced the Kamikaze. Suicidal attacks sank 36 American ships and damaged 369 —some of the heaviest American naval losses of the entire war.

By April, 1945, Japan was slowly being destroyed from the air. In July, plans were made for a full-scale invasion of the Japanese home islands, though it was realized that a successful invasion would be extremely time-consuming and bloody. But during the summer of 1945, the Manhattan Project had developed an atomic bomb. President Truman decided that its use would actually save lives by shortening the war considerably; this would also prevent the Soviet Union (now free from pressure in the west) from making heavy inroads in the Far East before the armistice with Japan.

On July 26, 1945, the United States in conjunction with England and China issued the Potsdam Declaration warning the Japanese to surrender unconditionally or face total destruction. Japan regarded the proposal as a bluff. On August 6 Hiroshima was bombed, followed by Nagasaki on August 9. On that day the U.S.S.R. declared war on Japan and launched attacks in Manchuria, Korea, and Sakhalin. On August 10 Japan offered to surrender, and hostilities ended four days later. On September 1, 1945, the official surrender took place and World War II was over.

The Lessons of the War

No single Allied nation won the war; it was a group effort. To assess the reasons why the Allies won is not a difficult task. As of December, 1941, no Allied power possessed an effective fighting force. The Axis powers had begun their preparation years earlier, and the Allies were attempting to bridge the gap. But the Axis powers had expanded their areas of conquest to the point where they

"All the News That's Fit to Print"

The New York Times.

LATE CITY EDITION

VOL. XCIV...No. 31,972   NEW YORK, TUESDAY, AUGUST 7, 1945.   THREE CENTS

FIRST ATOMIC BOMB DROPPED ON JAPAN;
MISSILE IS EQUAL TO 20,000 TONS OF TNT;
TRUMAN WARNS FOE OF A 'RAIN OF RUIN'

HIRAM W. JOHNSON, REPUBLICAN DEAN IN THE SENATE, DIES

Jet Plane Explosion Kills Major Bong, Top U.S. Ace

Flier Who Downed 40 Japanese Craft, Sent Home to Be 'Safe,' Was Flying New 'Shooting Star' as a Test Pilot

KYUSHU CITY RAZED

Kenney's Planes Blast Tarumizu in Record Blow From Okinawa

REPORT BY BRITAIN

'By God's Mercy' We Beat Nazis to Bomb, Churchill Says

Steel Tower 'Vaporized' In Trial of Mighty Bomb

Scientists Awe-Struck as Blinding Flash Lighted New Mexico Desert and Great Cloud Bore 40,000 Feet Into Sky

NEW AGE USHERED

Day of Atomic Energy Hailed by President, Revealing Weapon

HIROSHIMA IS TARGET

'Impenetrable' Cloud of Dust Hides City After Single Bomb Strikes

ROCKET SITE IS SEEN

125 B-29's Hit Japan's Toyokawa Naval Arsenal in Demolition Strike

ROOSEVELT AID CITED

Raiders Wrecked Norse Laboratory in Race for Key to Victory

MORRIS IS ACCUSED OF 'TAKING A WALK'

CHINESE WIN MORE OF 'INVASION COAST'

ATOM BOMBS MADE IN 3 HIDDEN CITIES

Secrecy on Weapon So Great That Not Even Workers Knew of Their Product

TRAINS CANCELED IN STRICKEN AREA

Traffic Around Hiroshima Is Disrupted — Japanese Still Have Havoc by Split Atoms

War News Summarized

TUESDAY, AUGUST 7, 1945

Turks Talk War if Russia Presses; Prefer Vain Battle to Surrender

Reich Exile Emerges as Heroine In Denial to Nazis of Atom's Secret

Ushering in a New Era in Warfare

were forced to dissipate their strength too widely. Part of their armies had to be used for occupation forces. And while the Axis was attempting to consolidate rapid gains, the Allies were afforded an opportunity to check them momentarily, giving the United States the time to gear up her tremendous industrial potential. By mid-1942 the United States was producing more than all the Axis powers combined, and her production rate continued to increase as the war progressed.

In the European theatre a combination of American industrial supremacy, British determination, and Russian territorial space and manpower were decisive factors. Russia was able to withstand an invasion which would have completely overrun any other European country. Then, with 3 million troops over a 2,000-mile front, well equipped with American supplies, she began her counteroffensive. Meanwhile Germany was losing her productive capacity. American bombers and industry were destroying her. On May 30, 1942, for instance, 1,043 bombers dropped 1,500 tons of high explosives on one single industrial center: Cologne.

In the Pacific the victory was mainly an American one. Japan was in a vulnerable position because she possessed few natural resources and no strategic reserves. To maintain wartime production she was forced to transport materials over thousands of miles of ocean. The United States was able to take full advantage of this situation.

But both Germany and Japan made serious strategic blunders. In 1941 Germany had brought England to one knee but did not throw the final punch. As a result, the United States was able to convert the British Isles into a giant warehouse, within air-striking distance from Germany. Germany's other major error was to invade the U.S.S.R. at a time when a non-aggression pact existed between the two countries. In the process she set herself up for attack from both sides.

Japan's major mistake was not to maintain her temporary advantage. Had she been able to bring the war to the American homeland, she could have delayed the development of American industrial potential and struck a deep psychological blow to the American people. But even though she was probably not capable of this move, she could have avoided extending her lines of communication deep into the South Pacific.

Throughout history every aggressor nation has suffered from the same drawbacks. To successfully hold and protect conquered territories, further conquests are necessary to provide "buffer" areas. Lines of transport are extended much too rapidly. Aggressors are too impatient; they are unwilling to consolidate their gains thoroughly before moving on. Perhaps Plato's observation on war leaders is correct. They maintain power only as long as they continue to provide victories. Peace is their destruction, but in the long run, so is war.

The Military in a Cold War World

The end of the war brought demobilization for America's armies. The men who had entered service first were the first to be discharged, but many were required to serve for some time afterwards because of the need for occupation forces in Germany and Japan. So there was not a complete demobilization, even though the draft was soon ended.

In 1947 Congress reorganized the military. A single Secretary of Defense was given complete authority over all branches of the service, instead of a Secretary of War and a Secretary of the Navy sharing authority. The new Defense Secretary would be advised by the military heads of the various services. The theory was sound but rivalry and friction developed between the service heads. To counteract this Congress authorized a

Chairman for the Chiefs of Staff, and the first one appointed was General Omar Bradley. But the group continued to be plagued with petty rivalries which limited its effectiveness.

Police Action in Korea

In 1945 Korea had been taken from Japan. The Soviets occupied the northern half of the country while the United States controlled the southern half. The Russians avoided unification, and when a United Nations truce team went into Korea in 1948, it was not allowed into the northern half. So elections were held in the south, and the Republic of Korea was created. American troops were pulled out of South Korea in June, 1949.

A year later, on June 25, 1950, North Korea launched an invasion of South Korea. The United States immediately took the matter to the United Nations Security Council, and by a 9–0 vote (Russia was absent), condemned the invasion. Truman ordered the Seventh Fleet to Formosa and sent military supplies to South Korea. Following a Security Council Resolution on June 27, calling for aid to Korea, Truman committed American ground forces to the conflict by dispatching two divisions from Japan.

The President managed to capture bipartisan support at home. The Security Council asked the United States to appoint a Supreme United Nations Commander, and General Douglas MacArthur got the job. Other nations began to contribute contingents of troops, and after bloody fighting, United Nations forces cleared South Korea; by the beginning of October they were preparing to move into North Korea.

Meanwhile, Congress was enacting various bits of legislation to create a semi-mobilized state. A new Selective Service Act had been passed in 1948, but since Congress had never authorized appropriations, the act only stimulated enlistments.

Funds were made available after the North Korean invasion and the draft was re-established. In June, 1951, the Universal Military Training and Service Act established the modern draft system. Males in the 18½-to-26 age group were liable for two years on active duty and six years in the reserves; as a result, by the beginning of 1953 the American armed forces included some 3.3 million men. Other legislative measures dealt with control of the economy and industry. And after Truman declared a National Emergency in December, 1950, Congress voted a $45-billion defense budget for fiscal year 1950–1951, which was funded by the reintroduction of World War II tax measures.

The Korean conflict had been regarded as a limited action requiring limited measures. In late October of 1950, however, American military personnel began to make contact with Chinese troops near the Manchurian border. In late November these "volunteers" launched a tremendous counteroffensive, and by the end of the year General MacArthur was advocating the bombing of China and a Chinese Nationalist invasion of the Chinese mainland.

It was not until late January, 1951, after United Nations forces had been almost driven out of Korea, that General Matthew Ridgway succeeded in halting the communist advance. At this point the United States officially endorsed the concept of fighting a limited war for a limited stated objective: the independence of South Korea. When MacArthur received word in March, 1951, that President Truman was about to attempt a negotiated settlement of the conflict, he again advocated bombing China and expanding the war. The military commander had openly challenged his commander-in-chief, and the American military has traditionally been considered subordinate to civilian authorities. Though MacArthur was exceedingly popular with the American people, Truman took the established constitutional view and fired MacArthur, replacing him with Ridgway. The immediate popular reaction was against Truman, but bitterness diminished with time. The war dragged on to become a political issue in the 1952 election. Dwight Eisenhower, the Republican candidate, promised to go to Korea to seek an end to the conflict. Renewed negotiations were initiated at Panmunjom in April, 1953, and an armistice was concluded on July 27, 1953. Some 55,000 Americans had lost their lives in this "police action," not to mention other losses. It was galling to many Americans that so much had been expended merely to return Korea to its prewar situation; the realities of the Cold War world were not easy to accept.

Vietnam

Just as Korea was divided following World War II, Vietnam (previously a part of Indo-China) was divided at Geneva in 1954, again with promises of elections to decide its fate. The United States was not a party to this agreement, but the Southeast Asia Treaty Organization, of which the United States was the guiding light, did promise protection for South Vietnam, and Laos and Cambodia as well.

In 1961, some time after the South Vietnam government had refused to allow the promised elections, communist guerillas from North Vietnam and their southern sympathizers began a terrorist campaign in South Vietnam. During this and the following year, irrefutable evidence was collected of North Vietnamese aggression. The United States had been providing military advisors for South Vietnamese forces, but they were nothing more than this. However, the attack on American vessels in the Gulf of Tonkin in 1964 led Congress to adopt the Tonkin Resolution, which gave President Johnson the authority to send fighting forces to the region.

Advisors multiplied rapidly, and the game of escalation was underway. Early in 1965 there was no longer any pretense of partial aid; American forces were fighting openly against the Vietcong, the military arm of South Vietnam's rebellious National Liberation Front. Bombing raids on North Vietnam began and progressively increased, both in number and in location. The United States claimed simply that it sought an opportunity for the South Vietnamese people to choose freely their own form of government without fear of terrorism. But in the process, the United States had become embroiled in another major military conflict, and by the spring of 1968, important officials were divided as to when and how it could end. The American people were even more divided; many added a *why* to the *when* and *how,* and anxiously watched the peace talks in Paris for a sign that the bloodshed could be ended.

The Role of the Modern Military

American public opinion has always viewed the military with distrust. At times this attitude has been expressed by government itself. In 1876, for example, Congress failed to appropriate revenues for the military, and military personnel served without pay. In jokes, in statements by ex-servicemen, by act and innuendo, Americans display their dislike of military life.

The basic tenet of American thinking is individual freedom. A product of the Enlightenment, this idea developed to a very high degree in America for two basic reasons. One was the preoccupation of the people with economic advancement. The other was the relative absence of a threat to national security, which avoided the need for a powerful military arm. The philosophy that guides the military stresses organizational rather than individual requirements. The individual must subordinate his identity to that of the group. The entire orientation of the military man is diametrically opposed to that of the American civilian. His job calls for violence, killing, and death. His civilian counterpart seeks life and peace; otherwise he violates the law. The civilian who has lived his life with positive goals and is suddenly thrust into a military situation is bound to experience a very serious readjustment problem, especially in American society. If the civilian lived in a dictatorial society, he would have no great problems in adjusting, for his goals would not have changed much.

Americans have worked out an unconscious compromise with a set of contradictory philosophies. It is recognized that huge military organizations are needed during time of war, but as soon as the war ends, the army must go. The 16-million-man army of World War II was down to 500,000 by the outbreak of the Korean War. The same situation has been witnessed after every other American war prior to Korea.

But since the Korean War a major change has taken place in America. International developments seem to have forced the United States to maintain a large military establishment, even though the nation is not technically at war. And as the military continues to exist over the years, the national economy has grown used to large military contracts; the American labor force has grown accustomed to having millions of its number removed from job competition (which helps bolster wages). To disarm and demobilize after two decades of such trends would require a great readjustment on the part of the American people and their economy. But there are some who feel that the cost of this constant military preparedness is already too great; if current international commitments require such a huge military machine, perhaps the United States should stop trying to protect the internal stability of those nations which are not directly vital to the American security.

Even so this does not answer the fundamental dichotomy between military and civilian life. As long as America continues to stand for the tenets of individual freedom upon which it is based, the civilian will experience great difficulty in adjusting to military life, but the military, by its very nature, cannot change its perspective lest it become totally ineffective. The conflict is ever-present in a democratic society. Americans do not like the military, but national self-preservation seems to require them to tolerate it.

For Further Reading

Baker, Newton D. *America at War*. 2 volumes. New York: Dodd, Mead, 1931.

Cook, Fred J. *The Warfare State*. New York: Macmillan Company, 1962.

Hammond, Paul Y. *Organizing for Defense: The American Military Establishment in the Twentieth Century*. Princeton: Princeton University Press, 1961.

Huntington, Samuel P. *The Soldier and the State: The Theory and Politics of Civil-Military Relations*. Cambridge: Harvard University Press, 1957.

Janowitz, Morris. *The Professional Soldier*. Glencoe, Ill.: The Free Press, 1960.

Millis, Walter. *The Martial Spirit*. Cambridge: Harvard University Press, 1931.

_____. *Road to War: America, 1914–1917*. Boston: Houghton Mifflin, 1935.

Pratt, Fletcher. *War for the World*. New Haven: Yale University Press, 1950.

Singletary, Otis. *The Mexican War*. Chicago: University of Chicago Press, 1960.

Stouffer, Samuel A., *et al.* *The American Soldier*. Princeton: Princeton University Press, 1949.

Swomley, John M., Jr. *The Military Establishment*. Boston: Beacon Press, 1964.

Tucker, Robert. *The Just War*. Baltimore: Johns Hopkins Press, 1960.

Chapter Fourteen
The Policy of Involvement:
Foreign Affairs

The United States is currently in an era when foreign affairs demand a large proportion of governmental effort and individual concern. Private citizens constantly discuss the wisdom of aid to other countries, United States involvement in Vietnam, solutions to problems with the Soviet Union and Red China, how to win the confidence and support of the new nations of Africa and Asia, plus a host of other issues.

There is an obvious reason for all this. Because of her strength, her ideological traditions, and her prosperity, the United States is a leader of nations. But her leadership is not going without challenge. Engaged in an ideological and sometimes military struggle with forces of revolution around the world, the United States must, for survival's sake, win the friendship of as many countries as possible. The nation cannot afford to "go it alone."

Through history a considerable evolution of American foreign policy has occurred. In keeping with President Washington's farewell warning against "entangling alliances," the United States developed in a state of near-isolation during the nineteenth century. It greeted the twentieth century with a brief period of international crusading spirit, only to become disillusioned and semi-isolationist two decades later. The events of World War II have created both a new world and a new America. Past times cannot be relived except in memory; current problems cannot be washed away except in fantasy. Like it or not, the United States is a world power, and as such she has been forced by circumstances to play out a leadership role on the international scene.

The present chapter will survey American diplomacy from the colonial period to the present. Major emphasis will be given to the twentieth century in an attempt to explain the reasons why America occupies her current role and why she adheres to certain positions in her foreign policy.

Why the United States is in Vietnam, why she gives away billions in foriegn aid, and why she makes commitments around the world, are deep and sometimes disturbing questions. An understanding of diplomatic history will not only cast some light on space-age diplomacy, but it will also, once again, reflect the evolving nature of the American system.

Eighteenth-Century Diplomacy

During the colonial period there was no American foreign policy as such, since the American colonies were subordinate to England. English diplomacy led the American colonies into a number of wars in which they had little natural concern; only the last of these wars, the French and Indian War, had American roots, but even this conflict was partly a result of the pre-conditioning of the principle combatants. Furthermore, English mercantilistic theory and its application to trade regulation had a direct detrimental effect on the economic development of the colonies. The first American-centered diplomacy came in the era of the Revolution.

Revolutionary Diplomacy

There were two primary aims to American Revolutionary diplomacy: to obtain foreign assistance and to obtain recognition of American independence. The nation quickly acquired unofficial aid from France through the "front" firm of Rodrique Hortelez et Compagnie, mainly because France was looking for ways to make England uncomfortable.

After the Battle of Saratoga, the French promised official recognition as soon as they could clear the issue with Spain (to whom they were obligated by the Family Compact of 1761). At this point the English offered home rule to America. Earlier, this offer would have been widely applauded in America, but not after Sar-

atoga. The American diplomat, Ben Franklin, rejected the offer, but made sure that France was not informed of his rejection. He intimated to the French that America would probably accept the English offer, hoping to force France into an immediate alliance.

The ruse worked and in January, 1778, France and the thirteen United States of North America signed a treaty. It included a recognition of American independence, a most-favored-nation commercial agreement (a promise to give no other nation better trade privileges than they gave each other); the treaty also stipulated that free ships made free goods (a neutral ship could carry war material through a blockade because it was neutral), that naval stores and foodstuffs were not military supplies, and that neither nation would make a separate peace with England. Also included was a mutual defense arrangement, whereby both countries promised to go to the aid of the other if attacked by England at some future date. The points on commercial treaties, free ships, and contraband of war remained basic tenets of American foreign policy well into the twentieth century.

The French minister Vergennes acquired concurrence from Spain, and in April, 1779, Spain declared war on England—not as an ally of America, but as an ally of France. She did this because she possessed numerous colonies and wanted to avoid the appearance that she was fighting for the freedom of rebellious colonies. In return for Spain's aid, France agreed to help Spain recapture Gibraltar (she had lost it in 1713), and to keep fighting until this aim was achieved. This tied the American war to strictly European issues, and complicated it with the no-separate-peace clause in the Franco-American treaty.

The Armed Neutrality of the North, an association of European powers opposed to English practices on the high seas, was formed in 1780. Led by Russia, these nations pledged themselves to enforce their neutrality to the point of waging war. England was walking a tightrope with Europe. And in the same year she declared war on "neutral" Holland for openly aiding France, Spain, and America; Holland was already the open enemy of England and welcomed the challenge.

In 1780 England was fighting the United States, France, Spain, and Holland, and there was a potential of war with the rest of Europe. This, more than Saratoga or Yorktown, explains her willingness to end the Revolutionary conflict. Peace negotiations opened in 1782. Spain had not recaptured Gibraltar, so France promised her the trans-Appalachian American West as a substitute. Americans heard of this, and in violation of the no-separate-peace agreement began separate negotiations with England. After a preliminary wrangle about the formal recognition of American independence, the United States won its point, and the Treaty of Paris was signed in 1783.

The Treaty of Paris

The treaty was more of a truce than anything else. Its terms were destined to be violated and some of them provided the basis for the War of 1812. England agreed to evacuate her troops from America, including those stationed on military posts in the Northwest territory; the forts were not evacuated until 1796. A problem concerned fishing rights off the banks of Newfoundland. As colonists, Americans had possessed this right, but independence brought certain disadvantages. The new nation did obtain the fishing rights but no shoreline privileges; this rendered the right useless since fish had to be processed ashore almost immediately to prevent spoilage.

The United States agreed to restore property confiscated from Loyalists during the war. She further promised that English merchants would be paid their just

debts. Neither one of these promises were kept. On her part, England agreed to return slaves which she had captured as "contraband of war," but this too, was not done.

An item of major concern was the use of the Mississippi River. It was agreed that both nations would have complete freedom of navigation. But the war was still in progress between England and Spain, and the latter nation owned territory on both banks at the mouth of the river. No nation possessed the right to pass through without Spanish permission. The United States did have partial claim to navigation rights since she owned most of the eastern bank of the river, but England had no legitimate claim. It was ironic that England, because of her naval strength, for some time had more freedom on the Mississippi than the weak United States.

Boundary settlements provided more problems. It was agreed that the Atlantic Ocean and the Mississippi would be the eastern and western boundaries of the nation. Over this there was no major dispute; it was the southern boundary that provided a major controversy. Since England and Spain were still at war, the fate of Florida was undecided. It was agreed that if Spain emerged from the war owning Florida, the southern boundary would be the 31st parallel; but if England owned it, the boundary would be farther north. (Florida at the time stretched to the Mississippi.) England emerged from the conflict in possession of Florida, but ceded the territory to Spain, and there remained a dispute over the Yazoo Strip, which lay between the two boundary lines.

A diplomatic problem facing the new nation was the establishment of commercial relations with the rest of the world. Americans discovered that there had been certain advantages to participation in the British system. The nation had to negotiate commercial treaties with Holland (1782), Sweden (1783), and with Russia, Spain, and Prussia (1785–86); there was already a treaty with France. Americans carried on some trade with Africa and Italy, but no treaties existed. No commercial arrangement was made with England, and that nation possessed a near monopoly on world trade.

Diplomacy in the Foundation Period

Relations with England and Spain

With the establishment of the Constitution, the nation was ready to tackle some of its outstanding diplomatic problems. With England there were disputes concerning evacuation of the Northwest forts and neutral rights. With Spain there were problems over Indians, navigation on the Mississippi, the Florida boundary, and port rights at the mouth of the Mississippi. And with France there was a host of difficulties arising from the French Revolution, the treaty of 1778, and neutral rights.

A partial settlement with England was effected by Jay's Treaty in 1795. England agreed to evacuate the Northwest forts and did so in 1796 (her fur trading interests were dwindling). It was also agreed that a commission would be appointed to settle the boundary dispute between Maine and Canada (destined to remain a standing issue). England paid the United States $6 million for damages to American shipping caused by English seizures during her wars with France. For her part the United States recognized Revolutionary war debts due to English merchants but not yet paid as promised in the Treaty of Paris (1783). A twelve-year, most-favored-nation commerical treaty was also negotiated. This was a major diplomatic success for America, but it did not include trading rights with English territories in the Caribbean. The treaty was silent on such items as search and seizure, and the impressment of American seamen—issues which could lead to war.

As a result of this treaty, Spain was anxious to win the friendship of the United States. She was an ally of France against England, and did not desire to add to the enemy's strength. She therefore decided to outdo England. The resultant Treaty of San Lorenzo (also known as Pinckney's Treaty) of 1795, was highly favorable to the United States. The United States received the entire Yazoo Strip and recognition of her right to navigate the Mississippi River. More important was acquisition of the right to use some port facility at the mouth of the river. Spain granted this right at New Orleans for a three-year period, subject to renewal. The settlement of these issues alleviated the Indian problem, since the United States gained control over the area, and no longer need suffer border raids. Spain gave much and received nothing concrete in return. European developments were working to the benefit of the young American nation.

Dealing With Revolutionary France

Relations with France came to a crisis in the Citizen Genet affair. Genet was the French diplomatic representative to the United States. He belonged to the Girondin (anti-monarchial) party in France. Landing in Charleston in 1793, he sought American aid for his revolution, began raising a "French Revolutionary Army of America," and collected contributions for the French government. He planned to use American ports to outfit French privateers. This would have constituted a definite un-neutral act, and Washington ordered him to desist. Genet ignored the warning and outfitted the *Little Democrat* as a privateer raiding ship. Washington demanded Genet's recall for this, and a new, more radical French government agreed. The guillotine was waiting; Genet petitioned to remain in the United States as a private citizen, and the petition was granted. The incident had placed a serious strain on American neutrality.

Difficulties were enhanced by the fact

that a mutual defense pact existed between the two nations. Alexander Hamilton argued that since the monarchy had fallen and there was no stable government in France, the treaty should not be recognized. Jefferson, on the other hand, rightly claimed that the treaty was between French and American nations, regardless of government, and must be observed. As a result of this, the French ambassador to the United States, Adet, openly campaigned for Jefferson's election to the presidency in 1796, and may have lost the office for him because of this interference in a domestic matter. Undaunted, France still showed their antipathy toward Jefferson's opponents, and this led to the XYZ Affair discussed in Chapter Thirteen.

Another pressing matter at the time concerned the definition of contraband. England and France, with their large navies, favored a broad definition of what constituted seizable contraband of war, whereas small nations like the United States desired a stricter interpretation of this concept. American ships were being seized by both England and France, but due to the XYZ Affair popular feeling was running strongest against France. It would shift shortly, but for the time being the result was an undeclared naval war with France in 1798.

Alexander Hamilton favored war with France as part of a three-point diplomatic program: first, seek an economic, military, and political alliance with England; second, stimulate the American economy by means of a major war effort; third, seek the independence of Latin American colonies and make them economic puppets of the United States. This marked the inception of an American policy toward her Latin neighbors which held throughout the nineteenth century and became known as Dollar Diplomacy at the beginning of the twentieth century. Also holding throughout the nineteenth century and lasting until American entrance into World War I was the goal of neutrality with respect to the

affairs of Europe (except for the brief War of 1812). This created the sentiment for isolationism which culminated in the promulgation of the Monroe Doctrine in 1823.

Napoleon came to power in 1799. He desired peace with America, agreed to abrogate the 1778 treaty and accepted the American concept that neutral ships make neutral goods. On her part, the United States waived any claims to indemnities arising out of French seizures of American ships during the 1790's. The agreement was known as the Convention of 1800, and with its signing the two nations entered upon a brief period of friendship. But also in 1800, Napoleon secretly acquired the Louisiana territory from Spain by means of the Treaty of San Ildefonso; the United States bought the huge region from France in 1803.

The War of 1812 and the Era of Good Feelings

At the opening of the nineteenth century the United States was diplomatically occupied with events leading to the War of 1812. These events centered around the enforcement of Napoleon's Continental System and England's Orders in Council. Napoleon closed Europe to English shipping, and England retaliated by proclaiming a blockade around Napoleon's Europe. Consequently, neutral nations like the United States were affected whether they traded with England or the Continent.

Both the effectiveness and the legality of England's blockade were questionable. All violating ships were supposedly subject to seizure, but most of them got through. Consequently, most shippers believed that the low risk of capture was worth the profits which would be realized if port was reached. Such an attitude led to many hostile encounters on the seas. In 1800 the British Admiralty Court, in the Polly decision, ruled that neutral ships could trade with belligerents in non-contraband goods during wartime if the goods were first imported into neutral nations by neutral ships. The decision meant millions to American shipping in the French West Indies trade.

But in 1805 England crushed Napoleon's navy at Trafalgar, and attained complete supremacy on the seas. Furthermore the Polly decision was altered by the Essex decision of 1805, which still recognized American rights to trade in the French West Indies, but required the United States to prove that the goods were truely "neutralized." Either a full tariff duty could be paid on the goods, or they could be unloaded and stored in America for a reasonable length of time. This would cut considerably into American profits. American shippers had been loading up in the West Indies and sailing directly for France. England believed, with considerable justification, that Americans were taking advantage of the Polly decision. The Essex decision proved to be the major maritime cause for the War of 1812; although few Americans were actually engaged in West Indies trade, that trade did contribute materially to American prosperity because it provided a nearby outlet for surplus crops. By curtailing western trade the decision curtailed western prosperity, and it was the West which prodded the nation into the War of 1812. (See Chapters Four and Thirteen.)

The War of 1812 ended with the Treaty of Ghent in December, 1814. It called for a *status quo ante bellum*, meaning a resumption of the pre-war situation, but the treaty did set up provisions for calling conventions later to deal with points of difference between the two nations. In July, 1815, a commercial convention ended all trade discrimination between the two countries except for the British West Indies. The Rush–Bagot Agreement of 1817 provided for a boundary between the United States and Canada, unguarded except for normal police forces.

An 1818 convention recognized American rights to the Newfoundland fisheries, and allowed shoreline privileges in uninhabited areas. Another 1818 convention extended the Canadian–American boundary line to the Rocky Mountains along the 49th parallel. Not solved at the time was the Maine boundary dispute.

In 1819 Spain and America negotiated the Adams–Onis Treaty. Spain ceded Florida to the United States, and the United States agreed to assume all claims of Spaniards living in Florida against their government. The Spanish Cortes refused to ratify the treaty, so the United States unofficially threatened to seize the region by force. This was no idle threat, since Spain was totally unable to police the area and it had become a refuge for pirates, escaped slaves, and renegade Indians. The treaty was ratified in 1821, and the United States rounded out her present southern boundary east of the Mississippi.

The Monroe Doctrine

The most important diplomatic incident in the period after the War of 1812 was the promulgation of the Monroe Doctrine, which had European backgrounds. After the defeat of Napoleon the victorious powers (including the French monarchy) formed the Concert of Europe to keep the peace and prevent the further spread of revolutionary ideas. In 1823, with Spain in the throes of a revolution against the recently restored monarchy, France sent her armies there to put down the revolt, with the backing of the Concert.

If a strong Spanish monarchy should somehow be established, Spain's newly rebellious New World colonies might be controlled again, and England could lose her highly profitable trade with those colonies. So the English minister, Canning, proposed to Secretary of State John Quincy Adams, a joint statement warning Spain and France not to interfere with the new Latin American republics. Adams liked the idea of preventing Spain from re-asserting herself in the New World, but he did not relish tying America's foreign policy to England's. He preferred a unilateral statement, knowing full well that the United States could not enforce such a policy, but that England would.

President Monroe's message to Congress in December, 1823—the policy statement which has since been named the Monroe Doctrine—embodied three basic points. The American continents were declared subject to no further European colonization. Moreover, since the political system of Europe was different from that of America, it would be detrimental to American interests if Europe extended her system to the western hemisphere. And finally, the United States promised not to interfere with existing European colonies, nor would she involve herself in the internal affairs of Europe.

The Monroe Doctrine could not have been backed up if challenged, but since it was nothing more than a statement in a presidential message, it was calmly accepted with little fanfare. Nevertheless it proclaimed the diplomatic independence of the United States in terms that have influenced American policy often since 1823.

Jacksonian Diplomacy

No other important diplomatic incidents occurred until the presidency of Andrew Jackson, when the President succeeded in opening the British West Indies to American trade simply by informing England that he stood ready to adopt new policies. This happened to be a violation of protocol, but American markets were nonetheless improved. Jackson settled the French debt issue in a similarly abrupt fashion. France had inflicted damages on American shipping during the Napoleonic era. Reparations payments had been arranged but not completed. Jackson denounced France and asked Congress for

the authority to make necessary "reprisals." Diplomatically, this action was tantamount to a war declaration. France broke off diplomatic relations, but cooler heads prevailed and the issue was successfully negotiated.

Texas provided another diplomatic point of contention. For twenty years American citizens had been settling in Spanish (later Mexican) Texas. To qualify for land ownership these settlers were required to accept Catholicism and Spanish land tenure laws. Problems arose as the number of Americans in Texas grew. American Texas revolted and successfully declared independence in 1836. The independence fight was actually a Mexican civil war; the United States should have remained neutral, but did not. Americans were highly sympathetic to their fellow Americans in Texas. Jackson allowed arms, men, and money to cross the border in aid of Sam Houston's forces. The United States recognized the independence of Texas, but Mexico did not. In fact, she warned that if the United States tried to annex the region, dire consequences would result.

Webster's Success

When John Tyler was inaugurated in 1841 he chose the extremely able Daniel Webster as his secretary of state. Webster provided an outstanding diplomatic achievement for the Tyler administration. His reputation in England was high, and he had visited the country. His appointment encouraged England to seek the restoration of friendly relations with the United States. With this in mind, she sent the talented Lord Ashburton to negotiate outstanding differences.

The two men negotiated the famous Webster–Ashburton Treaty of 1842. Its provisions included a settlement of the Maine boundary dispute with almost 60 per cent of the territory going to the United States, and two minor boundary adjustments in the Great Lakes area. This gave the United States her northern boundary as far west as the Rockies. Mutual extradition was agreed upon for seven major crimes. The United States agreed to police the African coast in conjunction with England in an attempt to halt the slave trade, but the United States did not keep her word. There were also a number of minor treaty provisions.

The Diplomacy of Manifest Destiny and Its Aftermath

Diplomacy became a very important factor in America during the era of the 1840's. At the time the American people were in an expansionistic temper, with their eyes on Texas, California, and the Oregon country. James Polk was elected to the presidency in 1844, on a platform favoring the annexation of Texas and the occupation of Oregon. But opinion on the Texas annexation issue was divided because of the rising slavery issue and Mexico's threats of war should annexation be attempted.

The Fight with Mexico

Tyler was still in office as a lame duck president. Recognizing the prevailing expansionistic mood, he hoped to salvage an undistinguished administration by acquiring recognition for Texas annexation. An annexation treaty would require a two-thirds vote in the Senate for ratification, and this would have been difficult. Instead, Tyler succeeded in passing a joint annexation resolution which required only a majority in each house of Congress.

According to the terms of annexation the Lone Star Republic would become a state when she submitted a constitution acceptable to Congress. She agreed to the eventual subdivision of her territory into as many as five states (thus creating ten slave-state senators instead of two). She

would pay her own revolutionary war debt, retain her own public lands, and have slavery protected by the Missouri Compromise. The joint resolution was approved and signed by Tyler just three days before he left office.

Polk was thus inaugurated with half of his expansionistic program completed. Mexico immediately protested the annexation and broke off diplomatic relations, but the impending war with Mexico arose from a number of factors, of which the annexation was only one. The weak Mexican government had repeatedly failed to protect American citizens in her country, and poor trade relations existed between the two nations. There existed also many unpaid American damage claims against the Mexican government.

But the most important difficulty between the two nations pertained to the southern boundary of Texas. From the days when she was a province, the southern boundary of Texas had been the Nueces River. But Texas, backed by the power of the United States, claimed the Rio Grande as her southern boundary. Polk backed the Texas claim, sent an army to occupy the disputed region, and dispatched John Slidell to Mexico to negotiate for the purchase of the area and also for the New Mexican and California territories as well. For obvious reasons, the Mexican government refused to receive Slidell, and war eventually came. (See Chapters Four and Thirteen.)

The war ended in 1848 with the Treaty of Guadalupe Hidalgo. It was a curious treaty in that the minister who negotiated it, Nicholas Trist, had been deprived of all authority to do so and ordered to return to the United States. Polk chose to accept Trist's treaty because of rising Whig opposition to the war. According to the treaty terms Mexico recognized the Rio Grande boundary. She ceded California and the New Mexican territories to the United States. In return for such a generous land cession, the United States paid Mexico $15 million. Furthermore, the United States assumed all claims of American citizens against the Mexican government, which amounted to approximately $3.2 million. The nation had added the Southwest to her domain.

When Polk was campaigning for the presidency, he had been quite militant about taking the entire Oregon country. The region was then held jointly by England and the United States. However, Polk mellowed considerably when war with Mexico commenced. Diplomacy solved the problem amicably in 1846 when the two nations agreed to extend the 49th parallel from the Rockies to the Pacific, exclusive of Vancouver's Island. This gave the United States a little over half of the disputed territory, including the much coveted Columbia Basin. By diplomacy the United States had achieved a very favorable compromise.

Cuba and the Slavery Issue

The acquisition of these vast territories and whether or not slavery would be allowed in them, created serious domestic strife in the 1850's, set off by California's petition to enter the Union as a free state. Part of this strife was of a diplomatic nature, especially during the administration of President Franklin Pierce, 1853–1857.

Spain and England were cooperating in an attempt to end the slave trade. Spain was enforcing this policy in Cuba, which was dangerously close to the slave-holding South. The South wanted the federal government to acquire Cuba for two reasons: to obtain an additional slave state, and to acquire the lucrative Cuban sugar industry. Pierce, too, was interested in the acquisition. The North claimed that he favored slavery, which was not true; the South cared little what Pierce favored, just so he acquired Cuba. Spain became hostile, and England became alarmed. The American ambassador to Spain, Pierre Soule, threatened military action if Spain

refused to sell the island.

Against this background occurred the *Black Warrior* incident of 1854. The *Black Warrior* was an American ship engaged in the coastal trade. In February, 1854, it docked in a Cuban port where it was immediately confiscated because it carried slaves. Soule demanded its immediate release from the Spanish government, and submitted his demand on Palm Sunday (in Catholic Spain absolutely no business was conducted during Holy Week). Spain considered the action as an insult to her religion. Soule followed with a forty-eight hour ultimatum, openly seeking war. Secretary of State Marcy and Pierce both refused to back their vociferous ambassador. The issue cooled to slightly below the boiling point.

Then came the Ostend Manifesto of October, 1854. The Manifesto was nothing more than a series of recommendations to the President as a private document, composed by three of his ambassadors: Buchanan (England), Soule (Spain), and Mason (France). The press managed to intercept and publish the letter, which called for the acquisition of Cuba at all costs. The result was an uproar which aggravated internal sectional conflict and aroused the fears of Europe, but no government action.

Civil War and Reconstruction Diplomacy

The Confederate Search for Allies

The military is the strong arm of diplomacy, but the latter does not cease when the military swings into action. And such was the case with the American civil conflict. Confederate diplomacy had three major aims. One was to secure a treaty of alliance with any country willing to do so. Another was to secure recognition of the Confederacy as a sovereign belligerent (this would mean that neutral nations could sell arms). And the third was to obtain any sort of unofficial aid possible. The North had only one diplomatic aim: to maintain the diplomatic status of the southern states as rebels against their legal government in a strictly internal affair.

When war commenced, the South felt confident that it could obtain European aid. It was believed that cotton was essential to the English economy. This had been true in the 1850's, but by 1860 England was obtaining cotton from India and Egypt and she needed northern grains more than southern cotton. It was also believed that English industrialists would desire to check rapid northern industrial growth; the English, however, were not prepared to risk war for this flimsy reason. Nor did the English landed gentry, a group which identified socially with the southern plantation owners, strongly back the rebels' political cause. The disappointment of Confederate hopes for English support was greatly aided by the existence of strong anti-slavery feeling and the presence of a capable Union ambassador to England, Charles Francis Adams. England's aid to the rebels remained slight and unofficial.

With France, as with England, the Confederacy mistakenly believed that southern cotton was essential to the economy. More plausible was the hope that France might desire to regain her colonial holdings in America. Napoleon III was experiencing considerable domestic difficulty, and needed other issues to occupy the attention of his people; he eventually settled on attempting the conquest of Mexico. Louis Napoleon's empty treasury and his fear of vulnerability to England, however, persuaded him to stay out of the American conflict. Similarly, Spain had too many of her own problems—civil wars, in fact—to interfere in the United States.

Union Diplomacy

Though Confederate foreign affairs were more notably bungled, several diplomatic problems arose between the North and Europe during the Civil War. Two of these were with England: the Trent Affair and the Alabama Episode. The third, the Maximilian Affair, was with France.

In 1862 the Confederacy sent James Mason as ambassador to England, and John Slidell as his counterpart to France. Because of the northern blockade the two men were smuggled to Cuba, where they boarded an English ship, the *Trent,* bound for Europe. The Union navy halted the vessel in neutral waters, and removed Mason, Slidell, and staff. In the North there was a favorable reaction to the incident. But England expressed considerable resentment and demanded the release of the Confederates. Charles Francis Adams was greatly embarrassed, and he feared military reprisals, especially when 8,000 redcoats were sent to Canada. Lincoln faced one of the most serious dilemmas of his presidency. To release the men would aid the Confederacy and appear to be knuckling under to England. But not to release them could drive the English into the Confederate camp—the end result of which would be a prolonging of the war or even defeat for the North. But Lincoln found an answer. He released the men, pointing to the traditional American position on search and seizure, and indicated that he was pleased that England saw fit to adopt the American viewpoint. With this adroit maneuver the Trent Affair concluded, but for a time it was quite critical.

The Alabama Episode arose from the fact that a Confederate agent named John Bullock had obtained shipbuilding contracts in his own name in England. These ships were then outfitted with armament in North Africa and used against the Union blockade. Great Britain claimed that she was not acting in an un-neutral manner because Bullock was a private citizen. Charles Francis Adams protested violently, and finally obtained an order prohibiting the release of further ships. The order was a tacit admission by England that she had been at fault.

One ship was practically completed when the order was issued, the *Alabama,* and it managed to set sail before the order was delivered. The *Alabama* inflicted over $7 million in damages against Union shipping; this frightened northern shippers and provoked sharp increases in maritime insurance rates. Whenever the *Alabama* damaged a northern ship, Adams presented a bill to the English government. He suggested that the issue be arbitrated, but England ignored the request.

In 1866 a more conciliatory government was elected in England. At the same time Americans were clamoring for action. Senator Sumner of Massachusetts claimed that England was responsible for the last two years of the war, and should either pay the United States $2 billion, or relinquish all of Canada. Eventually, Secretary of State Hamilton Fish, and British Foreign Minister Rose, agreed on a five-nation convention to settle the issue. This was the first truly international arbitration board. At the Geneva Convention of 1871, representatives from the United States, England, Switzerland, Brazil, and Italy, awarded $15.5 million in damages to the United States. The convention decided to settle all damage claims between the two nations, and awarded $2 million to England. The issue was finally resolved, and an important diplomatic precedent was established.

The Maximilian Affair with France had a complex background. Emperor Louis Napoleon desired a Mexican empire to draw attention away from his domestic problems, and to restore his nation's foundering prestige. Mexico owed large sums of money to England, Spain, and France. She had acknowledged this debt as early as 1842, but had failed to make most of her payments. In 1861, Mexican Presi-

dent Juarez completely suspended payments for a two-year period. After unsuccessful diplomatic attempts to collect their money, England, Spain, and France prepared for military intervention. This was a violation of the Monroe Doctrine, but the Civil War tied the hands of the United States. Secretary of State Seward proposed that the United States would make the payments for Mexico for a five-year period in exchange for land and mineral rights in northern Mexico. But all parties were against this idea.

The European powers claimed that they were only interested in collecting their just debts, and had no imperialistic designs on Mexico. With these assurances, and fearful that a strong protest might result in aid for the Confederacy by these powers, the United States agreed to the intervention, which took place in April, 1862. England and Spain kept their word, and withdrew within a matter of months. But France remained and increased her military forces. In July, 1863, French troops took possession of the Mexican capital. Thirty-five "leading Mexicans" chose a convention to determine the future Mexican government. The recommendation was that a hereditary Catholic monarch occupy the throne of a new Mexican empire. Personally picked by Louis Napoleon, this puppet emperor was the Archduke Maximilian of Austria. France next sought American recognition of the new government; the United States not only refused, but became exceedingly alarmed over the prospects of a Mexican–Confederate alliance.

Still, the nation was forced to wait until the end of the Civil War before taking definite action. Then, in 1865, with a million troops in the army's ranks, the United States issued an ultimatum—one of the very few the nation could have enforced in the nineteenth century. In the face of such potential force, France agreed to withdraw and did so late in 1867. Maximillian remained, mistakenly believing that the Mexican people loved him. As the last French troops departed, the Mexican people very impolitely removed Maximilian.

The Diplomacy of Imperialism

The nation emerged from the Civil War confident in its military strength, and the result was a series of minor territorial extensions, which have been adequately covered in Chapter Two. Until the 1890's, Americans took little interest in foreign affairs: they were primarily concerned with the rise of big business and with internal improvements. However, with internal growth there arose an increasing need for new foreign markets. Big business expected the government to aid in developing foreign trade, and diplomacy was geared toward this end. The State Department concentrated on the acquisition of commercial treaties.

It was with this in mind that Secretary of State James Blaine succeeded in forming the Pan-American Union in 1889. Such an organization had been unsuccessfully proposed by Simon Bolivar, the South American independence leader, as early as 1815. But through Blaine's efforts, the Union was formed as a loose regional organization concerned with economic cooperation and the peaceful settlement of disputes among hemispheric nations.

This not only satisfied big-business interests, but it fit in very well with the basic American diplomatic aim of the nineteenth century—to keep Europe out of the New World. Although the Pan-American Union did not perfectly serve this purpose, it was a step in that direction.

Interest in China

The diplomacy involved in the acquisition of the Hawaiian Islands, the territories arising out of the Spanish-American War, the Panama Canal Zone, etc., has been considered in Chapter Two. But there were related diplomatic maneuvers which reflected the expansionist mood of the period and the wishes of big business.

It is to be recalled that following the Sino-Japanese War of 1894–1895, the various nations of Europe began carving out spheres of interest in Chinese territory. England and the United States had not taken part in this, but both nations were fearful of losing their trading privileges in China. Both powers favored equal commercial opportunity—an "open door" policy.

Secretary of State John Hay sought assurances from England, Russia, Japan, Italy, and France, that no nation maintaining a sphere of interest in China would interfere with existing treaty rights, that only Chinese tariffs would be levied and collected by the Chinese themselves, and that no power would discriminate commercially within its sphere of interest. All nations except Russia agreed with various reservations. But Hay, on March 20, 1900, resorted to an elaborate ruse. He publicly announced that all nations had completely agreed with his request. And since each nation was unaware of what all other nations had agreed to, it remained silent. The main significance of this episode, however, was to indicate the frustrations and inadequacy of secret diplomacy.

The Latin American Problem

Involved in imperialism herself as a result of activities at the turn of the century, the United States became suspicious of other imperialistic powers, especially Germany. Most Latin American nations were heavily indebted to Europe and were defaulting. Venezuela was the worse offender, frankly refusing to pay her debts. The Monroe Doctrine was by now a venerable tradition but had never needed enforcement by arms. Europe was hesitant to force payment in violation of the Doctrine, in view of America's new position as an international power; but in 1902, Germany, England, and Italy decided to blockade Venezuela. That nation immediately agreed to arbitrate, so there was no crisis. But the United States was concerned over what course it would have taken had the blockade been initiated.

A firm American position was stated in 1904, when Germany was preparing to intervene in the Dominican Republic over another unpaid debt. Roosevelt issued the Roosevelt Corollary to the Monroe Doctrine. It stated that the United States was the police force of the western hemisphere, and if any European country had difficulties with a Latin American nation, it should deal through the United States. This pronouncement was followed by a 1905 treaty with the Dominican Republic which gave the United States permission to take over Dominican customs collections and financial management. The Corollary was a success for two reasons: Latin America was too weak to resist, and European nations were so balanced in military power that they could not afford to antagonize the United States without upsetting the equilibrium. There was therefore practically no reaction to the Corollary. Europe was preoccupied with the situation that would lead to World War I. Latin America remained quiet but eventually denounced the United States bitterly for her assumption of duties and powers.

Alaska and Japan

To the far north there was a boundary dispute over Alaska between Canada and the United States. In 1903 it was decided that three American and three British commonwealth jurists would jointly settle the dispute. Roosevelt appointed Secretary of War Elihu Root as a jurist, and caused a rumor to spread that if the United States did not receive what she desired, the entire area would be occupied militarily. Preoccupied with Germany, England wanted the United States as a future ally. So she "sold out" Canada, and gave the United States what was desired. Canadians were somewhat displeased.

The United States was losing popularity with the governments of many nations, but she did her best job in alienating Japan. By early 1905 Japan appeared victorious in the Russo-Japanese War, but she was near exhaustion. And Russia, faced with an anti-czarist revolution, wanted peace. Japan asked Roosevelt to arbitrate, and the result was the Portsmouth Conference of 1905. Japan demanded a large indemnity plus the Russian island of Sakhalin. Roosevelt convinced the Japanese to withdraw the indemnity claim and settle for the southern half of Sakhalin. Even though Japan emerged as the top power in the Far East, she was in poor financial condition. The tax-ridden people blamed the United States for their indemnity loss. A depression hit and Japanese workers sought employment on the West Coast of the United States. This was when the San Francisco School Board segregation issue took place. Somehow or other, Roosevelt got the feeling that his handling of the incident might be construed as a sign of fear of Japan by the United States.

To indicate otherwise, he sent the American fleet (then the second largest in the world) on a worldwide cruise, especially destined for Japan, to remind that nation that her fleet ranked fifth. The fleet was most cordially received in Japan. Afterwards, the two nations signed the Root-Takahira Agreement of 1908. They agreed to maintain the status quo in the Pacific, to respect each other's Pacific holdings, to uphold the open door in China, and to support the territorial independence of China. The agreement was indicative of a new era. It was between two new major powers, who were destined to come into increasing conflict in the Far

East. Disagreement on these basic points led directly to Pearl Harbor.

The Big Stick and Dollar Diplomacy

Roosevelt's diplomatic program was known as "Big Stick" diplomacy from his admonition that the United States should speak softly and carry a big stick in international affairs. Roosevelt's policy was crucial in creating the Panama Canal, but nowhere was it better exemplified than in 1904 when a supposed American citizen, Ion Perdicaris, was captured in Morocco and held for ransom by a chieftain named Raisuli. The United States demanded his release, ignoring strong evidence that he was not an American. Roosevelt sent the fleet to Morocco to force his release. He turned out to be a Greek citizen.

Scarcely had this incident passed when international tension flared up between France and Germany over spheres of interest in Morocco. Roosevelt called a conference of the powers at Algeciras in 1906, and used his influence to effect an agreement which was strongly favorable to France and England, and most anti-Germans.

International policy under Roosevelt's successor, William Howard Taft, was labeled "Dollar Diplomacy." It was formulated by Secretary of State Philander C. Knox, once a corporation lawyer, and aimed at the active aid of American industry in securing business opportunities abroad. This support extended to the point of armed intervention and monetary advances by the government to protect private investments. In Latin America, a number of military expeditions installed or protected governments favorable to American business interests.

A case in point was Nicaragua in 1909. A revolution broke out against dictator Jose Zelaya, and two pro-revolutionary Americans were executed. The United States solved the problem by taking over and stabilizing Nicaraguan finances, controlling customs, and threatening to use American troops if future revolutions occurred. Nicaragua had no choice in the matter; the United States forcibly carried out her wishes.

In 1911 there was another extension of the Monroe Doctrine—the Lodge Corollary. The State Department heard that a Japanese company was negotiating for a bay area in Baja California. Senator Henry Cabot Lodge introduced a resolution in the Senate expressing strong disapproval of the transfer of strategic areas in the western hemisphere to non-hemispheric companies, especially since they might be acting as agents of a foreign power. The Senate approved the resolution by a vote of 51–4. It was not a law or treaty, but simply a statement of American policy. The Japanese company did not obtain its land.

Mexico

Dollar Diplomacy was disapproved of but followed by Taft's successor, Woodrow Wilson. Despite his criticism of Taft's diplomacy, Wilson was responsible for more American armed interventions in Latin America than his predecessor. The most notable example occurred over difficulties with Mexico. In 1911 the Mexican dictator, Porfirio Diaz, was overthrown and exiled by Francisco Madero. The revolution was against corruption and the sale of Mexican natural resources to foreign powers, especially the United States. In 1912 Taft indicated American approval of Madero by selling arms to his forces only. But in February, 1913, a new revolution headed by Victoriano Huerta deposed Madero, who was personally murdered by Huerta a few days later. When Wilson took office he refused to recognize Huerta's government; he declared it illegal and demanded Huerta's resignation. Another revolution was in the making, headed by Carranza and Francisco "Pancho" Villa. Wilson supported these revolutionaries by selling them arms, while at the same time refusing arms sales to Huerta.

Latin America was extremely critical of the American policy of interfering in the domestic affairs of Mexico. The fact that the United States was against Huerta was his greatest asset. A vengeful stalemate lasted until April, 1914, when an American naval vessel landed at Tampico to resupply. Mexican authorities arrested the crew for allegedly violating martial law. The crew was almost immediately released with murmurings of regret, but Admiral Mayo issued an ultimatum to Mexico demanding a formal apology and a twenty-one–gun salute to the American flag. Mexico agreed to the apology but not to the salute. Two weeks later Wilson asked Congress for authority to send American troops into Mexico to restore order; the request was granted.

The very day Congress granted the request a German munitions ship was steaming toward Vera Cruz with munitions for Huerta. Wilson authorized the Navy to stop it. The result was the bombardment and invasion of Vera Cruz on April 21, 1914. American public opinion favored a second Mexican war. At this point the ABC powers (Argentina, Brazil, and Chile) proposed their services as mediators. Wilson accepted, and in May a conference was held at Niagara Falls, Canada. But Carranza, who had just overthrown Huerta, refused any plan of reconciliation. Nonetheless, a cooling-off period had been provided and war was averted.

But American problems with Mexico were not solved. In fact they grew worse as Carranza turned out to be more anti-American than Huerta had been. Quite naturally, another revolution was in the making. It was led by Francisco Villa. This colorful bandito realized that his only chances rested upon American intervention. On January 11 ,1916, at Santo Isabel, Villa halted a Mexican train and shot sixteen American passengers. On March 9, he raided Columbus, New Mexico, and killed nineteen more Americans. The United States demanded that Carranza maintain order in his country. Finally, American forces were allowed to enter northern Mexico to seek out Villa; this was the Pershing Expedition of 1916, a complete fiasco. In February, 1917, the United States had more important matters in mind; World War I was approaching. So the unsuccessful troops were withdrawn, and Latin America took a back seat until after the war.

There were many other interventions. American interests in protecting the Canal Zone brought more meddling in Nicaragua in 1913, armed intervention in Haiti in 1915, and in the Dominican Republic in 1914 and 1916. This interest also prompted the United States to purchase the Danish West Indies from Denmark in 1916.

Wilson and World War I

Neutrality

When World War I commenced in Europe, Woodrow Wilson immediately declared American neutrality and offered to mediate. Two weeks later, he urged the American people as individuals to remain neutral. But conflicting pressures were operating to sway American public opinion in three different directions: strict neutrality, intervention on the side of the Western Powers (England and allies), and intervention on the side of the Central Powers (Germany and allies). The United States possessed immigrant populations which tended to be sympathetic to their respective homelands, and most foreign-language presses purposely encouraged such patriotic feelings.

Both sides engaged in a tremendous propaganda campaign to draw the United States into the war. The Western Powers did the best job, both in quality and quantity. They appealed to a common tradition—England had founded America, and France had helped win American independence. The image developed for Italians was that they were easy going people who were victimized by aggressors. Playing on American sympathies for the underdog, a highly pro-Belgian feeling was created. English propaganda succeeded in establishing the stereotyped German as a cold military machine, complete with polished boots, monocle, and mustache; he was the brutal Prussian Hun. The presence of czarist Russia on England's side was not a great liability to it because Americans were not greatly interested in that nation.

A question of neutral rights existed almost from the beginning, pertaining to contraband of war. England claimed that foodstuffs were contraband and placed a "food blockade" around Germany. The latter responded by ordering a blockade around England. The United States protested and Wilson sent Colonel House to Europe to attempt to influence changes in policy.

In March, 1915, the English vessel *Fabala* was torpedoed and sunk by a German submarine, with the loss of an American life. In May came the sinking of the *Luisitania* with the loss of 1,200 lives, including 128 Americans. In August the British *Arabic* was torpedoed with the loss of two American lives. All along Wilson had been protesting strongly against unrestricted submarine attacks and the failure to provide for civilian safety. The resultant *Arabic* Pledge was a promise by Germany not to sink any more passenger ships without warning and without providing for passenger safety. But the Pledge was nothing more than a temporary truce.

Early in 1916 House was back in Europe. He obtained promises from England and France that they would attend a peace conference, with the understanding that if Germany refused, the United States would enter the war on the Western side. Wilson made no such promise, but House managed to deceive his listeners. He promised intervention, and when this was taken to mean military intervention, he made no attempt at clarification. He later claimed he was talking about diplomatic intervention.

While the peace attempt was progressing, Wilson and Secretary of State Lansing came close to a diplomatic break with England. That nation was beginning to arm her merchant and passenger vessels, and Wilson decided that this made them warships and they should be treated as such. Germany mistakenly took this to mean that in the eyes of the United States, they could be attacked. She announced that effective February 29, 1916, she would attack any armed ship. For obvious reasons England refused to disarm these ships and thus place them entirely at the mercy of German submarines.

In his attempt to play the role of the mediator, Wilson had established considerable friction between his country and England, and this had encouraged Germany to take a stronger position on submarine warfare. So he announced that American policy would not change, at the very time that Germany announced that her new policy would stand. This set the stage for an increase in the number of incidents on the high seas.

In March, 1916, a German submarine sank the unarmed French passenger liner *Sussex*. Wilson issued an ultimatum to Germany which in essence promised a diplomatic break if any similar incidents occurred. Not desiring war with the United States at the time, Germany issued the *Sussex* Pledge (May, 1916), promising to follow customary laws before sinking belligerent ships. But Germany warned that if the United States did not apply identical standards to other warring nations, she would repudiate her pledge.

The European war was beginning to intensify. England extended her blacklists of American companies dealing with Germany, and intimidated American shippers by withholding coal in her numerous worldwide ports. American hostility toward England was at its peak at the end of 1916. But Germany was also intensifying her submarine attacks, barely within the limits of the *Sussex* Pledge. Wilson became convinced that the only way to keep the nation out of war was to end the war, but the belligerents were not willing to negotiate.

The Transition to War

In January, 1917, Wilson made his "Peace without Victory" speech to the Senate. The aftermath of the war, he said, should bring equality for all nations, the right of all peoples to rule themselves, disarmament, freedom of the seas, and guarantees against future wars—a crude outline of the future Fourteen Points. Germany responded by announcing that effective February 1, 1917, all ships in the war zone, neutral or belligerent, would be sunk by submarines. One American ship per week would be allowed to pass, provided it was painted with red and white stripes. Wilson severed diplomatic relations on February 2.

Then came the Zimmerman note on February 25, 1917. A dispatch from German Foreign Minister Zimmerman to the German ambassador to Mexico instructed the latter to seek an alliance with Mexico if the United States went to war with Germany. If Mexico agreed, then Germany would aid Mexico in recapturing Texas and the territories lost during the Mexican War. The note also instructed the ambassador to sound out Mexico on a possible Japanese alliance, hoping to stir up the muddy waters of American-Japanese relations. England had intercepted the note and held it until Germany renewed unrestricted submarine warfare. Then she handed it over to the United States. The American nation was shocked; here

was unquestionable proof of hostile German intentions toward the nation.

Wilson proceeded on March 9 to arm American merchant ships, and announced that he would call Congress into Special Session on April 16. At this time the Russian Revolution was beginning. The Russian Czar had been overthrown and democracy became a possibility. This gave more validity to the notion that the side of the Western Powers was that of justice and virtue. The Special Session was pushed up to April 2, and on April 7, the United States went to war with Germany.

There were a number of economic factors which influenced American pro-war opinion, besides the destruction of lives and property by German submarines. The United States had become a wealthy nation. It had surplus goods and capital and interests around the world. It was the only nation in the world possessed of sufficient capital to purchase European war bonds, the value of which depended on the fate of the countries issuing them. American financiers invested in the bonds of all warring nations, but mainly in English bonds. There were two major reasons for this: the long-standing economic ties between England and America, and sheer geography—England was closest.

Prior to the outbreak of war there was a worldwide trade rivalry between England, Germany, and the United States. England and Germany were forced to absorb their surplus in the war effort, leaving the entire world market to the United States. And ultimately, America began selling civilian goods to her former competitors. The result was unbridled prosperity which most Americans hoped would continue. But as the war progressed both Central and Western powers began to lose the ability to pay cash for their goods. This created a dilemma for American business and government. The nation could either stop selling or start allowing credit. To stop selling would throw a damper on prosperity, and neither the government nor business wanted this. But to sell on credit meant the possibility of more incidents on the high seas and a deepening involvement in the fate of the European conflict. The most sound idea from a strictly economic viewpoint was for the United States to enter the war on the side of her biggest customer: England.

American shippers were more opposed to the English blockade than the German one, but they constituted a small portion of the population. The average American could only see German submarines blowing harmless vessels out of the water and killing American citizens. The British blockade was quite expensive monetarily, but unlike the German it did not take any American lives. This was a very crucial difference.

Wilson himself was a factor. The President sincerely wished to avoid war, but the introduction of his moral judgment into the causes and conduct of the war led him personally to desire a Western victory. The President developed a double standard of neutrality, far more tolerant of British than of German violations. In the process he indirectly encouraged both sides to assume more extreme positions: England because she knew she could get away with it, and Germany because she had to keep up with England.

The Fourteen Points

The avowed American war objective was to make the world safe for democracy. This generality was progressively broadened by George Creel, who urged the President to make a more definite statement. The result was the Fourteen Points of January, 1918. The Fourteen Points contain two major categories of provisions, dealing with geographical settlements and the easement of world conditions. Geographical settlements include Point 6 calling for the German evacuation of Russia, Point 7 calling for the restoration of Belgium, Point 8 calling for the restoration of France, Point 9 calling for a readjustment of Italian boundaries, Point 11 seeking the stabilization of the Balkans, Point 12 calling for the independence of Poland, and part of Point 13 calling for the reestablishment of Turkey. The easement of world conditions was touched upon by Point 1 calling for an end to secret diplomacy, Point 2 calling for freedom of the seas, Point 3 calling for free trade, Point 4 seeking armament reductions, Point 5 seeking an adjustment and lessening of colonial claims, Point 10 calling for self-determination for subject peoples, part of Point 13 calling for the internationalizing of the Dardenelles, and Point 14 calling for a League of Nations.

In February, 1918, Wilson issued his Four Principles, the basic idea of which was the promotion of self-determination for subject national groups. In July came his Four Ends, calling for government to be based on a reign of law at the consent of the governed, and sustained by the collective opinion of mankind. And in September, 1918, he listed his Five Particulars, which demanded an end to all discrimination and secret treaties. These statements were all elaborations on the Fourteen Points.

Germany, concerned about the consequences of defeat, was quite favorably impressed with Wilson's statements. The allies voiced support for the basic principles behind them, largely because the United States controlled the purse strings. Unofficially, they were opposed; Europe would solve Europe's problems after the war without America. American opinion generally was quite enthusiastic, but for partisan reasons, some Americans were against the League of Nations idea. Henry Cabot Lodge and Theodore Roosevelt, both of whom had supported the League in 1915, turned against it in an attempt to discredit the President.

Historical Pictures Service, Chicago

The "Big Four" at Versailles: George, Orlando,
Clemeanceau, and Wilson

The Versailles Conference

In November, 1918, Wilson announced that he would personally head the American peace conference delegation. It was a bold, controversial move; no previous president had left the country while in office. Many argued that he should stay at home and tend to the many pressing domestic problems that came with demobilization, and allow his diplomatic corps to handle diplomacy. Wilson took four special advisors and a large staff. His selections alienated many people. Secretary of State Lansing was a logical choice, but Wilson also took a military advisor named General Bliss, a competent career diplomat named Henry White, and Colonel House, his personal friend and advisor, who was not a public official. Not one Republican was included. And in the recent off-year congressional elections, the Republicans had gained control of both houses of Congress.

Any treaty would have to be referred to the Senate Foreign Relations Committee, headed by Lodge, who was against the Fourteen Points; the Senate would next have to ratify by a two-thirds vote. Had Wilson taken Lodge and several other ranking Republicans, he would have been in better position. Instead, he alienated a majority of the Senate, including the Democrats, since no senator was included, by his selections.

In December, 1918, Wilson went to Europe; he was treated by the French as their deliverer, but at Versailles he soon met with problems. The Allies were primarily concerned with punishing Germany, and a network of secret treaties had carved up German possessions among them. Most of Europe was in a hurry to arrange a peace, since civil conflict threatened most nations. The only Wilsonian concept which was universally accepted was the League of Nations.

Leadership at the conference was provided by Wilson, Lloyd George of England, Clemenceau of France, and Orlando of Italy, but the men rarely agreed. During the course of the negotiations Wilson made a trip home to report to congressional leaders on conference progress. He requested that they not discuss the report publicly, but Senator Borah blasted Wilson and his League. A Republican open letter, circulated and signed by thirty-nine Republican senators, condemned American participation in the League. Rather than negotiate, as the Republicans were demanding, Wilson retorted in a tactless manner and succeeded only in alienating more people.

The Ratification Fight

In June, 1919, the treaty was completed. It was a diplomatic victory for the United States because it officially recognized the Monroe Doctrine. But the treaty as drafted met with tremendous opposition in the United States. German-Americans protested against a victor's peace being imposed on their native land. Italian-Americans claimed that Italy had not received enough territory. The Irish claimed that England would dominate the League. Other opposition came from a growing number of isolationists who claimed that the nation was departing from a hallowed tradition. Republicans opposed the treaty because they had been ignored. And practically the entire Senate was affronted by the manner in which negotiations had been conducted. Also, the fact Wilson had salvaged only Point 14 of his Fourteen Points caused a number of sympathetic Americans to lose interest in the campaign for ratification.

Senator Lodge dictated the opposition strategy: to delay any action while organizing dissent, and then to propose numerous unacceptable amendments. After elaborate, time-consuming public hearings, Lodge's committee reported favorably for treaty ratification—with forty-

The Granger Collection

"The Accuser"—Contemporary Cartoon
Criticizing the Senate's Refusal to
Ratify the Treaty of Versailles

five amendments. Wilson undertook a nationwide speaking tour in behalf of his treaty—without amendments—but the strain caught up with him.

He collapsed, suffered a stroke, and partially lost his mental powers, but he still refused to compromise. Twice he managed to prevent amended versions of the treaty from being ratified. The treaty finally died in committee in March, 1920. The Knox Resolution was passed in May, 1920, repealing the war declaration, but Wilson vetoed it. The same resolution was passed under President Harding in July, 1921. Individual treaties were then negotiated, but the United States did not join the League of Nations, nor did she entangle herself in any way with Europe.

Diplomacy in the Inter-War Period

The nation did not desire participation in an international organization in 1919, though it might have in 1918. Yet staunch isolationism was dead in America. The nation did recognize some obligation to help solve world problems—if only out of self-interest—but not to the point of becoming entangled in military operations. This was the basis of American foreign policy throughout the Twenties.

Disarmament

National opinion, recoiling against the war, now strongly favored disarmament as a means of discouraging further worldwide conflict and reducing federal expenditures as well. And the government responded to this political force. In 1921 a Washington Armament Conference was called by the United States for the purpose of arranging naval disarmament and promoting peaceful relations in the Pacific. A number of treaties were negotiated at the conference.

The Five-Power Treaty set up a ratio of capital warships for the United States, England, Japan, France, and Italy, at a 5:5:3:1.75:1.75 ratio respectively. It provided for a ten-year naval holiday, during which no new battleships or aircraft carriers would be built, and limited the size of replacements. Also, England, Japan, and the United States agreed to maintain the status quo in the Pacific. A Four-Power Pact between these nations and France guaranteed each other's territorial possessions in the Pacific and promised the arbitration of all differences. A Nine-Power Treaty guaranteed the territorial integrity of China.

The treaties looked promising, but they contained serious flaws. The naval-armaments terminology was vague, and no enforcement provisions were established. There was a lack of good faith among the signers, especially Japan, who was displeased with her limits. Thus, when an attempt was made at Geneva, in 1927, to extend the provisions of the Five-Power Treaty to cover lesser vessels, the conference was a flop.

In 1928 the Kellogg–Briand Peace Pact was signed. Fifteen nations agreed to renounce war as a means of settling international disputes. But this did not cover wars of self-defense (all wars have been justified by self-defense). Besides, England excluded her colonial holdings, and the United States upheld the Monroe Doctrine as an overriding commitment. And again there were no provisions for enforcement or even censure.

Debts and Reparations

A major diplomatic issue during the Twenties concerned war debts and reparations. War debts were owed to the United States for wartime loans and post-war rehabilitation loans to other nations. They amounted to $7 billion for wartime loans, and $3–4 billion for reconstruction loans. "Reparations" referred to those indemnities levied on Germany by the victors, for having caused the war. The United States was owed no reparations.

The Allies objected to payment of their war debts. They argued that the war was a common effort; Europe lost lives and suffered material damage, so the United States should justly accept the loss of money. This argument was not credited. Europe then argued that since most of the money had been spent for American goods, a 90 per cent reduction in the debt was in order. Although this argument carried some weight, the United States did not accept it. Allies next fell back on their most practical argument: they did not have the money. France attempted to tie the war-debts issue with reparations. As Germany paid France, France would pay the United States—so why should the United States not collect directly from Germany? But the United States wanted no part of the reparations issue.

In 1924 the Dawes Plan provided that Germany would pay reparations of $250 million in 1925. The victorious powers would lend her $200 million in gold to revitalize her currency and industry. As the German economy improved, her payments were expected to go up, but it failed to improve; the Germans realized that they would, in effect, simply be working for the Allies. So in 1928 the Young Plan was devised. Germany would pay $153 million per year for fifty-nine years, plus bonuses in good years. The Allies would evacuate the Rhineland in 1930. The plan might have worked, but the world Depression hit in 1929 and all payments ceased. In 1932 a one-year moratorium was declared, and in 1933 the entire reparations affair was given up as a lost cause.

Wartime loans had been made informally, with the understanding that arrangements for repayment would be settled after the war and that the interest rate would be 5 per cent. In 1923 England agreed to pay $4.3 billion over a sixty-two year period at 3.3 per cent interest. The American public was pleased because England officially recognized her debt. Other debtors remained stubborn, and the United States finally placed an embargo on private loans to defaulting nations. The device was effective. In late 1925 Italy agreed to pay $1.6 billion at the extremely low interest rate of .4 per cent. In the spring of 1926 France recognized a $3.4-billion debt with a 1.6 per cent interest rate. Not one European nation, however, except Finland, paid off its full debt.

Latin American Affairs

The greatest diplomatic concern of the nation in the Twenties was Latin America. Relations with Mexico at the end of the war were fairly good. But in 1917 a new Mexican constitution contained a clause wherein Mexico claimed ownership of all subsoil resources. A number of American companies held leases on these resources, but they were generally recognized until President Alvaro Obregon took over in 1920. American refusal to recognize his regime

brought acceptance of the leases in 1923, but a new leader, Calles, restricted them in 1925. Relations deteriorated nearly to the point of war by 1926.

President Coolidge sent Dwight Morrow as ambassador to Mexico. Morrow knew absolutely nothing about Mexico, but he quickly learned the customs, traditions, and language of that nation; he spent much of his time talking to Mexican peasants in the streets. Also, Charles Lindberg (sponsored by the State Department) flew to Mexico City following his famous trans-Atlantic flight, fell in love with Morrow's daughter, and eventually married her. Especially given Lindberg's international popularity, this romance helped to soften the Mexicans' feelings toward the United States, and relations improved. The diplomatic disputes were negotiated and the United States refused to intervene in the 1929 revolution which established the regime of Pedro Gil.

American intervention in Latin America, however, had not completely subsided. For instance, the 1924 Nicaraguan elections were conducted under the auspices of American troops. When a new revolution broke out, the troops returned in 1926. But the United States was beginning to settle down in Latin America. She paid Colombia for the 1903 Panama intervention. American troops were evacuated from the Dominican Republic, and Cuba was given more self-rule. The nation successfully negotiated a settlement of the Tacna–Arica boundary dispute between Chile and Peru. She signed the Gondra Treaty of 1923, a hemispheric pledge for the peaceful settlement of disputes. A Pan-American Conference in 1929 reaffirmed the Gondra treaty and set up an arbitration board.

President-elect Herbert Hoover toured Latin America and set the stage for the future "Good Neighbor" policy. The Clark Memorandum of 1930 was indicative of the new policy. It repudiated the

Roosevelt Corollary and interpreted the Monroe Doctrine as a defensive measure for the protection of the western hemisphere.

The Depression Years

With the coming of the Depression, the American people lost all interest in foreign affairs. Rising European demagogues were not taken seriously. And the United States had developed the attitude that World War I had been fought in vain, and was further disillusioned over the debt issue. Neo-isolationism was the order of the day, but as usual the rest of the hemisphere was included in the sphere of involvement. Roosevelt's First Inaugural in 1933 mentioned the Good Neighbor policy.

At the Montevideo Conference of 1933 the Good Neighbor first came into action. War was outlawed as a means of settling disputes in the hemisphere. A mutual promise was made not to meddle in the internal affairs of other hemispheric nations. The groundwork for hemispheric reciprocal trade was established. The nation abrogated the Platt Amendment protectorate over Cuba in 1934, except for the lease on Guantanamo Bay, and renounced control over Panama. Marines were permanently withdrawn from Nicaragua and Haiti.

The Philippine issue was settled by the Tydings–McDuffie Act of 1934. The Philippines would gain their independence after a ten-year probationary period. During this period the United States controlled Filipino foreign affairs and could call on the Filipino army for defense. Arrangements about tariff and immigration matters were to be settled during the waiting period. Independence was delayed by World War II but it finally became a reality on July 4, 1946.

A major diplomatic issue concerned recognition of the Soviet Union. From 1917 to 1933 the Communist regime had not been officially recognized. But by 1933 American attitudes had altered significantly. The nation was looking for markets anywhere, and was not so confident of the perfection of capitalism any longer. The nation was still unhappy about the methods by which the Soviet government had attained and kept power, but was forced to admit that a stable government did exist. So the United States granted recognition in return for Russia's promise to refrain from propaganda and espionage in America, to negotiate the debt issue, and to guarantee freedom of conscience and fair trials to Americans in Russia. The United States also obtained some limited Soviet markets.

The Road to World War II

Isolationist Strategy

When Roosevelt took office no American desired war. For the next five years the nation attempted to avoid the mistakes which had led her into World War I. It was widely but erroneously held that business interests alone had brought about American intervention. So in 1935, with the invasion of Ethiopia by Italy under the Fascist Mussolini, a Neutrality Act was passed. The act made it illegal for Americans to sell or ship munitions to belligerents whenever the president recognized a state of war. The president was also authorized to forbid American travel on belligerent ships, and with this, the nation gave up her traditional championing of freedom of the seas. The act (which did not apply to Latin America) was renewed with additions in 1936. It forbade granting loans to belligerents once the president recognized a state of war. In early 1937, because of the civil war in Spain, this prohibition was also applied to revolutions. These measures were all temporary, but Congress was preparing permanent legislation of this type.

A fairly complete Third Neutrality Act was passed in 1937. It became a federal violation for an American to travel on a belligerent ship (previously he had simply traveled at his own risk). American ships were forbidden to carry war goods or to be armed. The president was authorized to forbid the use of American ports to belligerents. And civilian commodities could be sold to belligerents only on a cash-and-carry basis. This was the high point of American isolationism, but some Americans were beginning to disagree with it, pointing out that no distinction was made between aggressor and victim.

Hostilities Increase

But the bulk of Americans remained indifferent, as the *Panay* incident of 1937 indicated. Japanese airplanes strafed an American gunboat and three oil tankers off the Chinese mainland, then strafed the survivors in the water. She apologized for this "mistake," although the craft were clearly marked and visibility was perfect. Her apology, plus a promise to pay an indemnity, satisfied most Americans.

Conditions had worsened in the Far East throughout the Thirties. In 1934 the Vinson bill authorized the buildup of the Navy to treaty limits, but funds were not made available until 1938. As the Japanese expansion continued, a number of different responses were suggested in the United States—ranging from strict neutrality to unofficial aid for China. Roosevelt's Quarantine Speech of 1937, which suggested embargoes against all aggressors, was intended as a test of public opinion on how far he could push against Japan. The people evidently did not want to push. The ambassador to Japan, Grew, as well as most ranking government officials, clearly saw the Japanese menace, but with no backing from the people could do nothing.

Meanwhile the Good Neighbor policy was bearing dividends in Latin America. A 1936 Buenos Aires Conference made the Monroe Doctrine multi-lateral and espoused hemispheric neutrality. The Pan-American Conference at Lima in 1938 called for nonintervention, announced continental solidarity, outlawed war as a means of settling disputes, upheld peaceful relations between nations, and pledged mutual consultation if any American nation was attacked. The hemisphere was learning the advantages of cooperation.

Although he had broken the Versailles Treaty in 1935 by introducing compulsory military service, and again in 1936 by sending troops into the demilitarized Rhineland, most Americans were not greatly worried about Hitler. Even when he annexed the German-speaking areas of Austria and Czechoslovakia in 1938, it could wishfully be hoped that Hitler was sincere in claiming that he sought only to unite all Germans in one nation. It was with this hope in mind that France and England accepted Hitler's protestations at the Munich conference in September, 1938. But in 1939 Hitler violated his Munich pledge by taking the rest of Czechoslovakia, while Mussolini invaded Albania. Roosevelt attempted mediation, but both dictators refused his request that they foreswear further aggression and demobilize their armies. Roosevelt had anticipated this response and used it to sway public opinion to favor an arms buildup. He also began to move Congress to relax the terms of the Third Neutrality Act of 1937.

War in Europe

In August, 1939, Hitler made demands on Poland and signed a non-aggression pact with Russia. Poland was invaded on September 1, and two days later, England and France declared war on Germany. Soviet troops moved into Finland. Although the United States was strongly pro-Finn and the nation still desired official neutrality, public opinion clearly favored the English, French, and Russians. This was a major difference from World War I when public opinion had been divided between the contenders.

A Fourth Neutrality Act was passed in November, 1939. It authorized the president to sell munitions on a cash-and-carry basis (terms only England could accept) and to set up "danger zones" from which he could exclude American ships. This enabled Roosevelt to provide some aid to the Western Powers. Then came the Declaration of Panama in 1939. A 300-mile area around the western hemisphere was closed to the military vessels of all belligerents. The Declaration forbade the use of western-hemispheric territory by belligerents, and authorized the search and internment of violators. The measure was frequently violated since American republics did not enforce it rigidly.

In December, 1939, the warring European powers proclaimed blockades. The United States protested, but both sides knew who America favored. In 1940 Hitler smashed western Europe and France fell in six weeks. Americans became concerned. Congress announced that no transfer of New World territories would be permitted, and the Havana Conference of 1940 provided for hemispheric administration of the territories of conquered European nations for the duration.

The fall of France changed American neutrality to a rush for military preparedness and direct aid for the democracies of western Europe. In August, 1940, the Permanent Committee of Joint Defense between Canada and the United States was established. Since Canada was at war with Germany, this ended official American neutrality. The nation began to build up her defenses. English ships were repaired in American shipyards, and French pilots were trained on American soil. Congress authorized Selective Service and voted $18 billion for defense.

Now Roosevelt's major problem was how to grant more aid to the Allies, and his solution was the "Destroyer Deal" program. The United States "loaned" fifty destroyers to England in exchange for ninety-nine-year rent-free leases on eight Atlantic coast naval bases. (The leasing of these bases provided further aid to England, since it released English ships from protecting them.) Next came the Lend-Lease policy, according to which equipment was loaned to countries whose security was deemed essential to American security. The "borrowers" were required to pick up their goods and return them or their equivalent after the war. Roosevelt then asked Congress for $7 billion to re-tool American industry and to pay for Lend-Lease, and he obtained his request.

Canada and the United States began mobilization, and traded in war material. In March, 1941, the United States seized German and Italian ships in America. The exiled Danish government approved the American occupation of Greenland. When Germany began to attack American shipping, German assets in the United States were frozen, all German consulates were closed, and a blacklist of firms doing business with Germany was published. Germany then repudiated Russia and formed an alliance with Japan. Russia became the recipient of $1 billion in Lend-Lease, and the United States occupied Iceland.

In August, 1941, England and the United States signed the Atlantic Charter which showed the strong influence of Wilson's Fourteen Points. No Allied government was to seek new territories. The right of self-government and equal rights for all nations were upheld. Freedom from fear and want was proclaimed as a major goal along with improved economic relations among all nations. Freedom of the seas, disarmament, and world peace were all championed. The Atlantic Charter provided the basis for the future United Nations.

American warships began to escort Lend-Lease ships for part of their journey across the Atlantic, and following the Greer incident, when American and German ships exchanged fire, Roosevelt issued his "shoot first" order to protect American shipping (September 4, 1941). In October he asked Congress to repeal neutrality legislation, pointing to increasing naval incidents, German infiltration of South America, and the recent sinking of an American ship with the loss of 100 lives. Congress authorized the arming of American merchant ships, and allowed American ships to enter combat zones and belligerent ports. There was no longer any pretence of American neutrality. But war was to arise from events in the Far East.

Pearl Harbor

In 1938 the United States had placed a moral embargo on the shipment of sup-plies to Japan because of Japanese aggression in the Far East. The commercial treaty between the two nations was terminated January, 1940, but continued on a day-by-day basis. After France fell in 1940 Japan became interested in Indo-China. Moving into French Indo-China, she signed a pact with Germany and Italy in September, 1940, calling for concerted action against any neutral nation entering the war. This could refer only to the United States or Russia, and Germany's attack on Russia left only one possibility. The United States responded by banning more articles from shipment to Japan.

Early in 1941 German leaders tried to convince Japan to concentrate on a southern push and not draw the United States into open war. Konoye, the head of the Japanese government, wanted peace with America and suggested a conference at Hawaii. Roosevelt agreed provided a preliminary accord could be reached on

Historical Pictures Service, Chicago

The Japanese Attack on Pearl Harbor

Historical Pictures Service, Chicago

The Yalta Negotiators: Churchill, Roosevelt, and Stalin

fundamental issues, notably the status of China. Meanwhile, Tojo, head of the militarist faction in Japan, gained control of the government.

Nomura was the Japanese ambassador to the United States, and Tojo feared that he might actually arrange a settlement. Tojo therefore sent Kurusu to "assist" him. Japan demanded American recognition of her rights to the natural resources of the Dutch East Indies, an end to the moral embargo, and a cessation of supply shipments to China. Secretary of State Hull's reply came on November 26, 1941. He called for a non-aggression pact, demanded Japanese withdrawal from China and Indo-China, and recognition of Chinese independence.

The United States broke the Japanese diplomatic code and intercepted Japanese attack plans on Malaya, the Indies, and the Philippines. Hawaii was alerted to emergency possibilities, but no attack was anticipated there. Even though Secretary of

the Navy Knox and Ambassador Grew warned of such a possibility, it was felt that Japan would attack elsewhere.

On December 1, 1941, Japan decided to attack Pearl Harbor and her fleet set sail. The United States was aware of this, but anticipated an attack in Southeast Asia. At the last minute the nation deciphered a message indicating attack possibilities but Pearl Harbor was caught off guard. With the attack on Pearl, American isolationism suddenly halted; so did practically all criticism of Roosevelt's policies. The United States declared war on Japan. The Axis went into play, and Germany and Italy exchanged war declarations with the United States.

The United States as a Belligerent

Relations in Europe

Wartime diplomacy was governed by expediency. Considerable suspicion, distrust, and confusion existed between the United States and two of her allies: Russia and France. Russia was perturbed over the failure of the Allies to open a second western front until 1944, but deeper problems came into the open at the Yalta Conference of February, 1945. At this conference the basis for the post-war conflict between East and West was established.

Yalta produced a document known as the Crimean Charter, which provided for a division of the victors' pie. A new Polish state would be created, but with Russia receiving roughly one-third of the country. At the time the United States was dwelling on the heavy losses she would sustain by invading Japan, and felt that Russian manpower was needed. To obtain Russian aid (Russia was not at war with Japan) Roosevelt agreed that she would get the Kurile Islands north of Japan, along with Port Arthur and the southern half of Sakhalin (both of which she had lost in 1905). She would operate the Manchurian Railroad in conjunction with the Chinese. The U.S.S.R. had planned on fighting Japan as soon as the European war ended, but her silence enabled her to obtain a very favorable arrangement. Yalta set the stage for the Cold War by giving communism strong footholds in China and eastern Europe.

With France the problem concerned recognition of the proper government. Two-thirds of France was occupied by Germany, with the rest of the country in the control of the Vichy government, headed by Petain; Vichy was technically the legal government, but it was a German puppet. At first the United States had no choice but to deal with the Vichy government, but there were other forces at work. Charles DeGaulle headed the fighting French, but he lacked widespread support. The United States bounced from Petain to Darlan to Giraud to DeGaulle, and DeGaulle was not recognized as heading the French Provisional Government

until January 1, 1945. In the meanwhile American relations with France were quite unstable.

Latin America

The Declaration of Havana in 1940 had stated that an attack on one American republic would be regarded as an attack on all. Of the twenty Latin republics, nine declared war on Germany within three days of Pearl Harbor. Before the war ended all Latin nations had declared war on the Axis, although some nations waited until early 1945. At the Rio de Janeiro Conference of January, 1942, the United States came surprisingly close to developing a united front against the Germans and Japanese. With the exception of Chile and Argentina, all Latin nations broke off diplomatic relations with the Axis.

Mexico and Brazil were particularly warm allies. Mexico sent thousands of needed laborers to work in American plants. Brazil allowed air bases to be constructed on her soil from which to raid North Africa, and she was the only Latin American republic to contribute fighting troops to the global war. The United States pumped $6 billion in aid into Latin America. This was criticized but Latin America possessed natural resources which were essential to the war effort.

Argentina provided the only serious problem. Since her cattle and wheat were not needed by the United States, she continued to trade with Europe. Possessed of a fascist tradition, she was sympathetic to the Axis. At the Chapultepec Conference in February, 1945, the Monroe Doctrine was adopted multi-laterally against all aggressors. Argentina was the only hemispheric nation absent from the conference, and this left her out in the cold. And with Germany beginning to fall apart, she decided to join the cause and belatedly declared war on the Axis on March 27, 1945.

The United Nations

The only other war-era diplomatic issue concerned the development of an international organization. The United States was determined to avoid the fiasco which followed World War I. Both houses of Congress passed resolutions by overwhelming majorities in mid-1943, committing themselves to participation in a world organization. An eight-man Senate committee was created in April, 1944, to consult with the president on foreign affairs, thus keeping the Senate informed.

The first step was the United Nations Monetary Conference at Bretton Woods, New Hampshire, in July, 1944. About forty nations attended the conference and created a $9-billion international fund to stabilize world currencies; they committed another $9 billion to aid in post-war reconstruction. Some six weeks later, at Dumbarton Oaks in Washington, representatives from England, Russia, China, and the United States hammered out a rough draft of the future United Nations Charter for consideration at the San Francisco Conference of April, 1945.

Before the conference convened, notable changes occurred. On November 27, 1944, Secretary of State Cordell Hull resigned because of rapidly failing health and was succeeded by the relatively inexperienced Edward Stettinius. On April 12, 1945, Franklin Roosevelt died, elevating Harry Truman to the presidency. For a time there was some speculation over whether the conference would be held, but Truman announced that it would proceed as scheduled.

There was a great deal of friction at the conference over the Yalta promises, the veto power, the status of regional organizations, and the rights of small nations. Eventually, differences were compromised, and on June 25, 1945, the United Nations Charter was unanimously adopted. Fully realizing that the document pledged the United States to permanent international peace-keeping, the Senate ratified the charter by a vote of 89–2, with no reservations or amendments, on August 8, 1945.

While the United Nations negotiations were progressing, Truman went to Berlin to meet with Stalin and Churchill (later Atlee). The result was the two Potsdam Declarations. The first declaration was an unconditional surrender ultimatum to Japan, demanding complete disarmament, loss of all conquests since 1895, and deprivation of the economic resources needed to support a war effort. The second declaration dealt with European peace settlements. Besides the numerous territorial adjustments decided upon, it was agreed to try German leaders as war criminals and to require Germany to pay for the damage she had inflicted. Both declarations provided the basis for future peace treaties.

Contemporary America in World Politics

Post-War Adjustments

In the immediate post-war world the United States had one basic diplomatic aim: to punish Germany and Japan and rebuild them along American lines. The four occupying powers in Germany—the United States, England, France, and Russia—cooperated fully in the denazification and destruction of military potential. The American policy at this point was based on the vindictive Morgenthau Plan. It culminated in the Nuremburg War Trials, which lasted from November, 1945, until October, 1946. These controversial trials involved prosecuting top German officials for "war crimes."

In Japan the position of the United States was simpler in that she exercised complete control. Douglas MacArthur was placed in command of occupation forces. War crime trials were conducted, but on a smaller scale than in Germany. The nation was democratized, and a fairly thorough reform program was carried out, and quite soon Japan was on the road to cordial membership in the international community.

The problem-area was Europe and the culprit was the Soviet Union. Initial American policy called for bending over backwards to please Russia. Peace treaties were signed in February, 1947, with Italy, Hungary, Rumania, and Bulgaria. Italy passed over to the West, and the other countries fell under Soviet control. Russia blocked a peace treaty with Austria because she had not yet "sovietized" that country. In Germany nothing could be done because Russian policy called for maintaining a divided nation until such time as the Soviets won the allegiance of all Germans.

The existence of the atomic bomb immensely complicated disarmament. Until 1949 the United States was sole possessor of the bomb, but instead of using it for international blackmail, the nation sought to devote nuclear power to the peaceful needs of all. With this in mind the Baruch Plan was submitted to the United Nations in mid-1946, calling for an International Atomic Development Authority to exercise complete control over atomic power. Russia torpedoed the proposal.

As time went on, the Far East demanded more attention. The United States had kept the Nationalist Chinese government of Chiang Kai-shek from falling apart during the war. But the government was miserably weak and was under attack by Chinese communists. It was unclear which side was the strongest. The United States realized that the only way to maintain Chiang's government was by full-scale armed intervention, which the nation was unwilling to risk. A half-way measure was decided on; a coalition gov-

ernment would be negotiated, and General George Marshall was sent to effect it in December, 1945. He succeeded in arranging only a temporary truce. Full-scale civil war erupted in 1947 and Chiang's demoralized, undisciplined forces were driven to Formosa by December, 1949; the People's Republic of China became a reality.

Meanwhile, notable achievements were being made on the homefront. At the Rio de Janeiro Conference of 1947, there was drafted a treaty of reciprocal assistance, binding member nations to sever all economic and diplomatic ties with any violator of hemispheric peace, whenever two-thirds of the nations so voted. The treaty established a security zone around the American continents. The Ogdensburg Agreement of 1940 (between the United States and Canada) was reconfirmed in 1947, and provided that Canada would assume the responsibility for securing northern North America. At Bogota in 1948 the Organization of American States charter was adopted, and provided the machinery for enforcing the Rio treaty.

The Cold War and Foreign Aid

Meanwhile, the Truman administration was struggling to effect some understanding with the Soviet Union. Winston Churchill had made his historic "Iron Curtain" speech in May, 1946, but the United States was slow to redefine her policy. Prompted by Russian pressures in the eastern Mediterranean—notably in Iran, Turkey, and Greece, and by a British announcement that she could no longer support the Greek government—in February, 1947, the United States revised her policies. Truman asked Congress for $400 million in military aid for Turkey and Greece, which were threatened by communist-led revolution. His pronouncement that the United States had a duty to help people maintain their freedom was quickly labeled the Truman Doctrine. Over the next six years the United States poured $350 million into Turkey and $310 million into Greece. Both nations were preserved as American allies; had it not been for the Truman Doctrine, they probably would have fallen to Russia.

The nation came to the realization that even western European governments rested on shaky grounds. The former allies were also struggling to recover from the war, and failure could result in civil conflict. Secretary of State George Marshall proposed in June, 1947, that the United States should aid in the economic recovery of any European nation undertaking a well developed reconstruction plan. This Marshall Plan would lead to political and social, as well as economic stability.

Europe was overjoyed and submitted a plan calling for $22.5 billion in American aid. In March, 1948, after Czechoslovakia come under Soviet control, Congress appropriated $5.3 billion for the first year of the program. Within three years the United States expended $12 billion. Late in 1951 the Marshall Plan gave way to the Mutual Security Agency, which proceeded to give away $59 billion over the next six years.

Meanwhile, a frustrating German situation had developed. The Western Allies merged their occupied territories, and the German Federal Republic was created in October, 1948. The Soviet Union responded the next month with the Berlin blockade. At first it consisted of restrictions created by the introduction of bureaucratic red tape. Russia withdrew from the Four Power Military Council which was supposedly coordinating occupation policy. And finally, all western ground traffic into Berlin was halted (the Allied sector of Berlin lay well within Soviet-controlled East Germany). The Allied answer was the Berlin airlift of June, 1948–May, 1949, during which 2.5 million tons of supplies were flown into West Berlin. It was the American intent that if war came, it could only be the result of a Soviet attack on an American aircraft. Washington informed Moscow that the blockade would not be tolerated, so it was dropped.

The Berlin crisis brought Europe and America closer. In April, 1949, the North Atlantic Treaty Organization set up a defense structure among America and her European allies. Over $1 billion in defense aid was given to western Europe. Expediency and security had won over the suspicion of entangling alliances. A strong bipartisan vote committed the United States to leadership of the free world.

In the following years, Russia and the United States developed a standoff situation. Summit diplomacy was the supposed answer during the Eisenhower administration, but this personal diplomacy between heads of state failed to accomplish much. A serious confrontation with the Soviets occurred during the Kennedy administration over the placing of missile bases in Cuba, but it was a storm which, due to American firmness, passed over in short order. However, numerous minor incidents have developed regularly. It appears as if the two giant powers have learned to respect each other out of a recognition that the military potential held by both sides could bring worldwide destruction if unleashed.

Tension in Asia

The developments of the early fifties in Korea established a firm policy of containment against Red China (see Chapter Thirteen). In August, 1951, the United States signed a mutual defense treaty with the Philippines, and created the Southeast Asia Treaty Organization. In September, a peace treaty was signed with Japan, which stripped that country only of her former imperial possessions. A mutual defense treaty with Japan was then negotiated. Fissures had been created in the eastern communist bloc. The United States has consistently pursued a policy of non-recognition toward Red China, and has repeatedly succeeded in keeping that nation out of the United Nations. The Chinese government is teaching its people from the cradle to the grave to hate Americans, and the nation espouses a much more militant brand of international communism than do the Soviets.

The current crisis in Vietnam was largely the result of Red Chinese efforts to establish hegemony over Southeast Asia. America's Vietnamese military mission grew to a very large, highly active military machine in the Sixties. Yet the United States and Red China have not risked direct, open confrontation. Vietnam, like Korea before it, was caught between the United States and China. The American intervention in South Vietnam was based on the premise that a victory by the North could result in a complete communist take-over of Southeast Asia; the Philippines are not far away. There was much opposition at home, mainly because expediency (rather than idealistic policy) put the United States in Vietnam, and the cost was high in terms of blood, lives, and money. Added to this, the political situation in the country which America was defending was far from satisfactory.

Other international problems that will command America's attention for some time include the future of the United Nations, the fate of Chiang Kai-shek and Formosa, the keeping of the peace at the eastern end of the Mediterranean, the establishment of viable economies and stable governments in Africa and Latin America. One central issue lies behind all others, however: the rivalry between the East (particularly Red China) and West (particularly the United States) for the establishment of their governmental systems and political influence in the young and uncommitted nations of the world.

For Further Reading

Bailey, Thomas A. *A Diplomatic History of the American People.* New York: Appleton-Century-Crofts, 1955.

Bemis, Samuel F. *A Diplomatic History of the United States.* New York: Holt and Company, 1955.

Bloomfield, Lincoln P. *The United Nations and United States Foreign Policy.* Boston: Little, Brown, 1960.

Dulles, Foster Rhea. *America's Rise to World Power, 1898–1954.* New York: Harper, 1955.

Fulbright, J. W. *Old Myths and New Realities.* New York: Random House, 1964.

Gerberding, William P. *United States Foreign Policy: Perspectives and Analysis.* New York: McGraw-Hill, 1966.

Lerche, Charles O., Jr. *The Cold War—and After.* Englewood Cliffs: Prentice-Hall, 1965.

Molnar, Thomas. *The Two Faces of American Foreign Policy.* New York: Bobbs-Merrill, 1962.

Needles, Martin. *Understanding Foreign Policy.* New York: Holt and Company, 1966.

Pratt, Julius W. *A History of United States Foreign Policy.* New York: Prentice-Hall, 1955.

Radway, Lawrence I. *Foreign Policy and National Defense.* Glenview, Illinois: Scott Foresman, 1968.

Stromberg, Roland N. *Collective Security and American Foreign Policy.* New York: Praeger, 1962.

Tannenbaum, Frank. *The American Tradition in Foreign Policy.* Norman: University of Oklahoma Press, 1955.

Chapter Fifteen
American Intellectual and Cultural Traditions

People's behavior is usually based on what they think, even if their opinions are not articulated or consistent. Normally, people act according to what they think is proper and correct for them. They possess certain convictions and goals which they are attempting to implement in their behavior. Their values are derived from any number of sources. Education, television, newspapers, magazines, books, movies, billboards—all convey ideas which express and influence individual beliefs. Art, music, and oral traditions also reflect and influence people's values. It is much easier to identify the values themselves than to pinpoint their origins.

There are various ways of determining what values people hold. Politicians are one source of knowledge; in their dual role they both lead and follow public opinion. Desiring to remain in elected office, they attempt to discover and follow the wishes of their constituency, but try also to influence what the constituency wants. The media of print and electronics give voice to mass opinion as they lead it. Popular commentators often represent large blocs of votes and ideas, and news of public meetings, demonstrations, and popular movements reveals much about the feelings of the citizenry. The pronouncements of acknowledged thinkers and storytellers comprise another source. The simple fact that a particular idea is put forth by a given author does not in itself prove that the idea is influential; but when it can be determined that the work was widely read and favorably received, and that people acted in accordance with the idea, it becomes reasonable to assume that the idea was acceptable to and adopted by them.

The study of values is a difficult one, but it is obvious that ideas are very, very important in the modern world. Contemporary America is engaged in an ideological struggle with communism, and it is fighting a propaganda war. There is a great struggle for control over men's minds, not only by foes but by our own politicians and advertising men as well. People are constantly being manipulated by outside forces to control or influence what they think. The present chapter will attempt to survey the dominant intellectual themes of American history. The intent is to show the depth of the American mind (if there is only one), and ascertain what it stands for, in order to assess its function and influence on the contemporary domestic scene.

The European Intellectual Background

American intellectual history begins with European history. The Europeans who came to America were strongly influenced by two recent European developments: the Renaissance and the Reformation. Medieval cultural achievements had been found almost entirely in the religious realm. The Renaissance changed this: more concerned with man than with God, preferring earthly joys to unknown eternal pleasures, cultural achievements were being made in non-religious areas. But the Renaissance was not a purely materialistic movement. It was a rebirth of the ancient classical tradition, but with considerable emphasis on a long-neglected tenet of Christianity—man's essential worth and dignity. Here was the real germ-seed of American democratic thought.

One of the developments of the Renaissance was a church which became increasingly worldly and which, as a result, painfully cut its own medieval authoritarian moorings from beneath itself. Various local political leaders, with their new humanistic outlook, sought to break the power of the church over their political activities. And they coveted the vast landed estates which the church had accumulated during the Middle Ages. In the process, they broke the unity of medieval Christendom.

The Renaissance brought out a concern for the pleasures of this world, the Reformation attacked established authority and tradition, and the Calvinists had stated that a godly man should strive for earthly success. All of these ingredients were inherent in the geographical expansion of Europe. One result was mercantilism, one of the dominant ideas of the European rulers who were responsible for establishing colonies in America.

Mercantilistic Thought

Mercantilism was a theory whereby nations sought to accumulate economic advantages at the expense of all other nations. By establishing a favorable balance of trade, a nation sought to acquire stores of precious metals. It would be aided in this task if it could plant a worldwide network of colonies to serve as sources of raw materials and to provide markets for manufactured goods. The English colonies were established mainly by private capital, subject to restrictions and privileges specified by the Crown.

The money for colonial ventures came from the new middle class, the people who made their money out of trading and early industrial enterprises. Rulers in an age of growing nationalism required money more than anything else. So they gave select members of the middle class trading and self-governing privileges in exchange for some of their wealth. This was a highly significant contributory factor in the growth of democratic governments.

The Europe of around 1600 was a transitional Europe. It had just gone through a period of political, religious, and economic upheaval. It was still chaotic and unstable. In England, nearly half of the seventeenth century was taken up with civil war, as the Cavaliers fought the Roundheads for political supremacy. In the meantime, the newly founded American colonies were left to their own designs.

Religious Dissent

Of all the earlier settlers who came to America the New England Puritans were one of the most cohesive groups. Puritan thought was basically the thought of John Calvin as it had been picked up by exiled Englishmen in Switzerland and introduced to England during the Elizabethan era. The principle tenets of Calvinism as put forth by the Synod of Dort (1618 ff.) were: total depravity, man's innate inability to save himself; the doctrine of the elect, which held that God saved only some men and in His omniscience knew who would be saved and damned forever; limited atonement, which meant that Christ died only for the elect; irrefusable grace, meaning that those lucky souls destined for salvation had no choice in the matter; and perpetual sainthood, which held that those destined for salvation would not act wrongly while on earth since this would indicate a flaw in divine grace. This basically comprised the beliefs of such Puritans as John Endicott and John Winthrop, the founders of Massachusetts Bay Colony.

Puritanism left its mark on the New England mind. Since no one knew if he was one of the chosen few, as matters turned out many became obsessed with the threat of damnation. Puritans were commonly very intolerant of others, and lived to prove their own "elect" status. But the Puritans did develop the "Puritan ethic," which provided an ideological basis for American capitalism as it was practiced during the nineteenth century (see below).

Another New England religious group, the Pilgrims, had been very much in disfavor in England. Whereas Puritans hoped to change the Anglican Church from within, Pilgrims broke away to establish a new church with less formalism. Persecuted and seeking religious freedom, they sought a haven in America. They rejected the strict organization and authoritarianism of the Puritans, and advocated what eventually became known as Congregationalism: the idea that each religious body should elect its own ministry and be independent from all other congregations. There would be no institutionalized church hierarchy (important in a new land where there was a distinct shortage of trained clergy); select laymen would govern the church.

Puritans and Pilgrims alike, whether they realized it or not, championed the idea of the right to dissent by standing as examples. Both groups upheld the idea of government by written compact: the Puritan Fundamental Orders of Connecticut and the Pilgrim Mayflower Compact have both been regarded as the major precedents for the Constitution of the United States. Both groups manifested the humanistic orientation of the Renaissance, and both emphasized the value of education. They pursued public education, which was primarily religious in emphasis but which nurtured the idea that government had a responsibility to provide educational opportunities for its citizens.

Quakerism was another of the dissenting religions introduced to the American colonies. Quakerism was started by the Englishman George Fox in reaction against the growing influence of the European Enlightenment. Brought to America around 1650, it is best exemplified by William Penn, the founder of Pennsylvania. Quaker thought has exerted considerable influence on American ideas. According to John Woolman, a leading colonial Quaker, the key tenet of the religion was the doctrine of the Inner Light, which meant that every human being possessed a divine power by nature which enabled him to acquire spiritual truth through direct communication with God. This was not, however, an automatic process; each individual had to work to develop his own Inner Light. Thus any person might be in direct communication with God, and it would be wrong to disturb or do violence to a person who might be carrying on a conversation with the divine. Holding this attitude, it is not surprising that the Quakers believed in complete equality, both of races and of sexes, and were highly tolerant of other religious faiths. In all of these respects they were far in advance of other groups. Equalitarianism has prospered to become a major article of the American faith. The Quaker roots of pacifism are now obscure, but that idea, too, is becoming respectable and influential in modern America.

Seventeenth-century Europe is commonly referred to as the Age of Reason because of the growth of the Enlightenment—an attempt to discover and solve the problems of mankind through the use of the human intellect. Freed from the restrictions of an authoritarian medieval church and an attitude which regarded the world strictly as a waiting room for eternity, men were encouraged to concentrate on making the "waiting room" a more comfortable place. Quite naturally, the Enlightenment and such of its thinkers as Newton, Descartes, and Locke would influence thought in America. Seventeenth-century America was preoccupied with settlement; there was little interest in academic pursuits. No cities had yet developed which could act as centers for intellectual activities. But by 1700 America was ripe for her own Enlightenment. Some people were sufficiently settled to have time for reading and reflection. Cities were developing, new ideas were spreading, and Calvinism was beginning to lose its hold.

Enlightenment Thought in Early America

The American eighteenth century upheld the idea that human character was the product of environment. Improve the environment by first discovering and then implementing natural laws and human nature would also improve. Americans began their Enlightenment with a high degree of optimism. It was relatively easy to break with old traditions in a new geographical environment. But in the area of science, separation from the Old World proved to be a detriment to America, and American scientific contributions were destined to be sparse for generations.

Benjamin Franklin achieved world recognition for his scientific accomplishments and practical inventions, particularly his discovery that electricity charges and discharges. With this knowledge he was able to invent the lightening rod and thereby provide protection against one of the more feared natural phenomenon. Other American colonial scientists included David Rittenhouse in astronomy and mathematics, John Winthrop in astronomy, and Cadwallader Colden who made contributions in a number of fields. Christopher Colles built the first American steam engine, and Isaac Greenwood wrote the first arithmetic book.

Reason and Religion

Initially, the greatest effect of the Enlightenment on America was in the field of religion. Progressively more Puritans had modified their religious beliefs, aiming toward a religion based more on human reason and less on divine revelation. Gradually, Puritan clergymen were beginning to think that man was capable of divine truth by nature—quite a contrast to the doctrine of man's innate depravity. A strict brand of morality was still stressed, but the Puritan God became forgiving and shared part of his divinity with man. In the process the road was paved for the acceptance of Unitarian ideas during the latter part of the eighteenth century: Christ as subordinate to God, an example of the perfect man. And this was attributable to the fact that some clergymen became so thoroughly committed to the use of reason that they experienced considerable difficulty in explaining traditional Christian religious mysteries.

By the mid-eighteenth century American Enlightenment religion took the form of Deism. It was never widely accepted in America, and remained most popular only among the educated class. Reason was placed on the same level as revelation. God became the First Cause, a sort of divine watchmaker who, having completed his masterpiece, had set it in motion and now did nothing else to keep it functioning. The deistic God was a somewhat impersonal being. Ben Franklin, Thomas Jefferson, and Thomas Paine were all Deists.

The American synthesis of Enlightenment religious thought is well exemplified in the person of Ben Franklin, who accepted the values of Calvinism but refused to believe that life on earth should be austere. To him a person could lead a perfectly moral life but strive for earthly happiness at the same time. Being virtuous was a matter of common sense; it would be the best way of getting along in life even without the existence of a divinity. Reason demanded morality.

The Great Awakening

The Enlightenment did not lie behind every change in religious ideas in the colonies during the eighteenth century. There was a short-lived but highly effective antithesis. There were people in the colonies who were opposed to the emphasis on rationality, particularly as it was being applied to religion. The result was the Great Awakening, a period of religious revivalism which lasted roughly from 1720 to 1760. The movement was a popular one with an emotionalistic tone, though its leadership was provided by educated clergymen.

Membership in established colonial churches had brought various political, social, and economic privileges. The Calvinistic doctrine of predestination recognized only a select few as being among the

"elect." The average American settler wanted a direct and simple religion rather than obedience to an established, highly organized church, possessed of complex doctrines with just a few college-trained clergymen to expound and explain the rules.

The idea of an Inner Religion, one resting on personal belief and action rather than formalized church organization and doctrine, was brought to the colonies by such groups as the Quakers as early as the 1720's. Most immigrants were from the poorer economic groups by this time, and sought a religious experience appropriate to their status in life. The revivalist kind of emotional religion that attracted them was championed by Jonathan Edwards, the great figure in the New England phase of the Great Awakening. He blended inner religion with Calvinism, and stressed human emotion without formalized doctrine as the essence of religious experience. Organized and established religions did not molest the many revival preachers who followed in Edwards' wake, most of whom operated in the western regions of the colonies.

The Great Awakening produced a number of important effects. Some of the largest denominations in the modern United States received their impetus from this movement. Revivalism continued to spread partly because of the need for some sort of a religion in face of a distinct shortage of trained clergymen, but the Great Awakening also led to the establishment of some seminaries for the training of an American clergy.

Enlightenment and Revolution

The American Enlightenment exerted its most lasting influence in the political rather than the religious realm. Although the Enlightenment in general took a century to reach America, its political ideas arrived rather earlier. By the beginning of the eighteenth century (Locke had written in 1690), American clergymen were expounding the natural-rights doctrine that each man is entitled to life, liberty, and property. One of the first important figures in this respect was the Congregationalist minister, John Wise, who argued that God left the discovery of the best form of government to the reasoning abilities of man. By 1717 Wise had written and spoken in favor of democracy, equality, the contract theory (that government is validated only by agreement of the people), and the right of rebellion. Wise was very widely read and his works were republished in 1772 on the brink of the American Revolution. Building upon Wise's writings was a fellow clergyman, Jonathan Mayhew, whose real importance lay in his attempt to render revolution a rational and legitimate act. He did so by arguing that it was unreasonable to accede to an unjust government. The philosophical justification was thus established before the actual move toward a revolution occurred in America.

It is interesting to follow the development of natural-rights arguments through the Revolutionary period. Ben Franklin invoked the consent-of-the-governed theory when he called for colonial union in his Albany Plan of 1754. James Otis voiced the same argument in 1764 with reference to taxation without the consent of the governed. Both men insisted that colonials be allowed representation in Parliament. The Stamp Act Congress of 1765 took a more radical view. It argued against taxation without representation, but claimed that Americans could not effectively be represented in Parliament because of the intervention of the Atlantic. In effect these men were speaking out for more colonial independence, calling for local assemblies to handle the matters of Parliament.

In 1766 the New York assembly was suspended for refusal to submit to a long-standing law requiring colonial issuance of supplies to British redcoats. One result was a series of public letters by John Dickenson in 1767 and 1768, which claimed that compliance was a form of taxation, again without proper representation. To submit would mean to open the doors for any arbitrary curtailment of the liberty to which all men were entitled.

And in 1774 another colonial, James Wilson, went even further. Again arguing that government rested on the consent of the governed and must respect the natural rights of its citizens, he claimed that Parliament had absolutely no authority over Americans because Americans had no voice in Parliament—he did not stop at mere tax measures. Wilson did not, however, deny allegiance to the Crown. Alexander Hamilton and John Adams, writing in 1774 and 1775 respectively, reiterated this very position. Ideologically, American leaders had limited the tie between England and her American colonies strictly to an allegiance to the Crown, and this was a rather slender tie since Parliament claimed virtually all legislative authority.

Against this background, Thomas Paine published *Common Sense* in January, 1776. He argued that all men possessed equal political power, but were required to elect representatives to exercise that power for them, since their numbers were too large to be manageable in a single assembly. The King had not been elected. He did not rule with the consent of his people according to the contract theory. Therefore, there was no need for a tie with the English king. America by right should be free and independent. Paine had taken a very extreme position and his writings were viewed with mixed emotions in the colonies. But he found favor with colonial Revolutionary leaders.

Enlightenment political ideology found concrete expression a few months later in the Declaration of Independence. Placing faith in the reasoning abilities of man, the document stated that it was being written to justify the action to the rest of the world. The Declaration reiterated the contract theory, expounded upon the natural, inalienable rights of man, and upheld the right to revolution. Interestingly enough, in the closing list of American grievances against England, stress was placed on a tyrannical king, rather than (as usual) a usurping Parliament. Paine's influence was thus clearly demonstrated.

Rationalizing the Democratic Ideal

Unfortunately, the natural-rights doctrine was not applied equally to all men. And this points out a major characteristic of the American mind—its ambivalence. Negro slaves (and Indians) were somehow excluded from the protection of natural rights and the United States Constitution. This problem was initially a national blind spot—a subject best left undiscussed; but as time went on the South, under pressure from northern objectors, produced arguments to defend and even praise the institution of slavery.

The southern viewpoint was best exemplified by George Fitzhugh, a writer and thinker of the ante-bellum era. Like most southern writers, Fitzhugh preferred order and security over liberty. He developed the association theory to justify the southern social structure. Associations which existed over a long period of time became institutions. Such institutions reflected man's basic nature and long practical experience. Since slavery had existed throughout human history, this indicated that slavery was a basic trait of human society; reason and experience proved its necessity. According to Fitzhugh, freedom bred disorder and instability; individualism was not in the best interests of the public good.

This ideology suffered a setback at Appomattox. Ironically, the end of slavery weakened the crusading zeal of abolitionism. Although some individuals continued to press for human dignity for all, the Lockean doctrine of natural rights re-ceded slowly into the background. In the meanwhile, during the post–Civil War era, economic values replaced Lockean moral values. Southern elitist social theories were bolstered by the Social Darwinists and their conception of society as an arena for struggle. Basic individual rights were destined to receive much lip service but little realization in actual deed for some time to come.

The Spirit of Change in America

Transcendentalism

As abolititionist sentiment rose in New England against the embittered pro-slavery "reasoning" of the South during the early nineteenth century, some New England thinkers also grew dissatisfied with the Unitarian reliance on human reason in the religious realm. Inspired by such notables as Ralph Waldo Emerson and Henry David Thoreau, the transcendentalists held that man was capable not only of empirical knowledge (sense perception), but also of knowledge which transcended (went beyond) mere sense perception. Unitarians had been accepting as true in the theological realm only those concepts which could be known by observation. Such empiricism in religion often leads to scepticism, and renders it difficult to accept the supernatural. The Unitarians were looking for some rational proof for the existence of God, but with their insistence on sense perception to prove theological principles they were trapped in the material world.

Transcendentalism was intended as an answer to this plight. Although every transcendentalist had a different definition of transcendentalism, they agreed in the conviction that each and every man possesses the ability to arrive at spiritual truth intuitively. This intuitive power was part of human nature, though a man's spirituality varied depending on the degree to which he had developed his intuitive self. Christ had completely developed his intuitive powers; he was to be accepted as the perfect man (note this agreement with the Unitarians).

Since the ability to acquire profound truth was a birthright of every human being, most transcendentalists devoutly respected the dignity and integrity of each individual soul—no matter how humble and undeveloped its possessor might appear. This democratic attitude also involved both a sense of man's divinity and a belief in human progress. As man discovered more of himself and the spark of the divine within, he became more perfect. The human intellect was capable of advancing forever. One transcendentalist went so far as to claim that any man sufficiently motivated could equal Christ on earth. Mankind had made spiritual progress since the beginning of time, and this progress was insignificant compared with what the future held in store. Man was just beginning to discover his latent powers.

The idea that a close association with nature could bring about the development of the latent powers in man was also a leading tenet of transcendentalism. Man discovered himself by a careful observation of nature. He had to retire from the bustle of civilization occasionally in order to contemplate himself in nature. By identifying with nature, man could discover his transcendent self. This both encouraged and reflected the American attraction to the rural over the urban atmosphere.

Transcendentalists believed in a very active Divine Providence, which assigned various tasks and powers to races, nations, and individuals. In the Old Testament the Jews were made the Chosen People of God. In the 1830's the United States became the Chosen Nation. Providence did not assign a task without first providing the necessary equipment for achieving it. The United States had the fated role of up-

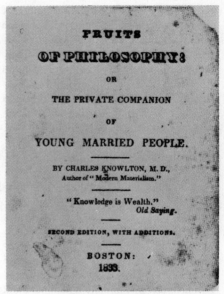

FRUITS
OF PHILOSOPHY:
OR
THE PRIVATE COMPANION
OF
YOUNG MARRIED PEOPLE.

BY CHARLES KNOWLTON, M. D.,
Author of " Modern Materialism."

" Knowledge is Wealth."
Old Saying.

SECOND EDITION, WITH ADDITIONS.

BOSTON:
1833.

Houghton Library, Harvard University

The Earliest American Book on Birth Control

lifting the rest of the world, of advancing the cause of democracy, and of championing individual integrity. This was very aptly brought out in the writings of George Bancroft, one of the nation's first great historians.

The transcendentalists were outspokenly dissatisfied with society as it existed. Being well educated people, they could readily see the inequities and barriers which hindered the realization of their perfect man. They enthusiastically worked for change and provided an ideological basis for the American reform spirit. Like the Quakers before them, and for essentially the same reasons, transcendentalists took an active role in abolition, prison reform, and temperance efforts.

The Ideology of Progress

It followed from Enlightenment ideas and also from transcendentalist thought that mankind could be quite optimistic about the future. The assumption that man—and society—improves as time goes on was relatively new in the eighteenth century, but has lain at the center of American thinking since then. The Enlightenment's confidence in the worth of human reason implied that human affairs could be measured against clear standards, and improved if they fell short of the mark. If mankind could discover the fixed laws of nature and work to regulate society accordingly, then why should there be any limit to human progress?

The French thinker, Condorcet, was largely responsible for introducing this attitude to America. He claimed that history demonstrated that progress resulted from the combined efforts of science and education. Intellectual progress would stimulate the growth of liberty, virtue, and natural rights. In the late eighteenth century, it was the United States more than any other nation which gave concrete expression to this doctrine. It was because he recognized this that the young Frenchman, De Tocqueville, visited America in the 1830's. His observations led him to claim that equality would bring about the perfectibility of humanity, and nowhere was this more evident than the United States. Americans agreed with him, and their interest in the view of history as progress was well demonstrated in numerous writings in journals throughout the nineteenth century. But the nation has always been more concerned with tangibles than with ideas, and it was natural that as time went on the American conception of progress would center not on intellectual and spiritual growth, but on the production and consumption of material goods. It was not the transcendentalists' perfected spiritual man, but the captain of industry that captured the imagination of America in the latter part of the nineteenth century.

The Ideology of American Industrialism

The Puritan Ethic

The ascendancy of the dream of material progress was nearly complete during the big business era, and the champions of big business in the post–Civil War period were able to draw upon a number of sources to develop an ideology which justified their actions. One of these sources was the Puritan ethic. The Puritans regarded the world as a place of temptation and spiritual danger, yet as members of the rising middle class, many Puritans were successful in economic ventures. Avoiding the potential conflict between worldly success and pious humility before God, the Puritans recognized that not every man could enter the ministry. If a man followed the Ten Commandments, he could lead a righteous and productive life in any number of ways—serving God according to his personal calling. Piety and utility thus went hand in hand. Wealth or success in one's vocation was taken as a sign of being one of the elect. The doctrine was thus little more than a blending of Calvinism with middle-class material values.

The real significance was that a halo of sanctification was given to the business of acquiring wealth. Idleness was the most deadly of all sins; not to seek wealth was to deny a talent offered by God. The good Puritan was not supposed to enjoy his wealth for its own sake; this would constitute a deadly moral danger. But by accumulating wealth he could promote the betterment of society and exploit his God-given abilities to the glorification of Providence.

Nowhere was the Puritan ethic better exemplified than in the writings of Benjamin Franklin. There are two key themes in Franklin's writings: industry and frugality. One should work as hard as possible at his calling and save every possible penny; this was the way to virtue —and wealth as well. Franklin's sayings remained popular in America and were very much alive during the age of big business, long after wealth had become its own reward. But the captains of industry rationalized their unscrupulous pursuit of riches by emphasizing the Puritan concept of virtuous industriousness as found in Franklin's writings, along with a new line of thinking that was called social Darwinism.

The Survival of the Fittest

In 1859 Charles Darwin published the first of his works expounding evolution. *The Origin of Species* touched off a controversy which lasted for over a half a century and which is still being waged in some fundamentalist circles. Darwin had arrived at a completely new understanding of nature's operations. Man had evolved over millions of years from lower animal-forms. Certain life-forms survived because they could adapt to changing environmental conditions; others died out because they could not. Thus, evolution occurs through a process of the survival of the fittest—the strongest thrive under conditions that extinguish the weak.

Darwin's theorizing held tremendous implications for theology and philosophy. He had reduced man, once held to be created in the image and likeness of God, to a creature who had developed not through righteousness or God's benevolence, but through good luck and impressive ability. Some individuals took this to mean that a scientific law had replaced God as the creator. And if man really was the product of natural selection and mutation, he was merely a transitory creature, destined to be superseded by a more advanced life-form in the future. The initial shock of Darwinian evolutionary thought encouraged disillusionment with religion. The effect was even more profound in philosophy, which then had to cope with a scientific explanation for man and the universe quite different from previous views, and could not so easily retreat into mysticism.

Gradually, various American thinkers picked up the Darwinian argument and attempted to square it with traditional religion. They pointed out that one need only accept survival of the fittest and the production of variation by random mutation as part of God's universal plan. By the end of the nineteenth century, religion was fairly well reconciled to Darwinism, and most religious leaders were able to accept basic Darwinian principles. But this was not so in the rural areas, where religious fundamentalism was in open conflict with evolution—even as late as the celebrated Scopes "Monkey Trial" of 1925, when a high school biology teacher in Tennessee was convicted of teaching evolution in violation of a state law.

During the second generation of Darwinian theorizing, a number of scientists were able to provide some scientific data to support the validity of the theory. This was done by arranging and classifying various fossils and plants in ascending order of chronological development. But the best support for the validity of Darwin's theory came when Luther Burbank, a California horticulturist, began to cross-fertilize and graft various plants to create new types of plants. He demonstrated the way mutations are propagated in his laboratories in the 1870's.

The arguments of the Darwinians and the support rendered by scientific experimentation made Darwinian thought quite acceptable to the upper and middle economic classes. It seemed to provide a means of explaining and coping with a rapidly changing way of life in industrial America—particularly the growth in the number of spectacularly wealthy people while unemployment and squalor continued unabated among the increasing urban masses. Herbert Spencer, a social theorist who applied Darwinian thinking to human society, made a triumphant tour of America in the early 1880's and told successful Americans exactly what they wanted to hear. Spencer felt that even though Darwin himself had written only about the slow process of the physical differentiation of species over eons of time, the concept of the survival of the fittest applied also to human relations. The laissez-faire doctrine could now be hailed as nature's way of sifting out the weaklings. And only by eliminating the unfit could the human race hope to improve. As the people who rose to the top of the heap victimized the rest of mankind—those whom the Puritans might have labeled too lazy or wasteful to succeed—the race was being improved.

It had once been argued that laissez faire maximized productivity by giving everyone an opportunity to better himself. But the majority of people had remained poor, and thus it could be argued that laissez faire had not provided the greatest good for the greatest number. But Spencer now proclaimed that it was natural and inevitable that the majority should be poor. It benefited the race to have some victors in a ruthless competition for survival. Those who survived should be honored, for these were the individuals most qualified to propagate the next generation. Social Darwinism, along with the Puritan ethic, thus provided a religious and scientific justification not only for the amassing of tremendous wealth, but also for an indifference to the plight of the poverty-stricken masses.

Another leading spokesman for this viewpoint was a Yale sociology professor, William Graham Sumner. Admitting that the system was quite ruthless, but also claiming that poverty existed by law of nature, Sumner was against aid to the poor. To give to the poor, one must take from the wealthy; one must penalize those who have done well and reward those who have done poorly. This would encourage the survival of the unfit, which hardly made sense in his opinion. In this same vein the eminent captain of industry Andrew Carnegie, writing in the mid-1880's, advanced the theory that industrialists were the stewards of God on earth (the Puritan ethic notion), and through the exercise of the laws of competition brought about the progress of the human race (Social Darwinism).

This justification for the rise of the American monied power was based on the assumption that ruthless competition was indeed free. The rules of acquiring wealth were the laws of nature. Change was seen as a manifestation of evolutionary process —but not always. To develop trusts, holding companies, and interlocking directorships was evolutionary; it aided the fit in the attainment of their ends (which in these cases was the curtailing of competition). But at the same time labor unions, which were actually copying big business organization and practice, were retrogressive because they aided the unfit.

This contradiction revealed a serious flaw in the entire big business argument because it implied that some of the successful needed the protection of anti-competitive devices to maintain their positions. It further showed that the analogy with Darwinian doctrine was false, since competition in economic matters was a struggle not for survival, but for wealth. The laborer or farmer who managed to feed himself and his family was certainly *surviving;* his economic status was an indication not that he was unfit to live, but that his opportunities and perhaps his preferences did not lead him toward material success. Social Darwinism could measure a man's worth only by the size of his bank account.

Pragmatism

There was another side to the intellectual activity of the age of big business. There appeared for the first time a native American philosophy: pragmatism, which was initially known as "instrumentalism." Pragmatism arose in part from the evolutionary concepts of the age, and in part from the practical-mindedness of the pioneers and industrialists who had set the tone of American life.

The American philosopher who originated the term "pragmatism" was Charles Pierce, who attempted to blend the old idealistic philosophy with new evolutionary theory. The operation of mutation and natural selection was acknowledged, but Pierce suggested that as time went by the influence of the selective process would lessen, until finally the universe would become orderly, unchanging. Hence, the universe would approach what it was traditionally held to be before the advent of Darwin, and there would be none of the insecurity associated with the struggle for survival. Pierce still thought in terms of the philosophical "universals," immutable truths, of pre-Darwinian philosophy. But he defined universals as ideas accepted on faith as true by the human community.

Pierce's concept of universals coupled with Darwin's theory of evolution provided the essentials for pragmatism as it was formulated by William James. The real heart of pragmatism centered around the definition of truth. James found unsatisfactory both the older concept of eternal, divinely-revealed verities, and Pierce's relativistic truth-by-consensus.

James accepted the notion that the universe was constantly changing in an unpredictable fashion. For him, truth was defined as an idea, applied to an actual situation, which *worked* in that situation. The truth or falsity of an idea was to be determined by whether or not experience verified it. And since reality was always changing—and with it, human needs and perceptions—so also was truth a shifting thing. In one sense, men thus created their own truths, but these had to be tested in action.

Though James' definition of empirical knowledge was not limited merely to the experience of the senses, it was true that God had lost his place as the necessary source of reliable knowledge and permanent laws of nature. The world and the future became uncertain. James had formulated for the American empire-builders a philosophy which they had long been practicing in their everyday affairs.

Equally important with James in any consideration of pragmatism is John Dewey. Dewey's major contribution to American thought was his practical application of James' pragmatic theory to contemporary social problems. He thereby made philosophy seem more relevant and useful to the mass of Americans. For Dewey, philosophy did not deal with abstract ideas, but with concrete realistic problems of everyday life. And at the base of his system, as with Jefferson long before him, there was a great insistence on the role of education in alleviating social ills. It was in the field of education that the practical-minded philosopher could best demonstrate his effectiveness and influence.

It is quite difficult to determine just what specific influences the thinking of Pierce, James, and Dewey had on American thought. Frontier situations had been forcing some Americans to think pragmatically all along. But many other Americans who had been employing the pragmatic method in their everyday affairs, and who greatly admired those individuals who achieved material success, still could not completely divorce themselves from the older natural-law doctrine as interpreted by John Locke. They were attempting to retain the old while accepting the new.

The net result is a continuing and fundamental dichotomy in modern American thought. The American people have retained the idealism of the Jeffersonian–Jacksonian tradition, but at the same time they respect "practicality." They would like to believe that sheer utility justifies all actions, but at the same time they are exceedingly reluctant to break completely with unchanging moral law.

Religion in the Gilded Age

Since big business had been successful by using new methods, in some quarters there was a feeling that perhaps traditional religion should also employ business methods. But there were also those who were appalled by contemporary industrial society, who repudiated social Darwinism, and who attempted to aid the poverty-stricken masses.

One such group was the Salvation Army, which had appeared earlier at a similar stage in England's industrial revolution. Founded as a practical religion, it concentrated not on dogma, but on real Christian charity. It concerned itself with social services, rehabilitation, and spiritual salvation, and attempted to fill the great social needs of the slums in the growing industrial centers. The group suffered a tremendous amount of belittlement, but accomplished an equally tremendous amount of good work.

The Christian Science sect, founded by Mary Baker Eddy, also made its appearance during the period. In a sense it was a reaction against the scientific, technological, and industrial advances of the age. At a time when science and technology ruled, it held that faith was superior to science, and prayer was superior to medical care (which was probably often true in view of the existing medical practices).

There also appeared a sizeable non-denominational, free-lance ministry. The movement embodied a blending of Great Awakening revivalist spirit with big-business era organizational techniques. Most free-lance ministers were uneducated but they were good organizers, and knew how to manipulate people through the medium of mass psychology. Free-lancing marked the beginning of revivalism as a big business. It combined entertainment, advertising, homemade theology and preaching, and showmanship, and it won huge profits for many of the preachers. It was popular in the rural areas where there was little other diversion, but it drew its largest crowds in the city slums. But in the process, the more unscrupulous of the free lancers succeeded in commercializing religion.

Most established churches started auxiliary services, such as youth groups and temperance societies. For the most part worship took second place to these new interests. Religion was in competition with commercial entertainment, a development which has maintained itself in America. A new type of religious ideology reigned supreme: the Gospel of Wealth. The Gospel was based on a forcible preaching of the old Puritan ethic and demanded that respect be shown to the wealthy since they were the earthly guardians of God's bounty. Clergymen and educators in this period tended to see only two possible alternatives in national economic structure: unrestrained capitalism (social Darwinism run wild) or European socialism, which was considered to be atheistic. Naturally, they chose the former as being the lesser of two evils. Besides, the wealthy industrialist was noted for his philanthropy; he was a good and generous man where many churches were concerned, and one dared not inquire into the means by which he acquired his riches. The wealthy helped encourage this notion, and most entrepreneurs attended church services faithfully—always in the front row.

The Ideology of Protest and Reform

Especially as industrialism took hold, there were more and more Americans who could not help but compare the libertarian ideals of the Declaration of Independence with what was being actually practiced in the nation. By the end of the nineteenth century there was a strong pressure for fundamental reform from some sectors of American society.

Suffragettes Petitioning the House of Representatives

Progress and Poverty

Henry George was one man who did not go along with the prevailing notion that poverty was the result of an unchangable natural law. Since the nineteenth century had witnessed great material progress he felt that the nation ought to be approaching some sort of utopia. George attacked existing economic theory in his *Progress and Poverty* (1879), by refuting two basic economic theories: David Ricardo's Iron Law of Wages, and the Malthusian theory of population.

The Iron Law of Wages held that a fixed amount of capital was available to pay wages. Competition among the vast number of workers seeking this limited capital would always keep wages at the bare subsistence level. Against this theory George argued that wages were not based on capital; rather, they were based on the value added to a product as a result of labor. Hence, wages were not static; theoretically, they could be raised indefinitely.

According to the thinking of Thomas Malthus, there was a limited food supply for which all men were competing. The food supply increases, but at an arithmetic ratio (1,2,3,4,5), whereas the population increases at a geometric ratio (2,4,8,16, 32) unless checked by war or famine. Poverty kept the world from becoming overpopulated by destroying the unfit. If wages were raised to provide everyone with the money to buy as much food as they desired, there would not be enough food to meet the demand. The result would be that people would continue to starve. George argued that, to the contrary, poverty and population were not inalterably related.

Traditional economic theory held that there were three basic factors involved in production: land, which earns rents, labor, which earns wages, and capital, which earns interest. The three were not supposed to be dependent on each other. But according to George, land had value only when labor and capital were applied to make it productive. Rents placed on land were unjust since land in itself possessed no value. The rent extracted from land was the great, unnecessary cause of poverty. Wipe it out through taxation, and labor and capital could prosper together.

George's importance rests in the fact that he claimed that economic inequality need not exist, a conclusion which ran counter to social Darwinism at a time when that theory was ascendant. George claimed that progress could only come through equality (recall De Tocqueville's observation on progress). He put his finger on a fundamental contradiction in the American scheme of things. On the one hand America upheld democratic principles and gave the common man the right to vote. On the other hand, the Gospel of Wealth condoned mass poverty. A poverty-stricken people possessed of political power might very well convert democracy into chaos unless their condition was improved (the riots of the late 1960's bear this out). Thus society had to be reconstructed, and this should be done by equalizing the distribution of land through taxation. To a large extent George was an impractical utopian, but his notions on taxation as a basis for social control have found widespread acceptance in the twentieth century. And today's War on Poverty program agrees with his central thesis that poverty need not exist in a land of plenty.

Edward Bellamy

Another dissenting thinker, Edward Bellamy, wrote *Looking Backward* (1888). In this utopian novel the author described a perfect society of the year 2000, in which there was no poverty, no aristocracy, and no ruthless competition. In his work Bellamy claimed that capitalism was a very inefficient system for several reasons. It produced for an uncon-trolled market. It was highly competitive and this in itself was very wasteful. And it was responsible for a great deal of idleness. Idle men looked for jobs while idle capital looked for a product and the labor to produce it. In the meantime there was poverty. Bellamy claimed that capitalism as an economic system was absurd and also morally abominable.

His solution was complete equality. He proposed a world quite close to pure communism—an economic order in which all property is owned by the community collectively. He said in a later work that class struggle was necessary to bring about these desired changes, but warned that he did not favor socialism. (Socialism is an economic order in which the workers, presumably through the government, own the means of production.) He did not believe that socialism would bring about the degree of equality which he felt was necessary.

The inequities of American society, as portrayed by George and Bellamy, were obvious to most American observers. Some people felt that minor adjustments in the system, with the mutual cooperation of all parties concerned, would solve its problems. This attitude was manifested in the Grange movement, the Populist Party, and by the leadership, but not the membership, of the Knights of Labor union organization (see Chapter Eight). But all of these attempts resulted in failure.

Progressivism and Socialism

A more far-reaching dissatisfaction gained social force in the late 1890's, after the collapse of Populism; its unifying idea was a belief in the necessity of class conflict. In part it was a response to European socialism, and in part it reflected the humanitarian impulse which was beginning to permeate the nation at the time. But the common American attitude about class conflict was unlike Marxian socialism in one essential way—even the militants were inclined to feel that bosses and workers could eventually learn to live with one another and respect one another.

The mainstream of American protest in the early twentieth century was called Progressivism. Its goal was the modification of the traditional capitalistic system in the direction of socialism. It did not advocate socialism as its ultimate goal. Progressivism has already been considered in the chapter on the American welfare state, but the influence of socialistic thinking in America's protest movements has not been considered and is deserving of attention.

Socialism exerted such a strong influence on the Progressive period that the first decade of the twentieth century has been termed the "golden age" of American socialism. Daniel DeLeon, one of the leading socialists of the era, believed that there would be an eventual revolution and overthrow of capitalism. Only in this way could class conflict be reconciled. But DeLeon's attitude was tempered by his American background; he insisted that the revolution would occur through the peaceful use of the ballot box, and would be attained by a combination of labor unions and the American Socialist Party.

DeLeon did not capture the leadership of the party. Instead it went to a man of even more moderate persuasion, Eugene Debs. Although Debs made no original contributions to American thought, he did serve as the major popularizer of socialist ideology in America. Because of his inherent faith in the democratic process, he championed a doctrine which was not only acceptable to millions of Americans, but which helped to create the climate of opinion for the passage of major reform measures during the Progressive era. Debs called for the use of the socialist ideology to provide some easing of the workingman's condition immediately, but with the ultimate public ownership and control of the means of production postponed for some more suitable time in the future.

His insistence on the ballot box, on peaceful means, and on proper education, made socialism palatable to Americans who were dedicated to individual liberty, for he emphasized the old American ideals of freedom and equality.

One other individual deserves mention for aiding immeasurably in the creation of the proper climate for a reform ideology: Thorstein Veblen and his famous work, *The Theory of the Leisure Class* (1899). His principle theme was that there were two interests in society: financial and productive. The upper class maintained its standards because it did not have to concern itself with productivity. Having nothing else to do and with plenty of money with which to do it, the member of the upper class attempted to outspend all other members of his class. This was what Veblen termed "conspicuous consumption." He thus attacked the basic values of the wealthy class—not just their economic practices, which were being so persistently publicized by other critics of the age.

Technology Creates New Social Values

The reform impulse was pushed into the background as a result of American participation in World War I. Reform was not dead; in fact the traditional American notions of equality, democracy, and economic betterment were very much responsible for American popular enthusiasm in the war. However, the post-war era brought major changes to American life and thought. Partly, these changes were due to the failure to "make the world safe for democracy" and resultant disillusionment. Partly, they were due to the unbridled prosperity of the Twenties, both real and artificial. And partly, these changes were wrought by new technological developments and by a radical alteration of the social structure.

Library of Congress

The Stereograph—Precursor of
Modern Media (1901)

Mass Communication and the Spread of Ideas

Of real significance in the cultural realm was the coming into its own of the automobile. The automobile was the status symbol of a prosperous age, and its impact is almost impossible for the modern generation to imagine. People were no longer trapped in the city; the cult of suburbia began. The farmer was no longer isolated, and small farming communities began to dry up. An interchange became possible between urban and rural dweller on a regular basis. Church attendance began to drop off, as many Americans preferred a Sunday drive and a picnic to a sermon. The mode of new transportation, forced the traditional one-room country school to give way to the consolidated school district.

The tight-knit family structure of the

past began to break down in the face of such easy mobility. The automobile replaced the home as a center of much social activity. There was much greater freedom for the nation's young people—and a relaxation of sexual mores as a consequence. The new mobility also created a new era for the professional criminal.

Another technological development which had a profound effect on American habits and attitudes was the infant motion picture industry. Starting in 1919 with the formation of United Artists Corporation, motion picture production increased throughout the decade of the Twenties until by the time of the stock market crash 100 million Americans were weekly attending motion pictures. The new form of entertainment enhanced the spirit of frivolity which characterized the era. The new radio industry helped in this development with the introduction of its soap operas. The audiences of the new mass

"And take care of mother and father, mother's husband and father's wife and mother's fiancé!"

Historical Pictures Service, Chicago

The Cultural Milieu of the Twenties

media were sometimes hard-pressed to separate fact from fantasy.

These communications devices—automobiles, motion pictures, and radio—tended greatly to break down the autonomy of the individual family unit. The American became fair game for the commercial advertiser, even in his own home. Commercials penetrated the living room, the kitchen, and even the bedroom—the radio saw to that. Catchy little phrases about a particular product (probably useless) would now be murmured unconsciously by the victims of saturation advertising. There was no escape. As a result of the new media, Americans became more cosmopolitan, but they also became the involuntary consumers of a commercially manipulated mass culture.

There was a certain wildness to the post-war nation, and it was due in large measure to the emergence of the modern American female. Women had won the right to vote in 1919; the victory marked the culmination of part of America's great crusade. But the young woman of the Twenties was disillusioned as well as free. The long-standing American ideal of equality had been realized for the fairer sex, but it quickly became confused with unbridled freedom. To enforce her newly acquired equality the young woman often felt that she had to do whatever men did—drink, smoke, break down the double-standard sexual code, and above all, throw off the shackling influences of convention. Hence, the Gay Nineties bustle dress was transformed into the flapper dress.

In a similar spirit, young Americans had no respect for a law which could not be enforced and was not wanted. Thus the nation's noble experiment with national prohibition produced mainly violence, crime, and corruption. The disrespect for this particular law was contagious, and consequently all unwanted laws and social conventions became fair game —not unlike the 1960's. Some of this sentiment wore off with the sobering ef-

fects of the Depression, but Americans have always exhibited a tendency to ignore unwanted laws, and sometimes to flaunt their violation.

Protest Reflects American Ambivalence

Though most Americans in the Twenties seemed to take an escapist attitude toward social problems, the spirit of dissent did appear in two separate realms. On one hand, the protest took the form of religious fundamentalism. And on the other hand, serious poets and novelists often spoke of the purposelessness and disillusionment of their age.

A struggle within Protestant ranks over the prevailing materialistic and hedonistic temper had resulted in a victory for conservative religious leaders. The fundamentalists (as these leaders were termed) gave no quarter to the supporters of the new national mood. They had little respect for new scientific discoveries and intellectual theories. For support, fundamentalists invoked various literally interpreted passages from Scripture. The Bible stated that the sun stood still; to the fundamentalists, any other theory of the universe, regardless of its substantial fact, was false and even blasphemous. The earth was created in exactly six days according to the book of Genesis, and geologists who claimed otherwise were devils. Above all, the theory of evolution was entirely immoral and totally false. Fundamentalism was a form of conservative protest from beneath the protective umbrella of religion.

The dominant theme of literature in the Twenties was disillusionment with the world, disgust with the United States, and a fear that life, after all, was without purpose. Men like Ernest Hemingway, Scott Fitzgerald, and John Dos Passos portrayed such feelings, each in his own way and with unique emphasis. They were joined by the incomparable Henry L. Mencken in their scathing denunciation of the false materialistic values and hopes of America. In the pages of the *American Mercury,* a magazine which he founded, Mencken took literary potshots at everything and everyone imaginable. He was particularly inspired in venomous discussion of his favorite subject: the hypocrisy and ignorance of fundamentalism.

The fact that only in literature and religion were there identifiable, influential movements of reaction against the status quo is more indicative than further discussion of protest in the Twenties could be. Earlier eras in American history had produced intellectual forces of lasting significance. American thought in the Twenties reflected the instability, the confused and restless dissatisfaction of most of the nation as it entered its modern era.

The American Character

One of the major intellectual struggles running throughout American history is an attempt to harmonize human rights with property rights. This was true during the colonial period, the Federalist period, Jacksonian America, the age of big business, but above all, during the contemporary era. Human rights are what civil rights are all about, and the struggle reflects one of the major problems of the nation: how to mix "life, liberty, and property" in proper proportions.

A related element in American intellectual history is preoccupation with the concept of equality. There has been a general trend, since colonial days, in the direction of greater equality (although at times they were serious setbacks), and this equality is seen as the root of the democratic ideal. The equalitarian trend has been complicated and partially arrested by conflict between various social and economic classes, by variation in talent and intellect, by the status of certain offices and professions, and by a general tendency on the part of many Americans to attempt to preserve some sort of a status hierarchy.

Equalitarianism has also been linked with certain negative attitudes. Insistence on equality, on the part of some Americans, has often meant suspicion of intellectual attainment—even though the gap between the average working man and the scholar is narrower and less insurmountable in the United States than in any other country in the entire history of the human race. In some measure this is partially due to another unique aspect of the American mind—its practical orientation, and scorn of the purely theoretical.

Yet Americans tend to live for an idealized future. Except for a tiny minority of individuals on the far right who seem to look forward to a nuclear holocaust, Americans generally regard a glorious tomorrow as being absolutely certain. Whatever may be the pains and anxieties of today, they can be suffered because tomorrow will bring another epoch. Americans work in the present, but they tend to live and dream in the future; the nation has always thought of itself as the land of opportunity. The American class structure is sufficiently flexible to allow for a rather high degree of social and economic mobility. Numerous examples of people who have "made it" continue to convince most Americans that they can be as successful. And it is an established and publicized fact that all but the very poorest Americans enjoy a living standard that is the envy of the rest of the world.

Despite the concern for material comfort, Americans are not soft creatures. Most of them are more than willing to work hard for what they get. In fact Americans are noted abroad for their superabundant energy. It is not accidental that there is, in the United States, a high incidence of mental illness, alcoholism, and social alienation. Americans have deliberately set a break-neck, pressurized pace for themselves, which they regard as necessary for achieving their ends. Energy, ingenuity, vitality, and industrious-

ness are all traits which fit into this pattern. To a large extent they simply reflect the dominance of the middle-class
Puritan ethic.

With all their commitment to material
success, Americans are not a selfish people. They produce not to possess, but to
consume—and they are often generous
with what they do not (or cannot) use for
themselves, though they may lavishly display their wealth as they are giving it away.
The need for retirement insurance programs is a clear sign that even the best-paid
Americans are likely to forget self-interest
in the use of abundance; it also indicates
their confidence in the future.

For Further Reading

Blau, Joseph. *Men and Movements in American Philosophy.* New York: Prentice-
Hall, Inc., 1952.

Commanger, Henry S. *The American Mind.* New Haven: Yale University Press, 1950.

Curti, Merle. *The Growth of American Thought.* New York: Harper and Row, 1964.

Ekrick, Arthur A. *The Idea of Progress in America, 1815–1860.* New York: Peter
Smith, 1950.

Ellis, Charles Mayo. *An Essay on Transcendentalism.* Gainsville: Scholar's Facsimiles
and Reprints. 1950.

Gabriel, Ralph H. *The Course of American Democratic Thought.* New York: The
Ronald Press, 1956.

Handlin, Oscar. *Race and Nationality in American Life.* Boston: Little, Brown, 1957.

Hofstadter, Richard. *Social Darwinism in American Thought, 1860–1915.* Philadelphia: University of Pennsylvania Press, 1945.

Logan, Rayford. *The Negro in the United States.* Princeton: D. Van Nostrand, 1957.

Persons, Stow. *American Minds.* New York: Henry Holt and Company, 1958.

Schlesinger, Arthur M. and White, Morton. *Paths of American Thought.* Boston:
Houghton Mifflin, 1963.

Warner, Lloyd. *Social Class in America.* New York: Harper, 1960.

White, Morton G. *Social Thought in America; the Revolt against Formalism.* New
York: Viking Press, 1952.

Wish, Harvey. *Society and Thought in America.* New York: Longmans, 1952.

Index